VISION AND MEANING IN NINTH-CENTURY BYZANTIUM

Image as Exegesis in the Homilies of Gregory of Nazianzus

The Byzantines used imagery to communicate a wide range of issues. In the context of Iconoclasm – the debate about the legitimacy of religious art conducted between ca. AD 730 and 843 – Byzantine authors themselves claimed that visual images could express certain ideas better than words. *Vision and Meaning in Ninth-Century Byzantium* deals with how such visual communication worked, and examines the types of messages that pictures could convey in the aftermath of Iconoclasm. Its focus is on a deluxe manuscript commissioned around 880, a copy of the fourth-century sermons of the Cappadocian church father Gregory of Nazianzus which was presented to the Emperor Basil I, founder of the Macedonian dynasty, by one of the greatest scholars Byzantium ever produced, the patriarch Photios. The manuscript was lavishly decorated with gilded initials, elaborate headpieces, and a full-page miniature before each of Gregory's sermons. Forty-six of these, including over 200 distinct scenes, survive. Fewer than half, however, were directly inspired by the homily that they accompany. Instead, most function as commentaries on the ninth-century court, and, carefully deconstructed, both provide us with information not available from preserved written sources and, perhaps more important, show us how visual images communicate differently from words.

DR LESLIE BRUBAKER is Senior Lecturer at the Centre for Byzantine, Ottoman and Modern Greek Studies, University of Birmingham. She has edited *Byzantium in the Ninth Century: Dead or Alive?*, and (with Robert Ousterhout) *The Sacred Image East and West*, as well as contributing chapters and articles to numerous publications in Byzantine studies.

Cambridge Studies in Palaeography and Codicology

This new series has been established to further the study of manuscripts from the middle ages to the renaissance. It includes books devoted to particular types of manuscripts, their production and circulation, to individual codices of outstanding importance, and to regions, periods and scripts of especial interest to scholars. Certain volumes will be specially designed to provide students in the field with reliable introductions to central topics, and occasionally a classic originally published in another language will be translated into English. The series will be of interest not only to scholars and students of medieval literature and history, but also to theologians, art historians, and others working with manuscript sources.

VISION AND MEANING IN NINTH-CENTURY BYZANTIUM

*Image as Exegesis in the Homilies of
Gregory of Nazianzus*

LESLIE BRUBAKER

CAMBRIDGE
UNIVERSITY PRESS

PUBLISHED BY THE PRESS SYNDICATE OF THE UNIVERSITY OF CAMBRIDGE
The Pitt Building, Trumpington Street, Cambridge CB2 1RP, United Kingdom

CAMBRIDGE UNIVERSITY PRESS
The Edinburgh Building, Cambridge CB2 2RU, UK http:www.cup.cam.ac.uk
40 West 20th Street, New York, NY 10011-4211, USA http:www.cup.org
10 Stamford Road, Oakleigh, Melbourne 3166, Australia

© Leslie Brubaker 1999

First published 1999

Printed in the United Kingdom at the University Press, Cambridge

Typeset in Adobe Garamond 11¼/13½pt in QuarkXPress™   [SE]

A catalogue record for this book is available from the British Library

Library of Congress cataloguing in publication data
Brubaker, Leslie
Vision and meaning in ninth-century Byzantium: Image as exegesis in the
homilies of Gregory of Nazianzus / Leslie Brubaker.
p.   cm. (Cambridge Studies in palaeography and codicology)
Includes bibliographical references and index.
ISBN 0-521-62153-4 (hb)
1. Bibliothèque nationale de France. Manuscript. Graecus 510–
Ilustrations.   2. Bible – Illustrations.   3. Gregory, of Nazianzus,
Saint – Art.   4. Illumination of books and manuscripts, Byzantine.
5. Orthodox Eastern Church – Sermons.   I. Title.   II. Series.
ND3385.B57B78   1999
745.6′7487–dc21   97-43385 CIP

ISBN 0 521 62153 4 hardback

For Christopher

Contents

Contents

Contents

Illustrations

x

Illustrations

PHOTOGRAPH CREDITS

Preface

The copy of the Homilies (sermons) of Gregory of Nazianzus produced in Constantinople for the Emperor Basil I and his family between AD 879 and 882 (Paris, Bibliothèque Nationale, codex graecus 510) was the subject of my 1983 doctoral dissertation. Since then, the discipline of art history has changed, and so have my conceptions of what art history is about and my areas of interest within the discipline. Few passages remain from the original dissertation; I have retained many of the themes that interested me years ago (though the words have been rewritten and the observations reframed), but have interwoven them with topics that now interest me more. The basic line of enquiry, however, remains the same. How and why was Paris.gr.510 made and used? What did Paris.gr.510 mean to the people who produced and used it? These issues – which boil down to questions of method, function, and meaning – are interrelated, but not simply.

Paris.gr.510 is not, in fact, a simple manuscript. It is arguably the most complex and internally sophisticated illustrated manuscript ever produced in Byzantium. Miniatures that expand upon the sense of Gregory's sermons rather than illustrating his narrative are normal. The relationship between image, text, and audience is often symbiotic and dialectical, and raises methodological problems of interpretation for us today. To circumvent the most obvious of these problems, comparisons and parallels have been drawn whenever possible from roughly contemporary images and texts or from works that scholarly opinion accepts as well known to the Byzantines during the last quarter of the ninth century. This restriction has one indisputable drawback: it excludes the evidence which no longer survives while privileging those ninth-century witnesses that have, for one reason or another, managed to endure. It seems important to signal this potential methodological pitfall, however inescapable.

The complexity of the manuscript also demands a reasonably detailed assessment of each miniature. These analyses are embedded in the following chapters; they provide the skeleton from which hangs the flesh of the surrounding discussion. Usually, each is set off by a subtitle giving the folio number of the miniature, and, in parentheses, its order in the manuscript. Each contains a brief description, an examination of the relationship between the image and the text it illustrates or originally illustrated, and a discussion of the imagery; it is intentional that the dialogue between text and image, which (as in most manuscripts) is very important in Paris.gr.510, introduces each discussion. Occasionally aspects of a miniature are treated in more detail outside this primary discussion; in these cases, cross-references appear in the notes. Formal characteristics that affect the meaning of the miniature – and, in Paris.gr.510, that especially includes composition – are also incorporated; signposts of individual painters ('hands') are noted as relevant.[1] The miniatures are not, however, considered in the order that they appear in the manuscript (an inventory of the miniatures, listing them in their present order of appearance, appears in Appendix A; Appendix B lists the textual bases for the scenes). Although the exegetical approach of the designer and painters matured as the manuscript progressed,[2] the conceptual development of particular themes is not linear. Many miniatures in Paris.gr.510 have multiple levels of meaning and all are essentially self-contained units; but most also correlate thematically with others, often far distant in the manuscript. To garner the collective evidence provided by these thematic groups I have assembled the miniatures around them. The reproductions of the miniatures, however, follow the order of the manuscript and, for ease of reference, are all grouped together between pp. xxiv and 1. The miniatures from Milan, Ambrosiana cod. E.49/50 inf. are grouped between pp. 18 and 19.

The interpretive role of many of the miniatures and the limited afterlife of the Homilies images in the Byzantine world – far more people are familiar with them today than were cognizant of the manuscript during its entire 600 years in Constantinople – suggested a focus on the original group of artisans, their employer, and the family for whom Paris.gr.510 was made. The intentions of this group are not recoverable, and in any event images convey socially constructed meaning within a constrained set of boundaries, in this case the parameters of what was visually thinkable around the year 880 in the élite circles of Constantinople. At the same time, however, Paris.gr.510 is a real object; it is part of, but not reducible to, the larger discourse in which it participated.[3] The particular people involved with the manuscript seem to have affected it, sometimes in unconventional ways. This issue, too, raises methodological problems. I am less concerned about over-interpretation – as Robert Taft pointed out long ago, ninth-century Byzantines preferred multi-level metaphors to simple allegory, and were happy 'to hold in dynamic tension several levels of meaning simultaneously'[4] – than with anachronistic interpretation, a tendency to impose (or to recognize only) meanings that are

---

[1] On the style of the miniatures as a whole, see chapter 2.   [2] See chapter 3.
[3] See the perceptive comments in Spiegel (1990).   [4] Taft (1980/1), esp. 60, 73–74 (quotation 74).

significant to us today. I have tried to balance the evidence of individual miniatures against the patterns revealed by groups of images, and to understand Paris.gr.510 as a dialogue, expressed in the language of images, between the people involved in its making and their world.

After introducing the manuscript, in the first chapter I have therefore turned immediately to a consideration of ways to understand the visual – and especially the colloquium between image, audience, and text in manuscripts – in ninth-century Byzantium.[5] Against this backdrop, chapter 2 turns to how this colloquium works in Paris.gr.510. In the following five chapters, the miniatures are arranged in thematic groups: the biographical miniatures, which focus on Gregory of Nazianzus and his fourth-century friends; the visual panegyrics that laud the Emperor Basil I; the exegetical miniatures that betray the involvement of the patriarch Photios; the group of miniatures that concentrate on saints and sinners; and the scenes that provide visual expressions of divinity. By then, we shall have considered most of the miniatures in Paris.gr.510; in chapter 8, the connections between Paris.gr.510 and other works are reconsidered, primarily from an iconographical point of view. Finally, in the conclusion, a number of sub-themes that run across chapters are addressed, along with the vexing question of why this curious manuscript was made.

I should note at the outset that neither I nor, apart from Charles Astruc, any scholar known to me has been permitted to see the manuscript, a ban that was apparently imposed before the Second World War; even the huge Louvre exhibition 'Byzance' in 1992 could not obtain the manuscript, though it appears in the catalogue. The paint is flaking so badly from the miniatures that Christian Förstel, the current Conservateur de la Section Grecque in the manuscript department of the Bibliothèque Nationale, has himself never opened the book.

Some technical notes. References specific to individual miniatures are collected into a bibliographical footnote near the beginning of the primary discussion of each miniature; here all secondary literature appears in chronological sequence. I have omitted clearly derivative descriptions or comments such as those in standard handbooks. References appear in abbreviated form (author and year of publication); full details appear in the Bibliography. English quotations from the Old Testament have been taken, with some modifications, from *The Septuagint Version of the Old Testament, Greek and English*, translated by L. L. Brenton (London, no date). Those from the New Testament are either my own translations from the Greek or follow the Authorized Version. The anglicization of Greek words and names follows current standard usage; it is not, therefore, entirely consistent (e.g. Makedonios and Romanos, but Macedonian and Lazarus).

[5] Parts of chapter 1 originally appeared as Brubaker (1989b).

Acknowledgments

This book has been a long time in the making, and I have acquired many and various debts to a huge number of people and institutions. My parents and family have been extremely supportive throughout. I am also happy to thank Anthony Cutler, who first introduced me to Paris.gr.510; the Johns Hopkins University, which granted me the Samuel H. Kress travel fellowship that enabled me to start this project; the Dumbarton Oaks Center for Byzantine Studies, where I have been accommodated as a Fellow or a simple scholar many times over the past fifteen years; the Getty Fellowship programme, which funded a year of released time when much of this book was written, and, later, a second year when much of it was revised; the British Academy for a generous publication subvention; and Wheaton College, which provided research funds during the years that I taught there. To my former colleagues Ann Murray, Dick and Jean Pearce, Mary Skinner, Sue Standing and especially Donna Kerner – who listened, criticized, recommended bibliography, and supplied unfailing intellectual and emotional support – I am grateful beyond words. My thanks, too, to the Centre for Byzantine, Ottoman and Modern Greek Studies at the University of Birmingham, my home away from home between 1987 and 1993 and since then my academic base, where much of this book was written under the inspiration and occasional prodding of A. A. M. Bryer and John Haldon.

Many libraries, and their staffs, have allowed me sometimes unprecedented access to manuscripts, and I should like particularly to thank Paul Canart at the Biblioteca Apostolica Vaticana for putting me in a room with every manuscript I wanted to examine in order that I might make comparisons between them. I must thank, above all, the staffs at the Biblioteca Ambrosiana in Milan and, especially, at the Bibliothèque Nationale de France in Paris; also the staffs at the Biblioteca Medicea-Laurenziana in Florence, the British Library in London, the Monastery of St John on Patmos, the Biblioteca Nazionale Marciana in Venice, and the Palazzo Venezia in Rome (where I was allowed to study the ivory casket reproduced here as figs. 84, 93, and 95). For helping me to understand manuscripts in the fullest sense,

xx

I thank Guglielmo Cavallo, who has discussed Paris.gr.510 with me for over a decade, and whose kindness has never faltered.

For help with securing photographs, I thank Anna Ballian for arranging contact with the Mount Athos monasteries, Monique Bourin for last-minute prints from Paris, and Sandro Carocci for sifting through hundreds of plates in the archives in Rome. I am also grateful for the assistance of Annemarie Weyl Carr, Graham Norrie, John Osborne, Lyn Rodley, Nancy Ševčenko, and Natalia Teteriatnikov.

At Cambridge University Press I especially thank William Davies, the 'anonymous' readers (John Haldon and Lyn Rodley), my copy editor, Rosemary Morris, my two editors, Kate Brett and Hilary Gaskin, and the editor of the series, Rosamond McKitterick, whose perceptive comments on the final draft of this book were immeasurably helpful.

Parts of what follow have been presented in various scholarly fora, and I have received so many valuable comments that to acknowledge them all here would extend this section beyond reason. I have tried to credit the ideas that I owe to others in the footnotes, but would like to single out here Annemarie Weyl Carr for convincing me that form was as important as content, if inextricably mixed with it; Justin Mossay for his generosity in sharing his knowledge of the textual tradition of the sermons of Gregory of Nazianzus; Ihor Ševčenko for his many kindnesses and especially for discussions of the *Vita Basilii* and the *Life of Tarasios*; and Susan Young for friendship and for arranging visits to the ninth-century churches on Naxos. Four people have been particularly important to me at various stages in the development of this book. Herbert Kessler directed my PhD dissertation on Paris.gr.510 and has been supportive ever since. Kathleen Corrigan first made me ask 'why?' in 1980 and has quietly continued to do so in the following years. Nancy Ševčenko has consistently reminded me of the importance of meticulous scholarship through her own example, which I can never do more than falteringly emulate. My final thanks are to my husband, Christopher Wickham, without whom a less nuanced book would have been published a long time ago and to whom this one is dedicated.

Since this book went to press in February 1997, a number of studies have appeared that could usefully have been incorporated. I signal four in particular: Marie-France Auzépy's *La Vie d'Etienne le Jeune par Etienne le Diacre. Introduction, édition et traduction*, Birmingham Byzantine and Ottoman Monographs 3 (Aldershot, 1997); Gilbert Dagron's *Empereur et prêtre: Etude sur le 'césaropapisme' byzantin* (Paris, 1996); Glenn Peers's 'Patriarchal Politics in the Paris Gregory (B.N. gr. 510)', in *Jahrbuch der Österreichischen Byzantinistik* 47 (1997), 51–71; and Christopher Walter's 'IC XC NI KA: The apotropaic function of the victorious cross', in *Revue des études byzantines* 55 (1997), 193–220. In addition, Shaun Tougher's PhD thesis on Leo VI, cited in chapter 5, has appeared as a monograph in the series The Medieval Mediterranean (Brill: Leiden, 1997).

Abbreviations

BHG	F. Halkin, ed., *Bibliotheca Hagiographica Graeca*. 3 vols. Brussels, 1957.
CLA	E. A. Lowe, ed., *Codices Latini Antiquiores. A Palaeographical Guide to Latin Manuscripts Prior to the Ninth Century*. 12 vols. Oxford, 1934–1971.
DACL	F. Cabrol and H. Leclerq, eds., *Dictionnaire d'archéologie chrétienne et de liturgie*. 15 vols. Paris, 1907–1953.
LCI	E. Kirschbaum, ed., *Lexikon der christlichen Ikonographie*. 8 vols. Rome, 1968–1976.
Mansi	J. D. Mansi, *Sacrorum Conciliorum Nova et Amplissima Collectio*. 53 vols. Paris, 1901–1927. Florence, 1759–1798.
MGH	Monumenta Germaniae Historica
NCMH 2	R. McKitterick, ed., *New Cambridge Medieval History* II, *c.700–c.900*. Cambridge, 1995.
NPNF	P. Schaff and H. Wace, eds., *A Select Library of Nicene and Post-Nicene Fathers of the Christian Church*, ser. 2, 7: *S. Cyril of Jerusalem, S. Gregory Nazianzen*. Grand Rapids, 1978 reprint.
ODB	A.P. Kazhdan, ed., *The Oxford Dictionary of Byzantium*. 3 vols. New York and Oxford, 1991.
PG	J.-P. Migne, ed., *Patrologiae Cursus Completus, Series Graeca*. 161 vols. Paris, 1857–1866.
RBK	K. Wessel, ed., *Reallexikon zur byzantinischen Kunst*. Stuttgart, 1963– .
SC	*Sources Chrétiennes*
SC 99	J. Grosdidier de Matons, ed. and trans., *Romanos le Mélode, Hymnes* I: *Ancien Testament (I–VIII)*. Paris, 1964.
SC 110	J. Grosdidier de Matons, ed. and trans., *Romanos le Mélode, Hymnes* II: *Nouveau Testament (IX–XX)*. Paris, 1965.
SC 114	J. Grosdidier de Matons, ed. and trans., *Romanos le Mélode, Hymnes* III: *Nouveau Testament (XXI–XXXI)*. Paris, 1965.
SC 128	J. Grosdidier de Matons, ed. and trans., *Romanos le Mélode, Hymnes* IV: *Nouveau Testament (XXXII–XLV)*. Paris, 1967.

SC 141   W. Wolska-Conus, ed. and trans., *Cosmas Indicopleustes, Topographie chrétienne* I. Paris, 1968.

SC 159   W. Wolska-Conus, ed. and trans., *Cosmas Indicopleustes, Topographie chrétienne* II. Paris, 1970.

SC 197   W. Wolska-Conus, ed. and trans., *Cosmas Indicopleustes, Topographie chrétienne* III. Paris, 1973.

SC 247   J. Bernardi, ed. and trans., *Grégoire de Nazianze, Discours 1–3*. Paris, 1978.

SC 250   P. Gallay, ed. and trans., *Grégoire de Nazianze, Discours 27–31*. Paris, 1978.

SC 270   J. Mossay, ed. and trans., *Grégoire de Nazianze, Discours 20–23*. Paris, 1980.

SC 284   J. Mossay, ed. and trans., *Grégoire de Nazianze, Discours 24–26*. Paris, 1981.

SC 309   J. Bernardi, ed. and trans., *Grégoire de Nazianze, Discours 4–5*. Paris, 1983.

SC 318   P. Gallay, ed. and trans., *Grégoire de Nazianze, Discours 32–37*. Paris, 1985.

SC 358   C. Moreschini, ed., and P. Gallay, trans., *Grégoire de Nazianze, Discours 38–41*. Paris, 1990.

SC 405   M.-A. Calvet-Sebasti, ed. and trans., *Grégoire de Nazianze, Discours 6–12*. Paris, 1995.

Fig. 1 Paris.gr.510, f. Av: Christ enthroned

Fig. 2 Paris.gr.510, f. Br: Empress Eudokia flanked by Leo and Alexander

Fig. 3 Paris.gr.510, f. Bv: cross

Fig. 4 Paris.gr.510, f. Cr: cross

Fig. 5 Paris.gr.510, f. Cv: Emperor Basil I flanked by Elijah and Gabriel

Fig. 6 Paris.gr.510, f. 3r: a. annunciation and visitation; b. scenes from the life of Jonah

Fig. 7 Paris.gr.510, f. 30v: a. crucifixion; b. deposition and entombment; c. chairete

Fig. 8 Paris.gr.510, f. 32v: martyrdom of the apostles

Fig. 9 Paris.gr.510, f. 43v: a. Gregory and his family; b. funeral of Kaisarios; c. death of Gorgonia

Fig. 10 Paris.gr.510, f. 52v: a.–b. creation and expulsion of Adam and Eve; c. Moses receives the laws; Gregory preaching in Nazianzus

Fig. 11 Paris.gr.510, f. 67v: a. vision of Isaiah; b. Gregory consecrated bishop of Sasima

Fig. 12 Paris.gr.510, f. 69v: a.–e. scenes from the life of Joseph

Fig. 13 Paris.gr.510, f. 71v: a. Basil, Gregory of Nyssa, and Gregory of Nazianzus; b. Job on his dungheap

Fig. 14 Paris.gr.510, f. 75r: transfiguration

Fig. 15 Paris.gr.510, f. 78r: a. hailstorm; b. Gregory preaching

Fig. 16 Paris.gr.510, f. 87v: a. calling of Peter, Andrew, James, and John; Christ and Zachias; calling of Matthew; b. Christ and the rich youth; conversion of Nathanael; c. conversion of Gregory's father

Fig. 17 Paris.gr.510, f. 104r: scenes from the life of St Basil

Fig. 18 Paris.gr.510, f. 137r: a. adoration and dream of the Magi; b. massacre of the innocents; flight of Elizabeth and John the Baptist; martyrdom of Zacharias; c. Presentation

Fig. 19 Paris.gr.510, f. 143v: a. Jeremiah raised from the pit; penitence of David; b. parable of the Good Samaritan; c. healing of the paralytic at Bethesda; healing of the woman with the issue of blood and the raising of Jairus' daughter

Fig. 20 Paris.gr.510, f. 149r: a. Gregory and Basil heal the sick; b. Dives and Lazarus

Fig. 21 Paris.gr.510, f. 165r: a. Christ among the doctors; b. temptation of Christ; c. multiplication of the loaves and fishes

Fig. 22 Paris.gr.510, f. 170r: a. healing of the leper; healing of the man with dropsy; healing of the demoniacs; b. healing of the centurion's servant; healing of Peter's mother-in-law; c. Christ walks on water

Fig. 23 Paris.gr.510, f. 174v: a. sacrifice of Isaac; b. Jacob's struggle with the angel; Jacob's dream; c. anointing of David

Fig. 24 Paris.gr.510, f. 196v: a. raising of Lazarus; supper at Simon's; b. entry into Jerusalem

*Fig. 25 Paris.gr.510, f. 215v: a. judgment of Solomon; b. conversion of the Samaritan woman;
healing of the ten lepers*

Fig. 26 Paris.gr.510, f. 226v: a. Moses strikes water from a rock; b. Joshua stops the sun and moon; Joshua meets the angel

Fig. 27 Paris.gr.510, f. 239r: a. Gregory and the Emperor Theodosios; b. Gregory leaves Constantinople

Fig. 28 Paris.gr.510, f. 264v: a. Moses and the burning bush; conversion of Saul; ascension of Elijah; b. crossing of the Red Sea with the dance of Miriam

Fig. 29 Paris.gr.510, f. 285r: vision of Habakkuk

Fig. 30 Paris.gr.510, f. 301r: Pentecost

Fig. 31 Paris.gr.510, f. 310v: a. healing of the man with the withered arm; healing of the two men born blind; b. healing of the bent woman; parable of the withered fig tree

Fig. 32 Paris.gr.510, f. 316r: a. healing of the blind man at Siloam; parable of the widow's mite; b. healing of the paralytic at Capernaum; raising of the widow's son at Nain

Fig. 33 Paris.gr.510, f. 332v: scenes from the life of Cyprian

Fig. 34 Paris.gr.510, f. 340r: martyrdom of the Makkabees

Fig. 35 Paris.gr.510, f. 347v: a.–b. scenes from the life of Samson; c. Gideon and the fleece; martyrdom of Isaiah

Fig. 36 Paris.gr.510, f. 355r: Council of 381

Fig. 37 Paris.gr.510, f. 360r: a. tower of Babel; b. Noah's ark

Fig. 38 Paris.gr.510, f. 367v: scenes from the history of the Arians

Fig. 39 Paris.gr.510, f. 374v: scenes from the life of Julian the Apostate, part I

Fig. 40 Paris.gr.510, f. 409v: scenes from the life of Julian the Apostate, part II

Fig. 41 Paris.gr.510, f. 424v: a. fall of Jericho; b. Israelites' victory over the Amalekites; c. Gregory writing

Fig. 42 Paris.gr.510, f. 426v: mission of the apostles

Fig. 43 Paris.gr.510, f. 435v: a. Daniel in the lions' den; three Hebrews in the furnace;
b. Manasses; Isaiah and Hezekiah

Fig. 44 Paris.gr.510, f. 438v: Ezekiel in the valley of the dry bones

Fig. 45 Paris.gr.510, f. 440r: scenes from the lives of Constantine and Helena

Fig. 46 Paris.gr.510, f. 452r: scenes from the life of Gregory of Nazianzus

Fig. 47 Paris.gr.510, f. 316v: headpiece to 'To Kledonios' II

Introduction

Gregory of Nazianzus, the fourth-century Cappadocian church father, was a prolific writer whose eloquence and theology so appealed to the Byzantines that they produced more copies of his sermons than of any other non-scriptural text. The ninth-century copy of his Homilies in Paris, Bibliothèque Nationale de France, codex graecus 510 provides the full edition of his forty-four orations,[1] as well as four of Gregory's letters (two each to Kledonios and Nektarios), two poems, and two texts not written by Gregory at all: the anonymous *Significatio in Exechielem*, and the 'Metaphrase of Ecclesiastes' now assigned to Gregory Thaumaturgos. The *vita* of Gregory of Nazianzus, written by Gregory the Presbyter, is partially preserved at the end of the manuscript, where an indeterminate number of leaves have been lost.

Paris.gr.510 is an unabashedly luxurious manuscript. It is large and long, and glitters with colour and gold leaf: most text pages (fig. 47) include at least two gold or painted initials and indicate important text passages with gilded marginal signs; painted headpieces originally introduced each sermon; and the forty-six miniatures – which incorporate over 200 distinct scenes – are full-page, full-colour, and surrounded by gold or decorated frames. The text itself was written in uncial rather than the faster and more economical minuscule.[2]

The evident expense involved, the coordination of labour implied, and the overall visual effect of the manuscript are, however, rarely noted in modern publications on Paris.gr.510: though the Paris Homilies has been cited more often than any other Byzantine manuscript (and probably more often than any Byzantine monument except Hagia Sophia), among the thousands of pages of discussion only perhaps fifty deal even tangentially with the material attributes of the book.[3]

---

[1] The textual tradition represented by Paris.gr.510 is considered later in this chapter.

[2] The actual cost of the manuscript is unknown; for comments on the expenses incurred in book production, however, see Kravari (1991).

[3] Kondakoff II (1891), 57–74, is the most notable exception, but see also Bordier (1885), 62, 89; Frantz (1934); Weitzmann (1935), 4; Nordenfalk (1970), 199; and Brubaker (1991). For the extent of the bibliography on Paris.gr.510, see the yearly listings of manuscript citations in *Scriptorium*, which

Paris.gr.510 has been accorded its position of prominence for reasons that have little to do with its quality: it remains one of the relatively few Byzantine manuscripts that can be localised and dated with precision, and it contains a vast repertoire of images.

Paris.gr.510 contains such a wealth of extended narrative sequences that one of its major roles has been to function as an iconographical repository for modern scholars to draw upon. The miniatures cannot, however, always be seen (as they sometimes have been) as representative of all-encompassing ninth-century iconographical traditions. Though the core groupings of many individual scenes repeat conventional formulae, the peripheral trappings are often unattested else-where; and while this may be an accident of survival, a genuine idiosyncrasy of the manuscript is that the shape of the page as a whole usually affects the presentation of the scenes pictured on it, with compositions adapted to complement other scenes on the page. The miniatures of Paris.gr.510 do not necessarily supply a reli-able iconographical stepping stone; instead, they reveal how and why the visual worked in quite specific circumstances. Paris.gr.510 was a private book, and its miniatures sometimes deliver personal messages.

It is perhaps for this reason that the meaning of the illustrations in the Paris Gregory only began to be deciphered in 1962, when Sirarpie Der Nersessian pub-lished her pioneering study of the relationship between the texts and images of Paris.gr.510 and demonstrated that the miniatures often acted as commentaries on – rather than direct illustrations of – Gregory's sermons. Standing on the shoulders of such a giant, I have pushed the material a little further; and, as this is a book rather than an article, I have also been able to consider the manuscript from more than one perspective. These perspectives all point back to the personalized mes-sages conveyed by Paris.gr.510. How and why these messages were formed and delivered is the subject of this book.

CODICOLOGICAL DESCRIPTION

In its present state, Paris.gr.510 consists of 464 folios (ca. 410 x ca. 300 mm) plus an introductory gathering (ff. A–C) of five miniatures.[4] The manuscript is too fragile

almost without fail note at least one new reference to the manuscript over the preceding six months. In Spatharakis (1981), 6–9, the select bibliography on Paris.gr.510 fills two densely packed columns of an oversized page; the only other manuscript even to approach this amount of citation is the Menologion of Basil II. Spatharakis included only discussions focused on Paris.gr.510; there are perhaps ten times as many passing references to the manuscript.

[4] Though the last folio of Paris.gr.510 is numbered (by a modern hand) 465, this same hand omitted 383. Published accounts of the size of the manuscripts vary. Omont (1929), 11 gives 418 x 305 mm; *Byzance* (1992), 346, gives 435 x 300. I have not been allowed to measure the manuscript; photographs containing scales, however, sugggest that page sizes range from 404 to 418 mm high, and from 272 to 305 mm wide.

to allow unrestricted access; as noted throughout this book, the Bibliothèque Nationale has never allowed me to handle it. But, because the amount of text written on each page is remarkably consistent, the amount of text missing – as revealed through collation of the Paris text (on microfilm) with editions of the Homilies published in Migne and Sources Chrétiennes – gives a clear and quite precise indication of how many leaves have perished. At least twelve folios, and probably thirteen, have been lost from the body of the manuscript; the end, abruptly cut off in mid-sentence, lacks an indeterminate number of pages. Probably during the fourteenth century, Palaiologan scribes replaced three of the lost pages, and inserted the apparently spurious thirty-fifth sermon. (See the diagram of quires: Appendix C.) With few exceptions, the gatherings are arranged in regular quaternions.

Quire signatures (numbers) appear on the first folio of all but five of the fifty-eight quires; eighteen of these, placed in the upper left margin, are in the ninth-century hand responsible for the marginalia of Paris.gr.510, and this same hand appended two small crosses, aligned with the rulings determining the left and right margins, at the top of f. 61r. At a later date – probably during the Palaiologan period – most of the quire numbers were rewritten. In some cases, the later signatures were placed below the original numbers; in others, the ninth-century numbers were over-written. When the manuscript was trimmed, possibly in conjunction with its rebinding in 1602, all but eighteen of the original signatures were excised; fortunately, most of the later numbers survived. In the quire diagrams that appear in Appendix C, the Greek number below each gathering refers to the quire signature. Those not enclosed by parentheses or brackets indicate a signature in the original ninth-century hand; parentheses denote a Palaiologan signature, brackets a hypothetical one. Quire 20 (K), for example, both retains its original signature and displays a later one, while quire 41 (MA) shows no signature.

The scribe carefully wrote the text on ruled leaves in two equal columns of forty lines each (Leroy's ruling 20C2),[5] using a regular uncial with a slight but pronounced slant to the right. Letter forms are generally consistent, though the pointed loop of the alphas does not always join the bar in the same place, the cross-bar of mu may be either pointed or curved, and two forms of xi are used interchangeably. Slanting uncial of the type found in Paris.gr.510 recurs throughout the ninth century; it is, however, not common after 870, by which time minuscule – a script introduced around 800 that was faster to write (and therefore cheaper to commission) – had become standard. The relative scarcity of uncial by the 880s may explain why palaeographers have not discovered the hand responsible for the Paris Gregory in any other manuscript: Werner Jaeger's attempt to link the Homilies with a group of texts associated with Vat.gr.2066 has not met wide

---

[5] Julien Leroy (1976).

acceptance,[6] and recent examinations of ninth-century script simply cite Paris.gr.510 as an example of slanting uncial.[7] The most similar script that I have found appears in Vat.gr.2625, ff. 216–219, a fragment of a text by Theodore of Stoudion.[8] The decision to use uncial rather than the more compact and less expensive minuscule presumably signalled two things to a late ninth-century audience: overt luxury and, by the 880s in Constantinople, the past. The old-fashioned script reiterated the authority of the tradition that lay behind Gregory's text.

Four of the marginal signs that had been associated with Gregory's Homilies since the sixth century supplement the text (fig. 47).[9] The original sigla are nearly all formed of gold leaf (a few were added in a dark ink by a later hand), and convey the same message as the uncial text: the patron of Paris.gr.510 followed tradition and spared no expense in doing so.

In addition to the traditional marginal signs, four homilies carry marginal numbers beside Gregory's references to mythology which correspond with a sixth-century commentary written by Pseudo-Nonnos.[10] The text, which exists in illustrated versions,[11] may once have followed the homilies. Sporadic (and unedited) scholia also appear in the margins.

One thousand four hundred and forty-five gold letters and 172 initials with painted decoration are distributed over the 433 ninth-century text folios; twenty sides – six falling at the ends of various homilies, with less than one column of text used – are without initials, while many pages have three or more: f. 123v contains eleven. In the quire diagrams (Appendix C), the arabic numbers along the side of each folio indicate the total number of painted or gilded initials on that page; if there are two numbers, the lower one signals how many of these received additional decoration. On f. 2v, for example, there are no enlarged initials (though there is a colophon, indicated by the letter C), while on f. 5r there are five; of these, one is elaborately decorated and the other four are gold.

Fifty-one headpieces remain; they are signalled by the letter H in the quire diagrams (Appendix C). All were originally numbered, and the (Greek) numbers are enclosed in parentheses immediately below the H marking; brackets indicate that the headpiece number no longer survives. Compare ff. 1r and 33r.

The forty-six miniatures – five prefacing the text (ff. A–C) and forty-one integrated or inserted within it – are indicated by the letter M in the quire diagrams (Appendix C). All will be considered in detail in subsequent chapters.

---

[6] Jaeger (1947), esp. 91–95. I have examined most of the manuscripts in Jaeger's group: their scripts are only generally similar to that of Paris.gr.510; the layout and decoration are quite different.

[7] E.g. Cavallo (1977), esp. 98–99.   [8] See Julien Leroy (1961).

[9] See Astruc (1974) and Mossay (1982).

[10] See Brock (1971); Declerck (1976, 1977, 1978/79); Accorinti (1990); Nimmo Smith (1992).

[11] Weitzmann (1951b), 87–88.

LOCALIZATION AND DATE

The localization and date of Paris.gr.510 depend on the disturbed first gathering of the manuscript (ff. A–C). Folio A, now a single sheet, originally had a blank recto; the manuscript apparently opened with the portrait of Christ on f. Av (fig. 1). Folios B and C form a bifolium which remains intact, but has been reversed.[12] The miniatures of the Empress Eudokia (d. 882; f. Br; fig. 2), a cross (f. Bv; fig. 3), a second cross (f. Cr; fig. 4), and the Emperor Basil I (867–886; f. Cv; fig. 5) are now in incorrect hierarchical order: Basil should come before Eudokia, an arrangement confirmed by the verse framing the empress's portrait which begins 'Basil, emperor of the Romans, precedes you . . .'.[13] The reversal occurred while the manuscript was in Byzantine hands, at some time after the middle of the tenth century – when the miniaturist of the Leo Bible copied the original disposition of two crosses framing dedicatory portraits[14] – but before the late fourteenth century, when the verse enframing f. Br was copied onto f. Av:[15] had the original order still been retained, the transcription would now appear on f. Cv. Folded correctly, the bifolium's original disposition of a cross (f. Cr), Basil (f. Cv), Eudokia (f. Br), and a final cross (f. Bv) resembles a commemorative diptych with exterior crosses enclosing portraits.[16]

Henri Bordier rightly rejected Bernardus de Montfaucon's opinion that the initial gathering constituted a later addition to the manuscript:[17] epigraphy, colour, and decorative details of ff. A–C match their counterparts in the rest of the book. Though all of the frontispiece miniatures are badly damaged, the frame on f. Av duplicates the alternating quadrilobes of headpieces on ff. 316v (fig. 47) and 427r, and the facial modelling of the two boys on f. Br is so similar to that of the frontal angels on f. 67v (fig. 11) that they must have been painted by the same hand.[18] We cannot divorce the frontispiece miniatures from the rest of Paris.gr.510.

The imperial portraits of the frontispiece sequence provide strong evidence that the manuscript was produced in Constantinople,[19] and allow us to date it with some precision. Leo and Alexander are designated *despotes* on f. Br,[20] a title that Leo attained in 870, and Alexander sometime before the middle of November 879; Basil's eldest son Constantine (crowned 867/8), who died in September 879, is not

---

[12] See Der Nersessian (1962), 198; she is wrong, however, in dating the reversal to the 1602 rebinding.   [13] See chapter 4.

[14] Vat.reg.gr.1, ff. 2r–3v: *Miniature* (1905), pls. 3–6; Dufrenne and Canart (1988), 19–20. This relationship has been noted by many previous scholars: see the discussion of ff. Bv-Cr in chapter 4.

[15] I would like to thank Nancy Ševčenko for her help in transcribing the inscription, and Ihor Ševčenko for his assistance in dating the hand to the second half of the fourteenth century; this dating has been confirmed by Charles Astruc, whom I thank for examining the inscription in December 1986.   [16] So too Kalavrezou-Maxeiner (1978), 24.   [17] Bordier (1885), 62.

[18] The imperial costume worn on f. Br, though not identical, recalls Helena's attire on f. 285r (fig. 29), too.   [19] Cf. Wilson (1967), 57.   [20] Kalavrezou-Maxeiner (1978).

included in the sequence. Eudokia, who died shortly after Leo's marriage to Theophano in the winter of 882, appears; Theophano does not. Folio Br must have been painted after Constantine's death and Alexander's coronation in the final months of 879, and before Leo's marriage in 882 and the subsequent death of Eudokia.[21] The frontispiece sequence thus indicates that Paris.gr.510 was completed between late 879 and 882.

A slightly earlier dating has been proposed by Ioannes Spatharakis on the basis of the underdrawing now visible beneath the badly flaked f. Bv (fig. 3), which shows a central imperial male figure jointly crowned by an archangel, standing on the (viewer's) right, and a third, barely revealed, figure on the left.[22] The underdrawing anticipates the final composition on f. Cv, and most scholars have assumed that it is a preliminary sketch for that page, a portrait of Basil flanked by Gabriel and Elijah.[23] Spatharakis, however, identified the underdrawing on f. Bv as a portrait of Basil's son Constantine, and redated the manuscript's commission to 879, arguing that Constantine's unexpected death led to the covering of his portrait by a cross.[24] Spatharakis' thesis was refuted by Ioli Kalavrezou-Maxeiner, who noted that Basil's son Constantine, unlike the man on f. Bv, was never shown bearded; that to place the heir-presumptive after his mother and younger brothers contradicted imperial protocol; and that the reverse of this leaf (f. Br) must anyway post-date September 879 because both the inscription and framing poem identify Alexander as *despotes*, a rank he attained only after Constantine's death.[25] Kalavrezou-Maxeiner is surely correct, and other arguments against an identification of the underdrawing with Constantine can be adduced: most basically, there is no reason to connect Constantine with Elijah and Gabriel, while there is ample reason to connect his father with them.[26]

---

[21] See Der Nersessian (1962), 198 and, on the implications of Theophano's absence, Mango and Hawkins (1972), 37. Eudokia appears with Constantine and Basil on what seems to be a commemorative coin struck after her death, and long after Constantine's (Grierson III,2 [1973], 481; for iconoclast parallels, see Grierson III,1 [1973], 8–9), but Constantine's absence here indicates that this is not a memorial sequence.

[22] Velmans (1974), fig. 7 (incorrectly labelled f. Av and with Gabriel identified as Michael) and Spatharakis (1974), fig. 5 reproduce details of the most visible underdrawing; a line drawing of additional traces appears in Kalavrezou-Maxeiner (1978), fig. 3. Velmans (1974), 141–145, noted the high quality of the drawing and speculated that a miniaturist otherwise unattested in Paris.gr.510 was responsible. This seems unlikely, as underdrawing visible elsewhere in the manuscript is equally fine; it was apparently simply more difficult to paint than to draw detail. The question of why detail soon to be obscured was drawn at all remains.

[23] See further the discussion of f. Cv in chapter 4.   [24] Spatharakis (1974).

[25] Kalavrezou-Maxeiner (1978). Spatharakis ([1989], 89–93) later speculated that Alexander might have been crowned before 879, that Constantine was of age by 879 and thus could have been shown bearded, and that Eudokia was placed before Constantine because – as is generally agreed (see e.g. Mango [1973]) – she was not his mother. He also suggests that the manuscript was commissioned by a donor in the circle of the empress. Spatharakis' proposed arrangement remains virtually unthinkable in terms of the Byzantine imperial hierarchy.   [26] See chapter 4.

Paris.gr.510 was, then, completed in Constantinople between 879 and 882 for the Emperor Basil I and his family. This locates the manuscript in the midst of a crucial half-century in the annals of Byzantium: years of economic recovery, and of religious consolidation following the end of Iconoclasm, the imperial policy that officially banned religious imagery between ca. 730 and 787, and again from 813 (or 815) until 843. The Paris Gregory is, in fact, the only securely dated Byzantine manuscript from the second half of the ninth century, and it is the first surviving illustrated book produced for a Byzantine emperor.

PRODUCTION AND DISTRIBUTION OF LABOUR

The production of Paris.gr.510 was well organized, and the same process was used consistently throughout the book. When an enlarged initial was to appear, the scribe paused to outline it before continuing with the text: the ink outline of the initial is clearly visible in several letters where the paint has flaked, and this outline must have been completed before the adjacent text was written, for the text flows smoothly around its contours. Further, we can still decipher exactly where the scribe dipped pen in ink, and the pattern formed by the progressive lightening and then abrupt darkness of the ink demonstrates that the scribe wrote the text continuously: there was no need to pause to block in an initial, for its outline was already there.[27] The enlarged letters are thus integrated within the text, a process that coincides with a change in the location (and importance) of the initials. In earlier Byzantine manuscripts, enlarged letters appear at the beginning of a naturally occurring line of text: to signal a particular passage, the scribe would enlarge the first letter of the next line of text.[28] In Paris.gr.510, with two exceptions among more than 1600 initials, the first letter of the passage to be marked received the enlarged letter; when an initial was required, the scribe began the passage to be marked on a new line.[29] The increased status of the enlarged letters is confirmed by their embellishment, in paint or gold leaf, in a separate process after the text had been completed: the paint on the far right edge of a painted initial is occasionally superimposed over the text. The writing and the painting were clearly distinct processes, and the scribes seem not to have anticipated elaborate ornament: even when initial terminal decorations are quite extensive, they never infringe on the text space, for no space was left for them by the scribe. The autonomy of the two processes, and the distinct approaches to the initials taken by the (conservative) scribes and the (sometimes flamboyant) illuminators, suggest that, in an apparent break from earlier Byzantine practice, the scribes were not responsible for the embellish-

[27] I thank Michael McCormick for this observation. [28] See Julien Leroy (1978), 52 note 4.
[29] See Brubaker (1991), 26–27.

ment of the enlarged initials. Paris.gr.510 seems to provide our earliest evidence of an autonomous group of illuminators. It is also the first datable and unquestionably Byzantine manuscript with painted initials. A detailed study of these initials has appeared elsewhere,[30] and will not be repeated here.

The illuminators also painted the decorative headpieces (fig. 47) that once prefaced each of Gregory's sermons: initials and headpieces share the motifs of the striped cable, multi-coloured rows of hearts, five-lobed leaf decoration, and an unusual palmette form, as well as more common jewelled panels. However, in only one instance – the miniature and incipit initial to 'On Easter' (ff. 285r–v) – are the non-figural decorations visually coordinated with a miniature. Furthermore, the visual vocabulary used by the miniaturists themselves differs from that used by the illuminators: the blessing hand of the hand-hasta epsilons (fig. 47) is, for example, invariably shown with the palm facing inward; in contrast, the miniaturists consistently elected to reverse the blessing hand, and drew them with the palm exposed to the viewer.[31] Not only, then, do the illuminators seem to have been distinct from the scribes; they also seem to have been distinct from the miniaturists.

There seem to have been at least three illuminators, most conveniently distinguished by a predilection for a particular type of terminal descender: trilobe (three small circles attached to the base of a letter), grape cluster, or foliate scroll. The trilobe decoration reveals a pattern of allocation in the first quarter of the manuscript, where trilobe initials appear in every third quire:[32] at least at the beginning of production, quires were farmed out to the illuminators following a fairly regular system, and the painter of the trilobe initials received every third quire. Collaboration between the illuminators was apparently loose, for initial forms are neither homogeneous nor consistent, and a variety of letter shapes (two forms of mu, for example) appear. There is no evidence that the illuminators formed part of an established scriptorium, nor do any other manuscripts reveal their contributions either solo or collectively.

THE PHYSICAL RELATIONSHIP BETWEEN TEXT AND MINIATURES

After the five-miniature frontispiece sequence that celebrates Christ's blessing of the Emperor Basil I and his family (ff. A–C), most of the illustrations in Paris.gr.510 are fully integrated into the fabric of the manuscript: the end of the preceding sermon or the beginning of the following one occupies the other side of thirty-two of the forty-one text miniatures. The continuity of the text ensures that these miniatures retain their original locations and preserve the intended disposition of text

[30] Brubaker (1991); here too earlier bibliography.
[31] See ff. 52v, 75r, 87v, 264v, 438v (figs. 10, 14, 16, 28, 44).
[32] Two in quires two and five, one in quire eight, three in quire eleven and two in quire fourteen.

and image. This arrangement simplifies matters for modern interpreters, but it has not been kind to the miniatures: painting on ruled parchment encourages flaking, and the images are often badly damaged.

Presumably for this reason, full-page miniatures were more normally painted on unruled leaves that were inserted into the text.[33] Apart from Paris.gr.510, the exceptions usually appear in manuscripts where most of the illustrations are not full-page: for example, pictures incorporated within the text dominate the early fifth-century Vatican Virgil, and the occasional full-page miniatures have text on their reverse.[34] Another exception is provided by the sixth-century Vienna Dioscorides, a herbal with each full-page plant miniature facing a page of explanatory text; the miniatures thus have the text belonging to the previous image on their reverses. The Vienna Dioscorides, however, was a deluxe presentation copy; herbals did not regularly contain full-page illustrations.[35] Like the full-page miniatures in the Vatican Virgil, those in the Dioscorides deviate from a tradition of smaller pictures inserted in the text.

Paris.gr.510 apparently continues this pattern. No other illustrated copies of Gregory's sermons use full-page illustrations; in all other copies, the image always shares a page with text (figs. 48–55, 79, 100). The integral miniatures in the Homilies perpetuate the integrated format normally used for illustrated copies of the text.

It is possible that in Paris.gr.510 the retention of the integrated format represents a bow to tradition, for the miniaturists demonstrably knew about painting on unruled and inserted sheets: the frontispiece sequence is unruled, and eight or nine miniatures in the body of the manuscript were painted on inserted single leaves, unruled, and with blank backs.[36] The first ten miniatures, in fact, follow this system: after the five frontispiece miniatures, five inserted leaves with miniatures on one side and a blank reverse appear in the first seven quires of the manuscript. There are no integral miniatures until the eighth gathering, where f. 67

[33] Few full-page miniatures produced in the eastern Mediterranean before (or during) the ninth century survive; those that do, however, usually share their leaf with another miniature (as in the sixth-century Rabbula and Rossano Gospels) or were painted on unruled leaves that remained blank on the reverse: e.g. the ninth-century miniatures of Princeton, Garrett 6 and the frontispiece to the Khludov Psalter. Later Byzantine examples, too, almost always follow this formula, as do pre-tenth-century Latin books: e.g. the sixth- or seventh-century Ashburnham Pentateuch, the seventh- and eighth-century insular gospelbooks, the eighth-century Vespasian Psalter, and the ninth-century Touronian Bibles.

[34] On the full-page death of Dido in the Vatican Virgil (*CLA* I [1934], no.11; Vat.lat.3225, f. 40r), painted in Rome ca. 400, see Weitzmann (1977), 36. In the ninth-century 'Christian Topography' (Vat.gr.699), eighteen of the sixty-one miniatures are full-page (ff. 15v, 38r, 43v, 45r, 49r, 52r, 59r, 61v, 63v, 66v, 74r, 75r, 76v, 82v, 83v, 89r, 114v, 115v); about half were painted on unruled sheets.

[35] Gerstinger (1979); Anderson (1977).

[36] See the next note. Quire 47 is problematic; it certainly has one, and possibly two, inserted miniatures.

contains the end of Gregory's sermon 'On Peace' on its recto and a miniature on its verso.[37]

The insertion of unruled leaves containing full-page miniatures into regular text gatherings is common in Byzantium,[38] but the combination of two systems of illustration found in Paris.gr.510, inserted and integral, is so unusual that the break between the two systems in the eighth gathering must indicate a decision to change the format at this point. It is however hard to imagine reasons for switching from inserted to integral miniatures: inserted leaves allow greater flexibility (scribes and painters can work independently) and provide a smooth surface that takes paint more easily, while the integrated format followed from f. 67 onward required the precise coordination of scribes and miniaturists and imposed an uneven ruled surface on the painters. The shift is unlikely to have resulted from an abrupt decision to trim production costs: in a book the length of Paris.gr.510, the sixteen folios (eight bifolia) saved by integrating the miniatures would have had little financial impact. Were cost-cutting the issue, full-page miniatures are unlikely to have been included at all and each new sermon would not begin on a fresh page, often leaving considerable empty parchment on the final page of the preceding homily. Instead – and especially given the care with which Paris.gr.510 was produced – the change in format seems to document a radical change in plans. This change occurred after the scribes had already begun work on the text and had completed the first six homilies, meticulously outlining the enlarged initials for the illuminators but neglecting to leave blank sides for miniatures. Since the scribes habitually left a blank side for a miniature before each sermon from the eighth quire on,[39] it seems reasonable to assume that they were only told to do so after they had completed the first seven quires. Either the designer of the manuscript at first forgot to tell the scribes to make accommodations for pictures, or the design of the manuscript itself was revised *in medias res*. Both possibilities are conceivable. The careful design otherwise evident throughout the manuscript suggests, however, that the shift in format reflects a genuine change in plans rather than the correction of an oversight. If so, the decision to illustrate Gregory's sermons was made only as the scribes began the eighth gathering. While the coherent and self-contained frontispiece sequence might or might not always have been intended, it appears that Paris.gr.510 may not originally have been conceived as an illustrated text. Whatever prompted the change in plans, miniatures were inserted into the first seven quires; thereafter, the

[37] All of the inserted leaves – f. 3 in the first quire, ff. 30 and 32 in the fourth, f. 43 between the fifth and sixth, f. 52 between the sixth and seventh, f. 347 in quire 44, f. 367 or (and?) f. 374 in quire 47, and f. 435 in quire 55 – disrupt the regular quaternion system used throughout Paris.gr.510. See Appendix C.   [38] See note 33 above.

[39] The exceptions are 'On himself' (Homily 26), which was unillustrated (see page 11), and the letter to Evagrios, now prefaced by an inserted miniature (f. 435v) that sustains no relationship to the letter and may well also originally have been unillustrated (see chapter 2). On the problematic quire 47, see Appendix C.

scribes left a side free for a miniature before most sermons and the traditional, integrated format of Homilies illustration was followed for the rest of the manuscript.

Once the die was cast with the first integral miniature on f. 67r, the following twenty-three miniatures share a leaf with either the end of the preceding sermon or the beginning of the next one. The system breaks down, however, in quire 44; though a space was left for a miniature (f. 346r is blank), f. 347 is an inserted leaf with a miniature on its verso. Inserted leaves can of course be moved without disrupting the text, and this may in fact not have been the original location of the miniature; its alternative site, however, follows the same pattern: it precedes a recto left blank for illustration (f. 319r in quire 41).[40] Whether the lapse in the integrated system occurred in quire 41 or quire 44, subsequent miniatures are integrated until quire 47, where again a page left blank for illustration (f. 366r) was ignored and a leaf with a miniature on its verso tipped in (f. 367). There is one more inserted miniature (now f. 435r in quire 55), the original location of which is unclear; the remaining seven miniatures that follow f. 367v are all integrated. If the miniatures were painted more or less in the order they appear, perhaps the three inserted miniatures that appear toward the end of the manuscript were painted separately in order that the scribes, illuminators and miniaturists could complete their work at roughly the same time.

SERMONS WITHOUT ILLUSTRATIONS AND 'LOST' MINIATURES

Of the homilies now without miniatures in Paris.gr.510, only one was clearly never illustrated: 'On himself' (ff. 231v–238v) could not even have supported an inserted miniature, for the text of preceding sermon ends on the recto of its opening text page.

Three texts, all in the third quarter of the manuscript, follow a blank page: the empty f. 249v faces 'On the nativity'; f. 308v, 'To Nektarios'; and f. 319r, 'On Athanasios'. These blank pages were apparently intended to receive illustrations that were never painted. It is possible that miniatures were once inserted before these three texts, for as we have just seen the inserted miniatures on ff. 347 and 367 follow blank pages, and the former may in fact have preceded 'On Athanasios', leaving the blank f. 346v before the sermon 'In praise of Heron' that it now prefaces.

Though there is no way of telling whether or not the illustrations were actually completed, the folios on which six additional miniatures could have been painted have been excised at the beginning of the following sermons:

'On peace': the original text now begins on f. 63r; the lost two paragraphs (sufficient for a single side, leaving a blank recto) were replaced in, probably, the fourteenth century.

[40] See chapter 2.

'On the Son' I: a folio is missing between ff. 187 and 188; its recto originally contained the final words of the preceding sermon; its verso could have contained a miniature.

'On the Holy Spirit': nearly six paragraphs from the beginning of the text are lost; with headpiece 23, this text would have filled three sides of the bifolium lost from the middle of quire 26 between the present ff. 204 and 205. The first of the four sides (originally facing f. 204v) was not needed for text and could have contained a miniature.

'On Virginity': a folio is missing between ff. 213 and 214; its recto originally contained the final words of the preceding sermon; its verso could have contained a miniature.

'On light': f. 256 is a fourteenth-century insert that contains the final words of the preceding sermon. The lost folio (half of a bifolium, with f. 261) would have accommodated this text on its recto; its verso could have contained a miniature.

'On New Sunday': a folio is missing between ff. 297 and 298; its verso once contained the opening paragraphs of the homily; its recto could have contained a miniature.

In all of these cases the relevant folios might have been removed to acquire the miniature. However, in each of the three cases where the end of the preceding text is lost, very little text – the final paragraph or only part of it – would have been written on the recto. Such almost empty pages were habitually pilfered for their blank parchment by later scribes, and this may be an equally plausible explanation for those leaf losses. If so, no miniature ever occupied the verso, and 'On the Son I', 'On virginity', and 'On light' were once preceded by a blank page meant for an illustration that was never painted.

HISTORY OF THE MANUSCRIPT

We know very little about the history of Paris.gr.510 after it was made. Neither its decoration nor its miniatures had a great effect on later Byzantine art outside of a small circle of manuscripts produced in Constantinople, and probably for members of the court and patriarchate: the Paris Gregory had limited and élite viewers. Yet the manuscript surely remained in the capital and was in at least occasional use until the late fourteenth century, the date of the latest Byzantine additions to the manuscript.[41] It had moved west by the early sixteenth century, and is variously listed as number 129, 18 and 132 in catalogues of the library of Cardinal Nicholas Ridolfi (nephew of Pope Leo X); Omont plausibly suggested that John

---

[41] See note 15 above.

Lascaris acquired the manuscript in the late fifteenth century on one of his buying trips to Constantinople after the Turkish conquest. From Ridolfi, Paris.gr.510 passed to Pietro Strozzi, and then, around 1558, to Catherine de Medici; it entered the Bibliothèque du Roi in 1594. Here it was rebound in 1602, and received its present cover bearing the arms of Henry IV. After a series of other appellations (no. 155 [CLV] in 1622, no. 1809 in 1682) it became graecus 510 in 1740.[42] It remains one of the most precious manuscripts owned by the French state (which took over the Royal Library after the revolution) and, because of its fragile state, is jealously guarded from use.

PARIS.GR.510 AND OTHER ILLUSTRATED MANUSCRIPTS OF GREGORY'S HOMILIES

Gospels and psalters, the primary biblical works used in the liturgy, make up the bulk of all Byzantine illustrated manuscripts. Though lack of wear suggests that many of the most heavily decorated were displayed rather than used, it was nonetheless putative service books that were normally produced as luxury items.[43] A selection of Gregory's Homilies, too, was recited over the course of the liturgical year in the orthodox church. Some are already incorporated in the ninth-century typikon of the Great Church (Hagia Sophia) and attested in a ninth-century collection of sermons associated with liturgical feasts, but the definitive selection and arrangement of sermons for liturgical use seems to have occurred in the tenth century.[44] Though the circumstances of their recital are not entirely clear, the so-called liturgical editions of the Homilies (called by the Byzantines the 'read words') comprise about half of all extant Gregory manuscripts.[45] This is also the group most commonly illustrated (figs. 79, 100): George Galavaris catalogued thirty-six copies of the 'read' Homilies with illustrations, the earliest of which date to the eleventh century.[46] In contrast, Paris.gr.510 is one of the three earliest examples of the full edition of Gregory's works, a group that makes up only about one per cent of all preserved manuscripts of the Homilies. Only two of the surviving copies of the full edition received illustrations: the Paris Gregory and a manuscript, also of the ninth century, in Milan, Biblioteca Ambrosiana, cod. E.49/50 inf. (figs. 48–55). Both illustrate the set of Gregory's sermons called the 'collection of fifty-two'

---

[42] Omont (1929), 10–11. On the export of Greek manuscripts to Italy in the fifteenth century, see R. Nelson (1995). [43] See Lowden (1990), 263–280. [44] See Galavaris (1969), 9–10.

[45] Here and in the remainder of this paragraph I rely on largely unpublished material provided by Father Justin Mossay, whom I thank for numerous discussions of the Homilies text tradition. The preliminary and basic study of this tradition remains Sinko (1917, 1923), whose conclusions are in the process of being revised as work progresses on the minor edition of the *logoi* in Paris (intermittently published in SC) and the major edition being prepared in Louvain.

[46] Galavaris (1969) reproduced most of the miniatures.

(known as 'family n' to text scholars); the other early group of Gregory manuscripts, the 'collection of forty-seven' ('family m') has no illustrated members.[47] The illustrations in these two manuscripts are quite different from those in the liturgical editions, the miniatures of which, like the pictures in many gospelbooks and psalters, responded to public rituals.

The so-called liturgical homilies differ from the Paris Gregory both textually and pictorially: in no case can a convincing parallel between a miniature from the liturgical editions and one from Paris.gr.510 be drawn.[48] The Milan manuscript is the sole copy of the Homilies with illustrations that ever resemble those of Paris.gr.510.

The connection between the two ninth-century manuscripts is not, however, straightforward. Their texts are far from identical. Though both belong to the 'family n', this family has a confusing stemma, and the Milan and Paris Gregories often present variant readings that are at odds with each other.[49] Generally speaking, the Milan manuscript is considered a better witness to the original text than is Paris.gr.510, and indeed the Paris Gregory often stands isolated from all other manuscripts in its readings and the order in which the sermons are arranged.[50] Someone (Photios?) extensively edited the text. In the opinions of its various editors, Paris.gr.510 nevertheless preserves, after the Milan Gregory, the best witness to the family; and it seems that a text very like that preserved in Milan was copied, with modifications, by the scribes of Paris.gr.510.

We do not know when Gregory's Homilies first received illustration, but the fact that the two oldest copies with miniatures belong to the same text family hints that if an earlier illustrated manuscript existed it probably belonged to 'family n'. While nothing in either of the ninth-century copies conclusively demonstrates the existence of an older illustrated text, comparison of the few scenes shared by Paris.gr.510 and the Milan Gregory suggests that the miniaturists of both were sometimes inspired by – or at least familiar with – similar pictures in more ancient copies of Gregory's sermons.

The Milan Homilies contains almost 250 marginal illustrations, nearly all composed as black ink drawings filled in with gold, with touches of red paint (figs. 48–55).[51] The miniatures respond directly to the text, though narrative episodes are often reduced either to their essential components or to a portrait of the major protagonist. The only images not inspired directly by Gregory's words are the extended author portraits that preface most of the sermons; these show Gregory delivering the homily (the first words of which are usually inscribed on a scroll he holds), often

---

[47] See Bernardi in SC 247, 53–68.   [48] The negative evidence is presented throughout this book.

[49] See the comments in SC 247, 54–68; SC 270, 25–26, 32; SC 309, 67–80; SC 318, 64–73.

[50] For Milan, see esp. SC 318, 64–65, 73; for Paris, see esp. SC 270, 25–26, 32 and SC 318, 70–73.

[51] Grabar (1943a) published nearly all of the preserved miniatures and connected them with the relevant passages in the *PG* edition of the Homilies (note, however, that pl. V,1 corresponds with *PG* 35:420–421, not 460; and pl. X,2 corresponds with *PG* 35:1156, not 115); for colour reproductions, see Cavallo (1982), figs. 464–467.

to a group of people and occasionally with the subject of the sermon pictured alongside. Though universally agreed to be of the ninth century, the Milan Gregory has never been dated with further precision; it has been attributed to a number of provincial locales, most recently to Byzantine Italy.[52]

The manuscript has been badly treated: rebindings have left the text disordered, and nearly as many of its marginal images have been excised as still remain. Sometimes we can still identify a lost figure or scene through its remaining inscription: for example, the titulus IC XC flanks excised medallions on pp. 506 and 662, Peter once appeared on p. 129, John the Baptist on p. 199, Moses on p. 639, Abraham and Jeremiah on p. 660, Cyprian's beheading on p. 351, Jacob's struggle with the angel on p. 422, and the anastasis on p. 544. Several times – as, for example, on pp. 69 and 133 – the shape of the excision and its location at the beginning of a new sermon suggest that a preaching scene was excised, and sometimes the location of an excision furnishes a clue as to the original subject matter presented. But most often there is nothing left to indicate the intended subject of the excised image; and when, as occurs throughout the manuscript, whole margins have been removed, there is no way of knowing whether the strip was removed for its unmarked parchment or for the images that may have been painted on it. While we may speculate that the Milan Gregory originally contained about twice as many images as now survive, we can determine the subject matter of only a handful of these now-lost pictures.

The Milan miniatures that are preserved differ radically from those in Paris.gr.510 in their style and function. While the Milan Gregory recalls the ninth-century *Sacra Parallela* (Paris.gr.923) in its marginal, gold forms arranged in abbreviated scenes or presented as portraits (figs. 58–60, 64, 88, 90, 91, 94, 105, 106, 113, 114, 123, 152, 153, 160, 172),[53] the technical quality of the Milan manuscript is far below that of the *Sacra Parallela* and, unlike that of the latter manuscript, its somewhat cursory style does not demonstrate even tangential ties with that of Paris.gr.510. Further, rather than presenting exegetical supplements to Gregory's sermons as does Paris.gr.510, the Milan miniaturist drew inspiration directly from the text. Though by their very presence the Milan images authenticate or validate textual descriptions,[54] and like all miniatures reframe the words that they accompany, they do not self-consciously expand the meaning of those words to create visual commentaries.

On the surface, it would appear that the only feature the two copies of the Homilies share is their 'family n' text. The differences between the ways that the painters of the two manuscripts handle images, however, make those visual parallels that do appear doubly significant. These parallels are of three types.

First, although most of the Milan marginal portraits accompany passages that

[52] Cavallo (1977), 101–103; Grabar (1972), 20–21; Cavallo (1982), 506–508.
[53] Weitzmann (1979a) reproduced the miniatures.
[54] See Corrigan (1992), 118–119, 138; and, on the use of images to validate a text, chapter 1.

did not inspire illustration in Paris.gr.510, these passages were often marked by the Paris scribe with an initial or marginal sign. This suggests either that these were simply the obvious passages to sign, or that the makers of both manuscripts had before them a copy of Gregory's Homilies that flagged these same phrases with an image – as in the Milan copy – or a marginal notation, as in Paris.gr.510. The marginal notations that habitually accompany Gregory's sermons from at least the sixth century have been catalogued, but not fully coordinated with the sermons.[55] Comparison of a selection of the homilies suggests that the correspondence between the passages marked in the Milan and Paris Homilies goes beyond the remit of traditional scribal notations, but only further work on the annotations will permit precision on this point.

The second type of parallel is found in instances where the Paris Homilies shows a narrative composition that centres on a figure who is represented by a portrait in the Milan copy: Abraham's aborted sacrifice of Isaac on f. 174v (fig. 23), for example, responds to a passage in Gregory's sermon next to which the Milan painter placed a bust of Abraham.[56] But because the function of the illustrations in the two manuscripts is so different, it is unusual to find the same passage illustrated with the same narrative scene in both books. The third type of parallel – formed of the images that survive in the Milan Gregory, where so many crucial narrative scenes have been excised, and recur in the Paris Homilies, a manuscript almost diametrically opposed to the Milan copy in its style and the role of its miniatures – thus takes on particular weight.

Five miniatures in Paris.gr.510 find echoes in the Milan Gregory, and five more illustrate scenes that inscriptions demonstrate were excised from it. The five scenes or groupings that the two manuscripts still share will be considered in detail in later chapters; they are simply listed here:

1 Gorgonia's death, illustrating Gregory's funeral oration to his sister in the Paris (fig. 9) and Milan (fig. 49) Homilies. Though much of the Milan image is missing and the figure of Gorgonia is reversed, the groupings and architecture at each end of the deathbed are the same in both manuscripts.
2 Gregory and his father, illustrating the historical circumstances that prompted the first oration 'On peace' in Paris (fig. 10) and Milan, Ambrosiana E.49/50 inf., p. 118. In the only biographical scene inserted on this page in Paris.gr.510, the two Gregories stand together as they do in the Milan manuscript. It is the inclusion of the pair at all in Paris.gr.510 that is notable; the surrounding composition does not appear in the Milan manuscript.
3 The triple portrait of Gregory, Basil, and Gregory of Nyssa accompanying 'To Gregory of Nyssa' on f. 71v (fig. 13) of the Paris Gregory and p. 138 (fig. 51) in the Milan text; here, again, it is the inclusion of the trio on f. 71v that recalls the

---

[55] Astruc (1974); Mossay (1982); cf. Brubaker (1991), 24 note 11.   [56] See chapter 5.

Milan manuscript. Paris.gr.510 frames the figures and joins them with an image of Job; both features are lacking from the Milan Homilies.

4 Julian's visit to the demon, illustrating the first 'Invective against Julian' in Paris.gr.510 (fig. 39) and Ambrosiana E.49/50 inf. (fig. 53). Both books present an extensive narrative scene that, aside from the reversal of the two major figures, is virtually identical in the two versions. The most important difference is that in Paris.gr.510 two historical details have been added.

5 The portraits of Basil and Gregory of Nyssa illustrating the second 'Invective against Julian' on f. 409v of the Paris manuscript (fig. 40) and p. 785 in the Milan Gregory (fig. 55). That the pair, seemingly unmotivated in the Paris scene – which relies on Pseudo-Amphilochios' Life of Basil rather than Gregory's sermon – appear in the Milan manuscript, where Gregory's oration is the sole textual inspiration, suggests a connection.

Except for Julian's visit to the demon, these are all biographical scenes or portraits of the sort habitual in the Milan Gregory but more rarely found in Paris.gr.510. Their duplication thus suggests some sort of affiliation, but this suspicion is strengthened only by the narrative of Julian's visit to the demon. This is by far the most significant of the shared images, for it is the only one that extends beyond portraiture; it is also – if only because it is a narrative scene with a relative wealth of shared incidental detail – the most convincing link between the two manuscripts.

The abbreviated nature of most of the scenes that the two manuscripts share makes the Milan excisions of narrative scenes that would help define the relationship between Paris.gr.510 and the Milan Homilies particularly frustrating. The scenes in Paris.gr.510 for which preserved inscriptions document lost images in the Milan Gregory illustrate:

1 'On the plague of hail': the incipit miniature in the Milan copy has been excised from p. 146. Most incipit miniatures show Gregory preaching to a group of monks, but sometimes the image is more specific. Gregory's sermon on the Makkabees in the Milan Homilies, for example, shows Gregory preaching beside two rows of figures: the bottom row represents the audience; the top row portrays the subjects of the sermon.[57] Elsewhere, Gregory preaches against Julian the Apostate in the centre of the composition, flanked on one side by his audience (in this case a group of monks) and on the other by his subject, Julian.[58] The excised miniature on p. 146 thus presumably showed either Gregory preaching or, as in Paris.gr.510 (fig. 15), Gregory preaching with his father by an image of the hailstorm.

2 'On theology': the miniature of Jacob's struggle with the angel, identifiable by its preserved inscription, once appeared on p. 422 of the Milan manuscript; the scene recurs, with an identical inscription, on f. 174v of Paris.gr.510 (fig. 23).

[57] Grabar (1943a), pl. XXIX.   [58] Ibid., pl. LXVII,1.

3 'On Pentecost': this scene, identified by inscription, most unusually once prefaced Gregory's sermon in the Milan copy (p. 577) as it does, on f. 301r (fig. 30), in Paris.gr.510.

4 'Against the Arians': all of the relevant scenes have been excised from the Milan Gregory, where the sermon fills pp. 591–602; the various scenes are collected on f. 367v of Paris.gr.510 (fig. 38).

5 The second 'Invective against Julian': two scenes of Julian's advance on the Persians have been excised from the Milan manuscript (pp. 763, 764); a single image of the advance appears in Paris.gr.510 on the first register of f. 409v (fig. 40).

The frustratingly frequent removal of narrative scenes shared by both manuscripts from the Milan Gregory is, presumably, coincidental. Many more than just these narrative scenes have been excised from the Milan manuscript, and it seems improbable that the Ambrosiana text was systematically physically pilfered for models by the miniaturists responsible for Paris.gr.510. The parallels are nonetheless suggestive and, combined with the evidence of the shared scenes, seem to indicate that buried beneath the miniatures of the Paris Homilies lies a manuscript with illustrations that resembled in some ways those in the Milan Gregory. The one narrative scene that both ninth-century manuscripts still retain – Julian's visit to the demon – reveals a constellation of unusual shared details that would be hard to understand without postulating that the two miniaturists relied on an older and similar visual tradition. It is this that makes me suspect that the other, more random, parallels between the books should probably be attributed to familiarity with an earlier illustrated Homilies; for unless the Paris miniaturists knew the Milan Gregory itself (a possibility that cannot be excluded), the tradition that they seem to share can only have been conveyed by an illustrated Homilies.

Although, as we have seen, Paris.gr.510 apparently was not originally intended to have illustrations, the correspondence between marginal notations in Paris.gr.510 and marginal portraits in the Milan Gregory, coupled with the witness of the motifs shared by the two manuscripts, suggests that the text followed by the Paris scribe could well have had them. It may, in fact, have been the presence of pictures in the text provided to the scribe that inspired the inclusion of miniatures in Paris.gr.510. Be that as it may, comparison of the Paris and Milan manuscripts suggests that the artisans responsible for Paris.gr.510 knew at least some pictures that resembled those of the Milan Gregory. If I am correct in supposing that the Paris miniaturists had before them a copy of Gregory's sermons with images that resembled those in the Milan copy, the 'modernization' apparent in Paris.gr.510 (to which we shall return in chapter 2) surely isolated it from any conventionally illustrated Homilies manuscript as much as if the miniatures had been compiled *de novo*.

Fig. 48 *Milan, Ambrosiana cod. E.49/50 inf., p. 510: Solomon, Moses, Manoe, Peter, Paul*

Fig. 49 Milan, Ambrosiana cod. E.49/50 inf., p. 100: death of Gorgonia

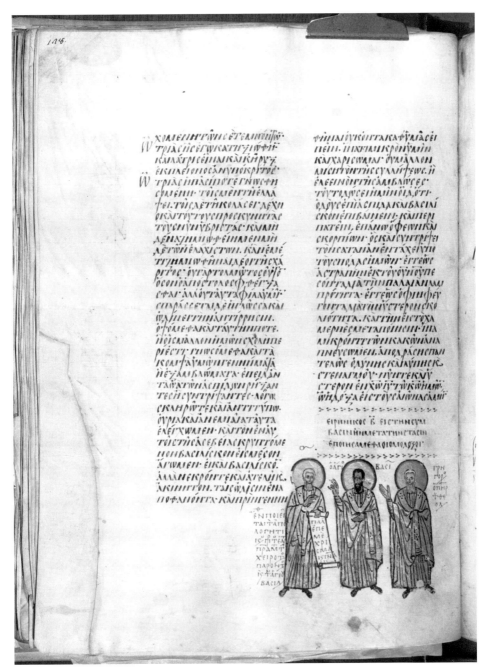

Fig. 50 Milan, Ambrosiana cod. E.49/50 inf., p. 128: Gregory of Nazianzus, Basil, and Gregory's father

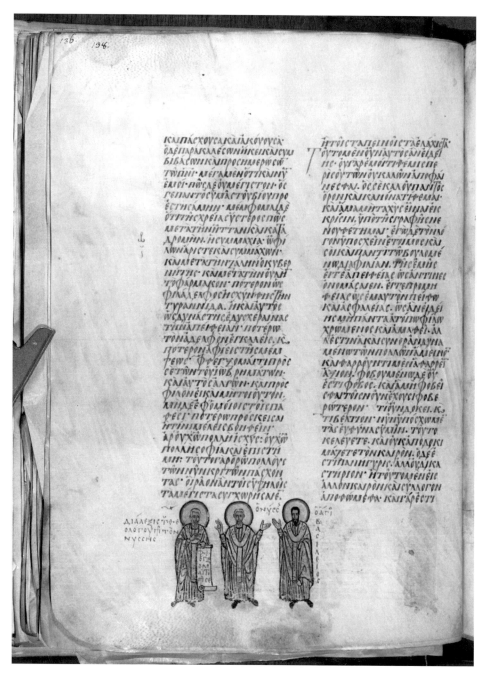

ΚΑΙΠΛΕΧΟΥΣΑΙΚΑΙΛΚΟΥΟΥΣΑ·
ΟΔΕΠΙΡΛΙΚΑΛΕΣΩΝΗΚΕΙΚΑΙΣΥΝ
ΒΙΒΑΣΩΝΚΑΙΠΡΟΣΗΛΔΕΡΩΣΕΩ
ΤΩΙΗΝ· ΛΙΕΓΑΛΕΝΟΤΙΚΑΛΜΥ
ΕΑΙΟΙ· ΠΩΣΛΕΟΥΛΙΕΓΙΣΤΟΙ· ΘΕ
ΓΕΙΝΑΤΟΣ·ΥΙΑΣΤΟΥΒΙΟΥΠΡΟ
ΕΣΤΙΣΚΑΛΗΝ· ΚΑΘΛΙΦΟΙΛΙΔΑΣ
ΟΤΙΤΗΣΧΡΕΙΑΣΥΣΤΕΡΟΣΙΠΩΣ
ΛΕΤΛΚΤΙΝΗΤΤΑΝΙΚΑΙΚΛΣΑ
ΔΡΟΜΗΝ· ΗΣΥΛΑΙΛΑΧΙΑ· Ω̄ΙΦΙ
ΛΩΝΛΡΙΣΤΕΚΑΙΣΩΜΛΧΗ·
ΚΑΙΛΕΤΚΤΗΓΛΛΗΝΟΙΚΥΒΕΡ
ΝΗΤΗΣ· ΚΑΙΛΕΤΚΤΗΝΟΥΛΗ
ΤΟΦΑΡΛΙΛΚΟΝ· ΠΟΤΕΡΟΝΩΣ
ΦΙΛΑ· ΕΚΦΟΣΗΧΥΙΦΗΕΣΤΗΙ
ΤΥΡΑΝΝΙΔΑ· ΉΚΑΛΛΥΤΟΣ
ΩΣΔΥΝΑΣΤΗΣΕΔΥΟΧΕΡΑΙΝΑΣ
ΤΗΝΛΛΕΙΨΕΙΑΝ· ΠΟΤΕΡΩ
ΤΟΝΛΔΕΟΝΕΓΚΑΛΕΙΣ· ΙΣ̄
ΠΟΤΕΡΟΝΑΦΕΙΣΤΗΣΛΛΕΑ
ΡΕΩΣ· ΦΘΕΓΧΟΛΙΤΙΠΡΟΣ
ΣΕΤΩΝΤΟΥΙΩΒ ῬΗΛΙΧΩΝ·
ΙΣΛΛΥΤΟΣΛΛΡΩΝ· ΚΑΙΠΡΟΣ
ΦΙΛΟΝΕΙΚΑΛΗΤΙΟΥΤΗΙ·
ΛΗΛΔΕΕ̄ΦΟΛΒΙΟΙΣΤΟΙΕΙΑ
ΦΕΕΙ· ΠΟΤΕΡΩΠΡΟΣΕΚΕΙΣΑΙ
ΗΤΙΝΑΚΕΚΕΙΣΕΒΗΙΦΕΙ·
ΑΡ̄ΟΥΧΩ̄ΠΟΛΗΙΣΧΥΕΣ· ΟΥΧ̄ῶ
ΠΟΛΗΣΟΦΙΑΙΣΝΕΗΙΣΤΗ
ΛΗΙ· ΤΟΥΤΩΑΡΟΘΟΛΟΛΟΓΟΥΣ
ΤΩΝΗΥΝΙΚΡΤΗΝΤΑΣΧΟΝ
ΤΑΣ· ΘΙΡΑΩΝΑΝΤΟΙΣΥΓ̄ΝΛΙΕ
ΤΑΛΛΕΓΙΣΤΑΣΥΓ̄ΧΩΡΙΕΣΝΕ·

ΉΤΟΙΣΤΑΠΕΙΝΟΙΣΤΛΕΛΛΧΙΣΤ̄
ΓΟΥΤΟΝΕΝΟΥΝΛΥΤΟΕΝΘΕΙΛΣΕΙ
ΝΕ· ΟΥΓΧΡΕΛΙΟΤΤΦΕΛΙΕΝΕ
ΡΙΣΟΥΤΩΝΟΥΚΑΛΩΝΛΠΟΦΛ
ΝΕΣΤΛΙ· ΘΕΣΕΚΑΛΟΥΠΛΝΤΟΣ
ΟΡΟΝΚΑΙΣΑΜΗΛΤΙΦΕΛΛ
ΚΛΜΛΜΛΗΤΛΧΣΕΗΜΕΝΕΙΣ
ΚΡΙΣΙΝ· ΥΠΟΤΗΣΓΡΑΦΗΣΕΠΕ
ΝΟΥΦΕΤΗΛΛΙ· ΕΓ̄ΩΔΕΤΗΝΟ
ΓΟΝΥΠΟΣΧΕΙΝΕΤΗΛΛΟΕΣΚΑΙ
ΕΟΗΚΛΜΛΝΤΙΤΩΒΟΥΛΟΛΙΕ
ΝΩΔΙΛΦΙΛΙΛΝ· ΤΗΣΕΛΛΗΣ
ΕΙΓΕΛΠΕΙΡΕΙΑΣΘΕΛΠΤΗΣΕ
ΟΝΟΛΙΛΣΑΙΕΝ· ΕΓΤΕΙΡΔΛΗ
ΦΕΙΛΣΘΕΛΛΥΤΗΝ· ΕΠΕΙΤΩ
ΚΑΙΛΣΦΛΛΕΙΛΣ· ΩΣΛΝΕΙΛΕΙ
ΗΣΛΛΠΛΝΤΛΧΤΙΝΟΝΦΙΛΗΝ
ΧΡΩΛΕΝΟΣΚΑΙΛΜΛΝΘΕΙ· ΛΛ
ΛΕΣΤΙΝΛΚΛΣΥΝΘΡΛΛΥΝΛ
ΛΕΗΙΩΤΩΠΟΛΛΩΝΛΛΛΕΙΝΟΤ̄
ΚΑΙΛΡΡΥΓΤΙΛΙΣΕΝΛΦΑΡΣΕΙ
ΛΥΙΟΝ· ΦΟΒΟΥΛΛΣΗΝΛΣΕΟΥ
ΕΣΤΙ ΦΟΒΟΣ· ΚΑΙΛΛΗΦΟΒΕΙ
ΣΘΛΝΤΙΣΟΥΗΕΧΟΥΣΙΦΟΒΕ
ΡΩΤΕΡΟΝ· ΤΙΟΥΝΛΔΟΚΕΙ·Κ̄
ΤΙΒΕΝΤΙΟΝ· ΜΗΜΗΠΟΣΧ̄ΛΣΕ
ΤΑΣΕΥΓΥΝΑΣΥΛΛΗ· ΤΟΥΤΟ
ΚΕΛΕΥΕΤΕ· ΚΑΙΟΥΚΛΠΟΔΡΚΙ
ΛΙΚΛΤΛΛΗΝΓΥΡΙΣ· ΛΛΛΟΥΔΛΙΚΛ
ΣΤΗΡΙΟΝ· ΗΤΟΥΤΟΛΙΕΝΕΙΣ
ΛΛΛΟΝΚΛΡΟΝΚΛΣΥΛΛΟΓΟΝ
ΛΠΟΘΩΛΕΘ̄· ΚΛΙΠ̄Ρ̄ΕΕΤΙ

ΔΙΛΛΕΞΙΣΤΟΥΘΕ
ΟΛΟΓΟΥΠ̄ΗΓ̄ΩΝ
ΝῩΣΣΗΣ

ὁνγες

ὁ·ἁγι
ΒΑΣΙΛΕΙ·ς

Fig. 51 Milan, Ambrosiana cod. E.49/50 inf., p. 138: Gregory of Nazianzus, Gregory of Nyssa, and Basil

I

Siting the miniatures: imagery in the ninth century

This chapter explores, from several different vantage points, how the makers of images reproduced and reinforced patterns of ninth-century Byzantine society, and how they contributed to the production of those patterns. It investigates ninth-century Byzantine images as indices of socially constructable meaning, and as constructors of social meaning.[1] My focus is on the presuppositions that conditioned the way the patron of Paris.gr.510 could envisage the manuscript, the way its producers could conceive it, and the way its original viewers could see it.

While the private meanings that an image could have for any Byzantine are irretrievable, we stand on slightly firmer ground when we try to understand the socially constructed meaning of images for certain defined groups. Even then, the ties that bind objects to their producers, context, and audience are seldom articulated; however imperfect, our best guide to how images could work and how people could understand them in the ninth century emerges from the assessment and comparison of recurring patterns in both verbal and visual communications. The following discussion of these patterns has been divided into a number of compartments which overlap inextricably; they are isolated only to clarify the arguments. Together, I hope, they will give a framework for ninth-century visual culture, inside which Paris.gr.510 can usefully be viewed.

BYZANTINE PERCEPTION OF THE VISUAL

Byzantium was not a monolithic culture, and the ways Byzantines wrote about what they saw depended on the situation and intent of the author, and differed as well over time and place. Nearly all, however, sound foreign now: Byzantine

---

[1] See Spiegel (1990); also Marx (1973), 146; Bechow (1975), 13–15 and (1976), 24–27; Ortner (1984), 158–159; Haldon (1986); Moreland (1991), 17–20.

responses to the visual as expressed in words are quite distinct from modern perceptions of Byzantine art.[2] Two examples illuminate the contrast.

The apse mosaic at Hagia Sophia (fig. 56) is one of the few surviving remains of
ninth-century monumental imagery, and it is the only one for which we have a contemporary reaction. The mosaic shows the Virgin Mary, seated, with the Christ
Child sitting upright on her lap;[3] the response was delivered in Hagia Sophia by the
patriarch Photios, who preached a sermon commemorating the completion of the
mosaic on Holy Saturday (29 May) in 867.[4] The sermon has agendas beyond the
description of a mosaic that Photios' audience could anyway see as they listened to
him. Were we to assume that Photios' intent was art-historical description, in fact,
it would be hard to reconcile his words with the mosaic preserved at Hagia Sophia –
and a number of scholars have duly argued that the mosaic we now see is not the
one Photios inaugurated.[5] But we cannot read Photios' sermon as if it were a
museum catalogue, nor can we suppose that the perceptions and expectations of
Photios and his ninth-century audience duplicated our own. As Liz James and
Ruth Webb noted, the type of text in which we normally find Byzantine descriptions of images – ekphrasis – was never intended to provide an objective record;
instead, ekphrasis focused on the meaning of the depiction.[6] They suggest,
convincingly, that Photios' aim was 'to express the Virgin herself, not to record a
particular image of her for posterity'.[7]

Photios nonetheless twice referred specifically to the quality of the image. The
first reference – 'for the painter's skill, which is a reflection of inspiration from
above, has thus exactly established the natural (life-like) imitation'[8] – reads oddly
to a modern viewer, for the mosaic is not, to our eyes, a 'natural imitation', and
Photios seems to deny the mosaicist the autonomy that we assume for artists. But
we follow different criteria from the Byzantines, who distinguished between idols –
which represented something imaginary – and icons, which had the original holy
figures as prototypes, and differed from them only in substance. Any religious

---

[2] For an early expression of the need to divorce ourselves from modern presuppositions when
dealing with Byzantium, see Lemerle (1952), 49–58.

[3] Mango and Hawkins (1965), 115–151.

[4] Homily 17: ed. Laourdas (1959), 164–172; trans. Mango (1958), 286–296. See too ibid., 279;
Cormack (1985), 146–160, esp. 153–154; Macrides and Magdalino (1988), 79–80; Sansterre (1994),
228–231. On Photios (patriarch 858–867, 877–886), see *ODB* 3, 1669–1670, and chapter 5.

[5] Most recently, Oikonomides (1985b), 111–115; for a thorough critique, Speck (1987), 302–312.

[6] James and Webb (1991).   [7] Ibid., 12–13; quotation, 13.

[8] Ὑπόκρισις ἄρα τῆς ἄνωθεν ἐπιπνοίας ἡ ζωγράφος τέχνη οὕτως ἀκριβῶς εἰς φύσιν τὴν μίμησιν
ἔστησε (ed. Laourdas [1959], 167); a similar translation appears in Mango (1958), 290. James and Webb
(1991), 13, supply an alternative: 'The art of painting . . . has set up such an exact imitation of her
nature'. However, because *eis phusin* follows normal, classicizing usage – *eis* plus an accusative singular
noun functions as an adjective – 'natural' or 'life-like' seems a preferable translation to 'of her nature'.
I thank John Haldon for help on this point.

image was thus by definition a reproduction of the original, and inspired 'from above'; if inspiration came from the artisan alone, the result would have been an idol, not an icon.[9] Byzantine texts thus almost invariably played down the 'art of the painter'. As expressed by the 787 Council, 'the idea, therefore, and the tradition are [the fathers'], not the painter's, only the art is of the painter'.[10] Photios' 'the painter's skill . . . is a reflection of inspiration from above' and, in a different sermon, 'a divine power superior to our own has formed its beauty'[11] continue the distinction between the inspiration and the execution. As Kenneth Parry observed, the Byzantine use of the term 'life-like' could simply mean that the image was inspired by a real person rather than representing, say, an imaginary mythological beast.[12] That Photios (among others) reacted within the accepted framework of orthodox image theory should not, however, blind us to his sympathy for, and response to, beauty and skill.[13]

Photios' second qualitative reference reads: 'To such an extent have the lips been made flesh by the colours, that they appear merely to be pressed together and stilled as in the mysteries, yet their silence is not at all inert neither is the fairness of her form derivatory, but rather it is the real archetype.'[14] The end of this sentence links image and prototype; the opening lines describe and then interpret: for Photios, the mosaic is a window to a real woman, and he is exploring his reactions to her as mediated through the image.[15] This is not the way that we normally respond to Byzantine images, and Photios' reaction to the visual suggests a different way of thinking and talking about what one sees – a different way of seeing – from the way we see and process the seen.

Photios' response to the Hagia Sophia mosaic is not unique. In his Life of Tarasios (patriarch 784–806), written between 843 and 847, Ignatios the Deacon comments on a lost (or imagined) martyrdom sequence that shares numerous points of resemblance with the martyrdom of the Makkabees painted less than forty years later in Paris.gr.510 (f. 340r; fig. 34).[16] As in virtually all Byzantine depictions of martyrdoms, the dying saints elicit little sympathy from most modern

[9] See notes 47, 48, and 50 below.

[10] Mansi XIII, 252C; trans. Sahas (1986a), 84. See also note 72 below; de Maffei (1974), 69–75; and Cormack (1977b), 155, 157, 162. The iconoclasts condemned painters for their greed: e.g. Mansi XIII, 248E; trans. Sahas (1986a), 81; and Mango (1972), 166.

[11] Homily 10,3: ed. Laourdas (1959), 100; trans. Mango (1958), 185.

[12] Parry (1989), 180–181. Kazhdan and Maguire (1991), 8–9, suggest that 'life-like' meant that an image followed recognizable conventions, and survey some of the earlier literature on Byzantine usage of the term. See now Maguire (1996).   [13] So too Maguire (1992), 137–138.

[14] Ed. Laourdas (1959), 167; trans. Mango (1958), 290.   [15] Cf. James and Webb (1991), 13.

[16] Ed. Heikel (1891); trans. I. Ševčenko (1984); a new edition of the text by Stephanos Efthymiadis is expected, see Efthymiadis (1991). On some of the interpretive problems it poses, Speck (1986); on the martyrdom sequence described, Walter (1980), Wolska-Conus (1980), Brubaker (1989a); on its possible location, Ruggieri (1991), 202. On Tarasios, *ODB* 3, 2011.

Fig. 56 Istanbul, Hagia Sophia: apse mosaic

viewers, to whom they appear remarkably detached. Yet Ignatios describes images of martyrs in highly emotional terms. He ignores even the names of the saints to concentrate instead on the viewer's response to their torments, as a typical sentence demonstrates: 'For who would see a man represented in colours and struggling for truth, disdaining fire . . . and would not be drenched in warm tears and groan with compunction?'[17] Ignatios' description is more directive than Photios' – though Photios too used rhetorical questions to channel the sympathies of his audience[18] – but both suggest that in the ninth century empathy was an accepted literary response to images that seem to us detached and static.[19]

Such literary conventions apparently reproduced the actual perceptions of ninth-century Byzantines, when the tears, fear, marvel and amazement inspired by

[17] Ed. Heikel (1891), 413; trans. I. Ševčenko (1984). See further the discussion of f. 340r in chapter 6.
[18] E.g. Homily 17,5: ed. Laourdas (1959), 170; trans. Mango (1958), 294.
[19] See further Brubaker (1989a). James and Webb (1991) conflate emotional responses in general with specific manifestations of emotion that the author assures the audience it will experience (e.g. projected tears), which do not become a standard of image writing until around the year 800.

images are recorded in numerous and disparate sources. The Acts of the Ecumenical Council of 787 cite the tears that contemplation of religious images generated as proof of the sanctity of such paintings.[20] The *Parastaseis Syntomoi Chronikai* (written sometime between 775 and 843, probably around 780), a guide to the antique statuary of Constantinople composed by less highly trained authors, fails to provide any real descriptions of the sculptures and instead concentrates on their effects on the beholder.[21] The spurious letter of Pope Gregory II to Emperor Leo III – probably, as Jean Gouillard argued, written around the year 800 by a Constantinopolitan monk – describes the compunction, emulation, and tears inspired by images on three separate occasions.[22] An account of the conversion of Boris of Bulgaria in 864, preserved in a text from the middle of the tenth century, records the king *demanding* an emotional response from imagery: Boris asks a certain Methodios to paint 'anything he might wish, on condition that the sight of the painting should induce fear and amazement in its spectators'.[23] Authors writing from a range of levels assumed the power of images to elicit emotional and person-alized responses.

As these texts make clear, ninth-century Byzantine writers saw images *as images* that were susceptible to qualitative remarks such as Photios'. But these authors also assumed that an image was not only a material depiction; their response was not only to the image, but also to the subject of that image. Texts dealing with monu-mental images and icons presume an interactive relationship, expressed in person-alized terms, that seems to parallel lived experience.

TEXT AND IMAGE IN NINTH-CENTURY MANUSCRIPTS

Miniatures in manuscripts were not usually exposed to public gaze, and they were not the subjects of ninth-century ekphrasis. Their cultural milieu is defined by two characteristic features, both of them required by the medium itself. First, and obvi-ously, viewers of miniatures had access to books; and secondly, most of them were almost certainly literate.[24] What proportion of Byzantines were literate, either functionally or actively, is unclear; it is not even certain to what extent literacy was

[20] Mansi XIII, 9, 11, 32. See Rouan (1981), 433–434; Sansterre (1994), 204. Tears had long been asso-ciated with piety and prayer (see, e.g., Cameron [1979], 20 and note 31; Auzépy [1987], 161); it is the overt association expressed here that is worthy of note.

[21] Ed. Cameron and Herrin (1984); on the date, I. Ševčenko (1992b), 289–293; Kresten (1994), 21–52. Cf. James (1996).

[22] Gouillard (1968), 285 lines 114–116, 289 lines 154–158, 289–291 lines 164–165. See also Stein (1980), 89–137. For another example, Corrigan (1995).

[23] Ed. Bekker (1838), 163–164; trans. Mango (1972), 190–191; see also Cormack (1977b), 160–162.

[24] A donor who gave a decorated book to a church might or might not be literate, but once the manuscript was housed in a church treasury its audience was automatically limited.

confined to particular groups in the ninth century.[25] But most Byzantines had at least passive familiarity with books as public vehicles of communication and authority, particularly the gospels and perhaps also the law codes: at the very least, Byzantines heard texts read aloud, and operated in a system that recognized the potential authority of the written word. It nonetheless remains unlikely that most Byzantines had frequent access to miniatures. Functional service books were rarely illustrated,[26] while illuminated manuscripts were expensive and often kept locked in libraries and treasuries, which restricted (and defined) their audiences. The small scale of miniature painting suggests, too, that viewers of miniatures were almost of necessity the actual readers (or viewers) of the text; it also assumes an intimate relationship between image and beholder. Miniatures cannot be seen as didactic tools meant to educate the unlettered or confirm broad truths to a general audience. Instead, they address a restricted group, most of whom could have written, read, and thought about texts. More than any other pictorial medium, miniatures speak to and for the same audience as do texts; they share a specific cultural niche with the authors of, and intended audience for, most of the texts that provide our written documentary evidence for the ninth century. Though words and images communicate differently, here each can legitimately be used to help understand the other.[27]

As expressed in written form, most statements about images throughout the ninth century appear in anti-Jewish polemic (later recycled into the anti-Islamic dialogues) or in texts generated by the iconoclast debate and its aftermath. The iconoclast debate, in particular, subjected one crucial component of illustrated manuscripts – the relationship between text and image – to intense scrutiny.

The miniatures in a manuscript usually presuppose a text; a text accompanied by them may presume images. The two can interact with each other: while miniatures would not exist without an enframing book, the way that they interpret the words can have profound implications on subsequent interpretation. Such interaction is evident in the extensively illustrated manuscripts preserved from the ninth century. In addition to Paris.gr.510, the manuscripts of concern here are the copy of the Homilies in Milan, introduced in the Introduction (figs. 48–55); the Paris *Sacra Parallela*; the marginal psalters now at Moscow, Mount Athos, and Paris; and the Vatican 'Christian Topography'.

---

[25] On Byzantine literacy, Browning (1978), 39–54, and Mullett (1990), 156–185. The prominence of tituli in Byzantine painting may suggest widespread pragmatic literacy; it may equally likely, and possibly at the same time, indicate the symbolic power of the written word – an avenue profitably explored by scholars dealing with the Latin west (e.g. Camille [1985], 26–49; McKitterick [1990], 297–318), though its application to Byzantium is problematic since a broader spectrum of the populace apparently read there than in the west, more diverse literature was produced, and silent reading seems never to have died out: see Moffat (1977), 85–92; Patlagean (1968), 109 and (1979) 264–278.

[26] See Lowden (1990).   [27] Cf. Diebold (1992); Brubaker (1995).

The *Sacra Parallela* (Paris.gr.923) contains a collection of quotations attributed to John of Damascus; like the Milan Gregory, it includes marginal illustrations in which the predominant colour is gold (figs. 58–60, 64, 88, 90, 91, 94, 105, 106, 113, 114, 123, 152, 153, 160, 172).[28] Also like those of the Milan manuscript, the miniatures of the *Sacra Parallela* include a large proportion of portraits, often in medallions, and usually reduce narrative scenes to their essentials. The miniaturist of the *Sacra Parallela* was, however, less constrained by the text, and was a more proficient painter. In fact, the *Sacra Parallela* is stylistically related to Paris.gr.510, and for this reason I am inclined to attribute it to Constantinople, and date it to the third quarter of the ninth century.[29]

The Khludov Psalter in Moscow (Historical Museum, gr.129), like the Milan Gregory and the *Sacra Parallela*, contains marginal illustrations, though in the psalter they are in full colour (figs. 57, 85, 103, 104, 110, 118, 122, 125, 131, 142, 143, 151, 166).[30] Some pictures illustrate the psalm texts directly, in a fashion analogous to the Milan miniatures; others provide instead a visual commentary on the text, and in this anticipate the Paris Homilies. Unlike those in the Paris Gregory, however, the commentary miniatures in the Khludov Psalter are usually at least partially explained by accompanying inscriptions. For this reason, among others, the psalter is believed to pre-date Paris.gr.510: it was probably produced between 843 and 847 in Constantinople.[31] Mount Athos, Pantokrator 61 (figs. 69, 102, 111, 120, 133, 144, 145, 158, 164, 173) is closely related, and was evidently made slightly later – but still apparently earlier than Paris.gr.510 – also in the capital.[32] A third, now incomplete, ninth-century marginal psalter, Paris.gr.20 (fig. 146), was probably produced in Constantinople as well.[33]

The 'Christian Topography' was compiled in the middle of the sixth century, apparently by Constantine of Antioch, known since the eleventh century by the invented name of Kosmas Indikopleustes.[34] It seems likely that the text was illus-

---

[28] Reproduced in Weitzmann (1979a); colour reproductions in Cavallo (1982), figs. 459–463; *Byzance* (1992), 190 with earlier literature.

[29] On the style, see further chapter 2. Weitzmann (1979a), 20–23, attributes the *Sacra Parallela* to Palestine. Grabar (1972), 21–24, 87–88 and Cavallo (1982), 506–508 argue for an Italian, and perhaps Roman, origin. Jaeger (1947), 101–102; Wright (1980), 8; and Cormack (1986b), 635 note 39 assign it to Constantinople. On the date, Osborne (1981a).

[30] Reproductions in Ščepkina (1977). Corrigan (1992) provides the most thorough study, with earlier literature.

[31] The association with the patriarch Methodios, first proposed by I. Ševčenko (1965), has been endorsed by Walter (1987), 220, and by Corrigan (1992), 124–134.

[32] Reproduced in Dufrenne (1966) and, partially, Pelekanides *et al.* 3 (1979), figs. 180–237. On the dating, Walter (1987), 220; for discussion and earlier literature, Corrigan (1992) and Anderson (1994).

[33] Reproduced in Dufrenne (1966); *Byzance* (1992), 349–350 with earlier literature; on the date, Walter (1987), 219.

[34] Wolska-Conus (1989), 28–30 provides the reidentification, which is based on the writings of Anania of Shirak.

trated from its inception: Constantine/Kosmas was convinced that biblical and scientific reasoning demonstrated that the world conformed with the shape of the ark of the covenant, an argument clarified by the use of diagrams, maps, and images that are introduced in the text itself.[35] For his thesis, Constantine/Kosmas was taken to task in the ninth century by the patriarch Photios.[36] The text was nonetheless copied and illustrated at this time, and survives as Vat.gr.699 (figs. 75–77, 138, 150, 156).[37] Close formal ties with the Paris Homilies suggest that the Vatican 'Topography' was produced in the capital during the last quarter of the ninth century.[38] The miniatures themselves are eclectic in both subject matter and format: all are painted in full colour, but may be framed or unframed, full-page or inserted in one of the two columns of text that run down each page, and they present both isolated figures and developed narrative sequences.

Two Job manuscripts – Patmos, Monastery of St John, cod.171 (possibly of the late eighth century) and Venice, Marciana gr.538 (dated by colophon to 905) – should also be mentioned here.[39] Though they will be only rarely cited in the following discussion, which focuses on manuscripts with a broader range of subject matter, it should be noted that their marginal miniatures allow the same kind of interaction between text and image that occurs in the marginal psalters and the Milan Gregory.[40]

The range exhibited by the manuscripts just introduced is not terribly surprising, for the Byzantines wrote (and presumably thought) more about imagery during the years immediately preceding the production of these books than at any other time in their history. Byzantine writings about images, some directed against Jews and others concerned with the iconoclast controversy, may resonate with deeper concerns: Averil Cameron has suggested that the controversy surrounding the use of sacred images formed part of a larger intellectual realignment, a battle to determine who had access to the truth.[41] However we interpret the debates, ninth-century miniatures illuminate an actuality: how painters really formed images while, and shortly after, Byzantine theories about images were being expounded and while, perhaps, the Byzantine world was redefining itself. Taken together, the words and the pictures allow us to examine the interface between theory and practice; between what the Byzantines wrote about images, and what the images themselves communicated.

---

[35] SC 141, 159, and 197; Wolska (1962).

[36] In his *Bibliotheke* (on which see chapter 5), codex 36: ed. Henry I (1959), 21; trans. Wilson (1994), 31–32.

[37] Reproduced in Stornajolo (1908); see also Wolska-Conus (1990), 155–191, with earlier literature. On some of the deviations of the Vatican manuscript from its model, Brubaker (1977).

[38] Julien Leroy (1974), 73–78, argued for an Italo-Greek origin.

[39] Weitzmann (1935), figs. 325–349; Cavallo (1982), 506–507, figs. 451–453.

[40] See Corrigan (1992), esp. 104–111.   [41] Cameron (1992b). See also Dagron (1979).

ICONOPHILE ARGUMENTS ABOUT IMAGES

The preserved eighth- and ninth-century texts that deal with imagery are almost all iconophile,[42] and they concentrate on four issues: the definition and justification of images; the role of tradition; the functions of images; and the relationship between images, texts, and speech.

I emphasize these issues with caution in the following discussion. The textual evidence has the advantage of providing words, which we think we can understand, about images, the understanding of which is more elusive and diffuse.[43] But the written word has its own distinct type of cultural imprint. What Janet Nelson has claimed so neatly with regard to the Carolingians – 'Literacy is a kind of technology: literacy is also a frame of mind, and a framer of minds'[44] – is, I suspect, equally true of ninth-century Byzantines, and particularly those Byzantines for whom miniatures were relevant. A change in medium reframes the message; it also reframes ways of thinking about messages. While the visual and the written are not antithetical (miniatures and texts were normally directed by, for, and at the same people, operating within the same cultural and historical formation), they are different, and their distinctions, as well as their shared features, are important.

The definition of images officially proposed by the iconophile Council of 787 reads: 'The [sacred] image resembles the prototype, not with regard to essence, but only with regard to the name and to the position of the members which can be characterized'.[45] The Council's distinction between image and prototype relied on earlier arguments;[46] coupled with the argument that Christ's incarnation had effectively destroyed the whole notion of idols,[47] it was meant to defuse the charges of idolatry levelled by, in this instance, the iconoclasts by demonstrating that the Christian image itself was not divine, because it did not partake of the divine

[42] The most recent theological summary is Giakalis (1994); see also e.g. de Maffei (1974); Rouan [Auzépy] (1981); Auzépy (1990); Parry (1996b). Iconophile refutations of anti-image tenets reveal, at least dimly, the other side of the argument, as does iconoclast imagery: see Grabar (1957), 115–180; Mango (1972), 152–153, 156–165; Cormack (1977a); Lafontaine-Dosogne (1987b); the description of how the iconoclast Emperor Constantine V 'lavished many allowances from the public treasury' on 'a great number of artisans skilled in construction' in Nikephoros' *Breviarium* (ed. Mango [1990b], 160–161); and the Vatican Ptolemy of 754 (Wright [1985], 355–362).

[43] See Miles (1985), 29–35.   [44] J. Nelson (1990), 262.

[45] Mansi XIII, 244B4–6, cf. 252D, 257D, 261D; trans. Sahas (1986a), 77, 84, 89, 92.

[46] E.g. by John of Damascus (see note 65 below) – 'An image is of like character with its prototype [πρωτότυπον], but with a certain difference. It is not like its archetype [ἀρχέτυπον] in every way' – in 'Against those who attack divine images' I,9: ed. Kotter (1975), 83–84; trans. Anderson (1980), 19. See further Alexander (1958), 23–53.

[47] Iconophile texts usually credit this formulation to the patriarch Germanos, whose resignation in 730 coincided with the introduction of Iconoclasm. See Grumel (1922), 165–175, esp. 169–171; and Schönborn (1976), 145. John of Damascus, among others, reiterated the differences between idols and images: 'Against those who attack divine images' II, 4–11: ed. Kotter (1975), 71–75, 79–80, 96–102.

essence of the prototype.[48] Further, divinity was adored, and received *latreia*, but images were only honoured, and received *proskynesis*. The Council that reinstated Iconoclasm in 815 obligingly dropped the charge of idolatry,[49] but – perhaps because the point was important in contemporary arguments directed against the Jews and Muslims, who also opposed religious images – around 820 the deposed iconophile patriarch Nikephoros continued to rebut the charge, arguing that idols were fraudulent images because, unlike images of holy figures, they had no archetype.[50] Nikephoros also countered the arguments presented by the Council of 815 that a picture of Christ either heretically circumscribed both his natures, human and divine, or separated them by only representing his human nature,[51] by vehemently refuting the equation of circumscription and painting.[52]

The iconophile separation of the divine essence from the image insisted that the viewer bridged the gap between the visual reflection of divinity and its genuine contemplation. The viewer, in other words, participated in the meaning of the image. Modern image theory has devoted itself to demonstrating that this interaction is inevitable – it is, for example, crucial to Ernst Gombrich's 1956 concept of the 'beholder's share' and to Victor Burgin's concept of the 'seeing subject' thirty years later[53] – but that the Byzantine viewer supplied the essence of the image is not a figment of modern speculation: it was acknowledged by the Byzantines themselves. In Byzantine terms, 'the power of sight...sends the essence of the thing seen on to the mind'.[54] It is no accident that recognition of this process and an emphasis on 'the power of sight' (to which we shall return later in this chapter) coincided with written definitions that demanded a separation between the essence of an image and its form. As the ekphrastic texts of Photios and Ignatios the Deacon have already been used to demonstrate, ninth-century Byzantines charged the beholder's share with singular importance.

The force of the beholder's share in the viewing of images is implicit in another major tenet of iconophile rhetoric. Following in the footsteps of St Basil, iconophile theologians continually insisted that 'the honour given to the image is

---

[48] See the Life of Michael Synkellos: Cunningham (1991), 68–71, 76–79; Ladner (1953), 3–34, esp. 14–16.   [49] See Alexander (1953), 40–41.

[50] *Antirrheticus* I, 28–29: *PG* 100:277; Mondzain-Baudinet (1990), 109–110; see also Alexander (1958), 199, and Travis (1984), 140–141. In the same passage, Nikephoros stressed that the image and its archetype differed 'in essence and substratum', and added that an image was 'an artifact shaped in imitation of a pattern but differing in substance and subject; for if it does not differ in some respect, it is not an image nor an object differing from the model'. On Nikephoros (patriarch 806–815), see *ODB* 3, 1477. See also a letter from Theodore of Stoudion (see note 115 below) to Plato: *PG* 99:500; trans. Mango (1972), 173–174. On the necessity of this argument in anti-Jewish and anti-Islamic polemic, Corrigan (1992), 37–40, 91–94.   [51] Alexander (1953), 40. Cf. Schönborn (1976), 161–168.

[52] Alexander (1958), 206–211. Other anti-iconoclast polemics – e.g. an anonymous refutation of John the Grammarian: Gouillard (1966), 179 – note that 'resemble' does not mean the same thing as 'be identical'.   [53] E.g. Gombrich (1969) (his 1956 Mellon lectures) and Burgin (1986), 69.

[54] Photios, Homily 17,5: ed. Laourdas (1959), 170–171; trans. Mango (1958), 294.

transferred to its prototype',[55] for anyone 'who swears by an image, swears by the one the image represents'.[56] The viewer prays to an image, realizing at least in theory that it is not the painted or sculpted form itself that receives veneration or supplicating prayers, but the person that the viewer understands is represented.[57] The association between image and prototype made by the beholder was intimate. The Council of 787 asked, 'Who does not know that when an image is dishonoured the insult applies to the person who is depicted?';[58] Nikephoros tells us that the Emperor Phokas' son-in-law hated him because 'he had been insulted on account of the removal of his own image [from] alongside that of Phokas';[59] and the miniature in the Khludov Psalter, visually equating the iconoclast John the Grammarian whitewashing an icon of Christ with Stephanos and Longinos tormenting Christ on the cross (fig. 57), expresses this same idea pictorially.[60] As Nikephoros' account demonstrates, the close affiliation between image and prototype did not apply only to religious images, and the iconophiles were careful to observe that 'dishonour shown to the emperor's image is dishonour shown to the emperor himself'.[61] The iconoclasts' denial of this quality of images was, we are told, tested by St Stephen the Younger. According to his *vita*, in an attempt to unmask the hypocrisy of the iconoclasts the saint threw coins bearing the effigy of the emperor on the ground in the presence of the court and it was only with great effort that Constantine V, comprehending the trap Stephen was laying for him, restrained his attendants from attacking Stephen forthwith.[62]

The iconoclast argument that an image of Christ heretically divided his divine and human natures by representing only the latter was apparently a favourite of the Emperor Constantine V. As the iconophiles were quick to point out in return, the disinclination to distinguish between Christ's two natures implicit in Constantine's thesis smacked of the Monophysite heresy.[63] The distinction between Christ's human and divine natures was, indeed, stressed by iconophiles from Germanos (patriarch 715–730) onwards, who saw in the incarnation a

---

[55] John of Damascus, 'Against those who attack divine images' I,21, 35 (= II,31, III,48), III,41: ed. Kotter (1975), 108, 147, 143; trans. Anderson (1980), 29, 36, 89. Life of Michael the Synkellos: Cunningham (1991), 92–93. For Nikephoros, see Travis (1984), 53. See further de Maffei (1974), 41–45.

[56] John of Damascus, 'Against those who attack divine images' II,21: ed. Kotter (1975), 120; trans. Anderson (1980), 65–66.

[57] In practice, such detachment was not always there, and individuals sometimes responded directly to the icon's material presence: see further Auzépy (1987); Dagron (1991).

[58] Mansi XIII, 325D; trans. Sahas (1986a), 145.   [59] *Breviarium* 1,1: ed. Mango (1990b), 34–37.

[60] It is also a polemical statement accusing the iconoclasts of denying Christ's human nature.

[61] John of Damascus, 'Against those who attack divine images' II,61 (citing Chrysostom), II,66 (citing Anastasios): ed. Kotter (1975), 163–165; trans. Anderson (1980), 68, 69–70. See also Ladner (1953), 20–22, and note 59 above.

[62] *PG* 100:1156D–1160B. Marie-France Auzépy's edition of this text is expected shortly.

[63] For discussion (relying primarily on Theodore of Stoudion: note 115 below), see Henry (1976), 21–25. Cf. Schönborn (1976), 171–172.

Fig. 57 Moscow, Historical Museum, cod.129, f. 67r: crucifixion; iconoclasts whitewash an icon of Christ

justification of religious images.[64] Both points were well expressed by John of Damascus (ca. 675–ca. 753/4), who wrote, on the difference between picturing the incarnate and the divine Christ, 'I do not draw an image of the immortal Godhead, but I paint an image of God who became visible in the flesh';[65] and, on the incarnation as justification for religious art, 'It is obvious that when you contemplate God becoming man, then you may depict him clothed in human form.'[66] It is difficult to assess how familiar the Byzantines clustered around the capital were with John's corpus (while the 787 Council defended his name from the abuse heaped upon it by the 754 Council without actually citing any of his iconophile writings,[67] this cannot be taken to imply that his works were unknown;[68] and certainly some of his writings were cited in the third quarter of the ninth century by Photios);[69] but the ideas that John expressed are echoed by contemporary sources written in Constantinople and its environs. The Council of 787, for example, argued the incarnation thesis even more strongly than had John: 'by making an image of Christ in his human form one . . . confesses that God the Word became man truly, not in conjecture'.[70] The iconoclasts' denial of imagery was therefore seen as a denial of the incarnation, as expressed by, among others, the 787 Council and reiterated in the Synodikon of Orthodoxy.[71]

The force of tradition and the witness of the Old Testament were also called upon to justify the production of religious images. Such statements derived their authority from the strength of Byzantine belief in the importance of the past, as exemplified by the Acts of the 787 Council: 'The making of images is not an invention of the painters but an accepted institution and tradition of the catholic Church; and that which excels in antiquity is worthy of respect.'[72] Old Testament references

[64] See Grumel (1922), 167; Henry (1976), 21–25; and note 71 below.

[65] John of Damascus, 'Against those who attack divine images' I,4: ed. Kotter (1975), 76; trans. Anderson (1980), 16. On John, see *ODB* 2, 1063–1064.

[66] John of Damascus, 'Against those who attack divine images' I,8; cf. I,16, 51: ed. Kotter (1975), 82, 89, 154; trans. Anderson (1980), 18, 23, 40.

[67] Mansi XIII, 356C-D, 357B-D; trans. Sahas (1986a), 168–170.

[68] See Cameron (1992c), 87–88; Sansterre (1994), 209–213.

[69] See *Amphilochia*, questions 80, 130, and 235 (ed. Westerink 5 [1986], 112–114, 139; 6,1 [1987], 18) and epistles 1 and 162 (ed. Laourdas and Westerink 1 [1983], 15; 3 [1984], 19).

[70] Mansi XIII, 344E; trans. Sahas (1986a), 160.

[71] 787 Council: 'they spoke iniquities against the nature of his incarnation' (Mansi XIII, 205E; trans. Sahas [1986a], 50); see further Parry (1989), 177–178, and Barber (1991), 57–60, who traces the idea back to Germanos, who built in turn on the Quinisext Council. See also e.g. a letter from Theodore of Stoudion to John the Grammarian (Grumel [1937], 185) and the Life of Michael the Synkellos (Cunningham [1991], 88–89). Kalavrezou (1990) has suggested that Mary's identification as *theotokos* shifted to *meter theou* in the ninth century because the new emphasis on Christ's humanity required a stress on Mary as mother.

[72] Mansi XIII, 252B (cf. 217D, 220E); trans. Sahas (1986a), 84 (59, 61). See also John of Damascus, 'Against those who attack divine images' I,56 (= II,52), I,60 (= II,56, III,53), I,66 (= II,69): ed. Kotter (1975), 158, 161, 166; trans. Anderson (1980), 43, 45, 47; and Nikephoros, *Antirrheticus* III,3, *PG* 100:380; Mondzain-Baudinet (1990), 186; Alexander (1958), 244; Travis (1984), 154–155.

were cited to demonstrate that God condoned imagery, as witnessed by the cheru-bim on the ark of the covenant (Exodus 25:18–20).[73] Iconophiles also latched on to the visions of divinity recorded in the prophetic books of the Old Testament, and argued that the ability of prophets to see an image of divinity was extended to all humanity through the incarnation, when ordinary people saw Christ.[74]

Many of the themes that run through the texts in defence of images were also communicated visually. Perhaps the best-known Byzantine work to stress the significance of the incarnation is the apse mosaic at Hagia Sophia (fig. 56); the Virgin and Child mosaic that replaced the cross in the apse of the Koimesis Church at Nicaea around the middle of the century also had the incarnation as its main theme.[75] The inclusion of many scenes from the infancy of Christ in Paris.gr.510 (figs. 6, 18, 21) may parallel this interest. In the Khludov Psalter, a sequence of scenes pictures David attesting to the meaning of the incarnation; still others visu-ally demonstrate that Christian images were not idols, for idolatry had been ren-dered obsolete by the incarnation.[76] An emphasis on the witness of the Old Testament, and especially of prophets, also runs through the ninth-century mar-ginal psalters,[77] and may have recurred in monumental form in the mosaics of the Church of the Holy Apostles, redecorated during the reign of Basil I.[78] Similar interests appear in the Vatican 'Christian Topography', which, unlike other Byzantine copies of the manuscript, includes an unprecedented group portrait of those who witnessed Christ's incarnation, and a full run of the prophets; it also incorporates a sequence of images of the ark of the covenant and tabernacle found in other 'Topography' manuscripts, but which had obvious relevance in the ninth century. Finally, passion imagery that stressed Christ's human suffering prolife-rated in the ninth century;[79] as did visions of divinity, which were transformed from timeless liturgical images into historical scenes.[80]

On one level, this collection of images reproduced the ideas of the texts defend-ing images in visual rather than in written form. But even from this restricted per-spective some of the differences between the ways words and images can communicate are apparent.[81] Pictures anathematized anti-image sentiments more

[73] E.g. the 787 Council (Mansi XIII, 285A; trans. Sahas [1986a], 110), and a letter from the patriarch of Jerusalem to Leo V as quoted in the Life of Michael the Synkellos: Cunningham (1991), 64–65, 147 note 86.   [74] See further chapter 7.   [75] Barber (1991).   [76] Corrigan (1992), 37–40.
[77] Corrigan (1992), 62–77.
[78] So Demus (1979), 241–245; but compare N. Ševčenko (1993/4), 164 and note 24. The Church of the Holy Apostles (the Apostoleion), built in the fourth century, rebuilt by Justinian and further dec-orated by Justin II, was repaired and apparently redecorated by Basil: Vita Basilii, 80; ed. Bekker (1838), 323; trans. Mango (1972), 192; on this text, see chapter 4 note 47. On the history of the church, see Malickij (1926), 123–151; Maguire (1974), 121–127; Epstein (1982), 79–82; Demus I (1984), 232–241; Mango (1990a). A tenth-century ekphrastic account was written by Constantine the Rhodian (ed. Legrand [1896], trans. Mango [1972], 199–201); a twelfth-century one by Nikolaos Mesarites (ed. Downey [1957]).   [79] See the discussion of f. 30v in chapter 7.   [80] See chapter 7.
[81] See further Cormack (1986a).

actively than any text ever could: they were self-validating, and they had the power of immediacy. Ninth-century Byzantines might know from texts that Christ's incarnation had entitled them to venerate his image or to share in the visions of Old Testament prophets; by dispensing with the intermediary of the written word, images enabled them to venerate and to participate directly and intimately.

NINTH-CENTURY PATTERNS OF IMAGERY

There is no homogeneous 'ninth-century manuscript style', nor are there consistent principles of layout and organization. There are, however, three patterns worth remarking. The first is, in fact, the heterogeneity of ninth-century manuscript illuminations, both as a whole and within individual manuscripts; the second is a general tendency to avoid elaborate settings; the third is the material splendour and brightness of so many of the miniatures.

The tendency to avoid complex settings is overt in the Milan Gregory, where most of the marginal scenes present figures in a minimal setting or without any backdrop at all. While there are several conceivable reasons for this – among them the technical ineptitude of the painter and the possibility that a model with equally minimal settings was followed – the *Sacra Parallela* and the Khludov Psalter, of higher technical quality and with many scenes created expressly for them, show the same lack of interest in backdrops and supplementary detail. The three manuscripts all contain unframed marginal miniatures, which may have constrained the miniaturists. However, two ninth-century Job manuscripts and the Paris Homilies,[82] all with framed pictures, display the same features. Though the miniaturists did indeed include backgrounds, these are normally flat washes of colour: a green strip for the ground below an unmodulated blue field. In the Paris Homilies and, still more, the Job manuscripts, the miniaturists also usually placed their figures in the front plane against this flat blue ground, which is only occasionally enlivened by a building or a column. The frame, in other words, may in these manuscripts be held responsible for a coloured backdrop to the scenes, but most of the miniatures in the Paris Gregory and the Job manuscripts are as lacking in supplementary details and complicated settings as are those in the books with marginal illustrations. The same is true of the framed miniatures in the Vatican 'Christian Topography', save that here the miniaturist omitted even the coloured background: figures and essential objects appear against the neutral parchment. Though the execution differs, a lack of interest in background and supplementary narrative detail remains characteristic.[83] Ninth-century miniaturists seem intent

---

[82] The Job manuscripts (see note 39 above), exceptionally, contain framed marginal miniatures.

[83] What remains of ninth-century monumental art in Constantinople resembles the miniatures in this respect: see chapter 2.

on displaying action or portraits without distracting paraphernalia; they concentrated on communicating the core content, not filling out the narrative with supplementary detail.

The various formats used by the miniaturists demonstrate that no single framework enjoyed hegemonic status in the ninth century, and the Paris Homilies and Vatican 'Christian Topography' indicate that formal eclecticism was acceptable even within a single product. The miniaturist of the 'Topography' used virtually every format available, from framed full-page pictures to unframed figures inserted between columns of text. The eclecticism of the Paris Gregory reveals itself less in the range of formats used – though here we do find great variety imposed *within* each of the invariably full-page framed miniatures – than in the absence of any formal homogeneity: several distinct approaches to representation are intermingled, apparently at random.[84] Even the usually consistent miniaturist responsible for the *Sacra Parallela* abandoned flat gold figures on occasion, as a series of painted and modelled fishes and animals in the manuscript demonstrates.[85] Formal unity was not, it appears, of prime importance.

Neither the emphasis on the essential nor the lack of attention to formal unity can be unilaterally attributed to material or technical limitations. The amount of gold used, the parchment-wasting preference for marginal illustration, and the sheer numbers of miniatures argue against material constraints; while the continuous production of painting and architecture in Constantinople during Iconoclasm presumably ensured technical continuity at least in the capital.[86] The status of ninth-century painters seems to have been reasonably high,[87] and there does not seem to have been a critical shortage of talent. The Ignatian Council of 869–870 banned painters who did not adhere to the canons of an earlier Council – a move that Cormack believes may have been intended to expel artisans who had earlier worked for Photios – and even if the ban temporarily removed all skilled painters from the scene (which seems unlikely), its enactment implics that more than a few artisans were active in the middle of the century, and that they had sufficient status to be noted by the Council. With the possible exception of the Milan Gregory, the patterns we have isolated within ninth-century style cannot be attributed entirely to the use of an unskilled labour pool. Coherent landscape and architectural settings, and complex poses, do in fact appear sporadically in Paris.gr.510 and the Khludov Psalter,[88] confirming that at least in these two manuscripts it was not lack of ability that conditioned the miniaturists' preference for reduced settings.

It is arguable that what underlay the miniaturists' (or their patrons') choices was a predilection for unambiguous presentation. Certainly each image is, in itself,

---

[84] See chapter 2.   [85] Paris.gr.923, ff. 199r-v, 200r-v, 247r-v: Weitzmann (1979a), figs. 546–558.
[86] See note 42 above.   [87] Cormack (1977b), esp. 160–162; Corrigan (1992), 6–7.
[88] E.g. Paris.gr.510, ff. 3r, 143v, 438v (figs. 6, 19, 44); Moscow, Hist.Mus.gr.129, ff. 46v, 88r–v (fig. 122): Ščepkina (1977).

direct. While format and composition often worked with, and underscored, meaning, only rarely were stylistic elaborations introduced that might distract from or dilute the essence of a scene. Perhaps because the miniatures often participated in complex dialogues between image and image, or image and word, or image and idea, their presentation remained straightforward; in their formal presentation, ninth-century miniatures provide a functional imagery of clear purpose.

A similar preoccupation with purpose (and appropriate context) affected literary criticism and ecclesiastical debate, where purpose became one of the ultimate criteria. As explained by the Seventh Ecumenical Council in 787: 'One should think of the purpose as well as of the means through which art accomplishes its result. If the purpose is piety, the result is acceptable; [if not,] it is despicable and to be rejected.'[89] In the same paragraph, we read: 'The same principle applies to books. If one describes in books shameful stories, these books are shameful and to be rejected.'[90] In the ninth century, Photios took much the same tack in his literary criticism: the correctness of content remained, for him, one of the most important factors in assessing a given author.[91] Thus, Photios sometimes observed that the content of a book made it worth reading, though the literary style was deplorable.[92] Photios praised books in which evil was punished and 'many innocent people exposed to great danger [are] saved'; while he condemned for their salacious content even works he judged well written.[93] Photios, in other words, recommended morally edifying books: the purpose, expressed by content, of the works he considered determined whether or not they were acceptable. We find the same privileging of content and effect in the text describing the statues of Constantinople, the *Parastaseis*, which focused on the subject matter, and the statues' effects on the populace, to the almost total exclusion of remarks on form.[94] Purpose and content were also important, and linked, during the 787 Council, when participants took earlier iconoclast councils to task for distorting the purpose of the church fathers by quoting them out of context. The same text could be interpreted either correctly or incorrectly;[95] it followed that the same image could be either acceptable or despicable, depending on its purpose. As expressed by John of Damascus: '[God,] who condemned the golden calf, now makes a bronze serpent . . . for a good purpose – to prefigure the truth.'[96] Personal responsibility was

---

[89] Mansi XIII, 241D; trans. Sahas (1986a), 76. The iconophiles here followed John Chrysostom; see further Travis (1984), 46–48. [90] Mansi XIII, 241C; trans. Sahas (1986a), 76.

[91] See Kustas (1962), esp. 152.

[92] See, for example, his comments on Maximus the Confessor in codices 192–195 of the *Bibliotheke* (on which see chapter 5): ed. Henry III (1962), 74–89, esp. 80–81.

[93] Quotation from codex 166: ed. Henry II (1960), 149; trans. Wilson (1994), 153; see also Treadgold (1980), 101–102. [94] Cameron and Herrin (1984), 46, 52–53; see note 21 above.

[95] See the references in note 202 below.

[96] John of Damascus (quoting Severianus), 'Against those who attack divine images' I,58 (= II,54, III,52): ed. Kotter (1975), 160; trans. Anderson (1980), 45.

assumed: 'concerning images, we must search for the truth, and the intention of those who make them. If it is really and truly for the glory of God . . . then accept them with due honour.'[97]

Such beliefs put a premium on purpose and function; the merit of an image resided in its content and use. Literary advocates of this perspective cluster in, and dominate, the eighth and ninth centuries; the spare and functional imagery characteristic of ninth-century manuscripts promoted (and demonstrated) the same attitudes in a concrete fashion. Practice and theory, in this case, were mutually reinforcing.

The third formal pattern observable in the ninth-century manuscripts is the material splendour and brightness of the miniatures. The dominant colour of both the Milan Gregory and the *Sacra Parallela* is gold, and though gold script appeared in deluxe early Byzantine manuscripts, the abundant use of gold to illuminate initials in the text – found in the *Sacra Parallela* and, especially, the Paris Homilies – seems to be a novelty of the post-iconoclast period. The palettes used by the miniaturists of the Paris Gregory, the Vatican Job, and the 'Christian Topography' included gold too, though it fails to eclipse the other bright and intense colours favoured in these manuscripts. As Nikephoros' punning reference to the iconoclasts as 'the persecutors of colour [*chromatomachoi*], rather, the persecutors of Christ [*christomachoi*]' suggests, the potential use of colour as an ideological concept was exploited in ninth-century Byzantium.[98]

Liz James has recently pointed out that the importance and the significance of colour to the Byzantines has been underestimated and misunderstood. Colour, she argues, was 'a crucial element in giving an image meaning'.[99] She also notes that, just as Byzantine perception of the visual was different from ours, so too was Byzantine response to colour. We concentrate on hue (a leaf is green, the sea blue); the Byzantines, following the Greeks and Romans, concentrated on brightness (a leaf is bright, the sea wine-dark). James concludes that this was one reason why written descriptions of colour stress words like 'glowing' or 'brilliant'.[100]

An important aspect of colour to the Byzantines was what James calls its 'light-bearing quality'.[101] This had theological implications, for light was equated with divinity. As Pseudo-Dionysios wrote, in a text well known to iconophile sympathizers: 'material lights are images of the outpouring of an immaterial gift of light'.[102] It is perhaps not surprising, then, that bright and clear colours character-

---

[97] Ibid., II,10 (= III,9): ed. Kotter (1975), 99–100; trans. Anderson (1980), 58. See also Photios, Homily 17,7: ed. Laourdas (1959), 172; trans. Mango (1958), 296 ('For it is thy [God's] wont to look not at the deficiencies but at the intention . . . ').

[98] 'Against the iconoclasts': ed. Pitra (1858), 282; trans. Travis (1984), 45.

[99] James (1991), 84. Compare, however, Kazhdan and Maguire (1991), 8–9.

[100] James (1991), 66–94, esp. 68, 72, 80–87.   [101] Ibid., 80.

[102] Quoted ibid., 80. On the iconophile use of Pseudo-Dionysios, see Cameron (1992b). The 'Celestial Hierarchy', from which the quoted passage comes, was cited, for example, by the 787 Council: Mansi XIII, 253E; trans. Sahas (1986a), 87.

ize most Byzantine manuscript painting (and mosaics), of whatever century. What is striking, and appears only in the ninth century, is the use of vast amounts of gold – the ultimate representative of light and sign of divinity[103] – to convey this brightness. May we assume that the miniaturists of, especially, the *Sacra Parallela* and the Milan Gregory meant to infuse their scenes with material expressions of divinity?[104] To a certain extent, I think we can: to invert and expand Nikephoros, as friends of colour (*chromatophiloi*), the friends of Christ (*christophiloi*) may well have found it especially appropriate to be friends of gold (*chrysophiloi*).

The lavish use of gold to express divinity fits a ninth-century context particularly well, and seems to correspond with the introduction of icon revetments which also associate precious metals with religious portraits.[105] But it must be said immediately that no simple equation can be imposed without caution or qualification. Since good and evil figures alike merit gold in both the *Sacra Parallela* and the Milan Gregory (although not in the Vatican Job, where gold is reserved for the good), it is the sanctity of the whole book (the manuscript as an object) or, more likely, the validity of imagery itself that is being given a divine *imprimatur*.

We cannot, however, impose a single meaning on the use of gold. It would not only be naive to suppose that the Byzantines ignored the material value of the gold; it would run against the evidence. Nikephoros, for example, approved of images that, to imitate the splendour of their prototypes, were 'made from the purest and most splendid material'.[106] The physical material (and its value) was an integral part of the object, and what we would call superficial appearance could convey vital meaning.[107] Nikephoros praised artisans who used 'the brighter materials and the clearer colours, which flower the appearance [of the prototype] to the utmost, and are artistically appealing and give glory to it'.[108] Material splendour enhanced immaterial glory, and this concept too may elucidate the profusion of gold in the *Sacra Parallela* and the Milan Gregory.

ICONOGRAPHY AND THE ISSUE OF TRADITION

Much ninth-century iconography falls into one of two rough categories: 'uncharacterized' imagery, by which I mean apparently generic iconographical formulae; and images that demonstrate 'single-instance adjustments', by which I mean motifs that serve such a particular purpose that they occur only in very specific cir-

---

[103] See James (1991), 82–83.   [104] See, for earlier explanations, Belting (1974), 8–14.

[105] See Anderson (1995), 37–38.

[106] *Logos*: *PG* 100:772; *Antirrheticus* II,8: *PG* 100:353; Mondzain-Baudinet (1990), 162; Travis (1984), 37. See also John of Damascus, 'Against those who attack divine images' III, 138: ed. Kotter (1975), 200; trans. Anderson (1980), 106–107.

[107] See further Parry (1989), esp. 169–170, 182–183; Cameron (1992b); Onians (1980); Rouan (1981), esp. 425–436; Cameron and Herrin (1984), 37 note 96 (the authors of the *Parastaseis* focus on the value of the material in question').   [108] *Logos*: *PG* 100:725; trans. Travis (1984), 44.

cumstances. The uncharacterized images are the more numerous, and show particularly well how the ways that miniaturists treated subject matter are related to the ways that they dealt with style.

Uncharacterized images are represented by many of the marginal scenes of the Milan Gregory, the *Sacra Parallela*, and the marginal psalters, where the absence of supporting figures or objects often results in images so reduced in content that they are sometimes incomprehensible to those unfamiliar with the more expanded narrative. These shorthand images incorporate only the material essential for their interpretation, and rely on conventional formulae to facilitate recognition. Sometimes, but not always, the full narrative was supplied by the adjacent text.

In the psalters, where many miniatures act as visual commentaries, meaning is often dependent on the interrelationship of the psalm text, commentaries on it, the image, and its inscription:[109] the picture itself carried only part of the burden. Recognition of the subject matter was, in these cases, important, and conventional formulae facilitated this. When this generic approach was interrupted by a characterizing detail – as in the caricatures of Jews – it stood out and thereby carried particular weight, often without any supporting inscription.[110]

In the *Sacra Parallela* the majority of images confine themselves to a portrait or to a single episode of a longer narrative related in the text; when narrative sequences appear, however, they repeatedly overstep the restrictions of the accompanying quotation. The Jacob and Isaac sequence illustrating the citation of Genesis 27:6–18, for instance, includes the episode of Isaac identifying his son that is not described until v. 22.[111] This characteristic feature of the *Sacra Parallela* has been cited as proof that the artist relied on a variety of visual models;[112] more important, however, is the attitude toward narrative. When sequential scenes occur, the miniaturist of the *Sacra Parallela* was interested in conveying a coherent visual narrative block rather than in providing either a detailed correspondence of text and image or an exegetical commentary. Particularizing iconographic details were less important than the completion of a recognizable narrative progression; and, even more than in the marginal psalters, such details were omitted in the *Sacra Parallela*. Though for different reasons, the *Sacra Parallela* confirms the evidence of the psalters that a generic, uncharacterized configuration that signalled a particular episode – an iconography reduced to its essentials – was often desired or at least sufficient; details for their own sake were superfluous.

The avoidance of particularizing iconographic details goes hand-in-hand with the formal insignificance of background and supplementary details; when such details appear, they are usually one-offs, single-instance adjustments to an estab-

---

[109] See esp. Corrigan (1992).   [110] Cf. Hahn (1990), esp. 12, 24.

[111] Weitzmann (1979a), 42; for other examples, see ibid., 38, 43, 76, 88, 92–93, 95, 101, 107, 116, 138, 148–149, 157, 159, 167, 169, 172, 174, 178, 183, 246.

[112] References in preceding note and ibid., 257–64.

lished formula. As such, they are important indicators of meaning, and we shall turn to them shortly. It is perhaps less obvious that the essential conservatism of the uncharacterized images represents an option; the use of traditional imagery, unencumbered by formal or iconographical flourishes, can convey meaning that goes beyond the subject matter itself.

Since similitude between image and archetype was a major feature of iconophile theory, conscious use of traditional iconography deflected the possibility of any criticism that the image was deviating from its prototype. It also provided an implicit defence against accusations of idolatry: as we have seen, orthodox Christians argued that Christian images had archetypes while pagan idols did not. Condemnation of innovation as 'pagan' appeared already in John of Thessalonike's seventh-century dialogue with a pagan about the difference between idolatry and the veneration of Christian images, where John observed that 'we do not invent anything, as you do'. John's remark was incorporated into the florilegion read during the fifth session of the Council of 787,[113] and this Council later expanded his sentiments: 'As for ourselves, we gain nothing but the certainty that we, who have come to a reverence of God, introduce no innovation, but rather remain obedient to the teachings of the apostles and fathers and to the traditions of the Church.'[114] Further reactions against novelty range from John of Damascus' 'stop your innovations' to Theodore of Stoudion's 'we have a command from the apostle himself which says that if anybody decrees or orders us to act contrary to tradition . . . he shall not be acceptable', to Photios' 'the memory of men who have used the brief time-span at their disposal for innovations is forever kept fresh by the eye of justice for the censure of their crimes'.[115] This attitude, joined with the insistence that art was not the invention of the painter,[116] led to Theodore of Stoudion's condemnation of innovative iconography: 'this deed was inspired not by God, but surely by the adversary, seeing that in all the years that have passed no examples of this particular subject have ever been given'.[117]

The importance of these condemnations becomes clear from echoes of the anti-image response. Describing an attempt to persuade the iconophiles to meet with the iconoclasts, the *Vita Nicetae* attributes to the Emperor Nikephoros I the statement 'if they [the iconophiles] are persuaded by you that their teachings are innova-

---

[113] Mansi XIII, 164–165; trans. Mango (1972), 140.

[114] Mansi XIII, 208C; trans. Sahas (1986a), 52. The Quinisext Council (692) had earlier suggested that bishops study the church fathers rather than produce new texts: see Parry (1989), 170 and note 36.

[115] John of Damascus, 'Against those who attack divine images' I,22: ed. Kotter (1975), 111; trans. Anderson (1980), 31. Theodore, letter to Theoktistos (epistle 1.24; ca. 808): *PG* 94:984A; trans. Alexander (1958), 90; on Theodore (759–826), see *ODB* 3, 2044–2045. Photios, Homily 17,1: ed. Laourdas (1959), 164 l. 18–165 l. 1; trans. Mango (1958), 287. For an earlier example, see the Emperor Julian's fourth-century defence of pagan imagery: 'Innovation I abominate above all things' (*Opera*: ed. Teubner, 453b).   [116] On which see references in note 10 above.

[117] Letter to Theodoulos of Stoudion (epistle I,19): *PG* 99:957; trans. Mango (1972), 175.

tions, let them stop their evil teaching'.[118] And Photios wrote of the iconoclasts: 'Accusing us of introducing daring innovations into apostolic teaching, they prided themselves on being, of all men under the sun, the only ones who had not deviated from it.'[119] To some, Iconoclasm was a battle for possession of the authority of the past, a battle that polarized the distinction between innovation and tradition.

Underlying this battle was an almost fanatical insistence on tradition as the best proof of truth.[120] John of Damascus eulogized tradition at least fifteen times in the course of his writings against Iconoclasm, often in the same breath with which he decried innovation: ' . . . stop your innovations. Do not remove age-old boundaries, erected by your fathers';[121] or 'We beseech the people of God, the holy nation, to hold fast to the tradition of the Church';[122] or, quoting Paul, 'stand firm and hold to the traditions which you were taught'.[123] For Nikephoros, too, tradition is the best guarantor of truth,[124] and one of his highest accolades is 'it bears the seal of the fathers'.[125] Further, of the three requirements for orthodox clergy, Nikephoros ranked preservation of the holy tradition second only to fear of God, and before honouring the sanctity of ordination vows.[126]

Faith in tradition as the best assurance of authority was widespread in the eighth and ninth centuries, and iconoclasts and iconophiles alike insisted that tradition supported their point of view.[127] The iconoclasts claimed that 'the images of false and evil name have no foundation in the tradition of Christ, the apostles and the fathers'.[128] The iconophiles, who had recent custom on their side, universalized from this – 'Nor can a single opinion overturn the unanimous tradition of the whole Church'[129] – and exploited iconoclast attempts at change: 'Let us not allow

[118] Commentary and trans. Alexander (1958), 130–132.

[119] Homily 17, 1: ed. Laourdas (1959), 165 ll. 23–25; trans. Mango (1958), 288.

[120] See also note 72 above; E. Martin (1930), 130-149, 191–198; Grant (1960); Schönborn (1976), 144–145, 148; Cormack (1986b), 615, 637 note 53.

[121] John of Damascus, 'Against those who attack divine images' I,22 (cf. II,15, III,41): ed. Kotter (1975), 111 (108, 141); trans. Anderson (1980), 31.

[122] Ibid. I,68 (= I I,71): ed. Kotter (1975), 168; trans. Anderson (1980), 49.

[123] Ibid. I,23 (cf. II,16): ed. Kotter (1975), 113; trans. Anderson (1980), 31.

[124] 'Everything, therefore, which has been handed over in the Church of God, both written and unwritten, is venerated and honoured, and sanctifies bodies and souls; and concerning these things there is no doubt among the faithful.' *Logos*: *PG* 100:617; trans. Travis (1984), 125.

[125] *Antirrheticus* III,3: *PG* 100:380; Mondzain-Baudinet (1990), 186; Travis (1984), 154–155.

[126] See Travis (1984), 107; cf. ibid. 124–157, 171–172.

[127] Though debates conducted almost entirely in traded quotations seem to be a phenomenon of the period, I do not mean to imply that tradition was ignored before the eighth century (see e.g. P. Gray [1982], 61–62); rather, I am highlighting its persistent significance in the debate about images. See Alexander (1977), 238–240; and Alexander (1958), 257–258, on the refutation of 'spurious' texts by quoting 'genuine' passages.

[128] Mansi XIII, 268C; trans. Mango (1972), 166–167; Sahas (1986a), 97. For Nikephoros' refutation, Alexander (1958), 245.

[129] John of Damascus, 'Against those who attack divine images' I,25: ed. Kotter (1975), 117; trans. Anderson (1980), 32–33.

ourselves to learn a new faith, in opposition to the tradition of the fathers'.[130] The measured tone of these statements could, however, slip easily into mild threats – 'it is no small matter to forsake the ancient tradition of the Church which was upheld by all of those who were called before us, whose conduct we should observe, and whose faith we should imitate'[131] – or, as it did with some regularity, blanket abuse. One of the great insults levelled on the iconoclasts by the iconophiles reads: 'Obviously they are unaware of what the fathers say.'[132] Or: 'It appears that they have never read what the fathers say. If they have, they have done so in passing and not diligently.'[133] The iconoclasts are accused of 'rejoicing . . . at distorting the traditions of the Church',[134] and characterized as 'like swine who have trodden on pearls – I mean the traditions of the Church'.[135] For 'the fabrication of [sacred] images is by no means new and recent, but was transmitted from the beginning and from on high, and confirmed in both the old and new covenants';[136] most definitively, the 787 Council assures us that 'all our holy fathers accepted the painting of images'.[137]

The ringing testimonials in favour of tradition and diatribes against innovation indicate how determined was the struggle for control of the past. Visual repercussions of this struggle can perhaps be seen in the uncharacterized iconography and the lack of formal embellishment found so often in ninth-century miniatures; in any event, these attributes reject innovation for its own sake. The rhetorical strategy employed by the churchmen does not, however, converge seamlessly with the visual evidence. Most of the manuscripts with which we have been dealing had pre-iconoclast ancestors, and the miniaturists of the marginal psalters and of the Vatican 'Christian Topography', and probably of the Paris and Milan Homilies as well, had before them illustrated early copies of these texts. Nonetheless, with the possible exception of the Milan painter the ninth-century miniaturists did not feel duty bound to duplicate exactly the subject matter contained in these witnesses to

[130] Ibid. III,41 (cf. I,26 and II,20): ed. Kotter (1975), 143 (117, 119); trans. Anderson (1980), 89 (33, 64).

[131] Ibid. I,2: ed. Kotter (1975), 67; trans. Anderson (1980), 14. Cf. I,16 (ed. Kotter [1975], 90; trans. Anderson [1980], 24): 'Either do away with the honour and veneration these things deserve, or accept the tradition of the Church and the veneration of images.' John also contrasted imperial edicts with church tradition, and found the former wanting (II,16: ed. Kotter [1975], 111–114); so too Theophanes, as noted by Sahas (1986a), 25.   [132] Mansi XIII, 257C; trans. Sahas (1986a), 89.

[133] Ibid. 248C; trans. Sahas (1986a), 81.

[134] Ibid., 268A; trans. Sahas (1986a), 96. See also Mansi XIII, 212D (where Epiphanios imagines the iconoclasts refusing to 'follow faithfully the tradition which existed from the beginning'); 217C (where the iconoclasts 'do not even come close to accepting the tradition admitted by so many saints throughout history'); 228C (where the iconoclasts refuse tradition 'with contempt'); 272E (where the iconoclasts are accused of 'speaking from their own belly' rather than from tradition); 273B (the iconoclasts 'have revolted against the fathers, they oppose the tradition of the church'); trans. Sahas (1986a), 55, 59, 66, 100, 101.   [135] Ibid., 325C; trans. Sahas (1986a), 145.

[136] Life of Michael the Synkellos, 11: ed. Cunningham (1991), 66–67.

[137] Mansi XIII, 269A; trans. Sahas (1986a), 98. See also note 72 above.

past tradition. While the iconography of individual scenes remains traditional, images not in the older versions of the text were added in the psalters, the 'Christian Topography', and the Paris Homilies, and new combinations of scenes appear as well. Nor do any of these manuscripts copy the miniature style of the earlier models, and most of them appear to have altered the format. Although all illustrated ninth-century manuscripts (except for the *Sacra Parallela*) were traditional in the sense that they copied early texts, the miniatures in them actually reframe tradition.

Another way that the miniaturists reframed tradition emerges in the second of the iconographical categories that dominate ninth-century miniatures. Smaller than the uncharacterized group, it consists of scenes (or details within them) that appear to have been invented *ad hoc* in the ninth century. Nearly all supplement rather than illustrate the text they accompany; and nearly all can be classified as 'single-instance adjustments': the miniaturists inserted details or scenes to make precise and time-specific points, tailored to a particular audience. Only rarely do single-instance adjustments become sufficiently generalized to enter mainstream ninth-century or later Byzantine iconography.

Examples of single-instance adjustments are frequent in the marginal psalters and also appear in the Vatican 'Christian Topography' and Paris.gr.510. For example, most of the specifically anti-heretical imagery grafted into the ninth-century marginal psalters was omitted from later copies, and even within the ninth-century group the anti-heretical additions are not consistent.[138] Single-instance adjustments personalized the manuscripts in which they appeared: they fine-tuned the miniatures to suit the tastes of the patron, miniaturist, or expected viewer. By virtue of the fact that they supplemented the written narrative, the single-instance adjustments essentially reinterpreted the text to reaffirm the beliefs of their creators. Such alterations have less to do with long-range rethinking of the significance of the scenes themselves than with the interpretation of certain episodes in a particular and time-bound context. They depend heavily on a three-way symbiosis between miniature, text, and informed audience; and the critical necessity of the latter is clear from the enigma that most of these images posed until recently, and that many still do.

We will examine a number of single-instance adjustments in the following chapters. Here, however, I should like to speculate on how we are to view them against the written strictures condemning innovation. Most obviously, the single-instance adjustments confirm the difference between the rhetorical strategies of texts and the visual strategies of images. Beyond this, however, Paul Magdalino's observation that 'new' did not necessarily mean 'innovative' to the Byzantines, but rather 'imitation of' or 'superior imitation of' (as in Constantinople the

---

[138] See Corrigan (1992).

New Rome),[139] suggests that what we frame as new or innovative in Byzantine iconography could have been viewed by its contemporary audience as superior reworkings of old themes, as clarifying improvements rather than as radical innovations.

It must, on the other hand, be stressed that although miniatures exhibiting single-instance adjustments are among the most fascinating products of the ninth century, they are far from the norm. Most of the pictures in the marginal psalters and the Paris Gregory, and nearly all those in the Vatican 'Christian Topography', the Milan Homilies and the *Sacra Parallela*, rely on iconographical formulae typified by their lack of characterization. We are confronted with a basic pattern of miniatures that are essentially pragmatic in their style and iconography, set against a small but significant group demonstrating single-instance adjustments.

THE FUNCTIONS OF IMAGES IN THE NINTH CENTURY

The ways that manuscript images were used to construct meaning in the ninth century show considerable latitude, and the results suggest considerable thought and effort on the part of the miniaturists and their patrons. Initially, it thus seems significant that the writings of the eighth- and ninth-century church councils and of the major proponents of the iconophile cause – John of Damascus, Theodore of Stoudion, Nikephoros and, later, Photios – stressed the function of images. When we look more closely, however, we find that while the uses of imagery listed in the texts rarely deviated from earlier theory, ninth-century miniatures often play roles quite different from those described and, sometimes, from those they had played before.

Byzantine religious imagery provided a visual interpretation of the past and on this level can always be defined as instructive or explanatory; even so, overtly didactic and polemical miniatures appear to have been singularly popular in the ninth century. The anti-iconoclast scenes in the Khludov and Pantokrator Psalters are probably the most famous examples,[140] but both manuscripts are rife with pictures interpolated in the ninth century that instruct the viewer in the proper interpretation of the psalms. In the Khludov Psalter, these interpretations are usually elucidated by concise inscriptions; following Kathleen Corrigan, we may identify most of the ninth-century additions as anti-heretical polemic, directed against the Jews and Muslims as well as iconoclasts.[141] The miniatures in the Paris Homilies have a broader focus, but most are equally intent on providing a visual interpretation of their accompanying text. Similarly, Wanda Wolska-Conus has argued that the

---

[139] Magdalino (1987), 53–54; see also Alexander (1962), 349–351.

[140] See the classic trio I. Ševčenko (1965), Grabar (1965), and Dufrenne (1965).

[141] Corrigan (1992).

miniatures in the Vatican 'Christian Topography' expand and explain the sense of the text.[142] The strength of didactic imagery, and especially of its offshoots, visual exegesis and visual polemics,[143] in the ninth century is clear.

No eighth- or ninth-century text known to me, however, includes argument or exegesis as a function of images.[144] The numerous specific functions attributed to images instead fall into three traditional groups: remembrance and honour, intercession, and instruction. The iconophile writers were not, of course, trying to classify images into function-defined groups (as classifications, all three of these groups are overdetermined: they encompass virtually all religious images, and certainly all miniatures in ninth-century manuscripts), but rather to explain the ways images worked within the structure of orthodox belief.

In discussions of honorific or commemorative images, the iconophiles stressed particularly the concept of imagery for the perpetuation of memory and as a reminder of historical presence. John of Damascus wrote that this 'kind of image is made for the remembrance of past events . . . in order that glory, honour and eternal memory may be given'.[145] He also quoted St Basil's sermon on the martyr Gordios to authorize the use of images as memorials – 'when we have his memory before our eyes it will always remain fresh' – and commented, 'obviously sermons and images are the best means of keeping it fresh'.[146] The idea of images as memory runs through many iconophile texts: 'Things which have already taken place are remembered by means of images, whether for the purpose of inspiring wonder, or honour, or shame, or to encourage those who look upon them to practice good and avoid evil.'[147] For, as Epiphanios the Deacon told the 787 Council, in reading about saints 'we are reminded of their zeal' but 'looking at their sufferings, we come to remember their bravery and their life inspired by God'.[148]

When put on the defensive, iconophiles sometimes restricted the legitimate roles of images (in response to the iconoclast Council of 754, for example, the Acts of the 787 Council claim that 'true worshippers . . . have iconographic representations only as a means of explanation and remembrance')[149] but normally the linked functions of intercession and salvation were not only included, but emphasized. The salvatory role of imagery relates to the redemptive value of the incarnation: as John of Damascus wrote, 'I saw the human shape of God and my soul found its

---

[142] Wolska-Conus (1990), 191. [143] On visual exegesis, see further chapter 2.

[144] Discussion of typologies comes closest to this function. See John of Damascus, 'Against those who attack divine images' I,12, II,20, III,22, 36: ed. Kotter (1975), 86, 119–120, 129, 140.

[145] Ibid. III,23 (cf. I,19, I,38 [= II,34], II,10–11): ed. Kotter (1975), 129 (94, 149, 99, 102); trans. Anderson (1980), 77 (26, 37, 58–59).

[146] Ibid. I,40–41 (= II,36–37): ed. Kotter (1975), 150; trans. Anderson (1980), 38.

[147] Ibid. I,13: ed. Kotter (1975), 86; trans. Anderson (1980), 21. On imagery to encourage imitation, see below; on the emotional impact of imagery implied in the first clause, see above.

[148] Mansi XIII, 348C-D (cf. 249D-E); trans. Sahas (1986a), 163 (83).

[149] Ibid., 277A; trans. Sahas (1986a), 104.

salvation.'[150] He explained: 'images are a source of profit, help, and salvation for us all, since they make things so obviously manifest, enabling us to perceive hidden things'.[151] Intercession was an equally important attribute: Nikephoros, for example, credited imagery with 'acknowledging memory and entreating intercessions'.[152] Later, Photios described the Virgin 'depicted in painting as she is in writings and visions, an intercessor for our salvation'.[153] The intercessory power of images was, in fact, one of their trump cards, and references to it are multiple, appearing even in the terse *Synodikon Vetus*.[154] As intercessors, images were called upon for protection,[155] and cited for their ability to terrify demons,[156] their efficacy at which is attested by miracles.[157]

The intercessory power attributed to religious art depends for its force on belief in the relationship between image and prototype, developed by St Basil, that was held by all known iconophile writers. It presumes that the image was, as Gary Vikan has put it, transparent – that the image bridged the space and time separating prototype and viewer.[158] This personalized and intimate conduit to the divine promoted, and in the orthodox church continues to promote, communication between human and divine that bypassed institutional control: by the eighth century the sacred portrait, which one could carry as an amulet or hang on the wall of one's house, put access to divinity at the disposal of the individual. Peter Brown suggested that the ability of holy men to intercede with God on behalf of the populace, and thus divert power traditionally controlled by the state and institutionalized church to the individual, was partially responsible for their persecution during Iconoclasm.[159] If we accept this model and apply it to images, we may understand one of the reasons why iconoclast bishops and the iconoclast Emperor Constantine V denied the power of images to intercede with God.[160]

The third role that iconophile treatises assigned to images was instruction or explanation. The churchmen did not mention visual exegesis or visual polemic under this rubric, but determined that an image could serve as a material aid to

[150] 'Against those who attack divine images' I,22: ed. Kotter (1975), 111; trans. Anderson (1980), 30 [with modifications]. See also the Acts of the 787 Council: Mansi XIII, 241A, 249E; trans. Sahas (1986a), 76, 83.

[151] John of Damascus, 'Against those who attack divine images' III,17: ed. Kotter (1975), 126; trans. Anderson (1980), 74.

[152] *Logos*: *PG* 100:589; trans. Travis (1984), 104. See also, on images of angels, *Antirrheticus* II,10–11: *PG* 100:353; Mondzain-Baudinet (1990), 164–167; Travis (1984), esp. 32.

[153] Photios, Homily 17,6: ed. Laourdas (1959), 171; trans. Mango (1958), 295.

[154] *Synodikon Vetus*, 150: ed. Duffy and Parker (1979), 124.

[155] E.g. John of Damascus, 'Against those who attack divine images' I,36 (= II,32): ed. Kotter (1975), 148; trans. Anderson (1980), 37.

[156] E.g. ibid. II,11, 17: ed. Kotter (1975), 102, 115; trans. Anderson (1980), 59, 64.

[157] E.g. ibid. III,135: ed. Kotter (1975), 198–199; trans. Anderson (1980), 105–106.

[158] Vikan (1989), 50–51.

[159] Brown (1973), 12–13, 33; see further Rouan (1981), 432.

[160] Gero (1977a), 147–151, and Wortley (1982), 253–279; on the bishops, Auzépy (1988), 5–21.

understanding immaterial concepts, as a model for imitation, or as a teaching device.

On the first of these themes, John of Damascus quoted Dionysios the Areopagite's 'we are led to the perception of God and his majesty by visible images',[161] and argued that 'It is impossible for us to think immaterial things unless we can envision analogous shapes.'[162] Nikephoros made the same point, and concluded that 'knowledge of the primary form [archetype] is obtained through the figure [image]'.[163]

The second theme, imitation, was a critical point in the iconoclast debate: both sides agreed on the value of imitating the lives of saints; they did not, however, agree on how one was to learn about the life to be imitated. John of Damascus asked, 'Shall we not make forms and images of things which are visible and perceptible to us, that we may remember them, and so be moved to imitate them?';[164] the iconoclasts promoted verbal or written understanding. In the so-called ethical theory of images, the iconoclasts denied the efficacy of visual *aide-mémoire* and admitted only the imitation of the virtues of saints and the eucharist as acceptable 'images'.[165] The iconophiles replied that the eucharist was not an image of Christ, but Christ himself. [166] Nikephoros argued that virtues are secondary actions of the (primary) bodies of saints – virtue cannot exist without a person to enact it – and proposed that while virtues expose capabilities, images reveal the saints themselves and are thereby more worthy of honour.[167] The critical distinction was between imitation of a life known through written and oral tradition (the iconoclast position) and imitation of a life known through both words and images (the iconophile position). The significance of this difference is clarified by iconophile arguments in favour of using imagery to teach.

The Seventh Ecumenical Council praised 'images placed inside the churches . . . for the purpose of teaching',[168] and championed imagery 'for the purpose . . . of

[161] John of Damascus, 'Against those who attack divine images' I,30–31 (= II,26–7): ed. Kotter (1975), 144–145; trans. Anderson (1980), 34–35 (with modifications).
[162] Ibid. III,21 (cf. I,11, 'the mind which is determined to ignore corporeal things will find itself weakened and frustrated'): ed. Kotter (1975), 128 (84–85); trans. Anderson (1980), 76 (20).
[163] *Antirrheticus* I,30: *PG* 100:277, 289; Mondzain-Baudinet (1990), 110–112; Alexander (1958), 200. Cf. *PG* 100:748D–789B; trans. Travis (1984), 49.
[164] John of Damascus, 'Against those who attack divine images' I,31 (= II,27): ed. Kotter (1975), 145; trans. Anderson (1980), 34. See also note 147 above.
[165] Anastos (1954), 151–160; Gero (1975), 4–22; Parry (1989), 171–172 and note 44; Cunningham (1991), 19–23; and Cameron (1992b). John of Damascus agreed that words – but not only words – could provide images: 'images are of two kinds: either they are words written in books . . . or else they are material images'. 'Against those who attack divine images' III,23: ed. Kotter (1975), 130; trans. Anderson (1980), 77–78.   [166] See Taft (1980/1), 72.
[167] On Nikephoros' points, see Alexander (1953), 49. On the iconophile response to the eucharist as an image see Sahas (1986b).
[168] Mansi XIII, 241A; trans. Sahas (1986a), 75. See also John of Damascus, 'Against those who attack divine images' I,18: ed. Kotter (1975), 94; trans. Anderson (1980), 26; and Photios, Homily 17,1: ed. Laourdas (1959), 164; trans. Mango (1958), 286–287.

reminding us of the gospel and explaining its story'.[169] While the explanatory role of images was sometimes grounded in the traditional topos of pictures as a text for the illiterate – 'What the book is to the literate, the image is to the illiterate'[170] – not all iconophiles accepted this formula;[171] unlike many of their western counterparts, eighth- and ninth-century Byzantine authors never endorsed what Parry has called a 'two-tier system' dividing the élite book-learner from the simple picture-learner.[172] On one level, in fact, those iconophiles who wrote that images functioned as a book for the illiterate simply conveyed their homage to earlier arguments.

A more prominent iconophile argument espoused the even older topos of the equality of texts and images.[173] Nikephoros, for example, noted that 'through calligraphic genius the teachings of divine history appear to us . . . by the excellence of painting, those same things are shown to us',[174] used the word 'graphe' for both painting and writing, and argued that only the scriptural written account and pictorial impressions represent 'what is factually true'.[175] Another earlier idea that recurs repeatedly is the belief that painting fulfils the purpose of writing: John of Damascus observed that 'images and sermons serve the same purpose',[176] and, in a famous letter, the iconoclast emperors Michael II and Theophilos wrote to Louis the Pious that 'those [images] that were displayed in high places they permitted to remain, so that *the picture might serve as scripture*'.[177] To Nikephoros, it followed

[169] Mansi XIII, 288C; trans. Sahas (1986a), 113.

[170] John of Damascus, 'Against those who attack divine images' I,17 (cf. I,47 [= II,43], II,10): ed. Kotter (1975), 93 (151, 99); trans. Anderson (1980), 25 (39, 58). Cf. the Life of Michael the Synkellos: ed. Cunningham (1991), 66–67, and for Nikephoros, Travis (1984), 48. On the topos: Kessler (1985a), esp. 75–76, 86; Kessler (1985b), esp. 18–20, 27–28; and, though his central argument fails to convince, Duggan (1989).   [171] E.g. Theodore of Stoudion: see Parry (1989), esp. 167–170.

[172] Parry (1989), esp. 166–167; see also Sansterre (1994), 209. For the western position, see McKitterick (1990), 297–318; J. Nelson (1990), esp. 264–265, 295; and Hahn (1990), 7–10.

[173] E.g. St Basil, as quoted by John of Damascus: 'Both painters of words and painters of pictures illustrate valour in battle; the former by the art of rhetoric, the latter by clever use of the brush, and both encourage everyone to be brave. A spoken account edifies the ear, while a silent picture induces imitation'. 'Against those who attack divine images' I,46; cf. I,32 (= II,28, III,44): ed. Kotter (1975), 151, 145; trans. Anderson (1980), 38–39. For the 787 Council: Mansi XIII, 277B-C; trans. Sahas (1986a), 104. See also note 148 above; Kessler (1985a), 84–87 and Barnard (1977), 11, 13.

[174] *Apologeticus Maior*: *PG* 100:748; trans. Travis (1984), 45. Similar sentiments appear in John of Damascus, 'Against those who attack divine images' I,17 and III,12 (ed. Kotter [1975], 93, 123; trans. Anderson [1980], 25, 72); Theodore of Stoudion (Parry [1989], 172–173); and the Acts of the 787 Council (Mansi XIII, 220E–221A, 232C, 280A; trans. Sahas [1986a], 61, 69, 105). Correspondingly, the Council countered invectives against painting by noting the illogic of condemning painters but not scribes: Mansi XIII, 249A; trans. Sahas (1986a), 82.

[175] *Antirrheticus* III,5: *PG* 100:381–384; Mondzain-Baudinet (1990), 188–190; Travis (1984), 48.

[176] 'Against those who attack divine images' I,45 (= II,41); cf. I,56 (= II, 52): ed. Kotter (1975), 151, 159; trans. Anderson (1980), 38, 44. See also the 787 Council: Mansi XIII, 269B, 280A, 312A (writings are 'animate icons'), 348C–D; trans. Sahas (1986a), 98, 105, 132, 163. For a fourth-century example, see Gregory of Nyssa, for whom the sacred image is 'silent scripture that speaks from the wall' (*PG* 46:737C–740A).

[177] Letter of 824 from Michael II and Theophilos to Louis the Pious: *MGH Concilia Aevi Karolini* I/2, 478–479; Freeman (1985), 100–105.

that anyone 'who accepts the written account will necessarily accept the pictures as well'.[178] Photios later continued in this same vein: 'Does a man hate the teaching by means of pictures? Then how could he not have previously rejected and hated the message of the gospels?'[179]

The specific relationship between images, speech, and texts thus became a significant issue of debate during Iconoclasm.[180] Iconoclasts such as John the Grammarian stressed the primacy of writing over sight,[181] while the iconophiles found images either equivalent to, or more powerful than, speech or texts. Superiority of visual over written witnesses was implied early by Cappadocian fathers such as St Basil,[182] and reiterated by, among others, Anastasios of Sinai in the seventh century,[183] and Nikephoros, Theodore of Stoudion, and Photios in the ninth. Nikephoros argued that 'we all know that sight is the most honoured and necessary of the senses and it may allow apprehension of what falls under perception more distinctly and sharply [than spoken words]'.[184] He held that while speech could be distorted, visual representations remained clear and distinct; images, therefore, were the more trustworthy documents.[185] Though less concerned with arguing this particular case, Theodore maintained that written accounts were of necessity based on what the author had seen; the visual thereby implicitly took precedence over the written.[186] Photios, who drew extensively on earlier discussions, presented an impassioned plea for the primacy of sight in 867:

Martyrs have suffered . . . and their memory is contained in books. These deeds they are also seen performing in pictures, and painting presents the martyrdom of those blessed men more vividly to our knowledge . . . These things are conveyed both by stories and by pictures, but it is the spectators rather than the hearers who are drawn to emulation . . . the comprehension that comes about through sight is shown to be far superior.[187]

He continued:

indeed much greater is the power of sight . . . . it sends the essence of the thing seen on to the mind, letting it be conveyed from there to the memory for the concentration of unfail-

[178] *Antirrheticus* III,3: *PG* 100:380; Mondzain-Baudinet (1990), 186–187; Mango (1972), 176.

[179] Homily 17,5: ed. Laourdas (1959), 170; trans. Mango (1958), 293–294; or, later in the same sermon: 'if he treats either one with reverence or with contempt, he necessarily bestows the same on the other' (Homily 17,6: ed. Laourdas [1959], 171; trans. Mango [1958], 295).

[180] See de Maffei (1974), 56–61.

[181] Gouillard (1966), 176. The Libri Carolini made the same point: Gero (1973b), 15. See also Alexander (1953), 54 note 21.

[182] As noted by iconophiles: e.g. John of Damascus, 'Against those who attack divine images' I,34 (= II,30, III,46): ed. Kotter (1975), 146. For other early examples, see Kessler (1985a), 84–85.

[183] See Kartsonis (1986), 42–44, 57–58.

[184] 'Refutatio' (unpublished): trans. Alexander (1958), 211. See also Alexander (1953), 49. Note that Nikephoros here describes texts as 'heard'.

[185] *Antirrheticus* III,5: *PG* 100:381–384; Mondzain-Baudinet (1990), 188–190; Travis (1984), 48. See also Parry (1989), 179–180.   [186] Parry (1989), esp. 172–173, 179–180.

[187] Homily 17,5: ed. Laourdas (1959), 170; trans. Mango (1958), 294.

ing knowledge. Has the mind seen? Has it grasped? Has it visualized? Then it has effortlessly transmitted the forms to the memory.[188]

Ninth-century arguments for the primacy of sight were, as Jean-Marie Sansterre has noted, part of the iconophile rhetorical arsenal; they should not be taken to indicate that images had more authority than the scripture.[189] It is nonetheless a measure of the power of the visual in ninth-century Byzantium, and of the force of the image–prototype equation, that images were by definition authentic; in contrast, texts (other than scripture) were susceptible to change, misinterpretation, and alteration.[190] The emphasis on tradition and the authority of the past fed into a concern with the authenticity of the texts that transmitted that past, and philological interests rose conjointly with the steadily increasing reliance on tradition as proof of truth. The Constantinopolitan Council of 680–681 has, indeed, been termed a council of antiquarians and palaeographers because of the zeal with which its members collated various copies of the same text to expose interpolations and determine correct readings, a process that also involved verifying the signatures and handwriting in, and carefully noting the physical properties and age of, relevant manuscripts.[191] Demonstration of the veracity of a text was a major concern, for falsification of documents was rampant in Byzantium; indeed, forgery seems almost to have been a closet industry by the seventh century.[192]

Certainly forgeries continued in the eighth and ninth centuries: Cyril Mango has cited an inscription fabricated in 781 purporting to convey the sentiments of a pre-Christian pagan and prophesying the luminous reign of Constantine and Eirene.[193] We have already noted the letter forged around the year 800 that pretended to express the pope's words to Leo III, and Marie-France Auzépy has argued that the legend of Leo's destruction of the icon over the Chalke gate was invented at about this same time.[194] That the Council of 869 could (apparently slanderously) accuse Photios of bribing people to forge bishops' signatures using both fine and coarse pens to vary the handwriting, and that Symeon Magister and Niketas the Paphlagonian could state, correctly or not, that Photios fabricated a false genealogy – intended to demonstrate Basil's illustrious lineage – in such a way that it 'looked ancient', demonstrates that spurious documents, and carefully crafted ones at that, remained an acknowledged fact of life.[195]

Problems of authenticity haunted even the authors of the secular *Parastaseis*;[196] they obsessed the Council of 787. Participants brought whole books with them to

---

[188] Ibid.   [189] Sansterre (1994).   [190] So e.g. Anastasios of Sinai: see Cameron (1992b).

[191] See Van den Ven (1955/57), 328–330; Bardy (1936), 290–291.   [192] Bardy (1936).

[193] Mango (1963), 201–207.   [194] Auzépy (1990); for the letter, note 22 above.

[195] For the Council, Mango (1958), 299; Symeon's *Annales*, ed. Bekker (1838), 689; for Niketas, *PG* 105:565–8. Other ninth-century implications in McCormick (1986), 191–192, 195. Forgeries were not restricted to Byzantium: see e.g. *Fälschungen* (1988).

[196] Cameron and Herrin (1984), 43–44, 87, 180, 199; see note 21 above.

ensure the accuracy and completeness of their quotations, and a second copy of each text was frequently consulted.[197] In corollary, the Council condemned the iconoclasts for violating the textual evidence. They were accused of effacing and excising passages favourable to images in books available to them (or even of burning the whole offending manuscript);[198] and of falsifying and corrupting texts.[199] The iconoclasts 'are fortified behind forged and intrusive writings'; they were 'forgers of the truth'.[200] The iconophiles charged their opponents with distorting,[201] quoting out of context,[202] inventing,[203] misquoting,[204] and plagiarizing;[205] they 'twist the knowledge of divine and true doctrine according to their own desires'.[206] The iconophiles claimed that the iconoclasts relied on heretical texts to buttress their arguments: they 'have ordained as their own fathers and have set up as teachers, [those] who of old had become defenders of impiety and atheism, and were driven out of reach from the catholic Church'.[207] Nor, according to the

[197] Sahas (1986a), 39; Van den Ven (1955/57), 332; Speyer (1971), 277. Documents read during the third session were also confirmed as authentic by personal witness: Mansi XII, 1145C–1154B.

[198] See Van den Ven (1955/57), 335–336.

[199] Mansi XIII, 225B–226C, 237D; trans. Sahas (1986a), 65, 74; the Council responded: 'every Christian, therefore, when happening to hear of spurious books, must spit upon them and not accept them in any way': Mansi XIII, 293B; trans. Sahas (1986a), 118. For similar sentiments from Nikephoros, see Grumel (1959), 127–135; Travis (1984), 144 note 27.

[200] Mansi XIII, 292E, 312B-E; trans. Sahas (1986a), 117–118, 133–134. For other accusations of forgery, see Alexander (1958), 254, 259.

[201] E.g. 'although they use the same words, they deceptively alter their meaning': Mansi XIII, 224A (cf. 281D, 288B); trans. Sahas (1986a), 63 (108, 112). For Nikephoros, see Alexander (1958), 255–256, 260–261; Travis (1984), 147.

[202] E.g. 'a characteristic of heretics is to present statements in a fragmented form' or 'they cut off a whole phrase deceitfully in order to lure the simpler ones': Mansi XIII, 301E, 285D (cf. 300E–301D); trans. Sahas (1986a), 125, 111 (124–125) and commentary at 133–134 note 54.

[203] E.g. 'having fabricated the accursed slogan . . . would that they had preserved his teachings, as well as those of all our holy fathers, unbroken': Mansi XIII, 212A, cf. 293B, 296D-E, 297B–300A; trans. Sahas (1986a), 54, 118, 120–122. John of Damascus, 'Against those who attack divine images' II,18 (ed. Kotter [1975], 116–117); for Nikephoros, who was fond of demonstrating that a passage was an incorrect interpolation by contrasting it with other quotations from the same author, see Alexander (1958), 257–259, 262.

[204] E.g. 'for they take as confessions what the orthodox Christians have never said': Mansi XIII, 260C; trans. Sahas (1986a), 91.

[205] E.g. 'having stolen statements from the fathers, which they put forth as their own, they say the following . . .': Mansi XIII, 221C; trans. Sahas (1986a), 62.

[206] Mansi XIII, 281B; cf. 289C, 292A-B, 300A-D, 325A; trans. Sahas (1986a), 107, 114, 115, 123–124, 144. See also Travis (1984), 147. On another front, Muslims and Christians flung the same charges back and forth: see Corrigan (1992), esp. 78–103.

[207] Nikephoros, *Apologeticus Maior. PG* 100:813 (here too Nikephoros condemned students studying heretical texts: ibid., 564–565). See also Travis (1984), 130, 136, 140, 160–161, 169–170 and, for similar arguments in Nikephoros' unpublished 'Refutatio', Alexander (1958), 252, 255. The 787 Council recognized this problem earlier: Mansi XIII, 253A, 313A–324C; trans. Sahas (1986a), 85, 134–143. In response, the Council ordered the destruction of all but one or two 'examples' of iconoclast writings, and recommended the same treatment for all heretical works: see Van den Ven (1955/57), 333.

787 Council, was this innocent behaviour: 'When those who deviate from the catholic Church are about to say something wicked, they begin with what everybody confesses. By being right on this, they hope not to be disbelieved on the rest. Thus, having stated a few things properly, they now mix gravel with the pearls.'[208]

The problems (real or perceived) with forged and adulterated texts, combined with the emphasis on tradition and the corresponding interest in texts that accurately conveyed that tradition, gave rise to authoritative lists of patristic citations – the florilegia. As early as the Council of Chalcedon in 451, a sort of proto-florilegion emerged, and the form was in full bloom by the 649 Lateran Council.[209] The florilegia became another of the critical nodes of the iconoclast debate,[210] and each side created versions promoting its own vision of the truth.[211] As his first overt step toward reinstating Iconoclasm, Leo V convened a committee to compile a florilegion of passages against religious imagery.[212] On the other side, lists of patristic 'proofs' supporting images appeared in the Acts of pro-image councils, and in polemics against heresy.[213]

The *Sacra Parallela* of John of Damascus is the only known illustrated florilegion.[214] That it was produced shortly after Iconoclasm is not, I think, coincidental. The text reproduced a collection of patristic and biblical citations, compiled by an iconophile hero, that had become the authoritative versions with the so-called restoration of orthodoxy in 843.[215] Nonetheless, the vicissitudes of the iconoclast conflict, which had favoured first one side and then the other for nearly 120 years, cautioned against complacency. The shape of intellectual dialogue did not change for some while; indeed, iconophile sentiments continued to be voiced until the early years of the tenth century. Long-standing and still intense preoccupations with tradition and, concomitantly, with florilegia merged with a contemporary reinterpretation of the role of imagery to make the *Sacra Parallela* a particularly appropriate text to embellish with pictures.

Ninth-century arguments for the primacy of sight joined with concerns about authenticity to fuel a growing consensus that images could confirm the historical

---

[208] Mansi XIII, 257B; trans. Sahas (1986a), 89.

[209] See Van den Ven (1955/57), 325–328; P. Gray (1982), 62.

[210] On which see Mango (1975), 33–34; Cameron (1990), esp. 206–207, 209, 217; Cameron (1992b); (1992c), 102–103; Alexakis (1994).   [211] See esp. Cameron (1992a), 254–255, 267–268.

[212] On this group and their work, see Alexander (1958), 126–127, 137.

[213] For a collation of the lists, see Martin (1930), 146–149, 194–195, 197–198; for a particularly extensive sequence of twenty-six texts in Nikephoros, *PG* 100:812–832. See also Alexander (1953), and, for the florilegion of Theodore Graptos, the Life of Michael the Synkellos, 30: ed. Cunningham (1991), 110–111 and 168 note 200.

[214] Though J. R. Martin (1950), 291–295, speculated that a hypothetical illustrated copy of the Sayings of the Fathers was one source for the illustrations in the *Sacra Parallela*.

[215] On the place of the *Sacra Parallela* within the textual tradition of iconophile florelegia see Alexakis (1994).

truth of a text. That a picture could take on the function and purpose of a 'seal of authenticity' is clear from a number of preserved passages. John of Damascus quoted Maximus the Confessor's 'they touched these [images] with their hands, in confirmation of what had been said'.[216] Theodore the Stoudite wrote that 'the true argument that Christ is a man is that he can be pictured'.[217] In his sermon of 867 inaugurating the mosaic of the Virgin, Photios noted: 'Christ came to us in the flesh. This is seen and confirmed and proclaimed in pictures, the teaching made manifest by means of personal eyewitness and impelling the spectators to unhesitating assent.'[218]

Images authenticated reality; what could be seen validated what could be read or heard.[219] In 1958, Paul Alexander noted this line of argument in the writings of Nikephoros and John of Damascus; he traced it to Aristotle, and saw it as an example of 'the scholastic type of reasoning' that, for him, characterized the last phase of the iconoclast debate.[220] Aristotelian in ultimate inspiration they may well be, but the references to the primacy of sight were not only scholastic exercises. Though the frequency with which the topos appears suggests that it had become an iconophile rhetorical device,[221] the number of references to it also argues that it was an important indicator of meaning. Ideas about the primacy of sight were ingrained in ninth-century Byzantine written culture, and conveyed to a wider audience through sermons.

MINIATURES AND AUTHENTICITY

The *Sacra Parallela* includes several hundred isolated portraits of the biblical and patristic authors quoted in the text. These are essentially author portraits, and as such find numerous ninth-century parallels.[222] In the *Sacra Parallela*, however, the authors pictured are presented in an unusual way. About half of them are enclosed in medallions (figs. 58, 59, 105), a format also used to isolate portraits of figures mentioned by Gregory of Nazianzus in the Milan Homilies (fig. 48); as Corrigan noted, this formula was probably meant to evoke icons and thereby provide a visual authentication to the biblical or patristic text quoted or paraphrased in the accompanying text.[223] As interesting here are the authors who, on over a hundred occa-

---

[216] 'Against those who attack divine images' II,65: ed. Kotter (1975), 164; trans. Anderson (1980), 69. For earlier examples and discussion, see Kessler (1985a), 86–87, and Kessler (1985b), 17.

[217] Epistle II,64: *PG* 99:1285A.

[218] Homily 17,5: ed. Laourdas (1959), 170; trans. Mango (1958), 293.

[219] See too Cormack (1985), 174–176; and, on the related use of seal images to validate the contents of letters, Mullett (1990), 183.   [220] Alexander (1958), 211–212.   [221] Cf. Sansterre (1994).

[222] E.g. in the *Sacra Parallela* itself (Weitzmann [1979a], figs. 2–7), the Milan Homilies (Grabar [1943a], pls. II, VI, IX, XII, *passim*), the Khludov Psalter (Ščepkina [1977], f. IV) and Paris.gr.510 (fig. 41).   [223] Corrigan (1992), 118–119, 138.

sions in the *Sacra Parallela*, point or gesture to their own words (fig. 58);[224] others hold pens that they direct toward the text as if they had physically just written the passages quoted (fig. 59);[225] while still others hold a book open toward the text column, as if disgorging their words into the ninth-century manuscript (fig. 60).[226]

Such figures are not unique to the *Sacra Parallela*: the Milan Gregory retains thirteen figures pointing at the text, and in a tenth-century lectionary at Mount Athos Matthew and Luke put pen to their gospels while John points to his.[227] There are, however, far more examples in the *Sacra Parallela* than in any other Byzantine manuscript. Why?

The person who commissioned the *Sacra Parallela*, and the miniaturists who illustrated it, were faced with a particular situation. In a world where questions of who had access to the authority of tradition, of correct usage, and of what constituted the truth had been the focus of acrimonious debate for over a century, the producers were faced with the task of presenting authoritative texts. But in the climate of debate that characterized the eighth and ninth centuries,[228] how was one to demonstrate conclusively that the texts quoted were indeed the authoritative versions rather than forgeries, excerpts taken out of context, misinterpretations, or worse? The makers of the *Sacra Parallela* called upon the authority of sight: the images provided the 'seal of authenticity' that demonstrated the accuracy of the quotations.[229] The pointing, writing, and book-holding figures visually confirm the text; their prototypes speak through them to verify their words. The authority of the text 'is seen and confirmed and proclaimed' by the portraits, and its lesson is indeed 'made manifest by means of personal eyewitness' that, it was presumably hoped, would 'impel the spectators to unhesitating assent'. Gold, the sign of divine

[224] Weitzmann (1979a), figs. 5 (John of Damascus himself); 66 (Moses); 190, 195, 198, 202, 207, 209 (David); 222 (Zophar, speaking); 225, 230 (Job); 233, 234, 240, 242, 244, 255, 258 (Solomon); 268, 272, 277–279, 284, 289 (Sirach); 292, 298 (Hosea); 306 (Micah); 312 (Joel); 329, 331 (Zechariah); 344–345, 350, 353, 354–357, 359 (Isaiah); 361–362 (Jeremiah); 377, 379 (Ezekiel); 400, 404, 413, 436 (Matthew); 453 (Luke); 484 (John and Peter); 493 (Peter); 503, 505–508, 511–514, 516–519, 521, 527–528 (Paul); 531 (James); 533 (Peter); 540 (Athanasios); 569, 571–572, 574, 576, 578–582, 587 (Basil); 601–602 (Clement of Rome); 613 (Didymos); 624 (Dionysios the Areopagite); 632 (Eustathios of Antioch); 648–649, 651–653, 655, 665–667 (Gregory of Nazianzus); 671 (Gregory of Nyssa); 698, 702–704 (John Chrysostom); 738–741 (Philo).

[225] Ibid., figs. 2–4, 6 (John of Damascus); 187, 202 (David); 520 (Paul).

[226] Ibid., figs. 7 (John of Damascus); 186 (David); 482 (John); 650 (Gregory of Nazianzus); see also fig. 515 (Paul holds an open book and looks to the text of Paris.gr.923). Authors also extend closed books toward the manuscript text: ibid., figs. 415, 437–440 (Matthew); 460, 463, 465–466 (Luke); 478 (John); 500, 510 (Paul); 542 (Athanasios); 573 (Basil).

[227] Mount Athos, Lavra, cod.86, ff. 94r, 110r, 254r: Weitzmann (1935), figs. 306–308. In the Milan Gregory, two of the pointing portraits show Gregory, once standing and once in a medallion; the remainder are standing Old Testament figures (mostly prophets) holding inscribed scrolls, and in four cases also adjacent to oboloi marking their quoted words in the text: Grabar (1943a), pls. III,1–3, IV,1–3, V,3, VIII,3, IX,3, XVII,1, XXV,3, XLVI,3, L,1.

[228] And had its roots in the seventh century: see Cameron (1992c), esp. 93–94, 98–100.

[229] On the medallion portrait as a seal, see Corrigan (1992), 74–75.

Fig. 58 Paris.gr.923, f. 44r: Gregory of Nazianzus

Fig. 59 Paris.gr.923, f. 16r: David writing, Hosea, Micah, and Jeremiah

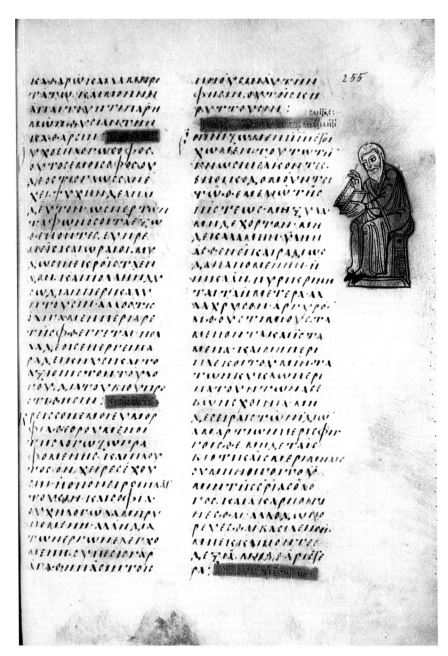

Fig. 60 Paris.gr.923, f. 255r: Gregory of Nazianzus

light, marked the images as infused with God's approval – as well as the connivance of a wealthy patron.

The portraits in the *Sacra Parallela* exemplify one form that the symbiotic relationship between words and images could assume in ninth-century Byzantium: the text generated the portraits; the portraits validated the text. The mutual reinforcement word and image could provide was expressed by the 787 Council thus: 'The representation of scenes in colour follows the narrative of the gospel, and the narrative of the gospel follows the narrative of the painting.'[230] As we have seen, the relationship played itself out in other ways as well: miniatures authorized interpretations of texts, and could provide autonomous visual commentaries on them. In the Khludov Psalter, for example, an author portrait of David was placed beside many images, accompanied by a caption wherein he explained the relationship between the psalm verses and their illustration. These images do not authenticate the text-in-itself (the psalms were evidently not in need of this); they verified a particular interpretation of it.[231]

The symbiotic relationship between text and image continued in the Paris Gregory. Although they lack the explanatory captions introduced in the marginal psalters, we shall see that many of the Homilies illustrations achieved sufficient authority to function as nearly autonomous exegetical commentaries on the text. It is probably significant that the autonomy of the pictures in Paris.gr.510 extended to their liberation from the confines of the text: they are among the earliest full-page miniatures in Byzantium.

Nearly every 'single-instance adjustment' to traditional iconographic formulae appears in the exegetic or polemic miniatures in the Paris Gregory and the marginal psalters. But in the *Sacra Parallela* and the 'Christian Topography', too, images supplemented the texts in important ways specific to time and place:[232] they changed, in fact, the way one interpreted and understood the text. The consequence of this chain of developments is that the texts of the manuscripts we have considered, as the Byzantines read them, cannot be fully comprehended without taking into account the pictures that the Byzantines saw at the same time. The miniatures document a reassessment of the texts, and reveal an attempt to visualize how old words could have meaning in a changed world; they exemplify how meaning was created and recreated in ninth-century Byzantium.

In the second half of the ninth century, words about art continued to focus on issues that had been raised by Iconoclasm. Whether or not various individuals had personal reasons to perpetuate these issues, acrimony and its progeny do not die quickly, and Iconoclasm was anyway symptomatic of a larger cultural realign-

---

[230] Mansi XIII, 269B; trans. Sahas (1986a), 98.   [231] Corrigan (1992).
[232] For the latter, see note 37 above and chapter 7.

ment.[233] In this realignment, words about images were a prime vehicle through which other ideas and conflicts could be expressed. That arguments about images often masked other issues does not mean that the images themselves were non-essential; indeed, it indicates their symbolic significance. But the texts in the end tell us less about ninth-century Byzantine images than about the thought system in which they participated. Some of the characteristic ways in which images communicated through and with this system have been explored in this chapter. How the process played itself out in Paris.gr.510 is what the rest of this book is about.

[233] Dagron (1979); Cameron (1992b), esp. 35–42.

2

The Miniatures: internal evidence

Paris.gr.510 contains forty-six full-page miniatures (figs. 1–46). Their contents are listed sequentially, folio by folio, in Appendix A, and by topic in Appendix B.

TYPES OF SCENES SELECTED FOR ILLUSTRATION

The subject matter included in the miniatures of Paris.gr.510 ranges from iconic portraiture to extensive narrative sequences picturing biblical, hagiographical, and historical episodes. Such iconographical diversity recurs in many illustrated copies of Gregory's sermons; Paris.gr.510 is distinguished by the quantity of its images.

The iconic images are restricted to the frontispiece sequence (figs. 1–5) and to portraits of Gregory and his family (f. 43v; fig. 9), of Gregory, Basil, and Gregory of Nyssa (f. 71v; fig. 13), and of Helena and Paraskeve (f. 285r; fig. 29). The portraits are formal, with passive figures confronting the viewer in strict frontality; all, aside from the enthroned Christ on f. Av (fig. 1), stand; most wear clothing indicative of rank and status. The interest in surface appearance reflected by this dignified display was at home in ninth-century Constantinople, and the emphasis on formality and hierarchy, signifying power and prestige, recurs in later Byzantine portraiture as well.[1]

Narrative images – historical, biographical, hagiographical, and biblical – appear both as single episodes and in sequences. The biblical scenes illustrate Old and New Testament episodes in roughly equal measure,[2] with isolated incidents and extensive sequences drawn from both. The most significant difference between the two lies in the way that the narrative is assembled: Old Testament sequences tend to be longer and relatively self-contained, while New Testament sequences are shorter and inclined to be grouped thematically.[3]

The miniaturists mixed disparate events and genres with abandon. Iconic por-

---

[1] See further Maguire (1989), esp. 221–227.   [2] See Appendix B.   [3] See Brubaker (1996a).

59

traits abut biblical scenes (f. 71v; fig. 13) and hagiographic images (f. 43v; fig. 9); Old Testament and New Testament scenes are often joined (ff. 3r, 143v, 215v, 264v; figs. 6, 19, 25, 28); hagiographical scenes coexist with episodes both from the Old Testament (ff. 52v, 67v, 424v; figs. 10, 11, 41) and from the New (ff. 87v, 149r; figs. 16, 20); history is injected with hagiography (f. 409v; fig. 40).

The variety and juxtaposition of scenes in Paris.gr.510 demonstrates that the idea of isolating genres was never entertained; nor were there 'appropriate' combinations. Instead, the over-riding consideration was evidently the meaning of the page as a whole.

THE CONCEPTUAL RELATIONSHIP BETWEEN TEXT AND IMAGE

It is possible to isolate four different ways in which scenes included in the text miniatures relate to their adjacent texts: they illustrate the historical circumstances under which Gregory delivered the sermon;[4] they picture the main theme of the homily as expressed in its title;[5] they depict scenes selected from among the episodes mentioned in the accompanying text;[6] or they parallel the theme(s) of the sermon exegetically, without relying on an example adduced by Gregory.[7] The scope admitted by these categories is large, and there is little attempt to segregate them. Only ten miniatures – all illustrating scenes never mentioned by Gregory[8] – restrict themselves to a single category; most blend two or even three ways of relating to the accompanying sermon. Folio 52v (fig. 10), for example, pictures the historical circumstances that inspired the accompanying sermon 'On peace' (the reconciliation of the Nazianzus community, pictured in the lowest register on the right); an episode mentioned in that sermon (Moses receiving the laws, on the left side of the same register); and an Adam and Eve sequence totally lacking from Gregory's text. The only generalization that can be extrapolated is that the theological orations and personal ruminations (including letters) usually received exegetical illustrations, while miniatures accompanying the biographical or historical sermons tend to picture scenes described in the text. The Homilies corpus includes five panegyrics (to Kaisarios, Gorgonia, the elder Gregory, Basil, and Athanasios),

---

[4] Folios 43v, 52r, 67v, 71v, 78r, 104r, 149r, 285r; figs. 9–11, 13, 15, 17, 20, 29.

[5] Folios 78r, 104r, 239r, 285r, 301r, 332v, 340r, 367v, 374v, 409v, 438v, 452r; figs. 15, 17, 27, 29–30, 33–34, 38–40, 44, 46.

[6] Folios 3r, 30v, 52v, 67v, 71v, 87v, 137r, 143v, 149r, 174v, 215v, 226v, 239r, 264v, 360r, 426v, 452r; figs. 6–7, 10–11, 13, 16, 18–20, 23, 25–28, 37, 42, 46.

[7] Folios 32v, 43v, 52v, 69v, 75r, 87v, 137r, 143v, 165r, 170r, 174v, 196v, 215v, 226v, 264v, 285r, 310v, 316r, 347v, 355r, 360r, 409v, 424v, 435v, 438v, 440r; figs. 8–10, 12, 14, 16, 18–19, 21–26, 28–29, 31–32, 35–37, 40–41, 43–45.

[8] Folios 32v, 69v, 75r, 165r, 170r, 196v, 310v, 316r, 355r, 440r. It is possible that ff. 347v and 435v should be added to this group; the problems connected with these two pages will be considered later in this chapter.

four praises (to Mamas, Cyprian, the Makkabees, and Heron), one *vita* (of Gregory), and two sermons against Julian the Apostate. The sermons dedicated to Athanasios and Mamas are not illustrated, and the miniatures now accompanying the funeral oration to Kaisarios and 'On Heron' are both on inserted leaves and may be misplaced. Of the remaining eight, only the miniature accompanying the funeral oration to Gregory's father pictures anything *but* episodes drawn from the subject's life.

The significant conceptual relationship between image and text, however, is dialectic: how each miniature worked with its accompanying text, and what the combined message of word and image might say to a circumscribed ninth-century audience. This can never be a simple relationship. When an image introduces a text, it predisposes the viewer/reader to think in certain ways about the words that follow, and that same audience sees an image embedded in a text. Efforts to decode the image–text–audience messages are obviously necessary when there is no overt connection between the sermon and its illustration, but even in those cases where Gregory specifically mentions an episode that appears in the accompanying miniature, we cannot simply presume that modest pictorialization was the goal. Gregory's references to the scenes pictured range from the rare explicit description (as for the scenes of Basil's life on f. 104r; fig. 17) to allusion (as when 'all must come into the net of God, and be caught by the words of the fishers' receives the calling of James, John, Peter and Andrew as an illustration on f. 87v; fig. 16). Often one episode of seemingly minor importance to Gregory's narrative receives illustration while other more central themes are ignored. The selection of episodes to picture was not, however, whimsical, but seems rather to have been carefully thought through. As illustrated by the examples that follow, the episodes selected were normally chosen to make a particular point, and they were frequently combined with scenes not mentioned by Gregory at all in order to focus the visual commentary even more sharply.

The inscriptions applied to individual miniatures do little to explicate the sense of the page as a whole,[9] but we are often guided to this point by markings in the text itself. As noted in the Introduction, Paris.gr.510 is the first preserved Byzantine book to incorporate painted initials, and it retains over 1600 of them (fig. 47).[10] While the quantity of decorated letters – nearly 90% of which are gilded – was presumably meant to underscore the luxurious quality of the manuscript, the particular circumstances that shaped the manuscript also made enlarged initials an asset in another way. Because the miniatures of the Paris Gregory often serve as visual commentaries on the sermons rather than as literal illustrations of their content, the connection between a picture and its text is sometimes not obvious, and at times a short digression – or even a single phrase – determines the subject of the miniature.

[9] The rare exceptions will be noted; see further Brubaker (1996b).
[10] Brubaker (1991); see also Appendix C.

These crucial lines are signalled, almost without exception, throughout Paris.gr.510 either by marginal quotation marks (*oboloi*) or, more commonly, by enlarged initials. Thirty-five of the text illustrations certainly retain their original location; of these, three are exegetical images with no direct connection to any specific passage in the accompanying homily, and one has lost its sermon. A relevant text passage could be marked only for the remaining thirty-one illustrations, and of these twenty-seven include annotation in their accompanying text to aid the reader in interpreting the picture.[11] Two rely exclusively on *oboloi* to mark the crucial lines, two use both *oboloi* and initials, and the remaining twenty-three depend entirely on enlarged letters to signal the vital passage. Some of the painted initials in the Paris Homilies thus have a specific function that is, to my knowledge, unique: they play the role of *lemmata*, tying the miniature to the text it interprets. It should nonetheless be noted that the *lemmata* initials conserve an older scribal practice of using marginal signs as a type of index. Further, not all initials serve as *lemmata*: the distribution is often governed by the layout and content of the Homilies text.[12]

The interaction between the miniatures and the sermons is straightforward in those cases where the miniature illustrates the circumstances under which Gregory delivered the sermon, or pictures the main theme of the homily as expressed in its title: f. 78r (fig. 15), for example, prefaces Gregory's sermon on a hailstorm and shows him delivering it below a representation of the storm; f. 301r (fig. 30) introduces 'On Pentecost', and duly depicts the biblical event. Miniatures that present scenes selected from among the many more episodes mentioned by Gregory in the text of the sermon involved either an element of chance or of choice: I shall argue for the latter, and use f. 137r to provide a paradigmatic example of how such selection could be used to provide a visual commentary on the text. Discussion of the fourth type of interaction, quasi-independent exegesis, follows.

Selection as commentary

Folio 137r (18)[13] (fig. 18)

Folio 137r shows scenes from the infancy of Christ: the adoration of the Magi shares the first register with the Magi's dream; the massacre of the innocents pairs with the flight of Elizabeth and the martyrdom of Zacharias in the second; and the presentation in the temple spreads across the whole of the lowest register.[14] The miniature introduces Gregory's nineteenth homily, 'To Julian the tax collector', the text of

---

[11] All are noted in the discussions of individual miniatures.   [12] See Brubaker (1991).

[13] The number in parentheses following the folio number indicates its placement: f. 137r is the eighteenth miniature in Paris.gr.510 as it is now preserved.

[14] Omont (1929), 20, pl. XXXII; Morey (1929), 95; Shorr (1946), 17–32; Der Nersessian (1962), 215–216; Bussagli (1985/86), 47.

which begins on the verso of the miniature and runs to f. 143r.[15] The picture is thus assuredly in its intended location, and Gregory mentions two of the illustrated scenes – the adoration of the Magi and the massacre of the innocents – in his twelfth paragraph. Both passages were signalled by the scribe: the only marginal *oboloi* in the homily mark the citation from Luke with which Gregory begins his brief account of Christ's infancy, while a gold initial introduces the passage on the massacre of the innocents later in the paragraph. The remaining scenes on the page, however, are not mentioned, and even the adoration and the massacre were selected because they complement the most important theme of the homily, not because Gregory devoted much time to them in his sermon.[16]

'To Julian the tax collector' concentrates on sacrifice and offering. Gregory counsels his audience to 'render unto Caesar those things which are Caesar's' (Matthew 22:21),[17] but admonishes Julian: 'you who are the registrar of our taxes … enrol my people in justice, in sanctity and benevolence, taking into consideration nothing but the fact that our Lord was born during such an enrolment'.[18] Gregory then briefly relates the events surrounding the birth of Christ, ending with the massacre of the innocents; he notes that most people cannot duplicate the costly gifts presented to Christ by the Magi, but argues that offerings from the spirit are more significant than material ones.[19] The theme of offering reasserts itself in references to the parable of the widow's mite and in lists of appropriate gifts to God paraphrased from Exodus 25 and 35.[20]

From among the infancy episodes mentioned by Gregory, the miniaturist pictured the two most relevant to the theme of offering and sacrifice: the adoration of the Magi,[21] and the 'sacrificial' massacre of the innocents.[22] The Magi's dream and the Elizabeth and Zacharias episodes continue the two narratives; more importantly, the slaying of Zacharias reinforced the theme of sacrifice, and linked the middle with the lowest register: following the Protevangelion (which identifies Simeon, the priest at the presentation, as Zacharias' successor[23]), the conjoint images present successive priests of the temple at Jerusalem.

The presentation fits well with the scheme of offering and sacrifice expressed in the first two registers. It represents the ritual offering of a firstborn male child to

---

[15] *PG* 35:1044–1064; on the context, Gallay (1943), 128.

[16] For this reason, neither the Milan Gregory nor the liturgical editions of the Homilies includes any of the scenes pictured on f. 137r: cf. Grabar (1943a), pls. XXI–XXII; Galavaris (1969), 42–46.

[17] *PG* 35:1056A9–10.   [18] Ibid., :1057A4–10; trans. Galavaris (1969), 43.

[19] Ibid., 1057A10–C9.   [20] Ibid., 1052B9, 13–20.

[21] For a classic expression, see John Chrysostom's eighth homily 'On Matthew': *PG* 57:81–84.

[22] Photios, for example, emphasized the sacrificial role of the massacred children (*Amphilochia*, question 26: *PG* 101:192–197; ed. Westerink 4 [1986], 96–99) while Theodore of Mopsuestia compared the massacre with the crucifixion (Reuss [1957], 99).

[23] Protevangelion 24: Hennecke and Schneemelcher I (1963), 388.

God, and the sacrifice of two turtledoves (prominently held by Joseph). The episode consummates the idea of offering and sacrifice inherent in the upper two registers and supplements the underlying theme of the homily. Visual parallels with the rest of the page confirm that the presentation was meant to continue the ideas expressed above it. Not only do the high priests and the temple of Jerusalem unite the lower two registers, but the presentation is also connected with the adoration at the top of the page. Joseph's stance is the same in both scenes, and he, Mary, and Christ line up in the third register directly beneath their portrayals in the first: though Mary sits with Christ in her lap during the adoration, the positions of the figures are otherwise virtually identical, and Christ turns to gesture toward the Magi as he reaches toward Simeon in the presentation. These compositional links parallel ninth-century commentaries, such as one written by Photios, that related the offerings of the Magi to sacrifices in the temple.[24] Liturgical associations may also be relevant. The presentation was celebrated on 2 February, with supplementary readings from Hebrews 7:7–17 that include a passage which dovetails with the sense of the homily: 'Here tithes are received by mortal men; there, by one of whom it is testified that he lives.'[25]

Folio 137r illustrates how scenes were selected from among those mentioned by Gregory, and then combined with other scenes to provide a unified visual commentary that supplemented the main theme of the accompanying sermon. Details within the miniature itself add density to the meaning of the page, and communicate a different series of messages as well.

As in virtually all Byzantine depictions of the adoration of the Magi (Matthew 2:1–11), f. 137r shows the enthroned Mary holding the Christ Child.[26] The exotic 'Persian' dress of the Magi conforms with standard practice, while the configuration of the trio, with the first Magus half kneeling and the other two looking at each other, recurs in an eighth-century fresco in Rome (Sta Maria Antiqua; fig. 61), and in an early tenth-century wall painting in Cappadocia (Old Tokalı).[27] Sta Maria Antiqua also anticipated the most unusual elements of the composition, the inclusion of Joseph and the half-figure of the angel hovering above Christ;[28] both also appear in tenth-century Cappadocian frescoes that are

[24] *Amphilochia*, question 306: *PG* 101:1148–1152; ed. Westerink 6 [1987], 104–105.

[25] Mateos I (1963), 220–225.

[26] For two of the rare exceptions, see Weitzmann (1951b), 59–62, figs. 6, 10; and Florence, Laur.plut.6.23, f. 6v (Velmans [1971], fig. 12). In Paris.gr.510, the scene is laconically titled in red on the frame ἡ προσκύνησις τῶν μάγων ('the worship of the Magi').

[27] Grüneisen (1911), fig. 83, pl. XXI; Epstein (1986), fig. 20; see also the marginal psalters London, BL Add.40.731, f. 115v (Dufrenne [1966], pl. 54) and London, BL Add.19.352, f. 92r (Der Nersessian [1970], fig. 150).

[28] On the angel, anticipated in John Chrysostom's seventh homily on Matthew (*PG* 57:78), see Bussagli (1985/86).

Fig. 61 Rome, Sta Maria Antiqua: adoration of the Magi

considered to be reliable witnesses to slightly earlier Constantinopolitan tastes.[29] As Charles Rufus Morey observed long ago, the Gregory adoration virtually duplicates that at Sta Maria Antiqua;[30] its painter was evidently familiar with a tradition current in eighth-century Rome which, as the Cappadocian wall paintings confirm, remained familiar in the Byzantine capital in the last quarter of the ninth century. Most important here, such close analogues suggests that the visual parallels drawn between the adoration and the presentation on f. 137r were not achieved through iconographic manipulation of the adoration; instead, modifications were imposed on the composition of the presentation in order to unify the page.

Unlike the familiar adoration, the dream of the Magi (identified as such by the legend O XPHMATICMOC TΩN MAΓΩN) makes its first preserved Byzantine

[29] Joseph recurs at Old Tokalı and Kiliçlar, the half-angel at New Tokalı (second quarter of the tenth century): Epstein (1986), figs. 20, 64; Restle II (1967), fig. 269. Vezin (1950), 85–88 and Bussagli (1985/86), 42–47 catalogue examples of the adoration that include the (normally full-length) angel. On the formal and iconographic relationship between the paintings in Old Tokalı and slightly earlier products from Constantinople, Epstein (1986), 18–19; on the same relationship between New Tokalı and Constantinople, ibid., 39–44 (though Thierry [1989], esp. 231, suggests instead links with Georgia).   [30] Morey (1929), 95.

appearance on f. 137r. The Magi sleep, uncovered and in a vertical pile on a hillock, as an angel strides toward them gesturing its warning. The biblical description of the episode (Matthew 2:12) makes no mention of an angel messenger; though this is a standard feature of apocryphal texts such as the Protevangelion,[31] the Homilies version of the dream has little in common with either contemporary western renditions or the few middle Byzantine images that survive.[32] Instead, the dominant figures of the angel and the central Magus duplicate a formula associated with a different dream, that of Joseph. Joseph's dream immediately follows the adoration and dream of the Magi in Matthew's account (2:13); illustrated gospelbooks, all later in date than Paris.gr.510, insert it between the adoration and the massacre of the innocents which follows on the next register of f. 137r.[33] It is possible that the Homilies miniaturist knew an infancy sequence that anticipated those preserved from later periods, with an image of Joseph's dream precisely where the dream of the Magi appears on f. 137r, and adapted the Magi's dream from a representation of Joseph's.

The middle register combines the massacre of the innocents (Η ΒΡΕΦΟΚ-ΤΟΝΙ[Α]) with Elizabeth and the infant John the Baptist hiding in the mountain, and culminates with the martyrdom of Zacharias. For the massacre (Matthew 2:16), Herod (ΗΡΟΔΗϹ) sits, flanked by two guards, and directs a single soldier. Though in its general morphology this group remains fairly consistent in Byzantium, earlier examples (fig. 62) anticipate Herod's gesture, and include both attendant guards, while later examples show but a single guard, or none at all.[34] The response of the mothers – who do not appear on f. 137r – and the manner of dispatching the children varies considerably.[35] In Paris.gr.510, the soldier raises a sword with one arm, and – unusually but dramatically – suspends a child by its hair with the other.[36]

The gospels omit the middle episode of the second register, but the

[31] Protevangelion 21:4: Hennecke and Schneemelcher I, 386.

[32] See Vezin (1950), 100–103. In the west, the Magi normally huddle together under a single blanket in a large bed: Schiller I (1971), 99–100; but compare the Metz ivory of ca. 850 discussed by Deshman (1989), 55, fig. 29. The middle Byzantine gospelbooks Florence, Laur.plut.6.23 and Paris.gr.74 omit the episode, nor does it appear in the Magi sequence in Vat.gr.1156. Mount Athos, Esphigmenou 14 and Jerusalem, Taphou 14 follow the Protevangelion account and show the Magi awake when the angel appears: see Lafontaine-Dosogne (1975), 216–217; Lafontaine-Dosogne (1987a), 211–224.

[33] See e.g. Florence, Laur.plut.6.23, ff. 6v–7r: Velmans (1971), figs. 12–14; and, for a similar dream image, the cathedra of Maximianus: Volbach and Hirmer (1961), fig. 230.

[34] E.g. the Rabbula Gospels of 586, a fifth-century ivory in Milan, and the sixth- or seventh-century frescoes at Deir Abu Hinnis (fig. 62): Florence, Laur.plut.1.56, f. 4v (Cecchelli et al. [1959]); Volbach (1976), no. 119; Clédat (1902), 9; Grüneisen (1922), pl. XXIX. For later examples, Millet (1916), 158–163.   [35] See Stavropoulou-Makri (1990), esp. 366–369.

[36] The motif recurs in a post-Byzantine gospelbook and, perhaps, at Deir Abu Hinnis: Der Nersessian (1926/27), fig. 57; Grüneisen (1922), pl. XXIX; Lafontaine-Dosogne (1975), fig. 57. The hair-grasping itself is common: e.g. Volbach (1976), no.186; Byzance (1992), 82–83; Velmans (1971), fig. 14; Omont (n.d.), pl. 7; Lafontaine-Dosogne (1975), fig. 60a; Stavropoulou-Makri (1990), fig.3.

Fig, 62 Deir Abu Hinnis: massacre of the innocents, Elizabeth and John the Baptist hiding in the mountain, Zacharias

Protevangelion describes the flight of Elizabeth with John the Baptist in detail.[37] As is often the case with apocryphal material, images of Elizabeth's flight appear with some frequency in pre-iconoclast and Palaiologan art, but more rarely during the middle Byzantine period proper, except in Cappadocia.[38] Two major variants appear: Elizabeth flees,[39] or, as on f. 137r, she hides in the mountain. The latter episode differs in the number (if any) and weaponry of the soldiers pursuing Elizabeth, in Elizabeth's position (standing or seated), and in whether she is fully exposed or half hidden in the mountain. Folio 137r shows a single soldier bearing a lance searching for Elizabeth who sits, half obscured by a rocky outcrop, safely within the mountain.[40] The closest comparison appears in the sixth- or seventh-century frescoes at Deir Abu Hinnis (fig. 62); a sixth-century pyxis now in the Louvre is also similar, but shows the full figure of Elizabeth.[41]

Parallels between f. 137r and Deir Abu Hinnis continue in the final scene of the middle register, the martyrdom of Zacharias, which, like the flight of Elizabeth, is missing from the gospels but appears in the Protevangelion.[42] Unlike the tenth-century Cappadocian wall paintings at Old Tokalı and Çavuşin, which show the discussion between Zacharias and Herod's henchmen, or the Menologion of Basil

[37] Protevangelion 22; Hennecke and Schneemelcher I (1963), 387.

[38] For a survey of the monuments, see Lafontaine-Dosogne (1975), 230–231.

[39] E.g. Grabar (1958), pl. LVI; Mount Athos, Esphigmenou 14, f. 410v: Pelekanides *et al.* 2 (1975), fig. 392. See also the Sinai icon reproduced by Lafontaine-Dosogne (1975), fig. 40.

[40] Both Elizabeth and John are identified by inscriptions: ΕΛΙСΑΒΕΤ and Ο ΠΡΟΔ[Ρ]ΟΜΟС (the forerunner).

[41] Clédat (1902), 9; on the pyxis, Volbach (1976), no. 186. Later examples such as the Rockefeller-McCormick New Testament show a half-figure of Elizabeth, but no soldier: Chicago, Univ.Lib.965, f. 9v (Willoughby [1932]).   [42] Protevangelion 23: Hennecke and Schneemelcher I (1963), 387.

II (ca. 1000), which portrays a conventional martyrdom of the 'sacrifice of Isaac' type, Paris.gr.510 and Deir Abu Hinnis picture a soldier lunging toward a kneeling Zacharias (ZAXAPIAC) stationed before an elaborate architectural backdrop in the forecourt of the temple.[43] A simplified version of this same formula recurs in the middle Byzantine tetraevangelion in Paris, where Zacharias' martyrdom is used to illustrate one of Christ's parables.[44]

Relatively close iconographic parallels with a single monument are unusual for the narrative sequences in Paris.gr.510; and the ties between the second register of f. 137r and Deir Abu Hinnis, coupled with the adoration's parallel at Sta Maria Antiqua, may suggest that the narrative of Christ's infancy spread out over the first and second registers followed a single – and relatively old – source, heavily dependent on the apocryphal Protevangelion. If so, however, the later witnesses to isolated scenes that we have seen in Cappadocia and the Paris tetraevangelion indicate that any sequence drawn on by the Homilies miniaturist continued to have currency well into the middle Byzantine period. The coherence of the upper two registers is, in any event, underscored by the manipulation of the composition of the lowest register to express visually the thematic and exegetic relationships among all of the scenes on the page.

The bottom register devotes itself to a single theme, the presentation in the temple (Luke 2:25–35). The composition is asymmetrical: in order to line up Joseph (IΩCHΦ), Mary and Jesus beneath their portrayals in the adoration of the first register, the action in the lowest tier shifts to the left. Simeon (CYMEΩN) thus stands dead centre – beneath the Magi of the adoration – and an ornate altar set before a structure evidently meant to represent the temple occupies most of the right side, beneath Zacharias' temple. The bottom register has been arranged to complement the scenes above it: the holy family reduplicates itself, Simeon's outstretched arms parallel those of the Magi, and the temple – outside and inside – lines up on the right.

The presentation does not seem to have been celebrated as a great feast by the orthodox church until the eighth century, and representations of it before that time are rare.[45] Dorothy Shorr argued that the elevation of the presentation resulted in a shift of attention from the narrative account of the priest Simeon recognizing the Messiah with great joy (the *hypopante* – which is in fact the legend attached to this scene on f. 137r: H YΠOΠANTH) to a more hieratic and symmetrical image focus-

---

[43] Epstein (1986), fig. 23; Restle II (1967), fig. 307; Vat.gr.1613, p. 14 (*Menologio* [1907]); Grüneisen (1922), pls. XXIX–XXX. For an unfortunately fragmentary sixth-century Constantinopolitan representation: Lafontaine-Dosogne (1975), 231, fig. 59.   [44] Paris.gr.74, f. 46v: Omont (n.d.), pl. 38.

[45] It is first cited in a list drawn up by John of Euboea: Millet (1916), 20, 23. The fifth-century mosaic at Sta Maria Maggiore in Rome is at best tangentially related to later presentations (Karpp [1966], pl. 13; for a different interpretation, Spain [1979]); the fragmentary seventh-century mosaic at the Kalenderhane Camii in Constantinople, however, generally anticipates the image on f. 137r: Striker and Doğan Kuban (1971), 251–258, fig. 11; Striker and Doğan Kuban (1997), 121–124, pl. 148.

ing on the presentation proper. A group of enamel reliquary crosses demonstrates the existence of the symmetrical 'liturgical' formula, with the figures grouped around an altar, by the ninth century, and it remained the most common way of depicting the presentation thereafter in Byzantium.[46] Folio f. 137r cannot, however, be slotted into this development as an example of 'archaic' retention of an earlier formula, for apart from the skewed composition the presentation in Paris.gr.510 corresponds closely with a group of roughly contemporary works. The ninth-century Martvili triptych, the Khludov Psalter, and two Cappadocian churches of ca. 900 (Kiliçlar and Göreme 6a) are strikingly similar; the Psalter even duplicates the somewhat lopsided disposition of the ciborium over Simeon's altar.[47] Of these, all but the Kiliçlar fresco join with the Homilies in portraying Jesus nearly in Simeon's outstretched arms, a motif that finds parallels in contemporary sermons and, according to Shorr, reveals the first tentative impact of the new liturgical importance of the presentation.[48] It is only the position of the altar that distinguishes Paris.gr.510 from these examples; the figures are practically interchangeable. While other ninth-century versions emphasize the central altar in accord with new liturgical requirements, Paris.gr.510 balances the presentation against the adoration of the Magi and martyrdom of Zacharias to consolidate the visual themes of offering and sacrifice.

Neither thematic nor compositional coherence, however, required the dream of the Magi, the flight of Elizabeth, or the stress on the temple of Jerusalem and its high priests. The dream and the flight may simply instance narratives continued despite the fact that the additional scene no longer sustained the point made by the first – a type of expansion familiar in the ninth century from the *Sacra Parallela*[49] – but Elizabeth's flight, and the emphasis on the temple and its priest, also introduce two currents that run throughout the manuscript. These stem from, and relate to, the audience rather than playing against or with the text, and they shift the ways selection may be used as commentary to a different level.

Elizabeth provides the female component of the middle register, a balance to Mary in the top and bottom tiers. Her inclusion fits a broad tendency in Paris.gr.510 to counterpose images of women and men;[50] Elizabeth's portrayal with the infant John the Baptist also conforms with a general emphasis on family rela-

---

[46] Kartsonis (1986), 102–103, figs. 25a, 26a. For a later example, see Mount Athos, Iviron 5: Pelekanides *et al.* II (1975), fig. 28. Further examples in Townsley (1974), 22–30. For an early asymmetrical composition see e.g. the (now lost) fresco from Sta Maria Antiqua (705–707), where Anna joined Joseph behind the Virgin (Grüneisen [1911], pl. IC.LXVII,2); for two rare later ones, the Bristol Psalter (London, BL Add.40.731, f. 263v; Dufrenne [1966], pl. 60) and an eleventh-century ivory plaque in St Petersburg (Goldschmidt and Weitzmann II [1930], no. 59), both of which omit Joseph and Anna.

[47] Kartsonis (1986), fig. 37b; Moscow, Hist.Mus.129, f. 163v (Ščepkina [1977]); Restle II (1967), figs. 58, 59, 97.   [48] Shore (1946); see too Maguire (1980/81), esp. 264–267.   [49] See chapter 1.

[50] Concomitantly, men and women are rarely presented in opposition, which may be one reason why the mothers have been omitted from the massacre.

tionships: mothers and children (especially sons, as Mary and Jesus in the enveloping registers) or husbands and wives. These themes will be considered in chapter 9, but I flag the pattern now to indicate that the significance of Elizabeth's presence on f. 137r probably goes beyond a desire to sustain coherent narrative blocks.

Folio 137r also introduces the apparent impact of the patriarch Photios, who stressed the sacrificial role of the massacred infants and linked the offerings of the Magi with sacrifices in the temple in a chain of connections that unites all three registers.[51] More idiosyncratically, Photios was interested in the high priesthood and the temple in Jerusalem. As Michael Maas demonstrated, his glosses of Josephus in the *Bibliotheke* ignored huge chunks of the texts in question and instead concentrated on Herod, the priests, and the temple.[52] The priests and the temple are, of course, exactly what receive exceptional emphasis on f. 137r, and it is this curious stress that suggests the guiding hand of Photios.

Photios was interested in these particular sections of Josephus for a specific purpose. In his summaries, Photios not only isolated the sections pertaining to Herod, the high priests and the temple; he also rearranged the material he selected in order to make it corroborate his argument that secular authorities should not intervene in religious affairs.[53] Photios was, in other words, using (or manipulating) older texts to buttress his own concerns. This pattern is not unusual in Photios' writings;[54] indeed, he was simply exaggerating a familiar characteristic of the eighth and ninth centuries.[55] But his interests here go beyond the use of past authorities to justify his own conclusions, for he reveals an almost obsessive fascination with the temple itself. As Maas put it, 'he lays on with a trowel technical specifics about its rebuilding. He loves numbers and precise measurements. [Photios] includes lengthy descriptions not essential to the development of his theme but nonetheless revealing of his own predilection for detail.'[56] While the focus on Zacharias and Simeon could be interpreted as underscoring Photios' interests in the status of religious authority, the emphasis on the temple – which, along with the alignment of the holy family in the first and third registers, resulted in a composition of the presentation that is without parallel – is both more unusual and more overtly reflective of the personal interests of the patriarch.[57]

The writings of Photios have strong bonds with the miniatures of Paris.gr.510; the nature of this relationship will be considered in chapter 5. Here, one additional point deserves mention. In his synopses of Josephus, Photios was not only selective of the material he summarized, he also added historical details. These included, for

---

[51] See notes 22 and 24 above.   [52] Maas (1990), 183–194. On the *Bibliotheke* see chapter 5.
[53] Maas (1990), esp. 183–187. See also Alexander's remarks, reported by Lemerle (1986), 209 note 15; and chapter 5.   [54] See, e.g., the discussion of f. 355r in chapter 5.   [55] See chapter 1.
[56] Maas (1990), 188.
[57] A parallel may be drawn with Photios' interest in Christ's tomb, discussed in connection with f. 285r in chapter 5.

example, the fact (omitted by Josephus) that Herod authorized the massacre of the innocents.[58] We shall find precisely this sort of almost offhand supplementary detail rampant, in visual form, in the miniatures of Paris.gr.510.

Image as exegesis

Exegesis literally means 'leading out'. Practically, it means interpretation, and usually the interpretation of biblical or patristic texts. In the miniatures of Paris.gr.510, image as exegesis – visual interpretation – works in a number of ways. Most basically, the miniatures interpret the past: like virtually all other Byzantine images, those in the Homilies create a visual memory of what past events looked like. Some of the miniatures not only construct or reconstruct the past, but envision links between the biblical past and the ninth-century present. Again, Paris.gr.510 is not alone in this: *vide* the page in the Khludov Psalter that juxtaposes Christ's torments on the cross with the defacement of his image by iconoclasts (fig. 57). Also like the Khludov Psalter, the Homilies miniatures interpret the text that they accompany. As we have just seen, the interpretation may be conveyed by the selection of particular passages for illustration. It may also, however, be conveyed by scenes not mentioned in the text at all. While all biblical images can be considered visual exegesis in the sense that they re-interpret a written narrative, and all miniatures sanction a particular reading of their accompanying text, this group presents image *as* exegesis. The following miniatures exemplify the process.

Folio 360r (37) (fig. 37)

The miniatures that parallel the theme(s) of the sermon without relying on the text for specific examples are often among the most difficult to understand, and can pose methodological problems for modern scholars. Sometimes, however, the visual analogy is reasonably clear, and seems to have been based on allusions made by Gregory himself in the accompanying sermon: such is the case with f. 360r.[59] Excision of the prefatory headpiece to Gregory's third oration 'On peace' on its verso has mutilated the upper register, which retains portions of the construction of the tower of Babel;[60] the lower register portrays Noah's ark. Though Gregory mentions neither episode – and the Milan Homilies includes a different sequence of images, all of which stem directly from the text[61] – the beginning of 'On peace' III on its verso demonstrates that the miniature was intended to introduce this sermon.[62]

---

[58] See Maas (1990), esp. 188.   [59] Omont (1929), 28, pl. LI; Der Nersessian (1962), 209–210.

[60] Bordier (1885), 83, misidentified this scene as Noah building the ark, an error that has been rectified in most, but not all, subsequent literature.

[61] Grabar (1943a), pls. XLIX,2–3, L,1, LI,4, LII,1.

[62] SC 270, 218–259. The sermon is sometimes incorrectly referred to as the second oration 'On peace', following an error in the Maurist edition reprinted by Migne in *PG* 35.

The loss of the headpiece means that we do not know the precise title given to Gregory's oration by the ninth-century scribe; in several medieval copies, it is aptly subtitled 'to the lovers of discord'.[63] The sermon contains a lament over the perilous condition of Christianity around the year 380, which Gregory blames on malice and trinitarian heresies.[64] He lists the disasters ensuing from God's displeasure at this state – 'countries devastated, myriads of fallen victims, the earth covered with blood and ruins, people speaking in barbarous tongues' – and wonders 'What person of good sense would not lament the present situation?'[65] But, he continues, even sensible Christians now fan the fires of discord, and he exhorts his listeners to strive for unity and peace, and to avoid that refuge of the enemies of orthodoxy, superficial language.[66] Gregory reminds his audience that though heresy rends the church, there is only one true battle, the struggle against evil, and that Christ became a human man in order to die a human death, be resurrected, and thus save them all.[67]

Gregory's complaints about the misuse of language, and especially his reference to 'people speaking in barbarous tongues', evidently suggested the image of the tower of Babel (Genesis 11:1–9). Beyond this, Sirarpie Der Nersessian argued that the image provided a visual parallel to Gregory's account of the destruction of unity within the church:[68] in other sermons copied in Paris.gr.510, the tower of Babel appears as a biblical analogue to fourth-century heresies, in contrast with the orthodox trinitarian view in which 'all speak the same language'.[69] Der Nersessian observed that similar oppositions appear throughout Byzantine exegesis and in the liturgy for Pentecost, where the bestowal of tongues on the apostles that enabled them to unify the world through Christ is set against the confusion of tongues imposed by God to disperse the gentiles. The tower of Babel acts as a visual encapsulation of the perils of ecclesiastical discord and particularly, in Gregory's writings, of discord brought about by trinitarian heresies – the subject of the oration.

As Der Nersessian noted, the pendant scene of Noah's ark complements the tower of Babel: while the latter symbolized discord, Noah's ark represented the concord of the unified church.[70] Most Byzantine commentators saw Noah's ark as a prefiguration of baptism,[71] but in the ninth century Photios appropriated a less common reading more relevant to f. 360r. In 'On the Annunciation', Photios addressed Mary as the 'living ark of God, in which the second Noah, having come to dwell, took in and saved well nigh our entire human race, that had been sub-

---

[63] See SC 270, 206–208.   [64] Ibid., 222.   [65] Ibid., 222–224.   [66] Ibid., 230, 234, 245.
[67] Ibid., 246–248, 250, 256.   [68] Der Nersessian (1962), 209–210.   [69] SC 270, 286 and note 1.
[70] Der Nersessian cited John Chrysostom's 'The ark is the church, Noah is Christ, the dove the Holy Spirit, the olive branch the divine philanthropy. As the ark in the midst of the waters protected those inside it, so does the church protect those who have strayed': *De Lazaro concio* VI.7 in *PG* 48:1037–1038.   [71] See Daniélou (1956), 75–85; Daniélou (1960), 69–102.

merged by the storm of sins, and afforded us models and examples of a second life and a more divine conduct'.[72] Here, the ark is a type of the Virgin, Noah is a type of Christ, and the waters of the deluge represent human sin.[73] Noah in his ark prefigures the advent of Christ as man, a theme that recurs in Photios' sermon 'On Holy Saturday', where Noah's ark is contrasted with the 'world saving ark of the saviour's body', the incarnate Christ.[74]

Photios' use of Noah's ark confirms and augments Der Nersessian's modern interpretation of f. 360r. Through the incarnation of Christ, prefigured by Noah in his ark, Christians escape the 'storm of sins' represented here by the tower of Babel. Belief in Christ's human nature remedied the discord caused by the trinitarian heresies railed against by Gregory in the third oration 'On peace'. The miniature is thus internally unified and, though evidently inspired by allusions in the text, presents a pictorial commentary on the sermon that relies on ninth-century interpretations of the scenes pictured.[75]

Folio 143v (19) (fig. 19)

In addition to scenes that visually pick up Gregory's implicit allusions, some exegetical miniatures incorporate scenes indirectly inspired by Gregory's reference to their main protagonist. Folio 143v does both in its upper register, which shows Jeremiah in a pit and the penitence of David. The lower registers, with the parable of the Good Samaritan above two healings (of the paralytic and of the woman with the issue of blood) and the raising of Jairus' daughter, provide an independent pictorial commentary.[76]

Folio 143v prefaces 'To the people of Nazianzus and the prefect' (Homily 17), which begins on the facing leaf.[77] Gregory delivered the sermon in 373/4 during a dispute between the citizens of Nazianzus and the provincial government; he assured the crowd of the relief the Lord brings to sufferers,[78] urged the prefect to be merciful, and likened his sorrow over the conflict to Jeremiah's suffering for Israel. Gold initials signal both sentences on f. 144r that deal with the prophet's trials,[79] presumabiy to link them with the opening image of Jeremiah on the facing page. Following Henri Omont, this scene has customarily been identified as Jeremiah being lowered into the pit (Jeremiah 38:5–6). In fact, however, we see the prophet

---

[72] Homily 7,7: ed. Laourdas (1959), 82; trans. Mango (1958), 148.

[73] The latter equation apparently relies on Revelation 17:15: see Daniélou (1960), 75–76.

[74] Homily 11,7: ed. Laourdas, 118–119; trans. Mango (1958), 209.

[75] On the iconography of the two scenes, see chapter 8.

[76] Millet (1920), 241; Omont (1929), 20–21, pl. XXXIII; Morey (1929), 36, 95; Buchthal (1938), 27–30; Gallay (1943), 123–124; Der Nersessian (1962), 215–216; Weitzmann (1979a), 175–176, 185; Ishizuka (1986), 3–22; Narkiss (1987), 425–426; Brubaker (1996a), 12–13; Brubaker (1996b), 105–106.

[77] PG 35:964–982.

[78] E.g. ibid. 969A11–16, marked with *oboloi* on f. 145r; numerous similar sentiments are signalled in the Paris text.   [79] Ibid., 964B4–965A6, 965B6–11.

raised out of the mire by two youths at the direction of King Zedekiah, who watches from a tower (Jeremiah 38:7–13). The inscription – 'Jeremiah in the mire' (IEPEMIAC EN BOPBOPΩ) – neither confirms nor denies this reidentification, which is based on the presence of King Zedekiah, who distanced himself from the lowering of Jeremiah into the pit but directed his release from it, and the 'old rotten rags' held by the two youths (one of whom looks to the king for directions), which replaced the cord that lowered Jeremiah into the pit during his removal from it.[80] We have, then, a portrayal of Jeremiah inspired by Gregory's text, but instead of the prophet's trials, we see the result of Zedekiah's clemency. The substitution results in a scene that augments Gregory's plea that the prefect of Nazianzus should be merciful; it supplements rather than illustrates the text.

The penitence of David shares the uppermost register with Jeremiah's release from the pit and, like it, illustrates the theme of forgiveness. Gregory does not refer to the penitence directly, but his frequent mentions of David's grief and release from sorrow by God's pardon – nearly all signalled by gold initials or marginal quotation marks[81] – presumably encouraged the image of David's confession of, and release from, sin. While Bathsheba (BHPCABEE) watches from behind the king's empty throne, David (ΔA[YI]Δ), prostrate at the feet of the archangel Michael (O APXHCTPATHΓOC), confesses to Nathan the prophet (NAΘAN O ΠPOΦHTHC). Although the image agrees broadly with Byzantine iconographic tradition, its exclusive emphasis on David's admission of sin finds few parallels.[82] The accompanying inscriptions – 'I have sinned against the Lord' (HMAPTIKA TΩ K[YPI]Ω) next to David, 'and the Lord has put away thy sin' (KAI K[YPIO]C AΦHΛE[N] TO AMAPTHMA COY) before Nathan – are unusually extensive for Paris.gr.510,[83] and the (written) spoken dialogue brings an immediacy to the episode that makes explicit the theme of penitence and mercy.

Because Gregory did not specifically describe the episodes pictured, the Milan Homilies includes neither.[84] Yet the Jeremiah and David episodes reinforce Gregory's descriptions of the relief the Lord brings to sufferers, and express the virtues of leniency in a way particularly appropriate to this sermon. Gregory

---

[80] No comparable example exists to cement this reidentification: f. 143v shows the only preserved Byzantine version of the pit episode in either of its versions, while the few medieval western examples (see A. Heimann, s.v. 'Jeremias' in *LCI* II [1970], 390–391) are far later, and do not resemble Paris.gr.510. Jeremiah, with long grey hair and beard, does, however, conform in type with his portraits in other ninth-century Greek books (fig. 152): see also Weitzmann (1979a), figs. 361–371; Grabar (1943a), pls. IV,3, IX,3, XLIX,3. The type persisted in many later Byzantine examples: Lowden (1988), 50–51, figs. 51, 69, 72, 107, 108.

[81] E.g. on f. 144r, which marks *PG* 35:965C9–11 (*oboloi*) and 968A10–12 (initial).

[82] See chapter 8.

[83] See Brubaker (1996b) and chapter 9; for later western examples of this type of dialogue, Camille (1985).

[84] Instead, the miniaturist depicted Zephaniah and two preaching portraits: Grabar (1943a), pls. XXII,4, XXIII,1–2.

exhorted the citizens of Nazianzus to obey their leaders, but he was most concerned to ensure that the prefect was merciful,[85] and both scenes selected for the upper register play to this theme: Zedekiah listened to Jeremiah's friends and freed the prophet, while God, through the intermediary Nathan, heard David's admission and delivered him from sin.[86]

The second register illustrates the parable of the Good Samaritan (Luke 10:30–37) in four scenes set against a unified landscape background. Gregory does not mention the parable, but its point – that the Good Samaritan, who showed mercy, was the best neighbour – underscores his message to the prefect. As depicted on f. 143v, the parable also graphically demonstrates the relief God brings to those who suffer: to emphasize that the Lord is the source of comfort, Christ replaces the Good Samaritan in the miniature, a substitution accented by his central location and the unusual placement of Christ and the rescued man on a separate, foreground plane.

Two of the scenes derive from Luke 10:30: 'A certain man went down from Jerusalem to Jericho, and fell among thieves, who stripped him of his garments, and wounded him, and departed, leaving him half dead.' The miniaturist visualized the journey by framing the register with walled cities, Jerusalem (ΠΟ[ΛΙC] I[HPOYCA]ΛHM) on the left, and Jericho on the right (ΠΟ[ΛΙC] IEPIXΩ). The 'certain man' departs from Jerusalem on horseback – a detail found in no other version – and in the ensuing scene, stripped of his clothes, he is beaten by three thieves.[87] Next, a priest (IEPEYC) and a Levite (ΛEYITHC) pass the bleeding man by (Luke 10:31–32); the two men, identical except for the headpiece worn by the priest, look back at the dying man and gesture in consternation but stride vigorously away toward Jericho. Finally, the Good Samaritan, as Christ, sets the reclothed man from Jerusalem on his own horse (Luke 10:34). While most versions of this episode show the Samaritan leading the horse on which the wounded man sits toward an inn in Jericho,[88] neither the Rossano Gospels (fig. 63) nor the *Sacra Parallela* (fig. 64) follows f. 143v in showing the wounded man clothed; on the other hand, Rossano provides the only other instance where Christ stands in for the Samaritan (a detail perhaps suggested by references to Jesus as a Samaritan such as

[85] *PG* 35:976–980A2.

[86] Another level of significance might be attached to these images. Photios built, and was later buried in, a Monastery of Jeremiah on the outskirts of Constantinople (Hergenröther II [1867], 713), a commission that suggests a fondness for the prophet on the part of the patriarch; Photios also linked Basil to David, here shown repenting (see chapter 4). The conjunction of the released Jeremiah (Photios?) and the repenting David (Basil?) is, therefore, intriguing, though its possible implications go beyond the confines of this chapter.

[87] Weitzmann (1979a), 176, erroneously credits the Gregory illustrator with uniquely showing both the stripping and the beating. The scene is inscribed O ΠΕΡΙΠECΩN EIC TOYC ΛHCTAC.

[88] For the *Sacra Parallela* and Rossano images, see note 91 below; for the tetraevangelia (Laur.plut.6.23, f. 128v and Paris.gr.74, ff. 131v–132r), Velmans (1971), fig. 221 and Omont (n.d.), pl. 116.

Fig. 63 Rossano Gospels, f. 7v: parable of the Good Samaritan

that in John 8:48),[89] and the *Sacra Parallela* is otherwise the closest comparison to the sequence in Paris.gr.510.

Weitzmann isolated seven distinct moments of the Good Samaritan narrative illustrated in the five manuscripts that include the cycle.[90] Within this group, Paris.gr.510 and the *Sacra Parallela* (fig. 64) favour a distinct manner of representing the parable that shares neither scenes nor details with the other versions. The two ninth-century sequences alone include the representation of both Jericho

---

[89] For patristic connections, see Cavallo *et al.* (1987), 144.   [90] Weitzmann (1979a), 175–176.

Fig. 64 Paris.gr.923, f. 320v: Christ defending the apostles; Christ relating the parable of the Good Samaritan

and Jerusalem,[91] the trio of thieves (brandishing identical clubs), the priest and the Levite, and the man straddling the Samaritan's horse rather than riding sidesaddle. Though the *Sacra Parallela* does not follow f. 143v in replacing the Samaritan with Christ in this last scene, the weight of the other correlations implies that both miniaturists adapted a sequence familiar in ninth-century Constantinople.[92]

The healings of the paralytic, the woman with the issue of blood and Jairus' daughter in the bottom register continue the theme of salvation through Christ, a connection stressed visually by repeating Christ's placement in the centre of the composition, where the healing Christ's halo extends into the top border of the reg-

[91] Paris.gr.923, f. 320v: Weitzmann (1979a), 175–176, fig. 457a. Jerusalem, but not Jericho, appears in the Rossano Gospels (f. 1r): Cavallo *et al.* (1987), 143–145; Weitzmann (1977), fig. 32.

[92] See chapter 8.

ister to meet the feet of Christ as Good Samaritan as they protrude down into the same frame.[93]

The miniaturist presents the first miracle simply: Christ blesses a man with a bed litter slung over his shoulders, who looks back at Christ as he walks away from him. The scene includes none of the narrative details that distinguish the healing of the paralytic at Bethesda (John 5:2–15) from the healing at Capernaum (Matthew 9:2–7, Mark 2:3–12, Luke 5:18–25), and no identifying legends remain; but f. 143v probably represents the paralytic at Bethesda, for the Capernaum healing appears on f. 316r. The abbreviated image repeats a widespread formula, and exemplifies Christ's healing and redemptive powers.[94]

The healing of the woman with the issue of blood and the raising of Jairus' daughter form part of the same narrative in the synoptic gospels (Matthew 9:18–26, Mark 5:22–43, Luke 8:41–56), and they are visually linked on f. 143v. As Christ turns to speak to the kneeling woman, Jairus prostrates himself at his feet; to the right, Jairus' daughter lies, apparently dead, surrounded by mourners.

Two different moments in the account of the healing of the woman with the issue of blood were pictured in the ninth century. The *Sacra Parallela* illustrates the first, when the woman crept behind Christ, touched his hem, and was cured (Matthew 9:20–21, Mark 5:25–29, Luke 8:43–44).[95] Paris.gr.510 illustrates the next episode – of which Mark 5:30–34 provides the fullest account – when Christ turned, asked who had touched him, and the woman fell down before him and confessed. Like the healing of the paralytic, the confession of the woman finds early Christian parallels; both also surfaced in anti-Jewish texts.[96] This connection does not, however, seem to be stressed on f. 143v, where the selection of the confession scene rather than the healing that preceded it suggests a return to the theme of the top register: compassion and mercy.

Christ, surrounded by Peter, James, and John (Mark 5:37, Luke 8:51), forms a strong central axis that is anchored by the prostrate woman on (our) left, and Jairus, in proskynesis, on the right. As Jairus begs Christ to save his daughter, the man behind him gestures as if to indicate that she has died. Again, an unusual moment was selected for illustration, for although the daughter and her attendants occupy the right quarter of the register, the actual raising of the child is not shown. This omission, coupled with the portrayal of Jairus in proskynesis, indicates that the image is less a healing scene than a visualization of the 'ruler of the synagogue'

---

[93] Jairus' daughter and the Good Samaritan are also tangentially linked in the liturgy: Luke 8:41–56 (Jairus) was read on the twenty-third Sunday after Pentecost, Luke 10:25–37 (Samaritan) on the twenty-fourth: Mateos II (1963), 160; Brubaker (1996a), 12–13.

[94] See Schiller I (1971), 169; Underwood (1975), 290. The episode was sometimes interpreted as an allusion to baptism, but the absence of a healing pool on f. 143v suggests that this meaning was not intended here.   [95] Paris.gr.923, f. 212r: Weitzmann (1979a), fig. 454.

[96] Schiller I (1971), 178–179; Hennecke and Schneemelcher I (1963), 457. On anti-heretical imagery in Paris.gr.510 see chapter 6.

beseeching Christ's aid. As in David's penitence, the accent is on the humility of authorities before God.[97]

The conceptual link between David's penitence in the top register and the vignette of Christ flanked by the woman and Jairus is cemented by the composition of the page. The two receive precisely the same amount of space, and Jairus lies exactly below David; the balancing females, Bathsheba and the woman with the issue of blood, are also aligned. Vertical alignments bind the second and third registers as well: the last scene of the Good Samaritan narrative reverts to the central foreground in order to associate Christ as Good Samaritan with the comforting Christ of the lowest tier. Folio 143v presents an exceptionally unified composition; its images of mercy and humility provide a coherent interpretation of Gregory's 'To the prefect' that supplements the themes of the sermon.

Folio 196v (24) (fig. 24)

The final two examples of exegetical miniatures included in this chapter incorporate scenes not alluded to in the accompanying oration even at second hand. Folio 196v, the simpler of the two, develops a coherent linear narrative that supplements the text on several interwoven levels.

While most miniatures in the first third of Paris.gr.510 are divided into three registers, f. 196v opens a series of ten miniatures preserved in the middle of the manuscript that show full-page pictures or, more usually, pages divided into two registers, as here. Three interconnected episodes appear: Christ raises Lazarus, and eats at the house of Simon, above the entry into Jerusalem.[98] Gregory mentions none of these in the accompanying sermon, his second homily 'On the Son',[99] which concerns the relationship between God and Christ, and was considered obscure (and important) enough in the ninth century for Photios to devote a lengthy section of his *Amphilochia* to its clarification.[100] Gregory's main thesis is that Christ acted as an intermediary between heaven and earth; he redeemed the sins of the world through the sacrifice of his crucifixion, and so reconciled humanity with God. It is precisely this theme that the miniature addresses.

The three scenes pictured were closely connected in liturgical and imperial cere-

[97] I am grateful to Anthony Cutler, who recently reminded me that proskynesis can imply forgiveness: Jairus' humility will be his salvation. See also Cutler (1975), 53–110.

[98] Omont (1929), 23, pl. XXXVIII; Morey (1929), 96; Der Nersessian (1962), 204–205; Dinkler (1970), 39–40; Weitzmann (1971b), 626; Brubaker (1985), 3–4; Brubaker (1996a), 15.

[99] SC 250, 226–275. Der Nersessian (1962), 204–205 connected f. 196v with the wrong sermon; the miniature is nonetheless certainly in its intended location, for the end of the preceding homily concludes on its recto. The Milan Gregory illustrates this sermon with its usual preaching scene, medallion portraits of Paul, Adam, and Christ, and two Old Testament groups in prayer: Grabar (1943a), pls. XXXIII,2–XXXV (excluding XXXIV,4).

[100] Question 78: PG 101:489B–493D; ed. Westerink V (1986), 101–108. On the *Amphilochia* see chapter 5.

monial, where the raising of Lazarus was associated with the Palm Sunday celebration of the entry into Jerusalem. The typikon of the Great Church (Hagia Sophia) entitles the sixth Saturday in Lent the 'Saturday of St Lazarus'; readings for the day commemorate Lazarus and anticipate Palm Sunday, celebrated the next day.[101] The same combination appears in the Book of Ceremonies, which entitles the ceremony for the sixth Saturday in Lent the 'Vigil of Palm Sunday'.[102] Photios, among others, explains the connection: human salvation depends on Christ's resurrection, and 'the resurrection was because of the death; and the death because of the crucifixion; and the crucifixion because Lazarus came up from the gates of hell on the fourth day'.[103] The Palm Sunday service itself describes the supper at Simon's house and the entry into Jerusalem and, in his two hymns 'On Lazarus', Romanos cemented the connection between all three episodes portrayed.[104] In aggregate, the scenes form an introduction to Christ's passion sanctioned by numerous sources and provide a fitting corollary to Gregory's second oration 'On the Son'.

This interpretation is reinforced by the presentation of the individual scenes. As a revelation of Christ's power to overcome death, the raising of Lazarus (John 11:1–44) was frequently depicted.[105] The image on f. 196v is unusually simple, showing only Mary (MAPIA) and Martha ([MAPΘ]A) prostrate at Christ's feet as he commands Lazarus to rise from the dead. Nearly all other examples of this scene include far more detail: even the abbreviated account at Old Tokalı incorporates a spectator, and most include a group of apostles and friends of Lazarus (fig. 65).[106] In the Homilies, Lazarus, wrapped in graveclothes, stands within a rectangular opening cut into a hillside, and the selection of such a gravesite is also uncommon in the ninth-century: contemporary (and later) versions normally substitute a narrow gabled building or a small mausoleum.[107] A final unusual feature of the scene on f. 196v is the size of Mary and Martha, who in other ninth-century and later Byzantine examples are almost invariably presented as diminu-

---

[101] The typikon, which describes the daily services observed in Constantinople, has been published by Mateos (1963) who dates its composition to the late ninth (post-878) or early tenth century; see also *ODB* 3, 2132–2133. See esp. the troparion and the evening lection (Mateos II [1963], 62–65), the latter citing Zachariah 9:9, a passage also quoted in the gospel accounts of the entry into Jerusalem.

[102] *De cerimoniis* I,40 (31): ed. Vogt I (1967a), 158–159.

[103] Homily 9,2: ed. Laourdas (1959), 90; trans. Mango (1958), 165.

[104] Mateos II (1963), 64–65; SC 114, 160, 214. On Romanos, who died after 555, see *ODB* 3, 1807–1808; and on hymnography, *ODB* 2, 960–961.   [105] See, e.g., Schiller I (1971), 181–186.

[106] For Tokalı, Epstein (1986), 64, figs. 31 and, for the New Church, 79. Other examples: Rossano, Diocesan Mus., f. 1r (Cavallo *et al.* [1987], 120–123; Weitzmann [1977], pl. 29); Cambridge, Corpus Christi College, cod.286, f. 125r (ibid., pl. 41); Mount Athos, Pantokrator 61, f. 29r (Dufrenne [1966], 23, pl. 4; Pelekanides *et al.* 3 [1979], fig. 185); London, BL Add.19.352, f. 31v (Der Nersessian [1970], 25, fig. 53); Florence, Laur.plut.6.23, f. 193v (Velmans [1971], fig. 288); Paris.gr.74, f. 192r (Omont [n.d.], pl. 165).

[107] Even the *Sacra Parallela*, which omits all details of the scene except the mummified Lazarus, places him in a small gabled building: Paris.gr.923, f. 388r (Weitzmann [1979a], fig. 481).

Fig. 65 Rossano Gospels, f. 1r: raising of Lazarus

tive figures.[108] While the hill-tomb and the full-sized women appear in earlier versions such as that in the Rossano Gospels (fig. 65), it may nonetheless be significant that both Romanos and Photios emphasize the role of Mary and Martha in the Lazarus episode: each stresses that Christ performed the miracle – itself indicative of his divinity – out of mercy and compassion for the two sisters.[109] Christ's sympathy with suffering humanity, his divinity, and even his power to raise the dead are all evoked by Gregory in the course of his second oration 'On the Son', though not in relation to Lazarus. The image in Paris.gr.510, with its emphasis on Mary and Martha, provides a visual parallel to these traits without relying on Gregory's text for its particularizing examples.

All four gospels narrate the next scene, Christ's supper in the house of Simon, here briefly identified by the inscription O ΔIΠNOC TOY CIMONOC ('the supper at Simon's').[110] The episode was invested with considerable importance in the ninth century: the typikon of the Great Church cited it on five different occasions, and Photios devoted two sections of his *Amphilochia* and two texts now preserved as catena fragments to it.[111] Photios viewed the occasion as an anticipation of Christ's death and an exemplification of the remission of sin through Christ,[112] both themes that correspond with Gregory's text. Though the supper at Simon's house appears in the middle Byzantine tetraevangelia in a form generally similar to that on f. 196v, the scene was not often illustrated; only the detail of the woman washing Christ's feet recurs with any frequency.[113] On f. 196v, the miniaturist suggests the interior of Simon's house by placing a triple portico in the background. Before this, Christ is seated upright at a semi-elliptical table shared by four other men, one of whom sits in front of the table in profile. A woman, her vase of ointment before her, kneels and dries Christ's feet with her hair; she is identified as H ΠOPNH ('the harlot'), but as her ochre robe duplicates that worn by Mary Magdalene in the preceding scene it seems reasonable to assume that f. 196v follows John's identification of the woman as Mary, in a passage read during the liturgy for Palm Sunday.[114] Christ motions to his

[108] In the Florence tetraevangelion, however, the women are depicted more or less normal size; the composition is otherwise dissimilar from f. 196v.

[109] Romanos, 'On Lazaros' II, refrain (SC 114, 198–219); Photios, 'On Good Friday', 3 (ed. Laourdas [1959], 16; trans. Mango [1958], 59).

[110] Matthew 26:6–13, Mark 14:3–9, Luke 7:36–50, John 12:1–8.

[111] Mateos I (1963), 34–37, 336–337; II, 64–67, 72–79; *PG* 101:357–368, 393–396 (ed. Westerink V [1986], 7–14, 34–35); Reuss (1957), 327–333. The *Amphilochia* is discussed in chapter 5.

[112] See esp. *PG* 101:357–368; ed. Westerink V (1986), 7–14.

[113] For the Florence tetraevangelion, Laur.plut.6.23, ff. 118v, 194v: Velmans (1971), figs. 206, 289. For the woman washing Christ's feet see e.g. the Khludov Psalter (f. 84v: Ščepkina [1977]) and the Pantokrator Psalter (f. 118r: Dufrenne [1966], pl. 18; Pelekanides *et al.* [1979], fig. 222).

[114] Mateos II (1963), 64–67. Matthew and Mark simply describe an unnamed woman pouring ointment on Christ's head, as illustrated in Florence, Laur.plut.6.23, ff. 53r, 91r: Velmans (1971), figs. 109, 174. Luke describes the scene as it appears on f. 196v, and calls the woman a sinner: see ibid. fig. 206.

dinner partners, named in John's gospel as Simon, Lazarus and two apostles; the figure in profile with whom Christ appears to exchange gestures may be Judas, who queried the woman's rash waste of anointing oil.

As noted earlier, the entry into Jerusalem (Matthew 21:1–9, Mark 11:1–10, Luke 19:29–38, John 12:12–15) in the lower register forms a liturgical whole with the scenes above it. Christ's capacity to redeem sin and to reconcile humanity with God, two significant themes of Gregory's sermon, were also associated with the episode by ninth-century authors. Photios, for example, wrote about the entry: 'Blessed is he that cometh to offer himself as a sacrifice for our sake, to expiate all our sins, and to reconcile us with the Father.'[115]

As one of the great events of the liturgical year, the entry into Jerusalem was depicted from an early period.[116] The iconography of the scene varies little; the version on f. 196v distinguishes itself primarily by the absence of the extra-biblical details common in many versions.[117] Christ, accompanied by a cluster of apostles, rides toward the walled city of Jerusalem, where a group of citizens bearing palm fronds (John 12:13) awaits him; immediately before Christ, a youth spreads a garment on the ground as described in the synoptic gospels. The most notable feature of the scene is the inclusion, for the first time, of a small child tugging at a woman's hand in the far right corner. This detail – perhaps inspired by the emphasis on children in the gospel accounts – had a long history in other contexts, nearly all of them, like the entry into Jerusalem, representations of processions. The Augustan Ara Pacis frieze provides an illustrious antecedent; a more direct connection may be provided by Exodus images, particularly the crossing of the Red Sea, in which, as Erich Dinkler noted, the 'Frau mit Kind' appeared on sarcophagi from the fourth century.[118]

Folio 196v provides one of the clearest examples in Paris.gr.510 of an exegetic rather than an illustrative accompaniment to Gregory's sermon. In this case, the exegesis is grounded in a multitude of contemporary interpretations; indeed, the compositional grouping had such resonance in its period that the selection of scenes seems almost over-determined.

Folio 165r (21) (fig. 21)

Folio 165r presents a thematic rather than a narrative selection of scenes, and these are used to underscore a particular motif in the sermon that follows. The top register pictures the young Christ among the doctors in the synagogue at Jerusalem; the second illustrates the temptation of Christ; and the bottom presents the multi-

[115] Homily 8,5: ed. Laourdas [1959], 88, trans. Mango (1958), 160 (as Homily 8,6).
[116] See Dinkler (1970). On the relationship between the entry and the imperial adventus ceremony – which is, I believe, often over-emphasized – see MacCormack (1981), 64–66; Catafygiotu-Topping (1977).   [117] In addition to Dinkler, see Schiller II (1971), 18–21; LCI I (1968), 593–597.
[118] Dinkler (1970).

plication of loaves.[119] Though the third paragraph of the accompanying sermon, 'On dogma and the installation of bishops',[120] contains several allusions to the temple at Jerusalem pictured in the upper two registers,[121] Gregory mentioned none of the episodes presented; he concentrated instead on definitions of doctrine and the proper role of the priest. The text in fact supplies few narrative details susceptible to direct illustration, and the Milan Gregory includes only a preaching scene and the death of Oza, alluded to early in the sermon.[122] The Paris miniature is, however, assuredly in its original location, for the text begins on its verso and the scenes pictured expand upon the theme of the sermon.

Christ's discourse with the doctors is considered to mark the beginning of his ministry, as it was the first occasion on which his knowledge was made public. Luke 2:41–49 explains that Mary, Joseph and Jesus went to Jerusalem to celebrate Passover; when his parents departed, Jesus tarried behind. Mary and Joseph noticed his absence, returned to the city, and after three days 'found him in the temple, sitting in the midst of the doctors', explaining the word of God. The episode exemplifies one of the major themes of Gregory's sermon, the contrast between true knowledge, given to humanity by God, and the false knowledge professed by 'the improvised sages, the self-elected theologians who, in place of the possession of wisdom, are content with the simple desire to possess it'.[123] Christ among the doctors purveying true knowledge provides a visual antithesis to this condemnation of false wisdom which, heralded by an enlarged and decorated initial, opens Gregory's sermon.

Three distinct moments unfold across the register from right to left. On the far right, the young Christ walks away from two jagged peaks toward the central temple. Here, Jesus sits amidst the doctors; this portion of the miniature has flaked badly, but its identification is confirmed by the inscription on the frame above: O X[PICTO]C MECON TΩN ΔΙΔΑCΚΑΛΩΝ ('Christ among the teachers'). On the left, Mary and Jesus embrace at their reunion while Joseph ([IΩ]CHΦ) watches.[124] The core components of the register appeared early: in the Augustine Gospels (fig. 66), a product of sixth-century Italy, the young Jesus sits frontally between two older doctors while Mary enters from the left.[125] Though f. 165r preserves the earliest recorded instance of the semi-circular grouping associated with Christ among the doctors, the compositional formula had long signified a forum

---

[119] Omont (1929), 22, pl. XXXV; Der Nersessian (1962), 205–206.   [120] SC 270, 56–85.
[121] See Mossay in SC 270, 62–63 note 1.   [122] Grabar (1943a), pl. XXX,1–2; SC 270, 60 (3:1–2).
[123] SC 270, 56 (1:1–3).   [124] TO OTI EZHTOYM[EN C]E is inscribed above their heads.
[125] *CLA* 2 (1935), no. 126; Cambridge, Corpus Christi College, cod.286, f. 129v: Weitzmann (1977), pl. 42. The Gospel's omission of Joseph was almost certainly due to the limited space available within the confined square of the composition, for he appears in virtually all other depictions of this scene: e.g. Florence, Laur.plut.6.23, f. 106v (Velmans [1971], fig. 188), Paris.gr.74, f. 110v and its Slavonic relatives (Der Nersessian [1926/7], figs. 48–50).

Fig. 66 Cambridge, Corpus Christi College, cod.286, f. 129v: Luke with scenes from his gospel

for learned discourse: it ultimately derives from semi-circular groupings of philoso-phers, and was appropriated for Christian use already in the catacombs.[126] Its retention here is particularly appropriate, and serves to stress Christ's role as the source of true wisdom.

While the image is badly damaged, what remains finds a parallel in a related but different episode painted on the walls of New Tokalı in Cappadocia during the second quarter of the tenth century (fig. 67).[127] The Tokalı scene immediately follows the presentation in the temple and precedes the calling of John the Baptist (it is thus located precisely where Christ among the doctors fits in the narrative structure), and it shows four figures arranged in a semi-circle around Christ. The arrangement, and even the positions, of the figures correspond closely with the image on f. 165r; however, the Tokalı Christ is represented not as a child but as middle-aged. Christopher Walter identified the scene as a representation of mid-Pentecost, for which service the gospel reading (John 7:14–30) begins, 'Now about the midst of the feast Jesus went up into the temple, and taught.'[128] The two gospel accounts of Christ teaching in the temple have evidently been conflated at Tokalı, but f. 165r and the fresco are nonetheless related; in whatever guise, the composi-tion was apparently familiar in the capital and is unlikely to be a *de novo* compila-tion by the Homilies miniaturist.[129]

Mary and Joseph habitually enter from the left to find Christ in the temple; f. 165r repeats this convention, adding only the twist of showing Mary embracing Jesus. The embrace, described in the apocryphal gospel of Thomas, appears only rarely.[130] Its inclusion here furthers the (right-to-left) narrative, emphasizes the emotional relationship of mother and son, and, with Christ's approach to the temple on the right, frames the central scene in the temple.

Christ's first teaching is followed in the second register by what Irenaeus called the triumph of divine pedagogy, the temptation of Christ in the desert.[131] In his *Adversus Haereses* – a text now preserved complete only in Latin but available in Greek in the ninth century, when it was read by Photios[132] – Irenaeus (among others) also saw Christ's struggle with Satan as analogous to the struggle of the

---

[126] Hanfmann (1951), 205–233; Mathews (1993), 109–111. See also the related mosaic of Moses and the Egyptian sages at Sta Maria Maggiore: Karpp (1966), pl. 85.

[127] Epstein (1986), 70, figs. 66–67.

[128] Walter (1979), 15–16; Epstein (1986), 70, 86; Mateos II (1963), 120–121. I thank Father Walter for further discussion on this topic.

[129] The elaborate exedra behind the central group on f. 165r (anticipated in the Moses mosaic at Sta Maria Maggiore: note 126 above) does not, however, appear here, and rarely recurs in later examples, which instead portray the group seated on a synthronon-like semi-circular bench: see e.g. Mount Athos, Dionysiou 587, f. 135r: Pelekanides *et al.* 1 (1973), fig. 252.

[130] Hennecke and Schneemelcher I (1963), 396; Lafontaine-Dosogne (1975), 237–238.

[131] Steiner (1962), 196.

[132] *Bibliotheke* (see chapter 5), codex 120: ed. Henry II (1960), 94–95; trans. Wilson (1994), 130.

Fig. 67 New Tokalı: presentation; mid-Pentecost

church against heresy.[133] Such an interpretation probably conditioned the decision
to picture the temptation on f. 165r, for it dovetails with the accompanying
sermon, wherein Gregory posed his definitions of doctrine as oppositions to the
great heresy of his own day, Arianism. Beyond this, Christ as representative of the
victorious holy wisdom of the orthodox church joins Christ among the doctors, the
source of true knowledge, to form a unified visual parallel to Gregory's condemnation of false wisdom.

The three temptations shown in Paris.gr.510 follow the order of Matthew
4:1–11.[134] Satan, standing on a hillock before Christ, challenges him to turn stones
into bread; following Irenaeus, commentators interpreted this temptation as
pitting a preoccupation with material goods against the virtue of being satisfied
with divine nourishment.[135] This temptation is not often illustrated, but the

[133] Steiner (1962), 205–206.

[134] Though innocent of Byzantium, Squilbeck (1966/7), 118–152, provides discussion and a catalogue of western examples.

[135] Steiner (1962), 206. Gregory roughly parallels this sentiment at the beginning of 'On dogma':
SC 270, 56 (1:5–7).

Fig. 68 Florence, Laurenziana plut.6.23, f. 109r: temptations of Christ

composition on f. 165r generally resembles an example in the middle Byzantine Florence tetraevangelion (fig. 68), save that the later manuscript shows Satan next to, rather than on, the hill.[136]

For the second temptation, Satan placed Christ atop the temple in Jerusalem and, with a mocking quote of Psalm 91:11, urged him to cast himself down, a suggestion represented by the devil's sweeping gesture on f. 165r.[137] Christ stands on a squat grey temple, its pinnacle rising high behind him; a thematic connection between the young Jesus teaching in the temple and the temptation on top of it was made by aligning them vertically. The second temptation is, however, distinct from that in the Florence tetraevangelion (fig. 68), which shows Christ and Satan planted firmly on the ground gesturing toward a tower. In this case, other Byzantine examples exist, for Satan's quotation of Psalm 91 assured for the second temptation a place among the miniatures of the marginal psalters (fig.

[136] Laur.plut.6.23, f. 109r, shows the three temptations in a single composition: Velmans (1971), fig. 191. In the *Sacra Parallela* the three temptations are so collapsed that comparison with Paris.gr.510 is futile: Weitzmann (1979a), 161, fig. 398.

[137] The inscription – O X[PICTO]C ΠΕΙΡΑΖΟΜΕΝΟC ΕΝ ΤΩ ΙΕΡΩ – is merely descriptive.

Fig. 69 Mount Athos, Pantokrator 61, f. 130v: temptation of Christ

69).[138] The psalter illustrations are closely interrelated, and share some features with the image on f. 165r, notably the position of Christ, his location on top of the temple, and the active stance of Satan. The marginal compositions are nonetheless far from identical to that in Paris.gr.510: the psalter miniaturists placed Christ on top of a large temple, omitted the backing tower, and located Satan at the base of the temple rather than beside Christ.

Finally, Satan took Christ to a mountain, and offered him 'the kingdoms of the world, and the glory of them'. On f. 165r, Christ stands frontally, while Satan, looking back at him, strides and gestures toward a gold casket representing the glory of all kingdoms of the world. The Gregory composition again differs from that in the tetraevangelia (fig. 68), but it resembles a mid-tenth-century wall paint-

---

[138] Moscow, Hist.Mus.cod.129, f. 92v (Ščepkina [1977]), Mount Athos, Pantokrator 61, f. 130v (Dufrenne [1966], pl. 20), London, BL Add.40.731, f. 154r (ibid., pl. 56), London, BL Add.19.352, f. 123v (Der Nersessian [1970], fig. 201).

ing in New Tokalı (fig. 70):[139] though the fresco reverses the positions of Satan and Christ so that Jesus strides away from, while looking back at, the devil, the stances of the figures are similar, and both images share the squat gold casket.

The lowest register illustrates the multiplication of loaves and fishes (Matthew 14:13–21, Mark 6:31–44, Luke 9:10–17, John 6:1–13). In the centre of the symmetrical composition, Christ stands frontally, arms outstretched to bless the two fish (Matthew 14:17) held in the draped hands of the flanking apostles. Despite the inscription – O [XPICTO]C EYΛO[ΓΩ]N [TOYC] ΠENT[E A]PTOYC K[AI T]OYC [Δ]YO IXΘY[A]C ('Christ blesses the five loaves and the two fishes') – the miniaturist has not shown the blessing of the bread. Rather, the twelve baskets of bread that remained after the meal (Matthew 14:20) float against the deep blue sky, above the multitudes grouped in clumps on either side of Christ. Though even the often conservative wall paintings at Old Tokalı (fig. 71) present the episode as a linear narrative of the type familiar from the tetraevangelia versions of this scene, f. 165r retains the symmetrical composition which was standard during the pre-iconoclast period.[140] Those responsible for these early representations – and the designer of f. 165r – apparently favoured the static format because they valued the miracle less for its narrative potential than for its symbolic weight as a type of eucharist.[141] On this interpretation, Romanos' hymn 'On the multiplication of loaves' is a typical informant.[142] Like most commentators, Romanos connects the miracle with the eucharist; the constant refrain of the hymn is 'Christ, the celestial bread of immortality'. For Romanos, the essence of the miracle is not the procurement of a meal for the multitudes, but the nourishment of all humanity with words of truth, knowledge of justice, and spiritual food.[143] The hieratic composition on f. 165r suggests that a similarly non-narrative interpretation, linking the miracle with the other scenes on the page and with the sense of Gregory's sermon, was envisaged here.

The theme of divine nourishment unites several scenes on the page. Jesus with the doctors opens the miniature speaking words of orthodox truth, the 'spiritual food' of Romanos' hymn. The victorious Christ of the temptation may implicitly continue the theme; although the words are not inscribed on the page, all Byzantines knew Christ's response to Satan: 'Man shall not live by bread alone, but by every word that proceedeth out of the mouth of God' (Matthew 4:4). The eucharistic nourishment – and the loaves and fishes that symbolically represent it – provides a literal equivalent to the divine 'food' dispensed in the uppermost regis-

---

[139] For the Florence tetraevangelion, see note 136 above; Paris.gr.74, ff. 7r (Matthew) and 65r (Mark) in Omont (n.d.), pls. 9, 59; for Tokalı, Epstein (1986), fig. 70.

[140] For Tokalı, Epstein (1986), figs. 29–30; for the tetraevangelia, Velmans (1971), fig. 213 and Omont (n.d.), pls. 26, 28, 70, 72, 112, 153. The Khludov Psalter also shows an asymmetrical composition: Moscow, Hist.Mus.gr.129, f. 30v; Ščepkina (1977).

[141] For commentary and examples, Underwood (1975), 260, 265–266, 285–288.

[142] SC 114, 110–131.   [143] See esp. strophe 9: SC 114, 118.

Fig. 70 New Tokalı: third temptation of Christ

Fig. 71 Old Tokalı: multiplication of the loaves and fishes

ter, a connection stressed by the vertical alignment of the young Jesus in the temple above Christ blessing the fishes. In a sense, the word becomes flesh as the viewer's eye travels down the page.

Folio 165r provides a coherent and multivalent commentary on Gregory's sermon that is literally independent of the text, although it parallels Gregory's concern with the nourishment of true knowledge. The miniature relies on analogy and metaphor; it functions as visual exegesis, rather than as illustration. The miniaturist accomplished this by juxtaposing and aligning scenes, and by selecting particular but apparently familiar iconographical formulae.

The text of Paris.gr.510 is stable in the sense that it is a copy of Gregory's fourth-century sermons; nonetheless, to the extent that the scribe marked passages relevant to the audience's understanding of the pictures, it was made to work explicitly with the miniatures. The miniatures also work with the text: though they would not exist without it, and though their ultimate inspiration rests on their role as adjuncts to Gregory's words, the pictures in an important sense have a life of their own, and infuse the words with new resonance. While the sermons provided what we might now call the control, the miniatures told their ninth-century audience how to read them: they interpreted the text for the viewer, and showed what could be gleaned from Gregory's words. The paradigmatic examples considered in this chapter demonstrate that, as Der Nersessian noted in 1962, the miniatures often complement and supplement Gregory's text. But I think that we can now extend that formula, and question its implication that images are necessarily subservient to words: in Paris.gr.510, the miniatures are active creators of meaning.[144]

The inserted miniatures

With one exception (f. 3r), the inserted miniatures occupy the verso of the folio so that the pictures face the opening paragraphs of the text they preface, and to that extent they are physically coordinated with the body of the manuscript. However, these miniatures are the only ones in Paris.gr.510 that could be moved without disrupting the text, and it is clear that some of them were. Given the often complicated relationship between Gregory's sermons and the pictures that accompany them in Paris.gr.510, the group as a whole thus presents a special set of problems.

Fortunately, some of the inserted miniatures certainly retain their intended locations: f. 3r (with the annunciation, visitation, and scenes from the life of Jonah; fig. 6) and f. 52v (Adam and Eve, Moses, and Gregory preaching; fig. 10) accompany sermons that refer to one or more of the scenes portrayed, as do f. 367v (the persecution of the orthodox; fig. 38) and f. 374v (Julian the Apostate; fig. 39), one of which has been inserted into the problematic quire 47. Two more are probably also still where they were intended to be: f. 32v (fig. 8) prefaces Gregory's funeral oration to his brother Kaisarios with the deaths of the apostles,[145] while f. 43v (fig. 9), picturing Kaisarios' funeral and the death of Gregory's sister Gorgonia, appropriately links the eulogy to Kaisarios with the funeral oration to Gorgonia. Folio 30v (passion sequence; fig. 7) originally prefaced the first sermon; it was moved – perhaps because its location caused considerable wear and tear on the page – to introduce Gregory's third homily, which has lost whatever miniature (if any) it ever had. The remaining two inserted pictures pose more difficult problems.

Folio 347v (35) (fig. 35)

The three registers on f. 347v contain five scenes from the life of Samson in the top and middle bands, while Gideon praying joins the martyrdom of Isaiah, sawn in two, in the bottom tier. The miniature, painted on an inserted half-leaf with a blank recto, now prefaces Gregory's 'On Heron the philosopher' in the damaged

[144] Cf. Cormack (1986a), 229; Kessler (1991/2), 57; Zoubouli (1995), 87.   [145] See chapter 6.

93

forty-fourth gathering. It is, however, difficult to see any relationship between this text and the images on f. 347v.[146] The sermon focuses on the role of the Christian philosopher, extolling Heron as a stellar example, with a number of digressions on fourth-century church history (these chiefly condemn heretical sects) and a long excursus on the Holy Spirit.[147] Gregory mentions the Nazirites (a group, though Gregory does not tell us this, whose members followed Samson in allowing their hair to grow untrimmed) but he neither names nor otherwise alludes to Samson; he speaks several times of martyrs (in the abstract), but never in a way that might suggest Isaiah.[148] Nor does the internal logic of the picture correspond in any obvious way with Gregory's theme. Samson, a well-known type of Christ, was also occasionally lauded as an early martyr;[149] his story might thus be linked tangentially with Isaiah's martyrdom below. Gideon praying for the dew to fall on his fleece, meanwhile, was habitually interpreted as foreshadowing the Virgin Mary,[150] with whom Isaiah too was consistently connected by Christian writers.[151] Gideon, the sixth Judge of the Old Testament, and Samson, the thirteenth Judge, were also connected in the New Testament.[152] Hebrews 11:32–40, in fact, could be read as weaving all three protagonists on f. 347v together in its listing of heroes of the faith and the suffering they endured.[153] Verse 32 reads: 'And what shall I more say? for the time would fail me to tell of Gideon, and Barak, and Samson, and Jephthae; David also, and Samuel, and the prophets'. Verse 37 returns to Isaiah: 'They were stoned, they were sawn asunder . . .'.[154] Gregory does not cite this section of Hebrews, but as he constantly extols Heron it could be that the illustration supplied a catalogue of Old Testament heroes to complement Gregory's subject by providing biblical parallels. Such a connection, however, seems tenuous, and given the disruption of the quire as a whole I suspect that f. 347v no longer retains its original location.[155]

Of the eight sermons now lacking illustration, only one suggests a plausible affinity with f. 347v. In 'On Athanasios', Gregory paints a sympathetic portrait of the beleaguered bishop.[156] He compares Athanasios' sufferings with those of Christ, and, in a paragraph introduced with a gold initial, explicitly connects him

[146] Other aspects of f. 347v will be considered in chapters 4, 6 and 8.   [147] SC 284, 156–205.
[148] On the Nazirites, SC 284, 158 and note 2; this section of the text, along with any markings that might once have aided in the miniature's interpretation, is lost from Paris.gr.510. Gregory refers to martyrs throughout the sermon.   [149] See W. A. Bulst, s.v. 'Samson', LCI 4 (1972), 30–38.
[150] E.g. John of Damascus, 'Against those who attack divine images' III, 22: ed. Kotter (1975), 129; trans. Anderson (1980), 77. Photios, Homily 5,5: ed. Laourdas (1959), 59; trans. Mango (1958), 119. The text describing the event appears in the typikon of the Great Church as a reading for Epiphany, also one of the principal days of baptism in the orthodox rite: Mateos I (1963), 178.
[151] See H. Höllander, s.v. 'Isaias', LCI 2 (1970), 354–359.
[152] And by Gregory himself in his first oration 'Against Julian': PG 35:548B.
[153] So Bulst (note 149 above), 35.
[154] On the universal association of this passage with Isaiah, see Bernheimer (1952), 32–33.
[155] See Appendix C.
[156] SC 270, 110–193. Photios, too, found Athanasios noteworthy; see esp. his remarks on the *vita*, codex 258 in the *Bibliotheke* (see chapter 5): ed. Henry VIII (1977), 18–40; trans. Wilson (1994), 231–244.

with Samson and likens the trials of his church to the cutting of Samson's hair.[157] Following this lead, the history of Samson may originally have provided a visual biblical antitype for the saint.[158] The martyrdom of Isaiah might also play to this theme, but as Athanasios was well known for his 'On the Incarnation', it is also possible that Isaiah, and the episode of Gideon and the fleece – both exegetically associated with the Virgin – pay tacit homage to the bishop's famed text. 'On Athanasios' begins on f. 319v; f. 319r remains blank. The same situation prevailed where f. 347v now sits: a blank side (f. 346v) preceded the opening of 'On Heron'. The blank page before 'On Athanasios' appears in quire forty-one; the next instance of a blank page was that preceding 'On Heron'. It seems plausible that during one of the manuscript's later rebindings the inserted leaf carrying the Samson miniature was relocated by someone who remembered that the miniature had originally accompanied a sermon prefaced by a blank page, but missed the correct location by one slot.

Folio 435v (43) (fig. 43)

On f. 435v, Daniel in the lions' den, the Hebrews in the furnace, the prayer of Manasses, and Isaiah with Hezekiah are arranged in a regular grid.[159] None appears in the accompanying letter to Evagrios,[160] and no typological or exegetical link between the letter and f. 435v is readily apparent.[161] An inserted leaf with a blank recto that now appears in a disturbed gathering, f. 435v may well no longer be in its intended location. But it is difficult to see what other text it might have been meant to illustrate. Elsewhere, Gregory mentions each of the episodes pictured, but never all four together and always in a sermon that retains its illustration.[162] Nor do any of the sermons currently without illustration offer an obviously appropriate home for the four scenes. More than for any other miniature in the manuscript, the text–image connection here remains opaque.

FORMAL CONSIDERATIONS

The style of the miniatures of Paris.gr.510 is not homogeneous. Miniatures display different ways of composing a page, of creating figures and the objects that are, in

[157] SC 270, 172, 164.

[158] The Milan Gregory and the liturgical Homilies preface the sermon with a portrait of Athanasios: Grabar (1943a), pl. XXVII; Galavaris (1969), 15–17.

[159] Other aspects of f. 435v will be considered in chapter 8.   [160] *PG* 46:1101–1108.

[161] So too Weitzmann (1947), 149 and Der Nersessian (1962), 218–219. The Milan Gregory shows Gregory handing the letter to a courier: Grabar (1943a), pl. LXXVIII,2.

[162] Habakkuk bringing food to Daniel and Hezekiah's repentance appear in Gregory's funeral oration to his father (*PG* 35:1021B, 1024A), illustrated on f. 87v; he cites both Daniel in the lions' den and the Hebrews in the furnace in his funeral oration to Basil the Great (*PG* 36:596C), illustrated on f. 104r; and he refers to the confession of Manasses in his sermon to the tax-collector Julian (*PG* 35:1052B), illustrated on f. 137r.

the Homilies, always supplementary to them, and of arranging those figures and objects in relationship to one another. This formal complexity makes it difficult to supply any coherent description, let alone analysis, of the miniatures taken as a whole, but the established date and Constantinopolitan origin of Paris.gr.510 have more or less compelled its inclusion in studies of Byzantine pictorial style.

In 1839, Gustav Waagen produced the first detailed formal analysis of the manuscript.[163] He divided the miniatures into two groups, one influenced by classical forms, the other less fluent but sometimes more accurate in its details. Waagen attributed the differences to the individual styles of two painters. In his description of the painted manuscripts in the Bibliothèque Nationale published nearly fifty years later, Henri Bordier simply summarized Waagen's remarks, as did others in different contexts.[164] In 1891, however, Nikodim Kondakoff reacted strongly against Waagen, and argued that the Homilies miniatures were stagnant; he suggested that they were painted by miniaturists incapable of new creations, and explained any 'antique' qualities the miniaturists managed to achieve as details grafted on to old traditional forms.[165] Kondakoff continued to divide the Gregory miniatures into two groups, but while Waagen segregated the classicizing images from the unclassical ones, Kondakoff drew the line between sacred images and 'vulgar' picturesque images: he perpetuated the two-tiered oppositional classification, but shifted the taxonomic basis from classicism to subject matter. In 1911, John Herbert merged Kondakoff's and Waagen's approaches: in his assessment, the best of the miniatures adopted Waagen's classical style; the worst exhibited an archaic style – Herbert's English transformation of Kondakoff's 'vulgar' genre – 'lacking all sense of dignity'.[166] Herbert added to these, however, yet a third style, the 'decorative', to which he assigned the imperial portraits. In France nine years later, Gabriel Millet made the first attempt to describe the characteristic features of the miniatures as a whole, which he defined as simplified compositions, admitting few accessory details, with large-headed figures all on a single plane.[167] The twenties ended, however, with Charles Rufus Morey reverting to the bifurcated classification scheme, though the two strains now bore the appellations 'Alexandrian' and 'Asiatic'.[168]

In 1935, Kurt Weitzmann produced an assessment of the earlier sources and later

---

[163] Waagen (1839), 202–215.

[164] Bordier (1885), 64; Vogt (1908), 411 note 1; and compare Schnasse (1869), 241–243. Schnasse accented Waagen's appreciation for the Ezekiel page by including it as his only illustration, thus initiating an emphasis on f. 438v that has continued unabated: see e.g. Tikkanen (1933), 89, who singled out the page and opposed its 'pseudo-illusionism' to the 'solidly medieval' character of most of the remaining miniatures.

[165] Kondakoff II (1891), 58–60. Paradoxically, the earlier manuscripts that Kondakoff held up as sterling examples of all the qualities he felt Paris.gr.510 lacked (for example, the Vienna Genesis) are precisely those with which Frolow (1962), 274–276, later adduced as close parallels with the Paris Gregory. [166] Herbert (1911), 40–42. [167] Millet (1920), 241–243. [168] Morey (1929), 96–97.

followers of Paris.gr.510 that considered neither bifurcation nor quality, but dealt morphologically with specific formal features of the miniatures.[169] In his 1936 review of Weitzmann's work, however, Ernst Kitzinger revived the interest in 'hellenistic' elements, and noted that the Homilies was not 'a first-class specimen of this tradition'; he concluded that it was 'doubtful whether the Paris Gregory represents Byzantine ninth-century art in its best form'.[170] Hugo Buchthal, in 1938, concentrated on the transitional nature of Paris.gr.510; in 1962, Anatole Frolow focused on the classicizing elements, but linked the 'robust humanism' and 'second hellenism' to Aristotelian theories of mimesis that, he argued, resurfaced during Iconoclasm.[171]

Recent scholarship has looked at Paris.gr.510 within the context of the ninth century, and has tended to homogenize its style: characteristic formal features have been identified in order more easily to compare and contrast the miniatures with other ninth-century paintings. Gary Vikan, for example, noted in 1973 that 'even the least accomplished miniatures of the Gregory codex show illusionistic tonal drapery modeling', and went on to contrast Paris.gr.510 with a group of manuscripts characterized by drapery conceived in a more linear fashion.[172] In contrast, Robin Cormack defined the Gregory miniatures as portraying 'stiff linear figures', and characterized the pictures as 'bold, linear, and flat'.[173] In the 1980s, the Gregory miniatures continued to be relied on for comparative purposes, and treated in a fairly monolithic fashion, but a new feature – the gestures of the figures – received emphasis. In addition, Annabel Wharton (then publishing as Epstein) pointed to the lack of interest in spatial depth, and the contrast between modelled flesh and 'geometricized' drapery;[174] while Anthony Cutler noted the prominence of 'isocephalic' groups, and suggested that Paris.gr.510 represented 'what might be called the Demonstrative Style of the late ninth century, in which motion and gesture serve to present complex narratives or single figures in an eminently legible, didactic manner'.[175]

That some of the interpretations summarized contradict each other illuminates the subjective nature of formal analysis; as important, their diversity suggests the inherent problems of defining the style of Paris.gr.510. The heterogeneous style of the manuscript does not lend itself easily to generalization, while attempts to isolate hands, or typologically to classify the individual miniatures, often tacitly assume that personal expression was valuable to the Byzantines, which is not neces-

---

[169] Weitzmann (1935), 2–4.

[170] Review of Weitzmann (1935) in *Journal of Hellenic Studies* 56 (1936), 118–119.

[171] Buchthal (1938), 73; Frolow (1962), 276–277, was influenced by Lemerle (1943), 96, 98.

[172] Vikan (1973), 16, 54. Cf. Weitzmann (1979a), 186, who suggested that the Gregory miniatures exhibited greater 'aristocratic restraint' than those of the *Sacra Parallela*.

[173] Cormack (1977b), 155; Cormack, 'Byzantine Art, 843–1453', in J. Strayer, ed., *Dictionary of the Middle Ages* 2 (1983), 440.　　[174] Epstein (1986), 40.　　[175] Cutler and Oikonomides (1988), 85.

sarily a productive assumption. I have attempted to circumnavigate these problems by using a somewhat different approach, and will consider the style of Paris.gr.510 from the outside in: from the relationship between the miniatures and the other text decoration, to the pages as a whole, and finally to patterns that criss-cross the various miniatures.

Comparison of the miniatures with the decoration in the manuscript – head-pieces and painted initials – reveals a sharp division of labour. As we saw in the Introduction, the scribe(s) did none of the painting; a group of illuminators, composed of at least three people, created the initials and headpieces; and another different group painted the miniatures. Modern flaking allows us to see clearly that this group began by blocking out the scenes and then painting the frame: the borders stop to accommodate large elements of the composition that overlap the frame, which must have been planned from the outset; the miniaturists, however, evidently expanded many of their compositions as they worked, and smaller protrusions were painted over the already gilded frames. It is possible that the illuminators were called in to decorate the most elaborate of the ten frames that are painted rather than gilded (ff. Av, 30v, 71v, 78r, 104r, 149r, 285r, 301r, 355r, 438v; figs. 1, 13, 15, 17, 20, 29, 30, 36, 44), most of which portray Gregory or fourth-century figures associated with him. There is, however, no evidence that the miniaturists themselves subdivided their task along specialized lines. Each miniature is internally coherent, and nothing suggests that backgrounds, faces, and drapery were the responsibility of different painters; nor is there evidence that particular types of subject matter were selected by or assigned to particular artisans.

Composition as a bearer of meaning

As the repeated figural groupings and significant vertical alignments of f. 137r intimated, the structure of the page is a crucial component of Paris.gr.510. The size, location, and disposition of figures and objects were habitually manipulated in order to make visual points. The care taken over the composition of the page as a whole is one of the most striking characteristics of the Paris Homilies, and reveals the coordination of process, form, and content.[176]

Folio 3r (6) (fig. 6)

As Paris.gr.510 is currently bound, f. 3r is the first narrative miniature of the manuscript. Painted on a half-leaf inserted into the first regular gathering, and with a blank verso, the miniature of the annunciation and visitation above a sequence of Jonah

---

[176] We might see a faint anticipation of this emphasis in the marginal psalters, where figures are often arranged in oppositional pairs: Corrigan (1992), 111–113.

scenes[177] is nonetheless certainly in its intended location. The homily it accompanies, 'In defence of his flight to Pontos', delivered at Gregory's reappearance before his congregation after a temporary escape to Pontos, refers both to the incarnation of Christ and to Jonah, whose flight from Joppa and subsequent return to Nineveh inspired Gregory to accept his responsibility to the church and come home;[178] the relevant passages are marked by decorated initials. Neither the Marian scenes nor the Jonah narrative appears, however, among the twelve miniatures to this sermon in the Milan Gregory, where only a portrait of the prophet carrying a scroll illustrates the paragraphs on Jonah.[179] As Der Nersessian observed, the decision to respond visually to these particular passages in Paris.gr.510 was apparently motivated by a desire to illustrate Gregory's overriding theme of hesitation or denial followed by acceptance. Gregory provided the Jonah analogy, but did not mention Mary's hesitation before Gabriel. This was, however, a familiar theme in ninth-century sermons: Photios, for example, has Mary respond 'I am troubled ... the messenger's rank and manner, and his seemly aspect indicate that the message comes from God. His words, however, which give the impression of being those of a suitor, prompt me to refuse assent.'[180] After a lengthy examination of this problem, in the course of which Gabriel tells Mary that Elizabeth has 'conceived a son in her old age: and this is the sixth month with her, who was called barren; for with God nothing shall be impossible',[181] Photios finally allows Mary to consent, saying 'Be it unto me according to thy word.'[182] Folio 3r thus pictures scenes analogous to or drawn directly from the ideas expressed in the sermon, selected to conform with its essential theme as it was understood in the ninth century. Even within the Jonah sequence, however, none of the episodes shown is explicitly described in the sermon.[183]

The Jonah narrative is apparently the densest early Christian or Byzantine example extant;[184] its circular composition is unprecedented and exceptional,[185]

[177] Mitius (1897), 79–81; Omont (1929), 13, pl. XX; Weitzmann (1929), 185; Buchthal (1938), 40–42; Nordstrom (1955/57), 505; Der Nersessian (1962), 211; Narkiss (1979), 64–65, 69. A later hand has transcribed the inscriptions in the margins.

[178] SC 247, 84–241 (NPNF, 204–227). For Christ, see esp. paragraphs 24 and 36; for Jonah, paragraphs 106 to 109: SC 247, 120–122, 134–136, 224–230 (cf. paragraphs 7, 25, 38, 98).

[179] Grabar (1943a), pls. II–V,3, the last of which reproduces Jonah; the text accompanying pl. V,1 should read PG 35:420–21; miniatures on pp. 33, 43, and 57 have been excised. The liturgical edition omits this sermon.   [180] Homily 5,3: ed. Laourdas (1959), 55; trans. Mango (1958), 115.

[181] Homily 5,5: ed. Laourdas (1959), 60; trans. Mango (1958), 120.

[182] Homily 5,6: ed. Laourdas (1959), 60; trans. Mango (1958), 120.

[183] On the iconography of the annunciation and the visitation, see chapter 8.

[184] For the extensive bibliography on Jonah iconography, see Narkiss (1979), esp. 71–72 notes 2–2a.

[185] Vague antecedents may perhaps be seen in the radially placed medallions encasing Jonah scenes on the ceilings of a few catacombs which the Homilies painter seems unlikely to have known; or in certain miniatures of the Vienna Genesis, such as the picture of Rebecca and Eliezer that progresses along a half-oval groundline (conveniently reproduced in Weitzmann [1977], pl. 24). Weitzmann (1929) speculated that f. 3r represents a unique phase in the development from column or strip pictures to full-page miniatures; I doubt this.

and is not repeated in the manuscript. The sequence begins in the upper left corner with Jonah leaving Joppa, shown as a walled city, for the shore, where he intends to board a ship sailing for Tarsis.[186] Sailors, approximately half the size of Jonah but still too large for the city gates of Joppa, struggle to unfurl the sails of the embarking ship (Jonah 1:1–3). A boat in full sail, slightly above the boat in port at Joppa, is manned by four sailors who appear to watch in some dismay as Jonah dives overboard toward the flickering tail of a sea-monster (Jonah 1:15). The arched body of the monster disappears into the frame; its torso must be imagined to complete the curve to reappear in the lower right corner, disgorging a fully clothed Jonah with his arms raised (Jonah 2:11). The lower left quadrant pictures Nineveh (ΠΟ[ΛΙC] ΝΙΝΕΥΙ): citizens peer from windows within the walls as their king bares his chest in grief and repentance at the words of Jonah, who stands between him and the shore (Jonah 3:1–6). Between Nineveh and Joppa, the sleeping figure of Jonah, compressed into a near-sitting position, rests his head on his left wrist (Jonah 4:5–6?); his position recalls the sleeping Constantine on f. 440r (fig. 45), rotated so that Jonah's axis is almost vertical.

Though these scenes all individually appeared earlier, the details do not coincide.[187] Jonah is usually bearded; he is a beardless youth on f. 3r. Jonah and the sailors are normally nude; all are clothed in the Homilies. The impact of Jewish texts has been seen in early Christian cycles; there is none here. Nor does the sequence correspond with the ninth-century miniatures in the *Sacra Parallela*, the Vatican 'Christian Topography', or the marginal psalters.[188]

On the other hand, later miniatures illustrating Jonah's Ode in the Paris and Vatopedi Psalters are clearly related to Paris.gr.510.[189] The mid-tenth-century Paris Psalter (fig. 72) shows a Jonah preaching to the Ninevites who is almost identical to the Homilies Jonah embarking; the city itself, with its inhabitants peering from behind the walls, recalls the Nineveh of f. 3r. The miniatures share the configuration of Jonah emerging from the sea-monster, the boat from which the sailors hurl Jonah, and the clothed prophet. The twelfth-century Vatopedi Psalter (fig. 74) follows f. 3r in its depiction of the king of Nineveh, though, as the later miniaturist ignored the chest-baring of the Gregory image, the king's hands hover ineffectually. In a second Jonah image, the Vatopedi miniaturist included four figures in the boat from which Jonah is thrown overboard (fig. 73), as in Paris.gr.510 but not the Paris Psalter; here too Jonah reclines beneath the gourd. The Jonah

---

[186] Inscribed ΙΩΝΑC ΦΕΥΓΩΝ ΕΙC ΤΑΡCΙC ('Jonah goes to Tarsis').

[187] See further Narkiss (1979).

[188] Paris.gr.923, ff. 15r, 29v (Weitzmann [1979a], figs. 316–317); Vat.gr.699, f. 69r (Stornajolo [1908], pl. 32); Moscow, Hist.Mus.gr.129, f. 157r (Ščepkina [1977]); Mount Athos, Pantokrator 61, f. 217v (Dufrenne [1966], pl. 32; Pelekanides *et al.* 2 [1979], fig. 236).

[189] Paris.gr.139, f. 431v and Mount Athos, Vatopedi 760, ff. 282v, 283r: Buchthal (1938), figs. 12, 80, 81; Cutler (1984) figs. 256, 389, 390; Christou *et al.* 4 (1981), 201–202.

Fig. 72 Paris.gr.139, f. 431v: scenes from the life of Jonah

Fig. 73 Mount Athos, Vatopedi 760, f. 282v: scenes from the life of Jonah

Fig. 74 Mount Athos, Vatopedi 760, f. 283r: scenes from the life of Jonah

scenes in the three manuscripts are closely related, and quite distinct from earlier examples.

Each psalter sequence finds parallels on f. 3r that do not recur in the other, but we cannot assume that the psalter miniaturists independently and exclusively consulted the Homilies composition, for the psalters share details not found on f. 3r, notably the location of the preaching Jonah and the inclusion of two sea-monsters, and neither replicates the circular composition. It seems most plausible that all three miniaturists presented versions of some now-lost sequence, though the miniaturist of the Paris Psalter seems to have studied f. 3r as well.[190]

Similarities between f. 3r and the psalters imply that the scenes of Jonah thrown overboard, his propulsion from the monster, his preaching to the Ninevites and his repose under the gourd appeared together in some form familiar to all three miniaturists. If Jonah's flight from Joppa was included, it has left no trace in the psalters: the Homilies miniaturist (or the designer of the page) obviously understood the importance of the episode to Gregory's analogy and, whatever the visual inspiration, included it. Aside from the tucking of the reclining Jonah behind and above the walls of Nineveh (a detail that recurs in the Vatopedi Psalter, which apparently preserves the least edited version of the composition familiar to the three miniaturists), the format of the putative source seems also to have been radically modified on f. 3r: the circular composition, as noted earlier, is unique. One effect of this change may be seen in the omission of the sea-monster about to swallow Jonah: while precedents for such telescoping of the narrative exist, the inclusion of two monsters in both psalters suggests that two appeared in the version that all three miniaturists independently knew. More curious is the displacement of Jonah preaching to the Ninevites from the left of the city to the right. The miniaturist of f. 3r did not reverse Jonah's body – he turns, as he does in both psalters, to address the Ninevites on the right – but as the Ninevites are on the left in the revised composition that appears on f. 3r, the painter portrayed Jonah looking back over his shoulder at the city and his audience.

The composition of f. 3r emphasizes and centralizes the two episodes most crucial to the theme of Gregory's homily: Jonah's flight from Joppa and his return to Nineveh, antitypes adduced by Gregory for his own flight and return. Jonah does not rise alone along the central axis of the miniature: the Virgin annunciate stands directly above Jonah as he flees Joppa. The miniaturist has aligned the three figures most relevant to the main oppositions developed in the sermon – hesitation and consent, flight and return – to highlight their importance as analogies to Gregory's

---

[190] Though the Vatopedi sequence is iconographically closer to Paris.gr.510, formal details in the Psalter corroborate Ioli Kalavrezou's observation that its illustrator studied, and borrowed motifs from, the Paris Gregory itself: 'The Paris Psalter', presented at the Eighth Annual Byzantine Studies Conference (Chicago, 1982); her study of the manuscript is awaited.

situation.[191] In the Jonah sequence, far smaller figures enact the monster and sleep episodes, which, although they had been the most frequently represented scenes in the past and were apparently included in a readily available source, were less important in this framework. The circular composition enabled the illustrator to centralize and focus on the two scenes most important in the context of the Homilies while retaining the expected narrative episodes; and it was the desire to single out Jonah's flight and return for special emphasis that evidently occasioned Jonah's placement to the right of Nineveh and led to his peculiar twisting form. I would argue, too, that the desire to align the three crucial scenes vertically on f. 3r inspired the development of the circular Jonah composition.

Folio 424v (41) (fig. 41)

In three registers, f. 424v illustrates the fall of Jericho, the defeat of the Amalekites, and Gregory writing.[192] The miniature retains its original location: the preceding homily ends on its recto and, though the scenes are not repeated in the Milan Homilies,[193] the illustrator nonetheless drew directly on the accompanying text. This sermon, 'On the consecration [of Eulalios as bishop] of Douris', exalts the faith of the priesthood.[194] In a series of passages, each marked with an enlarged gold initial or with *oboloi*, Gregory argued that though the struggle may be difficult, faith overcomes all adversaries: 'Armed with the shield of faith, we shall quench the fire of the wicked.'[195] The fall of Jericho and the defeat of the Amalekites represent the power of faith over 'the wicked', and Gregory refers to each more specifically: 'Through the calm stretching out of his hands he defeats the Amalekites. What many thousands of hands could not do, is done to the city through the prayers of the raised hands of the priests. Without struggle or attack, he demolishes fortified walls.'[196]

Gregory carefully selected his examples of Old Testament figures who were victorious through the intervention of God: he cited Moses (who defeated the Amalekites), Joshua (who captured Jericho) and David, all of whom were habitually interpreted as antitypes of Christ.[197] The episodes adduced by Gregory and pictured on f. 424v reinforced the christological interpretation: the battle for Jericho prefigured the spiritual struggle of Christians, and the city's fall represented the final victory of Christ; the victory over the Amalekites signified Christ's victory over Satan.[198]

---

[191] Jonah as an antitype of Christ (cf. Matthew 12:39–41) provides another potential level of meaning to this alignment.

[192] Omont (1929), 29–30, pl. LV; Weitzmann (1947), 197; Der Nersessian (1962), 214, 222.

[193] Here two preaching scenes suffice: Grabar (1943a), pl. LXXVII, 1–2.   [194] *PG* 35:851–856.

[195] Ibid., 856C; Paris.gr.510, f. 426r.

[196] Ibid., 853B; the last two sentences refer to the fall of Jericho: see ibid., 854 note 14.

[197] See e.g. Daniélou (1956), 93–96, 101–105.   [198] See Daniélou (1950), 145–148, 209, 246–256.

The fall of Jericho has been placed at the top of f. 424v, above and before the victory over the Amalekites that preceded it both chronologically and in the narrative of Gregory's sermon.[199] This arrangement underscores the scene's significance as a visualization of the imperial ideology of victory; but the important aspect here is that the structure of the page itself is used to make the point. Though in a slightly different way from the Jonah cycle, placement on the page nonetheless conveys meaning on f. 424v too.

The fall of Jericho provides one of the rare symmetrical (or virtually symmetrical) narrative compositions of Paris.gr.510, in the company of Isaiah's vision (f. 67v; fig. 11), the transfiguration (f. 75r; fig. 14), the multiplication of loaves and fishes (f. 165r; fig. 21), Pentecost (f. 301r; fig. 30), the ecumenical Council of 381 (f. 355r; fig. 36), the communion of the apostles (f. 426v; fig. 42), and the Hebrews in the furnace (f. 435v; fig. 43). None of these scenes is exactly mirrored, side to side, but all have a strong middle axis with roughly equal flanks, and the overriding impression in each case is of a focused and centralized composition. What they all share, too, is a scene in which it was important to signal the presence of the divine. On f. 424v, the symmetrical composition indicates that God is on the side of Joshua and has given him a divinely approved victory: the image here is one of the few Byzantine examples to show the city falling without human intervention.[200] As in the Jonah sequence, composition reinforces meaning.

The author portrait of Gregory in the third register was not derived from the descriptive passages of the homily text. Its inclusion was probably meant to suggest Gregory as the embodiment of the faith of the priesthood. In a sense, the portrait continues the christological theme of the upper registers, since the priest is Christ's representative on earth. Even were Gregory not the author of the sermon, the portrait would be particularly fitting in this context, for his medieval epithet 'the theologian' – shared only with John the evangelist – singled him out as the paradigmatic example of a priest able to transmit his understanding of the faith with clarity.[201] This is precisely what we see him doing: identified by inscription as Ο Α[ΓΙΟΣ] ΓΡΗΓΟΡΙΟΣ Ο ΘΕΟΛΟΓΟΣ ('St Gregory the theologian'), he sits in a high-backed chair outside a church and writes in a book supported on a lectern; behind him, a pedestal holds his inkpot. Curiously, though nearly every sermon in the Milan Homilies is accompanied by at least one miniature of Gregory displaying his words on an unfurled scroll, the Milan miniaturist never showed Gregory writing. Such portraits appear, however, in a number of copies of the liturgical

[199] On the iconography, see chapter 4; on the relationship between ff. 226v and 424v, see chapter 8.
[200] See chapters 4 and 8.
[201] Buchthal (1963), 81–90 suggested that the shared epithet accounts for the similarity between the portrait type of Gregory in Paris.gr.510 and contemporary portraits of John. See also Walter (1971), 202 note 70, and Walter (1978), 242–243.

Homilies,[202] and one is also found in the *Sacra Parallela* (fig. 60). In their basic configurations, these author portraits all follow conventions going back to antiquity, and numerous ninth-century examples still survive.[203] Only the expansive setting on f. 424v is unusual. This follows formulae found elsewhere in the manuscript: the two cypress trees on the left recur, for example, on f. 435v (fig. 43) behind Manasses and on f. 438v (fig. 44) behind Ezekiel; the church conforms with many others in the miniatures and, in its location to the right of Gregory, adheres to the pattern established by Basil writing beside a church on f. 104r (fig. 17). Whether this church is meant to represent Eulalios' new seat at Douris or Gregory's own church must remain a moot point. What is most striking about the structure is its size:[204] it takes up the whole right-hand side of the register, pushing Gregory off centre to the left.

After the symmetrical composition of the top register, this asymmetry strikes the eye. The prominence of the church, and its displacement of Gregory off to the left of the central axis, skew the internal compositional balance of the register and add nothing to its iconographic coherence. The size and location of the church seem, however, to have been motivated by the design of the page as a whole. Gregory could not occupy the centre of the register, for all of the main protagonists – Joshua in the top register, Moses in the middle, and here Gregory – occupy the left half of the page. The illustrator has arranged the types of Christ in descending hierarchical (rather than chronological) order, along a gentle diagonal from Joshua, antitype *par excellence*, to Moses, slightly more toward the centre and of lesser typological value here than Joshua, to Gregory, who represents the priestly and mundane representative of Christ on earth rather than a true antitype. As in the presentation on f. 137r (fig. 18), the bottom register seems to have been internally unbalanced in order to make a visual point vertically.

Cross-currents between miniatures[205]

The commentary-through-composition that is so important in Paris.gr.510 (as we shall see, the examples just adduced are the tip of the iceberg) and the diverse formats used for its miniatures – from full-page to five registers to grids – imposed formal requirements that varied from page to page. Nonetheless, the miniatures exhibit a broad coherence in their style, and I should like to continue this chapter's

---

[202] Galavaris (1969), 19–23, figs. 61, 78, 97, 98, 256, 275, 377, 428, 429, 435, 470, 473.

[203] Friend (1927), 115–147; Bergman (1973), 44–49. For ninth-century examples of authors other than Gregory, see f. 104r (Basil) and the *Sacra Parallela*: Weitzmann (1979a), figs. 186, 520, 731.

[204] Another large church, this time enveloping Gregory, appears in one of the liturgical manuscripts: see Galavaris (1969), 21–22.

[205] I thank Annemarie Weyl Carr for her perceptive comments on an earlier draft this section.

progressively narrowing focus by looking at the features that link the miniatures before considering those that divide them.

In the miniatures of Paris.gr.510, backgrounds rarely impinge on the action. They range from unmodulated expanses of deep blue to landscapes to ornate architecture, but invariably function as backdrops or frames for the all-important figures, who almost always act out their roles in the immediate foreground. The figures vary in proportion (some have large heads and squat bodies, some have small heads and long legs), but they are almost all active participants in whatever drama they enact, and there is very little repetition of any figure type on a single page: when such repetition occurs, as we saw in the discussion of f. 137r, the replication carries meaning and is worthy of note. The enlivenment of the figures seems to have been important: complicated poses were favoured by the Gregory miniaturists, as was the intermingling of figures seen in profile, from the rear, turning, and, less often (and sometimes awkwardly), *en face*.[206] Accoutrements – such as the saw used to martyr Isaiah (f. 347v; fig. 35), the well with a pulley-driven bucket at which Christ meets the Samaritan woman (f. 215v; fig. 25), and Cyprian's occult paraphernalia (f. 332v; fig. 33) – though never fronted, receive detailed attention. So do changes in status: when Cyprian and Basil (f. 104r; fig. 17) appear as philosophers they are bare-chested and togate; when they appear as religious, they wear the apostolic chiton and himation or ecclesiastical garb. The concern to provide each figure with appropriate dress coincides with a vigorous approach to drapery, which emphasizes line rather than tonal modelling. In general, the miniaturists describe drapery in three or four related tones, with the base garment colour shadowed with lines of a slightly darker hue and highlighted with shades of a slightly lighter hue. Sometimes, though, the *colora conjuncta* system – which juxtaposes different hues – appears: on f. 43v (fig. 9), for example, ochre and white model Gregory's ice-blue garment, while the purple robes of Christ and the Virgin normally show either red or midnight-blue shadows.[207] Though loose drapery such as the cloth between Abraham's legs on f. 174v (fig. 23) and between the archangel's on f. 438v (fig. 44) frequently appears as a mass of swirls, the articulation of drapery on a body is usually angular, with body parts segmented and constrained by the cloth.[208] Highlights and shadows are often abrupt: there is little sense of modulated rounded forms; instead, parts are broken up into ever smaller geometrical patterns. The overall impression of the figures, however, is not harsh, and this is in part due to the care with which most of the faces were painted; the rare ineptly painted face, such as Solomon's on f. 215v (fig. 25) or those of the two apostles on f. 310v (fig. 31), stands out and jars. Just as contemporary Byzantine mosaicists used smaller tesserae for faces in order to achieve more subtle modula-

[206] Compare Kalavrezou (1989), 380.

[207] These contrasts may be more evident to us than to the Byzantines: see James (1991).

[208] Again, compare Kalavrezou (1989), 380.

tions than was possible with the larger cubes found in other parts of a mosaic,[209] so too the faces in Paris.gr.510 are more smoothly modelled, and painted with smaller brushstrokes, than the drapery. Animation is achieved almost entirely through the eyes. Some figures look at us, some interact with each other, but only rarely do we encounter a blank stare: all of the techniques used to paint eyes ensure a lively gaze. The miniaturists sharply contrast the whites and the pupils, emphasize the upper lid, and either smudge the area between the eye and nose or do not let the upper and lower eyelids meet as they approach the nose: both alternatives achieve the same result of enlivening the eye. In short, the miniaturists join together in their presentation of active and differentiated figures, who are themselves invested with internal tension through the contrast between the essentially linear drapery and the modelled faces.

Notwithstanding this body of shared formal characteristics, the miniatures exhibit considerable variety. No emphasis seems, however, to have been placed on the individual 'signature' of a miniaturist: the Morellian method, which suggests that a painter's identity is revealed by study of small and seemingly insignificant details such as the structure of an ear or of a hand – and which was used successfully by Ihor Ševčenko in his analysis of the Menologion of Basil II, painted a century later[210] – hits a brick wall when confronted by Paris.gr.510. This is perhaps not surprising in a century dominated by a thought process that subordinated the skill of individual painters to divine inspiration, and from which the single named artisan known to us, Lazaros-the-painter, was recorded primarily as a symbol of iconophile resistance.[211] The manner of painting eyes demonstrates some of the problems. The most basic variant is the presence or absence of a lower lid; when present, its defining line may be either straight (and thus leave a gap in the contour of the eye, especially on the side toward the nose) or curved to join the upper lid. In either configuration, lower lids may be depicted with a black line (e.g. f. 43v; fig. 9) or with a red-brown one (e.g. f. 104r; fig. 17). Upper lids, meanwhile, either extend outward beyond the eye toward the ear (e.g. ff. 78r and 143v; figs. 15, 19) or stop at the edge of the white. Such details, however, do not allow us to isolate different hands: though a preference for a particular type of eye may go along with a set of other characteristic features, most miniatures mix the variants. Nor do particular eye configurations distinguish different types of figures or different head positions. The only consistent pattern is generated by the size of the figures. Small figures, such as those which enact the Joseph story on f. 69v (fig. 12) or the boatmen with Jonah on f. 3r (fig. 6), virtually always have a strong, dark, and almost straight line for the upper lid, and omit the lower lid entirely. Large figures, on the other hand, display all eye types, seemingly almost at random. In this instance, at least, scale has more bearing on formal details that any miniaturist's 'hand'.

---

[209] On which see Nordhagen (1965).　　[210] I. Ševčenko (1962).　　[211] See *ODB* 2, 1197–1198.

Another indication that the analysis of small details does not tell us very much about the process of painting Paris.gr.510 is provided by the depiction of haloes. Here the basic range of possibilities was more limited, and, with one exception (f. 239r; fig. 27), nimbuses are painted in one of two ways in Paris.gr.510: in roughly half of the miniatures they are surrounded by a white line, and in the other half they are not. Folio 143v (fig. 19), however, provides both versions: the Old Testament figures of the upper register carry haloes without a white outline, while Christ, pictured three times in the lower two registers, supports a nimbus framed in white. This suggests an attempt to differentiate Christ from Jeremiah, the archangel Michael, and Nathan on f. 143v, and indicates that formal details may serve iconographical functions. But, in the case of the framed or unframed nimbus, even this type of distinction does not always hold true. Folio 174v (fig. 23), for example, has many other formal features in common with f. 143v, but here, while all of the figures enact Old Testament narratives, all also wear the nimbuses outlined in white associated with Christ on f. 143v. Further, on f. 196v (fig. 24), Christ – the only nimbate figure on the page – three times supports a halo without a white border, while ff. 3r (fig. 6) and 215v (fig. 25) combine Old and New Testament figures all of whom bear the same type of nimbus.

We are not, in other words, dealing with a group of painters each of whom felt the need to work out an individualized personal style that encompassed small details. This apparent lack of self-consciousness coincides with the larger pattern evident in the manuscript as a whole, for despite the number of features common to all of the miniatures, and despite the variations in a particular motif that criss-cross through these miniatures without any apparent discrimination, no one has ever claimed that the miniatures of Paris.gr.510 present an entirely homogeneous formal ensemble. The miniaturists may not have felt compelled to create their own personalized styles, but neither are we dealing with a unified collective: there is no 'workshop style'. There is much variation within the broadly defined common framework.

The heterogeneous nature of the miniatures is brought forth clearly when we look at how constellations of features were combined. As we have seen, the decision to incorporate miniatures was apparently made only after the first seven quires of text had been written. The formal diversity of the early miniatures suggests that a group of painters was assembled at this point, and it seems reasonable to assume that whatever distribution system was selected was initiated during the assignment of the early miniatures. The miniaturists would, in this hypothetical reconstruction of events, have worked on the sheets to be inserted at the beginning as the scribe and illuminators continued with the text, and then picked up later miniatures as they finished their earlier paintings and as the text became prepared for them. I have selected the well-preserved miniatures at the beginning of the manuscript for paradigmatic analysis here because it seems most likely that any systematic apportioning of the miniatures to individual painters would not yet have broken down.

The first miniature in the manuscript proper, f. 3r (fig. 6), does indeed share various architectural, physiognomic, and drapery details with other miniatures in Paris.gr.510. The manner of constructing rooftops, doors, porticoes and furniture; the squared heads with heavy jaws, prominent ears, and slightly sad features suggested by the slant of the eyes and the shadows under them; the large expanses of unarticulated and body-hugging drapery bordered by thick fold lines that emphasize the groin at the expense of the waist and are set off by agitated folds between the legs; the sling-like drapery that constricts some of the arms; and, finally, the three-tone system used for drapery recur on ff. 78r, 87v, 170r, 316r (figs. 15–16, 22, 32) and, in somewhat modified form, on ff. 67v, 69v, 137r, 301r, and 310v (figs. 11–12, 18, 30–31). The second miniature, on f. 30v, is too flaked to sustain detailed formal analysis, but the third, on f. 32v (fig. 8), is reasonably well preserved. Here the apostles seem to float in front of a green strip of ground and a monochromatic blue landscape or architectural backdrop. Their heads, with eyes that glance to the side under heavy upper lids, are too large for their bodies. The eyelids, limbs, fingers, and toes are consistently outlined on one side only. Drapery, mostly conceived in two tones, hugs the figures' bodies. A head in profile appears in the seventh quadrant. These features recur on ff. 69v and 165r (figs. 12, 21), while ff. 67v, 104r, 137r, 226v, and 301r (figs. 11, 17, 18, 26, 30) display related formal motifs. In the fourth miniature, on f. 43v (fig. 9), the miniaturist arranged the figures on a two-tone strip of ground against an unmodulated blue backdrop. Excepting the idiosyncratic portrait of Kaisarios in the top register, rubbing or flaking has obliterated most of the faces. The drapery, however, is striking. Dark garments, such as the red tunics worn by the foremost two pallbearers in the middle register, are barely modelled. Instead, simple dark lines define contours. Light drapery, on the other hand, shatters into harsh geometrical segments differentiated by three or four tones, the darkest and lightest of which contrast sharply. This same drapery system, and many of the specific fold motifs, recurs on ff. 75r, 285r, 355r, and 426v (figs. 14, 29, 36, 42), and, somewhat modified, on ff. 310v, 316r, and 340r (figs. 31–32, 34).

The problem is clear: ff. 67v, 69v, 137r, 301r, 310v, 316r all appeared twice in the foregoing analysis, and from within the group already adduced we could include further apparent discrepancies. The flat-headed women of f. 3r (fig. 6), for example, recur on f. 137r (fig. 18), but the drapery patterns used in the two miniatures are only generically related. Details associated with one cluster of images recur in another one, and this interpenetration of motifs appears throughout the manuscript: one miniature can be connected with another,[212] yet no clear formal patterns emerge.

---

[212] Relevant examples will be noted in subsequent chapters; see e.g. the discussions of ff. 226v and 424v, and of ff. 52v and 174v, in chapter 8.

Though it would be useful to be able to determine how many painters were assembled to work on Paris.gr.510, it is simply not possible to group the miniatures by 'hands' in any convincing fashion without access to the manuscript.

It may be more practical to define the two extremes, the two most distinct approaches exhibited by the miniatures, while emphasizing that the majority of the images in Paris.gr.510 fall between them. The first of these 'extremes' surfaces in, for example, the martyrdom of the apostles on f. 32v (fig. 8), the Joseph sequence on f. 69v (fig. 12), and the legend of Constantine and Helena on f. 440r (fig. 45). Folios 32v and 69v share a number of details, and though several of these similarities resulted from the small scale of the figures included in both, they were nonetheless apparently painted by the same miniaturist; this painter may also have executed f. 440r, where the figures are larger. Whether or not this was so, the three display a cluster of similarities that recur throughout the manuscript in various configurations. All share a two-tone green ground beneath a blue backdrop;[213] background features are confined to elements essential to comprehend the narrative – such as the Milvian bridge on f. 440r[214] – or to a monochromatic landscape as on f. 32v.[215] Figures are stocky, and have large heads. There is a distinct preference for either frontal gazes or pure profile, though, as often in Paris.gr.510, complex poses are attempted. Neither the subject matter – in these examples we see an Old Testament, an apostolic, and a historical sequence – nor the iconographical sources of the miniatures are related: we are dealing neither with a formal 'mode' developed for a particular type of subject nor with images that faithfully copy any kind of related models.

Instead, we see in these miniatures a version of the style found in the *Sacra Parallela* (figs. 58–60, 64, 88, 90, 91, 94, 105, 106, 113, 114, 123, 152, 153, 160, 172).[216] Though we must look past the technical differences to see them – the gold leaf used throughout the *Sacra Parallela* made shading virtually impossible – there is a remarkable number of similarities between the *Sacra Parallela* and this group of miniatures in Paris.gr.510: heads are large, and while gestures are expressive, the bodies themselves are stiff; drapery is simplified and segmented to define body parts; faces show eyes made vivid by emphasizing the upper lid with a dark slash (in the *Sacra Parallela* lower lids are rare); mouths are formed of a single, and often swallow-shaped, line placed high above a prominent chin that is accented by a deep cleft. The Gregory miniaturists painted their scenes, and thereby minimized the

---

[213] The two-tone green ground also appears on ff. 3r, 30v, 43v, 310v, and 340r (figs. 6–7, 9, 31, 34).

[214] Compare the elaborate landscape setting for the bridge on f. 409v (fig. 40).

[215] Other monochromatic (usually blue on blue) backgrounds appear on ff. 52v, 71v, 78r, 239r, 426v, and 435v (figs. 10, 13, 15, 27, 42–43).

[216] On this style, sometimes called the double-fold style, see Weitzmann (1982), 190–193; (1978), 74–80; (1979a), 17–18. See also Brenk (1971), 408–411, who notes the widespread diffusion of this linear handling, and Bergman (1974), 169–171, who notes the 'double-stroke motif' in ninth-century Rome and its continuation into eleventh-century Amalfi.

linearity that the *Sacra Parallela* painters emphasized by relying on contour drawing filled in with gold leaf; but there are nonetheless fundamental similarities in the handling of figures in both manuscripts.

At the other extreme, the Homilies miniaturists reveal less interest in dramatic expression enacted in front of a neutral stage than in the interaction of figures. While the miniatures in this group are not in any obvious way united by discrete 'hands', the differences that distinguish them are better read as indications of variations on a common theme than as distinct formal statements. Folios 30v and 316r (figs. 7, 32), for example, were almost certainly painted by different miniaturists: the proportions of the figures are not the same, and the painter of the crucifixion page displays a propensity for fussy drapery that anticipates the so-called 'dynamic style' by three hundred years. Yet the common denominators outweigh these differences. Figures are placed before a setting and interact with each other; drapery is modelled in a three- or four-tone system (it is in this group that all examples of *colora conjuncta* modelling appear), and is articulated by very angular fold lines that produce geometrical shapes, many of which the two painters share: both, for example, combine a triangular shadow under the knee with two diagonal slashes across the thigh. Material clings to the figures' bodies, especially to their thighs, and its folds contain and constrain them: arms are held close to the body in sling-like folds; legs are restrained by a deep upturned hem. The miniaturists following this approach also employ the arrow highlight: a peculiar manner of emphasizing a fold by outlining it, in a lighter colour, on two sides with converging lines that meet to form a point.

As was true of the miniaturists using the first approach, those following this avenue find cohorts in contemporary manuscripts, and especially in the late ninth-century Vatican 'Christian Topography' (Vat.gr.699; figs. 75–77, 138, 150, 156). The portrait of Peter in the Vatican manuscript (fig. 75), for example, shows a triangular knee shadow surmounted by two diagonal folds outlined with arrow highlights exactly as in Paris.gr.510, while the angel feeding Isaiah his burning coal (fig. 76) displays the fussy drapery swirls between his legs so familiar in the Gregory miniatures; on this same page in the 'Christian Topography', Christ's robe reveals *colora conjuncta* modelling, and elsewhere in the manuscript sling-like drapery constrains arms and upturned hems restrain legs as in the Gregory miniatures (fig. 77). We also find many of these features, though in forms modified by their medium, in the contemporary monumental imagery of Constantinople. At Hagia Sophia, mosaics from the early 870s in the room over the vestibule – evidently the large sekreton of the adjoining patriarchal apartments – show facial types quite similar to those in Paris.gr.510, though here the drapery is more linear and the mosaicist left larger areas unarticulated than is usual in the Homilies.[217] In the chapel in the

---

[217] Cormack and Hawkins (1977), 237–240, figs. 26–49 and colour plates.

Fig. 75 Vat.gr.699, f. 81r: Peter

southwest buttress of Hagia Sophia, which was apparently decorated shortly after
the large sekreton, the drapery displays more segmentation,[218] but it is in the
mosaics of the north tympanum that we find the closest formal correlates to the
Paris Gregory (fig. 78).[219] Head types find virtually identical counterparts in
Paris.gr.510, down to such details as eyelids prolonged beyond the outer side of the
eyeball, and upper and lower lids that do not touch when they come together
toward the bridge of the nose; here too the drapery shatters into geometric shapes
with strong light outlines. When first published, the mosaics of the north tympanum were dated to the last two decades of the ninth century; more recently, they

[218] Mango (1962), 38–39, figs. 36–38.   [219] Mango and Hawkins (1972), 3–41, esp. 36–37.

Fig. 76 Vat.gr.699, f. 72v: vision of Isaiah

have been assigned to the late 870s or early 880s – precisely the years when the Homilies was in production.[220]

Paris.gr.510 reveals two approaches to painting that interacted fluidly: the extremes that I have described were hardly mutually exclusive, they simply illuminate the range of formal expression found in the manuscript. Neither approach was

[220] Ibid., 37–41; Cormack and Hawkins (1977), 239.

115

Fig. 77 Vat.gr.699, f. 83v: conversion of Saul

limited to the miniatures of Paris.gr.510 nor even to manuscripts, but instead both form part of the broader picture of ninth-century imagery. The loose and flickering brushstrokes that sometimes surface (the so-called 'illusionistic' elements) date back a long way and had most recently appeared across a sea: chronologically their closest precursors are to be found in some of the work done in Rome between 705 and 707 for Pope John VII at Sta Maria Antiqua. But the Roman frescoes do not show the hard linear highlights or the segmented and angular drapery folds that distinguish even the most 'painterly' of the Homilies, 'Christian Topography', and *Sacra Parallela* miniatures. Later eighth-century frescoes at Sta Maria Antiqua are more linear than those painted in 705–707, but even they do not display the almost

Fig. 78 Istanbul, Hagia Sophia: north tympanum mosaic, Ignatios Theophoros

fractured quality of the Gregory miniatures, nor do they share any of the formal vocabulary used in the drapery; for this, the closest Italian parallel I have been able to find is provided by the wall paintings at SS. Martiri in Cividale, roughly contemporary with Paris.gr.510 (ca. 900).[221] The schematization apparent in the Homilies images, which results in a predictable and regularized approach to drapery, appears in eastern Mediterranean works already in the eighth century: along with numer-

[221] Belting (1962); Belting (1968), 230–255.

ous other features of Paris.gr.510, it is for example found in the Vatican Ptolemy of 753/4.[222] During the ninth century, the most emphatic tendency toward schematized pattern produced the 'double-fold style' of the *Sacra Parallela*; in more modified form, it still proved influential enough to affect the most 'illusionistic' of painters.

Despite the fact that two approaches can be isolated in Paris.gr.510, it must be reiterated that the manuscript cannot simply be divided into the two 'styles'. Too many miniatures show both; too many are set, somewhat eclectically, between the two extremes. The two approaches I have set out are better seen as ideal types than as the distinctive signatures of single, or groups of, miniaturists; it is not even to be excluded that one miniaturist could, for whatever reason, use both approaches. To understand the production process of the Homilies, it is perhaps more useful to return to composition.

The coordination between scribes and miniaturists evident in the *lemmata* initials and marginal markings, the commentary role of many scenes, and the use of composition to convey carefully wrought meaning contrasts sharply with the almost haphazard combination of formal details in Paris.gr.510. The structure of the manuscript seems at odds with its execution, and this suggests that just as text, initials, and miniatures were the provinces of different groups,[223] so too the design and layout of the manuscript as a whole was determined by a specialist who conveyed requirements to various teams of scribes, illuminators, and miniaturists. The study of Byzantine manuscript production is in its infancy, and whether or not such a degree of sub-contracting was ever common is unclear. What is evident, however, is that Paris.gr.510 relied on meticulously directed teamwork, and it seems reasonable to suppose that the designer of the miniatures took on that job.

---

[222] Vat.gr.1291; on the date, Wright (1985).   [223] See the Introduction.

3

The biographical miniatures: toward image as exegesis

The episodes from the lives of Gregory of Nazianzus, his family, St Basil and St Cyprian illustrated in Paris.gr.510 were, with some notable exceptions, motivated directly by Gregory's sermons; in this respect, they resemble the miniatures in other preserved copies of Gregory's Homilies more closely than do most pictures in Paris.gr.510. But the group is not monolithic, and within it we can chart changes in the ways images were used as the production of the manuscript progressed: more clearly than any other category of pictures, the biographical miniatures reveal the growth of a system of visual commentary in Paris.gr.510.

GREGORY OF NAZIANZUS AND HIS FAMILY

Folio 43v (9) (fig. 9)

The three registers of f. 43v portray Gregory with his family, the funeral of Gregory's brother Kaisarios, and the death of his sister Gorgonia.[1] Painted on an inserted leaf that separates Gregory's funeral oration to his brother (homily 7) from his funeral oration to his sister (homily 8),[2] the miniature provides an appropriate bridge between the two eulogies and almost certainly retains its original location.[3]

The top register portrays Gregory flanked by his parents Nonna and the elder Gregory, in the place of honour on his right, and by his siblings Kaisarios and Gorgonia. All are identified by inscriptions.[4] Although the only other illustrated

---

[1] Omont (1929), 15, pl. XXIII; Der Nersessian (1955), 225; Der Nersessian (1962), 217; Buchthal (1963), 84–86; Walter (1976a), 120, 124; Weitzmann (1979a), 235–236; Brubaker (1996b), 98–99.

[2] SC 405, 180–245 (Homily 7; *BHG* 286; *NPNF*, 229–238), 246–299 (Homily 8; *BHG* 704; *NPNF*, 238–245). On the oration to Gorgonia, see also Cameron (1989), 197–198.

[3] For arguments against the thesis that the miniature has been moved, see the discussion of f. 32v (which prefaces the funeral oration to Kaisarios) in chapter 6.

[4] Nonna's inscription has flaked off; the others read: Ο ΑΓΙΟΣ ΓΡΗΓΟΡΙΟΣ Ο Π[ΑΤ]ΗΡ ΤΟΥ ΘΕΟΛΟΓΟΥ, Ο ΑΓΙΟΣ ΓΡΗΓΟΡΙΟΣ Ο ΘΕΟΛΟΓΟΣ, Ο ΑΓΙΟΣ ΚΑΙCΑΡΙΟΣ, and Η ΑΓΙΑ ΓΟΡΓΟΝΙΑ.

copy of the funeral orations, in the Milan Gregory, lacks a comparable group,[5] the Paris miniaturist has responded to Gregory's frequent mentions of his family in both funeral orations. The family portrait on f. 43v could in fact easily have been compiled *ad hoc*, for the painter has replicated details that appear elsewhere in the manuscript and the facial types of the male figures adhere to contemporary formulae. The gesture of the two women, for example, is repeated by a man on f. 104r (fig. 17), while Gorgonia wears the red and ochre in which she also appears on f. 452r (fig. 46), where Kaisarios recurs as well with the same facial type. On f. 43v, Kaisarios – a member of the imperial court until he quitted his post under Julian the Apostate – wears secular official costume that consists of a white mantle embellished with a large gold rectangle over a green tunic; when he appears in the Milan Gregory, he wears a simple belted tunic, but both the Milan and the Paris miniaturists portrayed him with dark hair and a short dark beard. Gregory and his father both wear bishop's vestments,[6] carry jewelled books in their left hands and gesture toward these with their right, have pointed grey beards, and grey hair that dips down over their foreheads: throughout Paris.gr.510, the two are, in fact, physiognomically indistinguishable.[7] The *Sacra Parallela* depicts Gregory of Nazianzus in the same way (figs. 58, 60), and sometimes in exactly the same pose.[8] Both manuscripts differ from later middle Byzantine portraits of Gregory, but resemble an eighth-century representation at Sta Maria Antiqua and drawings of a ninth-century mosaic at Hagia Sophia.[9]

The second register shows the funeral of Kaisarios (Ο Α[ΓΙΟC] ΚΑΙCΑΡΙΟC ΕΝΤΑΦΙΑΖΟΜΕΝΟC), with four youths carrying his body – still clad in the white mantle, which now covers his hands – on a bed toward a church. Gregory, swinging a censer, leads the procession; his remaining family follows, their hands raised to their faces in grief.[10] It is possible that a similar image has been excised from the Milan Gregory;[11] but in any event the composition on f. 43v presents an adaptation of standard funerary iconography.[12]

In the upper two registers, the miniaturist arranged the figures on a two-tone strip of ground against a blue backdrop; this format is retained for the death of Gorgonia, which is nonetheless presented as a domestic scene. Gorgonia lies on her deathbed,

---

[5] Grabar (1943a), pl. V,4 (Gregory and Kaisarios greet Nonna); VII,2 (Kaisarios returns to his parents during the reign of Julian); VII,1 (Kaisarios survives the Nicaea earthquake); VIII,1 (Gregory thanks God at the end of Kaisarios' funeral oration); VIII,2 (a partially excised miniature in which only Gregory, delivering Gorgonia's oration, survives); VIII,3 (Solomon speaks in praise of women); IX,1 (Gorgonia on her deathbed, also partially excised). The first miniature to Homily 7 (p. 71) has been removed but, as the text begins on p. 70, is unlikely to have been a prefatory family portrait.

[6] For the garments worn by the two Gregories throughout Paris.gr.510, see Thierry (1966), 308–315.

[7] See Buchthal (1963), 84–86.

[8] Weitzmann (1979a), figs. 648–670, esp. 651, 654, 656. The pose recurs in Gregory's portrait in Venice, Marciana gr.74, f. 1v, also attributed to the ninth century: Furlan (1978), 6–7, fig. 1.

[9] Buchthal (1963), 84–86; Weitzmann (1979a), 235–236; Mango (1962), 51, figs. 57, 59.

[10] See Maguire (1977), 141–142.   [11] See note 5 above.   [12] See Walter (1976a), 123–124.

murmuring her last words (a psalm verse) to the officiating priest, here identified as Gregory of Nyssa.[13] Gregory tells us that Gorgonia's family surrounded her as she lay dying, and singles out her husband and children for specific mention. Continuing the emphasis on Gregory's own immediate family evident in the top registers, however, Gorgonia's is omitted in favour of her parents and surviving brother, all of whom stand to the left, in front of a building presumably meant to represent the house in which she died. Nonna, still clad in green and pink, carries the burden of the grief: she leans over the bed and raises her covered hands to her face; the two Gregories, father and son, stand – only slightly inclined – behind her. Candles in decorated sconces burn to the right, before a structure with a central dome that may represent the church in which Gregory delivered the funeral oration. The scene adapts a common Byzantine formula to the requirements of Gorgonia's circumstances, and a parallel construction appeared in the Milan Gregory before much of the miniature was excised (fig. 49).[14] Aside from the reversal of Gorgonia, who lies with her head to the left in the Milan fragment, the composition duplicates that on f. 43v, with the feet of three figures to the left of Gorgonia's bed, and the legs of a figure before the substructure of a building to the right. However tenuous, the shared design at least hints that the Paris miniaturists may occasionally have been influenced by an illustrated Homilies that recalled the Milan manuscript.[15]

Folio 52v (10) (fig. 10)

Folio 52v illustrates Gregory's first oration 'On peace' (homily 6), which celebrated the reconciliation of the monastic community of Nazianzus in 364.[16] The two upper registers contain a long Genesis sequence that provides an exegetical comment on the sermon; Moses receiving the laws, the first scene in the lowest register, illustrates the text directly.[17] In the second scene of the register, Gregory delivers 'On peace', accompanied by his father. The pair, nimbed and holding gold and jewelled books in their covered left hands, stand in close-to-identical poses behind an altar draped in pink and surmounted by a baldachin. To the right, four pairs of men embrace in response to Gregory's entreaty to the monks to hug and kiss one another, and illustrate Gregory's observation to his father that 'All your children have come to you; they surround the altar.'[18]

---

[13] The inscription reads '[Gregory of] Nyssa hears Gorgonia's last words: I will lie down in peace' (Psalm 4:8): Ο ΝΥCCΗC [ΑΚ]ΟΥΩΝ ΠΑΡ[Α Γ]ΟΡΓΟΝΙΑC ΤΕΛΕΥΤΩCΗC · ΕΝ ΕΙΡΗΝΗ Ε[Λ]Ι ΤΟ ΑΥΤΟ ΚΟΙΜ[ΗΘΗCΟ]ΜΑΙ. The identification of Gregory of Nyssa as Gorgonia's confessor is unusual; see *PG* 35:789–790 (III), 815 note 78. On Gregory's description of Gorgonia's death, see Mossay (1973); on the inscription, Brubaker (1996b), 98–99.

[14] Grabar (1943a), pl. IX,1.   [15] See the Introduction.

[16] SC 405, 120–179. Omont (1929), 15–16, pl. XXIV; Gallay (1943), 80–84; Der Nersessian (1962), 208–209; Walter (1978), 238.

[17] On the relationship between the miniature and its accompanying text, see chapter 5; on the biblical iconography, chapter 8.   [18] SC 404, 174.

The Milan Homilies illustrates this passage with a portrait of the two Gregories, but the image does not seem to be related to that on f. 52v: no altar or monks appear, the gestures and vestments differ, the figures' hands are not covered, the younger Gregory holds a scroll rather than a jewelled book, and his father holds nothing.[19] On f. 52v, the physiognomic types displayed by Gregory and his father conform with those used for their portraits throughout Paris.gr.510, and the furniture finds numerous parallels as well;[20] as with the family portrait on f. 43v, the miniaturist could well have compiled this image *ad hoc*.

Folio 67v (11) (fig. 11)

The upper register of f. 67v depicts Isaiah's vision;[21] the lower shows Gregory's consecration as bishop of Sasima.[22] Appropriately, the miniature introduces Gregory's ninth homily, 'To his father, in the presence of Basil, on his consecration as bishop of Sasima'.[23] In the centre of the register, Gregory stands with slightly bowed head between two bishops who hold an open book over his head; in front of Gregory and separated from him by an altar draped in red, a third bishop – probably St Basil[24] – touches Gregory's forehead in blessing. A gold baldachin rises behind the figures, and a grey, semi-circular structure that presumably signifies an apse encloses the group; on this are four gold candlesticks, two on either side. Two groups of men stand to the left: those closest to the ceremony, deacons dressed in cream-coloured robes, swing censers and carry candles; the members of the second group also carry candles, but are dressed in brown, apparently to signal their status as monks. On the right is a green basilica with a curtained door and red-tiled roofs. Most details correspond with the orthodox liturgy for the consecration of a bishop as recorded in the euchologion, which specifies three officiating bishops and describes them holding the open gospelbook over the head of the new bishop as they stand in the sanctuary.[25]

While Gregory's consecration apparently recurs in the Milan Gregory (though there is nothing to confirm that the rite is being performed, Basil flanked by Gregory *fils* and *père* certainly raises his hand toward the younger Gregory in bless-

---

[19] Grabar (1943a), pl. X,1.

[20] The column decoration finds parallels on e.g. ff. 71v and 149r (figs. 13, 20); the front left column disappears into Basil's head on f. 104r (fig. 17) as it does into Gregory's here, and the design and decoration of the baldachin are generally similar; f. 104r also repeats the pink altar cloth. The relation between altar and baldachin finds a match on f. 367v (fig. 38). See too the baldachins on ff. 137r, 143v, 239r, and 332v (figs. 18–19, 27, 33).   [21] On which see chapter 7.

[22] Omont (1929), 16, pl. XXV; Der Nersessian (1962), 210–211; N. Ševčenko (1973), 40, 56–57; Walter (1978), 240–241; N. Ševčenko (1983), 82.

[23] SC 405, 300–315; Gallay (1943), 113–115. In Paris.gr.510, the first text page of Homily 9 has been lost; as it now stands, f. 68r begins at SC 405, 306 (3, l.3).

[24] So Omont (1929), 16; compare Basil's portrait on f. 71v (fig. 13).

[25] Goar (1730), 249–252. See also N. Ševčenko (1983), 81.

ing [fig. 50])[26] and appears in several later examples,[27] the consecration under a gospelbook finds only one parallel, and that later in Paris.gr.510 itself (f. 452r; fig. 46).[28] Here, Gregory's consecration is effected only by the two book-holding bishops and the blessing is, unusually, omitted.[29] The differences between the two miniatures are not clarified by their accompanying texts, nor by any written account of Gregory's life known to me. Presumably, the miniaturists varied the compositions either to distinguish the two occasions when Gregory was ordained bishop or to avoid monotony.

Folio 71v (13) (fig. 13)

The top register of f. 71v displays a series of autonomous portraits, rather like f. 43v (fig. 9), but in this case the figures accompanying Gregory – Basil the Great and Gregory of Nyssa – are not members of his family and are separated from each other by columns; Job on his dungheap appears below.[30] The miniature retains its original location: the preceding sermon concludes on the recto, and Gregory's eleventh homily, which follows on ff. 72r–74v, inspired the illustration. Gregory delivered 'To Gregory of Nyssa, brother of Basil the Great, who arrived after his consecration' shortly after he became bishop of Sasima in 372;[31] Gregory of Nyssa's arrival prompted the sermon, and Gregory of Nazianzus concentrates on his great love for him. Gregory reveals his friend's only flaw to be that he arrived too late to help with the decision to accept the episcopal seat; he recalls the words of Job to his friend Baldad, who arrived to comfort Job as he sat, covered with sores, on the dungheap (Job 25–26). The only marginal *oboloi* attached to the homily set off the relevant quotation from Job,[32] which clearly inspired the image in the lower register just as the title motivated the portraits above.

The church fathers stand in a gold and jewelled arcade. Although, as Charles Rufus Morey pointed out, they resemble figures arranged on a columnar sarcophagus, the architectural vocabulary employed is not so ancient. Details such as the columns with three bands of variable fluting, the quasi-ionic capitals, and the jewelled framing recur in the picture of Gregory and Basil ministering to the sick on f. 149r (fig. 20), while the spandrel ornament, in shades of blue with white details, is

---

[26] Grabar (1943a), pl. XI,1; Walter (1978), 240–241. The inscription to the left of Gregory gives the title of the sermon; the scroll contains its opening words.

[27] E.g. an illustrated commentary on Gregory's sermons written by Elijah of Crete ca. 1200, now in Basel (Bibliothèque de l'Université, gr.A.N.I.8, f. Ov): Walter (1972), 126, fig. 14.

[28] See N. Ševčenko (1983), 79–85.

[29] See Walter (1978), 240–241. The scenes carry the same inscription, Ο ΘΕΟΛΟΓΟΣ [ΧΕΙΡΟ]ΤΟΝΟΥΜΕΝΟC ('the ordination of the theologian'), save that, ironically, the χειρο has been lost or omitted on f. 67v. On *cheirotonia*, *ODB* I (1991), 417.

[30] Millet (1920), 242; Omont (1929), 17, pl. XXVII; Morey (1929), 95; Weitzmann (1947), 197; Ainalov (1961), 207; Der Nersessian (1962), 212. On the iconography of the Job image, see chapter 8.

[31] SC 405, 328–47 (*BHG* 716); Gallay (1943), 115–116.   [32] SC 405, 334 (3, ll. 17–19).

found on f. 438v (fig. 44). Many of the motifs enjoyed wide currency – the column form, for example, appears in Roman murals of the second half of the ninth century at S. Clemente and at the so-called temple of Fortuna Virilis[33] – and the portrait types of the three church fathers, all identified by inscription, conform with contemporary practice.[34] Even the variegated backdrop, with the central Gregory of Nyssa against a red ground and the flanking figures of Basil and Gregory of Nazianzus backed with green, finds analogues elsewhere in Paris.gr.510: the martyrdoms of the Makkabees on f. 340r (fig. 34), for example, are set against a grid of alternating blue and red squares.

The eleventh homily formed part of the liturgical readings for Gregory of Nyssa's feast day (10 January), and was incorporated in the liturgical editions of the Homilies with illustrations that stress the friendship between the two Gregories by picturing them talking, embracing, or praying together.[35] None of the liturgical manuscripts attaches any biblical scenes, however, and only once does Basil join the two Gregories (to form part of a historiated initial centred on Gregory of Nazianzus).[36] The Milan Gregory (fig. 51), on the other hand, resembles Paris.gr.510 in its inclusion of a triple portrait of the two Gregories with Basil, with Gregory of Nyssa in the centre and with Basil portrayed as younger than his brother and the author.[37] Both ninth-century miniaturists may have been independently inspired by the title of the oration, but they are joined in their similar interpretation of it.

Folio 78r (15) (fig. 15)

The miniature, with its ornate ribboned frame, is in complete harmony with the accompanying text, which begins on the verso of the folio.[38] Gregory delivered 'On the plague of hail and his father's silence' (Homily 16) in 373 after a serious hailstorm ruined the harvests of Nazianzus.[39] Gregory's father, who as bishop should have spoken, was so overwhelmed by the tragedy that he could not respond to the distressed citizens who flocked to the church. As his father's assistant, Gregory therefore delivered the sermon, and counselled penitence and prayer to atone for the sins that had provoked God's wrath and the storm.

In the top register, against a blue sky, balls of white hail descend from a grey-blue

---

[33] So Osborne (1981b), 277.

[34] Buchthal (1963), 86–87; Walter (1971), 205 note 81; Weitzmann (1979a), 219, 235. See also the miniature of Basil in Venice, Marciana gr.74, f. 2r: Furlan (1978). [35] Galavaris (1969), 11, 15, 53.

[36] Sinai.gr.346, f. 152v (eleventh century): ibid., 56 and fig. 350; Weitzmann and Galavaris (1990), fig. 331.

[37] Grabar (1943a), pl. XIV,2. The triple portrait appears at the end of the sermon; the opening image, anticipating the liturgical edition, presents the two Gregories; a third miniature portrays Moses and Aaron, mentioned in Gregory's second paragraph: ibid., pls. XIII,2 and XIV,1.

[38] Omont (1929), 18, pl. XXIX; Der Nersessian (1962), 199; Buchthal (1963), 63; Walter (1972), 121–122. [39] PG 35:934–944 (NPNF, 247–254); Gallay (1943), 122.

arc onto a landscape planted with wheat (on the right), vines (on the left), and shrubs (along the horizon line) that rise from a strip of green ground. A descriptive titulus, 'the plague of hail' (Η ΠΛΗΓΗ ΤΗΣ ΧΑΛΑΖΗΣ), appears on the gold frame between the registers. Significant as one of the few Byzantine images to depict a natural disaster,[40] the scene follows Gregory's description, introduced by a gold initial and expressed in the voice of God: 'I brought the hail upon you . . . I uprooted your vineyards and shrubberies and crops, but I failed to shatter your wickedness.'[41]

The lower register shows Gregory and his father (identified by a fragmentary inscription) standing in front of an aedicula, facing a central group composed of males, and a second group, on the right, of females.[42] As shown by his hand gesture and the inscription 'the theologian speaks' (Ο ΘΕΟΛΟΓΟΣ ΔΗΜΙΓΟΡΟΝ) Gregory is delivering the sermon; his father's silence is indicated by the concealment of both arms within his cloak. The gesture of the central male encapsulates the citizens' demand for an official response to the calamity, while the gestures of sorrow made by many of the group demonstrate the communal reaction to the storm.

In its specificity, f. 78r goes well beyond the illustrations to Homily 16 in other manuscripts of Gregory's Homilies. Though the incipit image to this sermon in the Milan manuscript has been excised,[43] of the six copies of the liturgical Homilies that illustrate the sermon only one pictures the hail.[44] The fourteenth-century Paris.gr.543 (fig. 79) shows Gregory preaching from a scroll (as he normally does in the Milan Gregory) while an arc confines the hail above the heads of the Nazianzus citizens; the composition bears little resemblance to f. 78r.[45]

'On the plague of hail' is not a biographical sermon; nor did its main theme present ideas so foreign to ninth-century Constantinopolitans that its meaning could only be translated verbatim rather than commented upon: Gregory's thesis that natural disasters were God's response to communal sins was compatible with ninth-century thought, and reference to God's use of natural calamities to punish sinners remained a common response to disasters.[46] Indeed, it is likely that the sermon struck a resonant chord, for a series of natural disasters (primarily earthquakes) hit the capital during the reigns of Michael III and Basil I.[47] The earth-

---

[40] See Brubaker and Littlewood (1992), 226–227.   [41] Folio 82v; *PG* 35:948B9–13.

[42] Omont (1929), 18, followed by subsequent scholars, mistakenly identified the figure who leads the group of men as Gregory.

[43] Only a portrait of the prophet Joel and a preaching scene related to a later section of the text remain: Grabar (1943a), pls. XV,3, XVI,3.   [44] Galavaris (1969), 36.   [45] Ibid., 68, fig. 469.

[46] See, for example, Photios, Homily 4,5 (ed. Laourdas [1959], 48; trans. Mango [1958], 105), and Mango's remark (ibid., 5–6) that 'nothing could have been further from the spirit of Photios than to have stated that natural calamities had no connection with our sins'. Though his focus is earthquakes, Vercleyen (1988), 155–173, provides many further examples of the moralizing use of natural disasters.

[47] For a summary of the source material, see Mango (1958), 5 note 4.

Fig. 79 Paris.gr.543, f. 342v: Gregory of Nazianzus and his father with the citizens of Nazianzus; Gregory preaching on the hailstorm

quake in 869 was sufficiently memorable to be incorporated into the cycle of liturgical commemorations;[48] and, as Gregory had done before him, the then-patriarch
Photios responded to it with a sermon (now lost) that almost certainly repeated
Gregory's points.[49] Gregory's specific subject, the plant-destroying storm, also presumably spoke to ninth-century Byzantines. The idea of the constructed landscape, represented by gardens and even fields, had great symbolic importance in
Byzantium, both as a romantic evocation of God's creation (this primarily for the
urban population) and as a means of demonstrating human control over the unruly
world of nature.[50] The destruction of cultivated vegetation brought into question
God's intentions and God's response to the agriculturalist who attempted to recre-
ate a paradisal and ordered landscape; on an even more fundamental level, it called
into question human authority over nature. The hailstorm on f. 78r, and the ago-
nized response of Gregory's flock to it, illustrated an issue that was basic and per-
ennial to the Byzantines, and remained as important in the ninth as in the fourth
century.[51]

Folio 87v (16) (fig. 16)

Folio 87v prefaces Gregory's eighteenth sermon, delivered in 374 on the death of his
father.[52] Omitting any conventional funeral scene, the miniaturist instead filled the
page with scenes of Christ's ministry and episodes from the life of Gregory's
father.[53] The uppermost of its three registers shows Christ calling the apostles Peter,
Andrew, James and John from their boats (Matthew 4:18–22); Christ conversing
with Zachias, who perches in a sycamore tree, before entering Jericho (Luke 19:1–5);
and the calling of Matthew (Matthew 9:9, Mark 2:14, Luke 5:27–28). The middle
register continues with Christ talking to the rich young man (Matthew 19:16–22,
Mark 10:17–22) and Christ converting Nathanael (John 1:47–48).[54] The lowest register chronicles the conversion of Gregory's father as described in the funeral
oration; enlarged initials in the text highlight two of the passages illustrated.

[48] Grumel (1958), 479; Mateos I (1963), 192; Dagron (1981), 96–98, 103; Vercleyen (1988), 161–167.
For an eleventh-century parallel, Cotsonis (1989), 11–13.　　[49] See the references in note 46 above.
[50] See Brubaker and Littlewood (1992) for discussion and bibliography.
[51] Cf. Kaplan (1992), 455–464. Bad weather may, however, have been a somewhat touchy issue – and
hence better treated with historical distance – for the night of Michael III's murder was, according to
Symeon the Logothete, particularly foul, and Basil had great difficulty crossing the water to get to the
palace (*Chronographia*: ed. [as Leo Grammaticus] Bekker [1842], 837–838; see also Tobias [1969],
153–156).
[52] *PG* 35:985–1044 (*BHG* 714; *NPNF*, 255–269); Gallay (1943), 124–125. The first leaf of the text has
been removed; the sermon now starts part way through the second sentence of paragraph four (see
Appendix C). The miniature itself retains its original location: the text of the preceding homily concludes on its verso.
[53] Omont (1929), 18–19, pl. XXX; Weitzmann (1942/43), 88; Weitzmann (1947), 100; Der
Nersessian (1962), 199–200; N. Ševčenko (1973), 39–40, 56–57; Weitzmann (1979a), 162, 181, 185;
Brubaker (1996a), 16; Brubaker (1996b), 98–99.
[54] On the iconography of the gospel scenes, see chapter 8.

The register opens with 'the vision of dreams that God often bestows upon a soul worthy of salvation'.[55] Gregory tells us that his father converted to Christianity after such a dream, in which he heard the words 'I was glad when they said to me, let us go into the house of the Lord' (Psalm 121:1); when he awoke, he repeated the words to his wife. The miniature shows Gregory's father waking from the dream – its divine inspiration indicated by a hand of God emerging from an arc of heaven in concentric bands of blue – and twisting round to speak to Nonna, here in red. The inscription written on the frame ('the father of the theologian [= Gregory of Nazianzus] saying to his wife, I was glad when they said to me') supplies the dialogue, though the viewer is left to complete the psalm verse.[56] The building behind Gregory's father may represent the house in which he awoke, or, as the ochre walls and red tile roof appear on a church in the following scene, 'the house of the Lord' that figured in the dream. We next see 'the wonder' when Gregory *père* fell to his knees rather than standing during his acceptance as a catechumen, and was thus accidentally ordained a priest.[57] The officiating priest, accompanied by a youthful assistant, stands before a church with his right hand raised in blessing; his left is open in a gesture of surprise as Gregory senior stumbles toward him, arms extended. Finally, Gregory's father – now nimbed – receives baptism from the same priest (his omophorion tucked over his left arm to keep it out of the water), who stands on dark green steps and lowers his right arm to touch the elder Gregory's head as it emerges from an ochre cruciform font that his son tells us was encircled by flashes of light and glory, here represented as a precise circular band of white that was evidently drawn with a compass.[58] In response, the priest repeats the gesture of surprise with his left hand: needless to say, this gesture does not recur in other baptismal scenes in Paris.gr.510 (e.g. f. 426v; fig. 42). Supernatural – or at least unusual – details thus mark all three episodes, in confirmation of Gregory's assessment that his father was 'called to himself by God'.

Unlike the scenes of Gregory's father's life, those of the upper registers are only tangentially related to Gregory's funeral oration. Still, as Sirarpie Der Nersessian observed, the theme of conversion unites much of the page,[59] and this association is underscored by the two *tituli* inscribed on the gold of the frame: the lower one, as we saw, invokes Psalm 121:1 while the top one reads 'the calling of the apostles' (H ΚΛHCIC TΩN AПOCT[OΛΩN]). The theme of apostolic conversion was in

---

[55] *PG* 35:1000A4–8 (introduced by a gold initial).

[56] O Π[AT]HP TOY ΘEOΛOΓOY ΛEΓΩN ΠP[OC] THN ΓYNEKA AYT[OY] · EYФPAN-ΘHN EПI TOIC EIPHKOCI MOI.

[57] *PG* 35:1000B14–C8 (introduced by a gold initial). The inscription on the miniature is laconic: O Π[AT]HP TOY ΘEOΛOΓOY KATHXOYMENOC.

[58] *PG* 35:1001A15–B9. The inscription ignores the wonders, and simply tells us that we see 'the baptism of the father of the theologian' (O Π[AT]HP TOY ΘEOΛOΓOY BAПTIZOMENOC). Another compass-drawn circle appears on f. 75r (fig. 14).   [59] Der Nersessian (1962), 199–200.

part suggested by the sermon, where, in a passage signalled by an enlarged gold initial, Gregory argued that his father's baptism came as no surprise, for 'all must come into the net of God, and be caught by the words of the fishers', a reference to Luke 5:10, part of the narrative describing the calling of James, John, Peter, and Andrew from their boats.[60] The dominant episode of the first register, the calling of Matthew the tax-collector, does not continue the fishermen metaphor directly, but contemporary exegesis confirms the obvious connection between the conversions: Photios, for example, quoted Matthew 4:19 – 'Come, he said, follow me, and I shall make you fishers of men' – and immediately added 'among tax-collectors' and other worldly but misguided professionals.[61]

Zachias, the rich youth, and Nathanael were none of them apostles; nor did the rich young man convert at all. On one level, the trio sets those who accepted Christ against those who did not. But the gospels list many men and women who could fill either of these slots: it was apparently the particular relevance of these three to Gregory's narrative of his father's life that suggested their inclusion on f. 87v.

Gregory *père* was not born orthodox; he converted later in life. His son put it more elegantly: in a phrase marked by an enlarged initial he wrote that his father 'was not planted in the house of God'.[62] Gregory was therefore at some pains to suggest his father's incipient goodness and stressed that his worthiness virtually predestined his conversion: 'Even before he was of our fold, he was ours . . . What greater and more splendid testimony can there be to his justice than his exercise of a position second to none in the state, without enriching himself by a single farthing? [. . .] For this do I term unrighteous wealth.'[63] The elder Gregory's predilection for conversion, and his intrinsic worth, may have suggested the parallel with Nathanael, placed directly above Gregory's baptism, whose similar qualities were immediately recognized by Christ (John 1:47). We might see Nathanael as a fitting parallel to Gregory's father: the scene of his conversion was rarely pictured in Byzantium, and such a thematic link would help explain its inclusion here.[64]

Gregory's allusion to his father's righteous use of money forms part of a discourse on wealth and its philanthropic disposal that runs throughout the homily.[65] In a passage marked by an enlarged gold initial, Gregory describes his father's attitude:

---

[60] *PG* 35:992A15–B3; Paris.gr.510, f. 88v. Returning to this metaphor, Gregory describes his father's death as the entry into a 'calm haven to men at sea': *PG* 35:988D2–989A1. He also cites James and John later in the sermon (ibid., 1013B5), in a passage that inspired portraits of both in the Milan Homilies, which otherwise shares no parallels with f. 87v: Grabar (1943a), pls. XVI–XXI. The liturgical edition omits Homily 18.

[61] Epistle 165 (= *Amphilochia* question 92): Laourdas and Westerink II (1984), 27, ll.55–7; *PG* 101:577C12–16. On the *Amphilochia* see chapter 5.   [62] *PG* 35:989D3.   [63] Ibid., 922B6–7, C5–11.

[64] The inscription simply says 'Christ speaks with Nathanael' (Ο Χ[ΡΙΣΤΟ]C ΔΙΑΛΕ-ΓΟΜΕΝΟC ΤΩ ΝΑΘΑΝΑΗΛ). None of the few other versions of the scene relates closely to this one: see chapter 8.   [65] See further Coulie (1985).

'Who was ... more bounteous in hand toward the poor? [...] For he actually treated his property as if it were another's, of which he was but the steward, relieving poverty as far as he could ... more pleased to dispose of his wealth than others we know are to receive it.'[66] Gregory's mother shared his attitude: 'She not only considered all the property which they originally possessed ... as unable to suffice her own longing but she would, as I have often heard her say, have gladly sold herself and her children into slavery, had there been any means of doing so, to expend the proceeds upon the poor.'[67] Gregory articulated a Christian response to wealth, and this theme recurs in three episodes pictured on f. 87v. On meeting Christ, Matthew the tax-collector simply 'left all, rose up, and followed him' (Luke 5:28), a dramatic inversion visualized by contrasting Matthew as tax-collector, his hands protecting a large pile of gold coins, with Matthew the evangelist, holding a book and walking away from the money table with Christ.[68] In this graphic portrayal of the rejection of wealth, Matthew seems to embody the attitudes of Gregory's parents. The rich youth, on the other hand, could not bear to part with his wealth, leading Christ to conclude that 'It is easier for a camel to go through the eye of a needle than for a rich man to enter the kingdom of heaven' (Matthew 19:21–24).[69] Beyond the simple contrast between the convertible and the unconvertible, the rich young man provides a specific antithesis to Matthew and to the elder Gregory. That this antithesis was intentional is corroborated by visual cues, for the rich youth, directly above Gregory *père* as he, unlike the youth, enters the church, replicates his half-stumbling position in reverse. Above the rich youth, the rich tax collector Zachias (who gave half of his goods to the poor; Luke 19:8), completes the centralized axial sequence by providing a biblical parallel to Gregory's father.

The upper two registers propound both philanthropy and conversion in their visual panegyric to Gregory *père*, themes that were both appropriate to the sermon and immediately comprehensible to the miniature's audience: the emphasis on conversion dovetailed with imperial and patriarchal preoccupations in the second half of the ninth century,[70] while philanthropy was a standard component of imperial panegyric. As Leo VI wrote in his funeral oration for Basil I, 'Who but he could have had so much concern for the poor? So much so that, for a little while, they did not even feel their fate, since the difficulties which arose from it had been swept aside by his generosity'.[71] The visual interpretation of the elder Gregory's life drew

---

[66] *PG* 35:1008C1–5, 10–11.   [67] Ibid., 1009B13–14; the passage is marked with a gold initial.

[68] The inscriptions identify Matthew the tax-collector (ΜΑΤΘΑΙΟϹ Ο ΤΕΛΩΝΗϹ) and Christ (ΙϹ ΧϹ), then tell us that 'the tax-collector follows Christ' (Ο ΤΕΛΩΝΗϹ ΑΚΟΛΟΥΘ[ΕΙ] ΤΩ Χ[ΡΙϹΤ]Ω).

[69] The inscription reads simply 'the rich youth questions Christ' (Ο ΠΛΟΥϹΙϹ ΕΠΕΡΩΤΩΝ ΤΟΝ Χ[ΡΙϹΤΟ]Ν).   [70] See chapter 6.

[71] Ed. Vogt and Hausherr (1932), 60. On imperial philanthropy and its shifting context, see Morris (1976), 3–27, esp. 20–21, whence the trans. of Leo's remarks.

from the sermon two themes familiar to the ninth-century Byzantine élite, and elaborated them to provide a miniature that eulogized Gregory's father as it reinforced contemporary ideology.

Folio 149r (20) (fig. 20)

A pearl and jewel frame encases the miniature on f. 149r, which shows Basil and Gregory healing the sick above a sequence illustrating the parable of Lazarus and the rich man (Luke 16:19–31).[72] 'On the love of the poor' (Homily 14) starts on the miniature's verso,[73] and inspired the depiction of Lazarus and the rich man, Gregory's reference to whom is introduced by a gold initial.[74] Though no other copies of the Homilies illustrate the parable,[75] it was presumably selected for illustration in Paris.gr.510 because it demonstrated both the value of Christian philanthropy and the consequences of uncharitable behaviour. The miniature broadly follows Luke's account, though the rich man – identified by inscription (Ο ΠΛΟΥ-CΙΟC), in the top centre of the register – rides toward Lazarus, as against the text which describes Lazarus sitting outside the rich man's gate.[76] Lazarus (Ο ΛΑΖΑΡΟC), however, conforms with Luke's description: he reclines on the grass, while a dog licks his sores. To the right, a figure wrapped in grave-clothes and laid out on a hillside represents Lazarus' death; below, angels deposit him 'into Abraham's bosom'.[77] Meanwhile, in the upper left, the rich man lies on a bier backed by an arcaded building in front of which stand two mourners: the painter carefully contrasts Lazarus' lonely demise on an empty hill in the upper left with the rich man's more comfortable death directly opposite, and pairs the living and dead men, with Lazarus (alive and dead) on the preferred right, the rich man (dead and alive) on the left. Continuing the bifurcation of the register, immediately below his bier the rich man sits in hell,[78] lifts his eyes 'and seeth Abraham afar off, and Lazarus in his bosom'. He points to his parched mouth, requesting water. A fragmentary relief from Antioch suggests that this scene appeared in the Christian east by the sixth century, but Paris.gr.510 contains the earliest fully preserved example.[79] A pale reflection of the core image – the rich man gesturing for water as he watches Lazarus

---

[72] Omont (1929), 21–22, pl. XXXIV; Der Nersessian (1962), 207, 227.

[73] PG35:857–909; Gallay (1943), 86–87.   [74] PG35:904B14–C3, on f. 162v.

[75] The Milan Gregory does not illustrate this sermon; the liturgical editions normally preface it with an image of Gregory preaching and gesturing to a group composed of the poor and sick: Galavaris (1969), 63–67.

[76] Similarly, on f. 143v (fig. 19) the man leaving the city in the parable of the Good Samaritan rides an otherwise unattested horse: the miniaturists evidently favoured this means of transport, perhaps because Basil I was a skilled horseman (see chapter 4).

[77] The scene is duly inscribed 'Lazarus on the bosom of Abraham' (Ο ΛΑΖΑΡΟC ΕΙC ΤΟΝ ΚΟΛΠΟΝ ΤΟΥ ΑΒΡΑΑΜ).

[78] As we are told by the inscription: Ο ΠΛΟΥCΙΟC ΕΝ ΤΗ ΚΑΜΙΝΩ.

[79] See J.M. Plotzek, s.v. 'Lazarus, Armer', in LCI3 (1971), 31–33.

in the bosom of Abraham – recurs in later Byzantine images,[80] but no comparable sequences survive. The careful and balanced arrangement of figures, so characteristic of Paris.gr.510, suggests that the narrative was compiled for f. 149r.

In the upper register, 'St Gregory and St Basil heal the sick' (Ο Α[ΓΙΟC] ΓΡΗΓΟΡΙΟC Κ[ΑΙ] Ο Α[ΓΙΟC] ΒΑCΙΛΕΙΟC ΘΕΡΑΠΕΥΟΝΤΕC ΤΟΥC ΑCΘΕΝΕΙC): four scenes of healing and nourishment appear between the columns of a basilica. Though Gregory mentions neither Basil nor any hospital in 'On the Love of the Poor', the mid-tenth-century Basil Elachistos tells us that Gregory delivered the sermon at the hospital built by Basil just outside Caesarea to house the ill, orphans, lepers, and the aged.[81] The scholia in Paris.gr.510 do not refer to the circumstances under which Gregory preached, and the miniature shows Gregory and Basil healing rather than the former preaching, but the miniature nonetheless anticipates Basil Elachistos' association of the homily with St Basil's hospital, which is described twice in Paris.gr.510, once in the *vita* of Gregory of Nazianzus at the end of the manuscript,[82] and once in a passage from Gregory's funeral oration for Basil. Here Gregory wrote that Basil

opened the stores of those who possessed them, and so, according to the scripture dealt food to the hungry, and satisfied the poor with bread, and fed them in the time of dearth, and filled the hungry souls with good things [. . .] Obtaining contributions of all sorts of food which can relieve famine, [Basil] set before them basins of soup and such meat as was found preserved among us, on which the poor live. Then, imitating the ministry of Christ, who, girded with a towel, did not disdain to wash the disciples' feet . . . he attended to the bodies and souls of those who needed it.[83]

On f. 149r, we see Basil washing the feet of one man, giving soup to the next, and serving meat to a group. Only the last vignette, which shows Basil feeding a man covered with sores (presumably a leper), refers directly to Basil's hospital; the rest come directly from Gregory's panegyric. Folio 149r provides the only preserved illustration to this passage, and the only image of Basil's hospital. The entire top register appears to have been created *ad hoc* in order both to supplement the theme of the oration, compassion, and to illustrate what were believed to be the historical circumstances that prompted Gregory's sermon, relying on Gregory's eye-witness account of Basil's charity.[84]

Folio 239r (27) (fig. 27)

The upper register of f. 239r shows Gregory 'conversing' with the Emperor Theodosios (Ο ΘΕΟΛΟΓΟC CΥΝ[ΔΙΑΛΕΓ]ΟΜΕΝΟC ΒΑCΙΛΕΙ ΘΕΟΔΟCΙΩ);

---

[80] E.g. Laur.plut.6.23, f. 144r: Velmans (1971), fig. 243.
[81] See Gallay (1943), 87; on Basil Elachistos, *ODB*1 (1991), 263.   [82] *PG*35:274B-C.
[83] Ibid., 544C–545A (*NPNF*, 407).
[84] Jolivet-Levy (1987), 454–455, suggested that the image may have been intended to reflect Basil I's philanthropy.

the lower shows his departure from Constantinople after he rejected the patriarchal seat in 381.[85] The miniature supplements Gregory's 'Farewell oration' (Homily 42) to the 150 bishops present at the Ecumenical Council of 381,[86] which begins on its verso. In the final two paragraphs, Gregory bids farewell to a long list of people, including, in a sentence marked with an enlarged initial, the emperor. The scene in the upper register pictures the actual farewell, after the sermon, when Gregory went to the palace to ask Theodosios' permission to leave the city; he takes his final leave of the bishops, just before sailing for Nazianzus, below.[87] Though inspired by the 'Farewell oration', both episodes occurred after Gregory delivered the sermon, and he described the audience with Theodosios in an autobiographical poem rather than in this sermon.[88] The information was, however, readily available, for the meeting is also recorded in the *vita* by Gregory the Presbyter that appears at the end of Paris.gr.510.[89] Both episodes were sufficiently familiar to be incorporated in later illustrated Homilies manuscripts, though not in the form that they take on f. 239r.[90]

Although most of the biographical miniatures in Paris.gr.510 appear in the first quarter of the manuscript, the intensely personal tone of the 'Farewell oration' evidently inspired a return to that genre midway through the book; the upper scene, too, harmonized with later ninth-century interest in the relationship between emperor and patriarch as expressed by Photios.[91]

The upper scene is set against an architectural backdrop painted in blue-on-blue that extends across the register and represents the imperial palace. Gregory, followed by two bishops, faces a frontal Theodosios distinguished by a pearled halo that perpetuates a motif more common in early Byzantine art and may suggest an attempt to provide historical flavour.[92] The emperor occupies the centre of the composition; on the right, an elaborate gold throne is flanked by two

---

[85] Omont (1929), 24, pl. XLI; Weitzmann (1942/43), 122–124; Lehmann (1945), 18–19; Der Nersessian (1962), 215, 223, 225–227; Galavaris (1969), 61–63, 117–118; N. Ševčenko (1973), 39–40, 56–57; Walter (1978), 241–242; Jolivet-Levy (1987), 464 and note 93.

[86] *PG* 36:457–492; Gallay (1943), 210–211.

[87] The destination is explained by the legend: Ο ΘΕΟΛΟΓΟC ΑΠΕΡΧΩΜΕΝΟC ΕΙC ΝΑΖΙΑΝΖΩ[Ν ΠΟΛΙΝ].   [88] Der Nersessian (1962), 215; for the poem, *PG* 37:1160–1164.

[89] *PG* 35:300C–301A; see further Gallay (1943), 210–211. Weitzmann (1942/43), 122–124, argued that the scene adapts a composition invented for an illustrated chronicle; Der Nersessian (1962), 215 corrected this hypothesis, and her views have been accepted by N. Ševčenko (1973), 40.

[90] Jerusalem, Taphou 14, f. 265r shows Gregory in a boat saying his farewells to a group of bishops; Paris.gr.543, f. 288v pictures Gregory and Theodosios: Galavaris (1969), 34–35, 61–63, 117–118, figs. 120, 467. The Milan Gregory illustrates the sermon (Grabar [1943a], pls. LIV,2–LVIII) but includes neither scene.

[91] On Photios' apparently unique formulation of this relationship, esp. in the *Eisagoge*, see Simon (1994), 16–18, and chapter 4. However, although Theodosios is one of the emperors with whom Basil I was later compared, the equation left no visual echo in this miniature.

[92] See Mango and Hawkins (1972), 27–28 and note 54. On the frontal imperial portrait: Maguire (1989).

bodyguards. Apart from the pearled halo, Theodosios is portrayed as elsewhere in the manuscript (f. 355r; fig. 36), and the jewelled throne presents a variation on a type seen in other miniatures as well.[93] The throne sits beneath a jewelled ciborium, supported by gem-encrusted columns with capitals in the shape of eagles, the imperial and cosmological significance of which was long ago noted by Karl Lehmann.[94]

An expanse of blue sea marked with darker blue waves occupies most of the lower register; it enters the harbour of Constantinople from the upper left, and is channelled between green shores along the top and left side of the frame. As in the image of Gregory's departure from his family (f. 452r; fig. 46), where the sea also takes up well over half of the composition, the Constantinopolitan dock appears on the right side of the page: travel to the capital by sea is always presented as a left-to-right journey. Here, the shoreline curves round to meet Gregory, who gestures farewell to a compact group of bishops and laity squeezed between him and the right frame. Behind him, three sailors man the boat on which he will depart: one steps ashore to help Gregory embark, one steadies the rudder, and the third is beginning to unfurl the sail.

Folio 285r (29) (fig. 29)

The miniature of Habakkuk's vision includes a portrait of Gregory, whose description of the vision in the adjacent second oration 'On Easter' inspired the image.[95] Gregory is an active participant in the scene: as will be discussed in chapter 7, through his gaze and gesture he invites the viewer to participate in the vision. Portraits of Helena and Paraskeve are also incorporated; these, as we shall see in chapter 5, introduce the interests of the palace and patriarchate into a miniature that otherwise fuses the subject of the sermon and its delivery in a manner somewhat reminiscent of ff. 52v and 78r (figs. 10, 15).

Folio 424v (41) (fig. 41)

The lowest register of f. 424v is devoted to an image of Gregory writing that, as noted in chapter 2, forms an integral part of the composition and meaning of the page as a whole.

Folio 452r (46) (fig. 46)

The final miniature in Paris.gr.510 presents scenes from Gregory's life in three registers; it prefaces the *vita* by Gregory the Presbyter, which begins on its verso and ter-

---

[93] With David on f. 143v and with the 381 Council on f. 355r (figs. 19, 36). This is not the so-called lyre-backed throne sometimes associated with the emperor, though that form is found occupied by Christ on f. 67v and by Julian the Apostate on f. 374v (figs. 11, 39); see also the discussion of f. Av in chapter 4.   [94] Lehmann (1945), 18–19.   [95] *PG* 36:624–664 (*NPNF*, 422–434).

minates in the middle of a sentence at the end of quire 58, the last preserved in the manuscript.[96]

In the top register Gregory, in episcopal regalia, turns toward his family as he steps aboard a ship indistinguishable from those on ff. 3r and 239r (figs. 6, 27); a sailor helps him embark, while another reaches out to unfurl the sail. The family, all nimbed, stand on a green shoreline that undulates vertically toward the top frame. Kaisarios has changed into a pink mantle over a blue robe; the rest are dressed identically to their portrayals on f. 43v (fig. 9). Two-thirds of the way across the register, the rippling water shifts to rolling waves to signal a change of scene. Here, in the right-hand corner, Gregory sits in a boat with a sailor, who seems to scan the distance; the boat has apparently just reached land, and a figure so rubbed that even its gender is indeterminable grasps the prow.

This sequence does not illustrate any passage in the accompanying *vita*; indeed, as anyone sufficiently interested in Gregory to plan a deluxe volume such as Paris.gr.510 would have known from reading his work, it is both historically and geographically inaccurate. Nazianzus was an inland Cappadocian town, and the only journeys that Gregory made by sea occurred either before his ordination in 361/2 or after the deaths of Kaisarios (in 369), Gorgonia (in the early 370s) and his father (in 374).[97] The register is nonetheless almost certainly meant to evoke Gregory's journey in 379 to Constantinople, the most important and distant of his bishoprics, and the only one requiring a sea voyage. But it is presented as a metaphorical journey, too: braving the dangers of travel – and sea travel was considered especially hazardous by the Byzantines – Gregory leaves the stability of his family, and thereby demonstrates his moral strength and his intellectual (and physical) courage.[98]

The middle register pictures Gregory's consecration, perhaps (since f. 67v [fig. 11], shows his consecration as bishop of Sasima in 372) his second, as bishop of

---

[96] *PG* 35:243–304 (*BHG* 723). Omont (1929), 31, pl. LX; Buchthal (1963), 85–86; Der Nersessian (1962), 210, 215, 219 note 103, 227; Walter (1972), 126; Walter (1976a), 124–125; Walter (1978), 240–241; N. Ševčenko (1983), 82. Der Nersessian ([1962], 219 note 103) observed in passing that f. 452r is preceded by three pages originally left blank but later written upon (ff. 450v–451v); in fact, however, f. 450v contains the end of the previous text, while f. 451, a smaller page, is a later insertion the stub of which is visible between ff. 457 and 458. It contains the so-called thirty-fifth homily, probably a spurious text, written in a Palaiologan hand: see Gallay (1943), 193–194.

[97] Gregory went to Alexandria and Athens as a student, and to Constantinople as a bishop in 379. He also visited his brother in Constantinople, but such a visit cannot be intended here since his brother bids him farewell. On the (disputed) location of Nazianzus, see Gallay (1943), 12–14 and, for a map, 249. Sasima, Gregory's first see, was close to Nazianzus.

[98] On fears of sea travel, see Kazhdan and Constable (1982), 42–43, and Galatariotou (1993), esp. 226. On the importance of families, and the difficulty of breaking from them, see Gregory's sermon on the Makkabees, in which family ties share the power of physical torture to sway uncertain souls (*PG* 35:917A); and Morris (1995), 79–80.

Constantinople in 381.[99] The two consecrations differ not only in the number of attending bishops, but also in the stances of the figures and in the architectural settings. On f. 67v, the rite takes place before a ciborium placed next to the church; on f. 452r, Gregory and the bishops stand within a bema (indicated by blue templon screens flanking a low gold door) that extends outward from the apsed church behind it, while a blue column, topped by a cross and swagged with red drapery, occupies the space remaining on the right. Two groups of men – one monastic and one clerical – witness the consecration on f. 67v; one group – the members of which are tonsured and therefore presumably monastic, though they do not wear the brown robes normal in Paris.gr.510 – appears on f. 452r. We have already seen that on f. 67v the officiating bishops effect Gregory's consecration both by hands and by book, while on f. 452r the consecration by book alone appears.[100] While it is possible that ff. 67v and 452r reflect different visual sources rather than (or as well as) picturing different consecrations or responding to a desire for variety, we must discard speculation that the column on the right of the 452r composition was inserted to expand the image to fill a wider space than it occupied in some hypothetical earlier model:[101] within the context of Paris.gr.510 the desire to align Gregory's portrayals vertically provides a more compelling justification for its placement.

The lowest register, 'The burial of St Gregory the theologian' (Ο Α[ΓΙΟΣ] Γ[ΡΗΓΟΡ]ΙΟΣ Ο ΘΕΟΛΟΓΟΣ ΕΝΤΑ[ΦΙ]ΑΖΟΜΕΝΟC), shows two men lowering Gregory into a sarcophagus – one holds his feet, the other grasps Gregory's halo as if it were an extension of his head – while a third swings a censer across it. Christopher Walter distinguished Byzantine representations of the deposition, which we see here, from images of the final illness (as of Gorgonia on f. 43v; fig. 9), and the funeral proper, as for Kaisarios on f. 43v and Basil on f. 104r (fig. 17). The remaining scenes of natural death in Paris.gr.510, Matthew's and Jude's on f. 32v (fig. 8), show the moment after the body has been placed in its sarcophagus, leaving Gregory's the only actual deposition in Paris.gr.510. His body is aligned with his two portrayals in the top register and the church of the middle tier, leaving room for a small aedicula in the left corner. This structure, which balances the column of the middle register, may represent a cemetery shrine or Gregory's mausoleum. A group of mourners would, however, have provided both a more usual accompaniment and vertical unity with the family cluster of the top tier and the crowd of clerics directly above; there may therefore be less significance attached to the aedicula than to the restricted number of three mourners standing around Gregory's bier, who are carefully (and unusually) differentiated as a beardless youth, a middle-aged man and an elderly priest with a

---

[99] See note 29 above.   [100] See Walter (1978), 240–241.   [101] Weitzmann (1948), 80–81.

long greying beard.[102] I do not know of any parallels from a comparably early period, but it does seem that the three ages of, in this case, man are here grouped with death.

The accumulation of details on f. 452r, especially in the top and bottom registers, provides a universalizing interpretation of Gregory's life. The way the page is composed follows a pattern well established in Paris.gr.510, but is equally hagiographic. The portraits of Gregory are all centralized, with the consecrated Gregory placed in the middle of the second register, the dead Gregory stretched out beneath this ceremony in the bottom tier, and the two images of the travelling Gregory placed above the dead man's feet and head. Other figures (or objects) consume the left and right edges of the folio. In the top register, these areas are filled with figures bidding Gregory farewell and welcoming him; in the middle register, with attending clergy and the column surmounted by a cross; in the lowest register, with the aedicula and a participant in Gregory's funeral. The predilection of the Gregory miniaturists for axial juxtapositions seems once again to have conditioned the compositions of the individual registers; it also trains the gaze on what the designer of the page considered to be the transitional moments of Gregory's life.

BASIL AND CYPRIAN

Folio 104r (17) (fig. 17)

The miniature prefaces Gregory's forty-third sermon, the 'Funeral Oration to Basil the Great', which was probably delivered in 381 on the second anniversary of the saint's death.[103] It is among the longest of Gregory's sermons – second only to the first homily against Julian – and was one of the most influential: around 888, for example, Leo VI modelled his eulogy of the Emperor Basil I on it.[104]

Gregory presents a detailed and affectionate account of Basil's life. Perhaps in memory of their student days together in Athens, Gregory sprinkled the oration liberally with allusions to classical mythology. These, together with the mythological references in three other homilies, inspired a sixth-century author now known as Pseudo-Nonnos to write an explanatory commentary that Byzantine manuscripts sometimes illustrate.[105] In Paris.gr.510, marginal numbers that correspond with sections of this commentary appear on ff. 105v, 107r, 108v, 113r–v, 114r–v, and 115v; we may probably assume that the Pseudo-Nonnos commentary originally fol-

---

[102] Three figures (usually clerics) often – though far from always – assist in images of Byzantine burials: see Walter (1976a), figs. 1, 10, 12. This grouping is presumably meant to evoke the trinity. The 'three-age system' found on f. 452r is, however, rare; on its application in other spheres of Christian art, see Sears (1986), 90–94.   [103] *PG* 36:493–605 (*BHG* 245; *NPNF*, 395–422).
[104] Adontz (1933b), 501–513.   [105] See Introduction note 10.

lowed the homilies, a not uncommon arrangement. If there was ever any visual reflection of this commentary, however, it too has been lost: the prefatory miniature to the 'Funeral Oration' concentrates entirely on Basil, and spreads ten episodes from his life over four registers set within a multi-coloured frame.[106]

The first register opens with Basil, flanked by his parents, hiding from Maxentius' persecution in a cave in the Pontos mountains: the three figures, visible from the waist up, look out from a dark cavern framed in pink rock that is set into a green hill.[107] To the right, four deer arrive to provide food for the starving fugitives; the three references to this episode begin with gold initials in the Paris text,[108] as do the two references to the cave.[109] Although the image illustrates a childhood experience, Basil is nonetheless presented as he appears elsewhere on the page, and throughout Paris.gr.510 (ff. 71v, 149r; figs. 13, 20): as a nimbed, middle-aged man with short dark hair and a long pointed beard.

Beyond the deer, a grey-blue cylindrical structure resting on a sculpted podium signals a shift in time and locale; it may, as Henri Omont suggested,[110] be meant to evoke a temple, for it introduces a scene of Gregory and Basil studying together in Athens, shown as a pink-walled city from within which a porticoed facade, a domed building, and two statues protrude. Gregory and Basil, their gold nimbs intact but their faces rubbed almost beyond recognition, sit on a low plinth in the foreground; they flank a philosopher, identifiable by the toga draped to expose half his chest, his long grey hair and beard, and his scroll. Basil seems to be the figure seated facing forward on the left in a brown mantle over a beige tunic; Gregory, with his back toward the viewer, wears green. Both hold scrolls, presumably in reference to the classical learning they absorbed in Athens. Gregory describes this happy period at length; the most important passage commences with a gold initial.[111]

The second register begins with Basil (Ο ΑΓΙΟC ΒΑCΙΛΕΙΟC), now clad as a bishop, seated on a red cushion over a gold bench, writing in a book supported on a gold lectern. Gregory refers to Basil's writing several times in passing, and at length in the forty-third paragraph.[112] Neither the image nor the oration suggests that we are meant to see Basil writing a specific text: the scene is perhaps best understood as

---

[106] Omont (1929), 19–20, pl. XXXI; Weitzmann (1951b), 7; Der Nersessian (1962), 198; Weitzmann (1979a), 230, 235; Walter (1982), 88; Brubaker (1992), 79–81.

[107] The inscription on the gold border immediately above the scene reads 'St Basil with his parents in the mountain' (Ο ΑΓΙΟC ΒΑCΙΛΕΙΟC CYN ΤΟΙC ΓΟΝΕΥCΙΝ ΕΝ ΤΩ ΟΡΕΙ).

[108] *PG* 36:502B2–5, 502D3–504A1, 504A4–6; Paris.gr.510, ff. 106v–107r.

[109] *PG* 36:500C, 502A3–6; Paris.gr.510, ff. 106r-v. The first passage is one of two in the entire manuscript interrupted mid-sentence by an initial – an indication of how important it was to signal this episode. [110] Omont (1929), 19–20.

[111] *PG* 36:513–525B; Paris.gr.510, ff. 109v–113v (paragraph 15 opens with the gold initial).

[112] Ibid., 552D–553B; 553A14–B1 appears as a separate paragraph in Paris.gr.510 (f. 121v), and is introduced with a gold initial.

a commemoration of Basil's prolific authorship. Behind Basil, a pink basilica leads to the central scene, which depicts the effect of Basil's orthodox service on the Arian Emperor Valens, as described in the fifty-second paragraph of the 'Funeral Oration'.[113] Basil, in full ecclesiastical regalia, stands before a gold and jewelled ciborium, accompanied by a censer-swinging deacon: he is officiating in the church that backs him. The emperor, in the purple mantle embellished with gold familiar from other imperial representations, was overcome by giddiness as he approached the altar; he twists as if staggering into a fall – the laconic inscription, ΟΥΑΛΗϹ ΠΕΡΙΤΡΕΠΟΜΕΝΟϹ, loosely translates as 'Valens twists round' – and Gregory says that he would have fallen had not an attendant, here represented as a youth in a blue tunic, supported him.

Valens then banished Basil, but the night before his exile was to begin, the emperor's son Galatias fell ill and Basil was summoned to the palace to pray for his recovery. The sickness subsided on Basil's arrival; but Valens also requested the prayers of the Arians, a perfidy that resulted in the boy's death. This entire episode, which the text highlights with two gold initials (one introducing the narrative; the other marking the passage wherein Gregory explains that Galatias' death was caused by Valens' recourse to Arian prayers),[114] is reduced in the miniature to Galatias, in purple and gold, lying dead on a gold and gem-encrusted bed that has been awkwardly inserted at an angle between the preceding and following scenes; the legend reads 'the death of the son of Valens' (Ο Υ[ΙΟ]Ϲ ΤΟΥ ΟΥΑΛΗ ΤΕΘΝΗΚΩϹ). Finally, Valens, seated on a gold lyre-backed throne decorated with pearls, signs an order of exile,[115] represented as a long scroll that unfurls down toward the ground, and Basil is pushed into the border of the miniature by a youthful courtier. The large pink and gold structure behind Basil may represent the palace.

Basil's protection of the widow introduces the third register.[116] The widow, whom a judge was attempting to force into marriage, fled to the church and put herself under Basil's protection: on f. 104r, enveloped in an ochre robe, she kneels before an altar draped in red on which sits a gold gospelbook. The altar sits before the arched opening of a grey-blue building; Basil stands behind it and gestures toward the widow. Behind her, the judge, in a red and blue garment embroidered with white, reaches his hands toward her: we are meant to understand that the action occurs in the church, and that the judge has violated sanctuary. Gregory expresses horror at the judge's disregard for ecclesiastical propriety, but the inscription accompanying the scene tells us only that 'the woman flees for refuge to St

---

[113] Ibid., 561C9–564A; Paris.gr.510, ff. 124r-v, introduced by a gold initial.

[114] Ibid., 564B12–565B3; Paris.gr.510, ff. 124v–125r.

[115] Though Gregory mentions the exile only once (*PG* 36:588A3–7), the inscription explicitly identifies the scene as Basil's exile (ΒΑϹΙΛΕΙΟϹ ΕΞΟΡΙΖΟΜΕΝΟϹ).

[116] Ibid., 568A-C5; the description opens with a gold initial (f. 125v).

Basil' (Η ΠΡΟΣΦΥΓΟΥΣΑ ΓΥΝΗ ΑΓΙΩ ΒΑΣΙΛΕΙΩ). The remainder of the register is filled with Basil's confrontation with the judge, who sits in the centre of the register behind a table, draped in a white cloth shaded with grey, in a white exedra presumably representing a court. The judge wears a pale blue garment with a purple inset; his long grey hair and beard are just discernible.[117] Basil stands to the right 'like my Jesus, before the judgment seat of Pilate' – a phrase introduced by a gold initial in the text.[118] An attendant, apparently the same figure who laid hold of the widow in the first scene, now tears off Basil's pallium, leaving the saint stripped to his long blue-grey undertunic. Basil offered to submit to torture and death but, as pictured in the final scene of the register, the citizens of Caesarea rushed to his aid brandishing clubs.[119] The episode is inscribed 'the people against the eparch' (Ο ΛΑΟΣ ΚΑΤΑ ΤΟΥ ΥΠΑΡΧΟΥ).

'The burial of St Basil (Ο ΑΓΙΟΣ ΒΑΣΙΛΕΙΟΣ ΕΝΤΑΦΙΑΖΟΜΕΝΟΣ) fills the bottom register. Badly flaked, and lacking its lower quarter, only the broad out-lines of the composition can be discerned. A crowd stands before the city walls at the left as Basil's body – in the vestments of a bishop and with a jewelled book on its breast – is carried on a gold litter by four youths toward a basilica on the right; two figures holding large gold candlesticks precede the cortège.[120] Though much has been lost, the remnants follow a common Byzantine pattern classified by Walter as the 'transportation of the remains'.[121]

The miniature on f. 104r connects as closely with Gregory's text as any in the manuscript, and more directly than most. Its reliance on the homily, emphatically underlined by the ubiquitous gold initials that signal nearly all passages illustrated, contrasts sharply with other Basil sequences. Cycles of Basil's life surface with some frequency in ninth- and tenth-century monumental decoration, but the pro-grammes at the so-called Temple of Fortuna Virilis in Rome, at New Tokalı, and at Balkam Deressi in Cappadocia rely on the apocryphal Life of Basil attributed to Pseudo-Amphilochios and offer no parallels to f. 104r.[122] The *Sacra Parallela* includes the episode of Basil protecting the widow, but here too, as Kurt Weitzmann observed, the image is unrelated to that in Paris.gr.510.[123] Even other manuscripts of the Homilies differ. The Milan Gregory includes two images related

---

[117] Omont reconstructed the barely legible inscription as Ο ΥΠΑ[Ρ]Χ[ΟΣ] ΕΠ[ΙΤ]ΡΕΠΩΝ [ΑΠΟΔ]ΥΘΙΝΕ Α[ΓΙ]Ο[Ν Β]Α[ΣΙΛ]ΕΙΟΝ.

[118] *PG* 36:568A-C5, quotation B11–14; ff. 125v–126r.   [119] Ibid., 568C6–569C5.

[120] Gregory stresses the large attendance at the funeral, as pictured; the sentence opens with a gold initial in the text: *PG* 36:601A13–604A14; Paris.gr.510, ff. 135v–136r.   [121] Walter (1976a), 123–124.

[122] On the Roman cycle: Lafontaine (1959), 35–40; Trimarchi (1978), 668–671. On the Cappadocian cycles: Jerphanion (1936), 52–53; Jerphanion (1938b), 153–173 (a slightly less detailed account appeared under the same title in *Byzantion* 6 [1931], 535–558); Epstein (1986), 26, 36–37, 77–78, figs. 108–109; Jolivet-Lévy (1989), esp. 278. A later icon in the Menil Collection shows scenes from Basil's life that also rely heavily on Pseudo-Amphilochios; though otherwise unrelated, the icon retains the only other image of Basil writing as part of an extended sequence known to me: Brubaker (1992).

[123] Weitzmann (1979a), 235.

to Basil's life, neither found on f. 104r,[124] while the liturgical manuscripts of Gregory's Homilies restrict themselves to a portrayal of Basil's funeral that is not in any significant way related to the scene in Paris.gr.510.[125] The Basil cycle on f. 104r is, in short, unique among the pictorial *vitae* in its close adherence to Gregory's account of the saint's life. Later in the manuscript, f. 332v reveals a rather different response to its accompanying sermon.

Folio 332v (33) (fig. 33)

Folio 332v presents a pictorial biography of St Cyprian of Antioch as a preface to Gregory's 'To Cyprian'.[126] Gregory did not know Cyprian – indeed, he intermingles the activities of Cyprian of Antioch and Cyprian of Carthage[127] – but the homily encapsulated such a stirring evocation of martyrdom that it was included in the liturgical editions, apparently for reading on the saint's feast day (2 October). In Gregory's version of Cyprian's life, the saint began as a practitioner of the occult arts. When he fell in love with a beautiful Christian virgin, Cyprian called on demons to aid in her seduction. The (unnamed) virgin invoked the protection of the Virgin Mary, the demon was thwarted,[128] and the failure caused Cyprian to burn his occult accoutrements and convert to Christianity. His enthusiasm incited the displeasure of the Emperor Decius, who had Cyprian's tongue cut out and exiled him. The saint continued to proselytize (in writing), and Decius ultimately ordered his execution by beheading.

This account motivated the miniature on f. 332v, though details from other sources were incorporated as well.[129] The upper register shows the Christian virgin, dressed in ochre and pink, nimbed, and identified by inscription as Justina,[130] before an altar draped in red and protected by a gold baldachin; she raises her hands and gaze to a gold medallion containing a bust of Christ while a winged demon, clad in a loincloth, returns daunted to Cyprian.[131] Cyprian (ΚΥΠΡΙΑΝΟC), clad as a pagan philosopher in a blue toga that leaves half of his chest exposed, sits amidst his occult paraphernalia, which include gold cult statues (the two in the basin may represent homunculi) and a blue globe banded in gold. A *scrinium* containing his rolled scrolls sits in the lower right corner; one of the minute foreground

---

[124] One shows the saint and his mother in a cave with birds overhead (*PG* 36:501C13–15), an episode distinct and conceived differently from the cave scene on f. 104r; the other presents a set of medallion portraits of the same pair: Grabar (1943a), pl. XXIV, 1–2.

[125] Galavaris (1969), 46–52, 127–130. A few details – notably the figures carrying torches – correspond, but they are of too conventional a nature to suggest an affiliation.   [126] SC 284, 40–85.

[127] See Delehaye (1921).   [128] SC 284, 62.

[129] Omont (1929), 26–27, pl. XLVII; Ainalov (1961), 22; Der Nersessian (1962), 198; Galavaris (1969), 103–105; N. Ševčenko (1973), 39–40, 56–57; Walter (1981), 317; Walter (1982), 88–89; Brubaker (1985), 11.

[130] Omont read H AΓIA [IOYCTINH] EYX[Ω]N TON K[YPIO]N, but in fact even now the 'I' of IOYCTINH is visible.

[131] The medallion of Christ also appears on f. 264v (fig. 28); see chapter 5.

buildings that are an intermittent characteristic of Paris.gr.510 appears in the centre as a small grey portico ending in a single column.[132]

The lower register presents Cyprian's life after his conversion to Christianity. To signal the change, he is nimbed and his hair and beard have gone grey. In the right third of the register, separated from the rest of the register by a cliff, appears a scene ignored by Gregory: a priest baptizes Cyprian by immersion in a body of deep blue water; beside them, a red fire consumes Cyprian's magic scrolls.[133] Behind the figures, on top of a high green hill, sits a white basilican church. A second scene that departs from Gregory's narrative occupies the left foreground: in the presence of a man who wears a small white fillet in his hair and is richly dressed in gold and red, the orant and nude saint boils in a blue cauldron surrounded by flames.[134] Again, a large building appears in the background, this time a blue, apparently secular, structure with an arched doorway. The sole post-conversion scene directly inspired by Gregory's panegyric concludes the sequence in the left background: an executioner in military dress beheads the saint, who kneels with bound hands on a hillside before a pale blue building embellished with relief sculpture, set against a variegated blue background that includes a leafless tree.[135]

While 'To Cyprian' determined the subject matter, f. 332v is clearly not based exclusively on this text: Gregory never names Justina, describes the woman as praying to the Virgin Mary rather than to Christ, and fails to discuss either Cyprian's baptism or his torture in the cauldron.

Only the first of these details recurs in other illustrated copies of the Homilies. In the Milan Gregory, a woman dressed as a Byzantine empress, holding a crown of martyrdom, is inscribed Justina;[136] one copy of the liturgical Homilies repeats the identification.[137] The identification of Justina was, however, well known: in the typikon of the Great Church, Cyprian and the virgin Justina (named) share a feast day; earlier, Theodore of Stoudion invoked their aid for the protection of suffering iconophiles.[138] Otherwise, neither the Milan nor the liturgical Homilies demonstrates any affinity with Paris.gr.510. The latter group includes five narrative episodes from Cyprian's life – Cyprian's attempted seduction of a Christian virgin by invoking demons, the saint before Decius, Cyprian writing, his martyrdom, and

---

[132] A close parallel recurs on f. 174v (fig. 23).

[133] The inscriptions read 'the magic scrolls burning' (ΧΑΡΤΑΙ ΜΑΓΙΚΟΙ Κ[ΑΙ]ΟΜΕΝΟΙ) and 'the baptism of St Cyprian' (Ο Α[ΓΙΟC] ΚΥΠΡΙΑΝΟC ΒΑΠΤΙΖΟΜΕΝ[ΟC]).

[134] The inscription reads 'St Cyprian in the cauldron' (Ο Α[ΓΙΟC] ΚΥΠΡΙΑΝΟC [ΕΝ] ΤΩ ΛΕΒΗΤΙ).

[135] The inscription reads 'St Cyprian dying' (Ο Α[ΓΙΟC] ΚΥΠΡΙΑΝΟC ΑΠΟΚΤΕΙΝΟΜΕ-ΝΟC).

[136] Two images of Gregory preaching, and two of Cyprian holding a cross, also accompany 'To Cyprian' in Milan: Grabar (1943a), pls. XXVII,2–3, XXVIII,1–3.   [137] Galavaris (1969), 216.

[138] Mateos I (1963), 58–59; Alexander (1977), 261. On the typikon, see chapter 2 note 101; on Theodore, chapter 1 note 115.

the saint posthumously revealing himself to a woman in a dream – but all follow Gregory's text closely and sometimes exclusively.[139] None requires a second textual source; none duplicates either of the episodes pictured on f. 332v that cannot themselves depend on Gregory's 'To Cyprian'. Nor do the scenes shared by the liturgical editions and Paris.gr.510 – the martyrdom and Cyprian invoking demons to aid in his seduction of Justina – demonstrate any affinity.

In short, the extra-homiletic scenes came to f. 332v from a source not used by other Homilies illustrators. This source was, as Omont recognized, almost certainly the three-volume verse account of Cyprian's life written by a certain Eudokia Augusta, probably the wife of Theodosios II.[140] The poem no longer survives intact, but it is attested in the ninth century by Photios, who was sufficiently interested in it to provide a lengthy summary in his *Bibliotheke*.[141] Photios' detailed description of the text suggests that it was not well known even in the ninth century, for he rarely mentions conventional works nor extensively describes familiar ones. Be that as it may, the relevant details of Eudokia's poem, as we know them from Photios, dovetail perfectly with the extra-homiletic features of f. 332v. According to Photios, the first volume of Eudokia's trilogy concerned the martyr Justina. Cyprian's attempt to sway the virgin by dispatching demons, the vanquishing of the demons by the sign of the cross, and, most important, the burning of Cyprian's books on magic and his baptism also appeared in the first volume and are duly described in the *Bibliotheke*. The second volume, Photios continues, recounted the youthful Cyprian's prowess in magic and the saint's zeal as a converted Christian, and the third told of the martyrdoms of Justina and Cyprian. In this account, Cyprian was first thrown into a bronze cauldron filled with wax and grease and set over a fire; his former friend Athanasios assisted in the torture. Athanasios' impiety was punished: he burned in the flame, while Cyprian miraculously escaped the boiling cauldron unharmed. Having thus failed to deter the saint, Diocletian (not, as in Gregory's sermon, Decius) ordered Cyprian's beheading. Photios' summary of Eudokia's poem thus not only identifies the richly dressed man standing beside Cyprian's cauldron as Athanasios, but also incorporates all episodes pictured on f. 332v – both those omitted from Gregory's panegyric and those described in it. While it is intrinsically unlikely that Eudokia's *vita* of Cyprian was illustrated, we cannot conclusively discount the possibility that an illustrated copy of the verse *vita* influenced the Paris miniaturist. It is, however, far more plausible that the poem itself prompted the image on f. 332v, a suggestion fortified by

[139] Galavaris (1969), 103–109; see also 40–41 for a koimesis of Cyprian; N. Ševčenko (1973), 39–40, 56–57.

[140] For the surviving fragments of this poem: ed. Ludwich (1897), 24–79. On Eudokia's authorship, see also Holum (1982), 118.

[141] Codex 184: ed. Henry II (1960), 196–199; trans. Wilson (1994), 174–176; on the *Bibliotheke* see chapter 5.

the absence of a comparable sequence in any other Byzantine representation of Cyprian's life.

In its incorporation of episodes not mentioned by Gregory, the life of Cyprian is quite unlike the hagiographical sequence devoted to Basil on f. 104r (fig. 17), though a similar pattern appears on one of the pages detailing the history of Julian the Apostate (f. 409v; fig. 40).[142] In that case, the additional scenes come from a text widely attested throughout the Byzantine world; f. 332v, on the other hand, provides the unique visualization of Eudokia's verses about Cyprian. This rarely attested work was of such interest to Photios that it is one of only two poems even to be mentioned in the *Bibliotheke.* Possibly his fascination was inspired by the association of Cyprian and Justina with suffering iconophiles recorded by Theodore of Stoudion; but whatever sparked Photios' enthusiasm, it seems likely that the Cyprian cycle was modified and expanded under his direction to include details motivated by Eudokia's *vita.*

TOWARD IMAGE AS EXEGESIS

The biographical scenes in Paris.gr.510 are by definition primarily illustrative rather than exegetical; in concept, they resemble most miniatures in other Homilies manuscripts. But the biographical scenes are actually less like illustrations in other manuscripts, and more like other images in Paris.gr.510, than one might anticipate. There are certainly occasional connections with other illustrated Homilies – most notably with the triple portrait of Basil, Gregory, and Gregory of Nyssa in the Milan Gregory, though perhaps the death of Gorgonia and the now-excised images of the funeral of Kaisarios and Gregory's sermon on the hailstorm in that manuscript were also once related – but many more scenes find no counterparts in other Gregory manuscripts, even when the same passage receives illustration. In the end, most of the biographical images stand alone; many seem to have been created specifically for the manuscript; and nearly all find structural parallels within, rather than outside, Paris.gr.510.

Over half of the pages that include biographical images appear in the first quarter of the manuscript (ff. 43v, 52v, 67v, 71v, 78r, 87v, 104r). The genre became decreasingly favoured as work on Paris.gr.510 progressed, and biographical scenes become more isolated: while seven of the first twelve text miniatures include biographical scenes (miniatures 9–11, 13, 15–17), the remaining six pages with biographical imagery are spread over the following twenty-nine miniatures (ff. 149r, 239r, 285r, 332v, 424v, 452r; miniatures 20, 27, 29, 33, 41, 46). As the number and density of biographical scenes diminishes, the relationship between the biograph-

---

[142] See chapter 5.

ical imagery, the texts and, when they appear, other scenes on the page also gradually shifts.

Six of the thirteen biographical miniatures restrict themselves to biography and are not combined with biblical or historical scenes. The first three of these are tied closely to Gregory's descriptions. Folio 43v (fig. 9) introduces Gregory's family and, inserted between funeral orations for his siblings, pictures Gorgonia's death and Kaisarios' burial; f. 78r (fig. 15) portrays the hailstorm that occasioned Gregory's sermon and shows him delivering it; f. 104r (fig. 17) illustrates the life of St Basil with episodes described in the accompanying eulogy. All of these appear within the dense cluster of biographical pages at the beginning of the manuscript; the final three full-page biographies are less dependent on the adjacent text. Folio 239r (fig. 27) pictures episodes that occurred after the accompanying sermon was delivered and that are not described in that text; f. 332v (fig. 33) includes scenes that contradict Gregory's *vita* of Cyprian and derive instead from a separate account of the saint's life. Folio 452r (fig. 46) mixes episodes recounted in the life of Gregory with scenes invented to display the theologian's virtues and with details designed to universalize his experience: the page as a whole is less informative about specific incidents in Gregory's life than about how the ninth century visualized the concept of sanctity. The first three miniatures illustrate Gregory's words; the final three supplement them or, in the case of f. 332v, provide an alternative interpretation.

The remaining biographical scenes or sequences form parts of larger compositions. When joined on a page, the biographical and biblical scenes form internally coherent miniatures: the two genres have been made to work symbiotically, but this process too changes over the course of the manuscript. On the first page to mix genres (f. 52v; fig. 10), the image of Gregory delivering his sermon provides a typological conclusion to the biblical scenes that precede it.[143] However, because the decision to illustrate Paris.gr.510 was evidently made after this sermon had been copied by the scribes, the precise chronological relationship between f. 52v and other biographical miniatures that mix genres is uncertain; it is in certain respects more similar to f. 87v than to the intervening ff. 67v and 71v. Folio 67v (fig. 11) combines Gregory's consecration as bishop of Sasima with Isaiah's vision, which supplies a biblical parallel to the feelings of hesitation and acceptance that Gregory tells us he underwent as he pondered the ecclesiastical see offered to him. On f. 71v (fig. 13), Job and his friends provide another biblical paradigm for Gregory's feelings about Gregory of Nyssa and Basil, pictured with him above Job. Both ff. 67v and 71v thus use biblical scenes to underscore the meaning of the biographical ones, and in each case the Old Testament paradigm pictured was provided by Gregory himself. By f. 87v (fig. 16) the relationship between biography and the bible has become more complex. While the scenes of Christ's ministry continue to reinforce

[143] See chapter 5.

the meaning of the biographical scenes of the conversion of Gregory's father, they were selected by the designer of Paris.gr.510 without the prompting of Gregory's sermon, and go beyond simple parallelism to become a commentary on the lives of Gregory's parents and on Christian ideas about wealth. The sermon is Gregory's funeral oration to his father, but direct illustration of the death and burial was avoided here (as it was not on f. 43v) in favour of an exegetical miniature in accord with many later pages of Paris.gr.510. Folio 149r (fig. 20) reworks this type of interaction, but with a difference: Basil's charity toward the poor is visually lauded through the parable of the rich man and Lazarus – but here the biblical parable appears in the sermon, while the biographical scene supplements it, and contextualizes the delivery of the sermon itself. Folio 285r (fig. 29) inserts Gregory into a prophetic vision: the biblical and the biographical are fused to promote a particularly ninth-century interpretation of visions of divinity. By f. 424v, the biographical scene has become complementary to biblical narrative: here again the biblical scenes pictured come from the sermon while the portrait of Gregory writing does not, but, though we may be meant to interpret the image as Gregory writing the relevant oration, this role is not expressed and the scene is generic; its primary function is exegetical rather than contextualizing.

It is an indication of the importance accorded the biographical scenes early in the manuscript that the biblical scenes with which they were joined expounded the significance of the biographical ones, rather than the reverse; this relationship in fact prevails until the last two instances of mixed genre (ff. 285r, 424v). The way in which the biblical complemented the biographical, however, changed from parallels already adduced by Gregory to more independent exegetic sequences as the manuscript grew. The general shift toward commentary miniatures – a development from illustrations that supplement (but remain tied to) the text, to visual exegesis – broadly documents an increasingly rarefied use of imagery in Paris.gr.510; it also suggests that the designer and the painters were learning on the job.

4

Basil I and visual panegyric

The miniatures of Paris.gr.510 respond to the manuscript's imperial recipient, the Emperor Basil I (867–886), with one series of images that reinforces the legitimacy of the new Macedonian dynasty and draws flattering connections between the emperor and Constantine the Great, and with another that equates Basil with Old Testament figures such as Joseph, Samson, David, and Joshua. These are familiar themes, and the use of images to perpetuate them had a long history in Byzantium. The visual vocabulary used to express the imperial messages, however, is sometimes unusual.

BASIL THE 'NEW CONSTANTINE' AND THE FOUNDATIONS OF THE MACEDONIAN HOUSE

Folio Av (1) (fig. 1)

As we have seen, the frontispiece miniatures in Paris.gr.510 opened with an image of Christ, followed by a bifolium that originally resembled a commemorative diptych with exterior crosses enclosing imperial portraits. The introductory miniature on f. Av sets the tone for the sequence.[1] Though partially reworked in ink – possibly in the fourteenth century, when a transliteration of the poem on f. Br was written at the top of the page[2] – some of the original paint remains, and the skeleton of the ninth-century miniature can still be deciphered: Christ, seated on a jewelled throne which may originally have resembled that occupied by Helena on f. 440r (fig. 45), blesses with his right hand and holds in his left an open book on which the opening words of John 14:27 are just visible. If it ever had one, the page has lost its conjugate leaf, and is tipped in with its stub pasted to f. C.[3]

Paris.gr.510 is the oldest extant manuscript to open directly with a miniature of

---

[1] Bordier (1885), 62; Millet (1920), 239–240; Ebersolt (1926), 21; Omont (1929), 12, pl.XV; Der Nersessian (1962), 198; Jules Leroy (1974), 224; Cutler (1975), 21; Breckenridge (1980/1), 248, 252. Part of the following discussion originally appeared in Brubaker (1994), 154–157.   [2] See Introduction.

[3] Der Nersessian (1962), 198, suggested that the leaf presumed missing 'perhaps represented the Virgin enthroned'.

Fig. 80 Nomisma, obverse (Dumbarton Oaks 2b.5) of 868–879: Christ enthroned

Christ.[4] The prominent location of an iconic image of the enthroned Christ may be understood on one level as a visual confirmation of the validity of sacred images and the legitimacy of representing Christ.[5] Certainly, the resurgence of images of Christ during the second half of the ninth century is well attested: the seals of Michael III introduced the bust of Christ, and the type continued under Basil I; both busts and standing figures of Christ also appeared on the patriarchal seals of Ignatios (847–858, 867–877).[6] An image of Christ was placed above the Chalke Gate in 843, and in 864 Photios noted a 'man-like' Christ in the dome of the recently completed Church of the Virgin of the Pharos.[7] Images of the enthroned Christ also proliferated: the impact of a mosaic version set between 856 and 866 above the throne in the Chrysotriklinos (a room reserved for important state ceremonies in the heart of the imperial living quarters of the palace) reverberated in royal commissions for several generations.[8] Basil I replaced the bust of Christ, reintroduced on coins by Theodora and continued by her son Michael III, with an image of Christ enthroned (fig. 80); all presumably indicate a self-conscious return to pre-iconoclast numismatic iconography (specifically to the coins of Justinian II) that may have been associated with Constantine: a legend, persistent throughout the ninth century and apparently started by the patriarch Nikephoros, claimed the survival of Constantinian coins bearing the effigy of Christ.[9] The depiction of the

---

[4] The Khludov Psalter (843–847) includes a medallion bust of Christ above its prefatory miniature of David, but not a full-length portrait (Moscow, Hist.Mus.gr.129, f. 1v: Ščepkina [1977]); sixty years earlier, and in the west, the Latin Godescalc Lectionary of 781–783 (Paris, BN, nouv.acq.lat.1203, f. 3r: Mütherich and Gaehde [1976], pl. 1) locates a portrait of Christ among the prefatory pictures, but not on the opening folio. The portrait of Christ in the Garrett Gospels (Princeton, Univ.Lib., cod.Garrett 6, f. 10v: Vikan [1973], 52–55, and Weitzmann [1935], pl. LXIII, fig. 374), which may be slightly earlier than Paris.gr.510, has been inserted into a later book and its original context is unknown.

[5] See chapter 1.   [6] Zacos and Veglery (1972), nos. 56–57, 59, pl. 18; Zacos (1984), no. 6, pl. 1.

[7] Frolow (1963), 107–120; for Photios, Homily 10,6: ed. Laourdas (1959), 102; trans. Mango (1958), 187.

[8] *Anthologia graeca* I,106; trans. Mango (1972), 184. On the potential impact, see Cormack and Hawkins (1977), 243–244.

[9] Basil's coins: Grierson III,1 (1973), 146, 154–156 and III,2 (1973), 476, 480–481, pl. XXX; Cutler (1975), esp. 7–9. Theodora's and Michael's coins: Grierson III, 1 (1973), 146, 153 (table 16), 454–455, 458, pl. XXVIII, nos. 2.1–4. Legend: Gouillard (1969), 10; Grabar (1957), 210.

Fig. 81 Istanbul, Hagia Sophia: room over the vestibule, mosaic of Christ enthroned

enthroned Christ persisted at the mints and recurs in two mosaics at Hagia Sophia which are closely related to the Homilies Christ. In the earlier mosaic (fig. 81), assigned to the 870s and associated with Photios by Robin Cormack and Ernest Hawkins, Christ forms part of a Deesis in the north tympanum of the room over the vestibule;[10] the later mosaic (fig. 82) shows Christ before a prostrate emperor – apparently Basil I or Leo VI – in the narthex.[11] The three representations of Christ are virtually identical save for the disposition of the book held by Christ, which is closed in the Deesis mosaic, but open and inscribed in the narthex mosaic and on f.

[10] Cormack and Hawkins (1977), esp. 241–244, pls. 30–31. Another contemporary example appears in the miniature of Isaiah's vision in the 'Christian Topography' (fig. 76); here, however, the throne is backless and the book closed. See also the Khludov Psalter (Moscow, Hist.Mus.gr.129, f. 90r: Ščepkina [1977]); a tile (ca. 900?) from Preslav that shows Christ seated on a lyre-backed throne, but with an apparently closed book (Totev [1987], 65–80); and a fragmentary fresco, probably of the late ninth century, at Vize (Ötüken and Osterhout [1989], 138–142, fig. 6, pl. XXXIIIc; I thank Robert Ousterhout for providing me with a colour reproduction).

[11] For a critical summary of the literature, see Cormack (1981), 138–141; see also Cormack (1986b), 621–622, where the mosaic is interpreted as Christ forgiving Leo VI.

Fig. 82 Istanbul, Hagia Sophia: narthex mosaic, Christ enthroned before Basil I or Leo VI

Av. The narthex text is the standard 'Peace unto you; I am the light of the world.' The text inscribed in Paris.gr.510 reads 'My peace I give unto you; not as the world giveth, give I unto you' (John 14:27a).[12]

John 14:27 is an unusual text for Christ to hold, but it conveyed two appropriate messages to ninth-century Constantinopolitans. For while the passage inscribed on Christ's book was not normally associated with images, it appeared on wedding rings, and it was the closing gospel reading for the birthday celebrations of the city on 11 May.[13] On wedding rings, as Gary Vikan has shown, it symbolized marital harmony and procreation through Christ,[14] an appropriate preface to the dynastic portraits that follow. The birthday celebrations of the capital were appropriate, too, to signal; the reference introduces the Constantinian messages conveyed by the frontispiece sequence as a whole.

[12] Much of the first half of this passage is still legible on f. Av (EIPHN[HN] THN EMH[N YMIN]); for the rest, I rely on Omont (1929), 12.

[13] As cited in the typikon of the Great Church (see chapter 2 note 101): Mateos I (1963), 288. The passage also occurs at least once in iconophile rhetoric: Mansi XIII, 276E; trans. Sahas (1986a), 104.

[14] Vikan (1990), esp. 161.

From the time of its inception under Constantine the Great, the capital's birth-day spectacle had combined religious rite and imperial ceremonial.[15] In the ninth century, the city's birthday occasioned one of the only three *encaenia* (consecration ceremonies) celebrated in Constantinople,[16] and the celebrations focused on the foundation of a Christian capital, the celebration of the founder, Constantine, and the perpetuation of imperial stewardship. The ecclesiastical procession described in the typikon of the Great Church moved from the church to the forum and then back to the church, stopping *en route* to pray for imperial continuity and divine protection. At one of these stops, in the forum, a deacon intoned: 'Deliver, Lord, our city . . . conserve always the imperial sceptre, by granting us, through the Theotokos, the repulsion of barbarians and distance from dangers.'[17] While the depiction of Christ rather than the Theotokos apparently responds to the ninth-century belief that Christ guarded Constantinople along with the city's traditional protectress,[18] his promise of peace on f. Av was associated with a ceremony that carried with it allusions to the ancient and continuing values of the imperial capital and its rulers. The interwoven mix of references evoked by John 14.27 must have seemed a particularly apt combination to attach to Basil I, an emperor who had not only usurped the throne – and was thus anxious to seem to blend into the seamless flow of imperial succession implied by the language and ritual of Byzantium – but had also won significant victories to bring temporary peace to the empire.[19] While the selection of John 14:27 does not specifically invoke Constantine's place in the birthday celebrations, Basil's restoration of the church of St Mokios, linked in the ninth century to Constantine and the foundations of Constantinople,[20] suggests that associations with the first Christian emperor also formed part of Basil's agenda; that the capital's 550th anniversary was celebrated in 880 may in fact have allowed Basil to focus particular attention on Constantinople's foundation and on Constantine, and to appropriate both by association. But whether or not this connection was emblazoned on the consciousness of the city's inhabitants, it is fur-thered by the frontispiece sequence in Paris.gr.510, where the portrait of Christ prefaces the imperial portraits of Basil and the Empress Eudokia flanked by those two of her sons who were in line of succession. In effect, we see Christ blessing the city, Basil, and Basil's dynastic successors; Christ assures the viewers of Paris.gr.510 that the capital rests in good hands, and that its noble heritage will be preserved and furthered by the new Macedonian house.

---

[15] See Krautheimer (1983), 61–62, and, for memories of the original foundation in the late eighth century, Cameron and Herrin (1984), 34–37, 172–173.   [16] See Magdalino (1987), 55.

[17] Mateos I (1963), 288.   [18] E.g. in Photios: see White (1981), 85.

[19] See Cameron (1987), esp. 134–135.

[20] *Vita Basilii*, 81: *PG* 109:340B (on this text see note 47 below); Mokios was commemorated on Constantinople's birthday, 11 May (Mateos I [1962], 290–291). The association with Constantine appears in the *Parastaseis*: ed. Cameron and Herrin (1984), 56–57. See Magdalino (1987), 56 and note 29.

The text inscribed on Christ's book projects a series of interlocked meanings; it connects beliefs about marital harmony and procreation – which, in an imperial context, may be equated with dynastic aspirations – with ideas about the Christian capital and its founder Constantine.[21] This chain of internal references deepens the meaning of the image itself, and of the frontispiece sequence that follows it. Folio Av seems to duplicate both the form of the Chrysotriklinos mosaic and its association of the temporal with the heavenly ruler.[22] Though in the ceremonial space of the throne room the visual demonstration that the emperor rules through and with Christ relies on the vertical alignment of the emperor's throne beneath Christ enthroned, while on the flat of the manuscript the association is sequential and linear, the miniature of Christ enthroned, like the mosaic to which it apparently refers (and probably drawing upon that association), introduces the ruling emperor and guides the viewer's response to him. Even without the text inscribed on Christ's book, continuity, tradition, and the relationship between emperor and Christ reinforced by imperial ceremony stands behind the image on f. Av. The text brings the sequence down to earth, for it grounds Byzantine imperial ideology in a specific ritual. Though a late entrant to the governing class, Basil has been affiliated with Constantinople by the birthday card held by Christ. All Byzantine emperors ruled through and with Christ: the swarm of meanings clustering around John 14:27 singled Basil and his family out as legitimate successors to Constantine. The frontispiece sequence inserted an upstart into the continuous river of tradition that Byzantine rituals and ceremonies insisted upon,[23] but it also indicated that he was special. Folio Av mingled religious and imperial themes to benefit one particular emperor and the fledgling Macedonian dynasty he did not know would succeed.

Folios Bv and Cr (3, 4) (figs. 3, 4)

Folios Bv and Cr, which once encased the imperial portraits that now envelop them on ff. Br and Cv, are virtually identical.[24] Both show a jewelled cross with flaring ends terminating in teardrop serifs;[25] gold cords and gems hang from the cross bar, just as they did on contemporary and earlier Byzantine processional crosses;[26] half-

---

[21] The Christian-ness of Constantine's refoundation of the city was emphasized from the seventh century, as noted by Cameron (1990), 217–218, and Cameron (1992a).

[22] See Cormack and Hawkins (1977), 243.   [23] See Cameron (1987), esp. 125–136 and, for Basil, 135.

[24] Millet (1910), esp. 104–105; Ebersolt (1926), 22; Omont (1929), 12–13, pls. XVII–XVIII; Morey (1929), 42; Grabar (1936), 32–39; Talbot Rice (1950), 72; Frolow (1956), 111; Der Nersessian (1962), 198, 220; Grabar (1969), 112–113 note 25; Kitzinger (1974), 17; Velmans (1974), 141–145; Spatharakis (1974), 102–105; Spatharakis (1976), 96–99; Kalavrezou-Maxeiner (1978), 20–24; Spatharakis (1989), 89–93; Teteriatnikov (1992), 103–104. Part of the following discussion originally appeared in Brubaker (1994), 139–145.

[25] Gemmed crosses appear regularly from at least the sixth century: see, e.g., London, BL Add.14591, f. 151v: Jules Leroy (1964), 114, 116, pl. 3,1. See note 38 below, and, for a summary of cross decoration in general between the fourth and ninth centuries, Cormack (1968), 49–54.

[26] See, e.g., Weitzmann and Ševčenko (1963), 385; Jules Leroy (1964), 114, pl. 3,2.

palmettes spring from the stepped base. The inscription IC XC NHKA flanks each cross and stands out against a deep blue ground.[27]

Folio Bv has flaked badly, uncovering part of a detailed underdrawing;[28] here, however, it is the cross that concerns us. When Paris.gr.510 was made, images of the cross carried three complementary messages, all of them represented on ff. Bv and Cr. First, the crosses represent the 'life-giving cross' of Christ's crucifixion, a standard formula visualized by the fronds and flowers that sprout from their bases, which embody the belief that the wood of the cross was given life to sprout new growth by the touch of Christ's blood at his crucifixion,[29] and equate the cross with the tree of life.[30] The palmette foliage of the crosses in Paris.gr.510 finds many parallels, particularly from the ninth century onward.[31] Second, the cross signalled God-given imperial triumph, as expressed by the inscription IC XC NHKA ('victory through Christ'), which refers to the voice saying 'in this sign conquer' that accompanied Constantine's vision of the cross before and during his victory at the battle of the Milvian bridge. The association of the cross with imperial victory, a commonplace of Byzantine rhetoric, was particularly clearly expressed in the ninth century by Photios, who specifically described the cross as a tropaion against all evil.[32] Finally, the gold and jewelled form of the crosses, and the steps on which they sit, refer to the cross that Constantine was believed to have set up after the victory.

Though I doubt that many Byzantines would have confused a relic of the cross with a representation of it in any form, the complementary meanings of written and pictorial *images* of the cross shifted easily between evocations of the 'true cross' of the crucifixion, the cross of the imperial vision, and Constantine's ex voto cross in the eighth and ninth centuries. The iconoclast poems and epigrams collected by Theodore of Stoudion, whatever their historical value, do at least record conventional attitudes toward the cross. One reads, in part, 'O Logos . . . [the cross] exalted your own glory, showing the potent force of faith. The rulers venerate it in a worthy manner; they make the subjected enemies fear by means of [its] power'; another, written in the shape of a cross, says simply 'I triumph over enemies and slay

---

[27] The variant spelling NHKA is not uncommon (see Frolow [1956], 107); NIKA, however, appears on the cross on f. 440r (fig. 45).   [28] See the discussion of f. Cv below, and the Introduction.

[29] Frolow (1961a), 329.

[30] This point is made by, among others, Photios in question 294 of the *Amphilochia* (ed. Westerink VI,1 [1987], 84; *PG* 101:1128A4–C3; on the *Amphilochia*, chapter 5). See Genesis 2:9; Frolow (1965), 178–186; Frazer (1973), 148; Kitzinger (1974), 7–8.

[31] See Sheppard (1969), 66–69. A slab of ca. 760–800 from Kurşunlu Monastery provides a somewhat earlier example (Mango and Ševčenko [1973], 276–277, fig. 153); a wall painting in the Chapel of St Basil, near Sinassos in Cappadocia, a (probably) roughly contemporary one: deemed iconoclast by Thierry (1982), 395–396, the Cappadocian cross has been dated ca. 900 by Epstein (1977), 105–106, fig. 23; its curious inscription is discussed by Pallas (1974), esp. 311–314. See too Pallas (1978), esp. 222–225. A slightly later example appears on the back of the Sinai icon B.52: Weitzmann (1976), 85, pl. CVIII, b.

[32] Westerink IV (1986), 93 ll.261–269 (*PG* 101:185D–187A). See also *De ceremoniis* II:78 (69) (ed. Vogt II [1967a], 126–129); Grabar (1936), 32–39; Gagé (1933).

barbarians'; a third tells us: 'O Logos, in order to strengthen the piety of mortals, and to show a clear and complete picture of yourself, you gave a law that only the cross be depicted . . . Behold, the great rulers depict it as a victory-bringing sign.'[33] Images of the 'victory-bringing sign' which provided both eternal salvation and temporal success appear throughout the eighth and ninth centuries; in most cases, as on ff. Bv and Cr, Constantine is implicit in the image without actually being depicted.

The interwoven meanings of the crosses on ff. Bv and Cr were not, then, first introduced in the Paris Gregory. The cross in the form of Constantine's ex voto – always recognizable by its stepped base – was in fact a sign of victory and triumph closely associated with the imperial house from, at the latest, 578, when Tiberios introduced it on his coins.[34] The association with imperial victory and Christian triumph – joined, perhaps, by the impact of the anti-Jewish and anti-Muslim dialogues that championed the cross – presumably cushioned the iconoclast acceptance of the cross when most religious images were condemned as idolatrous.[35] The inscription IC XC NHKA, which reinforced the imperial and Constantinian implications, is first documented during Iconoclasm: it appeared in an inscription commemorating the restoration of the walls of Constantinople in 740–741.[36] Here the apotropaic significance is clear: Constantine's cross helped the walls repulse the enemies of the city. The inscription also appeared with the stepped cross on iconoclast coins, thereby linking the relevant emperors with Christ, Constantine, and victory.[37] Further, if we believe the *Parastaseis*, Constantine's monument of triumph was duplicated in various media throughout Constantinople during the years of Iconoclasm.[38]

Theological arguments in favour of the cross, developed during the eighth century, apparently augmented the strength of the cross cult in iconoclast Constantinople.[39] In addition to the crosses that appeared on coins and seals, monumental crosses were either inserted or allowed to stand in the apse mosaics at

[33] All appear in Gero (1973a), 116, 121. On Theodore, see chapter I note 115.

[34] Grabar (1957), 27–29; Frolow (1961a), 336–337. Cf. Bernardakis (1901/2), esp. 199–200.

[35] See Frolow (1961b), 121; Cameron (1992a), 261–265; Reinink (1992), esp. 171–177, 183–186. On the impact of the anti-Jewish and anti-Muslim dialogues on ninth-century imagery, Corrigan (1992), esp. 40–42, 91–94.

[36] The abbreviated legend may, however, have been used as early as the reign of Heraklios: Frolow (1956), 104, 106; Grabar (1957), 31, 126.

[37] See Grierson III,1 (1973), 411, pl. XXII, nos. 1a.2–1c.2; Grabar (1957), 145, 153–155, and, for pre-iconoclastic usage, 27–30, 70. See also the standard, but outdated, Millet (1910). For a different (and I believe incorrect) interpretation of the steps as pieces of a broken pagan altar, see Ericsson (1968).

[38] Ed. Cameron and Herrin (1984), 94–95, 126–127 (cross with Constantine and Helena), 134–135 (the cross erected by Constantine; it is not clear from the text whether this cross was actually seen by the authors of the *Parastaseis*); cf. 208, 240, 246–247. On the *Parastaseis*, see chapter I note 21. In addition, the gemmed cross erected in Jerusalem by Theodosios II was transported to Constantinople in 635: on this, and gemmed crosses in general, see Frolow (1961b), 73–74; Frolow (1965), 187–204.

[39] On the cult of the cross during Iconoclasm, see, e.g., Gero (1977a), 34 note 55, 162–164; Lafontaine-Dosogne (1987b); Cameron (1992b). Concomitantly, Constantine also enjoyed increased popularity at this time: see Winkelmann (1978); Moorhead (1985); Kazhdan (1987).

Fig. 83 Istanbul, Hagia Sophia: sekreton mosaic, cross

Hagia Eirene in Constantinople and the Koimesis Church at Nicaea, while crosses replaced figural decoration in the sekreton at Hagia Sophia (fig. 83) in the capital.[40] At least some of these – like the frontispiece crosses of Paris.gr.510 – had multiple agendas, and fused references to Constantine's cross and the true cross of the crucifixion within a single image. When, for example, the crosses inserted in Hagia Sophia (fig. 83) replaced medallion portraits of saints, the encasing medallion was retained and filled in with concentric spheres of variously shaded light blue,[41] a configuration that signalled a vision of divinity;[42] we may presume that the iconoclast insertions invoked Constantine's vision of the cross along with the cross of Christ's crucifixion. The ideological importance of the cross, with its complex map of meanings, is clear from its immediate absorption by the new orthodoxy after

[40] See Cormack (1977a), 35–44.   [41] Cormack and Hawkins (1977), 204–205, 211–212.
[42] James (1991), esp. 82.

843: the image of Christ on the Chalke gate incorporated a cross, though we do not know in what form;[43] the stepped cross of iconoclast lead seals remained, in the words of Nicolas Oikonomides, 'particularly common between the middle of the ninth and the eleventh century';[44] and coins, too, retained the image.[45] The stepped crosses of ff. Bv and Cr, with their intimations of imperial triumph from the time of Constantine, had become conventional imperial attributes.

The combination of the stepped cross with the foliate living cross seems to be first presented in Paris.gr.510.[46] This twinned message of triumph and piety finds a contemporary parallel in the mosaic decoration of the Kainourgion (a structure built by Basil I in the Great Palace that is now known only through textual description), where a large 'victorious cross' dominated the gold ceiling, while portraits of the imperial family lined the walls, and seemed to be saying, in the words of the *Vita Basilii*: 'All that is good and pleasing to God [piety] has been accomplished and achieved in the days of our rule through this victorious symbol [triumph].'[47] The cross, symbol of victory and representation of God's approval, is linked, again, with portraits of Basil and his family.

While the crosses perpetuate older ideologies on the one hand, and embody contemporary propaganda on the other, the basic idea of introducing a manuscript with a cross devolved from a simpler past. Perhaps because of their apotropaic significance – and possibly in emulation of gospelbook covers where, like the crosses on Byzantine doors, they must be passed *en route* to the knowledge leading to salvation – single incipit crosses open numerous pre-iconoclast manuscripts.[48] The paired crosses of Paris.gr.510, however, are apparently unprecedented.

This anomaly was explained by Charles Rufus Morey as invention mothered by

---

[43] Grabar (1957), 134. Frolow (1963) argued that the cross referred to in descriptions of this image signified Christ's cruciform nimbus.   [44] Oikonomides (1985a), 12.

[45] For examples from Basil's reign, Grierson III,2 (1973), 482, pl. XXX; for iconoclast examples, ibid., III,1 (1973), 411, pl. XXII, nos. 1a.2–1c.2. For contemporary references to relics of the cross itself, see Frolow (1961b), 222–223; and on the continuing importance of the cross, Sansterre (1994), esp. 233–235.

[46] The leaved cross makes its first painted appearance here, but is found earlier in sculpture: see note 31 above.

[47] *Vita Basilii* 89: ed. Bekker (1838), 333. The description of the Kainourgion occupies all of chapter 89 (*PG* 109:348B–352A; trans. Mango [1972], 196–198). On the *Vita Basilii*, a mid-tenth-century text sometimes attributed to Basil's grandson Constantine VII Porphyrogennetos (but more likely by someone in that emperor's circle), see *ODB* III (1991), 2181; I. Ševčenko (1978); and I. Ševčenko (1992a), esp. 184–185. I have profited greatly from Ihor Ševčenko's new edition and translation of this text, as yet unpublished, from which all passages quoted in this book derive; and I am grateful to Professor Ševčenko for providing me with a typescript of the text in advance of publication, and for discussions of the *Vita*.

[48] Grabar II (1943b), 278; Jules Leroy (1964), 113–119; Kitzinger (1974), 3–17. Velmans (1979), 117–118, noted that when a cross appears in the opening miniatures it is often repeated on the cover, and suggests this possibility for Paris.gr.510. On doors, the foliate cross represented the gates of paradise from the sixth century: Frazer (1973), 145–162, esp. 154; Tsuji (1983), 28. If the inscription in Naples suppl.gr.12* can be trusted, which is questionable, another manuscript destined for Basil I opened with a single cross: Weitzmann (1959), 309–320.

necessity: the rejected underdrawing beneath f. Bv had to be covered up, so a second cross was painted. But there are obvious objections to this thesis. The underdrawing on f. Bv must have been produced before the rest of the bifolium was sketched out, for the underdrawings visible in other miniatures of this bifolium correspond with the painted images that cover them, which they would not do had the rest of the bifolium been designed before f. Bv and then altered when the under-drawing on f. Bv was found wanting.[49] Nothing but expense would have prevented the substitution of a fresh sheet of parchment should a blank page have been desired where the second cross now sits – and cost-cutting is not a notable feature of Paris.gr.510. Further, even granting Morey's belief that something had to be painted on what was then the last side of the opening bifolium, it need not have been a cross. Presumably, the double cross had meaning, a presumption reinforced by the repetition of the motif in the Leo Bible sixty years later.[50]

There are in fact so many possible justifications for the double crosses of Paris.gr.510 that the pairing seems almost over-determined. The cross–portrait, portrait–cross sequence emulated the precedents established by other sets of images, such as coins that combined imperial portraits on the obverse with a cross on the reverse or, more compellingly, diptychs where crosses encased portraits. The double crosses also emphatically signalled the ultimate sign of imperial Christian triumph; they might possibly even allude to Basil's defeat of the Paulicians (a heretical sect that denied the sanctity of the cross) in 872, an accomplishment announced with reference to the victorious cross: while slogans about the cross were traditional Byzantine battle cries, Byzantine sources particularly stress that the ultimate victory over the Paulicians was accompanied by the shout 'Conquer for the cross'.[51] Certainly the double image provided an overt sign of the Christian veneration of the cross, and made visible the reasons for that veneration twice over. Finally, the two crosses repeated a symbol of an imperial theophany, as Constantine's vision was viewed at the time,[52] and reiterated Basil's (and the new dynasty's) links with Constantine and his triumphs.

Whatever the way in which this combination of potential meanings was mixed in Paris.gr.510, the double crosses demonstrate that the cross had shed its brief and temporary role as a barometer of iconoclast or iconophile tendencies. It was too important an emblem to be limited by the iconophile position, which held that the cross had value as a symbol, but that images should be accorded equal or greater honour.[53] The subsequent frontispiece sequence depended upon and reinforced the messages dissolved within the images of the crosses themselves.

[49] On the underdrawing, see further the Introduction.

[50] Vat.reg.gr.1, ff. 2r, 3v: *Miniature* (1905), pls. 3, 6; Dufrenne and Canart (1988), 19–20.

[51] See Frolow (1956), 100; Tobias (1976), 52–54; on the Paulicians, Astruc *et al.* (1970) and Lemerle (1973). [52] Frolow (1956), 102–3; Thierry (1980/1), 206. On visions in Paris.gr.510, see chapter 7.

[53] E.g. Nikephoros, *Antirrheticus* 3,35: Mondzain-Baudinet (1990), 221–226; discussion in Travis (1984), 152–153.

Folio Cv (5) (fig. 5)

Folio Cv, originally the first of the imperial portraits, presents Basil I flanked by Elijah (viewer's left) and Gabriel (right).[54] Though the identifying inscriptions are still legible, little remains of the three nimbed figures standing against a gold ground on a jewelled podium; it is, for example, impossible to determine whether the portrait of Basil conforms with Pseudo-Symeon Magistros' description of him.[55] Virtually nothing remains of Elijah's robe save a few flakes of pale blue and white paint, but enough survives of the emperor and archangel to determine that they are clothed in the simple *loros* form also worn by Eudokia, Leo, and Alexander on f. Br (fig. 2), which once faced this page. Elijah passes a labarum to Basil, while Gabriel crowns him with his right hand and holds an orb in his left. The portrait is framed by a verse, the opening words of which are effaced; the remainder reads 'Elijah promises victory over [Basil's] enemies. But Gabriel, having predicted joy, crowns you, Basil, governor of the cosmos.'[56] A later hand has transcribed part of this verse in the margins.

Gabriel's crowning of Basil is among the earliest preserved examples of a Byzantine emperor so honoured by a member of the celestial hierarchy.[57] The concentration on divine sanction for Basil's rule apparent in the image and the inscription is evident as well from an innovation introduced at Basil's triumphal entries into Constantinople in 873 and 879. During the services held at Hagia Sophia as part of these celebrations, the patriarch bestowed the 'crown of victory' on Basil. Michael McCormick suggested that 'the circumstances of Basil's seizure of power' prompted this anomaly: 'Since venerable tradition had long associated crowns and victory, the triumphs of 873 and 879 may well have seemed apt moments for a new public display of the church's approval of the upstart emperor's authority.'[58] The image on f. Cv seems to participate in a campaign designed to demonstrate that Basil's ascent to the throne has been sanctioned by representatives of God: Gabriel in the miniature, and the patriarch on earth.

It also suggests, however, that Basil rules *through* God, and with the active cooperation of God's other representatives, a concept closely allied to the beliefs expressed by Photios in the *Eisagoge*. This work, a legal compilation, contains a

---

[54] Ebersolt (1926), 21; Omont (1929), 13, pl. XIX; Grabar (1936), 100, 116–117; Mango (1958), 178; Der Nersessian (1962), 198, 220–221; Guilland I (1969), 106, 305, 314, 321; Spatharakis (1974), 97–98; Corrigan (1978), 410; Kalavrezou-Maxeiner (1978), 22–23; Jolivet-Levy (1987), 445–446; Brubaker (1994), 149–152; Maguire (1995), 63–71. The location of the portraits at the beginning of the book follows Byzantine convention: Anderson (1975), 161–163; Jules Leroy (1974), 223.

[55] *Chronicle*: ed. Bekker (1842), 686. On Pseudo-Symeon, see *ODB*3 (1991), 1983.

[56] On the arrangement of the inscription: Follieri (1964), 452.

[57] The Palazzo Venezia ivory, which shows Basil and Eudokia *blessed* by Christ (fig. 79; Maguire [1988]), may pre-date Paris.gr.510; and some early Byzantine coins repeat that motif or show the emperor crowned by a hand of God (e.g. MacCormack [1981], 256–257). The ivory in Berlin which shows the Virgin crowning Leo VI in the presence of an archangel (fig. 177) provides a slightly later example: Corrigan (1978); Cutler (1994), 200–201.   [58] McCormick (1986), 157.

remarkable introduction which posits law (*nomos*), the emperor, and the patriarch as God's three agents on earth; it thus both relieves the emperor of certain powers (which he now shares with the patriarch and the concept of *nomos*) and elevates him as one selected by God to be 'initiated into divine truth'.[59] An allusion to this initiation perhaps appears on f. Cv where, as noted by Henry Maguire, Basil fully shares the divine space represented by Gabriel and Elijah – all stand on the same jewelled plinth – and is visually equated with Gabriel by stance and costume.[60] It is also possible that Photios' new conception of the relationship between the emperor and God lies behind the two earliest non-numismatic representations of an emperor with a divine agent: Basil with Gabriel here, and with Christ on the Palazzo Venezia casket (fig. 84).[61]

The belief that Basil was God's elect even before his coronation was also promoted.[62] As is well known, Basil was an emperor without an imperial past. He was born of (probably) Armenian parents, apparently entered the court milieu as a groom in the stables of Michael III, was made co-ruler in 866 under circumstances that are not clear, and achieved sole rule a year later by murdering his patron. Basil's career path was unorthodox and, just as his coronation is instigated by Gabriel on f. Cv, so too his rise to power was legitimized by accounts of visions and portents that foretold his rule; these, along with panegyrics and illustrious genealogies, accrued around Basil in his own lifetime, and continued to be composed for some time thereafter.[63]

The Old Testament prophet Elijah played a significant role in these accounts. The *Vita Basilii*, for example, describes a series of dreams in which Elijah appears to Basil's mother and tells her such things as 'God will hand over the sceptre of the Roman empire to your beloved son Basil; you should persuade him to go to Constantinople.'[64] Basil's active veneration of the prophet is recorded throughout the *Vita*, which also credits the emperor with several churches dedicated to Elijah. Of these, the most important was the Nea Ekklesia, where Elijah's sheepskin coat was kept as a relic.[65] The author of the *Vita Basilii* also recognized Basil as responsi-

---

[59] On the *Eisagoge*, see *ODB* 1 (1991), 703–704; Simon (1994), 16–18; Dagron (1994), 30; Lokin (1994), 78–80, discussion of the passage quoted at 78; cf. Gouillard (1969), 13. Compare the persistent complaints by iconophile writers that (iconoclast) emperors were usurping the rights of the patriarch and church: Alexander (1977), 259–262; Schönborn (1976), 149–150, 186–191.

[60] Maguire (1995) concluded that we might see the image as a visual vindication of Basil's murder of Michael III, and that the joy predicted by Gabriel in the framing verse referred both back in time to the annunciation, and forward in time to Basil's acceptance into heaven.

[61] See note 57 above, and the discussion of Basil and David later in this chapter.

[62] Moravcsik (1961) remains the classic study; see esp. 83.

[63] On the legends, see ibid., 59–126; on imperial topoi in accounts of Basil's life, Patlagean (1992); for the genealogy, note 220 below. On the prophecies that accrued around other ninth-century rulers, which provide a context for those associated with Basil, see Gero (1992), esp. 83–85.

[64] *Vita Basilii* 8: ed. Bekker (1838), 222; see note 47 above. For other texts, Moravcsik (1961), 90–91, 106 and Tobias (1969), 91–93, 100, 376. It is significant that dream interpretation was legalised at the end of the ninth century: see Calofonos (1984/5), esp. 218–219.   [65] Magdalino (1987), 51–64.

Fig. 84 Rome, Palazzo Venezia: ivory casket, lid

ble for the reintroduction of the feast of Elijah in Constantinople, and described the mosaic portrait of Basil in the sanctuary of the Church of St Elijah.[66] Elijah's elevated status in the later ninth century is further corroborated by the appearance of 'In Praise of Elijah', written by Photios' ally Theophanes of Caesarea.[67] In Paris.gr.510, as the framing verse explains, Elijah promises Basil victory. This is confirmed in the miniature, where the standard that Elijah hands to Basil is Constantine's labarum. In the first version of this scene, sketched beneath the cross on f. Bv (fig. 3), Elijah was already present, but he did not hand the labarum to Basil: the detail added to the final product thus takes on a certain significance. In both versions, Elijah represents the divine force that assured Basil's rule; the alteration in the final copy, however, seems to stress Basil's association with Constantine.[68] Constantine's labarum was a conventional imperial attribute on coins, but by showing God's representative Elijah actually presenting it to Basil – as if anticipating the prophet's statement to Basil's mother that 'God will hand over the sceptre of the Roman empire to your beloved son Basil' in the *Vita Basilii* – the miniaturist set the stamp of divine approval on Basil as a direct successor to Constantine.

A passage from the *Vita Basilii* suggests that this lineage may have been even more overtly promoted. The *Vita* is a panegyric, written in the tenth century probably at the suggestion of Basil's grandson, the Emperor Constantine VII. Some of the material it contains appeared in sources contemporary with Basil, and some occurs in no other preserved source. The following belongs to the latter category, and may therefore be more revealing about the tenth century than the ninth. Be that as it may, the *Vita* describes Basil's grandmother as a 'noble and seemly woman who dwelt in Adrianople and had led a chaste life of widowhood since the death of her husband (reports, not quite unreliable, circulated that she traced her lineage back to Constantine the Great)'. In the next sentence, Basil's mother 'proudly claimed descent from Constantine the Great [on the one side] and on the other side boasted the splendid ancestry of Alexander'.[69] By the tenth century, Basil's links with Constantine had moved from the conceptual to the actual. The image on f. Cv anticipates this leap of faith, but it encapsulates the same message. In so doing, the miniature reiterates the meaning of the opening portrait of Christ.

Gabriel, too, seems to have been favoured by the emperor. Though there is some doubt on the point, Basil apparently dedicated the Nea Ekklesia to him, along with

[66] *De Ceremoniis* I, 28(19): ed. Vogt I (1967a), 106, 109; see also Vogt I (1967b), 130–134, and Magdalino (1988).   [67] *BHG* 577c; Featherstone (1980), 95.
[68] So too Der Nersessian (1962), 220; cf. Kalavrezou-Maxeiner (1978), 22–23.
[69] *Vita Basilii* 3: ed. Bekker (1838), 215–216; see note 47 above. The exploitation of Constantine I evident here recurs in other texts associated with Constantine VII as well: e.g. in *De Administrando Imperio* 13 (ed. Moravcsik and Jenkins [1967], 66–67), Constantine advised his son to refuse to send imperial regalia to foreign dignitaries, using the excuse that they were brought to Constantine the Great by an angel; see also Shepard (1985), 240–241; Macrides (1992), 266–267.

Elijah and Christ and, secondarily, Mary and Nicholas. The *Vita Basilii* informs us that in his dedication of the Nea, Basil 'returned, as it were, the favour shown to him by Christ the Lord, by Gabriel, the first among the angelic hosts, and by Elijah the Tishbite, the votary – the one who had announced to his mother her son's ascent to the imperial throne . . . as well as to the Virgin and to Nicholas who holds the first rank among the hierarchs'.[70] Paris.gr.510 thus apparently pictures the three primary patrons of Basil's Nea Ekklesia in its frontispiece sequence: Christ on f. Av, Elijah and Gabriel on f. Cv. It seems unlikely that this replication is coincidental, for the manuscript was in production when the Nea was dedicated in May 880.

Folio Br (2) (fig. 2)

The miniature on f. Br presents the Empress Eudokia flanked by her eldest son Leo (on her right) and his younger brother Alexander (on her left), an order of precedence that reflects numismatic practice.[71] All wear the imperial *loros* in its simplest form, a type anticipated in the bema mosaics of angels at the Koimesis Church at Nicaea and repeated in Alexander's mosaic portrait of 912 at Hagia Sophia;[72] and each stands on a jewelled base, holding an orb in her or his left hand. Eudokia also carries a sceptre with a trefoil floral tip, while her sons both grasp a red akakia, a cylindrical container of dust carried by emperors on ceremonial occasions.[73] The three are frontal, nimbed, and surrounded by a framing verse that eulogizes Eudokia: 'Basil, emperor of the Romans, precedes you, the well-branched vineyard bearing the grapes of the empire, the gentle *despotes*. With them you shine forth, light-bearing Eudokia.'[74]

The Homilies portraits have been associated with those at the Kainourgion, where mosaics presented the emperor 'and his spouse Eudokia enthroned and decked out in imperial robes and diadems. The children of the couple are depicted all around the chamber as if they were bright stars; they too are resplendent in

---

[70] *Vita Basilii* 83: ed. Bekker (1838), 325; see note 47 above. Earlier in the narrative, we are told in passing that the Nea was dedicated to Christ, 'Michael the very first among angels', and Elijah (*Vita Basilii* 76: ed. Bekker [1838], 319); elsewhere, and again in passing, the dedication is described as being to Christ, Elijah, and the 'Chief Commanders of the Heavenly Host' (*Vita Basilii* 68: ed. Bekker [1838], 308–309). These brief allusions may reflect the dedication of the church when the *Vita Basilii* was written, but the fuller account quoted in the text probably accurately records the original patrons. Magdalino (1987), 56 note 26, suggested that Leo VI – who may have been Michael III's son, and rehabilitated his memory shortly after Basil's death – changed the dedication from Gabriel to Michael; cf. Epstein (1986), 36 note 21.

[71] Vogt (1908), 410; Millet (1920), 239–240; Ebersolt (1926), 22; Omont (1929), 12, pl. XVI; Morey (1929), 42; Grabar (1936), 27; Grabar (1960), 127; Underwood and Hawkins (1961), 191–193; Der Nersessian (1962), 197–198; Grierson III,i (1973), iii, 118 (table 12,G), 120, 141 and III,2 (1973), 474–476; Spatharakis (1974), 98, 104; Kalavrezou-Maxeiner (1977), 317 note 58; Kalavrezou-Maxeiner (1978), 21; Brubaker (1994), 152.   [72] Underwood (1959), figs. 7, 9.   [73] See *ODB* I (1991), 42.

[74] The final phrase implicitly equates the empress with Venus, a point I owe to Ihor Ševčenko. Plant metaphors were often associated with women; as we saw in chapter 1, for example, the Virgin 'puts forth in the way of fruit the most exact vision of truth' (Mango [1958], 290).

imperial robes and diadems.'[75] In the manuscript, however, only the sons in line for succession accompany Eudokia, giving f. Br 'the character of an official imperial representation' rather than of an extended family portrait.[76] As was recognized by André Grabar, f. Br is an unabashedly dynastic image.[77]

Folio 440r (45) (fig. 45)

Folio 440r presents Constantine's dream, his vision of the cross at the Milvian bridge, and Helena's discovery of the true cross in Jerusalem.[78] The top register, devoted to the dream, shows a nimbed Constantine, wearing a diadem surmounted by a small pearled cross, asleep on a red cushion laid on a gold bed draped with a purple and gold cloth. His purple mantle is drawn up around his upper body, revealing a pale blue undertunic with gold decoration worn over purple leggings. Constantine's position duplicates the standard sleeping formula found throughout Paris.gr.510: he reclines with crossed legs, his right arm thrown across his body and with his head resting on his left hand exactly like Jonah on f. 3r (fig. 6) and Jacob on f. 174v (fig. 23). On the right, two youthful guards, both in pale blue tunics decorated with gold under red cloaks, stand in relaxed poses, leaning on their lances and red shields. The inscription to the scene, in the upper left-hand corner against the blue sky, has been almost entirely effaced; fragments of Constantine's name are all that remain. In the middle register, Constantine, now wearing purple and gold under a red mantle that streams behind him, charges toward the Milvian bridge on his white horse and lances Maxentius, in blue, who falls from his black horse as his army flees off to the right.[79] The composition replicates, in reverse, that in the lowest register of f. 409v (fig. 40) showing Merkourios slaying Julian the Apostate, save that the Julian picture lacks the bridge and, of course, the gold cross that appears just above the head of Constantine's horse. A similar bridge does, however, appear in the top register of f. 409v, and a river, deep blue with paler blue striations, flows on either side of it. The river on f. 440r looks

[75] *Vita Basilii* 89: ed. Bekker (1838), 333; see note 47 above. Basil had at least one son (Constantine) and probably a daughter (Anastasia) by his previous marriage to Maria, while Eudokia may have borne Leo and Stephen to Michael III, whose mistress she may have been; Alexander, Anna, Helena, and Maria seem to have shared Basil and Eudokia as parents. Stephen, though older than Alexander, was groomed for the church and was therefore not included in the dynastic portrait in Paris.gr.510. See Adontz (1933b); Mango (1973); Kislinger (1983); and Karlin-Hayter (1991).
[76] Kalavrezou-Maxeiner (1978), 21.   [77] Grabar (1960), 127.
[78] Ebersolt (1926), 22; Omont (1929), 31, pl. LIX; Weitzmann (1942/3), 126–128; Porcher (1964), 275; Der Nersessian (1962), 219–221; Cormack and Hawkins (1977), 240–241; Walter (1982), 148–149; Schminck (1985), 217, 232; Jolivet-Lévy (1987), 457. Part of the following originally appeared in Brubaker (1994), 147–149.
[79] I here follow conventional identifications of the bridge and foe: the inscription to the scene identifies neither, but instead tells us that 'St Constantine pursues the foreigners' (Ο Α[ΓΙΟC ΚΩ]ΝCΤΑΝΤΙΝΟC [Φ]ΕΥΓΩΝ Τ[ΟΥC] ΑΛΛΟΦΥΛ[ΟΥC]). On f. 347v (fig. 35), the Philistines slain by Samson are similarly labelled 'foreigners': see note 156 below.

the same, but stops short at the bridge; the faint, dark blue undulating lines that appear to rise from the bridge suggest that the miniaturist may originally have intended to extend the river into the background as on f. 409v. The cross, with pearl serifs, sits against a pale green orb and bears the famous inscription EN TOYTΩ NIKA.[80] The lowest register contains two scenes. On the left, Helena sits on a jew-elled lyre-back throne. She is clad as a Byzantine empress, and retains the coiffure interwoven with pearls beneath a complex crown topped with a pearl cross that she wears on f. 285r (fig. 29); on f. 440r, however, a purple cloak with gold and jewelled borders hides her undergarments. Helena rests a blue orb surmounted by a cross on her lap, and gestures to a group of men who stand in the far left corner. Though badly flaked, the foremost of the men toward whom she gestures appears to wear clerical garb and may be identified as Makarios, bishop of Jerusalem, who helped Helena determine which of the three crosses she unearthed belonged to Christ.[81] Only Helena, however, is identified by inscription: H AΓIA EΛENH. To the right of the empress, two men carrying jewelled batons stand guard; they closely resem-ble the guards attending Theodosios on f. 239r (fig. 27). In the final scene, the standing Helena gestures toward a pit; a man identical with the one identified as Makarios in the preceding scene kneels alongside and reaches toward the cross within it, while a gesticulating group of onlookers cheer him on. The scene is identified by inscription as the 'finding of the true cross' (EYPECIC TOY TIMIOY CTAYPOY), and the same legend is repeated on the outer margin of the page in what appears to be ninth-century slanting uncial.

Despite his conceptual importance, Constantine does not appear elsewhere in Paris.gr.510. Helena, on the other hand, recurs on f. 285r (fig. 29) with Paraskeve in the vision of Habakkuk. There, although her physiognomic type remains the same, her costume is more elaborate; on f. 285r, her *loros* closely resembles that worn by the Empress Eudokia on f. Br. Folios 285r and 440r show different types of scenes: the former presents an iconic and formal portrait, the latter portrays Helena as a participant in a visual narrative. The affiliation of her formal portrait on f. 285r with that of Eudokia on f. Br was presumably intentional, and meant to solidify the links between Basil and his family, and Constantine and his.[82] On f. 440r, the miniatur-ist seems more concerned with connecting Helena and her own son: the dark purple garment, trimmed with jewelled strips of gold, that she wears provides a variant on Constantine's clothing in the register above; and Helena's location on the page complements the positioning of her son. The enthroned Helena sits

---

[80] See note 27 above.   [81] Weitzmann (1942/3), 126–128.

[82] Indeed, Der Nersessian (1962), 221, suggested that Helena's prominence in Paris.gr.510 might be explained as an attempt to promote her as a prototype of Eudokia, a point repeated by Jolivet-Levy (1987), 457. Eudokia, like many Byzantine empresses, was certainly called a 'new Helena' – e.g. in the Latin version of the acts of the eighth Ecumenical Council (*PL* 129:170) – but there may be other agendas visualized here as well: see the discussion of f. 285r in chapter 5. Note too that one of the couple's daughters was named Helena: note 75 above.

directly below the triumphant Constantine, so that the two most overtly imperial portraits on the page are axially aligned; and, in order to juxtapose the sleeping Constantine in the top register with the mounted Constantine and the enthroned Helena, the dream sequence has been pushed to the left half of the page, thereby requiring the miniaturist to fill the right with standing soldiers. As these manipulations might suggest, f. 440r is an *ad hoc* compilation: no convincing visual parallels to any of the scenes pictured exist; and, as we have seen, most of the miniature relies on stock details found elsewhere in the manuscript.[83]

The three episodes pictured on f. 440r were inextricably interwoven in Byzantine thought. By the sixth century, Constantine's conversion and Helena's discovery of the true cross were, for example, placed back to back in strophes 18 and 19 of Romanos' hymn 'On the adoration of the cross'.[84] By the seventh, when the various Lives of Constantine seem to have been developed, the history of Constantine almost invariably included an account of Helena and her discovery of the true cross.[85] Images, too, though mostly preserved from a later period, normally show the mother and son as a pair.[86] By around the year 800, the constellation of Constantine, his vision, his ex voto cross, and the relics of the true cross discovered by Helena had melted into one concept, a concept crucial to imperial authority, and especially to the triumph of the Christian Byzantine state. So strong was the association between these episodes and Byzantium's self-image that Greek authors sometimes moved both Constantine's vision and his dream away from Rome, and relocated them at specific sites in Constantinople.[87]

Images of Constantine and Helena also remained or were made during the years of Iconoclasm: according to the *Parastaseis*, their portraits, usually flanking the cross, appeared throughout Constantinople.[88] But iconoclast attempts to appropriate Constantine were countered immediately by their opponents.[89] The Khludov Psalter (fig. 85) provides an example from the years immediately following Iconoclasm: here Constantine, inscribed as a saint, dispatches his enemies with a cross-headed lance.[90] The miniature accompanies Psalm 59:6, 'Thou hast given a sign to them that fear thee'. The word 'sign' – glossed as 'the imprint of the life-giving cross' in the scholia at the bottom of the page – triggered the image,[91] and we see Constantine triumphant, defending the 'sign' against heresy. It was not the psalter miniaturist who made the connection between the psalm verse and the victory of orthodoxy over heresy: 'Thou hast given a sign to them that fear thee' was

---

[83] See too Walter (1982), 148–149.   [84] SC 128, 344–346. On Romanos, see chapter 2 note 104.

[85] Winkelmann (1978); Kazhdan (1987) argues for a somewhat later date (ca. 800).

[86] Grabar (1969), 112–120; Thierry (1980/1), 220–228.

[87] Ed. Cameron and Herrin (1984), 128, 134, and commentary 192.

[88] Ibid., 94–95, 126–127, 134–135; cf. 208, 240, 246–247.

[89] On the iconoclasts and Constantine, see Kazhdan (1987), who provides much earlier bibliography.   [90] Moscow, Hist.Mus.gr.129, f. 58v: Ščepkina (1977); Walter (1987), 209, fig. 1.

[91] Walter (1987), 209 and note 14; Corrigan (1992), 72.

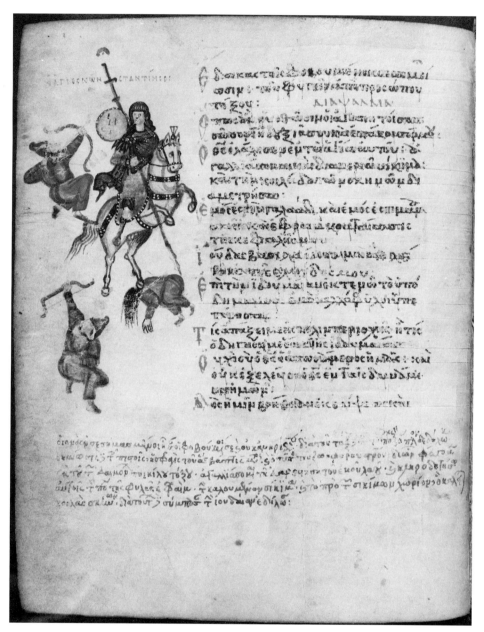

Fig. 85 Moscow, Historical Museum, cod.129, f. 58v: Constantine

cited in the polemics against heresy that proliferated in the eighth and ninth centuries, the preserved examples of which are fairly indiscriminately targeted against Jews, Muslims, and iconoclasts.[92] In the polemics, the psalm verse forms part of an arsenal of documentation meant to prove the authority of the cross and the authority of images. It is only, however, in the psalter image that Constantine represents the orthodox position. Here, in a miniature created almost immediately after the end of Iconoclasm, Constantine has been removed from iconoclast control, and used to exemplify orthodox victory. In the Khludov Psalter, the triumphant Constantine champions the new orthodoxy.[93]

During the reign of Basil I, more static portraits of Constantine (fig. 86) and, probably, Helena were incorporated into the mosaic decoration of Hagia Sophia. The surviving fragments, dated to around the year 870, seem to have been part of a fairly pointed visual statement directed against the old iconoclasts.[94] Certainly Constantine was shown in the company of other champions of the faith, some of whom – such as the former patriarchs Germanos and Nikephoros – were famous for their opposition to Iconoclasm. Like the cross, Constantine had been returned to the fold: he now served the iconophile orthodox.

The Khludov Psalter miniature and the Hagia Sophia mosaic provide a context of sorts for the sequence in Paris.gr.510. But, in contrast to these two works, on f. 440r Constantine is not explicitly set up as a champion of orthodoxy, triumphant against heresy. Instead, the Homilies miniature presents a visual narrative that emphasizes themes interwoven in earlier texts about Constantine and Helena. As with the crosses on ff. Bv and Cr, visual polemics have been abandoned on f. 440r; rather than promoting a particular cause, the miniature internalizes the ideological importance of Constantine and Helena to the Byzantine imperial system. Folio 440r provides a narrative version of the message conveyed by the crosses of the frontispiece sequence; the relationship between Constantine's cross of triumph and the true cross is here made manifest.

This relationship was demonstrably important to the imperial house under Basil I. But f. 440r has sometimes been singled out in attempts to link Basil I with Constantine for reasons that do not sustain detailed scrutiny. Its presumed importance has been based on two assumptions: first, that the miniature is unrelated to the text it accompanies, and hence can *only* be interpreted as imperial flattery; and second, that it was the penultimate miniature in the manuscript, followed only by Gregory's *vita*, and hence provided a strong visual conclusion. The first assumption is incorrect; the second is problematic.

---

[92] The 'Trophies of Damascus', which cites this verse, was directed specifically against the Jews; its relevance to the Khludov Psalter has been demonstrated by Corrigan (1992), this image at 72 and 178 note 54.

[93] On the orthodox reclamation of Constantine, see also the writings of Photios discussed in Mango (1975), 41.   [94] Cormack and Hawkins (1977), 230–231, 235–246.

Fig. 86 Istanbul, Hagia Sophia: room over the vestibule, mosaic of Constantine

The miniature on f. 440r introduces an extraneous text, the 'Metaphrase of Ecclesiastes' attributed to Gregory Thaumaturgos.[95] On first glance, the 'Metaphrase' sustains no relationship to the Constantine and Helena sequence spread over its frontispiece, and yet the picture is surely in its intended position, for the text begins on its verso. Sirarpie Der Nersessian argued that the selection of Constantine's vision and the invention of the cross relates to the programme of the manuscript as a whole, rather than to the 'Metaphrase in' particular, and functioned as a compliment to Basil I. She linked f. 440r with the prefatory crosses, and suggested that these miniatures formed a unified opening and (more or less) closure to the manuscript.[96] This last thesis is appealing, but unprovable, for the end of Paris.gr.510 has perished and we have no way of determining the original extent of the manuscript.[97]

More importantly, the scenes grouped together on f. 440r were not included merely to promote imperial interests: they also illustrate their accompanying text, though by analogy rather than by providing a literal picture of the report. The

[95] *PG* 10:987–1018 (trans. *Ante-Nicene Christian Library* 20 [Edinburgh, 1871], 7–29).
[96] Der Nersessian (1962), 197–198.   [97] See Introduction.

'Metaphrase', narrated by 'Solomon' in the first person singular, begins with a brief description of the pleasures the protagonist enjoyed before devoting himself to God. 'Upon awakening and recovering my sight', however, Solomon explains that he graduated from pursuit of sensate pleasure to pursuit of God's wisdom, the benefits of which he explores at length. The decision to illustrate this text with images of Constantine's dream and vision seems to have been motivated by the character of the 'Metaphrase's' protagonist, an ideal ruler type who saw the light, and awoke to forsake the profane for the God-fearing life. Constantine's conversion supplies a momentous parallel to this transfiguration, and Constantine also provided the most significant Christian example of a ruler who 'awoke' (literally, as portrayed in the top register of f. 440r) to a life believed, in the ninth century, to be thereafter one of unblemished orthodoxy and righteousness.[98]

But the fact that the connections between Basil and Constantine supposed to be demonstrated by f. 440r have been over-stated does not mean that they do not exist. Certainly a connection between Basil, Constantine, and the cross of victory fits contemporary imperial ideology – we have already seen this exemplified in the frontispiece sequence – and that in turn presumably had an impact on the selection of scenes for f. 440r. But it is worth noting that the imperial programme remains implicit rather than blatant. Constantine appears bearded,[99] and both he and Helena wear imperial costume; but Constantine has not assumed Basil's features as we know them from the scant remains of the frontispiece portrait, the Palazzo Venezia casket (fig. 84), or coins (fig. 87); nor does Helena here wear clothes identical to Eudokia's, though she does in her portrait on f. 285r (fig. 29). The association of contemporary with past rulers had not yet reached the stage observable in the tenth century, when both Constantine the Great and King Abgaros of Edessa apparently acquired the facial type of Basil's grandson, Constantine VII Porphyrogennetos.[100] The imperial associations of the episodes pictured on f. 440r are nonetheless clearly expressed in the Homilies miniature, as they were also at about the same time brought out in the typikon of Hagia Sophia in the prayers for the feast of Constantine and Helena on 21 May: 'Having seen in the sky the image of your cross and having received, like Paul, a call not human, your apostle among emperors, Lord, placed the imperial city in your hands; guard it always in peace, by the prayers of the Theotokos, and have pity on us.'[101]

If Constantine placed the imperial city in the Lord's hands, and God guarded it always in peace, the opening miniatures of Paris.gr.510 ask us also to believe that God nominated Basil, and his heirs, as worthy successors to Constantine.

[98] See note 93 above.
[99] Cormack and Hawkins (1977), 240–241, argued that the bearded portraits stress Constantine's imperial role.
[100] See Weitzmann (1972), 58–60; Weitzmann (1960), 163–184; Weitzmann (1976), 96.
[101] Mateos I (1963), 296–297. On the typikon, see chapter 2 note 101.

Fig. 87 Nomisma, reverse (Dumbarton Oaks AV 1) of 868(?): Basil I

Basil, Constantine, and the idea of dynasty

The Constantinian motifs are part of a larger fabric: the idea of dynastic continuity. The emphasis on imperial portraiture is in this respect noteworthy, and was not restricted to Paris.gr.510: the inclusion of a standing portrait of Basil, for example, parallels the reintroduction, after a two-hundred-year hiatus, of a standing figure of the emperor on coinage (fig. 87).[102] At the same time, imagery produced for Basil consistently reiterated the themes of family (and familial saints such as Elijah) and victory; the juxtaposition of crosses with family portraits in Paris.gr.510 and the Kainourgion seems designed to convey the same message: triumph, the Constantinian heritage, and the new Macedonian house were meant to be irrevocably linked in the eyes and mind of the late ninth-century viewer.

The Kainourgion mosaic and the frontispiece sequence in Paris.gr.510 accentuated, and attempted to legitimize, the dynastic aspirations of Basil I, but Basil did not invent the idea of dynastic continuity,[103] nor was he the first emperor to give it visual expression. Rather, he continued the conscious (and temporarily successful) efforts of iconoclast emperors to sustain stable hereditary dynasties, efforts that were also reinforced by the use of imagery.[104] A clear example of this is provided by coinage. Before the eighth century, emperors had sometimes shared the obverse with a portrait of their heir-apparent. In 720, however, Leo III (717–741) issued a new type of gold solidus with his own portrait on the obverse and a portrait on the reverse of his young son (crowned before he turned two), replacing the cross of his earlier coinage; the practice of depicting the junior emperor on the reverse of coins, which increased the visual autonomy and authority of the image, was followed by

[102] Grierson III,2 (1973), 476–477.

[103] But see Schreiner (1991), 183–184, 186–187, who believes that the idea of a dynasty with roots in the distant past was developed by Photios and Leo VI for Basil.

[104] See Herrin (1977), 15–20; Grabar (1957), 125–126. On the use of numismatic types to promote dynastic succession by the iconoclast emperors and Basil I, see also Bellinger (1956), 75, 79; and, on the use of names by the same emperors to achieve the same ends, Patlagean (1984), 27–28.

subsequent iconoclast emperors.[105] While the miniaturists responsible for the frontispiece portraits may have translated a long-standing numismatic conceit into tempera, the dynastic preoccupations of former emperors at least suggest that painted official imperial portraits may have anticipated Paris.gr.510 more directly.

Iconophile texts refer to iconoclast imperial imagery but without great specificity: for example, the pro-image Council of 787 made a list of imperial scenes allowed by the iconoclasts (portraits as such are not mentioned) but failed to mention whether (or where) such scenes actually existed;[106] Nikephoros accused the iconoclast Emperor Constantine V of being a new Nebuchadnezzar because he replaced images of Christ with imperial portraits, but Nikephoros seems to be speaking of coins.[107] Imperial donor portraits in mosaic were, however, certainly produced during the restoration of images under Eirene (780–802), as we know from a tenth-century description of the Church of the Virgin of the Source,[108] and other types of secular portraiture also continued during Iconoclasm: the *vita* of the iconoclast Philaretos, for example, refers to a (non-imperial) bridal portrait.[109] The perpetuation of other earlier imperial portrait types is suggested by a passage from the *Vita Basilii* that describes a pictorial sequence in the Kainourgion that portrayed Basil's exploits: 'in the ceiling above are depicted the Herculean labours of the emperor: his efforts on behalf of his subjects, his exertions in warlike struggles, and the victories granted to him by God',[110] a heroic narrative that seems to follow precedents such as the scenes of the Emperor Maurice's deeds painted in the Karianos portico at Blachernae in 587.[111] In any event, portraiture was not extinguished during Iconoclasm; just as the dynastic emphasis of the frontispiece portraits relied on a concept that was far from new, it may be that the dynastic portrait as a genre continued iconoclast patterns as well.

The overt Constantinian references in the miniatures of Paris.gr.510 bathe Basil in the golden glow of Constantine's legacy. These comparisons begin with the first miniature of the manuscript: the image of Christ on f. Av reinforces the ancient and continuing Constantinian values of the imperial capital and implicitly associates these values with Basil I. Further implications are worked out in the succeeding frontispiece sequence, where visual juxtaposition demonstrates that Christ blessed not only Constantinople, but also, on the following pages, Basil and his dynastic successors. The crosses that encase the portraits reinforce the Constantinian

---

[105] Herrin (1977), 18–19; Grierson III,1 (1973), 227, and see also 8–9 on the iconoclast practice of commemorating deceased family members, a mode of dynastic emphasis that was continued under Basil I (see Introduction).   [106] Texts and commentary in Grabar (1957), 143, 150, 160–161.

[107] See Grabar (1957), 143, 150–151. On Nikephoros, see chapter 1 note 50.

[108] The relevant passages from which are translated in Mango (1972), 156–157.

[109] I. Ševčenko (1977), 126; the evidence for other portrait sequences is summarized in Ruggieri (1991), 164–166, with bibliography.   [110] *Vita Basilii* 89: ed. Bekker (1838), 332; see note 47 above.

[111] Reported by Theophanes Continuatus: ed. Bekker (1838), 261; trans. Mango (1972), 128.

message, and stress the triumph of those who rule through Christ, points hammered home in the first portrait through the presentations of Gabriel and Elijah.

Paris.gr.510 is not the only place we can see the reworking of the Constantinian concept to legitimize Basil and his new dynasty. Basil's first son, born long before Michael III's death, was called Constantine. This is usually taken to indicate that he had been so named before Basil's elevation to the throne; it seems at least plausible, however, that Basil, like the Emperor Leo V before him, renamed his son Constantine on his coronation as co-emperor.[112] The eponymous bond between Basil's son and the earlier great emperor was, in any event, emphasized, and the young man was referred to as the 'new Constantine';[113] after his death in 879, Basil had him buried in the mausoleum of Constantine the Great, where no imperial burials had taken place since the death of Anastasius in 518.[114] Basil restored the adjacent Church of the Holy Apostles, also connected with Constantine, as well as the Church of St Mokios;[115] in his stage triumphs, he entered the city behind Constantine's gold cross (as his image does in Paris.gr.510).[116] His efforts were rewarded and recognized in his own lifetime by the pope, who duly addressed Basil as 'the new Constantine',[117] and later by his biographer who as we have seen fabricated a genealogy that purported to show Basil's direct lineage from Constantine and Alexander.

The visual links between Basil and Constantine the Great are surprising only in their extent and in their emphasis on the foundation of Constantinople. In addition to promoting the legitimacy of the upstart Emperor Basil I, the number of allusions to Basil as Constantine's true and legitimate successor demonstrates that the symbolic importance of Constantine as an ideal imperial model, nurtured throughout the eighth century,[118] had by now been fully absorbed within Byzantine imperial ideology. In some ways, both the affiliation of Basil and Constantine and the emphasis on dynasty visualized in the miniatures that we have just considered represent the culmination of processes initiated at least a century and a half earlier.

---

[112] See Patlagean (1984), 23–43, discussion of Leo V at 27–28. Patlagean does not refer to Basil; my hypothesis is based entirely on Basil's evident desire to identify with Constantine I.

[113] Κωνσταντίνῳ τῷ νέῳ is commemorated in the synaxarion and appears in texts associated with his grandfather: see Karlin-Hayter (1966), 624–626; Haldon (1990), 140 (the epithet is omitted from the translation on 141) and 270 for bibliography.

[114] Grierson (1962), 27–28. So too Magdalino (1987), 58.

[115] See note 20 above; on the Apostoleion, chapter 1 note 78. For references to the churches dedicated to Constantine built or restored by Basil, Magdalino (1987), note 43.

[116] See McCormick (1986), 155–157; Haldon (1990), 124–125, 245, who noted that by the tenth century Constantine's cross was kept in the Daphne palace, presumably because of its imperial associations (on which see further Thümmel [1992], 121–123).

[117] For Pope Stephen's reference, Mansi XVI, 425A and Kazhdan (1987), 246; cf. PL 129:170.

[118] See esp. Kazhdan (1987).

BASIL'S OLD TESTAMENT ANTITYPES

Basil and Joseph
Folio 69v (12) (fig. 12)

Folio 69v presents a detailed history of the Old Testament figure Joseph,[119] the peculiarities of which are evident from the scenes incorporated. The first four registers include ten scenes, all drawn from Genesis 37. In the first register Jacob, accompanied by his youngest child Benjamin, sends Joseph to his brothers (vv. 13–14);[120] Joseph (ΙΩCHΦ) journeys in search of his brothers (vv. 17–18); and Joseph's brothers, at table, see him coming and plot his humiliation (vv. 18–20).[121] In the second, Joseph's brothers lower him into a cistern (v. 24);[122] bloody his cloak (XITΩN ΙΩCHΦ) with kid's blood (v. 31); and, in a scene inscribed 'the sorrow of Jacob' (ΙΑΚΩΒ ΠΕΝΘΩΝ), show their father the bloody garment (vv. 32–33). In the third register, Joseph's brothers remove him from the cistern (v. 28);[123] then, again at table, they plot to sell Joseph to passing merchants identified as 'Ishmaelites' (v. 25).[124] In the fourth, we find 'the sale of Joseph',[125] and 'Joseph led to Egypt' by the merchants (both v. 28).[126] While the top four registers illustrate a mere fifteen verses (Genesis 37:13–28) with ten scenes, the fifth and final register presents a more compressed sequence: 'Potiphar buys Joseph' (Genesis 37:35 and 39:1);[127] Joseph flees Potiphar's wife (Genesis 39:12);[128] Pharaoh invests Joseph (Genesis 41:41–42);[129] and Joseph (ΙΩCHΦ) appears in triumph, standing in a chariot (Genesis 41:43).

The history of Joseph was translated into images often in Byzantium, but f. 69v omits many of the most familiar episodes – neither Joseph's ability to interpret dreams nor his reunion with his father and brothers, for example, are included – to focus on one particular aspect of Joseph's life: the obstacles he was made to overcome in order to emerge triumphant, finally, in the last two scenes. Folio 69v con-

---

[119] Omont (1929), 16–17, pl. XXVI; Der Nersessian (1962), 214–215; U. Nilgen, s.v. 'Joseph von Ägypten', in *LCI* 2 (1970), 427; Vileisis (1979), 58–85; Matthews (1980), 45; Riddle (1981), 75–76; Friedman (1989), 66; Gauthier-Walter (1990), 27, 32–33.

[120] The legend reads ΙΑΚΩΒ ΑΠΟCΤΕΛΛΩΝ ΤΟΝ ΙΩCHΦ ΠΡΟC ΤΟΥC ΑΔΕΛΦΟΥC ΑΥΤΟΥ ('Jacob sends Joseph to his brothers').

[121] Inscribed 'the brothers of Joseph eating and planning evil against him' (ΟΙ ΑΔΕΛΦΟΙ ΙΩCHΦ ΕCΘΙΟΝΤΑΙC ΚΑΙ ΒΟΥΛΕΥΟΜΕΝΟΙ ΚΑΚΑ ΠΕΡΙ ΑΥΤΟΥ).

[122] Inscribed 'Joseph let down into the cistern' (ΙΩCHΦ ΧΑΛΩΜΕΝΟC ΕΝ ΤΩ ΛΑΚΚΩ).

[123] Inscribed 'Joseph dragged from the cistern' (ΙΩCHΦ ΕΚ ΤΟΥ ΛΑΚΚΟΥ ΕΛΚΟΜΕΝ[ΟC]).

[124] Inscribed 'Joseph's brothers eating' (ΑΔΕΛΦΟΙ ΙΩCHΦ ΕCΘΙΟΝΤΑΙC) and ΙCΜΑΗΛΙΤΑΙ.

[125] ΙΩCHΦ ΠΡΑCΚΟΜΕΝΟC.

[126] ΙΩCHΦ ΑΓΟΜΕΝΟC ΕΙC ΑΙΓΥΠΤΟΝ.

[127] Π[ΕΤΕΦΡΗC] ΑΓΟΡΑΖΩΝ ΙΩCHΦ.

[128] Inscribed 'Joseph's mistress constrains him by force' (ΙΩCHΦ ΑΝΑΓΚΑΖΩΜΕΝΟC ΥΠΟ ΤΗC ΚΥΡΙΑC ΕΓΡΑΤΩC).　　[129] Inscribed ΙΩCHΦ and ΦΑΡΑΩ.

centrates on Joseph's betrayal by his brothers and his forced exile, with a brief aside on the treachery of Potiphar's wife.

The miniature prefaces Gregory's tenth homily, 'To himself, his father, and Basil the Great after his flight and return',[130] and is certainly in its correct location, for the quire is undisturbed and the text of the preceding sermon ends on its recto. The connection between the history of Joseph and Gregory's tenth homily has, however, raised problems. Der Nersessian found no link between text and image, and on this most subsequent commentators concur – though it has been suggested that the Joseph cycle might be read as supplying an Old Testament antitype to Gregory as the ideal bishop.[131] If so, the selection of scenes is curious and the juxtapostion of image and text strained: though the homily is autobiographical in the broad sense that Gregory speaks of his own situation and his feelings, it does not concern Gregory's attitude toward the priesthood or toward being a bishop. While reexamination of the sermon suggests that the miniature illustrates it by analogy, Der Nersessian's scruples are understandable, for the picture apparently comments as much on the relationship between Joseph and Basil I as on Gregory's homily.

Gregory delivered the sermon in 372 to set forth his reasons for accepting the bishopric of Sasima, chief among them his affection for Basil of Caesarea.[132] Much of the oration concerns definitions of friendship, and the responsibilities entailed by brotherly love.[133] Gregory describes the perils of such relationships in the second paragraph where, for the sake of elegant rhetoric, he condemns friendship, only to condone it in the antithetical third section: 'I said: No more shall I believe in friendship, and why should I place my expectations in men? For every man proceeds deceitfully, and every brother brings down others . . . Now I have changed my position.'[134] Although this passage is not signalled in the text, the sentiments of the paragraph parallel the Joseph sequence presented on f. 69v, which provides a classic example of brotherly deceit and yet in the end corroborates Gregory's conclusion that the advantages of friendship exceed its perils.

The imperial connotations of the final two scenes, however, seem designed to do more than provide a fitting finale to the commentary on Gregory's sermon established by the preceding scenes. The next to last image shows the enthroned Pharaoh leaning forward to fasten the purple robe of Byzantine emperors over Joseph's shoulders, in accord – as Der Nersessian observed – with Byzantine descriptions of

---

[130] SC 405, 316–327; Gallay (1943), 109. In the Milan Gregory, this text is introduced with a group portrait of Gregory, his father, and Basil: Grabar (1943a), pl. XIII,1

[131] Nilgen (as in note 119 above).

[132] In his funeral oration for Basil, Gregory called him 'a second Joseph' and drew out the parallel at some length: PG 36:545 (paragraph 36). Though the episodes from Joseph's life that Gregory adduced in the funeral oration are not those pictured on f. 69v, it may be that the comparison helped suggest that a Joseph cycle was appropriate here.   [133] On this theme, see further Mullett (1988).

[134] SC 409, 320 ll.13–16, 322 ll.4–5.

Fig. 88 Paris.gr.923, f. 12r: Joseph and Pharaoh

imperial promotions.[135] This detail, which grounds the image in Byzantine imperial ceremony, appears in no other Byzantine versions of the scene,[136] though the *Sacra Parallela* represents the scene as the coronation of a co-emperor (fig. 88).[137] While demonstrating that parallels between Joseph and contemporary rulers were current in ninth-century Constantinople, the differences between the *Sacra Parallela* and Paris.gr.510 suggest that the means of visualizing the concept remained *ad hoc*; the designer of f. 69v chose to interpret the 'fine linen robe' of the Genesis account as the Byzantine imperial purple.

The final scene is usually omitted from Byzantine Joseph cycles; the only sub-

[135] Especially the promotion of a caesar: Constantine Porphyrogennetos, *De Ceremoniis* I,43 (52); ed. Vogt 2 (1967a), 28.

[136] E.g. the Vienna Genesis shows Pharaoh gesturing toward Joseph (Vienna, Nationalbib. cod. theol.gr.31, f. 18r: Gerstinger [1931], pict. 36); the Constantinopolitan Octateuchs (e.g. the twelfth-century Smyrna, Evangelical School A.1: Hesseling [1909], fig. 130) and western relatives of the Cotton Genesis (see Weitzmann and Kessler [1986], 113) portray Pharaoh giving Joseph a ring.

[137] Paris.gr.923, f. 12r: Weitzmann (1979a), 46–47, fig. 46. For a similar image at Sopoćani, see Ljubinković (1965), 222–226 and, on Byzantine coronations, Walter (1975), 455.

stantial exceptions are the middle Byzantine Octateuchs, where the miniaturists stuck to the biblical account and portrayed Joseph, in imperial regalia, alone in a simple biga seen from the side.[138] The composition on f. 69v is, however, more closely related to Byzantine imperial portraits than to narrative Genesis illustrations. After the preceding scene, it is to be expected that Joseph should wear Byzantine imperial regalia, but here he also holds the orb and, apparently uniquely, Constantine's labarum:[139] the portrait is closely allied with that of Basil on f. Cv.[140] To reinforce Joseph's parallels with Byzantine emperors, he stands alone and frontal in a quadriga, a motif well known from imperial *solidi*.[141] Joseph is flanked by bodyguards, and a pair of small figures kneels before him: these elements, too, were borrowed from Byzantine imperial portraits.[142] Within the realm of Joseph iconography, the closest comparison with the scene – and it is not especially similar – is provided by the apotheosis of Joseph included in another anomalous sequence, that on a twelfth- or thirteenth-century ivory casket now at Sens (fig. 89), a work which, perhaps significantly, has been linked with imperial patronage.[143]

While a few other cycles or isolated images of Joseph connect him with the Byzantine emperor, in no case is the imperial accent so stressed as in Paris.gr.510. The question is whether the imperial details were incorporated only to salute the imperial status of the manuscript's recipient, or whether we are meant, by extension, to view the entire sequence on f. 69v as an analogy of Basil's life. While no text known to me draws an extensive series of parallels between the lives of Joseph and Basil,[144] several factors nonetheless favour such a connection.

Joseph was viewed as an ideal ruler by Philo, and as a model administrator by numerous early Latin fathers.[145] As both Der Nersessian and Margaret Riddle observed,[146] these associations were never as current in Greek literature as the pairing of Joseph and Christ. This lack of emphasis is not necessarily crucial, for Joseph's abilities as a ruler are clearly expressed in Genesis. We can never, anyway,

---

[138] E.g. the now-destroyed Smyrna Octateuch (f. 53v): Hesseling (1909), fig.130. The scene does not appear in the Vienna Genesis; for its rare illustration in members of the Cotton Genesis family, see Weitzmann and Kessler (1986), 113.   [139] So too Gauthier-Walter (1990), 33.

[140] On f. Cv (fig. 5) Elijah hands Basil the labarum draped with red cloth; it is gold on f. 69v.

[141] See Stern (1953), 156–157; Ross (1957), 254–256. The formula may ultimately derive from Sol-Invictus imagery, on which see L'Orange (1935). It was also a common way to represent triumphant charioteers, and may have been most familiar to many Constantinopolitans from its appearance on the bases of statues set up around the hippodrome: see Vasiliev (1948); Al. Cameron (1973).

[142] See Grabar (1936), 54–57, 85–88, 147–149.

[143] Goldschmidt and Weitzmann I (1930), no. 124y. Vikan (1976), 301, reinterpreted the Sens relief as Joseph's 'coronation', a problem to which we shall return in chapter 8. I thank John Hanson for fruitful conversations about the casket; on which see also *Byzance* (1992), 264–265.

[144] As the tenth homily was dedicated in part to Basil the Great, one might however speculate about a play on names between St Basil and Basil I.

[145] Philo, *De Josepho*: ed. F. H. Colson, *Philo* 6, Loeb Classical Library (Cambridge, 1935), esp. 157, 271. See also Schapiro (1952) and Fabre (1921/2).   [146] See note 119 above.

Fig. 89 Sens, Cathedral Treasury: ivory casket, apotheosis of Joseph

rely exclusively on surviving texts to tell us the full story of typological awareness: the visual association of Joseph with Byzantine rulers is clearly expressed in both the Homilies and the *Sacra Parallela* (fig. 88) and the concept of Joseph as ideal ruler was familiar to at least some later viewers as well. The thirteenth-century Joseph sequence at Sopoćani has, for example, been interpreted as a parallel to Stephen Nemanja's life, and the ivory casket at Sens – probably Italian but demonstrating strong Byzantine connections – pairs images of Joseph and David, the

Byzantine ideal of a ruler *par excellence*.[147] In ninth-century Constantinople there were also texts available that made the case: Philo's *De Josepho*, the major commentary to enumerate Joseph's qualifications as ideal ruler, is one of two treatises listed as codex 103 in Photios' *Bibliotheke*.[148]

If, however, the connection between emperor and Old Testament patriarch was meant to be confined to parallel examples of great rulers, it seems odd that episodes detailing Joseph's abilities were not stressed on f. 69v. Admittedly, the scenes of Joseph's betrayal by his brothers were necessary to illustrate (by analogy) Gregory's homily, but this aim could have been achieved with far greater brevity: Paris.gr.510 preserves the most extensive betrayal sequence in Byzantine art. The miniaturist seems to have dwelt intentionally on Joseph's personal travails before he attained power; the page recalls a sentiment encapsulated in Romanos' sixth-century hymn 'On Joseph': 'What sort of boast is there for the man who struggles hard, if not to win a crown by complete victory?'[149]

Whatever the truth of his background, Basil's status as a foreigner who was pre-destined to rule Byzantium, and overcame long odds to do so, is the underlying theme of the surviving texts that narrate his life.[150] As shown on f. 69v, Joseph also laboured hard against seemingly insurmountable odds for the imperial title in a distant land; his life was well suited to provide a parallel for Basil's as good as – or even better than – the more usual ideal rulers of Byzantine art and literature, David and Solomon, with whom Basil was also equated.[151] The Joseph scenes in the Paris Gregory can be understood as representing a general theme of ideal ruler; but, beyond this, the scenes seem to have been selected to personalize the miniature, and to imply a specific link between Basil and Joseph. The visual allusions worked out on f. 69v parallel the dominant theme of the written accounts of Basil's life by portraying Joseph, like Basil, as a foreigner who rose from agrarian stock to be made co-ruler after considerable personal struggle.[152] Joseph, unlike Basil I, never ruled alone; yet he is shown without his co-ruler on f. 69v, where Pharaoh serves an essentially menial function: I suspect that this is because Basil murdered his 'Pharaoh' – and Joseph's 'Michael III' is accordingly downplayed.[153] But whether or not I am correct on this particular detail, f. 69v provides an image that functioned as a com-

---

[147] Ljubinković (1965); *Byzance* (1992), 264–265.

[148] Ed. Henry II (1960), 71; on the *Bibliotheke*, see chapter 5. For the identification of the text, see Treadgold (1980), 135. [149] Strophe 27: SC 99, 231. On Romanos, see chapter 2 note 104.

[150] See Tobias (1969), 1–156; Adontz (1933a); Adontz (1934).

[151] On comparisons of Basil with David and Solomon see Photios in *PG* 102:582–584, the discussion of f. 174v later in this chapter, and of f. 215v in chapter 6; as we have just seen, Basil was also compared to Constantine.

[152] Riddle (1981), 75–76, observed that prophecies anticipated the rise of both Joseph and Basil I, but this connection is not made on f. 69v, where none of Joseph's dreams or apocryphal prophecies forecasting his elevation appears.

[153] It should be noted, though, that Joseph appears alone in a few later versions of this scene.

mentary on the tenth homily and a panegyric to the recipient of the volume, whose struggles, like Joseph's on f. 69v, were ultimately rewarded with the imperial diadem.[154]

Basil and Samson

Folio 347v (35) (fig. 35)

Folio 347v contains five scenes from the life of Samson in the top and middle registers; Gideon praying joins the martyrdom of Isaiah in the bottom tier.[155] The Samson sequence begins with the slaying of the thousand Philistines (Judges 15:15–16): Samson (CAMΨΩN) – a nimbless, beardless youth with long dark hair – wears a short blue tunic enlivened with a gold band under a red sash, which flutters behind him as he raises high the jawbone in his left hand while grasping the hair of a fallen Philistine he is about to despatch. Another Philistine has already fallen in the foreground, and a group flees toward the right.[156] Although the fleeing Philistines overlap it a bit, a tall and rocky mountain visually contains the action to the left side of the register. On the other side of the mountain, Samson recurs, framed by a second outcrop on the far right. Here he stands calmly, drinking the water that God caused to flow from the jawbone as a sign of divine favour; in response, he raises his right hand toward heaven (Judges 15:18–19). The legend reads 'Samson drinks from the jawbone' (CAMΨΩN ΠINON EK THC CIAΓONOC).

The second register opens with Delilah cutting Samson's hair (Judges 16:19). Delilah, her uncovered head indicating her status as a woman outside the norms of female decorum usually observed by the miniaturists, sits on a green slope in front of an extensive house, presumably to indicate that the action took place indoors. Her face has been almost totally abraded, perhaps a victim of intentional damage. Delilah wears a deep blue dress decorated in gold on which Samson reclines in sleep as she – and not the man described in the Septuagint text – trims his hair with a large pair of scissors, as described by the inscription 'Delilah shears Samson's head' (ΔAΛIΛAC ΞYPIZOYCA TON CAMΨΩN). Samson, now with very short hair indeed and with his arms bound behind him, reappears in the centre of the register,

---

[154] On the iconography of f. 69v, see chapter 8. Gauthier-Walter's article (1990) appeared after I had drafted this chapter; we are in substantial agreement about the interpretation of f. 69v.

[155] Omont (1929), 27–28, pl. XLIX; Weitzmann (1947), 197; Der Nersessian (1962), 218, 222; Weitzmann (1979a), 67–72; Jolivet-Levy (1987), 467. On the problems connected with the original location of this miniature, and the thematic coherence of the scenes it portrays, see chapter 2; on the iconography of the Isaiah scene, see chapter 6; and on Gideon, see chapter 8.

[156] All are covered by the blanket description 'foreigners' (AΛΛOΦYΛOI), the same term used to identify Constantine's foes on f. 440r (see note 79 above) and Samson's other enemies pictured on this page (see note 157 below)

walking toward the right. Behind him, Delilah, here with a brown mantle covering her hair and falling over her blue dress, lays a hand on his shoulder. A Philistine accompanies her, and four more confront Samson on the right. One of them raises his hand in a gesture of speech; another gouges out Samson's eyes with a large pin (Judges 16:21).[157] The final scene emblematically illustrates Judges 16:26–30. Samson, now without his red sash but with newly grown long hair, stands frontally between two pillars, resting a hand on each. The pillars support an arch, on which rests the house full of Philistines, portrayed as a diminutive conglomeration of buildings. As indicated by the inscription accompanying the scene – 'Samson brings down the house' (Ο CAMΨΩN ΡΙΠΤΩN THN OIKIAN) – but not shown in the miniature, the Lord granted his suicidal wish to destroy the Philistines by pulling out the foundations of the building under which he stood, 'and the dead whom Samson slew in his death were more than those whom he slew in his life' (v. 30).

The five scenes from Samson's life included on f. 347v were included in other, more extensive, Byzantine narrative cycles, notably those on a fifth- or sixth-century mosaic floor in Mopsuestia and in three of the middle Byzantine Octateuchs;[158] four also appear in the *Sacra Parallela* (figs. 90–91), though not as part of a single sequence.[159] The thirteenth-century Octateuch (Mount Athos, Vatopedi 602) is a copy of the twelfth-century Vat.gr.746;[160] otherwise the sequences seem to be largely independent of each other.[161] Not surprisingly, the Samson scenes on f. 347v find only loose affiliations within this group, and then with the ninth-century images in the *Sacra Parallela*.

The *Sacra Parallela* (fig. 90) provides a parallel to the first scene on f. 347v: Samson is nimbless, wears boots and a short tunic with a sash that blows behind

---

[157] Inscribed, on the gold frame, 'the foreigners blind Samson' (OI ΑΛΛΟΦΥΛΟΙ ΤΥΦΛΟΝΟΝ-ΤΕC ΤΟ[Ν] CAMΨΩN); see note 156 above.

[158] For Mopsuestia, Kitzinger (1973), with earlier bibliography. The Samson sequences in the two earlier Octateuch manuscripts – Vat.gr.747, ff. 247v–251r (eleventh century) and Vat.gr.746, ff. 488v–495v (twelfth century) – have never been fully published though a few images appeared in Lowden (1992), figs. 72–78; for the thirteenth-century copy (Mount Athos, Vatopedi 602, ff. 435v–445r), see Huber (1973), figs. 144–159; Christou *et al.* (1991), figs. 169–182. The remaining Octateuchs (Smyrna, Evangelical School A.1 and Istanbul, Topkapı Sarayı Müzesi, gr.8) never included the Samson sequence.

[159] Paris.gr.923, ff. 108v, 161v, 246v: Weitzmann (1979a), 68–70, figs. 96, 99–100, 102. Three Samson scenes (none relevant to this discussion) also appear in the Via Latina catacomb (ca. 350): Ferrua (1960), pls. XXX,1, CV, CIX.   [160] Lowden (1982); the arguments are repeated in Lowden (1992).

[161] The Mopsuestia mosaic is in such a fragmentary condition that iconographical comparison is impossible, but following Kitzinger's identification of the scenes it is evident that the mosaic and later manuscripts are not related; neither are the Octateuch sequences connected with the Samson scenes in the *Sacra Parallela* (Weitzmann [1979a], 67–70). Nor is Vat.gr.747 related to the later Octateuchs: it contains six scenes omitted from Vatopedi 602 and Vat.gr.746 and lacks fourteen episodes pictured in these manuscripts, while the fifteen scenes shared by all three Octateuchs preserve only the most general similarities.

Fig. 90 Paris.gr.923, f. 246v: Samson and the foxes; Samson slays the Philistines

him, grasps the kneeling Philistine with his left hand and raises the jawbone in his right in both pictures.[162] The two miniatures are, however, far from identical. Throughout the *Sacra Parallela*, Samson wears a beard, and here he looks up at the jawbone rather than down at the Philistine; also unlike Paris.gr.510, dead Philistines litter the ground behind Samson in the *Sacra Parallela*, and none flees the scene of carnage.

The next three scenes on f. 347v find no close Byzantine parallels: only Paris.gr.510, for example, shows Samson standing as the Philistines blind him, and only Paris.gr.510 omits the Philistine included in the Septuagint account of the hair-cutting episode. In this, Paris.gr.510 echoes Josephus, who described Delilah cutting Samson's hair; and the omission of the Philistine may not have been quite so unusual as it now appears: it is repeated in at least one later manuscript, the Arsenal Bible, a mid-thirteenth-century book illuminated in the crusader states at Acre by a painter who may also have worked in Constantinople.[163] The final scene again resembles the *Sacra Parallela* (fig. 91), and also the eleventh-century Octateuch Vat.gr.747 (fig. 92), in showing Samson between columns that support the house of the Philistines. Both the *Sacra Parallela* and Vat.gr.747, however, show a slightly later moment of the episode, when Samson wraps his arms around the columns, and in the *Sacra Parallela* pieces of the building and corpses already surround Samson. The novel formulation of this scene on f. 347v has two results: by halting the action at the moment before Samson brings down the house of the Philistines, the illustrator both implicitly stresses Samson's prayer to God and allows Samson to continue as a living hero. The emphasis on Samson's prayer for strength ties the scene to its counterpart in the top register – Samson's earlier request for water, which God fulfilled by making water issue from the jawbone[164] – and both of these scenes, in turn, relate to Gideon's prayer in the third register, an affiliation corroborated by the physical similarities shared by Samson and Gideon. The decision to portray Samson as yet unthreatened by his imminent death may also have been conditioned by factors beyond the internal coherence of the sequence.

Though Samson's usual biblical antitype was Christ, we have already seen Gregory linking him with bishop Athanasios, whose praise this miniature may once have accompanied.[165] Samson was also compared with Herakles and Constantine,[166] and his physical strength and ultimate triumph over the Philistines made him a suitable candidate for certain imperial programmes of decoration as well: for example, Samson joins Achilles and Joshua (among others) in the decora-

---

[162] Weitzmann (1979a), fig. 96; see also the relief at Aght'amar: Der Nersessian and Vahramian (1974), 82–83 (no. D–2). Samson's stance anticipates that in Vat.gr.747, but there he does not grab the hair of a fallen Philistine.

[163] *Jewish Antiquities* V, 312–313 (ed. Loeb, 140–141); Buchthal (1957), pl. 68; Folda (1976), 23, 67.

[164] So too Buschausen (1980), 298. The Septuagint account implicitly links the episodes: in both 'Samson wept before the Lord'.   [165] SC 270, 172, 164; see chapter 2.

[166] See W. A. Bulst, s.v. 'Samson', in *LCI* 4 (1972), 31–32.

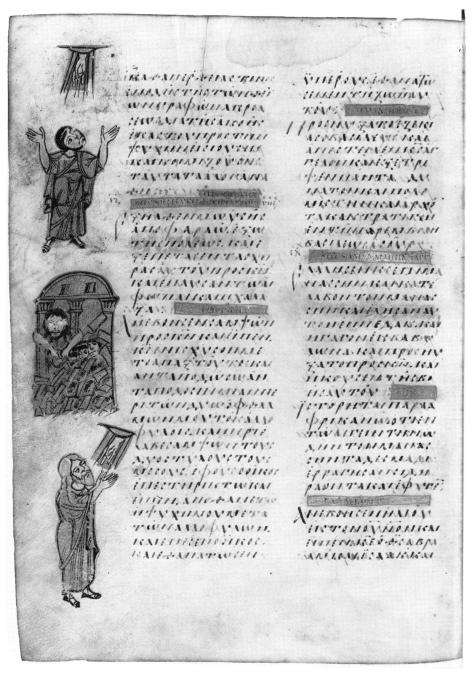

Fig. 91 Paris.gr.923, f. 161v: Moses praying; Samson destroys the house of the Philistines; Elijah praying

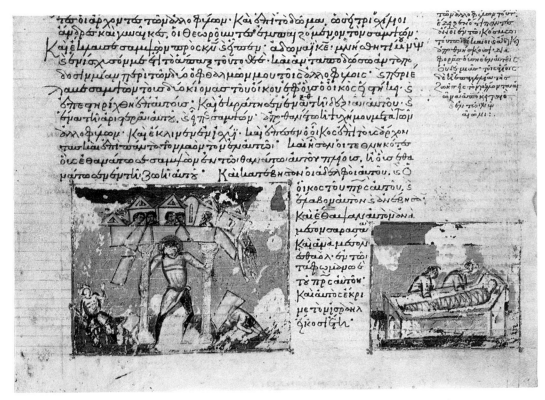

Fig. 92 Vat.gr.747, f. 251r: Samson destroys the house of the Philistines; burial of Samson

tion of the palace described in *Digenes Akrites*.[167] In the *Vita Basilii*, Samson is also connected with Basil: the author records Michael III's remark 'all he [Basil] has is valour, as did Samson of old'.[168] Basil's legendary physical strength may have suggested the comparison; it in turn suggests a consideration of the Samson scenes on f. 347v as potential metaphors of Basil's life.

The visual history of Samson has been carefully structured: it opens with a scene celebrating Samson's early feats of strength, followed by one demonstrating that he was favoured by God in his youth; next come the trials, by scissors and by nail, as Samson loses his hair and his sight; and, finally, in a scene which manages to imply Samson's victory without actually picturing his accompanying death, he triumphs. It is perhaps not too farfetched to see in this selection of scenes allusions to Basil's famed strength as a youth, the prophecies held to demonstrate that even then Basil was favoured by God, the setbacks he encountered on route to the throne, and his ultimate success.

[167] *Digenes Akrites* VII, ed. J. Mavrogordato (Oxford, 1956).
[168] *Vita Basilii* 15: ed. Bekker (1838), 234; see note 47 above.

Fig. 93   Rome, Palazzo Venezia: ivory casket, coronation of David; David and Goliath

Basil and David

David was one of the ideal-ruler types of the Old Testament most frequently associated with the reigning emperor in Byzantium, and Byzantine writers duly likened
Basil, also, to David.[169] How this equation was given visual form has been studied,
and attention has focused especially on an ivory box in the Palazzo Venezia in Rome
that depicts an imperial couple on its lid (fig. 84), surrounded by scenes from the
life of David (figs. 93, 95).[170] The emperor and empress are unfortunately not
named in the inscription on the box, but have been convincingly identified as Basil
and Eudokia.[171] Like the history of Joseph in Paris.gr.510, the scenes from the life of

[169] Moravcsik (1961), 69; also e.g. Tobias (1969), 22, 123. Most examples, e.g. *PG*102:581–584, come
from Photios who was also probably responsible for an anti-Paulician poem dedicated to Basil
wherein the comparisons with David are especially pronounced: see *ODB*1 (1991), 261; Markopoulos
(1992); and chapter 5.

[170] Cutler and Oikonomides (1988); Maguire (1988), 89–93; Kalavrezou (1989), 392–396.

[171] Guillou (1979); Maguire (1988), 89–92; and esp. Kalavrezou (1989), 392–396. Cutler and
Oikonomides (1988) argue for Leo VI; cf. Cutler (1994), 201.

David on the ivory box were apparently chosen to parallel events of Basil's life and to flatter the emperor by association. Maguire argued that a sanitized version of the conflict between Michael III and Basil I is metaphorically re-enacted by Saul and David; this pairing elevates Basil and, by using the analogy of Saul, implies that the murder of Michael III was just and inevitable.[172] On the ivory, David wears full imperial Byzantine regalia only in the scene of his coronation (fig. 93); he also holds the orb, and has suddenly acquired a beard. As Maguire observed, the addition of a beard was evidently meant to connect the coronation of David with the emperor on the lid of the casket;[173] in fact, the scene is very close to the painting of Gabriel bestowing the crown on Basil on f. Cv (fig. 5). I would suggest that the coronation of David on the Palazzo Venezia ivory (a scene apparently without precedents) provides another witness to the significance of coronation during the reign of Basil I,[174] and underscores the connections between David and the ruling emperor.

Within Paris.gr.510, on the other hand, the association between David and Basil remains muted. Only two scenes in the manuscript depict David, and while both of these seem to be linked with Basil, the opportunity to parallel visually the two lives in an extensive David sequence was – unless such a history appeared in one of the lost miniatures – not taken.

Folio 174v (23) (fig. 23)

The upper two registers on f. 174v illustrate episodes from the book of Genesis; the lowest is entirely occupied by the scene that concerns us here, the anointing of David.[175]

David's father, Jesse (IECCAI), in a pale blue tunic under a light brown mantle, stands in the centre. He turns to the right and urges the young David (ΔA[YI]Δ) forward toward Samuel (CAMOYHΛ), the only nimbed figure of the register. David wears a short blue and gold tunic over distinctive red leggings matched by the red sash flung around his upper body: this costume intentionally replicates that worn by Isaac and Jacob in the upper two registers.[176] Samuel, whose long and wavy grey hair provides a contrast with Jesse's short greying hair and neatly trimmed beard, wears a light tunic over his blue and gold chiton; with his right hand he holds the gold horn of anointing oil, point downward, above David's head.[177] Five of David's brothers, all in short tunics under sashes or short cloaks – in various combinations of blue, green, and red – and all named in

[172] Maguire (1988), 91–93; Kalavrezou (1989), 392–393, confirmed that the theme of David and Saul gained particular prominence during the reign of Basil I. For a possible western parallel, see Kessler (1992), esp. 662–664. Maguire (1995) also interpreted f. Cv in Paris.gr.510 as a visual exoneration of Basil: see note 60 above.

[173] Maguire (1988), 91; cf. Kalavrezou (1989), 396. Excellent reproductions of David's coronation and the blessing of Basil appear in Cutler and Oikonomides (1988), figs. 3, 7.   [174] See p. 158 above.

[175] On the page as a whole, see chapter 5; on the iconography of the Genesis scenes, chapters 7 and 8.

[176] See chapter 5.   [177] On the anointing horn see Stichel (1974), 169–170.

inscriptions,[178] stand behind their father Jesse. Their poses are varied, and the central brother, Nathanael, stands with his back to the viewer, his face turned in profile. On the other end of the register, part of a building is visible. The distinctive form of this structure, with only one column visible, resurfaces on f. 332v (fig. 33) and seems to form part of the standard architectural vocabulary of the Gregory miniaturists; the emphasis on the column, which sits on a plinth and appears separate from the rest of the building even as it seems to support the cornice, does not, however, recur.

Unlike the Genesis scenes above it, the anointing is not mentioned in the accompanying sermon; but, like the identically clad Isaac and Jacob of the upper registers, David was viewed as a type of Christ by Byzantine commentators, and Der Nersessian plausibly suggested that the designer of f. 174v selected the anointing of David as the culminating scene to provide yet another antitype of Christ: 'Instead of depicting Jacob anointing the pillar, which, as Gregory says, "significs the rock that was anointed for our sake," [the miniaturist] has painted the anointment of David, which has the same meaning.'[179] Even so, the decision to respond to Gregory's mention of Jacob anointing the pillar (a passage signalled with a painted initial), but with a different scene, suggests that the substitution furthered the point of the page in some way that the Jacob scene could not: Der Nersessian argued that David's anointing provided an example of imperial iconography inserted for the benefit of Basil I.

Although Christopher Walter found no clear visual connections between David's anointing and imperial unction before the eleventh century,[180] literary connections exist. David and the reigning emperor are affiliated in Byzantine texts from the middle of the fifth century,[181] and by the eighth the anointing is brought into the equation. The Barberini *Euchologion* (ca. 795) details a coronation ceremony in which, during the prayer over the chlamys, the patriarch says: 'O Lord our God, the King of kings and Lord of lords, which through Samuel the prophet didst choose David thy servant to be king over thy people in Israel, do thou now also hear the supplication of (name) . . . vouchsafe to anoint him with oil.'[182] As it happens, Basil is one of the emperors for whom the anointing of David seems to have had particular resonance.[183] Der Nersessian has already recognized the significance of the mosaic erected by Basil in the Kainourgion, in which, according to the *Vita Basilii*, Basil's sons held scrolls inscribed 'we are thankful to thee, o Word of God, for having raised our father from Davidic poverty and having anointed him with the unction of thy Holy Ghost'.[184] R. E. Brightman noted that one of the rare

---

[178] AMINAΔAB, CAMAA, NAΘANAHΛ, ACOM, and PAΔΔAI; the eldest, Eliab, is missing. See 1 Chronicles 2:13–15.   [179] Der Nersessian (1962), 203–204.   [180] Walter (1976b), esp. 61–62.   [181] See e.g. Dvornik (1966), 781, 784, 789, 797.   [182] Brightman (1901), 380.   [183] On this point, J. Nelson (1976), esp. 116–117.   [184] *Vita Basilii* 89: ed. Bekker (1838), 334–335; see note 47 above.

Byzantine references to anointing appears in a letter from Photios to 'the anointed and blessed king' Basil;[185] and Paul Magdalino has called attention to Basil's request to Photios for information on David's anointing, on the basis of which he argued that 'it was on [Basil's] initiative that the [Nea Ekklesia] acquired the horn from which Samuel had anointed David'.[186] The anointing of David resolves the typologies introduced by the upper two registers in a manner calculated to suit the emperor, and was evidently inserted in order to complement Basil's enthusiasm for the theme. This enthusiasm was not disinterested. Just as the coronation of Basil himself, on f. Cv, legitimized his claim to the throne, so too the anointing of Basil, like that of his precursor David, raised him from 'poverty' to divinely sanctioned rule.

The importance of the anointing in the latter part of the ninth century seems also to have affected the iconography of the scene. The modifications imposed did not, however, touch the core grouping of David and Samuel itself, which replicates a familiar compositional type found in the Milan Gregory (fig. 52) and the *Sacra Parallela* (fig. 94).[187] The *Sacra Parallela* even includes the brothers, crowded behind David, but the expansive composition found in Paris.gr.510 recurs only on the Palazzo Venezia ivory box (fig. 95) and in the later miniatures of the Paris Psalter (fig. 96) and the Leo Bible (fig. 97).[188] Though David bends slightly more toward Samuel in the psalter and bible miniatures, the anointing group is otherwise virtually identical in all three; further, Jesse shows the same physiognomic type, the brothers all wear short tunics, and, as Hugo Buchthal observed, the distinctive one-columned building on the far right of scene in Paris.gr.510 recurs in the left background of both later versions.[189] The condensed space of the psalter and bible compositions, which are even more closely related to each other than they are to Paris.gr.510, results in an overlapping cluster of brothers that nonetheless retains the figure seen from the rear with profile head of f. 174v. Notwithstanding differences such as the inclusion of an architectural backdrop, a sixth brother, and the personification of clemency (Praotes) in the later miniatures, the Paris Psalter, Leo Bible, and Paris Gregory reflect a single tradition later repeated in the eleventh-century Vatican Book of Kings.[190] The Palazzo Venezia

---

[185] '. . . χρῖσμα καὶ χειροθεσίαν βασιλείας', in epistle 98, l.3: ed. Laourdas and Westerink I (1983), 133; *PG* 102:765C. On Photios' use of the words *chrisma* and *cheirothesia*, see Vogt (1967b), 12 note 1.

[186] Magdalino (1987), 58, where he also observes that Photios often linked Basil and David.

[187] Milan, Amb.49/50 inf., p. 569 (Grabar [1943a], pl. XLIII,1); Paris.gr.923, f. 80r (Weitzmann [1979a], fig. 117).

[188] Cutler and Oikonomides (1988), fig. 2; Paris.gr.139, f. 3v; Vat.reg.gr.1, f. 263r: Buchthal (1938), 18–21, figs. 3, 27; Dufrenne and Canart (1988), 35–37.

[189] This, as we have seen, repeats a stock building type used by the Homilies miniaturist, and thereby provides further evidence of the unmediated links between Paris.gr.510 and the Paris Psalter and Leo Bible (see chapter 2 note 190).

[190] Vat.gr.333, f. 22v: Lassus (1973), 51–52, fig. 40 and colour plate.

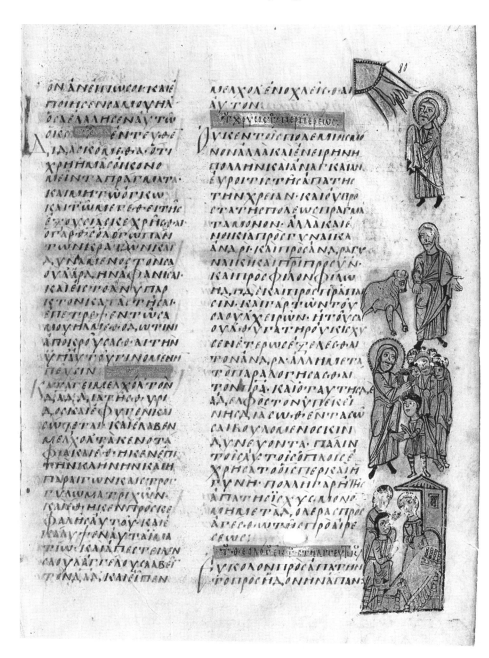

Fig. 94 Paris.gr.923, f. 80r: Samuel praying; Samuel with a heifer; anointing of David; Micah
deceives Saul's messengers

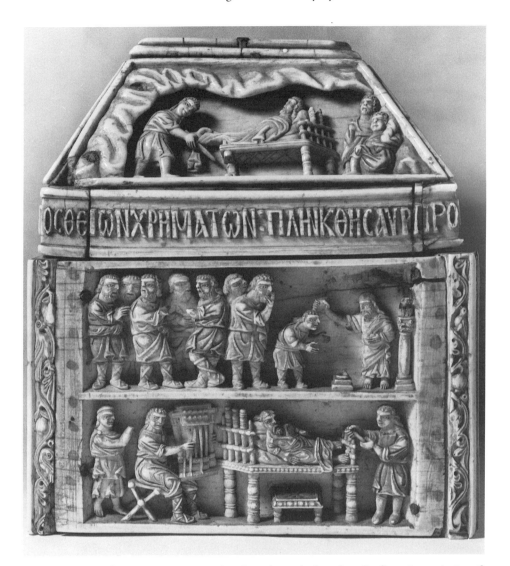

Fig. 95 Rome, Palazzo Venezia: ivory casket, David cuts the hem from Saul's tunic; anointing of David; David plays before Saul

ivory belongs with this group as well: despite some changes that may be in part attributed to the difference in medium, the ivory nonetheless shares with the miniatures a broad horizontal composition that allows, as in the Paris Psalter and the Leo Bible, all six brothers to be included; here too we find the same arrangement of David, Samuel, and the upturned horn of anointing.[191] Whatever the precise interconnections between these four versions of the anointing, they form a coher-

[191] The single column standing on the right was, however, apparently originally accompanied by a second one, the base of which is visible between David and Samuel; I thank John Hanson for this observation.

Fig. 96 Paris.gr.139, f. 3v: anointing of David

ent and distinctive group.[192] The formula that they share is not found in the mid-ninth-century marginal psalters;[193] the expansive composition may have been developed around the time of the Palazzo Venezia box and Paris.gr.510, inspired by Basil I's interest in the anointing.

[192] See the discussion of the Jonah cycles in the three manuscripts in chapter 2. As indicated in note 190 above, the later Vatican Book of Kings also belongs with this group.

[193] Moscow, cod.gr.129, ff. 79r, 89r (Ščepkina [1977]) and Mount Athos, Pantokrator 61, f. 125r (Dufrenne [1966], pl. 19) include only David and Samuel, who holds the horn upturned and gazes toward heaven.

Fig. 97 Vat.reg.gr.1, f. 263r: anointing of David

Folio 143v (19) (fig. 19)

On f. 143v, as we saw in chapter 2, the penitence of David and the adjacent scene of Jeremiah's release from the pit visualized the theme of forgiveness developed in the accompanying sermon; while Gregory did not mention the penitence specifically, he alluded to David's grief and release from sorrow by God's pardon in several passages that are signalled in the text. The inscriptions, unusually vivid for Paris.gr.510, spell out David's confession of sin and Nathan's assurance of God's forgiveness; and, while the penitence image itself has broad corollaries in Byzantium, the scene that it normally accompanies, Nathan's rebuking of David, has been omitted. The single-minded focus on God's pardon is extremely unusual,[194] and it is possible that the image was meant to imply, by extension, divine forgiveness for Basil's sins, notably the murder of Michael III.[195] If so, Nathan's role as intermediary – the prophet through whom God speaks – fell to Photios; as the *Eisagoge* demonstrates, the patriarch would have felt the part to be entirely appropriate.[196] The image may also respond to Basil's own formulation of David's penitence as the model for imperial humility, a point that the emperor developed in his address to the Council of 869.[197]

Basil and Joshua
Folio 226v (26) (fig. 26)

The upper register of f. 226v shows Moses striking water from a rock; the lower shows Joshua stopping the sun and moon, and Joshua confronted by the angel who is 'the captain of the host of the Lord' (Joshua 5:14).[198] The first of the Joshua scenes shows the nimbless hero striding toward the left before a green mountain that provides a compositional pendant to the pink peak from which Moses draws water in the top register.[199] Joshua's right arm is raised to grasp the top of his lance, and his left follows his gaze as he turns back toward the sun and the moon, both encompassed by an arc of heaven, represented as concentric bands of blue at the top of the scene. Joshua's cuirass is gold, as also are his leggings and the bottom of his helmet; its top, and the tunic under his armour, are blue; the fabric band protruding from beneath his shin guards is green. A red mantle, tied around his neck, blows out behind him and accentuates his turning movement. Two fallen Amorites lie beneath his feet; the rest of them flee on horseback toward the left. In his lack of a nimbus, the Gregory Joshua follows earlier precedents such as the mosaic at Sta Maria Maggiore and the Rabbula Gospels; these, however, omit the Amorites

---

[194] See chapter 8.   [195] As on the Palazzo Venezia casket: Maguire (1988) and note 172 above.
[196] See pp. 158–159 above.   [197] Mansi XVI, 94, 356; see Dagron (1984a), 311.
[198] Millet (1920), 242; Omont (1929), 24, pl. XL; Morey (1929), 95; Weitzmann (1947), 197; Der Nersessian (1962), 213–214; Brubaker (1996b), 103–104.
[199] Badly flaked; Omont could still decipher I[HCOY]C [O] Y[IO]C [N]AY[H].

entirely and lack the arc enclosing the sun and moon.[200] Most later examples, on the other hand, include the Amorites and the arc, but show Joshua nimbed.[201] No other version duplicates Joshua's stance.

In the second scene, Joshua, wearing the same costume and still nimbless, kneels and looks up at an angel who stands, blue sword in hand, on a small rocky outcrop that extends from the mountain of the first scene. The angel, like Joshua, wears military costume, with a gold cuirass and gold leggings; its undertunic and the material beneath its leggings are red, and its mantle purple. A red and blue shield, presumably Joshua's, lies in the foreground. While earlier versions of Joshua and the angel portray Joshua in civilian dress,[202] later Byzantine examples follow f. 226v in presenting him as a military figure but, unlike Paris.gr.510, picture Joshua twice, first standing (often before the city of Jericho), and then prostrate before the angel; also unlike f. 226v, in the later images Joshua usually looks at the ground rather than at the angel, and he is normally nimbed.[203] In part because it presents a scene condensed to fit a limited space, the version on the east wall at Çavuşin (fig. 98) from the third quarter of the tenth century recalls f. 226v most closely: though Joshua appears twice, he looks up, and Jericho does not appear. The Cappadocian scene has been linked with a victorious military campaign,[204] and this military flavour is anticipated on f. 226v.

The miniature illustrates Gregory's thirty-sixth sermon;[205] his autobiographical poem described the circumstances.[206] In November of 380 Gregory reclaimed the Church of the Holy Apostles from the Arians; under orders from the Emperor Theodosios, soldiers took possession of the church and guarded the procession of the orthodox, which proceeded under stormy skies while the displaced Arians, interpreting the weather as a sign of divine displeasure, rejoiced. At the moment Gregory arrived at the Holy Apostles, however, the sun broke through the clouds to great popular acclaim. The episode was immediately proclaimed a miracle, and the populace demanded that Gregory be made bishop of Constantinople. When the demands became tinged with violence, Gregory delivered the sermon. After reproving the crowd's behaviour Gregory wondered why the populace found him so exceptional: 'I have not smitten a new foundation for you, as Moses did on the journey out of Egypt.'[207] The sentence is marked by a decorated initial letter, and

---

[200] Karpp (1966), fig. 153; Florence, Laur.plut.1.56: Cecchelli *et al.* (1959); see also the Syriac Bible in Paris (BN syr.341): Jules Leroy (1964), pl. 44,1.

[201] E.g. the Octateuchs and the Joshua Roll: Weitzmann (1948), figs. 37, 42, 43.

[202] E.g. at Sta Maria Maggiore: Karpp (1966), fig. 133. The angel also carries a lance rather than a sword, on which see Künzle (1961/2), 162.

[203] For the Joshua Roll (sheet 4) and the Octateuchs, Weitzmann (1948), figs. 13–15; Mazal (1984), 48. For the Menologion of Basil II, Vat.gr.1613, f. 3r, *Menologio* (1907); Lazarev (1967), fig. 119.

[204] Rodley (1983), 322, fig. 5; see also Schapiro (1949) and Connor (1991), 64, fig. 94.

[205] SC 318, 240–269; Gallay (1943), 189–190. [206] *PG* 37:1120–1125 (vv. 1325–1391).

[207] SC 318, 242. The Milan Gregory does not, however, illustrate the episode, showing instead two preaching scenes and a portrait of the patriarch Alexander: Grabar (1943a), pls. LI,3, LIV,1 (the introductory preaching scene is not reproduced). On the iconography, see chapter 8.

Fig. 98 Çavuşin: east wall, Joshua and the angel; north apse, Nikephoros Phokas, Theophano, Caesar Bardas

Fig. 99 Vat.palat.gr.431, sheet 5: fall of Jericho

directly inspired the scene in the top register of f. 226v. Gregory, followed by ninth-century authors, understood this biblical episode as a type of Christ: Photios, for example, drew general parallels between Moses and Jesus, and equated the rock with Christ.[208] The christological typology continues in the second register: Byzantine exegesis cited Joshua as a type of Christ more frequently than any other person; he was, in addition, often contrasted with Moses as on f. 226v.[209] The image of Joshua stopping the sun and moon may also have been intended as a veiled reference to the miraculous appearance of the sun just before the sermon's delivery.

In the sermon, Gregory mentions the Gabaonites, who, though Gregory does not say so here, submitted to Joshua without a battle.[210] The two Joshua scenes selected for illustration in the second register were, however, probably chosen primarily to provide a visual interpretation of Gregory's long exhortation to emperors, a passage of sufficient importance (and familiarity) to be quoted in the *Sacra Parallela*:[211]

Emperors, respect your purple – for the word (*o logos*) lays out the laws even for legislators. You know what high mission has been conferred on you and what the grand mystery that concerns you is: the whole world is in your hand; an insignificant diadem and a piece of cloth control it. The things above are God's alone; those below are also yours. . . . 'The king's heart is in God's hand', as it says in the scripture and as you know. For your power comes from that, and not from gold or armies.[212]

[208] Photios is primarily interested in the crossing of the Red Sea, but also observes that 'the true rock is Christ'. *Amphilochia*, question 265: ed. Westerink VI,1 (1987), 56; *PG* 101:1088A–B; on the *Amphilochia* see chapter 5. For commentary, Daniélou (1960), 193–201.

[209] For commentary, Daniélou (1960), 229–243.   [210] SC 318, 256. See Joshua 9:1–27.

[211] *PG* 95:1289C-D; see Moreschini in SC 318, 264 commentary. Paris.gr.923 accompanied the passage with a medallion portrait of Gregory (f. 96v): Weitzmann (1979a), 234.

[212] SC 318, 264; quotation from Proverbs 21:1. In Paris.gr.510 the passage is studded with gold initials. That this passage would have found favour with the patriarch Photios is clear from his *Eisagoge*: see note 59 above.

Gregory stresses the subjugation of the emperor to God; the miniature presents a commentary on Gregory's words that shifts the emphasis somewhat. Both Joshua stopping the sun and moon and Joshua with the angel link divine approval and military success, but the first gives control to Joshua, and only the second depends entirely on God, mediated through the angel. The register presents a dialogue between Joshua and the divine. Perhaps for this reason, the combination of scenes is unusual; certainly it expresses a thematic rather than a chronological link.

Comparison of the biblical reports of each event makes their differences clear. The account of Joshua stopping the sun and moon (Joshua 10:12–14) asserts quite clearly that 'there was no day like that before it or after it, that the Lord hearkened unto the voice of a man: for the Lord fought for Israel'. Assurance that the Lord was on the Israelites' side is also the theme of the second episode (Joshua 5:13–15), which chronologically precedes the halting of the sun and moon. But here the balance of power has shifted, as is clear from the inscriptions to the scene, taken directly from the biblical account: Joshua asks 'art thou for us, or for our adversaries?' (HMET[E]PO[C EI] H TΩ[N] YΠ[E]NAN[T]IΩN); the angel responds 'I am the captain of the host of the Lord' (EΓ[Ω] APXI[C]TPATHΓO[C] K[YPIO]Y). Though not so identified on f. 226v, the captain of the host of the Lord was, from the fourth century on, habitually identified as the archangel Michael, whom Byzantine emperors increasingly called upon for aid in battle themselves. Whether or not we are meant to read the archangel as Michael here, the 'captain of the host of the Lord' is portrayed as totally in charge: Joshua's vigorous pose as he halts the sun and moon contrasts strongly with his kneeling position when confronted with the frontal and impassive angel. The contrast between Joshua and the angel in this narrative was brought out in contemporary texts as well: Photios cited the episode as an example of the difference between 'great men' of the Old Testament and divinity in an attempt to explain how the Father and Holy Spirit were both similar and different.[213]

Folio 226v contrasts a scene in which Joshua commands the Lord with a scene in which the Lord commands Joshua. The scenes together visualize an unusually equitable balance of power between God and a leader. I assume that Basil was meant to be implicated in this visual metaphor. The result of the symbiotic relationship pictured on f. 226v, victory for God's chosen people, was certainly an important theme of Basil's reign. Basil's successful military campaigns were heavily promoted in his lifetime; they were of course singled out for praise in his funeral oration, and left their stamp on the *Vita Basilii* as well.[214] The use of images of Joshua to corroborate imperial military triumphs is not well attested until the tenth century,[215] but to their Byzantine audience the underlying message of both of the

---

[213] *PG* 102:296B.

[214] Tobias (1976), 30–55; McCormick (1986), 152–157; *Vita Basilii* 36–42, 46–49, 52–70: ed. Bekker (1838), 265–274, 277–284, 288–312; see note 47 above.

[215] References in note 204 above; also Connor (1984).

Joshua scenes pictured on f. 226v was surely that as God fought for the Israelites, so the Lord now fought for them, and the Lord fought for them under the banner of Basil I. For victory depended on God's favour – 'the Lord hearkened unto the voice' of Joshua – and we are, I think, meant to understand that Joshua's voice has been reclaimed in the ninth century by the Emperor Basil I.

Folio 424v (41) (fig. 41)

The fall of Jericho, the third and last of the Joshua scenes, occupies the uppermost of the three registers on f. 424v.[216] The falling city occupies the centre of the register: buff-coloured towers and sections of wall collapse around the central core of small grey-blue buildings with red roofs. Four figures stand on either side of the city. Those on the right are soldiers blowing long narrow trumpets; on the left, three trumpet-blowing soldiers join Joshua, identifiable by his more elaborate costume. Joshua is nimbed, and in this, as well as in details of his military attire, he differs from his earlier portrayals on f. 226v, a shift that suggests that the Joshua scenes in Paris.gr.510 either carry different types of meaning or represent two distinct traditions.

The Old Testament narrative of the fall of Jericho unfolds over most of Joshua 6. For seven days, seven priests with trumpets, men bearing the ark of the covenant, soldiers, and the people circled Jericho; on the seventh day, 'the priests sounded with the trumpets', the people shouted, and the walls of Jericho fell (v. 20). On f. 424v, soldiers rather than priests blow the trumpets: the military has replaced the holy as an instrument of divine destruction. This interpretation of the destruction of Jericho finds no Byzantine parallels: the Octateuchs and the Joshua Roll (fig. 99), for example, follow the Septuagint in including the horn-blowing priests but, excepting Vat.gr.747, all also show a pitched battle for the city; in a sense, the soldiers usurp God's power.[217] The Gregory miniature is perhaps closer in spirit to the mosaic at Sta Maria Maggiore: though the mosaicist omitted Joshua and the trumpets, the panel shows a symmetrical composition, and the city, flanked by empty-handed warriors, falls without human contact.[218] On f. 424v, however, unlike the fifth-century mosaic or any other preserved version of the episode, the military and its leader enact God's will, but without arms;[219] divine agency works through the trumpet-blowing soldiers rather than being dependent on mundane weapons. This apparently unique manner of representing the fall of Jericho associates the idea of

---

[216] For further discussion of this miniature, see chapter 2; on the iconography of the victory over the Amalekites, chapter 8.

[217] Mazal (1984), 48; Weitzmann (1948), figs. 14, 16–18; Uspensky (1907), fig. 236. Vat.gr.746 lacks the fall of Jericho; Vat.gr.747 omits the battle. On the relationship between the Octateuchs and the Joshua Roll, see Lowden (1982), 122–123; Lowden (1992), 52, 105–115.

[218] Karpp (1966), fig. 138. In Paris.gr.510, these two features are probably linked, for the rare symmetrical compositions in the manuscript signal moments of divine grace or presence: see chapter 2.

[219] On the imperial implications of the fall of Jericho in the tenth century, see Schapiro (1949).

divinely predetermined victory with strong military leadership that works with God: rather than promoting victory under God's protection or leadership, f. 424v emphasizes military triumph *through* God. Though this is not precisely the attitude fostered by most Byzantine emperors – and, indeed, differs somewhat from the message conveyed by the Joshua scenes on f. 226v – it complements the meaning of the frontispiece sequence and might plausibly be interpreted as a reference to Basil's successful association with God. Folio 226v may, however, have more to do with Photios' conception of the relationship between God and emperor than Basil's – but that is the subject of the next chapter.

In the visual allegory characteristic of Paris.gr.510, which sometimes recasts biblical stories into metaphors of contemporary life, Basil has been made to embody the perfect mediating leader who rules both with and through God. There are also other basic structural similarities that run through the lives of the Old Testament figures associated with Basil as they are presented in Paris.gr.510. One obvious theme is the setbacks that the hero has to endure on the way to ultimate victory over adversity (as in the Joseph sequence on f. 69v, or Samson on f. 347v). Poor rural beginnings lead to urban success: David, a shepherd, became king as Basil, a rural Armenian, did; Basil, as strong as Samson and like him favoured while a rural youth by God, was equally destined for urban achievement; and Joseph's physical journey from his father's house to the pastures, and finally to the Egyptian capital, is emphasized far more than is normal in cycles of Joseph's life: like Samson, David, and Joseph, Basil was a provincial outsider.

Concomitantly, and again like David and Joseph, Basil was a ruler who rose from outside the traditional power structure to become the orthodox ruler of an established and great empire. It is evident from the justifications that now obscure Basil's elevation to the throne that questions surrounded his rise to power, and the images in Paris.gr.510 that stress his connections with great rulers of the past form part of a concerted campaign to provide Basil with an illustrious lineage, both literally and metaphorically. As is well known, both Niketas the Paphlagonian and Pseudo-Symeon Magistros attributed Photios' reconciliation with Basil in 877 to his fabrication of a spurious genealogy, made to 'look ancient', that purported to trace the emperor's lineage back to the Arsacids;[220] the later *Vita Basilii*, as we have seen, added Alexander the Great and Constantine to Basil's family tree.[221] The miniatures in Paris.gr.510 that parallel Basil with Old Testament figures fit into a larger pattern, apparently orchestrated in some way by Photios, of texts and images designed to legitimate the emperor by metaphorically providing him with an illustrious past.

---

[220] For Niketas, *PG* 105:565–568; for Symeon: ed. Bekker (1842), 689; see note 55 above.
[221] See note 69 above.

Paris.gr.510 has always slipped through larger analytical structures to remain an anomaly. Yet it is an internally coherent product. The miniatures that we have examined thus far have presented well-thought-out compositions, and have provided a set of inter-textual and inter-visual cross references that are at times staggeringly complex. The keystone that holds the miniatures in this chapter together is a sense of how to display the Emperor Basil I in the best possible light, and to that end unusual imperial antitypes are accorded apparently atypical prominence, while traditional imperial parallels receive strange twists. It is hard to believe that the fluent cross-fertilization of biblical and imperial and personal references was a coincidental product of the contemporary thought network.

The miniatures in Paris.gr.510 do not address a communal audience; they target a certain audience at a specific time and in a precise place. There is no doubt that the special audience for the manuscript was Basil: the frontispiece miniatures make this explicit, and the focus of the miniatures that we have discussed in this chapter is entirely explicable even if he were the only person who ever saw them. Beyond the visual panegyrics, other features of the miniatures also seem to respond to his personal interests. As noted earlier, Basil originally came into court circles as a groom. He was always a renowned horseman, and while the emphasis on his equestrian skills may play into the importance of the mounted hunt in Byzantine imperial ideology,[222] it remains true that the proliferation of horses in Paris.gr.510 is remarkable. In addition to the numerous depictions of horse warfare, many of which appear to be *ad hoc* expansions of conventional battle scenes,[223] we saw in chapter 2 that an unparalleled horseman was inserted into the parable of the Good Samaritan on f. 143v (fig. 19); in chapter 3, we found the same to be true of the parable of Dives and Lazarus on f. 149r (fig. 20). But I do not think that Basil had the tools at his disposal to design Paris.gr.510 himself.[224] The only person who was capable of coordinating the inter-textual and inter-visual references woven into the Homilies miniatures, and of directing this data toward a quite particular end, was Photios, the patriarch of Constantinople at the time Paris.gr.510 was made. He, too, had the resources to commission such a deluxe product, and a reason to do so. It is to Photios that we shall now turn.

[222] Patlagean (1992).
[223] See e.g. the discussion of ff. 226v (fig. 26) and 424v (fig. 41) in chapter 8.
[224] See further chapter 9.

5

The patriarch Photios and visual exegesis

Photios was patriarch of Constantinople twice, first from 858 until shortly after the death of Michael III in 867, when Basil I replaced him with Ignatios, and then again – with Basil's approval – from 877 until Basil's death in 886, when Leo VI removed him.[1] Though many questions about his background remain, Cyril Mango has established that Photios came from an eminent family characterized by its iconophile tendencies: his mother Eirene was related by marriage to the former Empress Theodora, under whose aegis Iconoclasm ended in 843; and he was related on his father's side to the former patriarch Tarasios (784–806), who presided over the council that restored the veneration of images in 787.[2] Photios himself was an important civil functionary, and held the office of *protasekretis* (head of the imperial chancery) before his rapid elevation to the patriarchate in 858.

After centuries of denigration by western (mostly catholic) authors – for whom, largely because of his opposition to the introduction of the *filioque* clause in the Nicene Creed,[3] Photios embodied what were seen by them as the evils of the orthodox Greek east – the modern intellectual appreciation of Photios is almost overwhelmingly positive: Paul Lemerle wrote that Photios must be 'counted among the greatest [figures] in the history of Byzantium . . . who perhaps most truly represents Byzantine civilization'; Dimitri Obolensky called him the 'greatest theologian and philosopher of his age', and 'one of the greatest Byzantine scholars of all time'; for

---

[1] Mango (1977b) is the best modern assessment of Photios; for the end of Photios' career, see now Tougher (1994), esp. chapter 2. Hergenröther (1867–1869) provides a dense biography, but is no longer easily accessible and is anyway out of date and essentially anti-Photian polemic; the latter tendency is continued by, e.g., Wieczynski (1974), 180–189. Dvornik (1948) remains the standard rehabilitation of Photios in English, supplemented by numerous articles which are conveniently collected in Dvornik (1974); White (1981) supplies a more recent, if hagiographic, biography. One of the most influential assessments of Photios appeared in Lemerle's 1971 *Le premier humanisme byzantin*; additional bibliography has been incorporated in the updated English edition: Lemerle (1986), 205–235. Most handbooks – e.g. Hussey (1986), 69–101 – supply summaries of Photios' life; publications dealing with more specific aspects of Photios' career will appear as relevant in the following notes.

[2] Mango (1977b), who relies in part on Grégoire (1933), 517–524, 530–531. Winckelmann (1987), 190, follows the family tree established by Mango.   [3] On which see the discussion of f. 355r below.

Nigel Wilson, Photios was 'the most important figure in the history of classical studies in Byzantium'.[4] The sheer bulk of Photios' preserved work (which of course demonstrates that at least some pre-moderns rated his writings highly, too) accounts for part of this enthusiasm, but, perhaps as importantly for the current appreciation of his abilities, Photios was a historian; though far from identical – Photios responded from a position bounded by the given beliefs of his chronological and social niche – his approach to the world anticipated modern interests and recent historians have reacted sympathetically.

It is, however, often difficult to determine to what extent Photios' writings echo more general ninth-century élite attitudes or, conversely, represent his personal response from within that framework. Legal historians agree that his *Eisagoge* departed radically from previous law codes in its formulation of the relationship between God, the emperor and the patriarch;[5] and Photios' particular approach to history and theology can also sometimes be isolated. But whether we read his works as generic or idiosyncratic, Photios covered a huge range of material; the way he frames the topics that he covers often allows us to speculate on how a well-informed ninth-century viewer could decipher the relationship between a miniature and its accompanying sermon. His voluminous writings include a series of book reports now called the *Bibliotheke*, a large number of sermons of which eighteen survive, a series of questions and answers about many different subjects collected as the *Amphilochia*, a book-length discussion of the Holy Spirit (the *Mystagogia*), the *Eisagoge*,[6] hundreds of letters, and a range of other texts most of which survive only in fragments. Photios provides the most extensive written documentation from the second half of the ninth century, and at least one example from each of his works has already been cited to witness verbal formulations current when the miniatures of Paris.gr.510 were painted.

The *Bibliotheke* is the modern name assigned to a collection of several hundred summaries and more or less critical reviews of books – each now commonly referred to as a codex – that Photios had read.[7] In its original and somewhat shorter form, the *Bibliotheke* was composed for Photios' brother Tarasios, probably around 845; it was, however, apparently updated sporadically by Photios, and the edition that now survives incorporates entries that were written later in the ninth century,

---

[4] Lemerle (1986), 205; Obolensky (1971), 103, 119; Wilson (1983), 89.
[5] See Simon (1994); Dagron (1994); and chapter 4.   [6] See note 5 above.
[7] Ed. Henry, in 8 vols., with a French trans. facing the Greek text; about a third of the entries appear in English in Wilson (1994). The most thorough study is Schamp (1987). Treadgold (1980) conveniently categorizes the various volumes; he breaks the 279 listed codices into 386 discrete books. The title *Bibliotheke* is not attested until the sixteenth century; another designation, the *Myriobiblos*, appeared in the fourteenth. Photios seems to have called the work 'Inventory and enumeration of the books I have read, which my beloved brother Tarasios asked me to make so that he might gain a general appreciation of them'. See Lemerle (1986), 219, and Mango (1975), 43 and notes 66–67, who suggests that Arethas might have been involved in the publication of the collection.

during Photios' patriarchate.[8] The *Bibliotheke* was widely quoted by later Byzantine authors, but is unlikely to have had a large audience by 880: it was not originally conceived for public distribution, and may not have been prepared for public release until after Photios' enforced retirement in 886.[9] The *Bibliotheke* is nonetheless useful both for its indication of what texts were available in Constantinople in the ninth century, and for its indication of how Photios read those texts. We may use Photios' reading list as a guide to what the informed and diligent Constantinopolitan élite reader could have known when Paris.gr.510 was produced, and for its indication of how one particular reader interpreted the available texts.[10] We cannot, however, assume that the *Bibliotheke* provides a catalogue of books easily available, or widely familiar, in Constantinople. Photios himself claimed that many of the books he listed were not readily to hand: he wrote notes on the books that his brother might not know. Apparently unusual details noted in the *Bibliotheke* were not universally familiar, nor were Photios' interpretations of the texts that he had read necessarily widespread.

The *Amphilochia* consists of essays, apparently written before Photios' second tenure as patriarch, framed as responses to questions posed by Amphilochios, metropolitan of Kyzikos.[11] The topics covered range from minute disquisitions on the properties of a magnet to broad considerations of various theological questions.[12] Like Photios' other letters, the responses collected in the *Amphilochia* mix references that Photios expects his reader to understand already with expositions of lesser-known ideas, some of which seem to represent Photios' personal ruminations.[13]

Of all Photios' preserved writings, his sermons provide the best insights into public expressions of ninth-century thinking;[14] and, in one form or another, they were heard by a far wider audience than had access to the *Bibliotheke* or the *Amphilochia*. They are useful indicators of what was acceptable patriarchal rhetoric

---

[8] Treadgold (1980), 16–36 provides the *terminus post quem* of 845; I would however agree with Mango (1975), 37–43 and Maas (1990), esp. 193–194, that revisions and additions continued after Photios became involved in patriarchal politics. Cf. Lemerle (1986), 209 note 15; Schamp (1987), esp. 37–41.   [9] See the references in the preceding two notes and, on later citations, Diller (1962).

[10] E.g. the *Bibliotheke* demonstrates that Irenaeus' *Adversus Haereses* (now preserved complete only in Latin), which provides keys to the interpretation of the temptation of Christ on f. 165r, was still available in Greek in the ninth century (see chapter 2); that a versified *vita* of Cyprian relevant to the miniature on f. 332v was of considerable interest to Photios (see chapter 3); and that Philo's *De Josepho*, the major non-biblical text to enumerate Joseph's qualifications as ideal ruler, was also accessible to him (see chapter 4). Another case will be considered in chapter 6: see the discussion of f. 32v.

[11] Ed. Westerink IV–VI,1–2 (1986/7); I have also cited the now outdated but more widely accessible edition in *PG* 101:45–1160 throughout this book, though it does not include all questions. A number of letters otherwise attested are repeated as questions in the *Amphilochia*; these have been signalled as relevant.   [12] For discussion of the *Amphilochia*, see Lemerle (1986), 230–233.

[13] For an example of the latter, see the remarks on the supper at Simon's in the discussion of f. 196v in chapter 2. The *Amphilochia* is not of couse the only place where Photios detailed apparently unusual interpretations: see the discussion of f. 75r in chapter 7, and of f. 52v later in this chapter.

[14] Ed. Laourdas (1959); trans. Mango (1958).

in the ninth century and often seem to exemplify contemporary interpretations, many of them relevant to the miniatures of Paris.gr.510.[15]

The writings left by Photios almost inevitably interact with the miniatures of Paris.gr.510: though words and images communicate differently, the production of Paris.gr.510 and of Photios' discourses overlaps chronologically, and both Photios and the people responsible for the manuscript operated not only from within the same system but also from within the same small cell within that system. To argue that Photios was personally involved with the Paris Homilies, as opposed to sharing an identical milieu, is more problematic. Sometimes, however, Photios deals with issues familiar from other preserved authors, and we can see how his thought differed. When Photios' apparently idiosyncratic interpretations appear in the miniatures in Paris.gr.510, I suspect the patriarch's direct intervention.

Nearly all Byzantine commentators, and all of those writing within the century of Paris.gr.510, interpreted Noah's ark as a prefiguration of baptism. Photios did too, but he also repeatedly expressed a far less common reading of the episode – for him, the ark was a type of the Virgin, Noah was a type of Christ, and the waters of the deluge represented human sin – and this interpretation defined and cemented the connection between Gregory's sermon and the miniature combining Noah's ark with the tower of Babel on f. 360r.[16] The combination and configuration of the adoration of the Magi, the massacre of the innocents, the martyrdom of Zacharias, and the presentation in the temple on f. 137r follow and elaborate this pattern. Photios emphasized the sacrificial role of the massacred infants, and connected the offerings of the Magi with sacrifices in the temple, thereby providing a typological link between the adoration, the massacre, and the presentation. The miniaturist's emphasis on the high priesthood and the temple in Jerusalem also points to the patriarch, who used the high priesthood as a historical exemplar in his arguments that secular authorities should not intervene in religious affairs, and betrayed an unusual fascination with the structure of the temple.[17] These two concerns are different, but both ecclesiastic status and personal preoccupations resurface in other miniatures of Paris.gr.510. This pattern suggests a patriarchal and an individual involvement in the manuscript, and that combination implicates Photios.

The emphasis on the high priests on f. 137r visually colludes with quite specific arguments about the relationship between ecclesiastical and secular authority; to develop these arguments, Photios manipulated an older text by Josephus. Photios did not invent the idea of manipulating earlier texts to his own ends – this conceit was anticipated by earlier authors and continued long after Photios[18] – nor is he the first person to be associated with a political use of images. But the way that the

---

[15] See e.g. the discussion of f. 196v in chapter 2. For a similar understanding of Photios' role as intermediary, this time in connection with the mosaics at Hagia Sophia, see Cormack (1986), 614–615.

[16] See chapter 2.   [17] Ibid.

[18] See chapter 1 on the use of earlier authorities to sanction present actions; and, for an example of outright manipulation of an earlier written source in 921, Baldwin (1988), esp. 176.

argument is structured both in Paris.gr.510 and in the writings of Photios is very similar, and is unlike other contemporary patterns of argument: the miniatures of Paris.gr.510 and the writings of Photios represent the same set of ideas, even though these have been developed in two distinct media. That Photios was somehow involved with Paris.gr.510 is suggested by the structure of the visual argument, which parallels the structure of his written argument; by the nature of the topical messages, which reflects concerns of the patriarchate; and by highly personal insertions such as that presented by the two images of the temple vertically aligned on f. 137r. Folio 137r does not present the only example of the impact of Photios' personal interest, or even the only example of his interest in the architecture of the Holy Land: a similar pattern may be seen on f. 285r, where Helena holds a version of Christ's tomb that visually replicates Photios' long and unique description of it.

Folio 285r (29) (fig. 29)

Folio 285r illustrates 'On Easter' with Habakkuk's vision, evoked by the first paragraph of the sermon; the miniature shows the Old Testament prophet and Gregory together presenting the vision to the viewer.[19] Gregory and Habakkuk stand in the right foreground; they are balanced on the left by two women, identified as Paraskeve and Helena (Η ΑΓΙΑ ΠΑΡΑΣΚΕΥΗ ΚΑΙ ΕΛΕΝΗ). The women do not, however, participate in the vision; unlike Gregory and Habakkuk, they stand in frontal immobility. Paraskeve, the personification of Good Friday, wears a simple brown garment and holds the instruments of Christ's passion: the lance, sponge, nails, and cup of vinegar with which he was tormented on the cross. Helena wears full imperial regalia and holds a small model of Christ's tomb, depicted as a jagged rock pierced by a door and surmounted by an outcrop that approximates a cruciform shape.[20] Both women are nimbed in gold.

The Milan Gregory includes a medallion portrait of Habakkuk among its four marginal illustrations to the homily, and several of the liturgical editions picture Habakkuk showing Gregory the angel of his vision (fig. 100).[21] No other Homilies manuscript, however, incorporates the figures of Paraskeve and Helena. Helena has no explicit connection with Gregory's sermon, although as the discoverer of the true cross she was implicitly associated with the crucifixion, and on f. 285r she holds Christ's tomb. Paraskeve, here making her first recorded visual appearance,[22] is portrayed as a rather generic female, distinguished primarily by her attributes. Through her association with Good Friday, she relates thematically to Gregory's opening paragraph, which celebrates Easter with the passage 'Christ is risen from the dead, rise ye with him. Christ is freed from the tomb, be ye freed of the bond of sin.' The tomb held by Helena was presumably inspired by this same passage; we

[19] Further discussion of f. 285r appears in chapters 3 and 7.
[20] Omont (1929), 25; Brubaker (1985), 10.
[21] Grabar (1943a), pls. XXXIX,2, XLI,2 (Habakkuk), 3; Galavaris (1969), 28–29, 120–125.
[22] U. Knoben, s.v. 'Paraskeve', *LCI* 8 (1976), 118.

Fig. 100 Oxford, Bodleian Library, MS Roe 6, f. 4r: Habakkuk's vision

are also told by Epiphanios the Monk (ca. 750–800) that three of the relics of the passion that Paraskeve holds (the vinegar cup, the lance and the sponge) were kept in Christ's tomb.[23]

Christ's tomb is normally represented in the guise of the Church of the Holy Sepulchre,[24] a formula ignored on f. 285r. The rock-hewn form pictured here instead follows the prescriptions recorded by Photios:

The saving tomb of the Lord is all of one bowshot away from the ancient Jerusalem. Indeed, blessed Helena, when she visited Jerusalem and cleared that holy place of the piles of rubbish and filth there, extended the buildings and the city wall . . . In fact, this tomb, though it is a natural rock, has been formed into a tomb by masons. The rock has been hollowed out from east to west, forming a narrow chamber . . . What one might call the entrance or mouth of the tomb, where the workman began to cut in, has its opening facing east . . . What we are now describing we learned from those who have taken the trouble to reside in that blessed place.[25]

Photios probably received his information either from emigrés from Palestine attested in Constantinople throughout the ninth century,[26] or from the Jerusalem delegates who attended the Council of 879–880 carrying letters (addressed both to him and to Basil I) asking for funds to help restore their churches.[27] While Photios was presumably not the only person to have received this information, he was certainly in a privileged position to do so; in any event, he provides the most extensive written description of the tomb extant.[28] As we have seen, Photios' interest in the monuments of the Holy Land extended to the temple of Jerusalem as well as to Christ's tomb; in both cases, Photios recorded his fascination in texts and, I believe, in the images of Paris.gr.510.

Folio 174v (23) (fig. 23)

Painted on the verso of the last leaf of the preceding oration, f. 174v certainly maintains its original location; it introduces 'On theology' (Homily 28),[29] the second of

---

[23] Epiphanios the Monk, 'The Holy City and the Holy Places' I.16–II.1: Wilkinson (1977), 117. Others were held in the Church of the Virgin of the Pharos in Constantinople, a ninth-century construction of Michael III: Janin (1969), 235.

[24] See e.g. Grabar (1965), 69–70; Corrigan (1992), 22–25, 66–68, 96.

[25] *Amphilochia*, question 316: ed. Westerink VI,1 (1987), 122–124, ll.6–16, 22–25, 30–32, 59–60; trans. Wilkinson (1977), 146. The text does not appear in *PG*; it has however been transcribed, often labelled as question 107, in a number of publications dealing with the Christian sites of Jerusalem.

[26] See now Corrigan (1992), 23, 96–97.

[27] Mansi XVII, 441–444, 461, 484; Magdalino (1987), 54–55.

[28] For other descriptions, see Wilkinson (1977). Earlier, John of Damascus referred to the 'tomb that was hewn out of rock by Joseph', but this takes us little further than the account in Matthew's Gospel: 'Against those who attack divine images' I,23 (= II,16); ed. Kotter (1975), 113; trans. Anderson (1980), 31; cf. Corrigan (1992), 167 note 67.

[29] SC 250, 100–175. One side of the text at the end of the sermon is lost, along with the miniature (or the space for one) to the following oration. Though Gallay and Jourjon (SC 250, 19–20) attributed the gap to scribal error, quire 24 (ff. 187–193) lacks a leaf precisely here: see Appendix C.

Gregory's five well-known theological orations. Perhaps because 'On theology' is the only one of these orations that deals exclusively with God the Father, all three registers show scenes from the Old Testament: the first two illustrate episodes from the book of Genesis – the sacrifice of Isaac and Jacob's struggle with the angel – while the third contains the anointing of David.[30]

In a passage introduced by an enlarged gold initial, the sermon evokes both Genesis episodes:

And Abraham, great patriarch that he was, was justified by faith, and offered a strange victim, the type of the great sacrifice. Yet he saw not God as God, but offered him food as man. He was approved because he worshipped as far as he comprehended. And Jacob dreamed of a lofty ladder and stair of angels, and in a mystery anointed a pillar, perhaps to signify the rock that was anointed for our sake . . . and wrestled with God in human form . . . perhaps this refers to the comparison of human virtue with God's; and he bore on his body the marks of the wrestling, setting forth the defeat of created nature.[31]

Even the visually laconic Milan Gregory preserves an echo of Abraham's 'great sacrifice' and Jacob's contest with 'God in human form': though a medallion bust of Abraham replaces the sacrifice of Isaac found in Paris.gr.510, an inscription preserved beside a large excision indicates that the Milan manuscript also once included the scene of Jacob's struggle with the angel.[32]

Gregory's reading of the Abraham episode as a prefiguration of the crucifixion followed Paul's interpretation in his letters to the Hebrews (11:17–19) and Romans (8:32), and remained standard in Byzantine exegesis. The expanded narrative on f. 174v, which shows Abraham taking leave of his servants while Isaac carries the wood for the sacrificial fire up the mountain in addition to the actual scene of sacrifice, visually strengthens this interpretation, for Isaac carrying the firewood was seen as a prefiguration of Christ carrying the cross to Golgotha.[33]

But if Gregory's commentary on the sacrifice of Isaac anticipates later Byzantine convention, his excursus on Jacob does not. The differences between Gregory's interpretation and that followed by most other commentators can be seen by comparing Gregory's reading with that of John of Damascus in the eighth century. John followed the standard equation of the angel with God, but conceived the episode in terms of a Marian typology: Jacob struggled with God, so the Virgin became the ladder by which God, as Christ, came to earth; Mary united that which had been

---

[30] Ebersolt (1926), 21, pl. XV,2; Omont (1929), 23, pl. XXXVII; Morey (1929), 95; Buchthal (1938), 18–21; Weitzmann (1947), 174–175, 197; Der Nersessian (1962), 202–204, 222; Walter (1976b), esp. 61–62; Jolivet-Levy (1987), 460–461; Cutler and Oikonomides (1988), 85; Kalavrezou (1989), 392–396. On the iconography of the sacrifice of Isaac, see chapter 8; on the anointing of David, see chapter 4; on Jacob and the angel, see further chapter 7.   [31] SC 250, 136–138 (18:7–18)

[32] Milan, Ambrosiana cod.E 49/50 inf., p. 422: the inscription IAKΩB ΠΑΛΑ[IΩN], which also appears in Paris.gr.510, can be seen at the bottom of Grabar (1943a), pl. XXXIV,4.

[33] E.g. by Romanos in his 'On the sacrifice of Abraham': SC 99, 138–165, esp. 162–164. See also chapter 8, and Daniélou (1960), 114–130, esp. 124.

separated.[34] Gregory's christological reflection is quite different from John's mariological reading; and it is the latter which encapsulated the standard Byzantine view: the typikon of the Great Church, for example, omits reference to Jacob's struggle with the angel, while including four readings of the passage on his dream, each of which falls on a feast dedicated to the Virgin.[35] Photios, on the other hand, followed Gregory's lead. He supplied a separate commentary on each event, and provided a christological rather than a Marian interpretation in both cases. In question 259 of the *Amphilochia*, Photios wrote that Jacob wrestled with the only-begotten son, that is, Jesus;[36] and in question 236, Photios, like Gregory, identifies Jacob's anointing stone with the 'rock that is glorious Christ, uniting two peoples'.[37] Whether or not Photios' christological interpretation of the Jacob episodes was inspired by Gregory, their agreement underscores the most unusual iconographic feature of the register.

Following the biblical account (Genesis 28:10–15), Jacob, wearing a pink mantle over a blue tunic striped with gold, reclines at the foot of a mountain, propped up by a deep pink rock. His right leg crosses over his left, his left arm cushions his head, and his right arm dangles in front of the rock. An angel stands before him; two more angels, one ascending and one descending, stand on a ladder (ΚΛΙΜΑΞ). All three are nimbed in gold and wear gold mantles over blue tunics. These details correspond closely with versions of Jacob's dream in the fourth-century Via Latina catacomb paintings and the twelfth-century Octateuchs (fig. 101):[38] though only Paris.gr.510 inserts a third angel speaking to Jacob (a detail which recurs in several Palaiologan examples),[39] all show Jacob in the same position, include two angels on the ladder, and lack the bust of Christ in an arc at the top of the ladder found in other representations of this episode. No other Byzantine representation of the dream, however, includes the altar that sits at the far right, directly below the altar prepared by Abraham in the top register. This feature, presumably added by the Homilies miniaturist in response to Gregory's association between the dream and the pillar that Jacob later anointed (v. 18), echoes Photios' interest in the anointed stone as a type of Christ, and ties the Jacob image not only to the sacrifice of Isaac above it but also to the anointing of David which appears below.

As if to cement the connection between them, the miniaturist clothed Isaac, Jacob with the angel, and David in identical garments: all wear a pale blue tunic hemmed in gold, with a red sash, red leggings, and blue boots. On one level, this pattern reinforced the typological associations of all three Old Testament figures

---

[34] For John's passage and further commentary: Der Nersessian (1975), 334–335. On John, see chapter I note 65.   [35] Mateos I (1963), 4–7, 18–21, 220–223, 368–373. On the typikon, see chapter 2 note 101.
[36] Ed. Westerink VI,1 (1987), 46–47; *PG* 101:1072A5–B.
[37] Ed. Westerink VI,1 (1987), 18; *PG* 101:1029B.
[38] Ferrua (1960), pl. XCVII and e.g. Smyrna, Evangelical School A.1, f. 41v (Hesseling [1909], fig. 99).   [39] See Der Nersessian (1975), 335–336.

Fig. 101 Vat.gr.746, f. 97r: Jacob's dream

with Christ; on another, it suggests that we are meant to view the page as a connected whole rather than as a collection of disparate scenes. A christological theme
is certainly present, but so too is the motif of anointing. Inspired by a sentence in
Gregory's text, the decision to include Jacob's altar unified the miniature visually
and thematically.

Photios is implicated in f. 174v in a number of ways, but always as a reinforcing
voice rather than as an instigator: he followed Gregory in his christological interpretation of Jacob and in his interest in the anointed pillar; and (as we saw in
chapter 4) his writings on the anointing of David were inspired by a request from
the Emperor Basil. The confluence of these interpretations, however derivative
each may have been on its own, nonetheless suggests that Photios was involved in
the planning of f. 174v.

Folio 355r (36) (fig. 36)

A full-page image of the Council of 381 prefaces Gregory's thirty-fourth homily
which, in Paris.gr.510, is incorrectly titled 'On the landing of the Egyptian

bishops'.[40] In fact, Gregory delivered the oration in honour of a group of Egyptian sailors who, landing in Constantinople with a load of grain at the height of the Arian controversy in 360, avoided the Arian churches and sought out instead Gregory's small orthodox church. Gregory praised the Egyptians for their unswerving loyalty to the orthodox position, and condemned the various interpretations of the trinity current among contemporary heretical groups:

the Father, the Son, and the Holy Spirit [are] neither so separated from one another as to be divided in nature, nor so contracted as to be circumscribed by a single person; the one alternative being that of the Arian madness, the other the atheism of Sabellios.[41]

The illuminator of Paris.gr.510 stressed the last clause ('the one alternative . . . ') by introducing it with a gold initial.[42] Without this clue, we would be hard pressed to explain the rationale behind the inclusion of the miniature, for Gregory made no reference to a council, much less the Council of 381, in his sermon, and Paris.gr.510 is the only illustrated copy of the Homilies to preface the oration with a conciliar picture.[43]

The image of the Council of 381 was of obvious importance to the designer of the manuscript: it occupies, exceptionally, the entire page, and a frame with rainbow-pattern cornerpieces and enamel-like sides replaces the standard gold border. The miniature shows Theodosios the Great (ΘΕΟΔΟ[CIO]C Ο ΜΕΓΑC),[44] nimbed and in full imperial regalia, seated with a crowd of bishops on a sigma-shaped bench against an architectural backdrop painted in shades of pink, green, blue, and ochre. A throne and an altar dominate the central axis. The throne, gold and jewelled, with a red cushion on top of a red and green protective cloth, bears an open gospelbook. The blue altar supports a closed red book tied with thongs that is flanked by two rolled scrolls; these presumably represent the acts of the first council, held at Nicaea. Above the throne, against a variegated blue backdrop, the scene is titled 'the second synod' (CYNOΔOC ΔΕΥΤΕΡΑ). Makedonios (ΜΑΚΕΔΟΝΙΟC), condemned by the Council of 381, crouches in the lower left corner; he has a short dark beard, closely cropped dark hair, and wears pink and blue. Apollinarios, also condemned by this council, originally mirrored him on the right: a seventeenth-century drawing (Paris.nouv.acq.lat.2343, p. 96) shows the inscription ΑΠΟΛΙΝΑΡΙΕC and appends a note saying that the page was already damaged.[45]

The miniature on f. 355r provides a fairly straightforward image of a council.[46] The semi-circular arrangement may, as Christopher Walter suggested, derive from

[40] SC 318, 198–227 (NPNF, 334–338). Omont (1929), 28, pl. L; Grabar (1936), 90–92; Weitzmann (1942/3), 124–126; Gallay (1943), 171–173; Bogyay (1960), 59, pl. IV; Ainalov (1961), 210; Der Nersessian (1962), 206, 221; Walter (1970b), 35–37, 253, 262; Brubaker (1985), 4–6; Cormack (1989), 'Additional Notes and Comments', 15.   [41] SC 318, 212.   [42] Paris.gr.510, f. 357v.

[43] The liturgical editions omit this homily; the miniaturist of the Milan Gregory introduced it with a preaching scene: Grabar (1943a), pl. XXXI,3.

[44] A darker ink has strengthened the name Theodosios.   [45] Omont (1929), 12.

[46] See Walter (1970b); Walter (1970a), 40–49.

antique scenes of Socrates and his disciples or from early Christian representations of Christ and his apostles, but it also seems to reflect contemporary reality, as elucidated in the Life of St Stephen the Younger, written by Stephen the Deacon in 807.[47] The enthroned gospelbook echoes ninth-century practice as well: texts document the solemn enthronement of the gospels at the Councils of Ephesus in 431, Nicaea in 787, and, most important here, Constantinople in 869.[48] Though it does not always appear in Byzantine representations of councils, the miniature of the iconoclast Council of 815 in the Pantokrator Psalter also includes the gospel (fig. 102),[49] which sits rather forlornly on a simple bench; whether or not the miniaturist was making a visual comment on the spiritual poverty of the 815 Council, the inclusion of the gospelbook in Pantokrator 61 suggests that the Gregory miniaturist followed pictorial as well as historical convention.[50] The enthroned gospelbook presiding over the council symbolized the guiding presence of divinity (and orthodox tradition) in much the same way as a portrait of the emperor guaranteed the authority of law courts;[51] more specifically, the book signified 'the presence in the council of the Holy Spirit who had inspired the scriptures'.[52]

However legible the miniature, it fails to illustrate the thirty-fourth homily in any direct way and, since Gregory was not himself present at the 381 Council, there is no biographical justification for its inclusion. As Gregory devotes much of the sermon to an attack on Arianism, the portrayal of a major church council on f. 355r was certainly an appropriate supplement to the accompanying text; following Gregory, however, one would expect to see the first Ecumenical Council (Nicaea I) and the downfall of Arius.[53] This is manifestly not the case: as the inscriptions make clear, we see the second Council (Constantinople I) condemning Makedonios and Apollinarios. Though there is a certain amount of uncertainty on the point, Makedonios apparently argued that the Holy Spirit was less important than the Father and the Son, and that it occupied a position midway between God and terrestrial humanity.[54] This was, in any event, how ninth-century Byzantium interpreted the Makedonian heresy: in Photios' words, Makedonios 'fought against the Holy Spirit'.[55] Photios was so concerned with Makedonios' heretical pronounce-

[47] Walter (1970b), 36, 233; see also Grabar (1936), 90–92. For Stephen the Deacon, *PG* 100:1140.

[48] For texts and commentary, Walter (1970b), 235.

[49] Mount Athos, Pantokrator 61, f. 16r: Dufrenne (1966), pl. 2; Pelekanides *et al.* 3 (1979), fig. 181. For commentary on this much-discussed image, Grabar (1957), 201–202; I. Ševčenko (1965); Corrigan (1992), 113–116. On the Pantokrator Psalter, see chapter 1 note 32.

[50] So too Grabar (1957), 202; and see also Corrigan (1992), 115.

[51] See Grabar (1957), 202; Walter (1970b), 148, 162.   [52] Crehan (1966), citation 210.

[53] As we find in Vercelli, Bib. del Capitolo, cod.CLXV, f. 2v, conveniently reproduced in Corrigan (1992), fig. 112.

[54] See G. Bardy, s.v. 'Macédonius et les Macédoniens', *Dictionnaire de Théologie Catholique* IX (1926), 1464–1478.

[55] Homily 16,5: ed. Laourdas (1959), 157; trans. Mango (1958), 267 (as Homily 16,7). See also the summary of the 381 Council read at the Council of 787: Mansi XIII, 233C-D; trans. Sahas (1986a), 71.

Fig. 102 Mount Athos, Pantokrator 61, f. 16r: Council of 815

ments that, in a letter to (Boris) Michael of Bulgaria describing the ecumenical councils, he devoted most of his discussion of the 381 Council to a condemnation of Makedonios and a justification of the orthodox position on the Holy Spirit.[56] Apollinarios, on the other hand, denied Christ's human nature. For this, he too was still being roundly condemned in the ninth century: the 787 Council mentioned the Apollinarian heresy briefly; Photios castigated him twice in the *Amphilochia* and again in two of his letters; Niketas the Paphlagonian (ca. 900) continued the attack.[57] The miniature on f. 355r, in other words, shifts its focus away from Gregory's condemnation of Arianism to emphasize instead the orthodox interpretation of the Holy Spirit and Christ's human nature. Given eighth- and ninth-century attention to the Arian heresy – which iconophiles cited as a historical precedent for Iconoclasm[58] – it is interesting that the opportunity to condemn Arius visually was not taken. But visual arguments against a different heresy were being marshalled here, and the realignment accords with other ninth-century preoccupations.

The courtly and patriarchal circle for which Paris.gr.510 was intended spent much of the second half of the ninth century in a struggle with the western church for authority over the newly converted Bulgarians.[59] Frankish, Roman, and Byzantine missionaries competed for the role, and the tense situation magnified the differences between Latin and Greek doctrine.[60] A major bone of contention became the wording of the Nicene Creed. The original formulation, followed by the Byzantines, stipulated that the Holy Spirit proceeded from the Father. For a variety of reasons, however, the Frankish missionaries in Bulgaria taught an interpolated Creed in which the Spirit proceeded from the Father 'and the Son' (*filioque*).[61]

The most eloquent Byzantine voice against the Latin position belonged, as one might expect, to the patriarch Photios. In his encyclical letter (867), his letters to Pope Nicholas and to the archbishop of Aquileia (883/4) and his *Mystagogia* (post-

[56] Epistle 1: ed. Laourdas and Westerink I (1983), 1–39, on the Council, ll. 123–71; *PG* 102:636B–637B; trans. White and Berrigan (1982). For an analysis of this letter, see Dujčev (1952).

[57] For the Council, Mansi XIII, 281B-C; trans. Sahas (1986a), 107. For the *Amphilochia* question 1: ed. Westerink IV (1986), 2–30, ll. 822–55 (*PG*101:89–92); question 48: ed. Westerink V (1986), 7–14, ll. 1–21 (PG 101:357C–360A). For Photios' epistle 248: ed. Laourdas and Westerink II (1984), 180–183; epistle 284, with over a dozen references: ed. Laourdas and Westerink III (1985), 1–97. For Niketas, Rizzo (1976), 46 (trans. 102). On Gregory's sermon against Apollinarios, illustrated with anti-heretical images on f. 316r (fig. 32), see chapter 6.   [58] See the discussion of f. 367r later in this chapter.

[59] On the political and cultural background, see Lemerle (1965); Browning (1975), esp. 145–153; Dölger (1943); Gjuzelev (1976); Gjuzelev (1986).

[60] Sansterre (1982); Haugh (1975); and the classic, if now rather dated, Dvornik (1948).

[61] The basic tenets of the *filioque* debate are discussed by the authors cited in the previous two notes; also useful are Rodzianko (1957); Jugie (1939); Schultze (1982); and D. Ganz in *NCMH* 2, 781–783.

886), Photios justified the orthodox position at length.[62] He cited the scriptures, provided logical rebuttals, and reviewed ecclesiastical case histories to discredit the Latin interpolation of *filioque*. The case histories are, for our purposes, most interesting. Photios termed the Latin teaching a 'semi-Sabellian monster', an epithet that takes on some significance in light of the enlarged initial that introduces Gregory's reference to the Sabellian heresy in Paris.gr.510.[63] Even more important, however, Photios relied on his knowledge of the condemnation of Makedonios by the Council of 381 to provide a historical precedent for his own condemnation of the Latin position, which he duly likened to the Makedonian heresy.[64] Photios found a resolution to the controversy with Rome about the Holy Spirit in the acts of the 381 Council, and he used the Council's condemnation of Makedonios as a justification for his own condemnation of the Latin position on *filioque*.

Gregory's trinitarian concerns, appropriate to the fourth century and clearly expressed in the homily accompanying f. 355r, were broader than those of the orthodox church during the patriarchate of Photios. The ninth-century orthodox church was involved in a dispute about only one aspect of the trinity, the role of the Holy Spirit. It is in this context that the miniature of the Council of 381 must be understood: the picture supplements Gregory's arguments against trinitarian heresies by supplying a corollary, the condemnation of Makedonios, appropriate to ninth-century problems. At this time, too, allusion to any aspect of the Holy Spirit was particularly appropriate in the context of Gregory's Homilies, for ninth-century authors cited Gregory of Nazianzus as a major authority on the definition of the Holy Spirit: 'It was Gregory alone and first before anyone else who clearly and most boldly proclaimed the Spirit to be God, equal to the Father and the Word [Christ].'[65] The miniature updates an appropriate text.

The decision to include a second heretic, Apollinarios, in the miniature was probably not based simply on a desire for compositional symmetry or historical accuracy. Apollinarios denied Christ's human nature, and this was one of the major

---

[62] Epistle 2 (encylical): ed. Laourdas and Westerink I (1983), 39–53, esp. ll. 101–192; epistles 288 and 290 (to Pope Nicholas): ed. Laourdas and Westerink III (1985), 114–120, 123–138; epistle 291 (to the archbishop of Aquileia): ed. Laourdas and Westerink III (1985), 138–152; *Mystagogia*: *PG* 102:279–398. In another letter, Photios approvingly cited Matthew's phrase 'a blasphemy against the Holy Spirit is never forgiven': White (1981), 93. See also Grumel (1936), nos. 480, 529, 566.

[63] *Mystagogia* 9, *PG* 102:289B. Photios also condemned the Sabellian concept of the Holy Spirit (but without reference to the *filioque* debate) in Homily 16,10: ed. Laourdas (1959), 161–162; trans. Mango (1958), 275–276 (as Homily 16,12).

[64] Encyclical: ed. Laourdas and Westerink I (1983), ll. 122–131 (PG 102:728B); *Mystagogia* 32 (*PG* 102:313B). See also Mango (1958), 22, 236–237; for an earlier, less developed, expression of this association see the Life of Michael the Syncellos: ed. Cunningham (1991), 54–57.

[65] Niketas the Paphlagonian: Rizzo (1976), 27 (trans. 124). Niketas refers to Gregory's sermon 'On the Holy Spirit', SC 250, 274–343. In his encyclical, Photios too cites Gregory of Nazianzus (along with Athanasios) as an authority on the Holy Spirit: see note 62 above.

heresies with which the iconophiles had charged the iconoclasts. As we saw in chapter 1, because the iconoclasts denied that Christ could be represented 'in material colours', the iconophiles accused them of denying that Christ had existed in truly human form.[66] It thus seems likely that Apollinarios appears on f. 355r for the same reason as does Makedonios: to provide a historical precedent that justified a contemporary orthodox position. To a certain extent, the entire image plays to this anti-iconoclast theme: according to the Life of St Stephen the Younger, the images of the councils on the Milion in Constantinople had been removed by the iconoclast Emperor Constantine V and replaced by hippodrome scenes; f. 355r implicitly redresses this defacement.[67] Both the page as a whole and the inclusion of Apollinarios sanction, by analogy, the recent iconophile victory just as the inclusion of Makedonios authorizes the orthodox stance on *filioque*.

This method of using earlier sources to condemn current heresies was a familiar one in the ninth century. The Paulician heresy, for example, was countered by the reissue of a fourth-century text by Alexander of Lykopolis against the Manichean heresy, brought up to date by an introduction dedicated to Basil I that was almost certainly written by Photios, explaining how Alexander's work was relevant to the ninth-century problem.[68] Photios made the same point in the opening paragraph of his *Contra Manichaeos*.[69] The parallelism between Apollinarios and Iconoclasm, and Makedonios and the *filioque* debate thus finds analogues in contemporary texts. Though more overt than in Paris.gr.510, several of the anti-iconoclast images in the marginal psalters supply the same kind of polemical parallelism: in the Khludov Psalter, for example, the iconoclasts whitewashing an icon of Christ are visually equated with Stephanos and Longinos tormenting him on the cross (fig. 57); later in the same manuscript, Peter tramples Simon Magus above an iconophile trampling an iconoclast.[70]

The image of the 381 Council can, then, be interpreted as a vindication of the orthodox Byzantine position on *filioque* and on Iconoclasm. It may also be linked with the Synod of 879/80, which reinstated the acts of the Photian Council of 867 that had been repudiated by the Pope and Ignatios after Photios' disgrace in 870.[71] As the 381 Council was called to reunite the church after the Arian schism, the 867 Council celebrated the unification of the church after the iconoclast controversy.[72] The 381 Council ratified the Nicene Creed; the 867 Council excommunicated the

[66] For a classic formulation of this favourite iconophile argument, see Mansi XIII, 205E, 344E; trans. Sahas (1986a), 50, 160.   [67] *PG* 100:1172A-B; trans. Mango (1972), 153.

[68] *Contra Manichaei opiniones disputatio*, ed. Brinkmann (1895), xxiv–xxvii. See further chapter 4; Markopoulos (1992); Vogt (1908), xxiii; Loos (1964), 54.   [69] *PG* 102:15.

[70] Moscow, Hist.Mus.cod.129, ff. 51v, 67r (Ščepkina [1977]). For commentary, Grabar (1957), 198–201; Corrigan (1992), 27–30. On the Khludov Psalter, see chapter 1 note 30.

[71] Haugh (1975), 123–130; Boojamra (1982); Meijer (1975).

[72] On the 867 Council, and Photios' sermon on unification at it, see Mango (1958), 297–306.

Frankish missionaries for teaching an interpolated version.[73] The 867 Council, in other words, condemned precisely the two heresies anticipated by the 381 Council and alluded to in the Homilies miniature: Iconoclasm and *filioque*. Certainly the image of the 381 Council could be related to contemporary Constantinopolitan concerns; it may also have visualized a historical precedent for the Photian Council of 867 or, more likely, the Synod of 879/80 that restored the acts of that Council.[74]

Whether or not f. 355r was so finely directed, however, the miniature visually replicates the structure of Photios' argumentative process as we know it from texts,[75] and uses this structure to condemn a heresy of primary concern to Photios himself.

Folio 264v (28) (fig. 28)

Folio 264v, unlike any other miniature in Paris.gr.510, joins together two separately framed pictures,[76] both of which have in addition a supplementary detail outside of the frame itself. The upper picture, bordered in gold banded with red, is subdivided into three individually framed scenes: Moses before the burning bush, the conversion of Saul (Paul), and the ascension of Elijah toward a hand of God that emerges from an arc of heaven above the frame.[77] The lower picture, isolated from the upper by a strip of neutral parchment and distinguished from it by the blue bands that frame the gold border, is twice as large and devoted to a single scene, the crossing of the Red Sea with the dance of Miriam. Once again, the miniaturist placed a hand of God above the frame; it continues the diagonal begun by the rays emanating from the hand of God above the top register.

The miniature prefaces Gregory's sermon 'On baptism', which begins on the following page, and the pictures are firmly linked with Gregory's text.[78] Gregory expounded the conventional equation between baptism and illumination or enlightenment at some length; he noted that 'God is light', and 'a second light is the angel, a kind of outflow or communication of that first light',[79] and then remarked:

And to mention more lights – it was light that appeared out of fire to Moses, when it burned the bush indeed, but did not consume it, to show its nature and to declare the power that was in it. And it was light that was in the pillar of fire that led Israel and tamed

[73] Ibid.; also Haugh (1975), 23–44, 91–99; Dvornik (1958), 30–31.

[74] Much of the material presented in the foregoing discussion originally appeared in Brubaker (1985), 4–6.

[75] On Photios' use of the past as a model for the present, see also Kustas (1964), esp. 37–48.

[76] Omont (1929), 24–25, pl. XLII; Morey (1929), 38, 41, 95; Buchthal (1938), 30–33, 67; Weitzmann (1947), 197; Weitzmann and Ševčenko (1963), 386, 388; Der Nersessian (1962), 200–201; Der Nersessian (1970), 102; Weitzmann (1979a), 54, 93; Brubaker (1985), 7; Jolivet-Lévy (1987), 462–463; Kessler (1990), 17; Brubaker (1996b), 104–105.

[77] Though otherwise of equal height, the outer two scenes are just over eight centimeters wide, the middle just under seven.   [78] SC 358, 198–311. In addition, the preceding homily ends on f. 264r.

[79] SC 358, 204.

the wilderness. It was light that carried up Elijah in the chariot of fire, yet did not burn him as it carried him . . . Light was the vision that blazed out upon Paul and by wounding his eyes healed the darkness of his soul.[80]

He concluded: 'Light besides these in a special sense is the illumination of baptism of which we are now speaking, for it contains a great and marvellous sacrament of our salvation.'[81] The three scenes of the top picture were thus specifically mentioned by Gregory, and though he never referred directly to the crossing of the Red Sea, he remarked on the pillar of fire that leads the Israelites in the lower scene. These episodes are, however, of only minor importance in the oration: the miniaturist of the Milan Gregory ignored them all to concentrate instead on the two narratives discussed at length, the miracle at Cana and the healing of the paralytic,[82] while the liturgical editions show either Gregory preaching or a scene of baptism.[83] By ignoring the obvious, the designer of f. 264v was not attempting to impose a new theme on Gregory's oration, for, as Sirarpie Der Nersessian observed, all the scenes relate more or less directly to baptism.[84]

Byzantine commentators habitually cited both the ascension of Elijah and the crossing of the Red Sea as types of baptism.[85] Neither the conversion of Saul (Paul) nor Moses before the burning bush, however, were normally cited in this connection; the burning bush episode was, in fact, usually interpreted as a prefiguration of virgin birth.[86] To Photios, though, Saul's conversion exemplified the rebirth of baptism, for, as he explained in a lengthy consideration of baptism included in the *Amphilochia*, the old Saul 'died' and was resurrected as Paul.[87] Photios did not literally connect the burning bush with baptism in the same concrete manner, but he did associate the two in such a way that the equation seems inescapable.[88] Again in the *Amphilochia*, Photios linked the burning bush with the Holy Spirit, and followed this immediately with a paraphrase of John the Baptist: 'I indeed baptize you with water, but . . . he will baptize you with the Holy Spirit and with fire.'[89]

---

[80] Ibid., 206–208; unusually, none of these passages received an enlarged initial.   [81] Ibid., 208.

[82] Grabar (1943a), pls. XL,1–2; the other marginal illustrations are all portraits, none of them relevant to Paris.gr.510: ibid., pls. XXXIX,1, XL,3–5, XLI,1.

[83] In the liturgical editions, 'On baptism' is Homily 11: Galavaris (1969), 15–17.

[84] Der Nersessian (1962), 200–201.

[85] For Elijah: Daniélou (1956), 107–108. The crossing of the Red Sea was interpreted already as a type of baptism in the New Testament (e.g. 1 Corinthians 10:2), and the typikon of the Great Church included the Exodus narrative among the readings for the Festival of Lights, the primary date consecrated for baptism in the orthodox church: Mateos I (1963), 174–185.

[86] See e.g. Mateos I (1963), 252–259; Der Nersessian (1975), 311–315, 336–338.

[87] Question 43 ('On baptism in the name of Christ'): ed. Westerink IV (1986), 159–180, esp. ll. 353–366, 593–602 (*PG* 101:301–330, esp. 317D, 329B).

[88] Photios sometimes more conventionally connected Moses before the burning bush with virgin birth as well. Question 300 of the *Amphilochia* (ed. Westerink VI,1 [1987], 90–92; *PG* 101:1136–1137) combines both interpretations.

[89] Question 300: ed. Westerink VI,1 (1987), 91, ll. 23–27 (*PG* 101:1136C-D); compare White (1981), 86.

However indirectly, Photios here constructed a baptismal interpretation for the Moses episode, and this reading of the scene brings it into conformity with the visual typology expressed throughout the remainder of the miniature.[90]

The message of f. 264v is not, however, carried by the typological selection of scenes alone: subsidiary themes of importance to the emperor and the patriarch leak into the whole page.

The way that Moses and the burning bush has been presented is unusual. Moses, his pink mantle flung over a light blue tunic, stands behind a small green hillock and has raised one leg to rest his foot on it; he leans forward, twisting his nimbless head to the side (perhaps to avoid looking at the angel on the right, perhaps to avoid hitting his head on his raised knee), and unties the laces of his sandal with both hands at the instruction of 'the angel in the bush' (O AΓΓ[ΕΛ]ΟΣ ΕΝ ΤΩ ΒΑΤΩ) who tells Moses to 'unfasten the sandals of your feet' (ΛΥΣΩΝ ΤΟ ΥΠΟΔΗΜΑ ΤΩΝ ΠΟΔΩΝ COY). The scene illustrates Exodus 3:2–5, when an angel appeared to Moses 'in a flame of fire out of the midst of a bush', and God told him to remove his shoes, 'for the place whereon thou standest is holy ground'. The gold-nimbed angel, in a pale brown mantle over a blue tunic and with one wing extending over Moses and the other tucked back, holds a lance in its right hand and stands in a relaxed contrapposto that contrasts with the contorted position imposed on Moses. Red flames mingle with green twigs about the angel's calves; both undulate up toward its waist; though following the Septuagint account, the presentation of the angel actually in the bush seems to be unprecedented. Moses is largely obscured by his position and his placement behind the hillock; it is the angel who dominates the scene and participates in the composition of the top register as a whole: it balances the identically clad Elijah on the right, and the smaller and slightly lower haloes of the angel and Elijah in turn frame the larger and higher medallion that surrounds a portrait of Christ in the central scene. The chevron shape described by the three haloes is counterbalanced by the more exaggerated reverse chevron formed by the repetition of costume colours: Saul, who kneels in the middle scene, wears the same combination as do Elijah and the angel. The scenes are further linked by the green hill which recurs in all three, and by the manifestation of divinity that appears, increasingly elevated, on the right side of each vignette. The form that the divine takes, however, differs.

In the middle scene, Saul, inscribed Paul (ΠΑΥΛΟΣ), kneels beneath a gold medallion that encloses a portrait of Christ, from which a stream of light blue light beams down to Saul. Christ's face has flaked off, but he is identifiable by the variegated blue rays that form a cross behind his head, and by the purple garment over his shoulders. A green hill frames Saul, and behind it rise the pink walls of a city, within which various blue buildings are visible. A small green structure with a

---

[90] The ideas expressed in this paragraph originally appeared in Brubaker (1985), 7.

purple door sits at the far right of the quadrant; two cypress trees rise behind it. The scene closely follows Acts 9:3–5, and Christ's question appears as an inscription beneath his portrait: CAYΛE, CAYΛE, TH ME ΔIOKEIC ('Saul, Saul, why persecutest thou me?'). The city behind Saul is presumably Damascus; the small green building before him may represent a rural shrine.[91] The conversion is far and away the most commonly illustrated event of Paul's life, and the version on f. 264v follows the conventional Byzantine formula, certainly established by the ninth century, as both this illustration and the Vatican 'Christian Topography' make clear (fig. 77).[92] This does not, however, mean that the conversion in Paris.gr.510 follows the 'Topography' pattern in all respects. Both ninth-century miniatures show Saul with his head raised rather than prostrating himself in full proskynesis with his forehead on the ground; in the 'Christian Topography', however, Saul appears twice, once standing and once fallen to earth,[93] a common duplication that was avoided on f. 264v – presumably because it was more important for the baptismal typology of the page to signal what Photios called the 'death' of Saul than to re-enact visually the narrative of the conversion story. The manner of depicting divinity also differs: the 'Topography' miniature shows divine rays emanating from an arc of heaven; other versions insert a hand of God.

The selection of a medallion of Christ for f. 264v, rather than a hand of God or an arc emitting rays, apparently conveyed meaning. André Grabar argued that the *imago clipeata* found here (a portrait in which Christ's halo is enlarged to act as a circular frame that encompasses his shoulders rather than simply sitting behind his head) was a symbol of victory; Kathleen Corrigan, who studied the frequent appearance of the formula in the marginal psalters, has suggested that it signified 'an icon of Christ'.[94] Christopher Walter, however, maintained that the use of this device in the marginal psalters was meant to indicate that Christ was 'physically present and visible', and proposed that this same meaning, which is linked with visions of divinity and has iconophile resonance, applied to f. 264v.[95] These interpretations have obvious relevance within Paris.gr.510, but a second layer of meaning seems to me equally important, and this layer lies not in the form of the image but in its content. The decision to depict Christ, rather than an arc or a hand of God, allowed the full panoply of the trinity to spread across the top register. Following Photios, the angel in the burning bush represents the Holy Spirit, Christ obviously is the Son, while the hand of God that rises above the ascension of Elijah in the next panel stands for God the Father. This layout is surely intentional: not only does it provide a final touch to the delicately balanced top register, it also and quite appropriately brings the trinity into the baptismal typology of the page as a whole. In addition, the format of the register visually confirms the equality of all

---

[91] Kessler (1990), 17, identified this as a milestone, a reading belied by the door.
[92] Vat.gr.699, f. 83v: Stornajolo (1908), pl. 48.   [93] Paul appears twice in the miniature as well.
[94] Grabar (1957), 218–221; Corrigan (1992), 74–75.   [95] Walter (1987), 214–216; cf. Kessler (1990).

members of the trinity that, as we saw in the discussion of f. 355r (fig. 36), was a pressing concern in the *filioque* debate. I suspect that the decision to portray Christ rather than either of the alternatives was the primary one; once the choice to complete the trinity was made, the form of the portrait took on its own weight.

Unlike the scenes of Moses and Saul, the ascension of Elijah and the crossing of the Red Sea had conventional baptismal typologies, and are presented in a relatively conventional way;[96] the prominence of the crossing of the Red Sea, however, merits brief mention here. The equation between Moses, who led his people to freedom across the Red Sea, and Constantine, who led his people to Christianity across the Tiber on the Milvian bridge, was an old and familiar one:[97] even Photios invoked the crossing of the Red Sea as an analogy for orthodox Christian victory.[98] The scene on f. 264v had, we may assume, imperial connotations;[99] it has been argued, in any event, that the rod held by Moses that features in the Homilies miniature was kept in the palace at Constantinople rather than at the patriarchate precisely for this reason.[100] The sheer size of the representation, which dwarfs the other typological pictures, smacks of preferential treatment and presumably respects the double layer of significance that the crossing of the Red Sea bore within itself: it played into the baptismal theme of the sermon and the miniature, and it stressed the religious importance of the emperor by calling on associations with Constantine the Great – associations that, as we saw in chapter 4, were not out of place in Paris.gr.510.

Folio 52v (10) (fig. 10)

Folio 52v shows scenes of the creation and fall in the upper two registers; Moses receiving the laws and Gregory preaching occupy the lowest.[101] The folio is inserted between quires six and seven, but nonetheless certainly retains its intended place, for (as we have seen) the scenes in the third register are closely related to the following sermon, Gregory's first oration 'On peace' (Homily 6), written to commemorate the reconciliation of the Nazianzus community after a period of strife.[102]

Gregory did not, however, write about Adam and Eve in the sermon; and the sequence that unfolds in the upper registers is in fact a curious one.[103] It opens with

---

[96] On the iconography, see chapter 8.

[97] For a recent discussion, with earlier bibliography, see Schminck (1989), 103 and note 2.

[98] See e.g. Mango (1958), 313.   [99] So too Jolivet-Lévy (1987), 462–463.

[100] Schminck (1989), 107; on references to the staff in the Book of Ceremonies see Thümmel (1992), 123–124.

[101] Omont (1929), 15–16, pl. XXIV; Morey (1929), 36, 95; Der Nersessian (1962), 208–209; Weitzmann and Ševčenko (1963), 386–387; Walter (1978), 238; Brubaker (1985), 8–10; Brubaker (1996a), 15–16.

[102] SC 405, 120–179; Gallay (1943), 80–84. See chapter 3 for additional discussion of the biographical scene; 8 for Moses.   [103] A detailed assessment of the iconography appears in chapter 8.

the creation of Adam, followed by the creation of Eve; rather than the temptation, the next scene shows God's cursing of Adam, Eve, and the serpent (Genesis 3:15–20), and this is followed by the expulsion from paradise. The second register begins with a representation of the cherub guarding the tree of life. Normally, following the sense of the biblical text, the cherub appears before the expulsion; were the top two registers of f. 52v collapsed into a continuous linear narrative, Adam and Eve would be propelled directly into the tree of life rather than out of paradise. An archangel handing Adam a two-pronged hoe follows the cherub, in reference to Genesis 3:24: 'So the Lord God sent him forth out of the garden of delight to cultivate the ground out of which he was taken.' A body of non-canonical literature elaborates on Adam's toils outside paradise, and at least two apocryphal texts intimate that the archangel Michael taught Adam how to till the soil.[104] Relevant visual parallels to this image do not, however, seem to exist.[105] Genesis 3:24 is normally illustrated by a depiction of Adam already at work or, closer in spirit to the Gregory scene but hardly identical, shouldering a mattock or spade as he is expelled from paradise.[106] Though the archangel's presence may presuppose knowledge of texts describing his role in the event, the picture of Michael handing Adam the mattock was evidently created for f. 52v to stress that physical labour was an important repercussion of the fall. The final scene of the second register, the lament of Adam and Eve outside paradise, returns to a standard iconographical formula.

However anomalous some details, the inclusion of the Adam and Eve sequence was not arbitrary.[107] On one level, the history of Adam and Eve signified schism: the temptation and fall, responsible for the original break between God and humanity, appear in the liturgy as antitheses to themes of peace and unity.[108] Juxtaposed with the scenes of the lowest register, representing reconciliation, the miniature as a whole thus provided a visual analogue to Gregory's sermon, and the

[104] The Apocalypse of Moses (*Vitae Adae et Evae*) 22:2 is most specific: 'And the Lord God sent diverse seeds by Michael the archangel and gave them to Adam and showed him how to work and till the ground' (Charles II [1913], 138; see also the Book of Jubilees 3:15, 32–35 [ibid., 16–17]). The tool appears to be a *dikellion*, on which see Bryer (1986), 70.

[105] Fourth-century sarcophagi on which Christ distributes a bundle of wheat to Adam and a lamb to Eve (Garrucci [1879], pls. 313,4, 381,5, 396,3–4) conceptually resemble f. 52v in showing Adam receiving an attribute of his earthly existence, but a direct connection appears implausible. The closest comparisons occur in a group of later, related Latin manuscripts – the Winchester Psalter (Wormald [1973], 70, fig. 44), the Psalter of St Louis (Omont [1902], pl. 3) and St Swithin's Psalter (N. Gray [1949], pl. 7) – but these shed little light on any possible antecedents for Paris.gr.510. An angel offers Adam a hoe on the twelfth-century bronze doors at Monreale (Boeckler [1953], pl. 51), and a spade in the voussoirs at Malmesbury (Galbraith [1965], pl. XVII,7), but both of these compositions differ markedly from that on f. 52v.

[106] For Adam at work: Kessler (1977), figs. 1–5, 29, 33; Demus (1949), pls. 29A, 98A. For Adam carrying a mattock or hoe, see Demus II (1984), pl. 32; Goldschmidt and Weitzmann (1930) I, nos. 84c, 86.

[107] Part of the following originally appeared in Brubaker (1985), 8–10.

[108] See e.g. the readings for Lent in Mateos II (1963), 18–19 (where Genesis 2:20–3:20 is coupled with Proverbs 3:23), and 24–25 (where Genesis 3:21–4:7 is coupled with Proverbs 4:2).

arrangement of the Adam and Eve sequence reinforced this interpretation by abandoning the chronological account of Genesis to set images of unsullied paradise, on the left, against images of dissent – the curse and expulsion – and its results (labour and lament) on the right. That the miniature was intended as a commentary on schism and reconciliation is signalled by the two passages marked by marginal *oboloi* in the text. The first of these paraphrases Ephesians 2:14: 'For he is our peace, who hath made both one, and hath broken down the middle wall of enmity.'[109] How this passage works with f. 52v is revealed in a sermon delivered in 863, when Photios expanded on it to write 'For Christ is our peace who has broken down the middle wall of enmity, and through him we have been reconciled with our Father and creator, from whom we had wickedly parted ourselves in former times.'[110] Beyond the general liturgical interpretation of the fall as an image of schism, the Adam and Eve sequence seems to have been more specifically stimulated by the paraphrase of Ephesians, conveniently marked to alert the reader to its significance.

But although the break between God and humanity is undoubtedly expressed by the Adam and Eve sequence, the moment of schism – the fall itself, which does not appear on f. 52v – was less important than the opposition between concord and discord as expressed through the vertical bifurcation of the registers. This not only parallels the dominant theme of the homily, but also, through the mediation of the second passage marked in the text, ties the sequence to the scenes of Moses receiving the laws and the Nazianzus priests and monks in the lowest register. The second marked quotation, from Romans 5:20, reads: 'where sin abounded, grace did much more abound'.[111] In the New Testament, this passage forms part of a discussion (vv. 12–21) in which Paul noted that sin entered the world through Adam, was understood as sin only with the introduction of the law to Moses (the first sentence of v.20 reads 'the law entered, that offence might abound'), and was redeemed by the new Adam, Christ. Paul's words provoked numerous medieval commentaries on original sin, and the verse marked in Paris.gr.510 served as a springboard for later exegesis on Adam as an antitype of Christ.[112] Most significant is a commentary on Romans 5:20, now preserved only as a lengthy catena passage, wherein Photios used Moses receiving the laws as a pivot around which he spun the contrasts between Adam and Christ,[113] an argument he returned to in the *Amphilochia*.[114]

---

[109] Paris.gr.510, f. 55v; SC 405, 140 ll. 7–8.

[110] Homily 8,2: ed. Laourdas (1959), 85; trans. Mango (1958), 156 (as Homily 8,3). See also Homily 6,10: ed. Laourdas (1959), 72; trans. Mango (1958), 136.

[111] Paris.gr.510, f. 56r; SC 405, 142 (9, ll. 3–4).

[112] Weaver (1983); Weaver (1985), esp. 243–247 for Photios. For commentary centred specifically on Romans 5:20, see also Cramer (1844), 53–56.

[113] Ibid., 55–56; cf. C.H. Turner, 'Greek Patristic Commentaries on the Pauline Epistles', in *A Dictionary of the Bible*, ed. J. Hastings, extra vol. (Edinburgh, 1904), 519–520.

[114] Question 24: ed. Westerink IV (1986), 85–94, ll. 270–281 (*PG* 101:187A-B). Treadgold (1980), 106, also noted Photios' 'particular interest' in the issue of original sin in the *Bibliotheke*.

Photios noted that until sin was defined by the Mosaic law, it could not be recognized; only after sin had been recognized could 'the king vanquish it through his sacrifice', that all might be released from the labourious existence imposed on humanity by Adam. In a homily on the annunciation, Photios continued in this vein, describing the redemption of original sin by Christ as a release from the 'toilsome life' awarded Adam for his transgressions – a reward pictured, as we have seen, on f. 52v.[115] While Mosaic law was necessary to understand original sin, it was superseded by Christ.[116]

The connection between Adam and Christ was a familiar one to ninth-century Greeks, but it is not critical to f. 52v, where the links between Moses receiving the laws, the reconciliation of the Nazianzus monks – both drawn from Gregory's sermon – and the Adam and Eve sequence require a more detailed chain of analogies. But while the connection between the miniature and Gregory's quotation of Paul's Epistle to the Romans is signalled by marginal *oboloi*, it remains the responsibility of the viewer to interpret the relationship between the marked words and the miniature; the tools to do so are provided by Photios' writings and by the composition of the page itself.

To Byzantines familiar with visual histories of Adam and Eve, it was presumably apparent immediately that the results of the fall were more significant on f. 52v than the core episode: while four scenes detail events that occurred after the fall, neither the temptation nor the fall appears. Further, the eight incidents included are grouped in clearly defined pairs: two scenes of creation, two of the immediate punishments for original sin, two of paradise lost, and two of the delayed consequences of the fall. This arrangement denies strict chronology, and instead seems to have been imposed in order to make a visual equation between the two registers. The two creation scenes, revealing Adam and Eve still in a state of grace, are directly above the tree of life and the cherub in paradise, while the curse and expulsion are vertically juxtaposed with God's second curse – the imposition of toilsome existence – and the lament. Grace informs the left half; the right side relays the consequences of original sin. This bifurcation continues and is resolved in the third register. Below the paradisal scenes, Moses receives the laws that first defined sin and thus made possible redemption; while below the punishments of Adam and Eve for their transgressions against God, unity is restored and reconciliation achieved. Folio 52v communicates with images the intersection of ideas that Photios' writings communicate with words.

---

[115] Homily 5,4: ed. Laourdas (1959), 56; trans. Mango (1958), 115–116. This theme resurfaces ca. 900 in Niketas the Paphlagonian's *Encomium*, 7: 'Thereupon [Adam] exchanged a painless and immortal life for sweat and toil and death' (trans. Rizzo [1976], 92).

[116] Compare Dagron (1994), 36. Part of this chain may have been presented earlier: Ignatios' *Vita Tarasii* joins scenes 'pertaining to the creation of the world' with Moses receiving the laws (I. Ševčenko [1984], 5; see chapter 1 note 16).

HISTORICAL MINIATURES

Folio 367v (38) (fig. 38)

Three miniatures devoted to historical subjects appear in sequence toward the end of the manuscript. The first, f. 367v, illustrates Gregory's sermon 'Against the Arians'.[117] The Arians, who regarded the Son as less important than the Father inside the trinity, flourished during the fourth century (ca. 320–380) and provided Gregory with his chief adversaries. The sermon consists of a litany of Arian crimes, the subject matter for the three registers of f. 367v.[118]

The first register shows a boat under full sail in the midst of a deep blue sea scarcely distinguishable in colour from the sky behind it. Six men – one a bearded bishop, one a young monk in a brown tunic, one huddled in a blue cloak, one a hooded monk wearing his brown *koukoulion* over a blue tunic, and two nondescript figures – cram the small vessel, which is engulfed in red flames (now badly flaked). The inscription identifies the scene as the orthodox burned in their boat by the Arians,[119] and corresponds with Gregory's rhetorical question: 'What priests have the contrary elements of fire and water divided, raising a strange beacon over the sea, and burning them up together with the ship in which they put to sea?'[120] Gregory refers to an event that took place during the reign of the Emperor Valens, who, enraged at an orthodox delegation, caused his prefect to set fire to their boat. The fifth-century historians Sokrates, Sozomen, and Theodoret all narrate this story in varying amounts of detail, and it was thus certainly familiar in the ninth century: Photios had not only read these three authorities but was well versed enough in the details of the Arian heresy to compose four (possibly five) accurate sermons on it himself. [121] Indeed, Photios' interest in the Arian controversy – presumably fuelled by the iconophile equation of the earlier heresy with Iconoclasm[122] – may account for the decision to illustrate Gregory's 'Against the Arians' in such a straightforward fashion. But while these histories give a detailed context for Gregory's almost offhand question about priests in a burning boat, they tell us no more than Gregory about the details of the scene as presented on f. 367v; none, for example, identifies the curious group of figures in the boat. The miniaturist seems

---

[117] SC 318, 156–197 (*NPNF* 328–334); Gallay (1943), 145–146.

[118] Omont (1929), 28, pl. LII; Weitzmann (1942/3), 91–100; Grabar (1953), 171–172; Der Nersessian (1962), 198; Anderson (1991), 74.

[119] ΟΙ ΟΡΘΟΔΟΞΟΙ ΕΝ ΠΛΟΙΩ ΥΠΟ ΑΡΕ[ΙΑΝΩΝ] ΚΑΙ[ΟΝΤΑΙ]. The fragments of the last word appear to the right of the sail.

[120] SC 318, 164.

[121] *Bibliotheke*, codices 28 (Sokrates), 30 (Sozomen), and 31 (Theodoret): ed. Henry I (1959), 16–18. Two of the sermons survive: ed. Laourdas (1959), 139–163; trans. Mango (1958), 244–278 (see also Mango's commentary, 236–243, and Mango [1975], 41). Gregory also mentions the episode elsewhere: see Moreschini in SC 318, 165 note 3.

[122] Found even in the *Parastaseis*, chapter 10: ed. Cameron and Herrin (1984), 68–69; commentary and additional references at 25–26, 167.

here to have furnished the standard boat type of Paris.gr.510 (see figs. 6, 27, 46) with a representative sampling of ecclesiastics, all in garments familiar and attested in the ninth century: the bishop and the young monk recur in the Paris Gregory – indeed, the bishop resembles portraits of Gregory himself – while the hooded monk finds parallels in the *Sacra Parallela* and the Milan Gregory.[123] As the relevant miniatures in the Milan copy have been excised, it is now impossible to determine whether the scene on f. 367v represents a free interpretation of the text or whether it once found a ninth-century parallel.

The inscription in the frame above the second register explains that the middle scene on f. 367v represents the Arians destroying the altars of the orthodox: [OI] ΑΡΕΙΑΝΟΙ ΚΑΤΑΣΤΡΕΦΟΝΤΕΣ ΤΑ ΘΥΣΙΑΣΤΗΡΙΑ ΤΩΝ ΟΡΘΟΔΟ-ΞΩΝ. Gregory alone alludes to this episode; in a passage introduced with a gold initial, he refers to the scene in a rhetorical question that contrasts his own behaviour with that of the Arians: 'What house of prayer have I made into a burial place ... Altars beloved, as the scripture says, now defiled.'[124] The passage was also considered significant enough to be illustrated in the Milan Gregory; once again, however, the relevant margin has been excised. On f. 367v, the register opens with a tightly massed group of laymen; those in the background carry pikes, while four of the figures closest to the centre extend long tapers toward a pale pink church (with, as usual in Paris.gr.510, blue roof tiles) and set fire to it. Two smaller blue buildings, identifiable as churches by the apses that extend from each of them, are already in flames in the foreground; all are carefully aligned with the burning boat in the top register. The altar mentioned in the inscription appears to the far right, covered with a red cloth and surmounted by a gold baldachin; it is enclosed by a green templon screen with a gold door, in a precinct about half the size of the central church. Kurt Weitzmann suggested that the composition was lifted from a copy of Sozomen's 'Ecclesiastical History' (no illustrated copies of which exist or are attested) that illustrated Julian's order to burn the churches in Miletus.[125] This is unlikely, for the miniaturist composed the scene on f. 367v from stock groupings found elsewhere in Paris.gr.510. Indeed, all details of the scene find parallels elsewhere in the manuscript: the tightly packed group of Arians conforms with the standard configuration of groups, and is particularly close to the huddle of Joseph's brothers in the fourth register of f. 69v (fig. 12); the altar duplicates in all essential features – including the curious perspective rendering – that on, for example, f. 52v

[123] On the former, see Anderson (1991), 74, and in general chapter 1 notes 28–29; on the latter, see e.g. Grabar (1943a), pl. XII and in general the Introduction. Weitzmann (1942/3), 94–97, suggested that the miniaturist copied Athanasios' escape, aided by monks, from Alexandria from a (hypothetical) illustrated copy of Theodoret's 'Ecclesiastical History'. Since the scene is composed of stock features, this seems unnecessarily complicated.

[124] SC 318, 160–162. The destruction of churches was also a concern of Photios', who complained (ca. 870) that during his exile 'They destroyed the houses of God, which we had established for the penance of our sins': see White (1974), 117.   [125] Weitzmann (1942/3), 97–98.

(fig. 10); the church sustains the tiny outbuildings that are such an eccentric feature of Paris.gr.510 (see, for example, the top register of f. 143v; fig. 19); and the placement of an altar alongside the church that we are meant to understand it to be inside recurs on f. 104r (fig. 17).

The bottom register is badly flaked, but one can still make out the nude body of an elderly man being dragged along with cords by two soldiers toward a building; the inscription reads 'the Arians drag along a saintly old orthodox man' ([OI] APEIANOI CYPONTEC AΓION ΓEPΩ[N]TA OPΘOΔOΞON). The scene illustrates another of Gregory's rhetorical questions – and, again, one in which he incorporates an episode ignored by other writers – wherein he sets the behaviour of the orthodox against that of the impious Arians: 'What bishop's aged flesh have we carded with hooks . . . and at last dragged away to death, to be crucified and buried and glorified with Christ?'[126] Based on this passage, we might speculate that the badly flaked building on the right, located directly beneath the altar of the second register, represents the tomb shrine destined to receive the saintly orthodox man. Unfortunately the relevant image in the Milan manuscript has been excised.

Folio 374v (39) (fig. 39)

Folio 374v presents the early history of Julian the Apostate,[127] and corresponds closely with the sermon that follows it, Gregory's first 'Invective against Julian'.[128] In the course of the sermon, Gregory alludes to a number of mythological figures, and marginal numbers collated with Pseudo-Nonnos' commentary on them appear in the margins.[129] The miniaturist, however, ignored the mythology and concentrated instead on events from the life of Julian the Apostate.

The top register shows Julian, in imperial red leggings beneath a long-sleeved pale blue tunic decorated with gold that stands out against his purple mantle, led away from a circular pink and white building toward a cave by a man with wavy grey hair and a short beard who wears a blue tunic beneath an olive-green mantle. Julian's head has nearly all flaked away, but it is still apparent that he averts his gaze from the man; this, along with his retracted right arm and gesticulating left one, make Julian appear to be resisting the man, who nonetheless strides forward grasping Julian firmly by the wrist as he looks back at the emperor, and gestures toward the cave with his left hand. Within the cave sits a large winged demon, painted in shades of white and grey, behind which float several pale heads; a grey sarcophagus rests on a pink outcrop of the otherwise grey-blue mountaintop above. A strip of

---

[126] SC 318, 164. The miniature is badly flaked, but Weitzmann (1942/3), 98–100, seems to be correct in seeing the cords attached to the old man's ears. Omont did not, however, note this feature in his 1929 description.
[127] Omont (1929), 29, pl. LIII; Weitzmann (1942/3), 100–108; Der Nersessian (1962), 198; Brubaker (1985), 2.   [128] PG 35:531–664.   [129] See Introduction note 10.

green ground forms the basis for the whole episode,[130] which Gregory described in detail:

[Julian] descended into one of those sanctuaries which are inaccessible for most people and regarded by them with fear . . . accompanied by the man who is worth about as much as most sanctuaries, the 'wise' man in such things, a 'sophist'; all this is a kind of divination amongst them, a meeting in a certain darkness and with subterranean demons about the future . . . But as the noble man proceeded, terrors dashed against him, continually more and more formidable ones, strange noises, as they say, unpleasant smells, fiery apparitions, and I don't know what kinds of nonsense and trifles. Being struck by the unexpected, for he was still a tyro in these matters, he takes refuge in the cross as an old remedy and in the sign thereof against the terrors and thus makes an assistant of him whom he persecuted.[131]

Though Gregory's text does not explain every detail, the passage reveals that the man dragging Julian is a sorcerer, and the cave a pagan sanctuary filled with apparitions.

Julian's descent into the cave is portrayed once outside of Paris.gr.510. As Gregory provides the sole description of the episode, it is to be expected that this second appearance should occur in the Milan Gregory (fig. 53), which accompanies the sermon with thirty-one marginal images, eight depicting events from Julian's life as narrated by Gregory.[132] Julian led to the cave is the only scene to duplicate an episode pictured in Paris.gr.510.[133]

In the Milan Gregory, the figures of the emperor and the sorcerer are reversed, so that Julian seems to be dragging the reluctant magician into the cave. Despite this, the two versions of the scene share telling details. Both show a winged demon – sitting in the same position and extending its arm toward the visitors – and both show dismembered heads behind the demon in the shadowy recesses of the cave. Within the Julian–sorcerer grouping, the position of the foremost figure is different, but as the sorcerer in Paris.gr.510 repeats a figure type found throughout the manuscript,[134] this distinction seems less significant than the fact that both images show the leading figure grasping his follower firmly by the wrist. As Gregory details none of these features, the miniaturists of the Milan and Paris Gregory manuscripts cannot have derived them independently from the text: either the designer of Paris.gr.510 adapted and corrected the Milan composition, or both miniaturists presented versions of a formula familiar to them from another source, presumably – since only Gregory recounts the episode – an illustrated Homilies.

---

[130] The fragmentary inscription was deciphered by Omont as ΙΟΥΛΙΑΝΟC ΧΗΡΑΓΩΓΟΥ-ΜΕΝΟC ΥΠΟ . . . ΒΑCΚΑΝΟΥ . . . ΒΛΕΠΟΝ ΤΟΥC ΔΕΜΟΝΑC.

[131] *PG* 35:557C–580A; trans. Weitzmann (1942/3), 101.

[132] In addition to the standard opening miniature showing Gregory preaching, the illustrator depicted five scenes or figures drawn from the Old Testament, seven mythological figures, and eighteen historical scenes; eight of the latter show Gregory addressing Julian, one portrays Gregory's lament over Julian's crimes, and one presents the emperor of India: Grabar (1943a), pls. LX,2–LXXII (excepting LXXII,2).   [133] Ibid., pl. LXVI,1.

[134] E.g. the angel on f. 174v (fig. 23) and Elijah on f. 264v (fig. 28).

Aside from the reversal of the protagonists, comparison of the Paris and Milan miniatures reveals two significant differences: neither the round building nor the sarcophagus appears in the Milan version. These do not derive from the first 'Invective against Julian', but both were described in fifth-century historical texts.[135]

In his 'Ecclesiastical History', Theodoret tells us that Julian 'met with a man who promised to predict these things, conducted him into one of the idol temples, introduced him within the shrine, and called upon the demons of deceit'.[136] Theodoret's account, though more abbreviated than Gregory's, suggests that the round building at the far left of the register represents the 'idol temple' in the precinct of which Julian visited the demon. Other historians were more specific. Sokrates wrote that 'Having ordered that the pagan temples at Antioch should be opened, [Julian] was very eager to obtain an oracle from Apollo of Daphne. But the demon that inhabited the temple remained silent through fear of his neighbour, Babylas the martyr; for the coffin which contained the body of that saint was close by'.[137] Sozomen relates the same story in greater detail, adding that

The demon did not openly admit that the hindrance was occasioned by the presence of Babylas, the martyr, but he stated that the place was filled with dead bodies, and that this prevented the oracle from speaking. Although many interments had taken place at Daphne, the emperor perceived that it was the presence of Babylas, the martyr, alone which had silenced the oracle, and he commanded his tomb to be removed.[138]

The histories of Sokrates and Sozomen allow us to identify the temple as that dedicated to Apollo at Daphne, and they also explain the sarcophagus mounted above the demon's cave: it belongs to Babylas, the Christian martyr – possibly the same Babylas whose bones were, by the ninth century, believed to have been transferred to the Chora monastery in Constantinople.[139] The ecclesiastical histories of Theodoret, Sokrates, and Sozomen explain certain details of the scene that could not have been known from Gregory's sermon alone; only Gregory, however, describes the cave and the sorcerer who drags the increasingly timid Julian into it.[140] While Kurt Weitzmann's suggestion that the scene was copied from an illustrated copy of Sozomen's 'Ecclesiastical History' is therefore improbable,[141] the historical texts clearly had an impact on the miniature. Knowledge of these texts in the ninth century is attested by Photios,[142] who also had reason to be particularly familiar with historical accounts of Julian's reign: he wrote an account of that

---

[135] So Weitzmann (1942/3), 100–108.   [136] III.1; trans. *NPNF* ser.2, 8 (1892), 94.

[137] 'Ecclesiastical History' III.18; trans. *NPNF* ser.2, 2 (1952), 88.

[138] 'Ecclesiastical History', V.19; trans. *NPNF* ser.2, 2 (1952), 341.

[139] Compare Cunningham (1991), 125 and 171 note 218 with *ODB* 1 (1991), 243.

[140] Theodoret refers to Julian's guide, but not to the circumstances of the emperor's meeting, and he omits nearly all other details of the scene.   [141] Weitzmann (1942/3), 100–108.

[142] See note 121 above.

emperor which is unfortunately no longer preserved.[143] It seems likely that the texts themselves, rather than some hypothetical illustrations of them, inspired the inclusion of the temple and sarcophagus; the form of Babylas' sarcophagus, in any event, was part of the miniaturists' repertoire and duplicates in all details that found in the scene of the demoniacs in the cemetery on f. 170r (fig. 22).

The scene painted in the middle register of f. 374v is less tightly bound to Gregory's text than are the other two images on the page. It shows Julian, clad in imperial regalia, watching the slaughter of a bull; the miniaturist then depicted the sacrificial animal burning before a circular flaming altar set within a niche topped by three gold statues. Two attendants stand behind Julian, and the sorcerer of the top register, still wearing a light brown mantle over a blue tunic, stands next to him, gesturing toward the sacrifice. The scene illustrates Julian's reintroduction of pagan ritual and, despite its generic titulus 'Julian sacrifices to the idols' (IOYΛIANOC ΘΥΩΝ TOIC EIΔΩΛOIC), seems in its specifics to have been inspired by one of the epithets Gregory bestowed on the emperor, 'burner of bulls'.[144] Although this epithet is only one of many that Gregory used, it epitomized an aspect of Julian's reign habitually noted by later historians: Sokrates explained that Julian 'sacrificed bulls continuously in front of altars of idols', and Sozomen claimed that 'They say jokingly that in the time of his reign the world itself had been destroyed quite as much as the supine bulls.'[145] Neither the ecclesiastical histories nor Gregory, however, provide an account of any specific sacrificial rite. The picture on f. 374v should be viewed as a general image representative of Julian's predilection for sacrifices – a visualization of Gregory's epithet 'burner of bulls' – rather than as an illustration of a particular episode.

No other representation of Julian observing a sacrifice survives, and this lack of visual comparanda, coupled with the conventional nature of the descriptive texts, makes it all but impossible to determine whether the Homilies miniaturist adapted the scene from an earlier image or compiled it from scratch.[146] Parallels exist, however, for the various components of the composition. The figures observing the

---

[143] As noted by Lemerle (1986), 233 note 72, Photios mentions this in epistle 187, which is itself mostly concerned with Julian: ed. Laourdas and Westerink II (1984), 76–87 (= *Amphilochia* question 101: *PG* 101:616–633). Photios was not alone in his interest in the Apostate: for obvious reasons Julian was often cited in iconophile polemic, and was roundly condemned in the *Parastaseis* (ed. Cameron and Herrin [1984], 25, 122–127, 235–237), which in chapter 47 both recounted his association with sorcery and included an account of a trick similar to the donativum episode pictured on the lowest register of f. 374v (ibid, 124–125).

[144] *PG* 35:608A. The Life of Michael the Synkellos called iconoclasts 'image burners', but there is no hint that any equation with Julian was intended: ed. Cunningham (1991), 58.

[145] Sokrates, 'Ecclesiastical History' III.17; Sozomen, 'Ecclesiastical History' V:19. See notes 137 and 138 above and Weitzmann (1942/3), 104. Photios noted that even Julian wrote against Christian animal sacrifice – epistle 211 (= *Amphilochia* question 109): ed. Laourdas and Westerink II (1984), 111–115, ll. 103–106 (*PG* 101:649D) – which implies familiarity with Julian's approval of (non-Christian) sacrificial ritual.   [146] But see Weitzmann (1942/3), 103–105.

sacrifice rely on standard types used throughout Paris.gr.510: Julian's attendant soldiers duplicate the pair found in the register below, and the stance of the emperor
mirrors that of St Basil on f. 409v (fig. 40). The sacrifice itself avoids the standard
Byzantine formula of throat-slitting and presents instead a simplified version of a
sacrificial type familiar on Roman imperial monuments such as the Arch of the
Argentarii in Rome (AD 204), which shows the bull's head being held down while
the executioner raises an axe above his turning body just as we see in Paris.gr.510.[147]

The scene of the lowest register is even more closely affiliated with Gregory's text
than was the opening image of Julian's visit to the demon. Julian, sitting on a jewelled lyre-back throne in front of a pink and blue building apparently meant to
represent the imperial palace, distributes coins to his officers. A large pot of gold to
the emperor's right, guarded by two henchmen, represents the source from which
Julian replenishes the small bowl of gold coins he holds in his lap. The emperor
cradles a badly flaked gold object – probably an idol or a censer – in his arms; a quatrefoil golden brazier, into which each recipient must throw incense and thereby
implicitly honour the pagan gods, obscures his feet. A group of soldiers and dignitaries crowd the right half of the register.[148] Gregory narrates:

It was the day of the imperial gift making . . . and the soldiery were ordered to be present so
that they might receive the donativum according to the merit or rank of each of them . . .
Now he presided in splendour, splendidly celebrating against piety and thinking about his
cunning contrivances . . . There was placed before him gold, there was placed before him
incense, the fire was close by and the exhorters near. And the scheme was so plausible
because it seemed to be the expected usage of the more ancient and the more honourable
donativum. What then? Each was supposed to throw incense upon the fire and to receive
from the emperor the recompense for their destruction.[149]

Gregory's text fully supports the illustration; as Weitzmann observed, 'a miniaturist
could have made up the composition from this text'.[150] However, because he
believed that the scenes presented in the upper two registers were borrowed from an
illustrated ecclesiastical history, Weitzmann suggested that since Sozomen and
Theodoret also described the donativum episode, its illustration was probably
copied from one of these texts.[151] Since, however, we have seen that his first
assumption is unlikely to be correct, there is no reason to trace any of the scenes on
f. 374v to an ecclesiastical history with pictures.

The Milan Gregory presents the sequel to the scene shown in Paris.gr.510, with

[147] Conveniently reproduced in Strong (1976), fig. 155.
[148] The inscription is, again, descriptive: ΙΟΥΛΙΑΝΟC ΡΩΓΕΥΩΝ ΕΝ ΔΟΛΩ ΕΧΟΝ Κ[Ε]Κ-
ΡΥΜΕΝΟΝ ΕΝ ΤΗ ΧΕΙΡΙ ΤΟ ΕΙΔΟΛΟΝ.
[149] *PG* 35:608C–609B; trans. Weitzmann (1942/3), 106. The sentence that invokes the episode pictured – 'There was placed before him gold . . . ' – is signalled by an enlarged gold initial.
[150] Weitzmann (1942/3), 106.
[151] Sozomen, 'Ecclesiastical History' V.17; Theodoret, 'Ecclesiastical History' III.12 (see notes 137
and 138 above); Weitzmann (1942/3), 105–108.

the (Christian) soldiers belatedly recognizing Julian's duplicity and returning the coins (fig. 54).[152] As in the Paris miniature, the Milan page shows Julian seated on a jewelled throne before his palace with soldiers entering from the right. Conventional though they are, the compositional similarities between the Paris and Milan scenes hint that if, as the cave episode seems to suggest, the miniaturists of both manuscripts were familiar with an earlier illustrated Homilies tradition, this might have included two pendant scenes – one of Julian distributing the donativum and the other of soldiers returning the coins – from which the two ninth-century miniaturists made different selections. Since the Milan Gregory extends the cave episode, restricted to a single scene on f. 374v – over three miniatures, a short narrative sequence cannot be excluded from consideration as part of an earlier illustrated Homilies reflected in the Julian sequences of the Paris and Milan manuscripts.[153] Like the image of Julian's descent into the cave, the donativum scene on f. 374v may preserve vestiges of an earlier narrative heritage.

Folio 409v (40) (fig. 40)

Folio 409v illustrates Gregory's second 'Invective against Julian'.[154] The first register shows the emperor advancing against the Persians at Ktesiphon, the second portrays St Basil addressing prayers against Julian, and the third depicts St Merkourios slaying him.

At the top Julian, in ornate gold military attire and astride a pale blue horse, leads his cavalry toward a bridge spanning a deep blue river. A walled city faces the troops across the river, and before it stand the defending Persians. The inscription tells us that 'Julian arrives in Persia' (ΙΟΥΛΙΑΝΟC ΑΠΕΡΧΟΜΕΝΟC ΕΝ ΠΕ[PCΙΔΙ]), and the image illustrates Gregory's text:

Now, having advanced in this way with the army and passed along the river's bank, with the ships on the river transporting corn and carrying baggage, he approached Ktesiphon after no small difficulty; so great was his longing for this city that even to be near it he considered as already a part of the victory . . . Ktesiphon is a strong fortress and hard to conquer, fortified with a wall of burnt brick and by a deep ditch and by lagoons coming from the river . . . [155]

It is unfortunate that the miniatures once accompanying this passage in the Milan Gregory have been excised.[156] An image of Julian's first manoeuvre after sighting the city, the burning of his ships to ensure a desperate fight for Ktesiphon by his soldiers, survives;[157] possibly Julian's arrival introduced the Ktesiphon campaign in

---

[152] Grabar (1943a), pl. LXVII,2.

[153] Ibid., pl. LXVI, 1–2; the third image, on p. 716, is almost totally excised and was not reproduced.

[154] PG 35:663–720. Omont (1929), 29, pl. LIV; Weitzmann (1942/3), 108–117; Galavaris (1969), 146–147; Walter (1978), 247–248; Walter (1982), 94–95; Der Nersessian (1987), 158; Anderson (1991), 74. [155] PG 35:676A-B; trans. Weitzmann (1942/3), 108–109.

[156] Milan, Ambrosiana 49/50 inf., pp. 763 and 764. [157] Grabar (1943a), pl. LXXIII,1.

one of the lost pictures. Be that as it may, the bridge spanning the Tigris on f. 409v contradicts Gregory's description of Ktesiphon's natural fortifications, and may perhaps be seen as an ironic inversion of the Milvian bridge on f. 440r (fig. 45), which it closely resembles. The Persians quietly facing the advancing Romans provide another curious detail, and Weitzmann is surely correct in seeing in them a visual corollary to Sozomen's description of Julian's halt at the sight of his enemy ranged along the riverbank.[158] With the loss of the Milan miniature, however, we will never know whether this historical detail had infiltrated the Homilies tradition more widely or whether it was inserted into f. 409v.

Despite the bridge and the passive Persians, the uppermost register on the whole remains true to Gregory's description. The same cannot be said of the lower two scenes, which depart radically from the sermon. In the middle register, St Basil, followed by another bishop, an acolyte or young monk, and two clusters of monks arranged according to age with the eldest closest to Basil, prays at a gold and green altar set before a pink church within a pink-walled enclosure. Only one element of this scene corresponds in any way with the second 'Invective'. Gregory refers, in passing, to the words of Basil and Gregory of Nyssa against Julian, and the illustrator of the Milan Homilies supplied this passage with an image of the two saints speaking to the emperor (fig. 55).[159] On f. 409v, the second register bears the inscription 'St Basil praying against Julian' (O ΑΓΙΟC ΒΑCΙΛΕΙΟC ΕΥΧ-ΟΜΕΝΟC ΚΑΤΑ ΙΟΥΛΙΑΝΟΥ), but here too the miniaturist supplied two bishops, the first with the dark hair and beard always accorded Basil in Paris.gr.510, the second with the grey hair and beard worn by both Gregory of Nyssa and Gregory of Nazianzus.[160] On the basis of the sermon and the Milan miniature, it seems likely that the former is shown here, and it may be that the Paris miniaturist has grafted a pair originally portrayed in another context in an older Homilies manuscript into a new scene, and one borrowed from another source entirely.

Basil leading prayers against Julian follows a widespread hagiographical narrative in which Merkourios appeared to Basil (either in a dream or as he meditated before an icon of the Virgin) to tell him that he had slain Julian; upon awakening, Basil assembled the clergy and led them to the church for prayer – the scene depicted here. In the lowest register, the miniaturist has depicted Julian's death. As explained by the inscription 'Julian slain by St Merkourios' (ΙΟΥΛΙΑΝΟC CΦΑ-ΖΟΜΕΝΟC ΥΠΟ ΤΟΥ ΑΓΙΟΥ ΜΕΡΚΟΥ[ΡΙΟ]Υ), Merkourios, in military dress, speeds toward the emperor on his white horse as Julian falls from his (black) horse to the ground in death. Though the colour of his horse has changed from the pale blue of the top register,[161] the miniaturist has nonetheless aligned the emperor

---

[158] Sozomen, 'Ecclesiastical History' VI.1; Weitzmann (1942/3), 110.
[159] *PG* 35:716A; Grabar (1943a), pl. LXXV,2.
[160] All three saints appear on f. 71v (fig. 13): see chapter 3.
[161] An indication, perhaps, of the switch from Gregory's account to another version of Julian's life?

in death beneath the living emperor above, and positioned the two praying bishops exactly between the two, as if their prayers were in truth responsible for Julian's fall.

This is not how Gregory described Julian's death in the second 'Invective'; indeed, Gregory admits to having heard several reports attributing the emperor's death variously to one of his own soldiers, a barbarian jester, or a Saracen.[162] The legendary account illustrated in f. 409v had surfaced by the sixth century, however, when it was recorded in the Chronicle of John Malalas.[163] It recurred in the seventh-century Paschal Chronicle and the Chronicle written around the year 700 by John of Nikiu; in the eighth century, John of Damascus paraphrased the legend as part of his defence of holy images; and a fully developed form had appeared by ca. 800 in a Life of Basil attributed to Pseudo-Amphilochios.[164] The principal difference between these accounts concerns Basil's state (dreaming or meditating) when Merkourios appeared to him, a matter not elucidated on f. 409v. But though all accounts note that Merkourios wore 'shining iron armour' as he set off to dispatch Julian, of the preserved texts only that of Pseudo-Amphilochios describes Merkourios 'unhorsing' the emperor;[165] it thus seems likely that, as Walter has already argued, the Life of Basil attributed to Pseudo-Amphilochios underpins the representations in the lower two registers of f. 409v.[166] An eighth-century cycle in Rome, two tenth-century sequences in Cappadocia, and an icon in the de Menil collection of ca. 1200 attest the visual impact of Pseudo-Amphilochios' Life; none of these, however, incorporates either scene pictured on f. 409v.[167] Nor did the Life affect the Milan Gregory; and, though an eleventh-century copy of the liturgical Homilies shows a nimbed horseman killing Julian, George Galavaris has argued that the image visualizes another tradition that credited Julian's death to one of his own (Christian) soldiers.[168] In short, while the scene on f. 409v suggests knowledge of the Merkourios legend as it was expressed in Pseudo-Amphilochios' Life of Basil, there is little evidence one way or another as to whether a text or an image conveyed this knowledge. As Photios rarely summarized saints' lives in his *Bibliotheke*, the absence of any reference to a Life of St Basil there is inconclusive;[169] he does, however, discuss the death of Julian in a manner that might suggest familiarity with the Pseudo-Amphilochios account: 'Some people attributed his death to one of the

[162] *PG* 35:680A–681A; trans. Weitzmann (1942/3), 114.

[163] *Chronographia* 13,25: ed. Dindorf (1831), 333–334; trans. Jeffreys and Scott (1986), 181–182.

[164] See Binon (1937a), 8–15; Binon (1937b), 11–29. For John of Damascus, 'Against those who attack divine images' I,60 (= II,56, III,53): ed. Kotter (1975), 161; trans. Anderson (1980), 45. See also Weitzmann (1942/3), 112–117.   [165] *PG* 29:ccciv-cccv.

[166] Walter (1978), 247–248; Walter (1982), 94–95.

[167] For the so-called Temple of Fortuna Virilis in Rome and the Cappadocian cycles, see the discussion of f. 104r in chapter 3 with Epstein (1986), 37. For the icon: Brubaker (1992). For independent images of Merkourios slaying Julian (none related to f. 409v): Weitzmann (1976), 78–79, pls. XXXI, CIV; Der Nersessian (1987), 158.

[168] Compare Grabar (1943a), pl. LXXIII,2, and, for the liturgical illustration (Mount Athos, Panteleimon 6, f. 242v), Galavaris (1969), 146–147, fig. 177.   [169] See Treadgold (1980), 107–108.

Persian deserters, others to a mercenary; but the general view, closer to the truth, informs us that he was led to the slaughter by God.'[170] Because the composition of Julian's death repeats stock figures found elsewhere in the manuscript – it is especially (and appropriately) close to the scene of Constantine unhorsing Maxentius on f. 440r (fig. 45) – text-based knowledge of the episode seems intrinsically more likely.

Paris.gr.510 is not the only illustrated copy of Gregory's Homilies to include historical miniatures: they appear throughout the Milan Gregory and also recur in a few versions of the liturgical edition. What distinguishes the historical miniatures in Paris.gr.510 is their incorporation of supplementary details or even whole scenes. Such additions are characteristic of the Paris Gregory, and underscore the conceptual unity of the miniatures: the question of an external visual source for the historical miniatures would not even pose itself were it not for Kurt Weitzmann's arguments in the 1940s that they provided evidence for now-lost copies of ecclesiastical histories with illustrations.

But, as we have seen time and time again, deviations from Gregory's sermons are not *prima facie* evidence for another visual source. While there is ample evidence throughout the manuscript that the designer of the miniatures knew other texts, in most cases it seems more plausible that it was the texts themselves, rather than any possible illustrations that they may have had, that precipitated the extra-homiletic features of individual miniatures.

In any event, seven of the nine historical scenes we have just considered find their fullest explanation in Gregory's sermons: all except the last two episodes from the life of Julian the Apostate depend on them for most of their details. While the repetition of stock figure types and motifs throughout the historical miniatures suggests that many of the scenes were compiled *de novo* for Paris.gr.510, I would nonetheless argue that some of them were adapted from an earlier illustrated Homilies manuscript with pictures that anticipated those of the Milan Gregory.[171] Such a hypothetical Homilies manuscript cannot, however, assume responsibility for all the details in the historical miniatures of Paris.gr.510, which incorporate supplementary elements that neither appear in the Milan copy nor derive from Gregory's text.

The most common textual sources for these details are the ecclesiastical histories written by Sokrates, Sozomen, and Theodoret. Iconoclasm had revived interest in the Arians and in Julian,[172] and though Photios was a more careful reader than many of his contemporaries he was not alone in his knowledge of earlier ecclesiasti-

---

[170] Codex 258: ed. Henry VIII (1977), 38; trans. Wilson (1994), 242.

[171] As Galavaris (1969), 146–149, observed, the liturgical editions are not related to Paris.gr.510; I cannot, however, agree with his conclusion that the liturgical historical images derive from illustrated ecclesiastical histories.   [172] See notes 122 and 143 above.

cal histories.[173] There is no evidence that any of these texts ever received illustration, but it seems likely that at least some other members of the élite Constantinopolitan circle with which we have been concerned, as well as Photios himself, were familiar with these histories. While only Photios, of this group, left a record of the books he had read, was demonstrably fascinated with history, composed a treatise on Julian, and wrote sermons on the Arian controversy,[174] it is, in the end, structural parallels between the way meaning is constructed in his writings and in the historical miniatures of Paris.gr.510 that provide perhaps the most compelling hint of his involvement in the manuscript. Just as Photios, in his synopses of Josephus in the *Bibliotheke*, was selective of the material he summarized, and added historical details,[175] so too the designer of Paris.gr.510 selected particular scenes from Gregory's sermons, and inserted historical details into them. The structure of the verbal and visual summary is the same: in both cases, particular episodes have been excerpted from a longer narrative, and then augmented with historical minutiae.

The ideas and thought patterns of Photios permeate Paris.gr.510. If the patriarch were not involved in the manuscript's production, we would have to invent his clone: an anonymous who had read, with Photios, the books cited in the *Bibliotheke*; who was thoroughly familiar with the exegetical twists and turns Photios favoured; who was as concerned with promoting the court and patriarchate as Photios was, and was as intimately associated with both; and who had apparently unlimited resources. It is simpler to confirm Der Nersessian's tentative speculations, and to identify Photios as the *éminence grise* behind Paris.gr.510.[176]

The patronage of imagery was a prerogative of Photios' position; we should not be surprised that he exercised it. Many previous studies have, in fact, linked Photios with other programmes, notably the new mosaic decorations installed in Hagia Sophia, part of which he eulogized in his sermon on the apse mosaic of 867.[177] Whatever his role in the Great Church, we know that as patriarch Photios controlled various teams of artisans; that these artisans may have been in sympathy with their former employer is suggested by one of the canons of the council that deposed him in 869–870, which forbade any painters who refused to go along with its decrees the right to work in churches, and thus seems to target Photian loyalists.[178] This canon may have some bearing on Photios' remark, during his exile, that

---

[173] E.g. Sozomen, Sokrates, and Theodoret are all cited (though often incorrectly) by the authors of the *Parastaseis*: see Cameron and Herrin (1984), 39.

[174] See e.g. Kustas (1964) and notes 121 and 143 above.

[175] See above, and chapter 2. On Photios' similar approach to Philostorgios' *History*, Nobbs (1990), 252–256; on his incorporation of the historical material he had read into his sermons, Mango (1958), 236–243; Mango (1975), 41. [176] Der Nersessian (1962), 227; see also Brubaker (1985), 7–13.

[177] See e.g. Grabar (1957), 196–198; Cormack (1986), 614–615, 618–620.

[178] See Cormack (1977b), 162.

churches were now being abandoned; certainly he complained that churches he had commissioned were being destroyed.[179] As patriarch, Photios urged Boris-Michael of Bulgaria to build churches; sometime between 868 and 871, during his exile, he wrote to Gregory Asbestos, bishop of Syracuse, encouraging him, too, to continue to erect and decorate churches.[180] Mango has in fact raised the possibility that Photios and Gregory collaborated in the design of decorative programmes.[181] Gregory does seem to have been transferred from Sicily (Syracuse) to Nicaea at about the time work began on Paris.gr.510;[182] he was therefore in reasonably close proximity to Constantinople. But Mango's intriguing hypothesis must, unfortunately, remain in the realm of speculation, for we have little further information about the bishop of Syracuse.[183] Another of Photios' letters written in exile may allude to a portrait painted of himself: 'Did not that good painter delineate our image with beautiful colours, he who maintains that he has said nothing bad about us?'[184] If it is a rhetorical flourish rather than a reference to an actual image, Photios' sentence at least indicates that he drew metaphors from the world of artisans.

Photios' association with a large and lavishly produced codex fits with the other information we can glean about the patriarch. His detractors portrayed Photios as having sold his soul to the devil in order to acquire his great learning,[185] and the controversy between Ignatios and Photios, as presented by their respective partisans, was often reduced to an opposition between culture (Photios) and piety (Ignatios).[186] Though the conflict was played out on other levels as well – for example, each side blamed the other for the great earthquake of 869[187] – the basic paradigm at least confirms the potential of Photian patronage. We know too, above all from the *Bibliotheke*, that Photios respected books; and in June of 870, when he was in exile from Constantinople and wrote to the Emperor Basil complaining about his treatment, he stressed the deprivation he felt from being denied them. Indeed, the entire letter concerns 'the fact that we have been deprived even of our books is novel and unexpected and a new punishment contrived against us', and includes such sentences as 'Eustathios, the admirable, endured the same treachery

[179] The first comment is contained in a letter to Gregory Asbestos, cited in the following note; for the second, see note 124 above. Cf. Magdalino (1996), 75.

[180] Epistle 112: ed. Laourdas and Westerink I (1983), 150–151 (*PG* 102:832D). See also White and Berrigan (1982), 59. [181] Mango (1977b), 140; cf. Cormack (1986), 614.

[182] Grumel (1936), no. 512. [183] See notes 184 and 189 below.

[184] Epistle 174: ed. Laourdas and Westerink II (1984), 47–61, ll. 127–129; trans. White (1981), 144. Photios may be speaking metaphorically; or he might be referring to Gregory Asbestos, an elusive figure who was, at least according to his enemies, a painter ('for this splendid fellow was also a painter in addition to his other vices': Niketas the Paphlagonian, *Vita Ignatii*: *PG* 105:540D; trans. Mango [1977b], 140; *pace* Oikonomides [1986], 47, Niketas' point is not that painting was beneath the dignity of a bishop). On Gregory, see also note 189 below. [185] See Gouillard (1971).

[186] This despite Ignatios' patronage of at least four monasteries and his imperial ancestry: see Ruggieri (1991), 201, 209; on the Mangana, Kaplan (1991), 353–357.

[187] See Vercleyen (1988), 168–169.

at the hands of the Arianizers, but his books were not, as in our case, taken away from him.'[188] As is well known, Photios' enemies claimed that he was involved with the production of other manuscripts. One of these was the famous parody of Ignatios, likening him to the anti-Christ, that was supposedly illustrated by Gregory Asbestos.[189] Another was a spurious genealogy of Basil I, designed to 'look ancient', that Photios' detractors asserted he had concocted in order to win back Basil's favour.[190] Whether or not these accusations have any basis in reality, they suggest that, to minds contemporary with his, Photios was associated with books, and with books that included pictures. Paris.gr.510, I believe, provides the surviving example. Why Photios chose to get involved with a manuscript of Gregory's Homilies is a question to which we shall return in the conclusions of this book.

[188] Epistle 98: ed. Laourdas and Westerink I (1983), 132–136 ll.17–19, 28–29; trans. White (1981), 161.
[189] Described by Niketas the Paphlagonian: *PG* 105:540D–541A; Grumel (1936), no. 497; trans. Mango (1972), 191–192. See e.g. Grabar (1957), 185–186, 196–198; Baldwin (1990). On Gregory, who seems also to have patronized church decoration, see Karlin-Hayter (1977), esp. 143; and notes 180 and 184 above. Photios was the victim of similar, though apparently unillustrated, attacks himself: Gouillard (1971).
[190] Niketas the Paphlagonian, *Vita Ignatii*: *PG* 105:565–568; Symeon Magister, *Annales*: ed. Bekker (1838), 689. See further Gouillard (1971).

6

Mission, martyrdom, and visual polemic

Both the Emperor Basil and the patriarch Photios encouraged the conversion of non-Christians, and sponsored extensive missionary activity. The 879–880 Council specifically praised Photios for this, while Constantine Porphyrogennitos devoted three sections of the *Vita Basilii* to his grandfather's conversion of Jews, Bulgarians, and Russians.[1] The other side of conversion rhetoric, anti-heretical discourse, had flourished for some time: the arguments that will concern us here were often first unleashed in the anti-Jewish dialogues, fanned by anti-iconoclast polemic, and kept smouldering by the anti-Islam broadsides and the conversion tracts aimed at the Bulgarians. But though programmes of conversion and diatribes against the un-converted are two sides of the same coin, in the miniatures of Paris.gr.510 references to missionary activity coexist rather than mingle with visual polemic directed against heresy: the two projects were kept visually separate, and mission was aligned with martyrdom for the faith rather than with condemnation of its opponents.

Folio 301r (30) (fig. 30)

Folio 301r contains within its jewelled red frame one of the five full-page text miniatures in Paris.gr.510, and, as is true of the other four,[2] the format signals a scene of particular importance: here a miniature of Pentecost introduces Gregory's sermon on the same topic, which begins on its verso.[3] The Byzantines held 'On Pentecost'

---

[1] Boojrama (1982), 18. *Vita Basilii* 95–97: ed. Bekker (1838), 341–343; see chapter 4 note 47. See further Dagron (1984), 307–309.

[2] The transfiguration (f. 75r), Habakkuk (f. 285r), the Council of 381 (f. 355r), and Ezekiel (f. 438v): figs. 14, 29, 36, 44. All but f. 75r also eschew the plain gold frames normal in Paris.gr.510 for decorated ones.

[3] SC 358, 312–355 (*NPNF*, 378–385). Millet (1920), 241; Morey (1929), 73–74, 91, 95; Weitzmann (1961), 480; Der Nersessian (1962), 199, 221 note 114; Walter (1971), 202–203; Weitzmann (1971b), 624; Weitzmann (1974), 35.

in great esteem: in the typikon of the Great Church, for example, Gregory's sermon is the *praelectio* – a reading normally derived from scripture – for Pentecost.[4] The significance of Gregory's text presumably accounts for both its expansive illustration in Paris.gr.510 and the inclusion of a similar image in nearly all other copies of Gregory's Homilies with pictures: even in the Milan Gregory a miniature of Pentecost (now excised) replaced the usual introductory preaching scene.[5] Folio 301r sits firmly within a coherent extra-Homilies framework as well, for images of Pentecost, rare before Iconoclasm, appeared with some frequency in the later ninth century, and continued into the tenth. The miniaturist of the Khludov Psalter added the scene to illustrate Psalm 65 (fig. 103); a drawing attests to its insertion in Hagia Sophia; and descriptive texts document an image of the Pentecost in the Church of the Virgin of the Source;[6] tenth-century examples proliferate in Cappadocia.[7]

The image of Pentecost on f. 301r replicates in most respects one of the two standard formulae used for this scene in Byzantine manuscripts.[8] Following the account in Acts 2:1–13, twelve apostles receive the 'cloven tongues like as of fire', badly flaked but still visible along streams of light issuing from a throne within a circle of blue light. The gold throne, backless but richly jewelled, supports a red cushion on which rest a gold and gemmed book, the dove of the Holy Spirit, and a crown; this crown, which is the only uncommon feature of the hetoimasia image, was apparently meant 'to signify [God's] royalty', a phrase from Gregory's description of Pentecost that the scribe of Paris.gr.510 marked with an enlarged initial.[9] Four of the apostles (presumably the four evangelists) hold books with jewelled gold covers; a fifth, identifiable by his physiognomy as Paul, carries a red book. The remaining seven hold scrolls. This manner of distinguishing the apostles appears frequently in ninth- and tenth-century images (in the Khludov Psalter [fig. 103], even the colours of the books held – gold for the evangelists, red for Paul – conform with f. 301r), and sporadically thereafter.[10] The manner of disposing the apostles is, however, unusual. Peter and Paul normally share the place of honour in Pentecost images – in the Khludov Psalter, for example, they flank the empty throne – and in Paris.gr.510 the pair duly sit together directly below the hetoimasia. But on f. 301r the axis is skewed slightly in Paul's favour, and this imbalance is emphasized by the

---

[4] Mateos II (1963), 136. On the typikon, see chapter 2 note 101.

[5] Only the explanatory caption on p. 577 remains; for the other illustrations to 'On Pentecost', see Grabar (1943a), pls. XLIII,2, XLIV, XLVI. Of the liturgical editions, all but one (Paris.gr.533) picture Pentecost: see Galavaris (1969), 29, 80–82.

[6] Moscow, Hist.Mus.cod.129, f. 62v (Ščepkina [1977]): Mango (1962), 35–38, figs. 22, 29–35. Baumstark (1904) is inevitably dated but still worth consulting.

[7] Cutler (1985) collects them all; see e.g. Epstein (1986), 60, 76, figs. 45–46, 93–97.

[8] See Ouspensky (1960). [9] SC 358, 340–342; f. 306r.

[10] E.g. all ninth- and tenth-century examples cited above (and St Petersburg 21, cited in note 12 below) follow this pattern, as do just over half of the images in the liturgical Homilies.

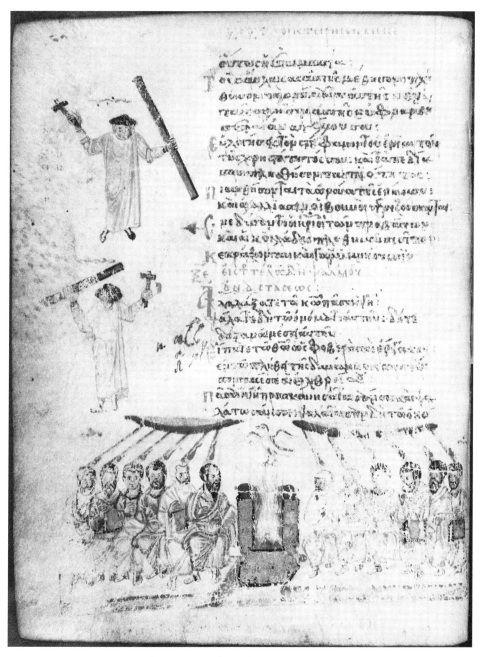

Fig. 103 Moscow, Historical Museum, cod.129, f. 62v: men singing in praise of God; Pentecost

fact that while Paul holds a book, Peter (on Paul's left) and a second apostle (possibly Andrew, on Paul's right) hold long staffs. They thus frame Paul as guards frame emperors, and ensure his dominance. Byzantine images of the Pentecost habitually give Paul the more important slot on the right side of God as represented by the empty throne (the viewer's left), and for obvious reasons: he was the apostle of the eastern empire, while Peter was associated with Rome.[11] What the Gregory miniaturist has done is make the ranking overt. The accent on Paul notwithstanding, the apostles otherwise sit conventionally on a semi-circular bench against an architectural backdrop, a habitual format found in numerous later examples.[12] The composition has suggested to some that f. 301r follows a monumental model designed for a curved surface, specifically a dome mosaic from the Church of the Holy Apostles;[13] no account of this church mentions a Pentecost dome, however, and it is anyway naive to think that curved shapes on a two-dimensional page were meant to replicate a three-dimensional dome: we see here a synthronon like that used for the church council on f. 355r (fig. 36). The wide distribution of the formula (without the slight realignment of f. 301r) does, however, suggest that it was well known in Constantinople.[14]

Perhaps in response to Gregory's reminder that the tongues of fire descended 'in an upper chamber . . . because those who were to receive it were to ascend and be raised above the earth',[15] the apostles and the hetoimasia – which extends above the frame of the miniature[16] – occupy the upper two-thirds of the page. The space below the inner curve of the semi-circular bench is filled with a green ground; on either side stand clusters of the 'devout men from every nation' described in Acts. The men recur in some later versions of the scene,[17] but their inclusion was never a prerequisite in Byzantine representations of Pentecost and f. 301r is the earliest image to include them. These 'devout men', many of whom chose to be baptized (Acts 2:38–41), emphasized a certain aspect of the pentecostal liturgy, the conversion and baptism of the multitude following the descent of tongues on the apostles.[18] The theme of conversion and baptism that underpins the episode narrated in Acts – reinforced on f. 301r by the inscriptions 'races' (ΦΥΛΑΙ) and 'tongues' (ΓΛΩCAI) – was not a motif that Gregory emphasized in his sermon, but (as noted above) it was a theme of considerable importance during the last third of the ninth century, with Photios' contributions officially lauded in the year that Paris.gr.510

---

[11] On Byzantine responses to St Peter, see von Falkenhausen (1988), esp. 642–643 (for Photios) and 652–657.

[12] E.g. St Petersburg, Public Lib. cod.21, f. 14v (*Lektionar* [1994]; Morey [1929], fig. 85; Weitzmann [1971b], fig. 4), many of the liturgical editions cited above, and the drawings of the Hagia Sophia dome mosaic (note 6 above).   [13] See Galavaris (1969), 80 note 178.

[14] Weitzmann (1974), 35, rather improbably suggested a lectionary model.   [15] SC 358, 342.

[16] See too the hands of God on ff. 75r and 264v (figs. 14, 28).

[17] E.g. the tenth-century lectionary in St Petersburg (note 12 above); see also Grabar (1968b) and Garidis (1969).   [18] On this liturgy and its relation to early Macedonian art, see Corrigan (1978).

was apparently commissioned.[19] Both André Grabar and Sirarpie Der Nersessian have already observed that the men awaiting baptism on f. 301r complement contemporary conversion campaigns;[20] their inclusion echoes a theme of the pentecostal rite that was particularly appropriate in the 880s.

Folio 426v (42) (fig. 42)

Folio 426v pictures the traditional mission of the apostles above twelve small vignettes that each show one apostle baptizing a new convert.[21] The miniature broadly illustrates the opening paragraphs of the accompanying sermon, 'On the Words of the Gospel' (Homily 37): 'Jesus who chose the fishermen, himself also useth a net . . . that he may draw up the fish from the depths, that is, man who is swimming in the unsettled and bitter waves of life.'[22]

These opening words have, however, little to do with the main thrust of Gregory's homily, an extended commentary on Matthew 19 that concentrates on the relationship between women and men. Indeed, the Milan Gregory ignores the fisherman theme altogether, interrupting the sermon only with its standard preaching scene and an image suggested by Gregory's citation of Matthew 19:19.[23] In Paris.gr.510 the decision to illustrate the first paragraphs rather than a passage more central to Gregory's theme was almost certainly dictated by Byzantine involvement with missionary work during the second half of the ninth century, which (as we have just seen) affected the Pentecost composition and which also informed Basil I's redecoration of the Apostoleion and the miniatures of the marginal psalters.[24]

Grabar noted the frequency of images of the mission of the apostles in the second half of the ninth and throughout the tenth century.[25] All of the early marginal psalters that retain Psalms 18 and 95 include versions of it, as do the tenth-century Cappadocian churches of Tokalı and Çavuşin; the Apostoleion portrayed specific missionary activities of individual apostles.[26] None of these, however, duplicates the format of f. 426v. Here a symmetrical longitudinal composition, with Christ in the centre of eleven (?) apostles ordaining them to 'Go therefore and teach all nations, baptizing them in the name of the Father, and the Son, and the Holy Spirit' (ΠΟΡΕ[ΥΘΕΝΤΕC ΟΥΝ ΜΑΘΗΤΕΥCΑΤΕ ΠΑΝΤΑ] ΤΑ ΕΘΝΕ ΒΑΠΤΙ-ΖΟΝΤΕC ΑΥΤΟ[ΥC ΕΙC] ΤΟ ΟΝΟΜΑ ΤΟΥ Π[ΑΤ]Ρ[Ο]C Κ[ΑΙ] ΤΟΥ Υ[ΙΟ]Υ Κ[ΑΙ] ΤΟΥ ΑΓΙΟΥ ΠΝ[ΕΥΜΑΤΟ]C; inscribed in red on the gold

---

[19] See note 1 above.   [20] Der Nersessian (1962), 221 note 114; Grabar (1968a), 160–163.

[21] Omont (1929), 30, pl. LVI; Morey (1929), 96; Gallay (1943), 194–196; Der Nersessian (1962), 206–207, 221, 226; Grabar (1968a), 160–163; Weitzmann (1971b), 640; Demus I (1984), 232–243.

[22] SC 318, 270–319 (*NPNF*, 338–344); quotation, SC 318, 270–272. As the text of the previous homily concludes on its recto, the miniature assuredly retains its original location.

[23] Grabar (1943a), pl. LXXVI, 1 and 2. An image between these two has been excised; it falls far too late in the homily to have depicted anything resembling f. 426v.

[24] See p. 257.   [25] Grabar (1957), 224.   [26] See notes 29 and 30 below.

frame), tops a grid composed of three tiers of four scenes each.[27] These nearly identical twelve frames each portrays an apostle baptizing in the presence of a white-
robed figure, presumably a catechumen awaiting his or her own baptism. The
apostles are not identified, though some can be named by virtue of their physiognomy (Paul occupies the second grid) or the physiognomy of those being baptized
(the black skin of the figure awaiting baptism in the final grid suggests Matthew,
credited with the conversion of the Ethiopians). Dark blue buildings against a
lighter blue ground provide an unobtrusive backdrop to all of the baptisms, which
themselves repeat a pattern. Reading from top left, the first apostle stretches his arm
toward the centre to baptize an initiate while the white-robed catechumen faces
him across the font. This format is reversed in the second grid, so that the catechumen stands at the left, facing the apostle across the pool at the far right. The formula
is reproduced throughout the page, resulting in lines of apostles ranging vertically
along the left and right margins and down the centre of the composition, while the
catechumens stand back to back along the lesser vertical axes. The shape of the fonts
provides a counterpoint: in the uppermost of the baptismal registers the fonts alternate between cruciform and round, in the middle register between round with an
inset quatrefoil and square. Only in the lowest register is this structural organization abandoned. While the first three compartments of this tier follow the formula
established in the top register, the last frame – already distinguished by its inclusion
of black candidates for baptism – shows a square font. The distinctions of this
section notwithstanding, compositional harmony dominates f. 426v and isolates
the Homilies mission sequence from other Byzantine monuments.

No other preserved Byzantine rendition of the mission of the apostles devotes so
much space to its unfolding. Nor, unless four baptism scenes were squeezed into
each of the three free tympana of the western arm of the Apostoleion,[28] did any
other Byzantine cycle concentrate on actual baptismal scenes. Most depictions
content themselves with the scene confined to the top register of f. 426v – Christ
commanding the apostles to 'go forth and baptize'[29] – and most early versions of
this scene present an asymmetrical composition, with Christ to the side of a
compact group of apostles.[30] The Gregory miniaturist apparently used the symmetrical arrangement to stress the importance of the episode and to maintain the
balance of the page – considerations that affect other compositions in Paris.gr.510[31]
– but may also have been nudged in this direction by one of the rare earlier exam-

[27] The grid format, which allows each apostle equal weight, was anticipated by the martyrdom of
the apostles on f. 32v (fig. 8).　　[28] For the arguments against this see Demus I (1984), 242–243.
　　[29] For New Tokalı, where Peter makes this pronouncement, see Epstein (1986), fig. 99.
　　[30] E.g. the marginal psalters: Moscow, Hist.Mus.gr.129, f. 96v (Šcepkina [1977]); Mount Athos,
Pantokrator 61, f. 137r (Pelekanides 3 [1979], fig. 225; Dufrenne [1966], pl. 20); London, BL
Add.40.731f. 4v (ibid., pl. 35). The eleventh-century Theodore Psalter portrays Christ ordaining Peter
and Paul only, while a compact group of 'the people of all nations' awaiting baptism stands below:
London, BL Add.19.352, f. 129r (Der Nersessian [1970], fig. 208).　　[31] See chapter 2.

ples such as the (now lost) apse of the Aula Leonina in Rome, which anticipated the symmetrical format of f. 426v by about eighty years.[32]

The marginal psalters illustrate Psalm 18:15 with images of the apostles preaching to the 'people of all nations'; while not iconographically related to Paris.gr.510, the version in the Khludov Psalter seems to parallel the intent of the Gregory page as a whole. While the eleventh-century (?) Bristol Psalter, which tends to avoid the topical features added in the ninth-century marginal psalters, simply portrays Peter and Paul preaching to two clusters of people,[33] the Khludov miniaturist responded to contemporary interest in missionary activity by depicting all twelve apostles preaching to discrete groups (fig. 104).[34] The mosaics in the Apostoleion also showed the missionary activity of the apostles: Mesarites' description notes Matthew with the Syrians, Luke preaching at Antioch, Simon among the Persians and Saracens, Bartholomew preaching to the Armenians, and Mark in Alexandria.[35] The descriptions given by Mesarites recall the apostles preaching to all nations in the Khludov Psalter, and both corroborate the importance of missionary imagery in the ninth century. It is also possible that the Apostoleion included a few scenes of apostles baptizing, one of which may be reflected at San Marco, where Matthew is shown baptizing the (white) Ethiopians.[36] But, in Byzantium, f. 426v appears to remain isolated in its emphasis on the actual rite of baptism; the only real parallel appears in the mosaic decoration of a mid-fourteenth-century dome mosaic in the Baptistery at San Marco, which Debra Pincus suggests may have been inspired directly by Paris.gr.510.[37]

Folio 32v (8) (fig. 8)

Like f. 426v, f. 32v is also constructed as a grid, with four rows of three squares, each containing the martyrdom or death of one 'apostle': Peter, Paul, and Andrew; James (son of Zebedee), Mark, and Matthew; John, Jude (Thaddeus), and Simon; and Philip, Bartholomew, and Thomas.[38] All are set against a monochromatic

---

[32] Davis-Weyer (1966), 124–125, fig. 5.

[33] London, BL Add.40.731, f. 31r: Dufrenne (1966), pl. 49; Dufrenne (1964), 159–182, esp. 163, 167 note 26. Anderson (1994), 212–217, argues that the Bristol Psalter copies Pantokrator 61; Corrigan (1992), 8–26, believes that they follow the same model.

[34] Moscow, Hist.Mus.gr.129, f. 17r: Ščepkina (1977); the image has been lost from Pantokrator 61 and Paris.gr.20. For the Theodore Psalter, where a similar composition spreads over ff. 19v–20r, see Der Nersessian (1970), figs. 34–35.   [35] Ed. Downey (1957), 905; trans. 875–877.

[36] Demus I (1984), 220, 234–243, and II (1984), pls. 360 and 371.

[37] Pincus (1996), 138, fig. 4; Tozzi (1933), 424, fig. 6.

[38] Millet (1920), 240; Omont (1929), 14–15, pl. XXII; Jerphanion (1930), 189–200; Der Nersessian (1962), 217–218, 221; Buchthal (1966), 43; Babić (1969); Kessler (1973), 213–214; Demus-Quatember (1974), 45–49 (see also Huskinson's review in *Art Bulletin* 58 [1976], 618–621); Weitzmann (1979a), 192; Demus I (1984), 219–225; Brubaker (1989a); Hahn (1990), 16. The identifications are Omont's: though the inscriptions he deciphered are often now illegible, physiognomic details and the types of martyrdom shown confirm his assessment.

Fig. 104 Moscow, Historical Museum, cod.129, f. 17r: apostles preaching

background, with darker blue trees and vaguely architectural shapes on a slightly lighter blue ground. Similar backdrops appear throughout the manuscript and sometimes, as on f. 71v (fig. 13), indicate that the scene took place outside the city walls.

Like all the text miniatures in the first sixty-six folios of Paris.gr.510, f. 32v is painted on a half leaf with a blank back, and it appears in the disturbed fourth quire.[39] Because the martyrdom of the apostles has no overt textual basis in the funeral oration to Gregory's brother Kaisarios that it introduces,[40] Gabriel Millet suggested that the miniature picturing Kaisarios' funeral (now f. 43v) once stood here, while f. 32v originally prefaced the homily that precedes it, 'To those who had invited him' (Homily 3).[41] That text is now preceded by a miniature of the crucifixion (f. 30v; fig. 7) which has almost certainly been moved forward from the first sermon; its theme is unappreciated preaching, and the deaths and martyrdoms of the apostles could be seen to visualize the consequences of rejected proselytizing. Disruption of the manuscript here is demonstrated by the loss of the first leaf of this short sermon; most of the homily is lost – the remaining text begins with paragraph 6 (of 8) – and with it any text markings that might have suggested a specific passage as the miniature's inspiration. Other copies of the Homilies provide no help: the oration is omitted from the liturgical editions, and the Milan Gregory accompanies it only with a preaching scene.[42] But the image Millet thought more appropriate to Kaisarios' funeral oration – his funeral on f. 43v – shares a page with an image of the death of Gregory's sister Gorgonia, and prefaces her funeral oration; there is no reason to think that the sequence would more fittingly precede than link the two eulogies. The death-of-the-apostles sequence might, in fact, be an appropriate introduction to a funeral oration for Kaisarios, a high government official who, in public debate, defied Julian the Apostate in declaring his Christianity, and was banished for his faith. Gregory's sermon never specifically connects his brother with the apostles, but it is full of phrases such as 'Such then was the arena, and so equipped the champion of godliness'[43] that rhetorically imply Kaisarios' affinity with the struggles of the earliest Christians. It remains at least plausible that the miniature retains its original location.[44]

The first square shows Peter's traditional reversed crucifixion.[45] An onlooker stands behind a balustrade to the left; his official dress suggests either the prefect Agrippa, who ordered Peter's execution, or Nero, during whose reign the saint's

---

[39] See Introduction and Appendix C.   [40] SC 405, 180–245 (*NPNF*, 230–238).

[41] SC 247, 242–255 (*NPNF*, 227–229).   [42] Grabar (1943a), pl. VI.

[43] SC 405, 211 (trans. *NPNF*, 233), signalled with a gold initial on f. 37r.

[44] Because it does not include any scenes from Kaisarios' life, however, I did not discuss it in chapter 3; as an inserted miniature, its time of execution is anyway uncertain.

[45] E.g. Hennecke and Schneemelcher II (1963), 319; Schermann (1907), 240–247.

crucifixion occurred. A round structure in three tiers balances the composition on the right; this represents the mausoleum of Hadrian, known in the ninth century as the Castrum S. Angeli, near which Peter was said to have been martyred.[46] Peter here lacks his familiar curly hair and is instead shown with a close-cropped light beard and straight short hair that dips down over his forehead, an alternative formula that also appears in the *Sacra Parallela* (fig. 105).[47] The composition resembles later images in menaia, menologia, and monumental cycles,[48] but I know of no earlier depictions of Peter's crucifixion.[49]

Rather than the canonically correct Matthias, Paul appears as Judas Iscariot's replacement in virtually all Byzantine lists of apostles. On f. 32v, he kneels in the second grid with his hands bound behind him; following the apocryphal Acts of Paul, he is about to be beheaded by one of Nero's soldiers, who raises his sword with his left arm while holding its scabbard with his right.[50] Paul's head type is standard; in the ninth century it recurs, complete with the tiny lock of hair on the otherwise bald pate, in the *Sacra Parallela* (fig. 106).[51] As Hugo Buchthal observed, Paul's martyrdom anticipates a conventional Byzantine formula;[52] f. 32v seems, however, to preserve the oldest example.

The third martyrdom, an upright crucifixion, is Andrew's. Contrary to the account in the apocryphal Acts of Andrew, which specifies that 'they came and bound his hands and his feet and did not nail him . . . in this way to torture him as he hung in that he would be eaten alive by dogs', Andrew is nailed to the cross.[53] The figure to the left speaking with the apostle, however, suggests that the miniaturist was familiar with an extra-biblical narrative of Andrew's life. On the basis of the preserved Acts, he might be identified as either Stratocles, Andrew's champion who conversed with him as he hung, or Aegeates, the proconsul who first condemned Andrew and later made an attempt (successfully resisted by the apostle) to unloose him from his cross.[54] Once again, there seem to be no older examples pre-

---

[46] Demus-Quatember (1974), 45–49.

[47] Paris.gr.923, f. 92r: Weitzmann (1979a), 198–199, fig. 534.

[48] E.g. Hagia Sophia at Ohrid, Monreale, and the Menologion of Basil II: Babić (1969), 116, figs. 80–81; Demus (1949), 119, 297, pl. 81a. The doors at San Paolo fuori le mura, Rome (fig. 107), made ca. 1070 in Constantinople, include the death of Peter, but here one executioner holds Peter's feet up with a rope while a second drives in the nails: Josi *et al.* (1967), pl. facing p. 8 and pls. 2–4; Frazer (1973), fig. 17; Cavallo *et al.* (1982), 417, fig. 318.

[49] On the lack of martyrdom scenes in early apostolic sequences, see Kessler (1979).

[50] Hennecke and Schneemelcher II (1963), 386; Schermann (1907), 290–292.

[51] Paris.gr.923, ff. 188v, 270v: Weitzmann (1979a), figs. 496, 502.

[52] Buchthal (1966), 43. The San Paolo doors (fig. 107), however, again differ from Paris.gr.510 in showing Paul led to his death by a rope tied around his neck (references in note 48 above). At Ohrid, Paul's head tumbles to the ground: Babić (1969), 112, figs. 78–79.

[53] For the Acts, Hennecke and Schneemelcher II (1963), 419. Most accounts simply specify a crucifixion: Schermann (1907), 247–253.   [54] Hennecke and Schneemelcher II (1963), 420–422.

Fig. 105 Paris.gr.923, f. 92r: Matthew, John, Peter

Fig. 106 Paris.gr.923, f. 270v: Paul (retouched)

served, though Andrew's crucifixion (with nails, as in Paris.gr.510) surfaces in numerous later menaia (fig. 109) and menologia.[55]

James, the first apostle to be martyred and the only one whose death is described in the canonical New Testament (Acts 12:2), appears fourth.[56] At the direction of Herod, seated on the left, an executioner pulls back James' head to expose his throat to the knife held in the soldier's left hand; James kneels with bound arms between the two officials. Though in the *Sacra Parallela* James has longer and more curly hair, his middle-aged physiognomy and dark hair are conventional attributes.[57] Later parallels to James' martyrdom appear in the Menologion of Basil II and in a twelfth-century Acts manuscript in Paris; reversed, and with the executioner's knife held to James' throat, the composition also recurs on the San Paolo doors (fig. 107).[58]

Though not listed among the apostles in the New Testament, Mark, like Paul, habitually appears as one in the Byzantine period. The fifth martyrdom shows him, prone before a colonnaded structure and a group of trees, being beaten to death by a young man brandishing a wedge-shaped club. His physiognomic details are standard,[59] and a similar compositional formula recurs in later images of Mark's death (fig. 108); f. 32v again provides the earliest preserved example.

The sixth apostle, Matthew, is simply shown in a sarcophagus, on to which two youths lower a lid decorated with a cross. This format anticipates the most common manner of representing Matthew's death in later works: for example, in the Menologion of Basil II and on the doors of San Paolo fuori le mura in Rome (fig. 107).[60]

John, the seventh apostle on the page, did not suffer martyrdom. According to the apocryphal Acts of John, when he knew his death was approaching he requested men with shovels to follow him outside the city wall of Ephesus, had them dig a pit and, after praying, lay down in it. He was then transported to heaven – the episode illustrated in Paris.gr.510, where two angels bear John upward.[61] The tradition of John's ascent is based on an interpretation of John 21:23, 'that disciple [John]

---

[55] E.g. a thirteenth-century menaion, Jerusalem, Patr.Saba 208, f. 91r (fig. 109): Weitzmann (1975), 102; Baumstark (1926/7), 72. The San Paolo doors (panel 19; fig. 107; references in note 48 above) and Ohrid (Babić [1969], 116, fig. 80) here deviate from Paris.gr.510 by showing Andrew nailed to a Y-shaped tree, a variant described in some apocryphal accounts of Andrew's death.

[56] Apocryphal accounts add no relevant details: Schermann (1907), 253–256.

[57] Paris.gr.923, ff. 115v, 175r, 287v: Weitzmann (1979a), figs. 529–531.

[58] Kessler (1973), 213–214. For other examples, Eleen (1977), figs. 9, 29–32.

[59] E.g. Paris.gr.923, ff. 148v, 301v: Weitzmann (1979a), figs. 446, 448.

[60] Vat.gr.1613, f. 186r (*Menologio* [1907]); for the doors see note 48 above. The Jerusalem menaion (Saba 208, f. 91v: fig. 109 and Weitzmann [1975], fig. 56) here deviates from Paris.gr.510 by picturing Matthew's death by stoning as described in some apocryphal accounts: Schermann (1907), 278. See also Demus I (1984), 224.

[61] Hennecke and Schneemelcher II (1963), 256–258; Schermann (1907), 257–266; and Duncan-Flowers (1990).

Fig. 107 Rome, San Paolo fuori le mura: bronze doors with the martyrdom of the apostles

should not die'. Apocryphal accounts frequently compare John with Enoch and Elijah, who also escaped death,[62] but John's ascent appears only rarely in later works, one example being the original mosaic (now destroyed) of the apostle's martyrdom at San Marco, which may reflect a mosaic contemporary with Paris.gr.510 in the Apostoleion in Constantinople.[63] The unusual depiction perhaps echoes iconophile interest in John's ascent, manifest in the Acts of the Council of 787 and reiterated by Photios, who recounts the episode in his *Bibliotheke*.[64] Later images sometimes show John without a beard, but in Paris.gr.510, as in the ninth-century *Sacra Parallela* (fig. 105), he is bearded.[65]

Jude (Thaddeus), brother of James, is ranked among the apostles by Luke and in

[62] Schermann (1907), 257–258, 262–263.   [63] Demus I (1984), 221.
[64] For the Council, Mansi XIII, 168D; for the *Bibliotheke*, codex 229, ed. Henry IV (1965), 139–141. Photios elsewhere disapprovingly cites another account of John's life (in an Acts of Peter, John, Andrew, Thomas, and Paul) which he claims was championed by iconoclasts: *Bibliotheke* codex 114, ed. Henry II (1960), 84–86; trans. Hennecke and Schneemelcher II (1964), 178–179, Wilson (1994), 126.   [65] Paris.gr.923, ff. 63r, 183v: Weitzmann (1979a), 199, figs. 536–537.

Fig. 108 Rome, San Paolo fuori le mura: bronze doors, detail, martyrdom of Mark

Acts, but is usually replaced by Luke in Byzantine lists.[66] On f. 32v, however, his funeral appears in the eighth quadrant complete with a censer-swinging attendant and a mourner. He was also depicted among the apostles at San Marco, where he has a youthful appearance as in Paris.gr.510.[67] In the *Sacra Parallela* Jude appears twice, once as a youth and once as middle-aged; the rarity of his portrayal perhaps militated against the creation of a standard type for the apostle.[68]

The last square of the third row contains the crucifixion of Simon in the presence of a soldier.[69] To the apostle's right is a small square structure on two steps. As for Jude, no standard type for Simon dominated Byzantine portraiture; a similar image appears, however, in the thirteenth-century menaion in Jerusalem (fig. 109).[70]

[66] Schermann (1907), 202–203, 282–283. [67] Demus I (1984), 224–225, fig. 362.

[68] Paris.gr.923, ff. 49r, 67r: Weitzmann (1979a), figs. 538–539.

[69] Apocryphal accounts vary in their descriptions of Simon's death; one tradition does, however, specify crucifixion: Schermann (1907), 280–282.

[70] Saba 208, f. 91v: Baumstark (1926/7), 72; Weitzmann (1975), fig. 56. The San Paolo doors (fig. 107) show Simon's crucifixion between two buildings with an executioner driving nails into the apostle's feet (note 48 above).

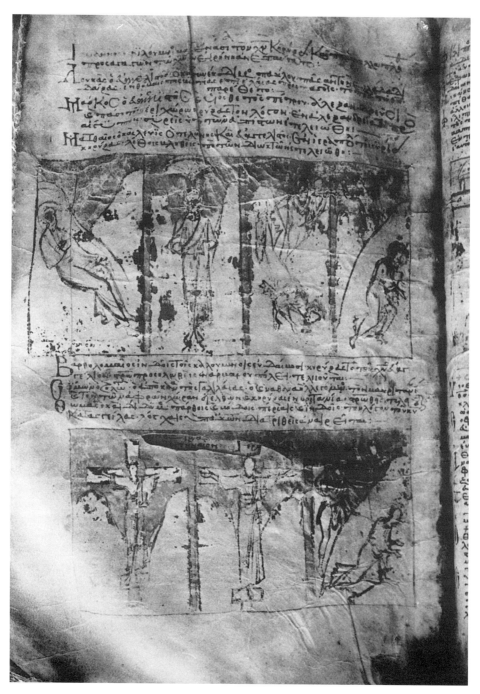

Fig. 109 Jerusalem, Greek Patriarchal Library, cod. Saba 208, f. 91v: martyrdoms of John, Luke, Mark, Matthew; Bartholomew, Simon, Thomas

Philip, the tenth apostle shown, meets his death by being crucified head downward, as specified in most apocryphal accounts.[71] Accompanied by an official, he appears as a beardless youth, his standard physiognomic description in Byzantine art; a similar martyrdom recurs on the doors at San Paolo fuori le mura (fig. 107).[72]

Following apocryphal accounts, the penultimate saint, Bartholomew, appears before an architectural backdrop, nailed to a cross.[73] Like Peter's, Bartholomew's portrait in Paris.gr.510 shows him with smooth rather than with the more usual curly hair.[74] Bartholomew's crucifixion figures in numerous later programmes (fig. 109) in similar form.[75]

The martyrdom of Thomas concludes the series. A soldier pierces him with a lance, as described in the Acts of Thomas.[76] Thomas appears, as always, beardless and youthful; his martyrdom is similarly depicted in the Menologion of Basil II and, complete with the detail of the apostle holding the lance as it enters his midriff, on the San Paolo doors (fig. 107). This gesture presumably refers back to Thomas' doubting probe of Christ's similarly located wound; it may also visualize Thomas' *request* to be lanced.[77]

The selection of apostles on f. 32v is unusual, and the order followed is apparently unique: it deviates from biblical and liturgical lists, adheres to no chronology, either actual (the years of the apostles' deaths) or liturgical (the order of the feast days of the apostles), and finds no visual parallels (even the mission of the apostles on f. 426v follows a different order).[78] In fact, however, few apostle sequences coincide: at San Marco, for example, only two of the numerous series of apostles correspond.[79] And while most middle Byzantine lists or depictions of the apostles substitute the evangelist Luke for Jude, Jude is cited as an apostle in the gospel of Luke, Acts, and the typikon of the Great Church;[80] since the latter was composed at about the same time as the Homilies, it seems clear that Luke had not yet entirely supplanted Jude.[81]

Evidence for the visual inspiration of the martyrdoms on f. 32v is cloudy. As noted earlier, the martyrdom of James has been associated with miniatures in the

[71] Schermann (1907), 268–269.

[72] Panel 28 (references in note 48 above). See also Babić (1969), 117, fig. 82 for an unidentified apostle in the martyrdom cycle at Ohrid nailed upside down to city walls in a manner reminiscent of Philip's crucifixion here.　　[73] Schermann (1907), 270–271.　　[74] See Demus I (1984), 178.

[75] Ibid., 362 note 48, lists other later examples.

[76] Hennecke and Schneemelcher II (1963), 529. Though the earliest texts specify death by natural causes, later ones agree that Thomas died by the lance: Schermann (1907), 274–275.

[77] Schermann (1907), 274–275; Lipsius (1883), 270–272.

[78] See the lists provided by Schermann (1907), 198–239; Jerphanion (1930); and Lipsius (1883), 16–25.　　[79] Demus I (1984), 220.

[80] Luke 6:13–16; Acts 1:13 (Thaddeus, conflated with Jude, is included in Matthew 10:2–4 and Mark 3:16–19); Mateos I (1963), 326 (30 June). The only other major Byzantine or byzantinizing cycle known to me in which Jude is not replaced by Luke appears at San Marco: Demus I (1984), 177, 220.

[81] As intimated in the previous note, however, Luke is celebrated as an apostle in Mesarites' description of the Church of the Holy Apostles: ed. Downey (1957), 905 (trans. 875–876).

Menologion of Basil II (ca. 1000) and in a twelfth-century Acts of the Apostles (Paris.gr.102). But if there was a direct source for f. 32v it is unlikely to have been an illustrated Acts. Illustrated Byzantine Acts manuscripts are rare, and the pictures in those which have been preserved are notoriously canonical and bound to the New Testament text, which ignores the deaths of all apostles save James.[82] Further, the miniatures closest in date to Paris.gr.510 that present narrative scenes described in Acts – those of the *Sacra Parallela* – portray John as dark-haired in the Acts illustrations and as light-haired, as he is in Paris.gr.510, elsewhere (fig. 105):[83] if a sequence of scenes from Acts was familiar in the 880s in Constantinople, it evidently deviated from the manner of depicting John represented by the isolated portraits in the *Sacra Parallela* and by the martyrdom scene in Paris.gr.510. But while f. 32v demonstrates little affiliation with Byzantine Acts sequences, it seems nonetheless to anticipate iconographic formulae found in later cycles. Its closest preserved parallels are the mid-eleventh-century frescoes of Hagia Sophia at Ohrid, the doors of San Paolo fuori le mura made in Constantinople in the 1070s (fig. 107), and the thirteenth-century menaion in Jerusalem (fig. 109).[84] All, like Paris.gr.510, isolate the deaths of the apostles from other events in their lives to form apostolic martyrdom sequences. Whether or not f. 32v was itself an *ad hoc* compilation, similar thematic sequences appeared elsewhere; it is possible that they were already in existence by the 880s.[85]

No visual evidence remains for an apostolic martyrdom sequence earlier than or contemporary with that on f. 32v; and since the apocryphal Acts that narrate the deaths were evidently familiar in ninth-century Constantinople the miniature could have been inspired by textual rather than pictorial accounts.[86] Textual corollaries nonetheless favour – but cannot confirm – the existence of such a sequence. Images of (unspecified) martyrs were often invoked in iconophile polemic, presumably in part because the iconophiles portrayed themselves as modern martyrs:[87] the Acts of the 787 Council, for example, beg all to accept 'the reproductions of the labours of the martyrs', and note that images of martyrs provide stellar examples to imitate.[88] As we saw in chapter 1, the *Vita Tarasii* (843–847) describes a

[82] Carr (1976); Eleen (1977), 264–265, 274.

[83] Compare Weitzmann (1979a), figs. 536–537, with figs. 483–487, 491.

[84] For Ohrid, Hamann-MacLean and Hallensleben (1963), 15 and Babić (1969), 110–117. For the doors, note 48 above; for the menaion, Baumstark (1926/7), 71–73, and Weitzmann (1975), 102, fig. 56.

[85] While it is possible that the scenes were independently extracted from an apostolic narrative cycle that utilized apocryphal legends, other groups of apostolic images – see Demus (1949), 297, 356; Demus I (1984), 221, 225–226 – are only sporadically related to Paris.gr.510: e.g. in the metaphrastian menologia, aside from the martyrdoms of Peter and Paul in Paris.gr.1528 and Moscow, Hist.Mus.9, simple portraits commemorate the martyrdoms (N. Ševčenko [1990]).   [86] See note 64 above.

[87] See e.g. the *vita* of St Stephen the Younger, written in the first decade of the ninth century, wherein Stephen the Deacon records a conversation about iconophile martyrs: *PG* 100:1164B–1168A; see Rouan (1981). For additional examples, I. Ševčenko (1977), 129 note 122; Gouillard (1960); Alexander (1977), 259–262.

[88] Mansi XIII, 240B, 301E–304D; trans. Sahas (1986a), 75, 125–126. These sentiments reflect old conventions: see e.g. Mango (1972), 36–39.

martyrdom cycle that Ignatios the Deacon claims was commissioned by Photios' uncle, the patriarch Tarasios (784–806).[89] Later, Nikephoros condemned the eradication of pictures of martyrs' acts from manuscripts, panels, and churches.[90] Though the images have perished, and though Nikephoros spoke in general terms and Ignatios rarely specified who was shown achieving martyrdom, evidently the idea of picturing martyrdoms was ideologically sound. It seems plausible that such images resurfaced in the years between the first and second Iconoclasms (787–815). That their importance continued is attested by the martyr cycle in the portico of Basil's Nea Ekklesia which, according to the *Vita Basilii*, 'contains the struggles and contests of the martyrs; it both offers nourishment to the eye and rouses the soul to the blessed and divine love, for the prowess of the martyrs draws the soul toward that love'.[91] Martyrs also appeared in the mosaic decoration at the Church of the Theotokos of the Pharos, probably completed in 864; whether these images were portraits or narrative scenes is not, however, noted by Photios in the inaugural homily that supplies our information on the church.[92] Linking martyrdom with the apostles may have paralleled a more general interest in the apostles that is evident in monumental programmes at Hagia Sophia – where busts of the apostles accompanied the four iconophile patriarchs in the mosaic decoration of the large sekreton, probably set in the 870s – and the Apostoleion,[93] and may especially have colluded with the emphasis on apostolic mission that began under Michael III and continued under Basil I: certainly the connection between apostolic mission and martyrdom is visually ensured in Paris.gr.510 through the shared compositional format of ff. 32v and 426v (fig. 42). The later apostolic martyrdom sequences intimate that f. 32v did not exist in isolation, and it is likely that similar but more accessible versions appeared during the latter half of the ninth century.

Folio 340r (34) (fig. 34)

The other martyrdom sequence in Paris.gr.510, that of the Makkabees on f. 340r, is also composed as a (nine-scene) grid: the series opens with the death of Eleazar and closes with that of Salomone, while the deaths of the seven sons range between.[94] Appropriately, the miniature prefaces 'On the Makkabees', which begins on its verso.[95] Here Gregory concentrates on the exalted status of martyrs, and celebrates

---

[89] Ed. Heikel (1891), 413,35–419,7: see chapter 1 note 16. An extract from this text appears later in this chapter in the discussion of f. 340r. Tarasios was buried in a chapel dedicated to all martyrs in a monastery he had founded on the Bosphoros; as I. Ševčenko (1984) observed, it is possible that the cycle described by Ignatios appeared there.

[90] *PG* 100:477B. More generally, Travis (1984), 100–104; on Nikephoros, see chapter 1 note 50.

[91] *Vita Basilii* 86: ed. Bekker (1838), 328–329; see chapter 4 note 47.

[92] Homily 10,6: ed. Laourdas (1959), 102; trans. Mango (1958), 188.

[93] Mango (1962), 44–45; Cormack and Hawkins (1977), 235. On the Apostoleion, see the *Vita Basilii* 80 (ed. Bekker [1838], 323; see chapter 4 note 47); chapter 1 note 78; and above.

[94] Omont (1929), 27, pl. XLVIII; Der Nersessian (1962), 198; Galavaris (1969), 109–117; Walter (1971), 203; Walter (1980), 258–259; Brubaker (1989a), 19–23.   [95] *PG* 35:911–934.

the rabbi Eleazar, the Makkabee brothers, and their mother – all of whom perished during Antiochos' persecution of the Jews in the first century – as protomartyrs whose importance, in Gregory's mind, equalled that of the first martyr, St Stephen. Gregory spends no time detailing the nature of the deaths, though he obliquely alludes to them in a list of obstacles that Christians must ignore in their efforts to uphold the true faith which includes cords to dislocate joints, torture wheels, hooks, the rack, iron nails, sharp swords, boiling cauldrons, fire, executioners, a threatening tyrant, the crowd, the sight of one's family, and mangled limbs.[96] Some of these items feature in the miniature on f. 340r, but the detailed visual record of the Makkabees' deaths can hardly be read as an illustration motivated exclusively by Gregory's list. The theme of the picture certainly correlates with Gregory's sermon, but the miniaturist has fleshed out the textual account.

Though the picture is badly rubbed, and the faces of the executioners seem to have been damaged deliberately, the salient details of each composition are clear. The first rectangle, in the upper left-hand corner, shows Eleazar (Ο Α[ΓΙΟC] ΕΛΕΑΖΑΡ), the elderly rabbi, being thrown to the ground and beaten with a club before Antiochos while, behind a balustrade, a guard pulls the hair of one of the Makkabee brothers in the presence of the other six. Antiochos (ΑΝΤΙΟΧΟC ΒΑCΙΛΕΥC) wears imperial regalia and a gold diadem; he sits on a jewelled throne and gestures toward the fallen Eleazar who, unlike the brothers, is nimbed. The backdrop of this scene is blue; on the rest of the page the miniaturist alternated between blue and purple grounds, producing a checkerboard pattern across the grid. Though Henri Omont, followed by Christopher Walter, found little connection between the sequence and the apocryphal books of the Makkabees,[97] this episode appears in II Makkabees 6:18–30 and IV Makkabees 5:4–6:30; five other scenes follow the books of the Makkabees as well.

The middle scene of the top register portrays two executioners flaying with iron claws one of the Makkabee brothers, who hangs suspended upside down from a catapult in the centre (IV Makkabees 9:26–10:1). Here, as in all remaining scenes, the tortured Makkabee is nimbed and wears a short blue loincloth.

The final scene of the top register depicts the second Makkabee suspended horizontally between two posts, to which he is bound by cords wrapped around his wrists and ankles. Two executioners beat him with large clubs. The image presumably visualizes IV Makkabees 9:11–12: 'the guards brought up the eldest of the brothers, and ripped off his tunic, and bound his hands and arms on this side and that with thongs . . . [and] flogged him with scourges until they were weary'. Though the text does not specify a horizontal position, this formula recurs repeatedly in Byzantine scenes of martyrdom and was apparently a conventional visual interpretation of flogging.[98]

---

[96] Ibid., 917A.   [97] Omont (1929), 27; Walter (1980), 258–259.
[98] E.g. in the Menologion of Basil II: Vat.gr.1613, pp. 27, 36, 71, 79, 217 (*Menologio* [1907]).

The middle register opens with an image of one of the Makkabee brothers being broken on the wheel (IV Makkabees 5:3, 8:13, 9:11–25, 11:1–13), with the cords pulled by two men in the short tunics habitual for executioners on f. 340r. In the central scene, two men beat a fallen Makkabee with iron mattocks, a form of martyrdom mentioned neither in the books of the Makkabees nor by Gregory. The last scene of the middle register pictures a bound Makkabee flung diagonally across the grid; two executioners crush his chest with a heavy plank while a third holds the martyr's head and appears to poke a nail in his eye. Again, this torment appears in neither of the relevant textual accounts.

The seventh rectangle contains a Makkabee, each wrist manacled to a separate ankle, being consumed by flames (IV Makkabees 8:13, 12:1–15?). Then follows a Makkabee crushed between two planks. Finally, Salomone, mother of the Makkabees, leaps into the fire (II Makkabees 7:41, IV Makkabees 17:1). Salomone (Η ΑΓΙΑ ΣΟΛΟΜΟΝΗ) was not so named in the books of the Makkabees, but her name was certainly widely known: she was listed in the typikon of the Great Church and specifically cited by Theodore of Stoudion, who called on her – along with Justina and Cyprian – to aid suffering iconophiles.[99]

As Omont noted, what little information Gregory provides about the martyrdom of the Makkabees was largely ignored by the illustrator of Paris.gr.510.[100] Nor did the miniaturist rely on a pictorial sequence that travelled with the text: the other Homilies present quite different images. In the Milan Gregory, two scenes have been excised from the margins; what remains is an image of Gregory preaching beside two ranks of standing figures. The lower group represents Gregory's audience, while the upper tier shows Eleazar and Salomone, both nimbed, followed by the seven brothers; in its iconic presentation, this formula recalls the earliest known image of the group, the early eighth-century fresco at Sta Maria Antiqua in Rome.[101] The liturgical editions follow Paris.gr.510 in supplying images of the martyrdoms,[102] but of the sixteen scenes that appear among the various manuscripts only four duplicate tortures shown in the Paris Gregory, and then the manner of representation differs.[103] While neither f. 340r nor the liturgical Homilies relied on Gregory's text for their visual enumerations of the tortures of the Makkabees, they supplemented the text in different ways.

Secondary textual descriptions, too, demonstrate considerable variation. Generally, the conceptual notion of torture opened a spectrum of possiblities that differed across time, and contemporary options seem often to have subsumed stale textual notations of no-longer-horrific tribulations: the synaxary of Constantinople, for example, lists a branding iron among the implements of torture – a detail more in line with Byzantine punishments than with the Makkabee text.[104] Given this, the

[99] Mateos I (1963), 356–357; Alexander (1977), 260. On Theodore, see chapter 1 note 115.
[100] Omont (1929), 27.   [101] Grabar (1943a), pl. XXIX; Romanelli and Nordhagen (1964), pl. 2.
[102] Galavaris (1969), 109–117.   [103] Compare Galavaris (1969), figs. 7, 37, 110, 208, 212, 392, 458.
[104] *Propylaeum ad Acta Sanctorum, Novembris*, ed. H. Delehaye (Brussels, 1902), 859–860.

degree of adherence to the Makkabee account revealed on f. 340r is actually rather surprising, all the more so since the ninth-century marginal psalters preserve other pictures of the Makkabees that deviate markedly from those in the Homilies.[105] But the martyrdom scenes on f. 340r also share certain curious features with a cycle of monumental paintings that, his *vita* tells us, the patriarch Tarasios sponsored. In his Life of Tarasios (843–847), Ignatios the Deacon includes the following description, apparently of a programme portraying martyrs and prophets:

For who would see a man represented in colours and struggling for truth, disdaining fire [scene 7] . . . and would not be drenched in warm tears and groan with compunction? Who, seeing a man . . . finally tortured to death, would not leave the scene beating his breast in the affliction of his heart? . . . Who, observing another man's flank and back being scraped with iron claws because he had refused to utter a word unworthy of piety [scene 2], would not be anointed with the emollient of compassion? Who is not filled with apprehension and subdued by fear? . . . Who would see a man tied to a straight board, his inner organs falling out because of heavy flogging and his suffering depicted in material colours [scene 8], and would not be wounded in his heart?[106]

Ignatios did not name the saints whose painted martyrdoms he described, for his main goal was not narrative biography.[107] But Walter convincingly argued that Ignatios here described episodes from the martyrdom of the Makkabees, and he connected the passage with f. 340r. This connection is appealing not only because three scenes described by Ignatios appear 'in colours' on f. 340r, but more importantly because the last torture enumerated is extremely unusual, appears in neither the Makkabees texts nor in Gregory's sermon, and seems to correlate with the penultimate martyrdom pictured on the page. Walter suggested that both Paris.gr.510 and the images described by Ignatios echo a standard series of scenes no longer attested elsewhere. If, however, the association of the two sequences is correct, the Gregory page may equally well, and more simply, adapt Tarasios' programme, which, assuming it survived the second wave of Iconoclasm, would have had particular prestige as a monument to an idolized iconophile patriarch who was also Photios' uncle.

Folio 347v (35) (fig. 35)

A final, isolated image of martyrdom appears as the lowest scene on f. 347v.[108] This shows the death of Isaiah, who sinks to the ground as two men saw his skull in half with a carefully painted two-handled saw, as described in the miniature's titulus (O HCAIAC ΠPIZOMENOC), various *vitae* of the prophet, the apoc-

---

[105] Moscow, Hist.Mus.cod.129, f. 79r (Ščepkina [1977]); Mount Athos, Pantokrator 61, f. 110r (Dufrenne [1966], pl. 16; Pelekanides 3 [1979], fig. 218).
[106] Ed. Heikel (1891), 414–415; trans. Ševčenko (1984). See chapter 1, esp. note 16, and the discussion of f. 32v earlier in this chapter.   [107] See Brubaker (1989a), 19–23.
[108] The martyrdom of Cyprian on f. 332v (fig. 33) was considered in chapter 3.

ryphal Martyrdom of Isaiah, and, later, the metaphrastian menologion.[109] Earlier examples survive, but these show Isaiah standing upright;[110] most late versions follow Paris.gr.510 in showing the prophet kneeling. It is possible that the Gregory miniaturist is responsible for the shift in Isaiah's position, for it represents a simple variant on that assumed by John in the transfiguration on f. 75r (fig. 14). More likely, however, the Homilies painter drew on another source already familiar in the capital, for a very similar illustration appears in a tenth-century Constantinopolitan Book of Isaiah, the painter of which does not seem to have been familiar with Paris.gr.510.[111] One thinks, again, of the series of martyrs and prophets the patriarch Tarasios is said to have had painted in Constantinople around the year 800 as a possible inspiration for both.[112]

The interest in the apostles manifest in Paris.gr.510, the sekreton mosaics at Hagia Sophia and the redecoration of the Apostoleion – where imperial funding and ancient associations made links between the orthodox emperor and the apostles explicit – represents another example of orthodox reclamation, a response to the iconoclast claim that their emperors were the new apostles: 'as in the past [Jesus] had sent forth his most wise disciples and apostles . . . so now he also raised his devotees, our faithful [iconoclast] kings – the ones comparable to the apostles'.[113] And the interest in martyrdom observable in the Homilies and in the portico decoration of Basil's Nea Ekklesia also had its roots in the iconoclast debate.[114] Both, however, also joined an apparently new enthusiasm for missionary activity during the reigns of Michael III and Basil I. Particularly under Basil, the new and resolutely orthodox Macedonian dynasty implemented the apostolic task of converting pagans to Christianity with an aggressive missionary campaign and the persecution of heretics.[115]

Grabar and Der Nersessian first observed the impact of Byzantine missionary

[109] T. Schermann, *Prophetarum Vitae Fabulosae Indices Apostolorum Discipulorumque Domini Dorotheo, Epiphanio, Hippolyto, Aliisque Vindicata* (Leipzig, 1907), 40, 68, 104; Charles II (1913), 159–162. The menologion reference was first observed by Omont (1929), 28. On the problematic relationship between this miniature and Gregory's sermons, see chapter 2; on the remaining images on the page, see chapters 4 (Samson) and 8 (Gideon).

[110] See Bernheimer (1952), esp. 30–31; Stern (1960), 111, fig. 5. For examples of this type of martyrdom imposed on saints other than Isaiah, see Walter (1972), 119.

[111] For the prophetbook (Vat.gr.755, f. 225r): Weitzmann (1935), 12–13, fig. 62; Lowden (1988), 68, fig. 37. The two compositions are so close that Weitzmann suggested that the later miniaturist copied the Gregory scene directly, a hypothesis countered by Lowden. A similar image once also appeared in the now-destroyed Smyrna Physiologos (Evangelical School 8, f. 21r), conveniently reproduced in Lowden (1988), fig. 117.   [112] See notes 89 and 106 above.

[113] Council of 754, quoted by the Council of 787: Mansi XIII, 225D; trans. Sahas (1986a), 65. See also Schönborn (1976), 152; Krautheimer (1983), 60, 64; Christou (1971), 284–285. On the mosaics, which align patriarchs and apostles, see note 93 above.   [114] For the Nea, see note 91 above.

[115] For Basil's development of innovative military tactics to subdue heretics, see Tobias (1976), 30–55.

activity on the miniatures of Paris.gr.510.[116] Both cited the images of the mission of the apostles (f. 426v) and the inclusion of the 'men of all nations' in the representation of Pentecost (f. 301r) as evidence of the importance of conversion themes in the Paris Homilies; the martyrdoms that the apostles, the Makkabees, Cyprian, and Isaiah suffered in consequence of their proselytizing could be added. But the emphasis on missionary work had another face: a sometimes fierce, and nearly always defensive, attack on heresy. Several miniatures in Paris.gr.510 visualize this other side of the coin.

IMAGES AGAINST HERESY

Some of the conversion imagery in the Paris Homilies is less positive than the apostolic scenes we have just considered, for rather than extolling the zeal of the apostles or representing those awaiting baptism, it condemns the unbaptized and specifically the Jews. Though the anti-Jewish polemic was sometimes a thinly veiled attack on iconoclasts, it was not just rhetoric: the severity of the anti-Jewish campaigns during Basil's reign was noted in contemporary texts.[117]

In general, the anti-Jewish miniatures accompany Gregory's sermons against heresy, which attacked fourth-century heresies that were, in the 880s, no longer in the forefront of theological debate; by then, Gregory's prime target, Arianism, was not a threat – it had become instead a pejorative label that could be conveniently attached to contemporary opponents. In common with many iconophile polemicists, for example, Photios equated iconoclasts and Arians, and reframed the fourth-century heresy into one resembling that of his own century.[118] Gregory's arguments were also transformed, and made relevant to ninth-century interpretations of heresy, by the pictures that supplemented them. In Paris.gr.510, the anti-Jewish miniatures contextualize the text; they work with and augment Gregory's anti-heretical sermons to clarify their meaning for a ninth-century audience.

Folio 170r (22) (fig. 22)

Six of Christ's miracles preface Gregory's twenty-seventh homily, 'Against Eunomians'.[119] In the top register, Christ heals the leper, the man with dropsy, and

---

[116] Grabar (1968a), 160–163; Der Nersessian (1962), 221, 226.

[117] See note 1 above and Starr (1939), 3–7, 127–140, for a collection of contemporary texts and commentary.

[118] Two of Photios' homilies nominally against Arianism, but in truth attacking iconoclasts, survive: ed. Laourdas (1959), 139–151, 152–163 (see esp. 154–156); trans. Mango (1958), 244–278 (esp. 264–266) and commentary 239–240.

[119] SC 250, 70–99. Omont (1929), 22, pl. XXXVI; Der Nersessian (1962), 205; Brubaker (1996a), 13–14.

the two demoniacs; the middle register shows the healing of the centurion's servant and of Peter's mother-in-law; finally, Christ walks on water and rescues Peter as his doubts cause him to sink.[120]

Though f. 170r is surely in its intended location, Gregory mentions none of these miracles in the sermon that begins on its verso,[121] which defends the doctrine of the trinity against the assertions of Eunomios, an Arian who denied Christ's equality with God.[122] Der Nersessian, however, persuasively argued that the miracle sequence functions as pictorial exegesis meant to corroborate Gregory's polemic against the Eunomians by emphasizing Christ's divinity. As she noted, almost any of Christ's miracles could serve this purpose; but the examples selected for illustration on f. 170r seem nonetheless to have been carefully chosen: the use of Arianism to condemn modern foes by analogy pointed to the contemporary relevance of Gregory's words, and this pointer was exploited in the miniature. Gregory's anti-Eunomian and anti-Arian text acquired pictures that seem to have been selected for anti-heretical interpretations appropriate to the ninth century.

The combined sense of the miniature as both expressive of Christ's divinity and anti-heretical is introduced in the first register. Following Old Testament indications that leprosy was the punishment inflicted by God for the worst sins, Christ healing the leper (Matthew 8:2–4, Mark 1:40–44, Luke 5:12–14) was broadly interpreted as signifying redemption.[123] More specifically, in the sixth century Romanos made a point of observing that the healing proved the Arians wrong by revealing Christ's divinity.[124] Photios reflected a ninth-century transference of anti-heretical rhetoric when, in a long section of his *Amphilochia* (question 60) that deals with the healing of the leper, he used the miracle as an excuse to harangue Jews.[125] The middle miracle, the healing of the hydrophobiac (Luke 14:2–4), was also associated with invectives against the Jews, for it was a Sabbath miracle against which the leaders of the synagogue protested.[126] Finally, Christ's healing of the demoniacs (Matthew 8:28–32), overtly revealed his triumph over the root of all heresies, Satan, for this healing was seen as analogous to Christ's victory over the devil during his temptations in the desert.[127] The scenes of the first register thus do double duty:

[120] For the iconography, see chapter 8.

[121] The text contains so little biblical narrative that the Milan Gregory does not illustrate it at all.

[122] The writings of Eunomios were still in circulation in the ninth century; Photios vehemently refuted them in his *Bibliotheke*: ed. Henry II (1960), 105–108; partial trans. Wilson (1994), 135–136.

[123] E.g. by Romanos: SC 110, 360–379 and commentary in SC 110, 255 and SC 114, 45.

[124] 'On the leper' (chanted on the third Wednesday after Easter): SC 110, 360–379, esp. 376 (strophe 16). On Romanos, see chapter 2 note 104.

[125] Ed. Westerink V (1986), 45–50. See also note 118 above and Mango (1958), 151–153.

[126] See e.g. John Chrysostom, 'Homily on John' 37:2 (*PG* 59:209–210). Commentary in Millet (1916), 65.

[127] E.g. Romanos, 'On the possessed' (for the fifth Wednesday after Easter): SC 114, 54–77, esp. 62 and 70 (strophes 9 and 19). On Christ's temptation (f. 165r), see chapter 2 above.

they demonstrate the divinity of Christ while simultaneously stressing his victory over heresies. The miracles selected to carry this message provide an appropriate corollary to Gregory's text, and the first and second of them also visualize anti-Jewish statements of specific relevance to the ninth-century conversion campaigns.

The second register also presents healings, but of acute rather than chronic diseases. The register opens with the healing of the centurion's servant (Matthew 8:5–13), here misidentified as the daughter of the leader of the synagogue (H ΘΥΓΑΤΗΡ ΤΟΥ ΑΡΧΙCΥΝΑΓΩΓ[ΟΥ]). Omont thus listed this scene as the healing of Jairus' daughter, illustrated quite differently earlier in the manuscript (f. 143v; fig. 19). As the main male figure is dressed as a centurion, and the ill figure is a male youth, this misidentification has been corrected in most subsequent references to this scene.[128] The healing of the centurion's servant is followed directly, as it is in the gospel of Matthew (8:14–15), by the healing of Peter's mother-in-law, though the details of the scene come from the version in Mark 1:30–31, 'and he came and took her by the hand, and immediately the fever left her . . .'. The two miracles are connected liturgically (falling respectively on the fourth Saturday and Sunday of Lent) and exegetically, as examples of Christ's impartiality toward men (the servant) and women (the mother-in-law).[129] Both of these healings, and especially the first of them, record the power of faith in Christ's divinity.[130] The same emphasis on the power of faith in Christ explains the selection of Christ walking on water and rescuing Peter (Matthew 14:25–31) in the third register, for Peter could only continue walking on water as long as he kept faith in Christ; the moment he doubted, he sank and had to be rescued.[131] As a unit, the lower two registers provide an antithesis to the anti-Jewish scenes of the top tier by demonstrating the recuperative benefits of belief in Christ.

Antithetical imagery was not characteristic of the polemicized marginal psalters made earlier in the century.[132] The anti-heretical miniatures in the psalters most often relied on inscriptions to make their points; when the polemic was expressed in fully visual terms, the psalters tended toward parallel images equating contemporary and biblical wrong-doers, or else resorted to caricature.[133] The miniatures of Paris.gr.510 moved away from the direct confrontation that characterized both the content of the psalter miniatures and their marginal assault on the text. What we seem to see instead on f. 170r is the internalization of the polemic process: a more

---

[128] E.g. Weitzmann (1979a), 164. The healings of the centurion's servant and of Jairus' daughter are sometimes painted next to each other (e.g. at New Tokalı: Epstein [1986], fig. 78); some similar situation may have instigated the scribal error. See further the discussion of this page in chapter 8.

[129] Mateos II (1963), 148–149; Millet (1916), 58 citing Kerameos, *PG* 132:828. See also Brubaker (1996a), 13–14.   [130] See esp. Matthew 8:10, 13.

[131] On Peter's status in Byzantium, see note 11 above.

[132] Corrigan (1992), 112 lists six examples, but interprets them, in the marginal psalters, as confrontations.

[133] Corrigan (1992), 62–77 (inscriptions), 27–33 (parallel scenes), 46–49 (caricatures).

subtle form of visual argument, antithesis, has replaced the broadsides of the psalters.

Folio 215v (25) (fig. 25)

Folio 215v illustrates Gregory's thirty-second oration, 'On moderation', with the judgment of Solomon above Christ speaking to the Samaritan woman and healing the ten lepers.[134] The scenes accord well with the homily,[135] which has as its introductory theme the question of who has the authority to judge trinitarian issues; the body of the oration then takes up the issue of wisdom in a more general way. References to Solomon, explicit and implicit, abound; Gregory repeatedly invokes the 'wisdom of the divine Solomon' and many of his references are marked with painted initials.[136] Gregory also observes that God alone imparts perfect wisdom; Christ, who passed this wisdom to the world, is humanity's only hope;[137] his wisdom should unite the church through 'One God, one faith, one baptism'.[138]

The combination of scenes on f. 215v, drawn from both the Old and the New Testament, echoes the contrast between the wisdom of Old Testament figures such as Solomon and the knowledge given by Christ. The judgment of Solomon was an obvious candidate for inclusion: as evident from Gregory's repeated references, Solomon embodied perfectly the spirit of Old Testament wisdom. The judgment of Solomon (3 Kings 3:16–27) was, however, rarely pictured; it does not even appear in the single illustrated Book of Kings preserved from the Byzantine period. On f. 215v, Solomon, dressed and enthroned as a Byzantine emperor, faces the two women and the sword-wielding soldier who holds the disputed child aloft by one arm.[139] The strong contemporary imperial flavour of the scene is not surprising, for Solomon had symbolic significance in Byzantine imperial rhetoric. Basil I seems, in fact, to have gone further than many emperors in his attempts to identify himself with – and, following the model of Justinian, to surpass – the Old Testament king: not only did he like being compared with Solomon, but he asked Photios for information on his wisdom, and is said to have buried a statue of the king (removed from a basilica near Hagia Sophia) in the foundations of his Nea Ekklesia.[140] As Gilbert Dagron has pointed out, however, the associations that both Justinian and

---

[134] SC 318, 82–155. Omont (1929), 23–24, pl. XXXIX; Gallay (1943), 143–145; Weitzmann (1947), 156, 197; Der Nersessian (1962), 207–208.

[135] Further, leaf losses in this section of Paris.gr.510 notwithstanding, the fact that the preceding text ends on its recto guarantees that f. 170v retains its original location. There is nonetheless no correspondence with the Milan Gregory: see Grabar (1943a), pls. LII,2–4, LIII, 1, 3.

[136] For an explicit reference, SC 318, 96–98; for an implicit one, SC 318, 130. Gold initials mark both.

[137] SC 318, 112, 146–148; gold initials mark both passages.

[138] SC 318, 152; marked with a gold initial.

[139] The inscription simply identifies the scene: Η ΚΡΙCΙC ΤΟΥ CΟΛΟΜΩΝΤΟC.

[140] *PG* 102:583–584; epistle 241 (ed. Laourdas and Westerink II [1984], 164–167). See Dagron (1984a), esp. 269, 307–309; Magdalino (1987), 58–59; Kazhdan (1984), 43.

Basil made with Solomon were weighted in favour of the Christian emperors rather than their Old Testament precursor: Solomon's wisdom, like his temple, must inevitably be surpassed by God's new chosen people, embodied in the orthodox emperor.[141] It is this undertone that links the image of Solomon, suggested by the text, with the New Testament scenes of the lower register, which supplement Gregory's oration and were selected with some care.

Ninth-century Constantinople knew three interpretations of Christ's conversion of the Samaritan woman: it provided a type of baptism, it referred to contemporary missionary work, and it functioned in anti-Jewish polemic. The most common interpretation predated the ninth century: already in the sixth, Romanos saw the episode as a type of baptism; that this reading continued into the ninth century is clear from the writings of Photios.[142] Gregory's concluding remarks on true wisdom uniting the church through God, faith, and baptism thus find a succinct illustration in the single image of Christ and the Samaritan woman. This interpretation was strengthened by the iconographical formula used by the Gregory miniaturist.

The image of Christ's conversion of the Samaritan woman (John 4:5–26) is most closely related to the illustration to Psalm 35:9 in the Khludov and Pantokrator Psalters (figs. 110–111).[143] Both duplicate the image in Paris.gr.510 with only minor variation: Christ sits on a jagged outcrop of rock rather than a bench, and an urn sits by the Samaritan woman's feet. All three share the distinctive form of Jacob's well, and freeze the action at the moment when the woman has drawn water (with her left hand on the pulley cord) and it spills over the sides of the bucket.[144] The emphasis on the well is not, perhaps, surprising, for a relic of this 'holy well' was kept along the path between the palace and Hagia Sophia; it would have been familiar to the viewers of the psalters and Paris.gr.510 alike.[145] But the overflowing bucket requires further explanation. The psalm verse illustrated begins 'For with thee is the fountain of life', and the adjacent inscription in the Khludov Psalter (fig. 110) – 'David says, Christ is the source of life' – makes clear its significance. The psalter verse has been interpreted as a typological allusion to baptism, and appropriately illustrated, for Christ identified himself as the well of living water to

---

[141] Dagron (1984a), esp. 294–301, 305–310.

[142] For Romanos, SC 110, 342; for Photios, *Amphilochia* 74: ed. Westerink V (1986), 81–85 (*PG* 101:457–464).

[143] Moscow, Hist.Mus.cod.129, f. 33r (Ščepkina [1977]); Mount Athos, Pantokrator 61, f. 42v (Dufrenne [1966], pl. 6; Pelekanides 3 [1979], fig. 191); see Walter (1986), 281. On f. 215v, the scene is inscribed O X[PICTO]C ΔIAΛ[E]ΓΩMENOC TH CAMAP[EI]TIΔH ('Christ talking to the Samaritan woman').

[144] The Theodore Psalter reverses the composition, and demonstrates a misunderstanding of the pulley device: London, BL Add.19.352, f. 41r (Der Nersessian [1970], fig. 71).

The Florence tetraevangelion follows the ninth-century examples save that, significantly, the well becomes a marble basin: Laur.plut.6.23, f. 174r (Velmans [1971], fig. 275).

[145] On the passage past the well, see Cameron (1987), 113–115.

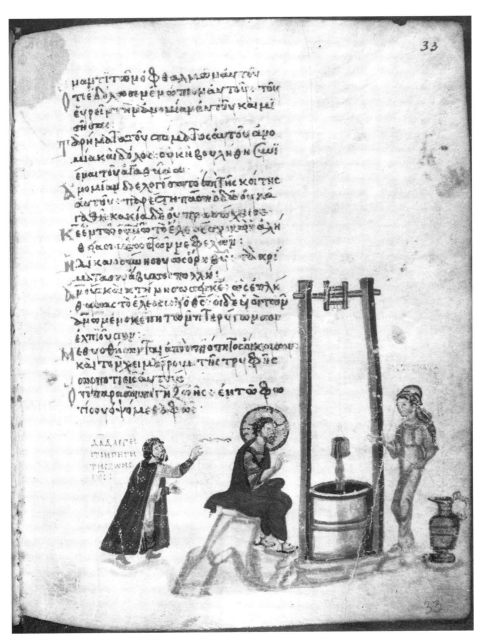

Fig. 110 Moscow, Historical Museum, cod.129, f. 33r: David with Christ and the Samaritan woman

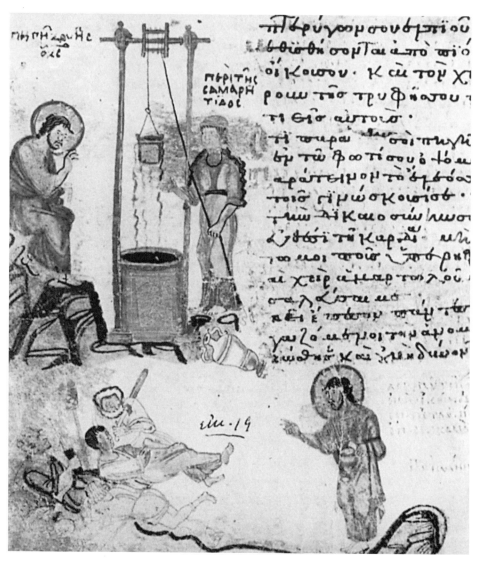

Fig. 111 Mount Athos, Pantokrator 61, f. 42v: Christ and the Samaritan woman; the Jews fall to the ground before Christ

the Samaritan woman (John 4:14); the overflowing bucket in the psalters and Paris.gr.510 underscores the typological reference to baptism.

On the Sunday of the Samaritan woman, the fifth after Easter, the typikon of the Great Church pairs the gospel account of her conversion with verses from Acts 11 narrating the missionary activities of Barnabas and Paul.[146] Following this association, the scene on f. 215v could also be seen as an example of the spreading of true wisdom through conversion, an apt interpretation during the intensive campaigns

[146] Mateos II (1963), 122–123.

268

of conversion directed at the Slav and Jewish populations that marked Basil's reign.[147] As an image of successful missionary activity against the Jews, the conversion of the Samaritan woman was, in fact, particularly appropriate, for the New Testament consistently contrasts the 'misguided' Jews with the Samaritans. Photios detailed their differences at length in various commentaries on the relevant New Testament passages, and continued the unflattering contrast.[148] The image of the Samaritan woman should probably, therefore, not be seen simply as an illustration of conversion to the true wisdom of Christianity, but also as a statement that some are more susceptible to receiving this knowledge than others. In this, the miniaturist followed the lead already provided by Pantokrator 61 (fig. 111). The Khludov Psalter portrait of David explaining the significance of the scene (fig. 110) has been ignored by the Pantokrator miniaturist; instead, below the Samaritan woman, who recognized and accepted Christ, is an image of the Jews who did not.[149]

An anti-Jewish interpretation of Christ and the Samaritan woman finds written confirmation as well. Byzantine exegesis habitually identified Christ as the Samaritan woman's sixth husband and Romanos, as Augustine before him, thus saw the woman as a type of *ekklesia*.[150] She receives 'the bridegroom who has come', and it is in this role that Photios used her in his eighth homily, where she is contrasted quite specifically with the Jews. The relevant passage appears as part of a lengthy discussion of the difference between wisdom and ignorance that shares numerous features with Gregory's 'On moderation'.[151] But while Gregory condemned the ignorance of heretical Christians, Photios condemned the Jews:

Thou sittest with long labour by the bridal chamber, but thou dost not receive the bridegroom who has come, seized as thou art by love of harlotry. Verily is your synagogue husbandless, brooding alone senselessly on bare words. Verily is this people foolish and unwise.[152]

Rather than pairing the Samaritan woman with an image of the Jews who did not recognize Christ, however, the Homilies miniaturist combined the episode with Christ healing the ten lepers (Ο Χ[ΡΙCTO]C ΙΟΜΕΝΟC ΤΟΥC ΔΕΚΑ ΔΕΠΡΟΥC). The scene may underscore the differences between the Samaritans and the Jews in a different way, for the gospel account of this healing (Luke 17:11–19) once again singles out a Samaritan – this time a male, so that the theme of Christ's impartiality to gender seen before on f. 170r continues – as the only one of the ten lepers who praised God on being healed. Iconographically, however, the

---

[147] Dvornik (1970); Mango (1958), 151–152.

[148] E.g. in question 74 of his *Amphilochia*: ed. Westerink V (1986), 81–85 (*PG* 101:457–464) and a catena fragment on John 4:13 (*PG* 101:1231). On Christ as Samaritan, see the discussion of f. 143v in chapter 2.

[149] So too Corrigan (1992), 65; the page provides a rare example of visual antithesis in the psalters.

[150] SC 110, 329–353, esp. 334–336, 340–342.

[151] Homily 8,1–2: ed. Laourdas (1959), 83–86; trans. Mango (1958), 153–157 (as Homily 8,1–3).

[152] Homily 8,2: ed. Laourdas (1959), 85; trans. Mango (1958), 155 (as Homily 8,3).

miniaturist has not distinguished the Samaritan leper from the other nine, but has simply reproduced the standard Byzantine formula with Christ gesturing toward the huddled mass of figures.[153]

The image on f. 215v illustrates the sense of Gregory's sermon in a manner particularly appropriate to the ninth century. While balancing the wisdom of the Old and New Testaments, the miniaturist departs from Gregory's words to depict scenes that stressed the foundations of orthodox belief. The Samaritan woman functions as a type of baptism, a type of the orthodox church, and as a piece of anti-Jewish polemic all at once; the healing of the ten lepers may reinforce the latter role, and thus further the use of visual antithesis to condemn the Jews by comparison with those who accepted Christ.

Folio 310v (31) (fig. 31)

Christ heals the man with the withered arm and the two blind men of Jericho in the first register of f. 310v; he heals the bent woman and delivers the parable of the withered fig tree in the second.[154] The miniature remains in its original location (the end of the preceding text occupies its recto), but sustains no direct connection with the text it illustrates, Gregory's first letter to Kledonios (epistle 101).[155] Gregory wrote to condemn the Apollinarian heresy, which held that the incarnate Christ had a divine rather than a human spirit.[156] The three healing miracles on f. 310v certainly function as visible proof of the dual nature of Christ – he is shown in his human form, performing divine miracles – but this rather generic connection between text and image neither illuminates why these miracles were selected nor encompasses the parable of the withered fig tree. Toward the end of the letter, however, Gregory hints at the subtext that all four episodes seem to complement: apparently because some adherents insisted on circumcision, he likens Apollinarianism to 'a second Judaism'.[157] Photios, too, whose interest in Apollinarios is well attested, saw him as an imitator of 'the madness of the Jews and [their] false teachings'.[158] The anti-Jewish implications of these passages, rather than their anti-Apollinarian messages, seem to have stimulated the illustration on f. 310v.

The healing of the man with the withered arm appears in the synoptic gospels

---

[153] See e.g. Florence, Laur.plut.6.23, f. 145v: Velmans (1971), fig. 244.

[154] Omont (1929), 26, pl. XLV; Morey (1929), 96; Der Nersessian (1962), 205; Weitzmann (1979a), 169, 185–186; Brubaker (1996a), 16. An explanatory inscription accompanies each episode: O X[PICTO]C IΩMENOC [TON] ΞHPAN EXΩNTA TH[N ΔEΞI]AN; O X[PICTO]C [IΩ]MENO[C TO]YC ΔYO TYΦΛ[OYC]; O X[PICTO]C IΩMENOC THN CYΓKYΠTOY-CAN; and O X[PICTO]C KATAPΩMENOC THN CYKHN.

[155] SC 208, 36–69 (*NPNF*, 439–443). In the Milan Gregory, Gregory hands the letter to a courier, and the courier then passes the letter on to Kledonios: Grabar (1943a), pl. LIX,1.

[156] Apollinarios was one of the two heretics shown condemned on f. 355r (fig. 36): see chapter 5.

[157] SC 208, 64, and note 1.

[158] Epistle 284, ll. 2562–2564: eds Laourdas and Westerink III (1985), 77. For Photios' other references to Apollinarios see chapter 5.

(Matthew 12:10–13, Mark 3:1–5, Luke 6:6–10) as part of a general condemnation of the Pharisees' attitude toward the Sabbath; all therefore stress that the healing occurred on the Sabbath in contravention of Judaic law, for 'the Son of Man is Lord even on the Sabbath day' (Matthew 12:8). Immediately below the man with the withered arm, the miniaturist – again juxtaposing genders, as on ff. 170r (fig. 22) and 215v (fig. 25) – placed his female counterpart, the bent woman. Again, Christ healed on the Sabbath, and was chastized by the 'ruler of the synagogue' (Luke 13:11–16). Following the lead of the gospels, Christian polemicists, Photios among them, used the Sabbath miracles as an excuse for invectives against the Jews.[159]

The conceptual unity of the two healings on the left side of the miniature is, to an extent, confirmed by their compositions: both have been reduced to the essential components of Christ, a witness, and the person to be healed. The top register shows Christ grasping the man's withered arm (he carries a staff over the wrist of his healthy one) in the presence of a youthful disciple holding a scroll.[160] A similar version of the healing appears in the mid-tenth-century wall paintings at New Tokalı (fig. 112),[161] where the man carries a staff in his healthy left hand while Christ grasps his withered wrist; at Tokalı, too, the man wears a short tunic over decorated leggings reminiscent of those he wears on f. 310v. Christ's position is virtually identical, and he is accompanied by a youthful disciple who, at Tokalı, duplicates the disciple immediately below Christ who witnesses the healing of the bent woman, down to the sling fold of drapery over his right arm.[162] Both may echo a fairly prominent Constantinopolitan source.[163]

The scene of the healing of the bent woman repeats the youthful disciple of the top register, here standing to the left. In essence, the male and female healings are mirror images of each other, an effect strengthened by the arrangement of the page where each takes up precisely the same amount of lateral space. The witness here gestures over the head of the bent woman, who gazes up to Christ. Christ moves slightly toward the right, but gestures and looks left; the stance is a familiar one in Paris.gr.510, and recurs throughout the manuscript.[164] Unlike most representations of this scene,[165] the bent woman does not walk toward Christ, but kneels on the ground; indeed, she resembles images of the woman with the issue of blood more closely than she does portrayals of the bent woman, and it seems plausible that the Gregory miniaturist modified the earlier image of that healing (f. 143v; fig. 19) here:

---

[159] E.g. John Chrysostom in *PG* 59:209–210; Photios, *Amphilochia*, question 60: ed. Westerink V (1986), 45–50, esp. ll. 24–25 (*PG* 101:409–416).

[160] The three healings of f. 310v recur in a sequence spread over ff. 211v–212r of the *Sacra Parallela* (fig. 113); the healing of the man with the withered arm is not, however, related: Weitzmann (1979a), 166, figs. 417, 435, 462. Nor are the tetraevangelia versions: Laur.plut.6.23, f. 67r (Velmans [1971], fig. 135); Paris.gr.74, ff. 23r, 68v, 117v, like Paris.gr.510, clothes the man in a short tunic (Omont [n.d.], pls. 23, 63, 104).   [161] Epstein (1986), fig. 77.   [162] At Tokalı, the disciple has an older companion.

[163] See chapter 2 note 29.   [164] E.g. on ff. 3r (Jonah), 87v (Christ), 174v (Abraham): figs. 6, 16, 23.

[165] E.g. Paris.gr.923, f. 212r; see Weitzmann (1979a), 177, fig. 462. Schiller I (1971), 178, described the two standard versions of this scene – both of them with the woman standing.

Fig. 112 New Tokalı: healing of the man with the withered arm

the women resemble each other closely – even their garment colours are the same – and Christ stands similarly in both.[166]

The scenes on the right half of f. 310v also form a thematic pair. The uppermost shows Christ healing the two men born blind, outside of Jericho (Matthew 20:30–34); the lower pictures the fig tree that, as it bore no fruit, Jesus caused to wither (Matthew 21:18–21, Mark 11:12–14, 20–25). This latter episode provided an antithesis to the opening image of the healing of the man with the withered arm – a connection visually emphasized by repeating the arrangement found in the opening scene, with the withered fig replacing the man with the withered arm –

---

[166] See also Paris.gr.923, f. 212r (where the two healings overlap each other): Weitzmann (1979a), fig. 454.

and contributed further to the anti-Jewish tone of the miniature. Photios, in his sixth homily, specifically equated 'the fig tree that has remained fruitless' with 'the barren and harsh synagogue of the Jews'.[167] If the withered fig tree signifies the synagogue, the two men of Jericho represent the triumph of compassion and faith in Christ. The use of this episode as part of an antithesis, setting those of faith against the synagogue, is not restricted to Paris.gr.510. In his hymn on the born blind, for example, Romanos too opposed the two men who had faith with the Jews.[168]

As were the two healings on the left side of the miniature, the two scenes on the right are compositionally connected. In the upper register, Christ stands as in the healing of the man with the withered arm, save that he now gestures toward the two blind men with his right arm. The two men, one in profile and one squatting *en face*, sit to the right and are separated from Christ by a tree that unifies this miracle with that of the withered fig tree below it. Not surprisingly, other versions of the scene lack the tree, but the *Sacra Parallela* (fig. 113) duplicates the squatting position of one of the men in the Paris Gregory, and this position, somewhat more elegantly rendered, recurs in the Florence tetraevangelion; in all three, Christ's position remains the same.[169] It thus seems likely that the Gregory miniaturist added the tree for compositional unity, while otherwise replicating a standard Byzantine formula.

In contrast, the miracle of the withered fig was rarely illustrated; when the scene appears in the densely packed middle Byzantine tetraevangelia, only the most general similarities surface.[170] It seems most likely that, like the adjacent healing of the bent woman, the miracle of the fig tree was compiled from stock figure types visible throughout the manuscript in response to Photios' polemic interpretation of the episode.

Folio 316r (32) (fig. 32)

Like f. 310v, to which it is thematically related, f. 316r presents four christological scenes in two registers. Each register maintains the balance of male and female; each combines a healing scene with an episode involving a widow: the upper tier pairs the healing of the blind man at Siloam with the story of the widow's mite, the lower joins the healing of the paralytic at Capernaum with the raising of the widow's son at Nain.[171]

---

[167] Homily 6,3: ed. Laourdas (1959), 65; trans. Mango (1958), 127–128.   [168] SC 114, 140.

[169] Paris.gr.923, f. 211v (Christ's scroll is omitted): Weitzmann (1979a), 169, fig. 435. Florence, Laur.plut.6.23, f. 41v: Velmans (1971), fig. 89. The healing of the two blind men formed part of the miracle cycle at New Tokalı, but is now too damaged to permit comparison: Epstein (1986), 71. In Paris.gr.74, f. 18r, the two men stand: Omont (n.d.), pl. 19.

[170] The tree is leafless in Florence, Laur.plut.6.23, ff. 43r, 85r (Velmans [1971], figs. 94, 164); leaved in Paris.gr.74, ff. 42r, 88v (Omont [n.d.], pls. 36, 78).

[171] Omont (1929), 25, pl. XLVI; Der Nersessian (1962), 205; Brubaker (1996a), 16. The inscriptions are, again, descriptive: Ο Χ[ΡΙСΤΟ]С ΙΩΜΕΝΟС ΤΟΝ ΕΚ ΓΕΝΕΤΗС ΤΥΦΛΟΝ and Η ΚΟΛΥΜΒΙΘΡΑ ΤΟΥ СΗΛΟΑΜ in the upper register; Η ΧΗΡΑ ΒΑΛΛΟΥСΑ ΤΑ ΔΥΟ ΛΕΠΤΑ and [Ο ΧΡΙСΤΟС ΕΓΕΙ]ΡΩΝΤΟΝ Υ[ΙΟ]Ν ΤΗС ΧΗΡΑС ΕΚ ΝΕΚΡΟΝ in the lower.

Fig. 113 Paris.gr.923, f. 211v: Christ healing the dumb man possessed by a demon, the man with the withered arm, four women, two blind men, the lunatic, and the two men born blind

None of these events features in the accompanying letter, Gregory's second 'To Kledonios'; as with the first letter, the Milan miniaturist restricted illustration to a portrait of Gregory handing the letter to a messenger, who forwards it to Kledonios.[172] The Paris miniature retains its intended location, however, for the text begins on its recto, and the illuminator indicated one level on which the miniature should be understood by signalling a phrase with a gold initial. Most unusually, the initial falls in the middle of a sentence, thereby underscoring the importance of the marked phrase, which (again) characterizes the Apollinarian heresy as a 'second Judaism'.[173] Indeed, like the miniature accompanying the first letter to Kledonios, that accompanying the second also includes anti-Jewish imagery.

Both of the healing miracles illustrated on f. 316r provided fuel for anti-Jewish polemic in the Byzantine period. The Siloam healing, which appears only in the gospel of John where it occupies most of chapter nine, is another of the Sabbath miracles for which the Jews condemned Jesus. It thus falls into the same group as two of the healings on f. 310v, a position confirmed by both Romanos and Photios.[174] Similarly, the healing of the paralytic at Capernaum (Matthew 9:1–8, Mark 2:3–12, Luke 5:17–26) evoked a vitriolic anti-Jewish passage from Photios, embedded in a commentary on Matthew now preserved as a catena fragment.[175] The anti-Jewish implications of the two healing scenes connect the miniature prefacing Gregory's second letter to Kledonios with that accompanying the first letter on f. 310v. Again, the anti-heretical slant of the second epistle has been redirected and focused on a specific 'heresy' of particular concern to the court and patriarchate in the 880s.

The two healing scenes selected for f. 316r were, in addition, both associated with baptism. From the time of the early church fathers, the Siloam healing exemplified the remission of sin effected by that rite. The reading from John 9 formed part of the baptismal liturgy – a connection reiterated by Photios in his *Amphilochia* – and the episode commonly appeared in the decorative programmes of baptisteries.[176] The miniaturist responsible for f. 316r stressed this aspect of the healing. While the left side of the scene closely follows the gospel narrative, showing Christ anointing the blind man's eyes with clay in a manner thoroughly consistent with earlier, contemporary, and later Byzantine versions of the scene,[177] some details on the right

[172] SC 208, 70–85 (*NPNF*, 443–445); Grabar (1943a), pl. LIX,2.

[173] SC 208, 76; Paris.gr.510, f. 317v.

[174] Romanos, 'On the born blind': SC 114, 140. Photios invoked the Siloam healing near the end of a long diatribe against the Jews that he puts in the mouth of Joseph of Arimathaea: Homily 11,4; ed. Laourdas (1959), 109–112 (for the Siloam reference, 111); trans. Mango (1958), 198–202 (200).

[175] Reuss (1957), 287.

[176] Commentary and discussion in Underwood (1975), 257–261; for Photios, ed. Westerink IV (1986), 33–34.

[177] E.g. the Rossano Gospel (Rossano, Diocesan Mus., f. 13r; Muñoz [1907], pl. XI; Cavallo *et al.* [1987], 140–143), the *Sacra Parallela* (Paris.gr.923, f. 212r; Weitzmann [1979a], fig. 480), the frescoes at Old Tokalı (Epstein [1986], fig. 31), the Florence tetraevangelion (Laur.plut.6.23, f. 188r; Velmans [1971], fig. 284).

side go beyond John's account. The man leans over to wash away the clay that Christ applied to his blind eyes and, as is clear from his open eyes, receives sight. According to both John and the legend accompanying the scene, the man washes his eyes at 'the pool of Siloam'; on f. 316r this pool is represented as a cruciform baptismal font identical to the one on f. 87v (fig. 16). In this detail, the Gregory miniaturist deviates from images such as that in the Rossano Gospels or at Old Tokalı, which show a rectangular pool, but may find a roughly contemporary parallel in the *Sacra Parallela* and certainly anticipates middle Byzantine versions such as the tetraevangelia miniatures, which repeat the font.[178] The baptismal implications of the Siloam healing are further emphasized by the inclusion of an angel, hovering over the font and gesturing toward it with a long staff. The angel 'troubling the water' belongs with an earlier episode in John's gospel, the healing of the paralytic at Bethesda (John 5:2–9), another passage that figured prominently in the Byzantine baptismal rite; commentaries specify that the angel represented the Holy Spirit descending at baptism.[179] Its anachronistic insertion in the Siloam scene leaves little doubt that the designer of the page intended the miracle to be read as a type of baptism.

The healing of the paralytic at Capernaum not only joins the Siloam scene in providing a piece of visual anti-Judaism, it also dovetails with the baptismal reading: the fullest gospel account of the Capernaum story (Mark 2:3–12), which is followed closely in the Homilies miniature, appears in the typikon of the Great Church as the reading immediately preceding the call to the catechumens on the second Sunday of Lent.[180] Christ, accompanied by the youthful disciple who repeatedly joined him on f. 310v, sits on the far left before a pink building that, in the context of Paris.gr.510, provides an unusually elaborate background. Two men lower the man sick with palsy through a hole in the roof with long cords attached to a hammock-like sling; to the right, in the middle of the register, a group of three men, presumably the critical scribes, stand behind their seated leader. The scene is far more specific in its details than the versions either at S. Apollinare Nuovo or in the middle Byzantine tetraevangelia,[181] but it is remarkably close to an eighth-century wall painting at the Church of San Saba in Rome,[182] which shares with f. 316r the open-roofed building through which two youths lower the paralytic, the disciples to the left, behind Christ (followed, in the more expansive fresco, by three more disciples), and the Pharisees to the right.

[178] References in preceding note; and cf. Weitzmann (1979a), 182.

[179] Discussion in Underwood (1975), 257–261; Daniélou (1956), 211–215.

[180] Mateos II (1963), 30–31.

[181] Deichmann (1958), fig. 175; Florence, Laur.plut.6.23, f. 65v: Velmans (1971), fig. 133. The architectural backdrop in Paris.gr.74, f. 67r (Omont [n.d.], pl. 62), however, recalls Paris.gr.510.

[182] Styger (1914), fig. 12; also Underwood (1975), fig. 31. The primary differences are that Christ stands in the wall painting, and the paralytic appears a second time, walking away with his bed on his shoulders.

The linkage of anti-Jewish and baptismal imagery in the two healing scenes on the left half of f. 316r suggests an implicit contrast between the true faith of the baptized Christian and the blindness of the unbaptized Jews. The two scenes on the right-hand side of the folio are also related to each other – as noted earlier, each portrays an episode from Christ's ministry that centred on a widow – but unless they are meant to provide a pictorial antithesis these two scenes have no evident connection with either the anti-Jewish or the baptismal programme of the left side of the page.

In the upper register, next to the Siloam healing, the parable of the widow's mite (Mark 12:41–44, Luke 21:1–4) appears as a narrative scene. Christ, repeating his stance in the adjoining Siloam scene, stands to the left of an arch placed behind a gold, three-tiered altar. The widow approaches from the right, and deposits her coins on the altar. No examples of this scene are preserved before the ninth century, when it appears both in Paris.gr.510 and in the *Sacra Parallela* (fig. 114).[183] The latter manuscript, anticipating the formula that later becomes dominant, shows a seated Christ explaining the significance of the widow's generosity to his apostles.[184] While the standing Christ recurs at New Tokalı and in one version of the scene in the middle Byzantine tetraevangelia (fig. 115),[185] in both cases the main grouping is of Christ and the apostles; the widow is either relegated to the margin of the scene or creeps to the altar on her knees. Unlike any other version of the scene, the image on f. 316r presents Christ witnessing the widow's action rather than recalling it for his apostles; the role of the widow is correspondingly increased. But if the focus of the Gregory scene finds no parallels, the detail of the altar set before an architectural structure recurs in the *Sacra Parallela* (fig. 114), suggesting that this, at least, repeats a familiar ninth-century motif.

Below the widow's mite, the miniaturist painted the resurrection of the widow's son at Nain. Gregory alluded to Christ's powers of resurrection in his second letter to Kledonios, though he referred specifically to the raising of Lazarus.[186] The raising of Lazarus had, however, already been depicted in Paris.gr.510 (f. 196v; fig. 24), as had all other examples of Christ raising the dead; the raising of the widow's son at Nain (Luke 7:11–16) was the only relevant miracle remaining. Save that the bier sits on the ground rather than being carried aloft, the image of this scene on f. 316r follows Luke's account faithfully. Christ stands to the far right, thereby completing, with his portrayal on the far left of the Capernaum scene, a frame to the lower register. Behind him, and extending toward the middle of the register, loom the massive city walls of Nain; the bier lies before Christ, and between it and the walls stands the widow, veiled hands raised to her face in a gesture of mourning, fol-

---

[183] K. Wessel, s.v. 'Gleichnisse Christi', *RBK* 3 (1970), 854–856.
[184] E.g. Florence, Laur.plut.6.23, f. 88v (Velmans [1971], fig. 171).
[185] Epstein (1986), fig. 76; Florence, Laur.plut.6.23, f. 154v: Velmans (1971), fig. 256.
[186] SC 208, 82.

Fig. 114 Paris.gr.923, f. 301v: Christ relates the parable of the widow's mite

Fig. 115 Florence, Laurenziana plut.6.23, f. 154v: Christ relates the parable of the widow's mite

lowed by a group of citizens bearing lit funeral torches. The scene finds no convincing parallels in Byzantine art: the Florence tetraevangelion, for example, shunts the city walls off to the side, and pictures two youths carrying the bier as Christ touches the dead boy.[187]

While the text of the second letter to Kledonios may have suggested, however obliquely, the inclusion of the raising of the widow's son at Nain, there is no textual justification for the widow's mite above it. This, apparently, served as a thematic balance to the aligned episode at Nain, for the two concerned widows and through their typological connection with the Old Testament widow at Sarepta, helped by the prophet Elijah (3 Kings 17:8–24),[188] provided examples of true faith.

The anti-Jewish miniatures are not the only anti-heretical miniatures in Paris.gr.510 but, with f. 355r (fig. 36),[189] they are tied particularly closely to contemporary missionary and conversion campaigns; in this context, the emphasis on baptism in the anti-Jewish pages may be associated with the unusual image of the apostles baptizing on f. 426v (fig. 42). What is perhaps most striking about the anti-Jewish miniatures, however, is how different they are from other ninth-century examples of the genre, and particularly from the outspoken anti-heretical miniatures of the marginal psalters.[190] While the psalters, especially the Khludov Psalter, present explicit attacks and confrontations enacted through coordinated inscriptions, textual notations, juxtaposed scenes and caricatured figures, the miniaturists of Paris.gr.510 – who, though they too relied on scribal notations to signal

---

[187] Laur.plut.6.23, f. 117v: Velmans (1971), fig. 204.

[188] See J. Paul and W. Busch, s.v. 'Sarepta, Witwe von', *LCI* 4 (1972), 45–46; and e.g. John Chrysostom's 'On Elijah and the Widow': J. Bareille, *Oeuvres complètes de S. Jean Chrysostom* V (1865), 514–515. Photios connects the Sarepta widow with all women raised by Christ: *Amphilochia* question 240: ed. Westerink VI,1 (1987), 20–25, ll. 96–99.   [189] On which see chapter 5.

[190] Corrigan (1992), 43–61.

relevant passages, painted images at a remove from the text – avoided explanatory inscriptions and caricature. The Homilies painters relied almost exclusively on juxtaposition; but rather than depicting confrontations, they compiled antithetical compositions. In the end, the anti-heretical images of Paris.gr.510 are less engaged in the intricacies of debate than are the comparative images in the marginal psalters, and they rely far less on the text; they have become quasi-autonomous visual commentaries on heresy as a system seen from late ninth-century patriarchal and courtly eyes.

7

Perceptions of divinity

Images of divinity, especially angels and visions, recur throughout Paris.gr.510, and are invariably accompanied by a portrayal of a human observer; often the human and the divine are shown in physical contact. Representations of human visions of divinity (theophanies) were recognized as important by André Grabar,[1] who argued these were favoured immediately after Iconoclasm because they demonstrated that humans could see the divine, and thus sanctioned religious art. Images of visions were not, however, invented in the ninth century; nor are the visual manifestations of human interaction with divinity in the Homilies restricted to theophanies. Grabar's thesis remains fundamental, but the real significance of the images showing human contact with divinity in Paris.gr.510 is that they are not presented as isolated and timeless icons: they are narrative depictions of historical realities.

OLD TESTAMENT VISIONS

Folio 67v (11) (fig. 11)

Gregory opened his ninth homily, 'To his father, in the presence of Basil, on his consecration as bishop of Sasima', with an analogy between his position and Isaiah's, whose response to a vision of God enthroned and surrounded by seraphim was to decry his worthiness.[2] Appropriately, Isaiah's vision (OPACIC HCAIOY) appears in the top register of f. 67v above an image of Gregory's consecration:[3] the miniature joins the two scenes to encapsulate the sermon's central theme of a man protesting his unworthiness but ultimately accepting God's choice. Even the Milan Gregory provides a faint echo: Isaiah appears in the series of portraits accompanying the sermon.[4]

---

[1] Grabar (1957), 247–248.

[2] SC 405, 300–315. Omont (1929), 16, pl. XXV; Der Nersessian (1962), 210–211; Brubaker (1989b), 40–42, where some of the following points originally appeared.

[3] On the consecration, see chapter 3.

[4] Grabar (1943a), pl. XI,2; two additional figures have been excised from the right margin. The liturgical edition does not include this homily.

At the top of the composition, a nimbed Christ sits enthroned on a gold and jewelled lyre-back throne draped with a red cloth. The head is badly abraded, but compare f. Av (fig. 1); discussion of that folio in chapter 4 intimates how neatly the portrait on f. 67v fits with contemporary images of Christ enthroned. Christ carries a closed gold book, wears a deep blue mantle over a blue-violet tunic, and is set against a gold medallion framed by a rainbow border.[5] Below, a curving row of six seraphim, each with six gold and white wings framing a small white face, is painted against a curved red strip on which flaming wheels have been drawn. Below the seraphim are six cherubim, distinguished by their two pairs of gold and white wings covered with small eyes, as well as by their larger heads and the hands and feet that emerge from the sides and bottom, respectively, of their wings. More angels, nimbed in gold, cluster in the centre foreground. Only the front pair is fully visible: both wear white mantles over pale blue tunics and extend their covered arms beneath the medallion of Christ. On either side, in strict frontality, stand four nimbed figures in deep blue and gold mantles over deep blue leggings; their white tunics are exposed only on their right arms, which emerge from their mantles to grasp the long gold lances that identify the figures as archangels. On the far left, imposed on the gold frame, kneels the prophet Isaiah (HCAIAC), a white mantle over his pale blue tunic. Isaiah has long and wavy grey hair, and a grey beard; he raises his hands and gazes toward Christ. The cherub closest to the prophet extends red pincers toward his mouth: we see the purification of Isaiah's lips with a burning coal that allowed the prophet henceforth to speak without sin. The inscription that flanks Christ – [ΕΙΔΟΝ or ΕΙΔΕ?] ΤΟ[N ΚΥΡΙΟ]N ΚΑΘΗΜΕΝΟΝ ΕΠΙ ΘΡΟΝΟΥ ΥΨΗΛΟΥ: '[I *or* he] saw the Lord sitting on a high throne' (Isaiah 6:1)[6] – as most of the details of the scene, comes directly from the biblical account, Isaiah 6:1–7. The subsidiary details that embellish the Homilies miniature – notably the cherubim and the wheels of fire, both of which derive from Ezekiel's rather than Isaiah's vision – are absent from the two miniatures of Isaiah's vision closest in date to Paris.gr.510, one in the *Sacra Parallela*, the other in the Vatican 'Christian Topography' (fig. 76), both of which restrict Christ's retinue to two seraphim.[7] The addition of the accumulated host in Paris.gr.510 presumably responds to the orthodox liturgy. Following the lead of John Chrysostom (ca. 350–407), as early as the sixth century seraphim and cherubim became linked and began to take on each other's characteristics.[8] Under the influence of Chrysostom's liturgy, most of the features that recur on f. 67v had already been combined to form a 'liturgical

---

[5] On the rainbow border, see James (1991).

[6] Omont neglected the ΤΟ still visible at the far left despite the bad flaking, and substituted an H for the N at the end of Κύριον and again for the ON at the end of καθήμενον. The accusative endings suggest the addition of εἶδον (as in the Isaiah text) or εἶδε at the beginning of the inscription.

[7] Paris.gr.923, f. 39v (Weitzmann [1979a], 146, fig. 349); Vat.gr.699, f. 72v (Stornajolo [1908], pl. 37).

[8] Pallas (1971).

Majestas' before Iconoclasm; appropriately, most of these early versions decorated church apses, where they supplied a fitting backdrop to the liturgy itself.[9] Similar ensembles, which Cyril Mango termed 'Old Testament theophanies',[10] continued after 843. One appeared in a late ninth- or early tenth-century mosaic in the south gallery of Hagia Sophia now known only through drawings;[11] around 890, in a sermon delivered at a church built by Stylianos Zaoutzas, Leo VI described another such composition.[12] Though by the 880s even the inclusion of Isaiah had liturgical resonance – the patriarch Germanos (715–730) had invoked the purification of Isaiah's lips in his exegesis on the orthodox liturgy, likening the prophet's purification with the sanctification of the eucharist[13] – the preponderance of monumental examples of the core formula suggests that the miniaturist of Paris.gr.510 may have transposed the composition from the wall to the page, awkwardly inserting Isaiah over the left frame in order to make a monumental 'liturgical' format appropriate to the ninth homily.[14] But whether or not a monumental image supplied a formal source, the inclusion of the prophet suggests a change in the significance of the image.

Grabar observed three Old Testament prophetic visions among the miniatures of Paris.gr.510.[15] He argued, and his theories were later elaborated by Jacqueline Lafontaine-Dosogne,[16] that the frequent mention of Old Testament visions in iconophile writings predisposed post-iconoclast artisans to depict them. Essentially, the iconophiles argued that the prophets saw an image of divinity, that this privilege was extended to all humanity through the incarnation, and that what can be seen can be depicted.[17] John of Damascus, for example, listed the visions recorded in the Old Testament, then quoted Hebrews 11:13 – 'These all died in faith, not having received what was promised, but having seen it and greeted it from afar' – and asked, 'Shall I not make an image of him who was seen in the nature of flesh for me? Shall I not worship and honour him, through the honour and veneration of his image?'[18] The iconophiles insisted that visions were historical

---

[9] Ihm (1960), 42–51.   [10] Mango (1962), 34.

[11] Ibid., 29–35, figs. 22–27. Fragments of a mosaic of Ezekiel, possibly originally paired with Isaiah, are preserved at Hagia Sophia in the room over the vestibule: Cormack and Hawkins (1977), 228, fig. 38. The mosaic is too badly damaged to permit further precision.

[12] See Mango (1972), 203–204.   [13] See Taft (1980/1), 56–57.

[14] So too Grabar (1953), 171, and Weitzmann (1979a), 147 (reversing his earlier opinion that f. 67v borrowed from an illustrated prophet book: Weitzmann [1942/3], 90–91). In the *Vita Tarasii* (843–847), Ignatios the Deacon mentions scenes of 'the conduct of the prophets', but does not specify episodes: ed. Heikel (1891), 416,21; trans. I. Ševčenko (1984); see chapter 1 note 16.

[15] Grabar (1957), 247–248; ff. 285r and 438v (which is not, strictly speaking, a vision) are discussed below.   [16] Lafontaine-Dosogne (1968).

[17] Gouillard (1969), 8–9; Elsner (1988), 479. Visions of angels, prominently depicted on f. 67v, are included among the visions of divinity in iconophile discussions: see Travis (1984), 30–40, 154.

[18] 'Against those who attack divine images' III,26 (cf. III,24 and 36): ed. Kotter (1975), 133, 131, 140; trans. Anderson (1980), 80, 79, 87. On John, see chapter 1 note 65.

and visible realities, not symbolic events;[19] in iconophile polemic, Old Testament visions justified images. In order to make this point visually, the prophet had to be present: the vision was important because divinity was recorded by human eyes. The insertion of Isaiah on f. 67v, however awkward it may look, transforms a time-less 'liturgical Majestas' into a historical event. Isaiah's presence changed the meaning of the scene, and altered the relationship between an image of a vision and its viewer.

Folio 285r (29) (fig. 29)

Folio 285r forms part of an ensemble where, alone in Paris.gr.510, the miniaturist and illuminator coordinated the prefatory picture, the headpiece to the text, and its opening initial; all repeat the star motif that, in the miniature, surrounds Habakkuk's vision. The miniature itself is ornately framed, with rainbow-pat-terned cornerpieces separated by white double-heart motifs against a red ground. All this introduces a particularly influential homily, Gregory's second oration 'On Easter'.[20] Its powerful opening paragraph inspired the miniature on f. 285r and, before Paris.gr.510, John of Damascus' canon for Easter; through John's quotation of Gregory's text, the sermon influenced much later liturgical imagery as well.[21] The beginning of this passage, introduced by the most ornate initial in the whole of Paris.gr.510 and studded with other painted letters, reads:

I will stand upon my watch, saith the venerable Habakkuk; and I will take my post beside him today on the authority and observation which was given me of the Spirit; and I will look forth, and will observe what shall be said to me. Well, I have taken my stand, and looked forth; and behold a man riding on the clouds and he is very high, and his counte-nance is as the countenance of an angel, and his vesture as the brightness of piercing light-ning; and he lifts his hand toward the east, and cries with a loud voice. His voice is like the voice of a trumpet; and round about him is as it were a multitude of the heavenly host; and he saith, today is salvation come into the world, to that which is visible, and to that which is invisible. Christ is risen from the dead, rise ye with him. Christ is freed from the tomb, be ye freed of the bond of sin.[22]

The full-page illustration to this passage on f. 285r pictures Gregory – who con-forms with his other depictions in Paris.gr.510 – standing in the lower right-hand corner holding a gold and jewelled book with red pages.[23] He looks out as if he were speaking to the viewer, and raises his right arm, perhaps to shield his eyes from the divine light of the vision. Gregory is accompanied by a youthful

---

[19] E.g. 'Those who know and admit that divinity itself gave the visions of the prophets forms and contours . . . eternal be their memory': Gouillard (1967), 51.   [20] *PG* 36:624–664 (*NPNF*, 422–434).
   [21] See S. Der Nersessian, 'Note sur quelques images se rattachant au thème du Christ-Ange', *Cahiers Archéologiques* 13 (1962), 209–216.   [22] *PG* 36:624A-B (*NPNF*, 423).
   [23] Millet (1920), 241; Omont (1929), 25, pl. XLIII; Grabar II (1943b), 204 note 1; Der Nersessian (1962), 201–202; Brubaker (1985), 10–11; Walter (1989), 257.

Habakkuk,[24] also nimbed, in a pink mantle over a blue tunic striped with gold. The prophet gestures upward toward the 'man riding on the clouds', here represented as an angel standing within a mandorla formed of concentric green bands. The mandorla seems to float just above the green hill that provides a backdrop for Gregory and Habakkuk; the blue sky against which it is set has been divided into two bands, the darker of which, below, is studded with gold stars. The angel, in an ochre mantle over a blue and gold tunic, carries a lance in its left hand; its outstretched wings are painted in shades of purple and blue, highlighted with gold. The angel 'lifts his hand toward the east' (our left, the angel's right), and the 'multitude of the heavenly host' appears as ten angels, variously clad but all with gold nimbs outlined with broad red bands, who stand among the stars. Paraskeve and Helena, identified by inscriptions, stand in the left corner and provide a balance to Habakkuk and Gregory.[25] The red inscription set against the gold border of the frame above the head of the angel reads 'Today is salvation come into the world' (CHMEPON CΩTHPIA TΩ KOCMΩ). Taken directly from Gregory's sermon and marked with a gold initial in the text of Paris.gr.510, this line was one of those borrowed by John of Damascus that later appeared in commentaries and images.[26]

Unlike Isaiah's vision, Habakkuk's was never narrated by the prophet himself; the image on f. 285r finds its only textual counterpart in Gregory's sermon. The strength of the opening paragraph guaranteed Habakkuk a place in many illustrations to the oration: the Milan Gregory includes a medallion portrait of Habakkuk among its four marginal illustrations to the homily,[27] and several of the liturgical editions picture Habakkuk and Gregory with the angel. But although the liturgical Homilies are here generally similar to Paris.gr.510 (fig. 100) – each of the seven manuscripts that include the scene, for example, presents the angel in a mandorla, with Gregory gazing up at it – none of them duplicates Habakkuk's active participation in the event: all separate Gregory and Habakkuk; most show the prophet standing passively to one side, and one omits him entirely.[28] The miniaturist responsible for f. 285r is alone responsible for the active interaction of Habakkuk and Gregory.[29]

---

[24] Habakkuk had no single canonical portrait type in Byzantium, but the youthful prophet of f. 285r, beardless and with short dark hair, follows one of the more common variants, found also in the Vatican 'Christian Topography', the Turin Prophetbook, numerous later psalters, and elsewhere in Paris.gr.510 (f. 435v; fig. 43). Vat.gr.699, f. 69v (Stornajolo [1908], pl. 33); Turin Bib. Naz. B. I.2, f. 12r (Lowden [1988], pl. V, fig. 17); London BL Add.40.731, f. 250r (Dufrenne [1966], pl. 59); and for other psalters, Cutler (1984), figs. 204, 262, 329, 353, 405. See also Weitzmann (1979a), 140; Walter (1989).

[25] See chapter 5.   [26] *PG* 36:625A; see note 21 above.

[27] Grabar (1943a), pls. XXXIX,2, XLI,2 (Habakkuk), 3.

[28] The manuscripts are Mount Athos, Dionysiou 61, f. 4r; Mount Athos, Karakalou 24, f. 6v (without Habakkuk); Moscow, Hist.Mus. 146, f. 4v; Oxford, Bodl. Lib. Roe 6, f. 4r (fig. 100); Paris.gr.533, f. 7r; Paris.gr.543, f. 27v; and Sinai.gr.339, f. 9v: Galavaris (1969), 28–29, 120–125, esp. 124–125, and figs. 357, 453, 2, 437, 236, 455, 379.

[29] Walter (1989), 257, suggested that the gestures of these two figures may have been inspired by images of the ascension.

The activity of the two males singles them out for attention on f. 285r: while all of the other figures on the page are frontal and impassive, these two look out at us, and Habakkuk's gesture leads our eyes to the angel. Gregory and Habakkuk do not themselves look at the vision; instead, they invite whoever sees the page to participate in it: the vision is presented neither as a metaphor nor as a symbol, but rather as a real event in which we are asked to involve ourselves. The collapse of time that allows Gregory to share the prophet's vision encompasses the viewer too. On an ideological level, the composition demonstrates that when divinity manifests itself in ways visible to humans it can be portrayed in this guise and made accessible; through images the faithful may become full participants in the prophet's experience.

Folio 438v (44) (fig. 44)

One of the best-known images in Paris.gr.510, f. 438v shows the prophet Ezekiel in the valley of the dry bones (Ezekiel 37:1–14).[30] The miniature introduces the *Significatio in Ezechielem*, a short discourse on Ezekiel's vision of God by the river Chebar and the first of the three texts not written by Gregory that now close Paris.gr.510.[31] While the *Significatio* concentrates on a different episode in the prophet's life, narrated in Ezekiel 1, the title clearly inspired the choice of protagonist on f. 438v, for, as the last lines of the preceding homily appear on its recto, the picture demonstrably retains its original and intended location.

Folio 438v carries the most elaborate frame of any miniature in Paris.gr.510. Gold and green cornucopias, jewelled roundels, and foliate motifs form an elongated oval surrounding the central image; gold bands of the sort that normally border the miniatures in Paris.gr.510 square off the corners. Blue fills these corner spandrels, and a green triangle (bordered in white and terminated by trilobes) surrounding a gold fleurette sits in the centre of each spandrel. Though Gabriel Millet argued that this unusual frame indicated that the prototype for the whole page was a monumental image or an icon, the lack of any comparable examples in either of these media – coupled with the similar, if less sumptuous, frame applied to the top register of f. 71v (fig. 13) – suggests instead that the Gregory miniaturist embellished the frame to emphasize the importance of the scene it surrounds.[32]

This central composition combines two distinct moments of the narrative, which – as in the Jonah sequence on f. 3r – flow together within a single unified setting. A green ground, interrupted by spare trees, rises to cliffs on either side that encase the first portrayal of Ezekiel, standing against a pink sky that segues to blue at the top of the page. At the prophet's feet and continuing up the mountainside are human skulls and bones, following Ezekiel 37:1–2. On the far left, two cypress trees

[30] Neuss (1912), 185–188; Millet (1920), 241; Ebersolt (1926), 20–21; Omont (1929), 30–31, pl. LVIII; Morey (1929), 95; Weitzmann (1947), 197; Grabar (1953), 171; Der Nersessian (1962), 216–217; Weitzmann (1979a), 157; Narkiss (1987), 427–428; Brubaker (1989b), 40–42; Cutler (1992), 51–52; Brubaker (1996b), 100–103.   [31] *PG* 36:665–669.   [32] Millet (1920), 241.

rise, as if to underscore that the prophet stands in a valley of death. Ezekiel (IEZE-ΚΙΗΛ), clad in blue and pink, and with shaggy hair extending in wisps against his gold nimb, raises his arms to a hand of God that emerges in a gesture of blessing from a deeper blue arc of heaven set within the upper blue streak of sky. Between the two lies the inscription 'Lord, Lord, will these bones live?' (K[YPI]E K[YPI]E HZHCETAI TA OCTA TAYTA). Ezekiel, in other words, asks God the question that in the Septuagint the Lord asks him (v. 3).

Ezekiel (IEZEKIΗΛ), clad as above, recurs in the lower right. Here he stands next to an archangel, which wears a white ribbon in its hair and the familiar white mantle over a blue tunic striped with gold; it also carries the long staff always associated with archangels in the Homilies and is identified, as usual, as [O AP]XI-CTPATHΓOC. The scene evokes Ezekiel 37:9, when God instructs the prophet to call upon the winds to 'breathe upon these dead, and let them live'. The dead, re-formed from the bones of the valley at Ezekiel's command, appear as a group of small figures to the left of the archangel; painted in grisaille, they evidently have yet to receive the life-giving breath. Ezekiel does not seem, however, to call upon the winds specified in the Septuagint to fill the spectres with breath; rather, he points to his own mouth and looks to the archangel, which, while looking back toward the prophet, strides forward and gestures downward to the grisaille figures. Ezekiel appears either to be requesting that the archangel breathe life into the dead, or to be receiving this instruction from the angel. Finally, a small and badly flaked building, reminiscent of many others in Paris.gr.510, appears at the bottom of the frame. This may represent the tombs of the house of Israel (v. 13) or, metaphorically, the house of Israel itself.[33] The latter is perhaps more likely, for the leafless tree that rises behind the building seems to underline the dry and hopeless state of the bones that are identified with the house of Israel (v. 11).

To the Byzantines, Ezekiel in the valley of the dry bones signified, above all, resurrection, and had done so from the time of the early church fathers;[34] for this reason, most images of the scene produced before Paris.gr.510 – none of which bears any resemblance to the miniature – were carved on sarcophagi.[35] The episode was invoked in the morning liturgy for Holy Saturday, following a chant exalting Christ's resurrection from the tomb,[36] and preceding one of the four baptismal

---

[33] So too Cutler (1992).

[34] See Der Nersessian (1962), 216–217. Gregory himself presents this interpretation elsewhere: SC 284, 190–192.

[35] An image modelled on Moses striking water from the rock appears during the early Christian period (Neuss [1912], 141–154) and recurs in the Syriac Bible in Paris (probably ca. 600): Omont (1909), 95, fig. 10; Jules Leroy (1964), 210. The more broadly narrative treatments at Dura Europos (third century), Dara (sixth century), and even in the Milan Gregory are equally unrelated to f. 438v. For Dura, see Kraeling (1956), pls. LXIX–LXXII; Weitzmann and Kessler (1990), 134–135. For Dara, see Mundell (1975), 209–227. For the Milan Gregory, Grabar (1943a), pl. LVI,3. See also Cutler (1992).

[36] Der Nersessian (1962), 217; Mateos II (1963), 82; Brubaker (1996a).

ceremonies performed by the patriarch each year.[37] When Paris.gr.510 was made, baptismal implications had become intertwined with the interpretation of the episode as a prefiguration of resurrection:[38] as Ezekiel, long understood as a type of Christ, saved his people, so Christ saved orthodox Christians through baptism. The typological use of Old Testament prophets to demonstrate the truth of orthodox Christianity is familiar from the polemics against the Jews and the Muslims, and was visualized, above all, in the marginal psalters;[39] we may see a continuation of that debate here.[40]

It is nonetheless surprising that the miniature presents this episode rather than Ezekiel's more famous vision of God by the river Chebar; the *Significatio* concentrates on the latter, and the Chebar vision was more commonly depicted than the scene shown on f. 438v: at least two versions are known from the ninth century, one (now lost) in Hagia Sophia, the other in the Vatican 'Christian Topgraphy'.[41] Whatever the reason for the selection of the miracle rather than the vision, Ezekiel in the valley of the dry bones has been modified, in a way that finds no Byzantine parallel, to make a point.

The Ezekiel miniature has been claimed as an example of the prophetic visions of God believed to have been especially popular in the years immediately following Iconoclasm.[42] Unlike the prophet's vision by the river Chebar, however, the narrative of Ezekiel in the valley of the dry bones does not describe a theophany: it records, instead, a conversation between the prophet and God. But the miniature in Paris.gr.510 makes the same point as an image of the Chebar vision could have made, for by incorporating the archangel – which has neither biblical justification nor visual precedents – the miniaturist was able to show a divine being appearing to the prophet. Ezekiel communicates, if mutely, with an obviously corporeal figure. Folio 438v, whatever its other agendas, perpetuates a theme familiar from the previous two miniatures: the archangel confirms, visually, the orthodox dictum that the prophets saw divinity.[43] In the miniatures of Paris.gr.510, it seems to have been of paramount importance to portray human and divine figures acting together in historical narratives.

Despite the importance of prophetic visions in the rhetoric of the eighth and ninth centuries, Jacqueline Lafontaine-Dosogne and Jean Gouillard have both pointed

[37] See Mateos II (1963), 84, 287.

[38] On this common linkage, see the discussion of f. 264v in chapter 5, and Kartsonis (1986), 173–175.

[39] Corrigan (1992), esp. 62–77.

[40] For a different interpretation of a tenth-century ivory that depicts the scene, see Cutler (1992).

[41] For Hagia Sophia, Mango (1962), 29–35, 85–86; this was a liturgical Majestas, but contained elements of Ezekiel's vision. Vat.gr.699, f. 74r: Stornajolo (1908), pl. 39.

[42] As suggested in the introduction to this section, such an assumption is problematic; we shall return to it in the remarks immediately following our discussion of this page.

[43] See note 17 above.

out that there was no significant increase in the number of visions depicted.[44] But while the number of representations of visions varies little, their setting and function shifted in the ninth century. Most earlier Old Testament visions that have been preserved appear in monumental (liturgical) settings – that is, church apses;[45] after the ninth century, most Byzantine examples are found in manuscripts.[46] During the ninth century itself, book images were on the rise. In addition to the Paris Gregory, the *Sacra Parallela* incorporates Isaiah's vision, and the ninth-century copy of the 'Christian Topography' in the Vatican added three visions – Isaiah's (fig. 76), Ezekiel's, and Daniel's – that do not seem to have been in its sixth-century model.[47] Unlike Old Testament visions painted in church apses, the ninth-century miniatures are not liturgical images: the relevant manuscripts were not produced for church use, and, while pre-iconoclast 'liturgical theophanies' rarely included the prophet who saw the vision, post-iconoclast images of visions in manuscripts nearly always do. Although the number of theophanies did not increase dramatically in the ninth century, the context in which they were viewed shifted from a liturgical to a historical (narrative) one. By including the prophet, ninth-century images stressed the narrative and historical validity of the prophet's visions; in this, they collude with orthodox written polemic.

The shift from monumental to miniature format during the course of the ninth century is also significant. By virtue of their small size and the close contact with the viewer which they required, miniatures of theophanies allowed the beholder to witness the vision individually, along with the prophet. The ninth-century Byzantines who had access to the Homilies, *Sacra Parallela*, and 'Christian Topography' presumably knew that Christ's incarnation had entitled them to participate in the visions of Old Testament prophets; but whether or not these viewers formulated their dogma so neatly, the miniatures of prophetic visions – dispensing with the intermediacy of the word – invited their participation either implicitly or blatantly. As the significance of a theophany changed, and as the messages that an image of a prophetic vision could carry thickened, so too (one assumes) did the viewer's response to such images. In Paris.gr.510, the historicized visions that invite the viewer's participation and emphasize the interaction of human and divine agents almost inevitably had another consequence as well: they coloured the viewer/reader response to the text that followed. While narrative images are nearly always dependent on texts for their plots, once seen, the images themselves shape the way that a viewer/reader receives and remembers the details of that narrative. The visual interpretation provided by the miniatures in

---

[44] Lafontaine-Dosogne (1968), 135–143; Gouillard (1969), 8–9. Some of the following discussion appeared in Brubaker (1989b), 40–42.   [45] See Ihm (1960), 42–51.

[46] For a representative selection of examples, see Weitzmann (1979a), 146–147.

[47] Paris.gr.923, f. 39v: Weitzmann (1979a), fig. 349. Vat.gr.699, ff. 72v, 74r, 75r: Stornajolo (1908), pls. 37, 39, 40.

Paris.gr.510 charged the texts they accompanied with new (and in these cases topically relevant) meaning.

PERCEPTIONS OF DIVINITY

In Paris.gr.510, visual manifestations of human interaction with divinity are not restricted to theophanies. In addition to interactions that form an established part of the Byzantine repertoire – the angel propelling Adam and Eve from paradise on f. 52v (fig. 10), Christ and a hand of God respectively directing Saul/Paul and Elijah on f. 264v (fig. 28), and Constantine's dream/vision on f. 440r (fig. 45) – there are several less common conjuctions. In chapter 4, for example, we saw that f. Cv (fig. 5) most unusually presents the archangel Gabriel and the Emperor Basil as equals (f. Cv): they stand on the same level, and wear the same costume.

Another example is provided by the second register of f. 174v (fig. 23), which opens with Jacob's struggle with an angel (Genesis 32:24–30).[48] The gold-nimbed angel looks like most other angels in Paris.gr.510: it wears a whitish mantle over a blue tunic striped with gold and supports a white diadem in its short dark hair. Here, its wings, painted in tones of white, blue, and pale purple and tinged with gold, are fully extended. Jacob, in clothes identical to those Isaac wears in the top register of the page, stands with his back to the viewer and grasps the angel by its shoulder and elbow; the angel pulls up Jacob's right leg. The major distinction between pictorial accounts of the episode lies in the manner in which the two men wrestle: Jacob and the angel either lean toward each other and appear to embrace, or the two physically grapple and the angel puts its hand on Jacob's thigh (as specified in Genesis). In no other image known to me, however, does the stance of the angel on f. 174v, coupling a striding position with a sharply raised right elbow, recur. This position, which simulates the effect of a real struggle, appears elsewhere in the manuscript;[49] its application here emphasizes the physicality of the struggle between Jacob and the angel and distinguishes the scene on f. 174v from all other versions.[50] Here too the active stances of both figures, but especially Jacob, are highlighted by the way the drapery has been painted: it seems to shatter into small whorls and jagged pieces.

The angel appearing to Joshua (f. 226v; fig. 26) could not replicate the physical contact of Jacob's struggle with the angel, but the relationship between the human Joshua and the divine messenger was stressed in another way: the two have a conversation, recorded in one of the rare inscriptions in Paris.gr.510 that goes beyond a simple identification.[51] There are, in fact, only nine such inscriptions in

---

[48] Other aspects of this page are considered in chapters 4, 5, and 8. [49] E.g. f. 374v (fig. 39).
[50] Closest is Vat.Ross.251, f. 5r: Martin (1954), 108–109, 184–185, fig. 227. [51] See chapter 4.

the Homilies,[52] and four of the nine are devoted to demonstrating divine–human communication: in addition to the conversation between Joshua and the angel on f. 226v, one is Ezekiel's question to God on f. 438v (fig. 44); the other two have God telling Moses to 'unfasten the sandals on your feet', and Christ asking 'Saul, Saul, why do you persecute me?' (both on f. 264v; fig. 28). In all of these cases, of course, divinity is pictured, as well as represented by words.

Most of these examples – Basil and Gabriel, Constantine and the cross, and Saul/Paul and Christ excepted – focus on Old Testament witnesses. Two miniatures that we have not yet considered present New Testament narrative variations on the theme.

Folio 30v (7) (fig. 7)

Folio 30v, among the most extensively discussed pictures in Paris.gr.510,[53] shows the crucifixion in the top third of the page, the deposition and entombment in the middle register, and the chairete at the bottom. Though it is really only the last scene which plays to the theme of this chapter, the chairete cannot be divorced from the page as a whole; the full picture is therefore presented here.

The miniature covers one side of a single leaf, the recto of which remains blank; it has been inserted in the midst of the irregular fourth quire as a frontispiece to Gregory's third homily. The passion sequence does not, however, sustain any links with that sermon, and Sirarpie Der Nersessian, followed most recently by Anna Kartsonis, plausibly suggested that the miniature originally prefaced the first homily (ff. 1r–2v), which no longer carries an illustration.[54] Although other illustrated copies of the Homilies are no help here – the Milan copy carries no illustrations to the first homily and the liturgical editions almost without exception preface the sermon with an image of the anastasis[55] – Der Nersessian's thesis is almost certainly correct: the theme of the first homily, 'On Easter and his [Gregory's] reluctance [to preach until now]', is of obvious relevance to the sequence on f. 30v,[56] and the association seems to be confirmed by the text of Paris.gr.510, where the two passages most directly related to the scenes pictured are introduced by enlarged initials. The first of these relates to the last scene on the page, the chairete, and is the opening line of the sermon: 'It is the day of the resurrection.'[57] The second appears in the fourth paragraph: 'yesterday I died with him, today I am quickened with him; yesterday I was buried with him, today I rise

---

[52] Brubaker (1996b).

[53] Vogt (1908), 412; Omont (1929), 13–14, pl. XXI; Morey (1929), 69–73, 87, 96; Martin (1955), 191–192; Weitzmann (1961), 479–480; Der Nersessian (1962), 217–218; Weitzmann (1971b), 629; Cormack (1977b), 153; Maguire (1977), 144, 154, 169; Parker (1978), 15–23; Kartsonis (1986), 140–146; Kazhdan and Maguire (1991), 11; Brubaker (1995), 159; Brubaker (1996a), 11–12; Brubaker (1996b), 99.

[54] Der Nersessian (1962), 217–218; Kartsonis (1986), 140–146.   [55] Galavaris (1969), 14–16.

[56] SC 247, 72–83 (*NPNF*, 203–204).   [57] SC 247, 72; Paris.gr.510, f. 1r.

with him'.[58] This passage joins together all three phases illustrated – death, burial, and resurrection – and would seem to cement the affiliation between the first homily and f. 30v. The dislocation of a miniature early in the manuscript accords with codicological evidence that the introductory gathering was disturbed already in the Byzantine period;[59] it may have been at this time that the initial text picture was moved, perhaps because it was even then displaying the flaking paint that now allows us to discern the underpainting.

While 'On Easter and his reluctance' seems to have inspired the selection of scenes, Gregory's terse account could hardly have suggested the details of the individual scenes; rather, the miniaturist evidently adapted current formulae. The process of adaptation – and alteration – is particularly obvious in the uppermost scene, where sections of the upper layer of paint have flaked off to reveal an image different from the final version.

The upper register presents an expansive crucifixion (Matthew 27:33–56, Mark 15:22–41, Luke 23:33–49, John 19:18–34). The crucified Christ dominates the composition. The miniaturist placed the figure exactly in the centre, and portrayed Christ on a larger scale than the remaining figures in the register; he stands nearly as tall as the interior picture space. The cross itself overlaps the frame: the base of the suppedaneum on which Christ stands rests on the strip that divides the top from the middle register; below the suppedaneum, the cross juts into the middle register where it rests on the floating green hill of Golgotha with a flaked dark half-ellipse in its centre that probably originally contained the skull of Adam. The upper portion of the cross, carrying a crossbar without a legend, also extends above the top frame, which consists of a band of gold rimmed with blue and green strips filled with gold diamonds.

Christ remains erect with straight arms on the cross, though his head tilts to the left. His head is badly rubbed and, though his eyes appear to be closed, even Henri Omont, who was able to examine the manuscript closely at the beginning of the twentieth century, could not tell for certain whether or not they actually were. As an indication of Christ's condition, this point is of less relevance than one might assume, for the Byzantines were well aware that the eyes of the dead remained open. In his account of Joseph of Arimathaea's removal of Christ's body from the cross, for example, Photios constructs a monologue for Joseph that begins: 'Shall I close with my hands the eyes of him who by means of clay and speech planted eyes in the blind?'[60] This is not to deny the symbolic value of Christ's closed eyes, but at least in the case of Paris.gr.510 – so closely associated with Photios – whether or not Christ appears with open eyes in the top register may not be of critical importance for the interpretation of the scene. If Christ is here presented as already dead, the

[58] SC 247, 76; Paris.gr.510, f. IV. This paragraph was influential, and was connected with orthodox Easter services: Strunk (1955), esp. 82; see also Kartsonis (1986), 142.   [59] See chapter 2.
[60] Homily 11,4: ed. Laourdas (1959), 111; trans. Mango (1958), 200.

inscriptions on either side of him – which Omont could still decipher as Christ's dying words to his mother (IΔE O Y[IO]C COY) and to John (IΔOY H M[HTH]P COY) as recorded in John 19:26–27 – are anachronistic, but conventional: the same legends flank a clearly dead Christ on an early ninth-century icon at Mount Sinai and in the tenth-century programme at New Tokalı in Cappadocia.[61] Christ wears a purple kolobion, most of which has flaked off to reveal that originally he wore a white loincloth, shaded in blue. This alteration was apparent to Albert Vogt in 1908 and was noted by Omont in his 1929 publication of the manuscript;[62] it has occasioned a great deal of comment since. As is well known, early eastern Christian representations of the crucifixion usually pictured a living Christ wearing a kolobion, and we may guess from Gregory of Tours' sixth-century account of an image of Christ in a loincloth which asked to be clothed that these older versions clad him in a kolobion out of respect.[63]

As Kartsonis demonstrated, the christological controversies of the seventh and eighth centuries made explicit representation of Christ's human nature imperative; he was increasingly shown dead, and in a loincloth that revealed his corporeal body, on the cross.[64] As variants of this argument – directed against iconoclasts, Jews, and Muslims – proliferated in the ninth century,[65] it might be expected that by the second half of the century images of the living and kolobion-clad Christ would have disappeared. But they did not. Instead, ninth-century representations of the crucifixion exhibit nearly all possible variations on the theme. The living Christ on the cross wearing a kolobion, the standard pre-iconoclast formula, continued (fig. 57), conterminously with pictures of the dead Christ wearing either a loincloth or a kolobion; indeed, in the Khludov Psalter all three types appear in the same manuscript,[66] which suggests that the different iconographical types did not simply correspond with distinct theological positions.[67] It is, however, clear that the Homilies miniaturist originally painted the semi-nude Christ on the cross and then later covered him with a kolobion, a process also observable in the second register, and on a seventh- or eighth-century icon now at Mount Sinai.[68] Perhaps the station of the audience – imperial in the case of Paris.gr.510, monks in church in the case of the icon – suggested a more

[61] For the icon, Sinai B.50, Weitzmann (1976), 80, pl. XXXII; for Tokalı, Epstein (1986), 73–74, figs. 83–87. On the importance of Christ's words in the ninth century, see Kalavrezou (1990), 168–170.

[62] Vogt (1908), 412; Omont (1929), 13–14.

[63] Gregory of Tours, *Glory of the Martyrs*, trans. R. van Dam (Liverpool, 1988), 41 (*Liber in Gloria Martyrum* 22; ed. B. Krusch, *MGH Scriptores Rerum Merovingicarum* I.2 [Hanover, 1885], 51). Kartsonis (1986), 128 note 8, and Corrigan (1995), 48–49, also cite this account.

[64] Kartsonis (1986), 33–68.   [65] Corrigan (1992), esp. 81–90.

[66] Moscow, Hist.Mus.gr.129, ff. 45v (dead, kolobion), 67r (alive, kolobion), 72v (dead, loincloth): Ščepkina (1977).

[67] This position, taken by Kartsonis (1986), 144–146, was criticized on other grounds by Corrigan in a review of Kartsonis in *Art Bulletin* 71 (1989), 312–315.

[68] Sinai B.32: Weitzmann (1976), 57–58, pl. XXIII.

traditional approach to the image after its initial design, and on f. 30v an emphasis on Christ's imperial purple kolobion might have on reflection seemed a better choice in a manuscript destined for the emperor.[69]

On f. 30v, the crucified Christ is flanked by two men, one piercing his side with a lance so that it spouts a stream of blood (John 19:34), the other proffering a sponge laden with vinegar (Matthew 27:48, Mark 15:36, Luke 23:36, John 19:28–29). All of these features recur in other ninth-century depictions, including the miniatures in the Khludov Psalter mentioned above, one of which (f. 67r; fig. 57) in fact provides the closest parallel to the central grouping on f. 30v. Mary, head bowed and covered hands outstretched, stands on the left; John, turned toward the right but gazing back at Christ, stands on the right. A red sun hangs above Mary, a blue moon floats above John. Mary, John, the sun, and the moon appear in numerous ninth-century versions of the crucifixion: the two images on the cover of the Fieschi-Morgan reliquary (fig. 116), and that on the obverse of the related Vicopisano reliquary cross (both made in Byzantium earlier in the century) provide close parallels, save that Mary, as is indeed true of most images other than that in Paris.gr.510, does not cover her hands and raises one of them to her face; the inscriptions also recur here.[70] A similar grouping, complete with the lance- and sponge-bearing soldiers, appears in Old Tokalı (though here Christ wears a loincloth) and many other examples could be adduced.[71] Finally, at the lateral ends of the register, two women – presumably Mary Magdalene and Mary mother of James (Matthew 27:56, Mark 15:40, John 19:25) – stand in an arched structure behind the Virgin, and two men stride toward the edge of the miniature on the far right. The men balance the two Marys on the left, and, like them, stand before an architectural backdrop, which here apparently represents a basilican structure splitting into two halves, its gold rear section apsed, its blue porch fronted with columns. This seems to pictorialize the events immediately following Christ's death, as narrated in Matthew 27:51, Luke 23:45 and, quoted here, Mark 15:38: 'And the veil of the temple was rent in twain from the top to the bottom'. The two men, who flee while looking back at Christ, apparently refer to Matthew 27:54;[72] they also recall apocryphal accounts that refer to the healed paralytic defending Jesus before Pilate, for the foremost man wears a small diadem while the rear figure, in a short tunic, carries a red pallet on his back.[73] There is rarely room to include additional figures such as these in other Byzantine representations of the crucifixion, but similarly expansive compositions are not unknown. At New Tokalı (fig. 117), for example, two women

[69] On the possible implications of the loincloth, see Corrigan (1995), 52–57; cf. Kazhdan and Maguire (1991), 11.
[70] Kartsonis (1986), figs. 24f-g, 25a. For another similar version, this time also with the skull beneath the cross, see ibid., fig. 26c (the internal Pliska cross).   [71] Epstein (1986), fig. 37.
[72] So too E. Lucchesi Palli, s.v. 'Kreuzigung Christi', LCI 2 (1970), 614. See also Mark 15:39, Luke 23:47.   [73] Acts of Pilate, 6; Hennecke and Schneemelcher I (1963), 456–457.

Fig. 116 Fieschi-Morgan reliquary: exterior, lid, crucifixion

Fig. 117 New Tokalı: crucifixion

follow Mary, as on f. 30v, and the centurion and friends huddle before the split temple on the right.[74] Though more extensive than many examples, most features of the crucifixion image in Paris.gr.510 find thematic parallels in ninth- and tenth-century Byzantine art.

The same cannot be said for the two images spread across the middle register, the deposition and the entombment. John 19:38–42 recounts both events, telling us that Joseph of Arimathaea and Nikodemos 'took [they] the body of Jesus, and wound it in linen clothes with the spices'; they then laid it in a new sepulchre in a

---

[74] Epstein (1986), figs. 83–86. The two groups recur in the later Florence, Laur.plut.6.23, ff. 59r, 162v, 208r (here only the centurion and a companion appear, but they stride as in Paris.gr.510): Velmans (1971), figs. 121, 264, 297.

garden. To this account, the synoptics (Matthew 27:57–60, Mark 15:42–46, Luke 23:50–53) add only that the tomb was cut into rock.

On f. 30v, the deposition (Η ΚΑΘΕΛΚΥCΙC) occupies the left half of the register. Christ, his head tilted to the right, still has one hand nailed to the cross; Nikodemos, standing on the ground and turning toward the left, extracts the nail from this hand while Joseph of Arimathaea supports Christ's body by grasping him about the hips. As in the top register, Christ wears a kolobion, which has flaked to reveal the original loincloth underneath. The Virgin, still with raised covered hands, stands to the left, accompanied by John, who occupies the centre of the composition. John stands in the same position as he does in the top register: the only significant difference between the two figures is the disposition of drapery over the saint's arms – a sling-like fold now encases his right arm and a swath of material covers his left hand. All five participants are nimbed, and the sun and moon of the crucifixion remain over the cross. The scene clarifies the biblical narrative by providing some logistical details ignored by the gospel authors, and by adding Mary and John.

The deposition is barely mentioned, and never represented, before the ninth century: f. 30v preserves the first recorded image in Byzantium. And while the liturgical importance of the deposition was first developed by Germanos in the early eighth century,[75] it is only in the ninth that the theme became an important topic of sermons: Photios, for example, devoted a long paragraph of his eleventh homily to the deposition, and in it concentrated not on the theological implications of the event, but on Joseph's emotional reactions to Christ's body.[76] Another ninth-century account appears in a homily on the death and resurrection of Christ by George of Nikodemia, who stressed the role of the Virgin and described her presence at the deposition.[77] The ninth-century elaboration of both visual and written descriptions of the deposition seem to reverberate from the impact of orthodox arguments about the significance of the incarnation;[78] representing perhaps the most mundane moment of the passion sequence, the deposition emphasized the reality of Christ's human nature.

The entombment, which follows the deposition on the right side of the middle register, shows Nikodemos (identified by inscription) and Joseph carrying the wrapped Christ to his tomb.[79] Nikodemos, standing on a raised groundline, bends over Christ and grasps him around the thighs; Joseph stares out at the viewer and clasps Christ's torso to his own chest. Behind the figures looms a rough-hewn tomb carved into a hillside. Though Paris.gr.510 preserves one of the earliest known

[75] Taft (1980/1), esp. 55.
[76] Homily 11,4: ed. Laourdas (1959), 109–112; trans. Mango (1958), 198–202.
[77] See Maguire (1981), 97–101, and Ratkowska (1964).
[78] See Corrigan (1992), 69–71, 81–90; Kartsonis (1986), 137, 229.
[79] The titulus describes the scene as Ο ΕΝΤΑΦΙΑCΜΟC, 'the laying out for burial'.

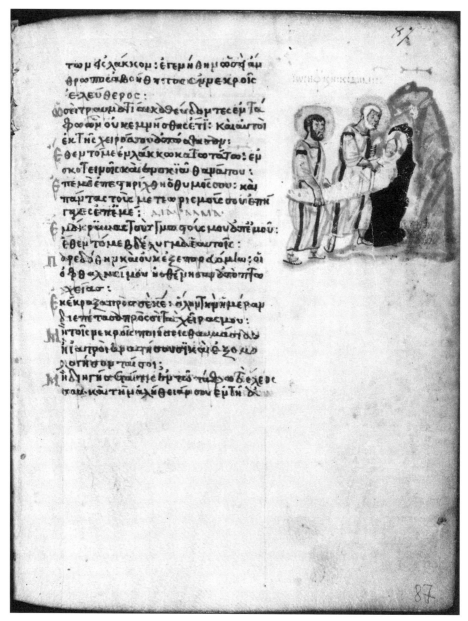

Fig. 118 Moscow, Historical Museum, cod.129, f. 87r: entombment

examples, the iconography of the entombment may have developed in the late seventh century, along with the anastasis and the dead Christ on the cross, in response to Monophysite denials that Christ was fully human.[80] But whether or not some (now lost) anti-Monophysite image stands behind it, the entombment on f. 30v corresponds with earlier ninth-century depictions in the marginal psalters. In the Khludov Psalter (fig. 118), the two men, differentiated by age and hair colour and with, as on f. 30v, Joseph leading, carry the wrapped Christ to his tomb, visualized as a rough-hewn cave in a mountain.[81] The most notable difference between the psalter image and that in Paris.gr.510 is the relative positions of the figures and the tomb: by placing the trio of men in front of the cave, the Homilies painter has arrested the narrative, and Nikodemos and Joseph display Christ's body to us, a shift underscored by Joseph's gaze, aimed directly out at the viewer. A similar composition, with Nikodemos and Joseph holding and displaying Christ in front of the (here minute) tomb, recurs in Old Tokalı (fig. 119), where it is paired with the deposition as in Paris.gr.510; it also appears in the slightly later lectionary in St Petersburg.[82] As with the deposition, the Homilies miniaturist stressed the human aspects of Christ's death: rather than glossing over the entombment as part of a narrative sequence, it is made into an important, indeed almost iconic, scene.

The final image occupies the whole of the bottom register and shows the chairete (XAIPETE), the risen Christ greeting Mary Magdalen and Mary mother of James (Matthew 28:9–10). Christ stands in the centre of the composition, flanked by the prostrate figures of the two women. The scene takes place in the garden that housed Christ's tomb, pictured below its counterpart in the second register. Earlier examples of the chairete, which are numerous, normally show the two women huddled in proskynesis both on the same side of Christ; later images frequently repeat the symmetrical grouping of f. 30v.[83] But few other representations include the tomb displayed so prominently: the only other roughly contemporary version to picture the tomb – here represented as a building rather than as a cave – illustrates Psalm

---

[80] See Kartsonis (1986), 52–57, 68–69. She suggests (56 note 42) that in question 168 of the *Amphilochia* Photios 'largely paraphrases' one of the anti-Monophysite responses, but this is actually an excerpt from codex 277 of the *Bibliotheke* summarizing one of Chrysostom's sermons: ed. Westerink V (1986), 221–222; ed. Henry VIII (1977), 151.

[81] Moscow, Hist.Mus.gr.129, f. 87r: Ščepkina (1977).

[82] Epstein (1986), fig. 38; *Lektionar* (1994); Morey (1929), fig. 100.

[83] For earlier asymmetrical examples from a variety of media, see the Rabbula Gospels (Florence, Laur.plut.1.56, f. 13r: Cecchelli [1959]), the gold marriage ring at Dumbarton Oaks (Weitzmann [1979b], 496) and icon B.27 at Mount Sinai (Weitzmann [1976], 50–51, pl. XXI); for a later symmetrical version, see the ivory diptych from Milan (conveniently reproduced by Kartsonis [1986], fig. 70) and the St Petersburg lectionary (*Lektionar* [1994]; Morey [1929], fig. 83); for a later asymmetrical version – here, probably significantly, part of an extensive narrative cycle – see Florence, Laur.plut.6.23, f. 60v (Velmans [1971], fig. 124).

Fig. 119 Old Tokalı: deposition; entombment

77:63 in the marginal psalter, Pantokrator 61 (fig. 120).[84] The Pantokrator image retains a more narrative flavour than we find in Paris.gr.510: the two Marys both kneel to the right of Christ and the sleeping soldiers still lie at the base of the mausoleum. This latter detail makes explicit the significance of the scene: it is, as Kartsonis pointed out, a narrative analogue to the resurrection.[85] On f. 30v, the

---

[84] Folio 109r: Dufrenne (1966), pl. 16. The chairete from the Church of the Virgin of the Source (Pege) is lost: see the discussion in Kartsonis (1986), 146–147.　　[85] Kartsonis (1986), 21, 143.

Fig. 120 Mount Athos, Pantokrator 61, f. 109r: chairete

miniaturist could of course have evoked Christ's resurrection by picturing the anastasis – and in fact that image prefaces nearly all later copies of this sermon[86] – but elected to present the chairete instead. Though Kartsonis views this as indicative of a conservative approach to imaging Christ's resurrection,[87] other considerations seem more important. The decision to picture the chairete probably responded at least in part to interest in Christ's tomb found elsewhere in Paris.gr.510; it also complemented the composition of the page: just as the crucified Christ of the first register is aligned with the risen Christ of the third, so the tomb awaiting Christ's dead body in the second register and the tomb emptied of it in the third axially correspond.

The decision to picture the chairete rather than the anastasis may also respond to the impact of contemporary liturgy, where the crucifixion, entombment and

---

[86] See note 55 above.   [87] Kartsonis (1986), 141, 150.

301

deposition, and chairete figure in the gospel lections for holy week while the anastasis does not.[88] Another difference between the chairete and the anastasis is that in the former two women witnessed the risen Christ on this earth, while the anastasis, enacted in Hades, had no terrestrial witnesses. As we have seen, there is a consistent emphasis on human perception of, and interaction with, divinity throughout Paris.gr.510, for such episodes proved that divinity could take on tangible material form, and could – indeed, should – therefore be depicted. I suspect that the chairete appears on f. 30v at least in part because it made a point that the anastasis could not: the ability of human witnesses to see divinity. The importance attached to this point may be at least partly responsible for the large amount of space allotted to the chairete on f. 30v: while the entire passion sequence is crammed into the upper two registers, the chairete extends over the whole lower third of the page.

As an opening text image, f. 30v would have been particularly well suited to the political climate of the orthodox church in the second half of the ninth century. The image as a whole conclusively demonstrates the humanity of Christ, for even if alive in the crucifixion scene he is certainly dead in both the deposition and the entombment. Such an emphasis on the humanity of Christ accords with the orthodox insistance that the incarnation justified religious imagery, for, as we have seen repeatedly, this position demanded that to deny pictures of Christ was to deny his human nature.[89] Depictions of the dead Christ thereby confirmed and reinforced the orthodox position, and to this extent inevitably functioned in part as visual polemic.

The image also may have been arranged to correspond with contemporary liturgical ideas. The central axis of the page follows a dominant line from the crucified Christ on Golgotha to the figure of John in the central tier, and thence to the risen Christ of the bottom panel. The painter – as with the aligned tombs, and in many other miniatures in Paris.gr.510 – overlaid the horizontal narrative strips with a vertical comment. As Kartsonis first observed, the figure of John ties together the crucifixion and the resurrection, the 'cause' and the 'effect'. She argued that this alignment was particularly apt, because John's gospel was seen as a significant account of the resurrection and played a major role in the Easter liturgy, just as Gregory's sermon 'On Easter' did.[90]

Folio 75r (14) (fig. 14)

Uniquely among miniatures in Paris.gr.510, the transfiguration on f. 75r shares a page with the last lines of the preceding homily's text. The twelfth sermon, 'To his father, when he had entrusted to him the care of the church at Nazianzus', begins

---

[88] Mateos II (1963), 72–91; Brubaker (1996a), 11–12.

[89] This is an iconophile topos; see, for example, the Acts of the 787 Council: Mansi XIII, 205E; trans. Sahas (1986a), 50. Further, Martin (1955), and, for an assessment of how this topos centres ninth-century theology, Elsner (1988), 479.   [90] Kartsonis (1986), 144–145.

on its verso; bracketed by these texts, the image assuredly retains its original location.[91]

Gregory delivered the oration after leaving the bishopric at Sasima to return to Nazianzus as bishop-coadjutor. He begins with an invocation to the Holy Spirit, and continues to refer to the Spirit throughout the homily. In a passage marked by an enlarged initial on f. 76v, he admits that he is:

torn asunder with regret and enthusiasm. The one suggests . . . that the mind should retire into itself, and recall its power from sensible things, in order to hold pure communion with God, and be clearly illuminated by the flashing rays of the Spirit, with no admixture or disturbance of the divine light by anything earthly or clouded . . . The other wills that I should come forward . . . and publish the divine light.[92]

Though he never refers specifically to the transfiguration, Der Nersessian rightly connected Gregory's recurring use of light imagery with the image on f. 75r. Further, the narrative of the metamorphosis – when a cloud overshadowed the divine light, to protect 'sensible things' (e.g. Luke 9:34–6) – lies behind the textual imagery of the passage marked in Paris.gr.510. But if we can unravel the connection between text and miniature with relative ease, the transfiguration nonetheless illuminates rather than illustrates Gregory's sermon: in the Milan copy the marginal images accompanying the sermon are restricted to two portraits of Gregory holding a scroll inscribed with the adjacent words of his sermon.[93]

On f. 75r, Christ stands along the central axis of the page beneath rays of light coming from an arc of heaven; he blesses with his right hand and holds a scroll in his left. An aureole of ochre light (which, like that on f. 87v [fig. 16], describes such a perfect circle that it must have been traced with a compass) surrounds him, and encompasses most of the youthful Moses (MΩYCHC) on the left and the older Elijah (HΛIAC) on the right. Though their arms are confined by constricting sling-like drapery, Moses and Elijah turn and gesture toward Christ. All three stand on a light brown mountain, which also supports the two date palms that frame the upper half of the miniature. Below, on a strip of green ground, the apostles Peter, John, and James alternate with tiny rocky outcrops. Peter (ΠΕΤΡΟC), with the unusual light-brown straight hair he also wears on f. 32v (fig. 8), stands at the left. He turns toward and looks up at Christ, raising his right arm in greeting. John (IΩANNHC), here bearded as he is on f. 32v (but not on f. 30v), is placed directly below Christ; he falls forward with extended hands, his right leg flung behind him. James (IAKΩBOC) has fallen on one knee; he faces forward, but looks back up at

---

[91] SC 405, 348–361 (*BHG*, 730v; *NPNF*, 245–247). Millet (1920), 241; Malickij (1926), 147–148; Omont (1929), 17–18, pl. XXVIII; Morey (1929), 89, 96; Gallay (1943), 117; Weitzmann (1961), 480; Der Nersessian (1962), 211–212; Weitzmann (1969), 415–421; Weitzmann (1971b), 638; Maguire (1974), 123–124; Weitzmann (1974), 35; Elsner (1988), 474–475.   [92] SC 405, 355.
[93] Grabar (1943a), pls. XV, 1–2; in the former, Gregory's father accompanies him. The liturgical editions do not include Homily 12.

Fig. 121 Mount Sinai, Monastery of St Catherine, apse mosaic: transfiguration

Christ, raising his right hand to shield his face. All figures are nimbed in gold. The distinction between the Old and New Testament figures is conveyed by costume: all wear a pale blue undertunic, but the mantles worn by Moses and Elijah are beige highlighted with white, while those worn by Christ and the apostles are white shaded with pale grey. The scene is identified as 'the holy metamorphosis' (Η ΑΓΙΑ ΜΕΤΑΜΟΡΦΩCIC) on the gold frame; the identification Η ΜΕΤΑ-ΜΟΡΦΩCIC is repeated in white below Moses' feet.

Matthew 17:1–10, Mark 9:2–9, and Luke 9:28–32 recount the episode, and f. 75r conforms to these accounts. Nonetheless, the Gregory transfiguration differs in a number of important respects from the famous sixth-century mosaic at Mount Sinai (fig. 121),[94] where only Christ occupies the aureole of light, Elijah (in skins rather than chiton and himation) and an older Moses are reversed, and, though Peter kneels in an exaggeration of the posture assumed by John on f. 75r, the apostles are arranged differently. The differences between Paris.gr.510 and the Sinai mosaic suggest a changed conception of the scene.[95]

The transfiguration, as proclaimed by the Council of Nicaea in 325, proved

---

[94] Forsyth and Weitzmann (n.d.), pl. CIII. For other early examples, see e.g. Elsner (1988), 474–477.
[95] So too Elsner (1988), 474–477.

Christ's divinity; as important in the 880s, it also demonstrated that the divinity of the Son could be seen by mere mortals.[96] The renewed significance of the transfiguration resulted in a spate of images; of those preserved, the Khludov Psalter is closest in date to Paris.gr.510, and anticipates the Homilies image in most details (fig. 122).[97] Christ stands on a mountaintop in a nearly circular aureole which also encloses a youthful Moses (left) and older Elijah (right); as on f. 75r, the Khludov miniaturist used different-coloured costumes rather than different types of costume to distinguish the Old and New Testament figures. The Psalter miniaturist has reversed the apostles, but Peter stands and gestures up toward Christ and James repeats the pose he holds in the Homilies miniature. Only John differs: in the Psalter he huddles close to the ground.

For other roughly contemporary images of the transfiguration we have written evidence, but the only detailed account concerns the scene in the Apostoleion.[98] Constantine the Rhodian supplied a tenth-century description;[99] and, around 1200, Nicholas Mesarites provided a fuller report on what is apparently the same mosaic.[100] From these narratives, it appears that the Apostoleion disciples looked as they do in Paris.gr.510 or the Khludov Psalter (the description is not sufficiently precise to indicate John's exact position, the major difference between the two miniatures) and, assuming Mesarites described the disciples from left to right, followed the order of f. 75r rather than the psalter. Apparently, too, Moses and Elijah stood to the left and right, respectively, of Christ, all three of them in the bright cloud. Also as in Paris.gr.510 (but not the Khludov Psalter) rays of light, signifying God's voice, streamed down from heaven. The major difference seems to be in the attributes of the prophets: the Apostoleion Moses carried a book and Elijah wore rough skins. Despite this discrepancy, Paris.gr.510, the Khludov Psalter, and the Apostoleion mosaic are more closely related to each other than any of them are to the earlier Sinai mosaic.[101] All seem to reproduce, with individual variations, a new formula for the transfiguration familiar in the capital from the middle of the ninth century.[102]

Two details on f. 75r nonetheless stand out. The date palms, which replicate the tree included in the Adam and Eve sequence (f. 52v; fig. 10) and evidently refer to the tree of life, appear in neither the Khludov Psalter nor in the descriptions of the

---

[96] McGuckin (1985), esp. 336–337, notes that the main concern of Greek theologians writing about the transfiguration was its theophanic character.

[97] Moscow, Hist.Mus.gr.129, f. 88v: Ščepkina (1977).

[98] On the Apostoleion, see chapter 1 note 78. Leo VI's mention of a transfiguration in the church of Stylianos Zaoutzas provides little iconographical information: see Mango (1972), 203–205.

[99] Ed. Legrand (1896), 60; trans. Mango (1972), 200–201.

[100] Ed. Downey (1957), 902–903, trans. 871–873.

[101] It has, in fact, been suggested that Paris.gr.510, and the Khludov Psalter as well, here follow the Apostoleion: Weitzmann (1969); cf. Demus I (1984), 238 and, for arguments against this thesis, Malickij (1926), 147–148.

[102] So too Elsner (1988); his liturgical explanation is not, however, entirely convincing.

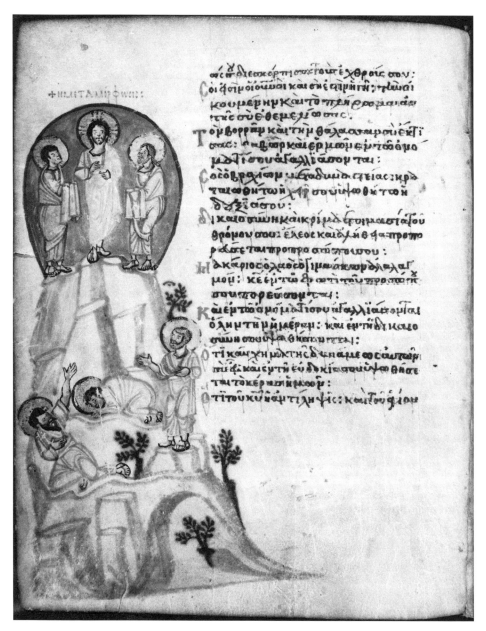

Fig. 122 Moscow, Historical Museum, cod.129, f. 88v: transfiguration

Apostoleion mosaic. Their inclusion was presumably intended to impart an eschatological flavour to the miniature[103] – Christ's divinity was revealed on earth to the apostles as it will be revealed to all at the Second Coming – familiar from early Byzantine commentators such as John Chrysostom.[104] This association was certainly accepted in the ninth century, when Photios repeated it in his Commentary on Matthew.[105] But the visual combination is unusual; while the trees may signal a patriarchal intervention, it is as important that their paradisal implications underscored Christ's divinity. The transfiguration visualized the orthodox belief that divinity was seen and could therefore be pictured; the trees underscore the point.

The hand of God emerging from an arc of heaven to fill Christ with the Holy Spirit provides a second unusual feature of f. 75r. Not only does this motif provide a rare instance of a compositional element appearing outside the framed miniature, but a hand of God hardly ever appears in images of the transfiguration at all: God's presence was evidently important enough that the designer of Paris.gr.510 deviated from the conventions both of the manuscript and of traditional iconography. The rays emanating from God's hand accord with the emphasis on divine light manifest in Gregory's sermon; and we might also see God imbuing Christ with the Spirit as a divine parallel to the transfer of power from Gregory *père* to Gregory *fils* that the adjacent homily commemorates. As important, however, the hand of God stressed the divinity of the transfigured Christ.

All of the images considered in this chapter have shown humans, on earth, viewing and interacting with divinity; in some cases the viewer is invited to participate. In a sense, one could argue that all of the miniatures that picture Christ or saints extend the same invitation: the whole concept of figurative religious art recognizes the ability of the earth-bound beholder to witness representations of the holy. The miniatures considered in this chapter simply take that equation a little deeper, and show either supernatural divinity – angels and visions of God or Christ – or the incarnate Christ revealing his divine nature, as in the chairete and the transfiguration. All demonstrate the human ability to perceive divinity; all demonstrate that what past humans saw can be visualized and experienced anew through the medium of images. That three of the five full-page miniatures in the body of the manuscript are found within this group suggests that this message was important.

[103] See Dinkler (1964), 87–100.   [104] *PG* 58:554.   [105] *PG* 101:1205A.

8

Iconography

'Iconography' is a weighted term, and the baggage that it carries depends on one's time and place of training, and on the discipline in which one was trained. It is used here as a shorthand reference to the constellation of features that determined how a particular episode was depicted. These features include, but are not restricted to, morphology (the shape of the scene) – the traditional object of iconographic study.

The primary aim of this book has been to examine how images worked in Paris.gr.510. Hence, iconographic analysis has so far focused on elucidating how (and sometimes why) apparently familiar formulae were modified, and on isolating features that seem to have had particular meaning around 880, when they were combined with Gregory's sermons. This exercise required a focus on what surviving sources suggest was normative ninth-century iconography in order to provide a general picture of what the miniaturists were likely to have known; there has been no attempt to pinpoint precise sources.

The visual sources with which the Homilies miniaturists were familiar are important to our understanding of the manuscript as a whole. The precisions about image-patterns potentially available in Constantinople that can be wrung from these associations are less important for an analysis of Paris.gr.510 than they are for an understanding of Byzantine visual culture in general. Since chapter 1, which pictured the context with which Paris.gr.510 interacted, I have concentrated on the internal workings of the manuscript. This chapter is about what Paris.gr.510 tells us about other works.

ICONOGRAPHY BY THE BOOK

The Old Testament
Genesis

In Paris.gr.510, twenty-eight scenes from the book of Genesis are gathered into four miniatures. Two of these pages picture the densest narrative sequences in the manuscript, and we shall therefore rely on the Genesis scenes as a model for subsequent discussion.

Three of the pages containing Genesis scenes (ff. 52v, 69v, and 360r; figs. 10, 12, 37) present exegetical illustrations; the fourth (f. 174v; fig. 23) pictures scenes mentioned but not described by Gregory. Though the sermons cannot have provided the direct or descriptive inspiration for the Genesis scenes in Paris.gr.510, one would not expect them to have in any case: Genesis spawned more narrative sequences than any other Old Testament book; in an important sense the visual narrative of Genesis had a life independent of the biblical chronicle.

Folio 52v (10) (fig. 10)

The top register of f. 52v shows scenes in paradise, represented as a green meadow studded with red flowers and gold leaves; the background is of variegated blue. The first scene, the creation of Adam (Genesis 1:26–27, 2:7), presents the creator as a badly flaked hand of God in the upper left corner. The nude Adam (AΔAM) lies with his eyes closed on a diagonal in the left corner. Several distinct episodes in Adam's creation appear in extensive Genesis cycles,[1] and both the illustrated Octateuchs – a half-dozen interrelated manuscripts dating from the eleventh, twelfth and thirteenth centuries that contain the first eight books of the Old Testament – and a group of works sometimes called the Cotton Genesis family include a similar prone Adam among their scenes.[2]

In the next image, a nude Eve (EYA) and Adam (AΔAM) sit side by side in the garden of paradise. This is probably meant to represent the creation of Eve, with the creative force coming from the hand of God used in the preceding scene. Though Eve's creation is most frequently indicated in Byzantium by the creator drawing a half figure of a woman or a rib from Adam's side, the fully formed Eve recurs in the fourteenth-century frescoes at Dečani, and possibly in the badly flaked miniature showing Eve's creation from the mid-fourteenth-century Manasses Chronicle.[3]

The third scene shows Adam (AΔAM) and Eve ([EY]A) standing next to an upright serpent, covering their genitals with large green leaves. The absence of a tree and lack of fruit indicate that this is not a conventional image of the temptation or the fall; the prominence of the serpent suggests more than the covering of

---

[1] See Weitzmann (1947), 176–178.

[2] The bibliography on these somewhat artificial groups is extensive. Most of the Octateuch material is collected in Lowden (1992); on the Cotton Genesis group see Weitzmann and Kessler (1986). For the prone Adam: Hesseling (1909), figs. 9, 13; Lassus (1979), fig. p. 117; Bernabò (1978), pl. IV; Kessler (1977), figs. 1, 2, 4; Weitzmann and Kessler (1986), 52.

[3] For Dečani, Petković (1941), pl. CCLV; Marković and Marković (1995), 351: I thank Zaga Gavrilović for the latter reference. Despite the image, the inscription above the scene ('And God brought a trance upon Adam, and he slept . . .') implies the rib-drawing episode: I thank Slobodan Ćurčić for translating the Serbian inscription. For the chronicle, Filov (1927), 33; Dujcev (1962), pl. 4.

nakedness: the three participants in the drama of original sin seem to be receiving the curse of God (Genesis 3:15–20), emanating from the hand in the upper left-hand corner, that condemned Adam and Eve to a life of toil outside paradise and doomed the serpent to crawl on its belly ever after. The same moment is illustrated in the *Sacra Parallela* (fig. 123) where, as in Paris.gr.510, Adam and Eve turn toward each other, gesturing, and the serpent is still upright.[4] In the *Sacra Parallela* the snake is inserted between the two figures, but the asymmetrical grouping of the Paris Gregory recurs in the tenth-century dome paintings at Aght'amar and in several later manuscripts such as a fourteenth-century copy of the liturgical Homilies now in Paris.[5]

The upper register closes with Adam and Eve, still clad in leaves rather than the garments of fur that the Genesis narrative has given them by this time, cast out of paradise by an archangel. An angel expeller is not specified by Genesis, but is common in both literary and artistic interpretations of the 'casting out' narrated in Genesis 3:25.[6] The anachronistic retention of the fig-leaf garments is less conventional, but recurs on several tenth-century Byzantine ivory boxes, in the paintings at Aght'amar, and in numerous manuscripts, including the eleventh-century Vatican *Klimax*, both twelfth-century copies of the Homilies of James of Kokkinobaphos (fig. 124), the Manasses Chronicle, and a fourteenth-century liturgical roll on Mount Athos.[7]

The second register begins with a representation of the cherub guarding the tree of life (Genesis 3:25). As noted in chapter 5, most narrative sequences locate the cherub before the expulsion; but the Kokkinobaphos Homilies repeat the pattern found on f. 52v and picture the cherub guarding paradise on a later page from the expulsion.[8]

The tree of life, its location in paradise clearly indicated by the words O ΠΑΡΑΔΕΙCOC inscribed above it on the gold frame, is represented as a date palm. Although Genesis does not identify the species – and most apocryphal texts specify

[4] Paris.gr.923, f. 69r: Weitzmann (1979a), 34–35, fig. 9.

[5] Thierry (1983), fig. 5. Grishin (1985) suggested an early eleventh- rather than a tenth-century date for the dome paintings but this has not met wide acceptance; I thank Lyn Jones for discussion of this point. Paris.gr.543, f. 116v: Galavaris (1969), fig. 462.

[6] The expulsion is narrated in two parts, with Adam and Eve 'sent forth' in Genesis 3:24 and 'cast out' in verse 25; without exception, Adam and Eve are 'sent forth' by the creator and 'cast out' by an angel: see Kessler (1977), 21; Weitzmann and Kessler (1986), 57–58. For the apocryphal literary sources of the angel expeller, see Charles II (1913), 140, 148.

[7] Goldschmidt and Weitzmann I (1930), nos. 67d, 69c, 73, 115; Thierry (1983); Martin (1954), 69, fig. 106; Stornajolo (1910), pl. 11, Omont (1927), pl. V, and Hutter and Canart (1991), 30–31; Filov (1927), 33–34 and Dujcev (1962), pl. 6; Brehier (1940), pl. II,2 and Pelekanides *et al.* 3 (1979), 259–261. The motif also appears in medieval Roman works: Waetzoldt (1964), fig. 334 (San Paolo); Garrison (1961). Compare Bernabò (1979), 277–278, with Corrigan (1995).

[8] Vat.gr.1162, ff. 33r (expulsion), 36r (cherub): Stornajolo (1910), pls. 11, 13; Paris.gr.1208, ff. 47r (expulsion; fig. 126), 50r (cherub): Omont (1927), pls. V, VI.

Fig. 123 Paris.gr.923, f. 69r: curse of Adam, Eve, and the serpent

Fig. 124 Paris.gr.1208, f. 47r: scenes from the history of Adam and Eve

a fig – the date palm is sanctioned by the Book of Enoch[9] and, more importantly, by artistic convention.[10]

The guardian cherub stands against a red backdrop suggesting flames, set within a blue-grey doorway that represents the gate to paradise. The cherub has six blue wings covered with eyes and is tetramorphic: in addition to its human head and feet, a lion's head extends to the left, a bull's head to the right, and an eagle emerges from behind the cherub's gold nimb. The creatures are light brown; they, along with the eyes on the wings, derive from Ezekiel's description of the cherubim as tetramorphs 'full of eyes'; the number of wings follows Isaiah's portrayal of seraphim as six-winged.[11] This conflation conforms with ninth-century practice: the Vatican 'Christian Topography' combines the attributes of cherubim and seraphim in the same manner (fig. 76), presumably in response to their conjoint description in the anaphora of the Chrysostom liturgy.[12] Despite the inscription 'the fiery sword' (Η ΦΛΟΓΙΝΗ ΡΟΜΦΑΙΑ) on the gate, the cherub carries a red lance rather than the sword of Genesis 3:25; this, and the gate in which the cherub stands, duplicate the image in the Khludov Psalter (fig. 125), while the lance recurs in the Paris Kokkinobaphos of the 1130s.[13] Usually, the gate appears before or within the garden of paradise, but the isolation of the tree of life found in the Homilies recurs at San Marco.[14]

To the right of the cherub, an archangel, clad as in the top register, hands Adam a two-pronged hoe. Though the scene alludes to Genesis 3:24, we saw in chapter 5 that it finds no Byzantine visual parallels.

The final scene of the Adam and Eve sequence shows the couple's lament outside Paradise. Adam, still wearing only his green fig leaf, sits on a large grey rock resting his head on his hand with his fingers wrapped around his beard; Eve's head and shoulders appear behind him. Genesis does not describe the lament, but the episode appears in numerous apocryphal texts, including a version of the *Vitae Adae et Evae*: 'And we sat together before the gate of Paradise, Adam weeping with his face bent down.'[15] The lament was being pictured by the fourth century and it continued to be represented throughout the Byzantine period.[16] Usually Adam and Eve are shown in garments of fur, but several variants – a group of ivory caskets, the Kokkinobaphos manuscripts (fig. 126), and a copy of the liturgical Homilies – follow Paris.gr.510 in clothing the lamenting couple in fig leaves, or

---

[9] And some editions of the Apocalypse of Moses: Charles II (1913), 146 note 5, 204–205.

[10] See J. Flemming, s.v. 'Baum, Bäume', in *LCI* 1 (1968), 260–264.

[11] Ezekiel 1:5–24, 10:8–17; Isaiah 6:2–3.

[12] Vat.gr.699, ff. 72v, 74r (Stornajolo [1908], pls. 37, 39); Pallas (1971), 59.

[13] Moscow, Hist.Mus.gr.129, f. 119v (Ščepkina [1977]); Tsuji (1983), 23–25; Anderson (1991).

[14] Weitzmann, in Demus II (1984), 116, pls. 32, 130.   [15] Charles II (1913), 134.

[16] See e.g. the fourth-century Via Latina catacomb paintings (Ferrua [1960], pl. XCV) and the Smyrna Octateuch (Hesseling [1909], figs. 22, 23).

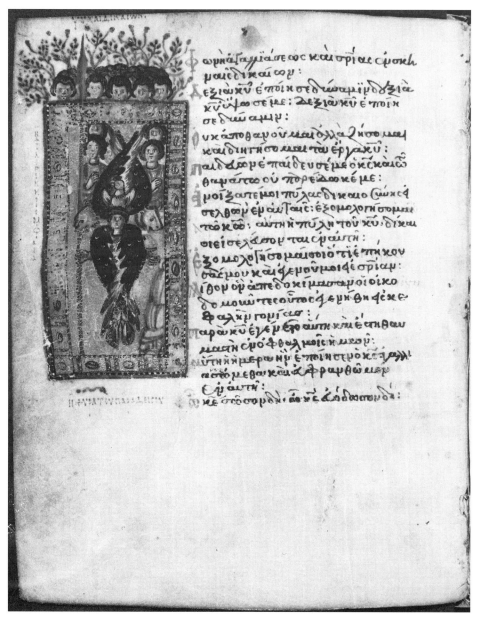

Fig. 125 Moscow, Historical Museum, cod.129, f. 119v: cherub guarding the gate of paradise

Fig. 126 Paris.gr.1208, f. 49v: scenes from the history of Adam and Eve

show them nude; in all of these examples, as on f. 52v, Adam seems to tug at his beard.[17]

The Adam and Eve sequence on f. 52v provides a visual commentary on the sermon it accompanies, and specific episodes from the narrative of the creation and fall were chosen with care;[18] it is perhaps not surprising that neither the selection of scenes nor their arrangement is precisely duplicated elsewhere. Nonetheless, six of the eight scenes relate standard themes of the Genesis narrative, many of them influenced by apocryphal accounts. These do not correspond with the narrative sequences incorporated in illustrated Genesis manuscripts. There are virtually no similarities between f. 52v and the Vienna Genesis; and the hallmark of the Cotton Genesis group, the anthropomorphic creator, is not found in Paris.gr.510.[19] In the Octateuchs Eve's creation is represented by a half-length figure emerging from Adam's side, and both are correctly clad in fur after the expulsion; the curse appears only in Vat.gr.747, where it has been so heavily repainted that its original form is uncertain.[20] Rather than associations with illustrated books of Genesis, the Homilies scenes find visual parallels in a seemingly diverse assortment of other works, notably the Kokkinobaphos manuscripts and a group of ivory caskets, which share with f. 52v the iconography of the expulsion, the cherub guarding the gate, and the lament.[21] All, like the sequence on f. 52v, present selected scenes from the history of Adam and Eve divorced from a narrative textual context.

Folio 69v (12) (fig. 12)

Fourteen scenes spread over five registers detail a history of Joseph that concentrates on Joseph's triumph over adversity.[22] In the opening image, Jacob instructs Joseph to join his brothers in Sychem. Between the two stands a small figure which Henri Omont, followed by subsequent scholars, identified as a female.[23] The uncovered head, short brown hair and simple red tunic with gold collar, however, signify a youthful male in Paris.gr.510. Comparison with the centurion's servant on f. 170r (fig. 22) or the rich youth on f. 87v (fig. 16) allows the re-identification of the figure as Benjamin, Jacob's youngest son, who remained at home when Joseph departed. Genesis does not specify Benjamin's presence here, but he appears fre-

---

[17] Goldschmidt and Weitzmann I (1930), nos. 67c, 68c, 69d. In the Kokkinobaphos manuscripts, the lamenting couple appears twice, once in fig leaves and once in skins: Vat.gr.1162, f. 35v (Stornajolo [1910], pl. 12, Hutter and Canart [1991], 31–32); Paris.gr.1208, f. 49v (fig. 128 and Omont [1927], pl. VI). Paris.gr.543, f. 116v (marginal image): Galavaris (1969), fig. 462; cf. ibid., fig. 102, where Adam appears alone in Jerusalem, Taphou 14, f. 111r.   [18] See chapter 5.

[19] Vienna, Nationalbib. cod.theol.gr.31, ff. 1r–v (Gerstinger [1931], pict. 1–2); Weitzmann and Kessler (1986), 37.   [20] See note 2 above; Hutter (1972); and Lassus (1979), fig. p. 136.

[21] The form taken by the creator varies: an anthropomorphic creator alternates with the hand of God on the ivory caskets; an angel appears in the Kokkinobaphos manuscripts. I am unconvinced by the tentative association of these images with the Cotton Genesis family: Weitzmann and Kessler (1986), 29.   [22] See chapter 4, where inscriptions and biblical citations are noted.

[23] Omont (1929), 16; hence the misidentification of this figure as Bilhah: Friedman (1989), 66.

Fig. 127 Rome, Sta Maria Antiqua: Jacob and Joseph

quently in works as disparate as the Vienna Genesis, the Octateuchs, and the frescoes at Sta Maria Antiqua (fig. 127).[24] Though badly damaged, the latter relates closely to the Gregory image: traces of a figure's foot and the silhouette of a long garment appear between a seated Jacob and standing Joseph virtually identical to their counterparts on f. 69v.[25]

The remainder of the register shows Joseph, walking behind a donkey, greeted at Dothaim by his brothers, who sit around a semi-circular table. Donkeys rarely appear in depictions of this episode,[26] but even more unusual is the portrayal of the brothers feasting. Genesis 37:17 does not specify the circumstances of the brothers' reunion, but Jacob had sent his elder sons off to tend the flocks, and Byzantine representations of this scene almost without exception present Joseph coming

[24] Vienna, Nationalbib. cod.theol.gr.31, f. 15r (Gerstinger [1931], pict. 30); Smyrna, Evangelical School A.1, f. 50r (Hesseling [1909], fig. 120); Grüneisen (1911), 363–364, fig. 89 (identifying the scene as Joseph telling Jacob his dreams; for the correct identification, Vileisis [1979], 58–61). See also the Cotton Genesis (Weitzmann and Kessler [1986], 103; Vikan [1979], 101) and Sopoćani (Ljubinković [1965], fig. 1).

[25] I thank John Osborne for allowing me unrestricted access to Sta Maria Antiqua during the summer of 1984. The similarity between the Roman fresco and Paris.gr.510 was also noted by Vileisis (1979), 58–64; cf. Weitzmann and Kessler (1986), 27.

[26] For another example, see the post-Byzantine Rumanian miniature where, however, Joseph rides the donkey: Pächt and Pächt (1954), 38, pl. 12; Vikan (1976), 55–59.

Fig. 128 Sens, Cathedral Treasury: ivory casket, Joseph approaches his brothers at Dothaim; David
and the lion

upon them in a pasture:[27] the feasting brothers depart from a widespread and near-
ubiquitous tradition. The same anomaly recurs, however, on an eleventh- or
twelfth-century Byzantine or Italo-Byzantine ivory casket at Sens carved with
scenes from Joseph's life (fig. 128).[28] In both versions, Joseph approaches from the

[27] E.g. the Vienna Genesis and the Octateuchs (references in note 24 above), and works related to
the Cotton Genesis: Weitzmann and Kessler (1986), 103. See also Vikan (1979), 102.
[28] Goldschmidt and Weitzmann I (1930), 64–66, no. 124a. See also note 57 below.

left, supporting himself with a staff held in his right hand; the brothers sit around a sigma-shaped table supporting a large platter. But there are differences. On the casket, Joseph leans back on this staff and gestures in greeting toward his brothers, who remain unaware of his presence; on f. 69v the brothers gesture or gaze toward Joseph, but there is no indication that Joseph has yet sighted them. More important, in each case the scene echoes another: on f. 69v, it duplicates almost exactly the brothers at table in the third register (even the curious position of the right foreground figure is identical); on the casket, it replicates Joseph's banquet, carved immediately above it.[29] In both cases, internal compositional pairings seem to have inspired the unusual banquet at Dothaim. On f. 69v, the feast was included primarily to secure the link between two episodes involving Joseph's plotting brothers.

The second register opens with Joseph's brothers casting him into a cistern as they remove his cloak, thus telescoping the events of Genesis 37:23–24 into a single action. Such a compression appears to be unique in Byzantine art, if only because the removal of Joseph's cloak was rarely portrayed. Divorced from the descent into the well, it may once have appeared in the Cotton Genesis;[30] it recurs on the Sens casket – which, however, differs utterly from Paris.gr.510 in showing Joseph on his hands and knees as the brothers unfasten (rather than pull off) the mantle[31] – and in two later manuscripts, which also differ from f. 69v.[32] Depictions of Joseph being cast into the cistern (or the sometimes indistinguishable scene of his removal from it) are as common as images of the removal of his cloak are uncommon. The significant features of the Gregory version – the irregular, almost conical mound of earth that surrounds the cistern and the symmetrical groups composed of an active brother backed by several passive ones that flank it – anticipate the composition found in the Octateuchs (fig. 129).[33]

The middle scene of the second register shows one of Joseph's brothers cutting the throat of a goat while a second brother holds Joseph's cloak before the gushing wound. Genesis 37:31 does not specify the manner of dispatching the goat, but most representations follow Paris.gr.510 in showing Joseph's brother approaching

---

[29] Goldschmidt and Weitzmann I (1930), no. 124u.   [30] Weitzmann and Kessler (1986), 103.

[31] Goldschmidt and Weitzmann I (1930), no. 124b. For late western examples of this format: London, BL Royal 2,B.VII, f. 14v (Warner [1912], pl. 26) and Rovigo, Accademia dei Concordi, cod.212, f. 28v (Follena and Mellini [1962], pl. 56).

[32] One is a fourteenth-century English paraphrase of Genesis in London (BL Egerton 1894, f. 18v: James [1921]) that Pächt (1943), esp. 62–66, first associated with the Cotton Genesis family. The other is a post-Byzantine Rumanian copy of Pseudo-Ephraim's Life of Joseph (Virginia Beach, Helen Greeley Collection, cod.M [McKell], f. 8r: Vikan [1976], 61–62). Both obscure Joseph's head beneath his mantle.

[33] E.g. the now-destroyed Smyrna Octateuch (f. 50v): Hesseling (1909), fig. 121. Many of the features shared by Paris.gr.510 and the Octateuchs recur in the Sopoćani Joseph cycle, though here the passive brothers stand to the left: Ljubinković (1965), 214–215, fig. 2. For the cistern presented as a raised well, see Weitzmann and Kessler (1986), 103–104; Goldschmidt and Weitzmann II (1930), no. 94; Graeven (1900), 110–111. In the *Sacra Parallela* version of this episode, two brothers put hands on Joseph's head as if to push him down; the form of the abbreviated cistern may allude to a mound: Paris.gr.923, f. 391r; Weitzmann (1979a), fig. 39.

Fig. 129 Vat.gr.746, f. 116v: Joseph cast into the cistern, Joseph's brothers bloody his coat

the animal from the rear and pulling its head backward against his knee to expose its throat. The second brother bending forward with Joseph's cloak also recurs in such disparate monuments as the Octateuchs (fig. 129) and the cathedra of Maximianus.[34]

The biblical narrative describes the bloodying of Joseph's cloak after his sale to the Ishmaelites, an episode that waits until the beginning of the fourth register on f. 69v. This inversion is not, however, uncommon. Manuscripts wherein the relationship between the text and its illustration remains literal and strong – such as the eleventh-century Octateuch in the Vatican – usually retain the episodic order prescribed by Genesis.[35] But when the bond between word and image weakens, as in works physically divorced from the biblical text such as Maximianus' cathedra or a group of Coptic textiles showing Joseph scenes, the order followed on f. 69v prevails.[36] Jane Timken Matthews has argued that Philo's *De Josepho* may have influenced the reversal, for here too the order of the Septuagint narrative is inverted.[37]

The final scene of the second register shows a single brother displaying Joseph's bloody cloak to Jacob, who sits chin-in-hand in a characteristic Byzantine posture of sorrow,[38] a pose that occurs in many images of the episode – though not in two works that have displayed other similarities with the page, the Cotton Genesis and the Sens casket.[39] Joseph's many-coloured cloak is here, and throughout f. 69v, presented as a white tunic with green collar and hem.

The third register opens with two brothers pulling Joseph – clothed in what are presumably meant to be interpreted as his undergarments – by his arms from the cistern, preparatory to his purchase by the Egyptian merchants. Compositionally the scene resembles the depiction of Joseph lowered into the cistern directly above it; the miniaturist has, however, lowered the hillock in which the cistern sits and thus allowed more of Joseph to be seen. Despite the apparently intentional use of echoing images, the second cistern scene on f. 69v nonetheless finds a number of visual corollaries and seems to adapt a reasonably familiar pattern.[40]

[34] E.g. the Smyrna Octateuch (f. 50v; Hesseling [1909], fig. 121); Cecchelli (1944), pl. XVII. See also Weitzmann and Kessler (1986), 105. The centre of the image in Paris.gr.923, f. 353r (Weitzmann [1979a], 44–45, fig. 40) is badly flaked but the scene sustains no obvious parallels with f. 69v.

[35] Vat.gr.747, f. 58v (unpublished).   [36] Cecchelli (1944), pl. XVII; Vikan (1979), 102.

[37] Matthews (1980), esp. 36–42, whose suggestion that Philo's paraphrase was known through its incorporation in the marginal *catena* does not apply to Paris.gr.510 (see chapter 4, where we saw that this text was familiar in ninth-century Constantinople), but may suit the twelfth-century Octateuchs, which diverge from Genesis (and Vat.gr.747) to present the scenes as adjacent images: see e.g. Smyrna (f. 50v): Hesseling (1909), fig. 121.   [38] See Maguire (1977), 132–140.

[39] Weitzmann and Kessler (1986), 105; Goldschmidt and Weitzmann I (1930), no. 124f.

[40] E.g. a fresco at Sta Maria Antiqua, though here the nude Joseph rises from a low well: Grüneisen (1911), 364–366, pl. XXII. That this is the removal from the cistern is clear from the presence of the Ishmaelites, whose arrival prompted Joseph's release. The Sens casket is similar in its depiction of the symmetrical groupings of the brothers, the position of Joseph (though he wears a loincloth on the

Fig. 130 Venice, San Marco: Joseph's brothers feasting

The feast scene that follows Joseph's removal from the cistern finds parallels in the Octateuchs and in works sometimes affiliated with the Cotton Genesis; it also recurs in the *Sacra Parallela*.[41] Closest to Paris.gr.510, the San Marco mosaic (fig. 130) shares with f. 69v the sigma-shaped table supporting an ornate oval dish, the peculiar posture of both the leftmost and rightmost brothers, and two Ishmaelites astride camels rather than the more common single figure on foot.[42]

What is most unusual about the third register is that the scene of Joseph's removal from the cistern precedes the feast and arrival of the merchants. In the biblical narrative followed by other pictorial cycles, Joseph is cast into the cistern, his brothers then sit down to feast and while eating sight the approaching Ishmaelites, after which they remove Joseph from the cistern and sell him to the merchants. On f. 69v the narrative has been adjusted in order to provide a visual correlation between the two cistern episodes, best achieved by their vertical juxtaposition.

ivory), and the low rim of the cistern from which Joseph emerges: Goldschmidt and Weitzmann I (1930), no. 124c. Weitzmann (1979a), 44 note 65, later suggested that the panel represents the descent into rather than the ascent from the pit. The Cotton Genesis, followed by the San Marco mosaics, differs from f. 69v: Joseph throws his leg out of the well as he escapes (Weitzmann and Kessler [1986], 104). Neither the Vienna Genesis nor the Octateuchs includes the scene.
[41] Hesseling (1909), fig. 121; Weitzmann and Kessler (1986), 103–104; Weitzmann (1979a), fig. 39. The Vienna Genesis lacks this scene.   [42] Demus II (1984), colour pl. 55 and pl. 251.

The penultimate register shows Joseph's sale to the Ishmaelites and the journey to Egypt. Joseph's eight brothers crowd together by the left frame; the foremost lays one hand on Joseph's shoulder and gestures toward the two Ishmaelite merchants – wearing red garments and turbans, and backed by two camels – with the other. Between the two groups, Joseph stands passively, gazing directly out at the viewer. For the journey to Egypt, the Gregory illustrator depicts Joseph sitting quietly on a camel led by a turbaned Ishmaelite who looks back at his charge and gestures forward; a second camel interposes itself between the viewer and Joseph, and a second trader follows behind. The Homilies images retain general similarities with most other versions of this episode,[43] and the entire fourth register is also related to a sequence preserved in some of the marginal psalters as an illustration of Psalm 104:17 (fig. 131): 'He sent a man before them, even Joseph, who was sold for a servant.' Paris.gr.20 and the Bristol Psalter show only the textually justified sale of Joseph, but both the Khludov (fig. 131) and Theodore Psalters append another trader leading away a camel.[44] The depictions of the sale agree with the Homilies image in all details, and even the trader leading the camel seems to be a highly abbreviated version of the journey to Egypt found in Paris.gr.510: though Joseph is omitted, the relationship between the camel and the trader who gestures forward while looking back is identical in all three examples.

The final register contains four scenes, the first of which is Joseph's sale to Potiphar. Joseph stands passively between two Ishmaelite traders (badly flaked) and a standing Potiphar, who extends his right arm over Joseph's head toward the traders. While most versions of this episode show Potiphar enthroned,[45] a panel on Maximinanus' cathedra, a fresco at Sta Maria Antiqua (fig. 132), a mosaic at San Marco, and possibly the Cotton Genesis show Potiphar standing.[46] Potiphar's gesture, extensively flaked in the miniature, is presumably one of payment.

The next scene shows the attempted seduction of Joseph by Potiphar's wife, who sits on a gold stool, leaning on her left arm while grasping Joseph's shoulder with her right hand. The inscription reads 'Joseph's mistress constrains him by force', a simplification of Genesis 39:12 ('And she caught hold of him by his clothes and said, Lie with me . . .') that accords better with the picture than does the biblical text.

[43] E.g. a mosaic in San Marco (Demus II [1984], pl. 253; cf. Weitzmann and Kessler [1986], 104–105), the McKell Life of Joseph (Vikan [1976], 73–75, cf. 236–237 note 95); and, for the journey, the middle Byzantine Octateuchs (e.g. Hesseling [1909], figs. 121, 124). The Sens casket is quite distinct: Goldschmidt and Weitzmann I (1930), no. 124d.

[44] Moscow, Hist.Mus.gr.129, f. 106r (Ščepkina [1977]); London, BL Add.19.352, f. 140v (Der Nersessian [1970], fig. 225).

[45] For the now-destroyed Smyrna Octateuch (f. 51v), Hesseling (1909), fig. 124; for Sopoćani, Ljubinković (1965), 219–221, fig. 2; for Sens, Goldschmidt and Weitzmann I (1930), no. 124g.

[46] Cecchelli (1944), pl. XVIII; Grüneisen (1911), pl. XXIII; Demus II (1984), pl. 265; Weitzmann and Kessler (1986), 105, 107–108. The latter believe that the Cotton Genesis differentiated between the biblical accounts of the sale in Genesis 37:35 and 39:1 by showing a standing figure for one verse and a seated figure for the other.

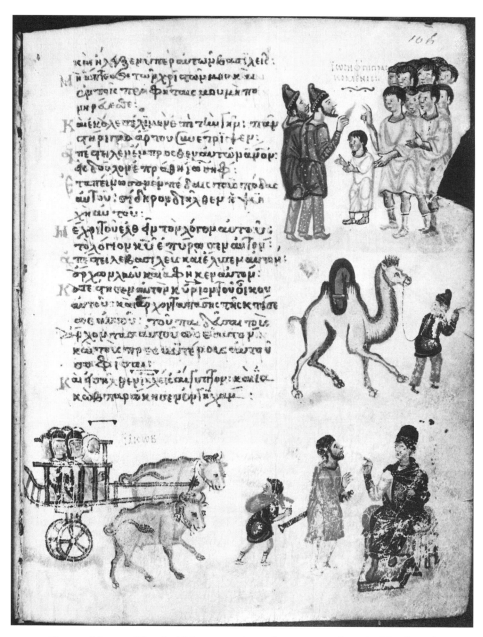

Fig. 131 Moscow, Historical Museum, cod.129, f. 106r: scenes from the life of Joseph

Fig. 132 Rome, Sta Maria Antiqua: Joseph sold to Potiphar; Joseph and Potiphar's wife

Most depictions, however, follow Genesis in showing Potiphar's wife clutching Joseph's cloak as it streams behind him while he runs from her.[47] In two of the Byzantine Octateuchs, the standing woman exceptionally holds Joseph's wrists;[48] even closer parallels are provided by Maximianus' cathedra, perhaps the Cotton Genesis fragments and, especially, by a fresco at Sta Maria Antiqua (fig. 132), in which Potiphar's wife, seated, clasps Joseph's shoulder as he flees, looking back at her over his shoulder exactly as on f. 69v.[49]

The iconography of the last two scenes, which deviates from all other known Byzantine variants, has already been considered:[50] presumably neither the investiture of Joseph nor his triumph finds close parallels elsewhere because each carries additional imperial meanings linking the life of Joseph with that of the emperor.

[47] See Weitzmann and Kessler (1986), 108–109; Gerstinger (1931), pict. 31.
[48] Vat.gr.746, f. 121v (unpublished); Istanbul, Seraglio 8, f. 127v (Uspensky [1907], pl. XVI).
[49] Weitzmann and Kessler (1986), 108–109; Grüneisen (1911), 369–371, pl. XXIII.
[50] See chapter 4.

Nonetheless, a significant number of the scenes on f. 69v find counterparts in other extant Joseph sequences: however much adaptation and modification occurred[51] – and whether the sequence ultimately relies on a precise source, on the visual memory of its painter, or on a combination of the two – the miniaturist did not invent the iconography of the sequence entirely from scratch. Though the miniaturist selected episodes, and adjusted the subject matter to sustain the exegetical function of the illustration (as in Joseph's investiture) as well as its compositional coherence (as in the duplicated banquet, and the cistern episodes), the iconography of many scenes on f. 69v did not require this type of modification. The illustrator had fairly simple tasks: to pictorialize the concept of brotherly deceit – achieved by the selection of scenes from within an established repertory of Joseph imagery – and to eulogize Basil I, accomplished by the selection of (standard) scenes and by stressing imperial formulae in the final two episodes presented.[52] With few exceptions, the scenes shown on f. 69v could have been adapted from existing and apparently familiar images.

But as was true of the Adam and Eve scenes on f. 52v, the Joseph scenes adapted to f. 69v do not seem to have been familiar from an illustrated Genesis or other Old Testament manuscript with monolithic narrative sequences resembling any still preserved today. Matthews claimed that f. 69v 'adheres entirely to the Octateuch tradition',[53] perhaps because twelve of the thirteen episodes pictured recur in the Octateuchs, which lack only the removal from the well. Only five, however, resemble the analogous images in Paris.gr.510: the brothers bloodying Joseph's cloak (fig. 129), Jacob's sorrow on being shown the coat, the two pit episodes (fig. 129), and the Ishmaelite leading Joseph into Egypt who appears in a composition otherwise distinct. Most of these are familiar compositions, not the exclusive property of the Octateuchs. In the end, f. 69v shares with the Octateuchs only one unmatched detail, the depiction of the cistern as a hole sunk into a mound of earth, and the condensed *Sacra Parallela* miniature suggests that even this motif had an independent existence.[54] A connection with the Cotton Genesis family, suggested by Mira Friedman,[55] suffers the same problems. Joseph's sale to the Ishmaelites, his journey to Egypt, his sale to Potiphar, and the bloodying of Joseph's cloak are indeed similar; again, however, equally compelling parallels for these scenes appear in works that have never been associated with the Cotton Genesis tradition. Only the scene of Joseph's brothers at table sighting the approaching Ishmaelites exhibits an apparently unique tie with a member of this group, the mosaic representation at San Marco (fig. 130).[56] Nor, despite the conceptual similarities, do the Joseph scenes in Paris.gr.510 demonstrate specific iconographic links with the Sens

---

[51] As Vikan (1979) observed, the popularity of Joseph cycles was such that intrusions are to be anticipated; for an example, see note 36 above.   [52] See chapter 4.   [53] Matthews (1980), 45.
[54] See note 33 above.   [55] Friedman (1989), 66 note 9.   [56] See, however, note 62 below.

casket.[57] Of the three scenes that reveal certain features in common, Joseph's removal from the pit sustains a pattern widely found elsewhere, while Joseph's arrival at Dothaim to find his brothers feasting (fig. 128) and the concluding scene of Joseph in triumph (fig. 89) share only their unusual subject matter, the iconographical details of which differ.[58] The closest parallels with f. 69v come from the Joseph sequences closest in date to Paris.gr.510: in the frescoes at Sta Maria Antiqua and in the marginal psalters.[59]

The eighth-century Genesis frescoes at Sta Maria Antiqua retain seven scenes from the life of Joseph.[60] Four of them recur in Paris.gr.510; all are similar to their counterparts on f. 69v and two provide the closest parallels extant. The portrayal of Jacob's instructions to Joseph (fig. 127) is virtually identical in both; and they also share the non-biblical motif of Potiphar's wife grasping Joseph's shoulder rather than his cloak as he flees from her, gazing back over his shoulder (fig. 132). Joseph's removal from the cistern, and his sale to Potiphar,[61] are also related, though in the former a low well replaces the earthen mound of f. 69v and in the latter the fresco reverses the composition. Further, in both sequences the episode with Potiphar's wife directly follows, without intervening scenes, Joseph's sale to Potiphar.[62] The sale of Joseph is even more closely related to that image in the mid-ninth-century marginal psalters (fig. 131), where remnants of Joseph's journey very similar to the scene on f. 69v also appear. Both the frescoes and the marginal miniatures are earlier than Paris.gr.510,[63] and together suggest that the Homilies miniaturist was familiar with a sequence of episodes from the life of Joseph that were once more widely attested than they are now. The selection and arrangement of the scenes, however, remains particular to Paris.gr.510, and the Homilies miniaturist should also be credited with the image of Joseph's brothers feasting at Dothaim, perhaps

---

[57] *Byzance* (1992), 264–265, with colour plate; Vikan (1976), 299–301, significantly emends Goldschmidt and Weitzmann I (1930), 64–66, and correctly notes four episodes ignored in the earlier publication; for reproductions, ibid., nos. 124a–d, f, g, y; see also Weitzmann (1979a), 44. Seven of the twenty-eight scenes from the life of Joseph on the ivory appear (condensed into six scenes) on f. 69v: Joseph's reunion with his brothers at Dothaim, Joseph's brothers removing his coat, the brothers taking Joseph out of the pit (the latter two collapsed on f. 69v), Joseph sold to the Ishmaelites, Jacob's lament, Potiphar's purchase of Joseph, and Joseph in Pharoah's chariot. Gary Vikan first noted the parallels; I thank him for allowing me to read in typescript his lecture 'Pictorial Recensions in their Cultural Settings', delivered in 1980 at McMaster University, and for numerous profitable discussions. I thank John Hanson for the same; publication of his study of the casket is awaited.

[58] Neither scene recurs elsewhere: see Pächt and Pächt (1954); Blum (1969); and Vikan (1976).

[59] The close links between f. 69v and Sta Maria Antiqua have been noted already by Grüneisen (1911), 366–369, and Vileisis (1979), 58–85.   [60] Grüneisen (1911), figs. 89, 90, pls. XXII–XXIV.

[61] So too ibid., 366–369.

[62] The Sta Maria Antiqua sequence may be distantly related to the Cotton Genesis family: Vikan (1976), 249 note 155; see the more cautious remarks in Weitzmann and Kessler (1986), 27.

[63] Corrigan (1992), 20, suggests that the Joseph scenes may have been included in a pre-iconoclast psalter.

with the combination of the removal of Joseph's cloak and his descent into the cistern, and with the modifications imposed on the final two scenes.

Folio 174v (23) (fig. 23)

The top two registers of f. 174v illustrate the sacrifice of Isaac and Jacob's struggle with the angel.[64] Gregory briefly mentions both events, but this in no way circumscribes their depictions: both were widely pictured in Byzantium and the presentations here adhere to standard iconographical types. The sacrifice of Isaac sequence opens with Abraham (ABPAAM), shown with long grey hair and a near-grey beard, instructing his servants to remain behind while he and Isaac continue on alone (Genesis 22:5–6). Abraham, nimbed in gold and wearing a white mantle over his blue tunic, stands turned slightly to the right, gesturing with his left hand toward Isaac, but looking and motioning back toward his two servants, dressed in short tunics, who are seated on the ground before a horse tethered to a tree. Isaac, youthful and unnimbed, wears a short blue tunic trimmed in gold and wrapped with a red sash, red leggings, and white boots. Placed in the centre of the register, he has started up the mountain with a bundle of wood on his back. This mountain, painted in shades of grey and brown, looms up in the background, and separates the two scenes of the register. For the sacrifice, Abraham (ABPAAM) stands almost in a striding position and looks back over his shoulder at a hand of God, painted outside the frame above the mountain, as he pulls back Isaac's head by the hair to bare his son's throat for the knife poised in his right hand. Isaac (ICAAK) kneels, facing away from his father, with his hands bound behind his back. A tall grey altar surmounted by fire closes the register on the right; the ram ultimately to be sacrificed on it peers out from behind the mountain. This image differs in numerous details from the account in Genesis 22:9–13: the Homilies miniaturist showed Isaac's arms, rather than his feet, bound together, placed Isaac before rather than on the altar, and substituted the hand of God for the angel specified in Genesis.[65]

The Homilies formula of sacrifice comes indirectly from antique schemes, but it entered the realm of Christian imagery early: a sixth-century pyxis in London, for example, shows Menas undergoing his martyrdom in precisely the same position as that held by Isaac.[66] Isaac kneeling on the ground rather than on the altar also appears early in representations of the sacrifice as, for example, in the Via Latina catacomb paintings.[67] The early Christian representations do not, however, duplicate Abraham's stance. For this the closest parallels occur in the marginal psalters and the middle Byzantine Octateuchs.

Three of the marginal psalters illustrate Psalm 104 with the sacrifice of Isaac (fig.

---

[64] See further chapter 5 with, for Jacob, chapter 7.
[65] For iconographical surveys, Speyart van Woerden (1961), and Gutmann (1984).
[66] Weitzmann (1947), 174–175; Volbach (1976), no. 181.   [67] Ferrua (1960), pl. XCIX.

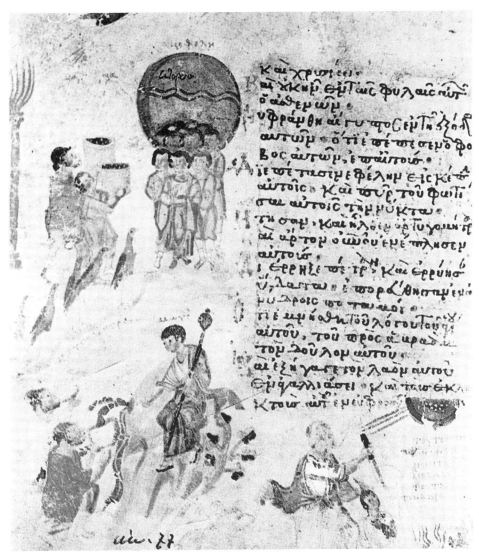

Fig. 133 Mount Athos, Pantokrator 61, f. 151v: miracles of the manna and quails; Moses strikes water from a rock; sacrifice of Isaac

133).[68] The versions differ slightly, but consistently present Abraham striding forward and grasping Isaac, who kneels before the altar, by the hair. And while the Khludov and Theodore Psalters show an angel halting the sacrifice, and Abraham brandishing a sword, Pantokrator 61 (fig. 133) duplicates the composition found in

[68] Moscow, Hist.Mus.gr.129, f. 105v (Ščepkina [1977]); Mount Athos, Pantokrator 61, f. 151v (Dufrenne [1966], pl. 23; Pelekanides *et al.* 3 [1979], fig. 227); London, BL Add.19.352, f. 140v (Der Nersessian [1970], fig. 225).

Fig. 134 Vat.gr.746, f. 82r: Abraham and Isaac

Paris.gr.510: Abraham gazes over his shoulder at an arc of heaven, and points a knife directly at Isaac's exposed throat.[69]

The same composition recurs in the twelfth-century Octateuchs, where it forms part of a three-scene sequence that is closely linked with f. 174v (figs. 134–135).[70] The preceding image (fig. 134) shows the two servants seated before a tethered donkey to the left of Abraham, who is securing a bundle of wood on Isaac's back. Despite illustrating slightly different moments of the Genesis narrative, the Homilies and Octateuch images share several features lacking in other versions. The servants sit (as directed in Genesis); Abraham has not been given the textually prescribed knife; and Isaac supports the wood on his back, secured with long thongs that he holds in his hands. Paris.gr.510, the Pantokrator Psalter, and the middle Byzantine Octateuchs ultimately perpetuate the same formula, variants of

[69] Corrigan (1992), 20, suggested that most of the miniatures illustrating Psalm 104, as this scene does, were retained from a pre-iconoclast psalter. She noted some modifications imposed on the Khludov Psalter; it seems that here Pantokrator, too, updated the earlier formula.

[70] E.g. Smyrna, Evangelical School A.1, ff. 34v, 35r: Hesseling (1909), figs. 78–80; also Weitzmann (1947), 141–142, figs. 126–128.

Fig. 135 Vat.gr.746, f. 83r: sacrifice of Isaac

which also appear in the mid-ninth-century Khludov Psalter and the somewhat later Vatican 'Christian Topography'.[71]

Jacob's struggle with the angel, in the second register, was considered in chapters 5 and 7 where we saw that while the core of the composition replicated a conventional formula, for which the closest comparisons were provided by the eleventh-century Vatican *Klimax* and Octateuch manuscripts, the Homilies image was distinguished by its emphasis on the physical interaction between Jacob and the angel.

The second scene of the middle register illustrates Jacob's dream at Bethel (Genesis 28:10–15), and was considered in chapter 5. As we saw there, the altar was added to a core composition that otherwise corresponded closely with versions of the scene in both the fourth-century Via Latina catacomb paintings and twelfth-century Octateuchs.

[71] Vat.gr.699, f. 59r: Stornajolo (1908), pl. 22.

331

Folio 360r (37) (fig. 37)

The tower of Babel and Noah's ark were juxtaposed on f. 360r to create a piece of pictorial exegesis: like the Adam and Eve sequence on f. 52v and the history of Joseph on f. 69v, the scenes on f. 360r were not mentioned in the accompanying sermon 'On peace'.[72]

About one-third of the upper register was destroyed when the headpiece on its verso was excised. What remains of the tower of Babel reveals an incomplete wall that extends across the page: the paint has flaked badly, and lines ruled for the text on the verso now show through, allowing us to see that the miniaturist used them as levels on which to line up the light brown stones of the wall. Sections of a brown zig-zag ladder on which a figure, now mostly lost, originally stood remain to the left of the excision. Both the ladder and the prominent brick wall find parallels in works associated with the Cotton Genesis – notably the mosaics at San Marco – that allow us to reconstruct the image as the building of the tower; following the Venetian mosaic, the ladder zig-zags because it was once supported by scaffolding.[73] Above, remnants of an arc of heaven presumably once enframed the hand of God responsible for the tower's ultimate collapse; to the right of the cut-out section, a badly rubbed shape that is apparently a brick kiln spouts red flames.

The image of Noah's ark (Genesis 8:6–11) is better preserved. In the centre of the scene, inscribed 'the flood' (O KATAKΛYCMOC), a three-tiered ark floats on a sea strewn with five corpses.[74] Noah's ark (KHBOTOC NΩE) is made of brown wooden panels; again, flaking reveals that some are aligned with the page rulings. Each of its three tiers is topped by a dark blue roof. While Genesis 6:15–17 describes the ark as having three levels, few representations follow this prescription: normally, the ark appears as a monolithic box-like structure or as a conventional boat.[75] Closest to Paris.gr.510 is the version found in the Vienna Genesis (fig. 136), where the ark is presented as a series of gabled forms superimposed on each other.[76] Other details of the Gregory miniature – notably Noah's release of a dove and its return from a tall green mountain in the right-hand corner, bearing an olive branch in its beak – are omitted from the Vienna Genesis,[77] though they appear in numerous other versions of the scene.[78] The raven (the bird originally sent by Noah) that feeds on one of the bodies floating in the water is not described in Genesis, but is a

---

[72] See chapter 2.

[73] Weitzmann and Kessler (1986), 69, fig. 144; Demus II (1984), 81, pl. 180. See also Bucher (1970), pl. 24.

[74] *Pace* Gutmann (1953), 65 note 51, these are not the giants recorded in Midrashic commentaries on Genesis, a hypothesis belied by the size of Noah's hand emerging from the ark.

[75] E.g. Hesseling (1909), fig. 32; Ferrua (1960), pl. CXVIII; Weitzmann and Kessler (1986), 64–66, figs. 109–126; see also the articles cited in note 79 below.   [76] Gerstinger (1931), pict. 3.

[77] Bianchi Bandinelli (1961), 354–355, emphatically and correctly denies any connection between the two miniatures.   [78] E.g. Weitzmann and Kessler (1986), 65–66, figs. 118–119.

Fig. 136 Vienna, Nationalbibliothek, cod.theol.gr.31, pict. 3: Noah's ark

commonplace of patristic and medieval exegesis and habitually appears in representations of Noah releasing the dove.[79] In short, nearly all elements of the Gregory image find parallels in earlier representations of Noah's ark – but the precise combination does not. The eclectic combination of features suggests that the scene was so familiar that the Gregory miniaturist neither required nor relied on a specific model, but instead combined familiar motifs *ad hoc*.

The most – and perhaps the only – uncontestable conclusion to be drawn from the Genesis scenes in Paris.gr.510 is that they do not all stem from a single source, or at least not from one otherwise attested. Noah's ark seems to be a generic compilation; the Adam and Eve sequence clusters with a diverse assortment of short sequences; the history of Joseph recalls Sta Maria Antiqua and the marginal psalters; and what remains of the tower of Babel seems reminiscent of the Cotton Genesis. The sacrifice of Isaac finds close ties with one of the marginal psalters and the twelfth-century Octateuchs, to which Jacob's dream also seems to be related; while Jacob and the angel may modify a composition of the type found later in the Vatican *Klimax* and Vat.gr.747.

The mix of iconographic patterns that have been sorted into different 'families' (sometimes called pictorial recensions) by some scholars suggests that even for biblical narratives which are as frequently visualized as Genesis, the iconographic traditions adapted in Paris.gr.510 derived not from monolithic visual cycles but from smaller, independent narrative sequences. It is also evident from Paris.gr.510 that what modern scholarship has defined as different iconographic traditions were not conveyed by an artisan's training. The miniaturist responsible for f. 174v (fig. 23) has a distinct style characterized by a love of fussy drapery with certain peculiar details. While the teardrop highlights on the knees and angular white highlights elsewhere are familiar features of late ninth-century style, the transformation of the loop of drapery that falls from the waist over the rear hip into a fairly sharply defined narrow rectangle is unusual, as is this painter's predilection for twisting positions that enable a high proportion of profile figures and figures viewed from the rear with buttocks defined by a nearly spherical swirl of fabric. The Genesis scenes on f. 174v are most closely associated with those in the marginal psalters and the later Octateuchs, but all the features characteristic of this miniaturist – plus others such as the way the landscape is treated and the use of olive skin tones for angels in contrast to the ruddy flesh of humans – recur on f. 52v (fig. 10), in the Adam and Eve sequence that has but one scene paralleled in the marginal psalters and is barely related to the Octateuch images at all. What we distinctly do not find, then, is a combination of iconographical traditions carried into Paris.gr.510 by artisans trained in different ways. What we have instead is an indication that the

[79] See Gutmann (1977); Gatch (1975).

modern concept of pictorial editions was neither relevant nor obvious to the Byzantines who made and used Paris.gr.510.

Before turning to the Exodus scenes, one final feature of the Genesis images rates brief comment. Despite the fact that the scenes and sequences pictured in Paris.gr.510 cannot be viewed as autonomous creations, only the mutilated f. 360r lacks details apparently specific to the manuscript. The image of Michael and Adam on f. 52v, the composition and selection of scenes used on ff. 52v and 69v, the iconography of the last two scenes on f. 69v, and the emphasis on the altar in the portrayal of Jacob's dream on f. 174v all represent modifications imposed on and for Paris.gr.510.

Exodus

The Exodus selections are less extensive than were those from Genesis. Kurt Weitzmann noted the same discrepancy between the number of Genesis and Exodus scenes in the *Sacra Parallela* and in the later Octateuchs; he suggested that both the relative shortness of Exodus and its long prescriptive passages made it less susceptible to illustration than Genesis.[80] The thesis is problematic and in fact does not always apply: in the 'Christian Topography' manuscripts, for example, there are more scenes drawn from Exodus than from Genesis. In Paris.gr.510, episodes from Genesis appear on four pages; so too do episodes from Exodus (ff. 52v, 226v, 264v, and 424v), but – unless one isolates the dance of Miriam from the crossing of the Red Sea into which it is incorporated in Paris.gr.510 – none are developed into multi-scene sequences. Perhaps because the five episodes pictured had sufficiently familiar exegetic resonance to convey a point without additional narrative embellishment, the five episodes from Exodus stand on their own. Throughout this sequence, Moses is presented consistently: he wears a light blue chiton under a white himation, has short dark hair and is beardless; except on f. 264v, he is nimbed.

Moses receiving the laws (Exodus 34:4–5), the penultimate image on f. 52v (fig. 10),[81] shows Moses, nimbed and with his head averted, striding up the mountain to receive, in his outstretched and covered hands, the two tablets proffered by a hand of God. Behind him, a crowd of Israelites watch. The most unusual feature of the scene is that the viewer is presented with the back of Moses' head: he turns his face away from us as he deflects his gaze from God. Moses' modesty here presumably reflects an earlier episode, when, confronted by the burning bush, 'Moses hid his face, for he was afraid to look upon God' (Exodus 3:6). The image is often compared with its counterparts in the Leo Bible (fig. 137) and the Paris Psalter, with

[80] Weitzmann (1979a), 56–57.
[81] For the primary discussion of this miniature, see chapter 5; the iconography of the upper two registers was discussed earlier in this chapter, and the biographical scene has been considered in chapter 3.

Fig. 137 Vat.reg.gr.1, f. 155v: Moses receiving the laws

which it shares all features except the averted head.[82] The Gregory scene also resembles that on a sixth-century cross at Sinai where, while there is no room for the Israelites, Moses ducks his head to avoid looking at God.[83] The formula recurs in the ninth-century copy of the 'Christian Topography' (fig. 138), which maintains both the Israelites and Moses' averted gaze, though here the patriarch's face is visible to the viewer.[84] We have, then, a persistent iconographical formula, one variant of which is whether or not Moses looks at God; in those cases where he does not, the position of his head is itself mutable.

Moses striking water from the rock (Exodus 17:1–7) occupies the upper register of f. 226v (fig. 26).[85] Moses stands to the right and lifts a baton that ends with a large round knob toward the top of a pink hill that rises steeply in the centre of the register; at its base is a small flat outcrop that in scale and location recalls the minuscule foreground buildings we have seen throughout the manuscript. A stream of blue water pours down the hill and curves off to the left, where three men in garments of solid blue, ochre, and green, respectively, kneel to drink from it with cupped hands. A male figure, dressed in a light brown cloak over a pink chiton and shown in profile, stands behind Moses at the far right of the register, and a crowd of Israelites – within which four male faces and the tops of several more heads may be deciphered – peers at the drinkers from behind the rock on the far left. The blue sky behind the scene is badly abraded; Omont was able to decipher the inscription as [M]Ω[YC]HC [TYΠTΩN] THN [ΠE]TPAN ('Moses striking the rock').

Contemporary comparisons for the scene are provided by the marginal psalters (fig. 133),[86] which share with f. 226v the pink hill, Moses' knobbed staff, and (usually) the restriction of the number of drinking Israelites to three men, who often kneel on the ground. The relationship is not tight – the stance of Moses never recurs in the psalters, where the Israelites drink from goblets, and the water often leaps in an arc from the top of the hill – but it is closer than any other.[87]

The most striking feature of the image of Moses and the burning bush on f. 264v

[82] E.g. by Morey (1929), 36, 95. Vat.reg.gr.1, f. 155v (*Miniature* [1905], pl. 10; Dufrenne and Canart [1988], 31–32); Paris.gr.139, f. 422v (Buchthal [1938], fig. 10). The Milan Gregory illustrates the fourth homily with an image of Moses receiving the laws; it is not, however, related to that on f. 52v: Grabar (1943a), pl. LXIII,1.   [83] Weitzmann and Ševčenko (1963), 386–387.

[84] Vat.gr.699, f. 45r: Stornajolo (1908), pl. 11. We may also see a remnant of Moses' ducked head in the marginal psalters: Moscow, Hist.Mus.g.129, f. 108v, and Paris.gr.20, f. 16v: Ščepkina (1977), and Dufrenne (1966), pl. 40.

[85] The primary discussion of f. 226v appears in chapter 4; on Joshua and the angel see also chapter 7.

[86] Moscow, Hist.Mus.gr.129, ff. 76r, 82r, 107r: Ščepkina (1977). Mount Athos, Pantokrator 61, ff. 104r, 114r, 151v: Pelekanides *et al.* 3 (1979), figs. 212, 219, 227; Dufrenne (1966), pls. 14, 17, 23. London, BL Add.40.731, f. 137v: ibid., pl. 56. Paris.gr.20, f. 15r: ibid., pl. 39. The scene also appears in copies of the 'Christian Topography', but this version is even more unlike that in Paris.gr.510 than are those in the marginal psalters.

[87] Two of the twelfth-century Octateuchs show the figure(s) drinking from cupped hands, but the painters compiled the images *ad hoc*: Anderson (1982), 99, figs. 30, 32.

Fig. 138 Vat.gr.699, f. 45r: Moses with the Israelites in the wilderness; Moses receiving the laws

(fig. 28) is the inclusion of the angel, an unusual addition that responds to ninth-century concern with the distinct natures of the three members of the trinity.[88] Moses himself, who bends down to remove his sandals, sustains general similarities with the figure in the mid-tenth-century Leo Bible (fig. 137).[89] The relationship between this manuscript, Paris.gr.510, and the Paris Psalter is convoluted: on the basis of other shared scenes, we can only say that sometimes the Bible seems to copy Paris.gr.510 directly, while at other times the two adapt a common source.[90] Which

---

[88] See chapter 5. The angel appears in some later versions of the scene, e.g. in the twelfth-century Kokkinobaphos manuscripts (see Hutter and Canart [1991], 40–41).

[89] So Buchthal (1938), 67. Vat.reg.gr.1, f. 155v: *Miniature* (1905); Dufrenne and Canart (1988), 24–26. [90] See chapter 2, and note 92 below.

alternative is preferable here is difficult to say, though the predilection of the Homilies miniaturist for complicated poses at least suggests that the figure of Moses was created for f. 264v.

The crossing of the Red Sea (Exodus 14:21–31) with the dance of Miriam (Exodus 15:20–21) fills the lower two-thirds of the page, and the large format reflects the typological and imperial significance of the scene.[91] Numerous variants of this episode coexisted in Byzantium, and the version in Paris.gr.510, conventionally entitled – despite the presence of Miriam and several women – 'the exodus of the sons of Israel' (H ΕΞΟΔΟC TΩN YIΩN I[CPA]HΛ), can be tied to a particular group the lineage of which Hugo Buchthal traced back to early Christian sarcophagi.[92] The stance of Moses is the most immediately recognizable and distinguishing feature of the set: he strides to the right, front leg forward, while gazing down and back toward the drowning Egyptians, toward whom he also extends a long staff held in his outstretched right arm. He would be hard to miss on f. 264v, and is identified by inscription (MΩCHC). A tightly massed and large cluster of Israelites accompanies him, the foremost of whom stands in profile, facing right with both arms extended toward the column of fire (identified by inscription: CTYΛOC ΠYPOC). The drowning Egyptians, among whom Pharoah (ΦAPAΩ) and his horse are prominent, occupy the lower half of the picture, descending on a diagonal from left to right. A personification of the Red Sea, portrayed as a half-nude female carrying a rudder over her shoulder, occupies the lower right-hand corner. The versions of the scene most closely related to f. 264v – in the Leo Bible (fig. 139), the Paris Psalter (fig. 140) and its derivatives[93] – all postdate Paris.gr.510, but do not blindly copy the Gregory picture. Miriam (MIPIAM), for example, who spins with timbrels held above her head between the Israelite in profile and the column of fire, recurs in the Leo Bible but not the Paris Psalter. The later manuscripts also share details that do not appear on f. 264v. Neither of these points demonstrates conclusively that the miniaturists of the Paris Gregory, the Leo Bible, and the Paris Psalter independently consulted a third image, for the iconography of the crossing of the Red Sea was being revised in the ninth century, and iconography in flux is susceptible to random accretions. While the complicated relationship between these three manuscripts does not always unravel in the same way, I suspect that in this case the later two followed the lead provided by Paris.gr.510, but added other details also known in the ninth century.

The crossing of the Red Sea appears as well in the marginal psalters (figs.

[91] See chapter 5.

[92] Buchthal (1938), 30–33; here too further comments on f. 264v, and its relationship with the Paris Psalter and Leo Bible.

[93] Paris.gr.139, f. 419v: Buchthal (1938), 30–33, and pl. 9. Vat.reg.gr.1, f. 46v: *Miniature* (1905), pl. 7; Dufrenne and Canart (1988), 24–26. See also Morey (1929), 38, 41, 95.

Fig. 139 Vat.reg.gr.1, f. 46v: Moses and the burning bush; crossing the Red Sea

Fig. 140 Paris.gr.139, f. 419v: crossing the Red Sea

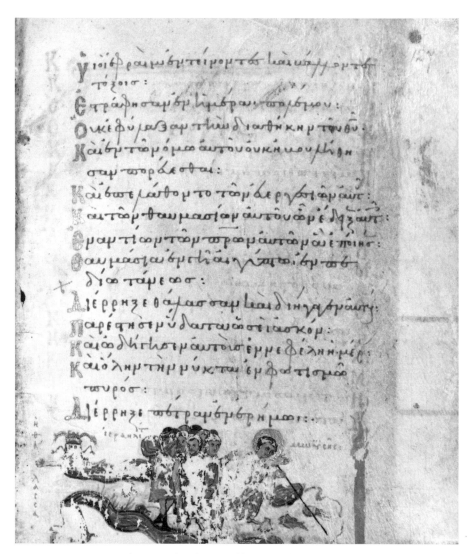

Fig. 141 London, British Library, Add.40.731, f. 127r: crossing the Red Sea

141–146) and the *Sacra Parallela*,[94] and the psalters provide a better context for f. 264v in some ways than do the later Paris Psalter and Leo Bible. The Bristol Psalter, an eleventh-century manuscript that often omits ninth-century additions to the psalters, preserves only one image of the crossing of the Red Sea (fig. 141): this differs in most respects from that on f. 264v, most notably in its absence of Egyptians and personifications and in the location and stance of Moses (who leads his people and looks forward), but does portray an unbearded and nimbed

[94] Paris.gr.923, f. 369r: Weitzmann (1979a), 54, fig. 55. *Pace* Weitzmann, the scene is too contracted to compare usefully with other compositions.

Moses who leads his people toward the flaming column.[95] The Khludov Psalter includes two depictions of the scene, the first of which (fig. 142) generally resembles that in the Bristol Psalter, but omits the column of fire and adds women to the crowd of Israelites, one of them (at the far left) in sharp profile and the other towing along a child; the second (fig. 143) includes the dance of Miriam.[96] Pantokrator 61 also illustrates the episode twice. The first depiction (fig. 144) modifies aspects of both the Bristol and Khludov Psalters: the column of fire recurs here, as does the profile figure to the left, but now as a male; in addition, a personification of the Red Sea – portrayed as a female head wearing a crustacean crown – appears at the front of the water.[97] The second version (fig. 145) shows Moses behind the Israelites, and Miriam dancing.[98] The final ninth-century psalter, Paris.gr.20, retains only one picture of the Red Sea crossing (fig. 146), and it differs somewhat from the other manuscripts of its group: while the two women familiar from the Khludov Psalter recur, the drowning Egyptians are new, Moses stands behind the Israelites and turns back toward the Red Sea, and the profile figure – one of the two women, who grasps the hand of a child – now leads the crowd. The scene has been cropped, so it is impossible to determine whether or not Miriam or the column of fire were included: there may have been room for the latter, but it is unlikely that the former could have been inserted.[99] What we see happening in the ninth-century psalters, then, is an accumulation of details attaching themselves to the crossing of the Red Sea – the column of fire, Miriam, the child, the women, the profile figure, the Egyptians, the personification of the Red Sea – in various combinations. Whatever the precise relationship between the psalters, it is clear that the iconography of the scene was fluid in the ninth century, and that virtually all of the features included in Paris.gr.510 were possible elements. What remains striking about f. 264v is the expansive composition that incorporates these details, and that, as we have seen, seems to be a response to its imperial message.

The final scene from Exodus fills the second register of f. 424v (fig. 41), and shows the decisive moment in the Israelites' victory over the Amalekites.[100] On the left, accompanied by a descriptive inscription (ΜΩCΗC ΥΠΟCΤΙΡΗ-ΖΟΜΕΝΟC ΥΠΟ ΑΑΡΩΝ Κ[ΑΙ] ΩΡ), Aaron and Hur support the (anachronistically) young Moses' arms aloft, as described in Exodus 17:8–13. The hill on which Moses stands in the biblical narrative here rises steeply behind him, and

---

[95] London, BL Add.40.731, f. 127r: Dufrenne (1966), 61, pl. 55.

[96] Moscow, Hist.Mus.gr.129, ff. 108r, 148v: Ščepkina (1977).

[97] Folio 103v: Dufrenne (1966), 29, pl. 14; Pelekanides et al. 3 (1979), fig. 211.

[98] Folio 206r: Dufrenne (1966), pl. 29; Pelekanides et al. 3 (1979), fig. 233.

[99] Folio 16r: Dufrenne (1966), pl. 40. It is this miniature, which of all the marginal psalter versions of the scene in fact most closely approximates the later images in the Paris Psalter and the Leo Bible, that Weitzmann attached to the *Sacra Parallela*: see note 94 above.

[100] The primary consideration of this miniature, with bibliography, appears in chapter 2, additional discussion in chapter 4.

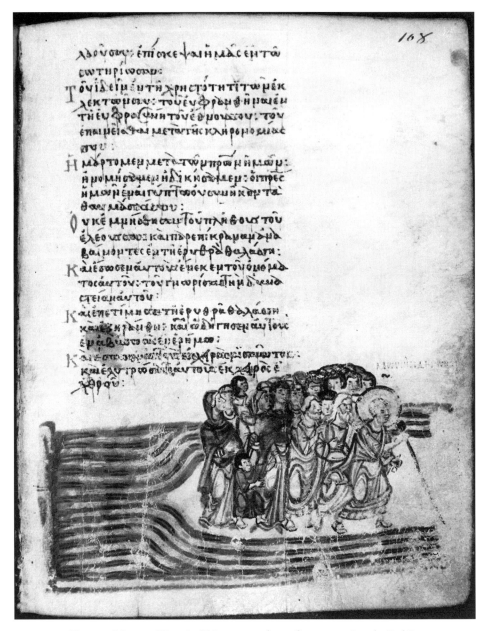

Fig. 142 Moscow, Historical Museum, cod.129, f. 108r: crossing the Red Sea

Fig. 143 Moscow, Historical Museum, cod.129, f. 148v: crossing the Red Sea, the dance of Miriam

Fig. 144 Mount Athos, Pantokrator 61, f. 103v: crossing the Red Sea

from it Joshua's army pours forth toward the fleeing Amalekites (ΑΜΑΛΗΚΙΤΑΙ), two of whom have already fallen to the ground.

The core group of Moses, Aaron, and Hur admitted very little variation – especially as the cross formed by Moses' arms became an important topos of exegetical literature – and examples from the fifth-century mosaic at Sta Maria Maggiore to the middle and late Byzantine Octateuchs present the trio in much the same fashion as they appear on f. 424v.[101] The cavalry charge, on the other hand, seems to have been an insertion of the Gregory miniaturist.[102] Indeed, the Gregory miniatures on the whole include cavalry skirmishes of one sort or another whenever possible: they appear on the earlier Joshua page (f. 226v; fig. 26), during Julian's assault on the Persians (and at his death at the hands of Merkourios) on f. 409v (fig. 40), and in Constantine's victory at the Milvian bridge (f. 440r; fig. 45). This last example provides a reasonably close parallel to the attack on f. 424v – both reproduce variations on the same compositional formula – and there are even closer ties between f. 424v and Joshua's defeat of the Amorites on f. 226v (fig. 26). These two pages share a predilection for steep hills that rise almost vertically in jagged tiers;

---

[101] Karpp (1966), fig. 133; Uspensky (1907), fig. 128; Hesseling (1909), fig. 185.
[102] So too Gaehde (1974), 379.

Fig. 145 Mount Athos, Pantokrator 61, f. 206r: crossing the Red Sea, the dance of Miriam

the attacking soldiers emerge from behind the hills, and chase the enemy toward the frame of the miniature, over which the legs of the retreating horses extend into the margins of the page. The retreats on both folios are represented by four horsemen, the foremost of whom looks back at his attackers, his profile face foiled by a green cap that itself contrasts sharply with his red garment. The two folios were almost certainly painted by the same miniaturist: in addition to the shared details evident in the scenes of attack, drapery on both pages is presented with little highlighting except on light blue and beige garments, and falls in angular pleats, often with an unmotivated tuck over the calf; further, hands are emphasized, and smudgy 'rouge-spots' enliven faces bereft of cheekbones. The addition of the cavalry charge that supplements the conventional grouping of Moses, Aaron, and Hur did not, in other words, require great powers of invention: the same miniaturist simply reversed the formula used earlier on f. 226v and inserted it into the victory over the Amalekites on f. 424v. This insertion may be in part explained by the desire to align the protagonists (Joshua, Moses, and Gregory) along a diagonal moving from the left side of the page, which necessitated the expansion of the compositions to the

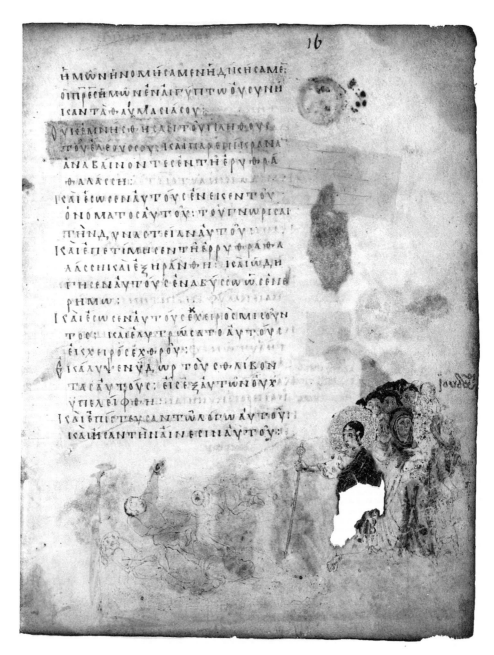

Fig. 146 Paris.gr.20, f. 16r: crossing the Red Sea

right. The selection of a victorious cavalry charge – and the proliferation of horse warfare in Paris.gr.510 in general – may also respond to military practices in the ninth century.[103] But as noted in chapter 4, the equestrian emphasis evident throughout Paris.gr.510 may respond to Basil's status as a renowned horseman as much as to contemporary military practices.

Three of the five Exodus scenes in Paris.gr.510 – Moses striking water from the rock, the victory over the Amalekites, and Moses receiving the laws – retain early compositions that remained standard throughout the middle Byzantine period. Excepting the addition of the cavalry charge to the Amalekite scene, these are essentially conventional images, and it is difficult to slot them into some developmental scheme of Byzantine iconography. The fourth scene, Moses and the burning bush, was modified to suit exegetical requirements to such an extent that iconographical affiliations are scarcely tenable. Only the depiction of the crossing of the Red Sea seems to participate in the shifting flow of Byzantine iconographical revision: with the marginal psalters, it demonstrates a changing conception of the scene, and in this case the version adopted by the miniaturist of Paris.gr.510 had famous progeny in the Leo Bible and Paris Psalter.

Joshua

Three scenes from Joshua appear on two pages in Paris.gr.510; the two episodes on f. 226v (fig. 26) bracket that on f. 424v (fig. 41) in the biblical narrative. The iconography of these scenes was considered in chapter 4. Two points are worth reiterating here. First, Paris.gr.510 documents the increasing importance of Joshua in imperial victory commemorations, and may well provide one of the earliest visualizations of Joshua's role in imperial military symbolism. Second, though the same miniaturist painted the two Joshua pages, this does not result in iconographical consistency:[104] on f. 424v, Joshua is nimbed, and his red leggings, white boots, blue cloak, red shield with gold border, and lack of a helmet all contrast with f. 226v, where an un-nimbed Joshua wears no leggings at all beneath gold boots with a green top band, a red cloak, carries a red shield with a blue border and is helmeted.

Judges

The two selections from Judges both appear on f. 347v (fig. 35), and this is not coincidental; as we saw in chapter 2, the passage that links them together with the third image on the page, the martyrdom of Isaiah, emphasized Samson's and Gideon's roles as judges.

---

[103] This does not, of course, mean that cavalry actually dominated the ninth-century Byzantine army: see e.g. the review of middle Byzantine warfare techniques in McGeer (1988) which suggests that, in the tenth century at any rate, military tacticians were particularly concerned with the use of infantry.　　[104] Thus repeating the pattern seen in the Genesis miniatures.

Gideon (ΓΕΔΕΩΝ) appears on the left side of the third register, standing beneath an arc of heaven. A beardless youth like Samson, he also wears a similar short blue tunic decorated with gold; Samson's red sash has, however, become a red mantle. A whitish lump, now badly flaked, rises from the ground; inscribed ΠΟΚΟΣ, it represents the fleece of Judges 6:36–40. This passage was habitually interpreted as an allusion to the Virgin Mary, an association stressed in the only other ninth-century version of the scene, that in the marginal psalter Pantokrator 61.[105] The two miniatures preserve the earliest known images of Gideon and the fleece, but the portrayals are quite different. In the psalter, a small blue hillock supporting a medallion portrait of the Virgin replaces the fleece of f. 347v, and Gideon is shown as a mature man, with dark hair and a short dark beard, in long pink garments; rather than raising his hands toward heaven, he gestures toward the Virgin. Both the psalter and the Homilies images are commentary pictures rather than narrative illustrations of Judges – in the former, Marian typology prevails;[106] in the latter, Gideon is visually paralleled with Samson – but even the narrative excerpts incorporated in the *Sacra Parallela* portray Gideon in different ways: once with short dark hair and a short dark beard, and twice as an old man.[107] None of these three scenes portrays the fleece episode, but they do serve to demonstrate that the ninth century allowed considerable latitude in portrayals of Gideon. By the eleventh or twelfth century, the portrayal of Gideon as an old man with white hair and beard seems to have become standard, and he appears in this guise in the Octateuchs and the Kokkinobaphos manuscripts (fig. 147), which include the fleece episode as part of their mariological programme.[108] The composition of the first of the three Gideon scenes in the Kokkinobaphos manuscripts recalls that on f. 347v: Gideon stands before the lump of fleece and raises his hands to an arc of heaven. The twelfth-century Kokkinobaphos miniatures, unlike Paris.gr.510, add the dew raining down on the fleece, but despite this, and the shift in Gideon's age (and therefore costume), they nonetheless provide the closest comparisons with the scene on f. 347v.

As we saw in chapter 4, two of the five scenes incorporated in the Samson sequence that occupies the upper two registers of f. 347v (Judges 15:15–16:30) sustain some affiliation with marginal images in the *Sacra Parallela*, but the remaining three remain quite distinct from all other Byzantine portrayals of the Samson story. Indeed, as with the images of Gideon, no coherent tradition of Samson illustration predominated in Byzantium: even the Octateuchs differ one from another.

---

[105] Folio 93v: Dufrenne (1966), 28, pl. 12; Pelekanides *et al.* 3 (1979), fig. 206. For discussion, see Der Nersessian (1970), 80; Walter (1986), 274, 282.

[106] See Walter (1986), 274, 282; Corrigan (1992), 77.

[107] Paris.gr.923, ff. 90v, 101r, 248v: Weitzmann (1979a), 65–66, figs. 86–88.

[108] Vat.gr.747, f. 242r; Vat.gr.746, f. 478v (unpublished). Paris.gr.1208, f. 149v (Omont [1927], pl. 18); Vat.gr.1162, f. 110v (Stornajolo [1910], pl. 46; Hutter and Canart [1991], 59–60).

Fig. 147 Paris.gr.1208, f. 149v: Gideon

On the basis of the admittedly limited selection of scenes from Judges in Paris.gr.510, it appears that the creation of Judges imagery in the ninth century was essentially an *ad hoc* process, though smaller narrative units sustained images familiar enough to be repeated in several works across three hundred years.

Kings

There are four scenes from the books of Kings in Paris.gr.510: they surface on four different folios, and one comes from each of the four books of Kings. Following biblical order, the Kings episodes appear on ff. 174v, 143v, 215v, and 264v; I shall, however, consider them in the order in which they appear in Paris.gr.510.

The penitence of David occupies two-thirds of the top register of f. 143v (fig. 19).[109] The second book of Kings 12 narrates the rebuke and penitence of David together; Psalm 51 ('a psalm of David, when Nathan the prophet came to him, when he had gone in to Bathsheba' in most Greek editions), is David's hymn of repentance. The eleventh-century Book of Kings illustrates both the rebuke and the penitence; the *Sacra Parallela* presents Nathan's rebuke.[110] All other Byzantine miniatures (aside from Paris.gr.510) that picture either event appear in psalters.[111] Few restrict themselves to simple illustrations of the biblical texts: like Paris.gr.510, nearly all include an angel mentioned in neither Kings nor Psalm 51, and most show David prone before Nathan, though David's prostration is not specifically mentioned until 2 Kings 12:15–17, which describes David's solitary penance. David's proskynesis visualized Byzantine confessional practice and need not require an extra-biblical source, but the inclusion of the angel does: both of these details in fact come from a ninth-century (?) paraphrase, the *Palaia historica*.[112] The broad outlines of the penitence image on f. 143v thus fit comfortably into ninth-century Byzantine iconographic possibilities; the exclusive emphasis on David's repentance, however, finds few parallels.[113]

The penitence image begins with Bathsheba, peering over the back of David's empty throne from within a gold and jewelled ciborium-like structure. Though David's desire for Bathsheba unleashed the events leading to his repentance, and

---

[109] How the penitence of David worked with the other images on f. 143v to provide a commentary on the accompanying sermon was considered in chapter 2; the imperial implications were examined in chapter 4.

[110] Vat.gr.333, f. 50v (Lassus [1973], fig. 92); Paris.gr.923, f. 231v (Weitzmann [1979a], fig. 132).

[111] E.g. the Theodore Psalter, London, BL Add.19.352, f. 63v: Der Nersessian (1970), fig. 102. Ishizuka (1986) provides the most complete listing of examples. I thank Mr. Ishizuka for sending me an offprint of his article, which is difficult to find in this country.

[112] Cutler (1976), 248 and note 47 (crediting Ihor Ševčenko); a fuller consideration appears in Ishizuka (1986), esp. 8–9, 14–15.

[113] The Bristol Psalter (London, BL Add.40.731, f. 82v: Dufrenne [1966], pl. 52), two psalters on Mount Athos (Stavronikita 57, f. 32v; Vatopedi 760, f. 96v), the Spencer Psalter (New York, Pub. Lib. Spencer gr.1, f. 126v), and the Psalter of Basil II (Venice, Marc.gr.17, f. IVv) provide the only other examples: Cutler (1984), figs. 60, 377, 208, 413. The group does not form a coherent iconographic set.

Fig. 148 London, British Library, Add.40.731, f. 82v: penitence of David

she is specifically named in the title of Psalm 51, aside from Paris.gr.510 only the
marginal psalters include her; the Bristol (fig. 148), Theodore, Barberini, and
Walters Psalters follow Paris.gr.510 in showing her through a window.[114] Structures
similar to that in which Bathsheba stands recur throughout Paris.gr.510 over imperial thrones;[115] here an empty throne sits in front of the ciborium, and the structure

[114] In Khludov, Bathsheba stands behind the enthroned David: Moscow, Hist.Mus.gr.129, f. 50r:
Ščepkina (1977). Corrigan (1992), 16, implies that the Khludov miniaturist omitted the architectural
frame present in earlier psalter images. For Bristol, see note 113 above; for the later Theodore Psalter,
note 111 above.   [115] On, for example, ff. 104r (fig. 17) and 239r (fig. 27).

apparently does double duty as a representation of the imperial palace, the outlying buildings of which extend to the right and behind Bathsheba. The empty throne and ciborium return in the Psalter of Basil II, though here they are separated by a wall;[116] the empty throne recurs in the Bristol Psalter (fig. 148).[117] Both resemble f. 143v in showing gold and jewelled thrones padded with a cushion; Bristol even shares the latticed throne back with Paris.gr.510. On f. 143v, the archangel Michael is simply identified as *archestrategos*: in a manuscript destined for Basil I, wherein David allegorically stood in for the emperor, the archangel chastizing David could hardly have been overtly identified as Michael, whose namesake Basil had murdered. The figure exaggerates a type found elsewhere in Paris.gr.510 (see, for example, Habakkuk on f. 285r; fig. 29); the turning pose may have been selected in response to the *Palaia historica*, which tells us that the angel deflected its sword from David at the moment of his confession. Over half of all preserved images of David's rebuke and/or repentance include the angel, but usually as a small figure hovering between the king and Nathan. Large angels planted firmly on the ground appear only in the later marginal psalters, Dumbarton Oaks 3, and Vatopedi 760.[118] The prostrate figure of David, however, admits only minor variations; still, the version in the Bristol Psalter (fig. 148) is virtually identical to that on f. 143v. Between David and Nathan sits a small building, variously identified as Rabbath (by Omont) or David's palace (by Ishizuka). It could equally well represent the 'walls of Jerusalem' that David prays for in Psalm 51:18,[119] or, more likely, the city Nathan mentions in his parable (2 Kings 12:1) condemning David. The final figure, Nathan, differs from nearly all other portrayals: his short dark hair recurs only in the Vatican Kings, the Paris Psalter (fig. 149) and the related Taphou 51.[120] Indeed, the Paris Psalter Nathan resembles the Gregory prophet in nearly every detail, from his stance down to specific garment folds. The Psalter illustrator here, as elsewhere, seems to have copied directly from the Paris Gregory;[121] unusual details shared by f. 143v, the Psalter of Basil II and Dumbarton Oaks 3 suggest that the Homilies may have been more widely available to the upper echelons of Constantinopolitan miniaturists.

Folio 143v presents the earliest known Byzantine image of the penitence of David; the Khludov Psalter and the *Sacra Parallela* preserve the oldest extant rebukes. Later, the two episodes become conflated, but distinct forms for each seem to have been maintained in the ninth century: the Khludov Psalter, for example,

---

[116] See note 113 above. The ciborium and the wall recur in Washington, Dumbarton Oaks 3, f. 27r: Cutler (1984), fig. 323. In the Khludov Psalter, a ciborium frames the entire scene.

[117] Stavronikita 57, Vatopedi 760 and the Spencer Psalter also show a backless throne, covered by a swag of drapery (see note 113 above): these images are related to each other, but not to Paris.gr.510.

[118] See notes 111 and 113 above.

[119] If so, however, it diverges from the representation of Jerusalem in the next register.

[120] For the former, see note 110 above. Paris.gr.139, f. 136v; Jerusalem, Taphou 51, f. 108v: Cutler (1984), figs. 145, 252. [121] See chapter 2 note 190.

Fig. 149 Paris.gr.139, f. 136v: penitence of David

lacks a developed penitence scene but shows an isolated and humbly dressed David prostrate in the left margin, far distant from the rebuke that appears to the right of the text.[122] Further, ninth-century depictions of the rebuke are in no significant way related to the penitence in Paris.gr.510. The distinction, and the formula presented by the Homilies miniaturist, were evidently short-lived: later versions unite the two scenes, and those that share telling details with f. 143v nearly all seem to borrow from Paris.gr.510 directly. The Gregory miniaturist does not, however, seem to have invented the scene *de novo*, but rather to have adapted an earlier version of the penitence to include new elements introduced by the *Palaia historica*. Folio 143v's closest relative appears in the Bristol Psalter (fig. 148), an insufficiently studied manuscript which appears to retain older motifs than the other marginal psalters but adds an overlay of tenth-century details (as if it had somehow skipped

[122] Moscow, Hist.Mus.gr.129, f. 50r: Ščepkina (1977).

the ninth-century accretions on the group);[123] the only significant difference between the two scenes is that a personification of Metanoia – possibly inspired by the Paris Psalter (fig. 149) – replaces the archangel Michael. It has long been speculated that some hypothetical Kings cycle included two distinct images for 2 Kings 12: the rebuke and the penitence.[124] Both the Bristol Psalter and Paris.gr.510 do indeed seem to transform the same image of the penitence, while the *Sacra Parallela* and the Khludov Psalter preserve the rebuke. Bristol probably added the personification of Metanoia;[125] Paris.gr.510, under the influence of the *Palaia historica*, added the archangel Michael. Both miniaturists imposed modernizations on the skeleton of a dying iconographical unit.

The anointing of David (1 Kings 16:3–13) occupies the lowest of three registers on f. 174v (fig. 23). The miniaturist expanded and modified a composition that, on the witnesses of the Milan Gregory and *Sacra Parallela* (figs. 52, 94), seems to have been widely known in the ninth century. The enlarged formula found on f. 174v found a parallel on a contemporary ivory casket also made for Basil I (fig. 95); it was presumably inspired by the importance of David's anointing to the emperor. The format recurred in two later Constantinopolitan products, the Leo Bible and the Paris Psalter (figs. 97, 96).[126]

The judgement of Solomon (3 Kings 3:16–27) on f. 215v (fig. 25) was so rarely depicted in Byzantium that it is impossible to determine to what extent Paris.gr.510 conforms with, modifies, or diverges from earlier practice.

With the ascension of Elijah (4 Kings 2:11–13) on f. 264v (fig. 28) we return to a scene that replicates a common ninth-century formula. The small vignette has a strong diagonal accent, running from Elisha (ΕΛΙCΑΙΟC) in the lower left through Elijah in his ascending red quadriga, and culminating in a hand of God that emerges from a blue arc outside the frame. The diagonal is reinforced by a green mountain that fills the right side of the composition; this itself contains a triangular blue body of water that holds, in the corner, a nude male personification of the river Jordan (ΙΟΡΔΑΝΗC ΠΟΤΑ[ΜΟC]). The upper left corner of the scene carries the inscription 'Elijah's ascent' (ΗΛΙΑC ΑΝΑΛΑΜΒΑΝΟΜΕΝΟC). Elisha and Elijah are both nimbed, and wear identical blue tunics decorated with gold bands under white mantles; as he ascends, Elijah passes what appears to be a (third) mantle to his follower on the ground.

The ascension of Elijah was often pictured in Byzantium, and several ninth-century versions survive. The Vatican 'Christian Topography' (fig. 150) retains the diagonal axis of the Gregory version: Elisha, nimbed and dressed as in Paris.gr.510 – even the mantle flutters behind him in the same way – reaches up to receive the mantle passed to him by the nimbed Elijah, who here rides in a brown biga and stands between the two red horses that pull it up toward the hand of God emerging

---

[123] See chapter 6 note 33.   [124] See Cutler (1974), 139–142.
[125] Walter (1990), 47; cf. Buchthal (1938), 27–30.   [126] See chapter 4.

Fig. 150 Vat.gr.699, f. 66v: ascension of Elijah

from a blue arc of heaven. In the lower right, as on f. 264v, is a personification of the river Jordan; the mountain, curiously, is tucked into the corner beneath the personification.[127] The two versions are closely related, and are joined by that in the Khludov Psalter (fig. 151), where the figure of Elijah is identical to that on f. 264v even in its colouring: four red horses pull a red quadriga up toward the arc of heaven; Elijah (dressed in a white chiton under a blue himation with a piece of loose fabric blowing like a tail behind him) turns back to pass his mantle to Elisha.[128] The miniature in the *Sacra Parallela* (fig. 152), gilt as normal in that

[127] Vat.gr.699, f. 66v: Stornajolo (1908), pl. 27.
[128] Moscow, Hist.Mus.gr.129, f. 41v: Ščepkina (1977).

357

Fig. 151 Moscow, Historical Museum, cod.129, f. 41v: ascension of Elijah

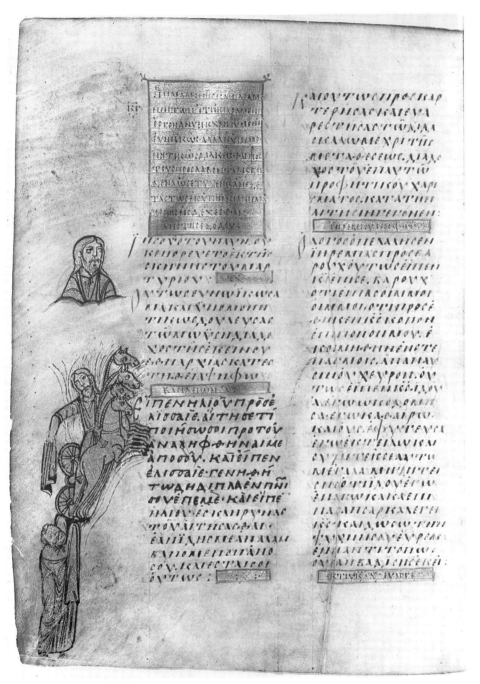

Fig. 152 Paris.gr.923, f. 268v: Jeremiah; ascension of Elijah

manuscript, preserves the same configuration of quadriga and prophet, but here Elijah lacks a halo and, correctly but uniquely, wears only his chiton in the chariot, as he passes his himation on to Elisha.[129] Both the psalter and the *Sacra Parallela* show Elisha without a nimbus; in other respects he resembles his counterpart in Paris.gr.510 save that his hands are not covered in the Khludov Psalter, and, like Elijah, he wears only his tunic in the *Sacra Parallela*. The mountain up which Elijah ascends – green in Paris.gr.510, pink in the psalter, green and brown in the 'Christian Topography', and indicated by two sketchy lines in the *Sacra Parallela* – replaces the whirlwind described in 4 Kings 2:11; it stands above the river Jordan beside which Elisha stood after the ascension (v. 13) on f. 264v and in the Khludov manuscript. The personification of the river in the Homilies, the Khludov Psalter, and the 'Christian Topography' rarely appears in other Byzantine images of the ascension of Elijah.[130] Its appearance in three ninth-century miniatures confirms some connection between them, but the manner of depicting the personification differs: the Khludov Psalter shows a huge male, the 'Christian Topography' a reclining figure, and Paris.gr.510 a torso emerging from the water. The striking similarities between other features shared by these three versions of the scene, many of them evident in the *Sacra Parallela* as well, suggest that the composition as a whole replicates a standard ninth-century formula; the variations imposed on the personification, on the other hand, suggest that this detail was seen as less 'canonical' and was therefore amenable to modification. Psalm 41:7, which inspired the picture in the marginal psalters, specifically mentions the Jordan and presumably sparked the addition of the personification.[131] In Paris.gr.510, its inclusion was perhaps recommended by the baptismal typology visualized throughout the miniature, which encouraged an emphasis on the river Jordan.

By now it comes as no surprise that the three scenes from the books of Kings that appear with sufficient frequency in Byzantium to make iconographical affiliations feasible are not iconographically tied to a single source. The penitence of David (f. 143v) links most closely with the Bristol Psalter; the anointing of David (f. 174v) is related to a contemporary ivory panel and to miniatures in the Milan Gregory and *Sacra Parallela*; and the ascension of Elijah (f. 264v) finds its closest relatives in the Khludov Psalter, the Vatican 'Christian Topography' and, again, the *Sacra Parallela*. As a group, the Kings miniatures in Paris.gr.510 provide no evidence for an earlier illustrated Kings manuscript: the two images emphasizing David had great imperial resonance and had been depicted in this context for centuries, while the ascension of Elijah was equally important in typological equations. Whether or not Jeffrey Anderson's thesis that, apart from illustrated Genesis manuscripts, dense narrative cycles in Byzantium only began to appear in the early eleventh century is

---

[129] Paris.gr.923, f. 268v: Weitzmann (1979a), 93, fig. 175.

[130] It does not appear, for example, in the Vatican Kings: Vat.gr.333, f. 109 (Lassus [1973], fig. 104).

[131] Cf. London, BL Add.19.352, f. 51v: Der Nersessian (1970), fig. 87.

correct,[132] the evidence provided by Paris.gr.510 certainly suggests that the lone Greek Kings manuscript with miniatures – Vat.gr.333 – did not copy some now-lost early exemplar, but rather compiled its sequence by supplementing then-popular cycles, such as that of David, with additional scenes familiar from earlier sources.

Job

As we saw in chapter 3, the image of Job on f. 71v (fig. 13) illustrated Gregory's reference to the Old Testament figure and supplemented the accompanying sermon. The scene itself compresses several events narrated in Job 2 into a single composition. Job (IΩB), sits on the dungheap specified by the Septuagint (Job 2:8), which is distinguished from the green ground by its brown colour; it rises gradually toward the right frame. Job is nimbed,[133] nude and covered with boils; he turns his head to address his wife. She, identified as 'the wife of Job' (Η ΓΥΝΗ ΤΟΥ ΙΩB), covers her nose with her pink mantle in response to the stench, and extends toward Job a stick from which dangles a potsherd with two handles; with this he will 'scrape away the discharge' from his boils (Job 2:8). Behind them rise the walls of a large house, painted a monochromatic blue that blends with the background. Between Job's wife and the frame sits a free-standing pier supporting an ochre urn and tied about its middle with a swag of pink drapery. These motifs recur elsewhere in the manuscript;[134] as there, they are apparently included here to signify Job's exile from the city and civilization, as bewailed by his wife (Job 2:9). To the left stands a badly flaked group of Job's friends. Omont was able to make out six figures here, three of whom he interpreted as the kings of Job 2:11, in large part because the foremost, who wears red leggings and an imperial purple and gold mantle over a blue and gold tunic, is identified by inscription as CΩΦΑΡ Ο ΜΙΝΩΝ ΒΑCΙΛΕΥC, 'Sophar, King of the Mineans' (Job 2:11).

Byzantine miniaturists developed two distinct ways of showing Job sitting on his dunghill. The Vatican Job and the related image in the *Sacra Parallela* (fig. 153) picture Job encased by the hill, clothed in a loincloth, and seated frontally with his knees drawn up.[135] Paris.gr.510 instead follows the formula found in the Patmos and Venice Job manuscripts (fig. 154): all show Job seated on the hill, usually with extended legs; the Venice manuscript, as the later Leo Bible (fig. 155), also resembles Paris.gr.510 in portraying Job nude.[136] This group also places Job's wife to the right,

---

[132] Anderson (1991), 95–96.   [133] See R. Budde, s.v. 'Job', *LCI* II (1970), 408.

[134] The monochromatic blue architectural backdrop appears throughout Paris.gr.510; see e.g. f. 32v (fig. 8), where it indicates that the martyrdom scenes occurred outside city walls. A similar pier recurs on f. 143v (fig. 19); a column swagged in cloth on f. 452r (fig. 46). Cf. Weitzmann (1948), 80–81.

[135] Vat.gr.749, ff. 26r, 27r, 28v, 30r, 119r, 126r, 152r, 153v, 157r, 179v, 190r (in a few miniatures, he turns slightly and appears to sit in a more conventional fashion: ff. 138v, 144v, 181v); for both variants, Weitzmann (1935), figs. 533, 534. Paris.gr.923, f. 257r: Weitzmann (1979a), fig. 214.

[136] E.g. Patmos, Mon. of St. John, cod.171, pp. 53, 75: Jacopi (1932/3), figs. 104, 106; Grabar (1972), fig. 43. Venice, Marc.gr.538, f. 23r: Weitzmann (1935), fig. 346. Vat.reg.gr.1, f. 461v: *Miniature* (1905), pl. 17; Dufrenne and Canart (1988), 46–49.

Fig. 153 Paris.gr.923, f. 257r: Job's wife with Job on his dunghill

and she extends a potsherd to him on a stick as in Paris.gr.510.[137] The Patmos Job is of uncertain date and origin; it has most recently been assigned to Italy and placed in the ninth century.[138] At the very least it is contemporary with Paris.gr.510, and it may well be earlier. The Venice Job, on the other hand, is certainly later, for it bears an inscription dating it to 905, though again its place of origin is not specified. No one would argue, however, that the illustrator of the Venice Job was influenced by Paris.gr.510, and so we may assume that the Gregory miniaturist knew the image of Job and his wife from the tradition represented by the Patmos and Venice manuscripts. We may, however, hold the Gregory illustrator responsible for the inclusion of Job's friends, for this episode is never conflated with the scene of Job and his wife in the Job manuscripts proper. The addition was almost certainly suggested by the accompanying sermon, wherein Gregory acknowledges the support of his own allies, Gregory of Nyssa and Basil (pictured in the top register), by invoking the Old Testament parallel of Job and his friends. Only in the Leo Bible (fig. 155) do we find a similar combination and, as Buchthal has already remarked, the whole miniature

[137] References in preceding note; see also Jacopi (1932/3), fig. 105.
[138] Grabar (1972), 24–25, with further bibliography.

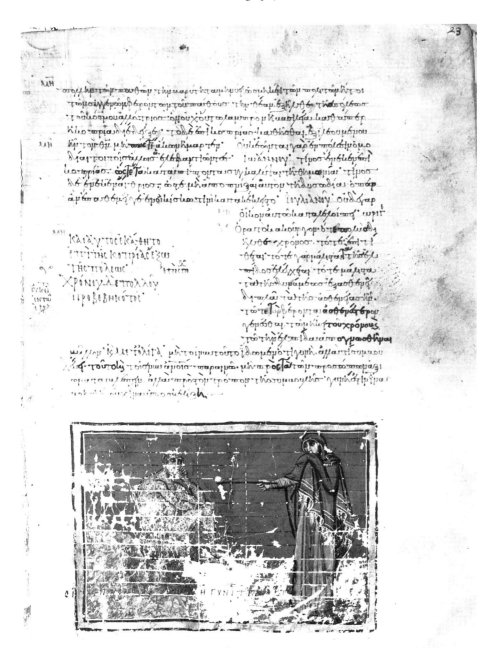

Fig. 154 Venice, Marciana gr.538, f. 23r: Job's wife with Job on his dunghill

Fig. 155 Vat.reg.gr.1, f. 461v: Job's wife and friends with Job on his dunghill

in the Bible resembles that in Paris.gr.510 so closely that it seems most likely that the later painter drew directly from the Gregory page.[139]

Prophets

The three scenes portraying Isaiah recall contemporary Constantinopolitan work. We saw in chapter 7 that the vision on f. 67v (fig. 11) may modify a formula originally devised for mural decoration – it may echo lost wall decorations at Hagia Sophia and the (later) Zaoutzas church – but, as with all visions of divinity in Paris.gr.510, Isaiah's stressed the mediating role of the prophet as a means both of involving the viewer in the theophany and of stressing the historicity of prophetic visions in ways not obviously applicable to wall painting. The second Isaiah scene – the prophet with Hezekiah (fig. 43) – finds its closest counterpart in the *Sacra Parallela* and recurs in the Paris Psalter; it will be considered along with the rest of f. 435v later in this chapter. The martyrdom of Isaiah (f. 347v; fig. 35) does not depend on the bible, but comes instead from the apocryphal Martyrdom of Isaiah. Like the previous two scenes, however, Isaiah's martyrdom may replicate a formula standard in Constantinople: we saw in chapter 6 that it recurs in a later and apparently otherwise unrelated prophetbook made in the capital.

The single scene from Jeremiah, which shows the prophet raised from the pit on f. 143v (fig. 19), finds no parallels in Byzantine art, and we saw in chapter 2 that it seems to have been compiled as part of the visual commentary provided by the miniature as a whole. The lone Ezekiel page, presenting the prophet in the valley of the dry bones on f. 438v (fig. 44), was discussed in chapter 7.

Two scenes from the book of Daniel appear on f. 435v (fig. 43): the three Hebrews in the furnace (Daniel 3:26–88) and Daniel in the lions' den (Daniel 14:31–39). We shall see later in this chapter that both scenes find parallels in contemporary Byzantine miniatures.

Finally, as discussed in chapter 2, the Jonah sequence on f. 3r (fig. 6) is a pastiche that rearranges a composition that later influenced the Paris Psalter and Vatopedi 760 while introducing a new scene (Jonah's flight from Tarsis) in the process. The new composition was compiled in order to augment the accompanying sermon; while many of its constituent parts had a long history, the combination on f. 3r remains unique.

The prophet miniatures in Paris.gr.510 almost all relate more or less directly to contemporary Constantinopolitan products. While a mural cycle may underlie some compositions, the proliferation of scenes from the lives of the prophets seems primarily to offer a visual corollary to the increased interest in them that we also find in

---

[139] Buchthal (1938), 67.

texts during the eighth and ninth centuries, a theme that has been considered already in chapter 7.

Old Testament Apocrypha

The Makkabees sequence on f. 340r (fig. 34) may have been inspired by an earlier cycle commissioned by the patriarch Tarasios; it was discussed in chapter 6.

Paris.gr.510 and the Ode miniatures of the 'aristocratic' psalters
Folio 435v (43) (fig. 43)

The four scenes arranged in a regular grid on f. 435v – Daniel in the lions' den approached by Habakkuk, the three Hebrews in the fiery furnace, the prayer of Manasses, and Isaiah with King Hezekiah – betray no obvious connection with any of Gregory's homilies.[140] It has been generally assumed that the internal logic of the miniature, at least, is nonetheless straightforward, for all four scenes appear in Byzantine psalters as illustrations to the Odes that follow the Psalms.[141] The parallels are, however, only superficial; there are serious problems with the 'Ode thesis'.

The apocryphal last chapter of Daniel (14:31–39) narrates the episode of Habakkuk bringing food to Daniel in the lions' den. In Paris.gr.510, the orant Daniel (ΔΑΝΙΗΛ) stands in the centre of the quadrant flanked, as is normal Byzantine practice, by two rather than the seven lions described in the textual account. The prophet is nimbed, and clad in standard 'Persian' costume: a white cap with red stripes, a red cloak with a gold collar, a blue tunic decorated down the front with a panel of gold, green leggings, and white boots with golden cuffs. He stands in front of a dark cave carved into a green hill, which frames the central trio. A badly rubbed angel in blue and beige garments hovers above the den, holding Habakkuk – his pink mantle bunched around his neck over his blue tunic – firmly by the scruff of the neck. Only Habakkuk's upper torso is visible; he appears as a dark-haired youth, and carries a basket full of pottage on his left shoulder, a gold ewer in his right hand.

Daniel in the lions' den was a popular motif in Byzantium; in the ninth century, a virtually identical version appears in the 'Christian Topography' (fig. 156).[142] Here, however, Habakkuk and the angel have been omitted, though an un-identified youth walks toward Daniel and four beasts that the Vatican miniaturist

---

[140] Millet (1920), 242; Omont (1929), 30, pl. LVII; Buchthal (1938), 43–45, 68; Weitzmann (1947), 149–151, 162, 197; Der Nersessian (1962), 218–219, 222–223; Walter (1989), 252–254; Walter (1990), 48, 51; Brubaker (1996b), 105–107. On the relationship to the text, see chapter 2.

[141] Millet (1920), 242; Buchthal (1938), 68; Weitzmann (1947), 149–151, 197.

[142] The colours of the leggings and undergarment have been reversed, but the two images share all other details, including the red mantle and the chest band. Vat.gr.699, f. 75r: Stornajolo (1908), pl. 40; Weitzmann (1947), fig. 155.

Fig. 156 Vat.gr.699, f. 75r: Daniel in the lions' den

transposed from another section of the 'Topography' text stand below.[143] After the early Christian period, when the pair appeared frequently as an image of salvation, Habakkuk and the angel are in fact rarely seen.[144] In the tenth century, they join Daniel in the lions' den at Aght'amar;[145] in the eleventh, they appear above the

[143] The accompanying text is Book V:173–174 (SC 159, 262–265); the beasts are described in Book II:66–67 (SC 141, 380–383).

[144] *DACL* 6,2, 5510–5515; H. Schlosser, s.v. 'Daniel', *LCI* I (1968), 469 and Jeremias (1980), 45–47, 130–131 note 162 collect and discuss the relevant examples.

[145] Der Nersessian and Vahramian (1974), fig. 54.

Fig. 157 Paris.suppl.gr.610, f. 252v: Habakkuk's Ode

prophet in prayer as an illustration of Habakkuk's Ode in two psalters, one of which (Dumbarton Oaks 3) apparently copies the other (Paris.suppl.gr.610; fig. 157).[146] The angel and Habakkuk resemble their counterparts in Paris.gr.510; the combination with the praying figure, itself a familiar component of Odes illustrations, is however otherwise unknown. Habakkuk's Ode (Habakkuk 3:1–19) makes no mention of the angel episode, and Sirarpie Der Nersessian plausibly suggested that the motif was inserted into the psalters because it represented the only known event from Habakkuk's life.[147] There is nothing to suggest that the combination was anything other than *ad hoc.*

Conversely, an image of the three Hebrews in the fiery furnace consistently appears in Byzantine psalters, and accords fully with the relevant Ode text (Daniel 3:26–88).[148] Very nearly all of the psalter images share with Paris.gr.510 a symmetrical composition, with the angel behind the central Hebrew and extending its arms to encompass the two flanking figures; as on f. 435v, the psalters normally show the Hebrews as orant youths in 'Persian' costume. Without exception, however, the miniaturists of the aristocratic psalters place the Hebrews in a rectangular furnace which obscures their lower bodies,[149] whereas in Paris.gr.510 the Hebrews are shown in full, surrounded by flames, with only traces in blue monochrome behind the embracing angel to hint at the structure of the furnace itself. The two ninth-century marginal psalters that preserve the Ode, Khludov and Pantokrator 61 (fig. 158), follow the pattern of Paris.gr.510, and locate the full figures of the Hebrews and the angel within a furnace full of flames, with no obstructing wall; the Pantokrator image is particularly close to that in Paris.gr.510.[150] Like Daniel in the lions' den, the Hebrews in the fiery furnace preserve a ninth-century iconographical type. They also represent an iconographical variant that, even more definitively than Habakkuk and the angel, is foreign to the later 'aristocratic' psalters.

The third quadrant pictures Manasses (MANACCH[C]), standing orant in imperial gold and purple regalia behind a bull; painted in ochre with brown shading, like the lions above, the animal is represented as a living creature. The monochromatic blue background shows two cypress trees on the left and a circular columned building on the right. Manasses appears in 4 Kings 21:1–18 and 2

---

[146] Cutler (1984), 72, 94, figs. 262, 329; Der Nersessian (1965), 158, 171. In an unpublished MA thesis (Pennsylvania State University), Judith Cave demonstrated that the Washington manuscript relied directly on Paris.suppl.gr.610.   [147] Der Nersessian (1965), 171.

[148] E.g. Cutler (1984), figs. 18, 86, 96, 126, 135, 142, 151, 186, 203, 218, 243, 279, 332, 356, 391, 408.

[149] The Spencer Psalter differs slightly because the scene appears as a historiated initial: Cutler (1984), fig. 218. The menologion Mount Athos, Lavra Δ 51 (f. 431r) follows the psalters: N. Ševčenko (1990), 97, 100. See also the *Sacra Parallela* (Paris.gr.923, f. 373v), though here the angel is omitted: Weitzmann (1979a), fig. 385.

[150] Moscow, Hist.Mus.129, f. 160v (Ščepkina [1977]); Mount Athos, Pantokrator 61, f. 222r (Dufrenne [1966], pl. 33; Pelekanides *et al.* 3 [1979], fig. 237).

Fig. 158 Mount Athos, Pantokrator 61, f. 222r: three Hebrews in the fiery furnace

Chronicles 33:1–20, but no text known to me describes this image, which seems to represent the king's penitence after years of sin, and to foreshadow his sacrifice 'of peace offering and praise' on 'the altar of the Lord', represented by the bull and the circular building respectively (2 Chronicles 33:16). The sacrifice itself is apparently represented in a twelfth-century psalter in Athens as the illustration to the Ode of Manasses (fig. 159).[151] The Athens and the Paris miniaturists may have

[151] Ethnike Bib. 7, f. 256v: Cutler (1984), 16, fig. 12. The Manasses Ode (Charles I [1913], 620–623) appears in only a few psalters, and is normally illustrated by the king in prayer: Moscow, Hist.Mus.gr.129, f. 158v (Ščepkina [1977]), London, BL Add.40.731, f. 261v (Dufrenne [1966], pl. 60), Washington, Dumbarton Oaks 3, f. 82v (Cutler [1984], fig. 339), Athens, Benaki 34.3, f. 191v (ibid., fig. 357); the same formula appears in Paris.gr.923, f. 231v (Weitzmann [1979a], fig. 209). The Spencer Psalter follows 2 Baruch 64:8 (Charles II [1913], 515), and shows Manasses praying inside of a brazen horse: New York Pub. Lib. Spencer gr.1, f. 395v: Cutler (1974), 146–148, fig. 26; Cutler (1984), 58, fig. 223. Compare Pantokrator 61, f. 220r, where the praying king is bound with rope: Dufrenne (1966), 37, pl. 32.

been independently, and indirectly, inspired by images of martyrs burning in bulls, which show half-figures of saints emerging from the bull's back surrounded by flames;[152] in the Athens Psalter, however, Manasses is an elderly man and the sacrificial bull reclines on a flaming altar.[153] Though both miniatures record Manasses' acts of penitence, the psalter portrays an older king at a later moment in the narrative.

The final scene on f. 435v illustrates Isaiah 38:1–3. As described in the titulus written on the frame above the scene – 'Isaiah said to Hezekiah, Give orders concerning thy house' (ΗCΙΑC ΛΕΓΩΝ ΤΩ ΕΖΕΚΙΑ · ΤΑΞΕ ΠΕΡΙ ΤΟΥ ΟΙΚΟΥ COY) – the prophet addresses the sick king inside his palace, represented by an architectural backdrop. Smaller outbuildings flank a large gold door preceded by two prominent steps, which evidently allude to the steps along which God later caused shadows to move as a sign that Hezekiah would recover (Isaiah 38:7–8). Isaiah (ΗCΑΙΑC), whose flowing dark hair oddly contrasts with his grey beard, stands to the far left; his covered left hand may once have held a scroll (the area is now flaked), while with his right hand he gestures toward Hezekiah in speech. Hezekiah (ΕΖΕΚΙΑC) reclines on a red and gold mattress in a richly decorated bed; his shoes rest on a low footstool. He leans his head on his covered left hand and faces the viewer – perhaps in response to the Septuagint description of the king turning his face to the wall – as he gestures to Isaiah with his right hand.

A similar composition appears in the *Sacra Parallela* (fig. 160) – which shares the obliquely aligned bed, the king's averted head, and the architectural setting incorporating a prominent set of steps – and the Khludov Psalter shows Hezekiah in bed, gesturing toward the Ode text, but by far the closest comparison is provided by the Paris Psalter (fig. 161).[154] While apart from Khludov all other illustrated psalters follow the Ode of Hezekiah (Isaiah 38:9–20) and show the king in prayer,[155] the miniaturist of the Paris Psalter added to this the scene of Isaiah and Hezekiah. The grouping is strikingly similar to that found on f. 435v, and even small details correspond: the prophet's two-toned hair, the tiny bed finial, the king's flanged gold pectoral, his discarded red and gold shoes,[156] and the drapery wadded around his left hand all recur in the later psalter. In both miniatures, too, grey-blue steps rise to a palace door. As with the anointing of David and the history of Jonah, the psalter miniaturist here again appears to have consulted Paris.gr.510 directly.[157]

---

[152] E.g. Vat.gr.1613, p. 96 and Mount Athos, Esphigmenou 14, f. 52v: *Menologio* (1907); Pelekanides *et al.* 2 (1975), fig. 330. Cf. Cutler (1976), 240–241.

[153] Cutler (ibid.) suggested that this represents a moment before Manasses' repentence, and shows him 'praying behind his bull-idol', but in the context of the penitential Ode itself the king's sacrifice to God seems more likely.

[154] Paris.gr.923, f. 252v: Weitzmann (1979a), 148–149, fig. 357. Moscow, Hist.Mus.gr.129, f. 157v: Ščepkina (1977). Paris.gr.139, f. 446v: Cutler (1984), 69–70, fig. 258; Buchthal (1938), 43–45, fig. 14.

[155] See e.g. Dufrenne (1966), pls. 32, 60; Cutler (1984), figs. 8, 222, 338.

[156] This detail recurs in Paris.gr.510 on f. 440r (fig. 45), in the scene of Constantine's dream.

[157] So Ioli Kalavrezou: see chapter 2 note 190. See also chapters 2 and 4.

Fig. 159 Athens, Ethnike Bibliotheke, cod.7, f. 256v: sacrifice of Manasses

Fig. 160 Paris.gr.923, f. 252v: Isaiah and Hezekiah

Fig. 161 Paris.gr.139, f. 446v: Isaiah and Hezekiah

While all four scenes collected on f. 435v appear as illustrations to the Odes in Byzantine psalters, only the three Hebrews in the fiery furnace recur with any frequency, and here Paris.gr.510 is connected with the marginal rather than with the 'aristocratic' psalters.[158] Far from being conventional Ode illustrations, the remaining three scenes do not feature in the Ode texts at all, but were more or less one-off pictorial supplements to them in the related psalters in Washington and

[158] See too Khludov's putative affiliation with the Hezekiah scene, noted above.

374

Paris (Habakkuk), a psalter in Athens (Manasses), and the Paris Psalter (Hezekiah). The Habakkuk and Manasses scenes reflect middle Byzantine elaborations rather than isolated survivals from earlier and unattested models, and though the image of Hezekiah in the Khludov Psalter indicates that portraits of the king in bed were not unknown to psalter illustrators, the connections between f. 435v and the marginal psalters repeat a pattern found throughout Paris.gr.510 that seems to have more to do with the ninth-century iconographic vocabulary than with any distinct genre of psalter imagery: certainly the miniaturist of the Paris Psalter borrowed the Hezekiah image directly from f. 435v.

But if f. 435v is not really an 'Ode page', what holds it together? Der Nersessian noted that the four scenes all concern royalty: cruel kings victimized Daniel and the three Hebrews, while below we see two rulers saved through faith. She suggested that the combination in some way reflects the imperial dedication of Paris.gr.510 to Basil I – although, if so, it was not entirely complimentary to the emperor.[159] But other features, too, link the scenes. First, the upper two scenes both derive from Daniel, while family ties connect the lower two scenes, for Manasses was Hezekiah's son (4 Kings 20:21; 2 Chronicles 32:33). Second, the four scenes emphasize salvation: through faith in the upper half of the page, and through prayer and repentance in the lower half. The miniaturist seems, in fact, to have stressed this interpretation by including details often omitted in parallel images. By far the majority of representations of Daniel in the lions' den lack Habakkuk, but to focus on the theme of salvation through faith the miniaturist portrayed him coming to Daniel's aid. To highlight the theme of salvation through repentance, Manasses prays with his peace offering before him; while the last quadrant shows Isaiah forecasting Hezekiah's imminent doom, from which – as the viewer is reminded by the central steps – he will ultimately be saved by prayer and tears.

The New Testament
Gospels

Nearly seventy scenes from the gospels appear in Paris.gr.510, and the iconography of many of them has already been discussed. Three sets of scenes that have not yet been analysed will be considered here as paradigmatic examples leading to the assessment of the gospel iconography in the manuscript as a whole.

Folio 3r (6) (fig. 6)

The top register of f. 3r contains two scenes: the annunciation (O XAIPETIC-MOC) and the visitation (O ACΠACMOC).[160] The archangel Gabriel, in a white

---

[159] Der Nersessian (1962), 222–223.
[160] The primary discussion of this miniature appears in chapter 2.

mantle shaded with beige over a blue tunic decorated with gold, enters from the left. Nimbed in gold, with a white band in his short dark hair and with wings painted in shades of blue with gold highlights, Gabriel holds a lance with one hand and gestures toward the Virgin with the other. Mary, swathed in purple (but with red shoes) and also nimbed in gold, returns the archangel's gesture with her right hand; she holds two knitting needles in her left. Between the two figures, a small green plinth supports a bowl containing balls of blue wool. The Virgin stands on a gold and jewelled footstool, set before a gold bench covered with a red cushion. A white building with a red cornice, its door half covered by a green curtain, forms a backrop; a red curtain decorated with small dots hangs from the roof and extends over a small ochre and red outbuilding with a shuttered window.

The gospel description of the annunciation (Luke 1:26–38) identifies the archangel and indicates that the building in the background is Mary's house. The Protevangelion added the detail, nearly ubiquitous in Byzantine depictions of the episode, that Mary was seated spinning when Gabriel arrived;[161] though she stands on f. 3r, the wool and needles indicate familiarity with this account or representations derived from it.

Presumably because of the impact of the Protevangelion, the standing Virgin of f. 3r is less common in scenes of the annunciation than a seated figure.[162] Exceptions include the Rabbula Gospels of 586,[163] and, particularly close to the version on f. 3r, two wall paintings of the annunciation at Sta Maria Antiqua in Rome, one painted ca. 650 (fig. 162), the other between 705 and 707 (fig. 163).[164] The ninth-century Khludov Psalter and Pantokrator 61 (fig. 164) reverse the figures of Mary and Gabriel and omit the architectural backdrop, but Pantokrator 61 in particular otherwise resembles f. 3r.[165] Constantine the Rhodian's tenth-century description of the now-lost mosaic cycle at the Church of the Holy Apostles in Constantinople, probably set during the reign of Basil I, simply describes 'Gabriel bringing to a virgin maiden [tidings of] the incarnation', but Mesarites' twelfth-century ekphrasis indicates that Mary stood, interrupted from her spinning, when Gabriel arrived.[166] Such an important monumental analogue might explain why the closest well-preserved parallel to f. 3r occurs in Cappadocia, in New Tokalı, painted in the middle of the tenth century (fig. 165).[167] Here, Gabriel strides more forcefully and

---

[161] Protevangelion 11: Hennecke and Schneemelcher I (1963), 380.   [162] See Millet (1916), 67–92.

[163] Florence, Laur.plut.1.56, f. 4r: Cecchelli (1959).

[164] Romanelli and Nordhagen (1964), pls. 20–21.

[165] Moscow, Hist.Mus.gr.129, f. 45r (Ščepkina [1977]); Mount Athos, Pantokrator 61, f. 55v (Dufrenne [1966], pl. 8; Pelekanides et al. 3 [1979], fig. 194).

[166] For Constantine: ed. Legrand (1896), 58; trans. Mango (1972), 200. For Mesarites: ed. Downey (1957), 905–906; trans. 877. On the Church of the Holy Apostles, see chapter 1 note 78. The Church of the Virgin of the Source (869–879) and the Church of Stylianos Zaoutzas (886–893) also included the annunciation, but extant descriptions provide no details.

[167] Epstein (1986), 29–32, 39–44, fig. 58; see also chapter 2 note 29. Cf. chapel 15a in the Göreme region: Restle III (1967), fig. 553.

Fig. 162 Rome, Sta Maria Antiqua: annunciation

Fig. 163 Rome, Sta Maria Antiqua: annunciation

Mary lacks a throne, but the archangel carries a staff, the casket of wool rests to the left of Mary's jewelled footstool, and the Virgin's gesturing right arm is restrained by a sling-like garment while she clasps her knitting needles in her left hand exactly as in Paris.gr.510.[168] Whatever its relationship to the Apostoleion, however, the Sta Maria Antiqua frescoes demonstrate that the type was inaugurated before

[168] In Old Tokalı (first quarter of the tenth century) the annunciation recurs, but here Mary retreats from Gabriel (Epstein [1986], fig. 16); the use of two iconographically different annunciations in the same chapel confirms the introduction of a new type, and others have argued in favour of a Constantinopolitan import: see note 167 above and Cormack (1967).

Fig. 164 Mount Athos, Pantokrator 61, f. 55v: annunciation

Iconoclasm; and Pantokrator 61 indicates that the annunciation in Paris.gr.510 replicates a formula familiar in the capital in the second half of the ninth century.

The annunciation is followed by the visitation (Luke 1:40–45). As in nearly all Byzantine examples, the miniature shows Mary and Elizabeth embracing before Elizabeth's house.[169] Mary, dressed as in the previous scene, is placed to the left of Elizabeth, who wears red shoes and an ochre mantle over a light brown robe; the house, with a half-drawn red curtain in the doorway, is beige with a red cornice. Close parallels include the Khludov Psalter (fig. 166) and Cappadocian wall paintings at Kiliçlar (ca. 900) and Old Tokalı (first quarter of the tenth century).[170] The

[169] See Schiller I (1971), 55–56.
[170] Moscow, Hist.Mus.gr.129, f. 85r: Ščepkina (1977). Epstein (1986), fig. 17 (see also chapter 2 note 29); Restle II (1967), fig. 262.

Fig. 165 New Tokalı: annunciation

Gregory visitation is particularly close to its counterpart in the psalter – even the colours of the women's garments are the same – suggesting that, as was the case for the annunciation, the visitation drew on a contemporary source familiar in the capital.

Folio 87v (16) (fig. 16)

The gospel episodes on f. 87v appear in the top two registers: the uppermost shows Christ calling the apostles Peter, Andrew, James, and John from their boats (Matthew 4:18–22); Christ conversing with Zachias, who perches in a sycamore tree, before entering Jericho (Luke 19:1–5); and the calling of Matthew (Matthew 9:9, Mark 2:14, Luke 5:27–28). Christ talking to the rich young man (Matthew

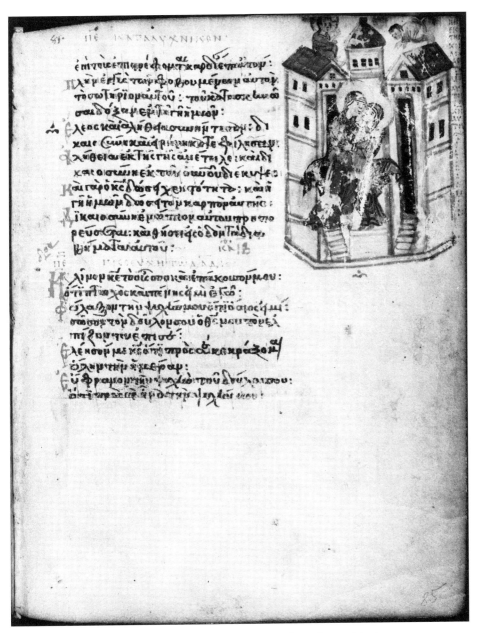

Fig. 166 Moscow, Historical Museum, cod.129, f. 85r: visitation

Fig. 167 New Tokalı: calling of Peter, Andrew, James and John

19:16–22, Mark 10:17–22) and Christ converting Nathanael (John 1:47–48) follow in the middle register.[171]

Christ calling the four apostles from their boats all at once apparently represents a new iconographical formula: though the calling of Peter and Andrew appeared earlier at S. Apollinare Nuovo in Ravenna, James and John first join them here.[172] Later versions, however, share only particular details with Paris.gr.510: the vertical pile-up of boats recurs in the tenth-century frescoes at New Tokalı (fig. 167), while

[171] For primary bibliography and the relationship between f. 87v and its accompanying text, see chapter 3; the inscriptions not transcribed there simply identify the figures: IC XC for Christ, throughout, with ΠΕΤΡΟC, ΑΝΔΡΕΑC, ΙΩΑΝΝΗC, ΙΑΚΩΒΟC, and ΖΑΚΧΑΙΟC.

[172] Schiller I (1971), 155.

Fig. 168 Florence, Laurenziana plut.6.23, f. 9r: calling of Peter, Andrew, James and John

in the Florence tetraevangelion one figure in each boat replicates John's raised hands and backward glance (fig. 168).[173]

The Zachias episode that follows in the top register often appears in Byzantine compositions as part of the entry into Jerusalem, but only rarely stands as a scene in its own right. The sixth-century Augustine Gospels provides the earliest example (fig. 66); two ninth-century marginal psalters – Khludov and Pantokrator 61 – use it to illustrate Psalm 84:3; and it recurs in the Florence and Paris tetraevangelia.[174] Paris.gr.510 follows the Augustine Gospels in the main lines of its composition: Christ, accompanied by a group of disciples on f. 87v and a single representative in the gospelbook, gestures to the youthful Zachias perched in a tree. In the Gospels, however, Zachias grasps the branches of a bifurcated tree dotted with random leaves, while in Paris.gr.510 he is encased in the tree's leaves. The marginal psalters

[173] Epstein (1986), 71, fig. 72; Laur.plut.6.23, f. 9r (Velmans [1971], fig. 18): both reverse the composition and locate the shoreline on the left. The other extensively illustrated Byzantine gospelbook, Paris.gr.74, is quite different (Omont [n.d.], pls. 10–11, as is Paris.gr.923 (f. 145v; Weitzmann [1979a], 161–162, fig. 399).

[174] Cambridge, Corpus Christi College 286, f. 129v (*CLA* 2 [1935], no. 126; Weitzmann [1977], pl. 42); Moscow, Hist.Mus.gr.129, f. 84v (Ščepkina [1977]); Mount Athos, Pantokrator 61, f. 118r (Dufrenne [1966], pl. 18; Pelekanides *et al.* 3 [1979], fig. 222); Florence, Laur.plut.6.23, f. 149r (Velmans [1971], fig. 249); Paris.gr.74, f. 149v (Omont [n.d.], pl. 129).

repeat the tree form initiated in the gospelbook, though they differ from this manuscript (and from Paris.gr.510) in showing Christ unaccompanied and Zachias as an old man. The tetraevangelia return to a youthful portrayal of Zachias and envelop him in leaves as on f. 87v; though the miniaturist of the Florence tetraevangelion omits the disciples, they appear in the Paris copy, which seems to be the Gregory scene's closest relative.

The calling of Matthew fills the right half of the top register, and is presented as a two-scene sequence. The future evangelist, identified as Matthew the tax-collector, sits before an aedicula, guarding a pile of coins heaped on the draped table in front of him with his hands; he turns to face Christ, who stands nearly frontally on the right and gestures toward Matthew with his right arm. The miniaturist has crammed a group of Pharisees between Matthew and the left edge of the scene. The second scene, inscribed 'the tax-collector follows Christ', shows Matthew, now carrying a jewelled gospelbook, doing exactly that; both move off toward the right. Byzantine painters depicted the calling of Matthew even more rarely than the preceding two scenes. The earliest known representation appears, once again, in the Augustine Gospels (fig. 66), which shows Matthew, accompanied by a second disciple, following Christ; later versions surface at New Tokalı – which pictures only the calling of Matthew (fig. 169) – and in the Florence tetraevangelion (fig. 170), which includes both scenes.[175] Though the three versions of Matthew following Christ are generally similar, the scene reproduces such a simple composition that the rough parallels tell us little. In contrast, the presentation of Matthew the tax-collector incorporates a wealth of detail, none of which recurs in the Florence tetraevangelion; at Tokalı, however, an architectural backdrop (unusual in these frescoes) suggests an interior, and Matthew sits behind a table backed by a crowd of Pharisees. As the New Tokalı painters apparently often followed Constantinopolitan models,[176] the parallels suggest that the Homilies scene reproduces a composition familiar in the capital.[177]

The second register opens with the rich young man asking Christ about the kingdom of heaven in the presence of Philip, a scene that finds few parallels. Surprisingly, the Khludov Psalter depicts the rich youth with Christ twice, once as an illustration to Psalm 13:2, and again with Psalm 52:3–4;[178] here, however, the youth is bearded and stands straight. As with the scene of Zachias in the top register, Christ and the rich youth find their closest relative in the Florence tetraevangelion (fig. 171), which follows Paris.gr.510 in portraying the beardless youth leaning forward intently as he listens to Christ's words.[179]

---

[175] Epstein (1986), 43, 71, fig. 71; Florence, Laur.plut.6.23, f. 17r (cf. f. 113r): Velmans (1971), figs. 28, 199.   [176] Epstein (1986), 39–44; see also chapter 2 note 29.

[177] Though neither Constantine the Rhodian nor Mesarites mentions the scene in his description of the Apostoleion, the apostle cycle there provides a possible candidate for its location.

[178] Moscow, Hist.Mus.gr.129, ff. 11r, 52r: Ščepkina (1977).

[179] Florence, Laur.plut.6.23, f. 39r: Velmans (1971), fig. 84.

Fig. 169 New Tokalı: calling of Matthew

Philip recurs in the next scene, where he is a central character. Inscribed 'Christ talks with Nathanael', the image illustrates John 1:44–49. To the left of the figures, dividing this scene from the preceding one, stands the fig tree mentioned by John. Nathanael stands under it, looking at Christ and gesturing his amazement at Christ's recognition. Philip, nimbed and wearing the blue tunic and green mantle of the preceding scene, stands frontally but turns his head to look at Nathanael and gestures in speech toward him, as he points out Christ with his other hand. Christ stands on a small hillock and extends his arm toward the pair in blessing. A few other versions of this episode are known, but – though the Florence tetraevangelion and the *Sacra Parallela* repeat Nathanael's gesture of surprise[180] – none relates

[180] Florence, Laur.plut.6.23, f. 170r (Velmans [1971], fig. 270); Paris.gr.923, f. 275r (Weitzmann [1979a], 181, fig. 477). Compare Paris.gr.74, f. 170r: Omont (n.d.), pl. 147.

Fig. 170 Florence, Laurenziana plut.6.23, f. 17r: calling of Matthew

closely to this one, which conflates two moments to produce an image relevant to the theme of the miniature.

Folio 170r (22) (fig. 22)

Folio 170r concentrates on images of healing: Christ heals the leper, man with dropsy, and demoniacs in the first register; the centurion's servant and Peter's mother-in-law in the second. The third register contains a single scene, Christ walking on the water.[181]

The three healings of the top register are presented simply. In order to accommodate all three, Christ performs alone, without the accompanying disciple(s) familiar in other healing sequences. In each case, he stands to the (viewer's) left of those he heals, clad in purple robes enlivened with gold; the men to be healed are barefoot and wear pale blue loincloths tied at the waist. Each is accompanied by an identifying inscription: 'Christ heals the leper' (O X[PICTO]C I[O]MENOC TON ΛEΠ[PON]), 'Christ heals the man with dropsy' (O X[PICTO]C IOMENOC TON Y[Δ]PΩΠ[IKON]), and 'Christ heals the demoniacs' (O X[PICTO]C IOMENOC TOYC ΔAIMONI[ZO]MENOYC).

The gospel accounts of the healing of the leper are brief. Matthew 8:2–3 tells us that Jesus healed the leper by touch; to this, Mark 1:40–44 and Luke 5:12–14 add only that the leper knelt down to beseech Christ. On f. 170r, the leper stands and turns toward Christ with his arms hanging at his sides, palms outwards, as if to display the red sores which cover his entire body; his face has flaked, but he appears

---

[181] For further discussion and bibliography, see chapter 6.

Fig. 171 Florence, Laurenziana plut.6.23, f. 39r: Christ blesses the children; Christ with the rich youth; Christ tells the apostles about the kingdom of heaven

to be a beardless youth. Christ gestures toward, but does not touch, the leper with his right hand; he holds a scroll in his left. The healing of the leper is, in later Byzantine examples, often presented in a broader narrative context.[182] Closest to Paris.gr.510 is the equally abbreviated image in the *Sacra Parallela* (fig. 172), which restricts the scene to the two figures found on f. 170r and, except for the slightly more active stance of the leper, presents them in the same way: Christ, on the left, gestures toward the leper, who wears a loincloth and stands with his right leg forward as he displays his arms.[183]

Luke 14:2–4 briefly relates the healing of the man with dropsy, in an account that stresses its enactment on the Sabbath rather than narrative details. Save that the man with dropsy has, instead of leprous spots, an extended belly, the weight of which he supports on straight legs, and extends his right arm toward Christ, the two figures duplicate those in the previous healing. The scene of the healing of the man with dropsy in Paris.gr.510 anticipates, in its general outlines, the version found in the Florence tetraevangelion.[184] The image on f. 170r is, however, simpler

---

[182] E.g. Epstein (1986), fig. 75; Velmans (1971), figs. 20, 132, 197.

[183] Paris.gr.923, f. 211r: Weitzmann (1979a), 163, fig. 408.

[184] E.g. Velmans (1971), fig. 236. In the Paris version, the man with dropsy leans over backwards, supported by a stick: Omont [n.d.], pl. 122.

Fig. 172 Paris.gr.923, f. 211r: Christ healing the leper, the centurion's servant, Peter's mother-in-law, and two blind men

than most later versions, which normally show Christ accompanied, and the man with dropsy supported either by a stick or another figure.[185]

The healing of the two demoniacs must ultimately rely on the narrative preserved in the narrative preserved in Matthew 8:28–32, as Mark 5:1–14 and Luke 8:26–36 describe only one man possessed by demons. The two, hands bound behind their backs, emerge from the tombs, two of which – in pale blue to simulate marble – appear behind them on a grey-green hill. The rear demoniac stands facing Christ, but the foremost lunges forward and bends sharply down from the waist so that his hair flies toward Christ and his face is invisible. An identical figure throws himself before a standing Christ in Pantokrator 61 (fig. 173);[186] and both features recur in the Florence tetraevangelion (fig. 174), which also shares with Paris.gr.510 the two tombs resting on the mountainside.[187]

The healing of the centurion's servant (Matthew 8:5–13, Luke 7:2–10) opens the second register.[188] Christ, depicted as above, addresses the centurion, a middle-aged man with a short dark beard, who – visualizing his own self-description as 'a man under authority, having soldiers under me' – wears gold armour and boots and is backed by four soldiers. The centurion's house appears as a rectangular niche in the centre of the register behind the soldiers. Within the house, the centurion's youthful male servant lies ill on a green mattress set into a golden bed hung with red and blue undercurtains; he is fanned by another youth dressed in red and gold. The scene recurs in the *Sacra Parallela* (fig. 172) directly beneath the healing of the leper, precisely the same vertical juxtaposition that obtains on f. 170r; below this, the healing of Peter's mother-in-law has been depicted.[189] Despite the similar combination of scenes and the shared details of the leper healing, the healing of the centurion's servant in the *Sacra Parallela* does not resemble that on f. 170r: in contradiction to the gospel accounts, the *Sacra Parallela* shows Christ at the bedside of the servant while the centurion, here an old man in civilian clothes, stands by. Nor is the scene closely related to the versions in the middle Byzantine tetraevangelia.[190] The painting at New Tokalı (fig. 175), on the other hand, incorporates the group of friends who accompany the centurion in Paris.gr.510, and locates them in an architectural frame similar to that enclosing the servant on f. 170r. Further, the next scene in the church – the healing of Jairus' daughter (fig. 175) – is very close in composition to the following scene on f. 170r, the healing of Peter's mother-in-law. It is conceivable that both the wall painting and the miniature

[185] For the stick, see the tetraevangelia; for another figure, New Tokalı: Epstein (1986), fig. 78.
[186] Folio 144r: Dufrenne (1966), 33, pl. 22; see also Vaccaro (1967), 116–118. Other ninth-century psalters omit the demoniac from this scene.
[187] Florence, Laur.plut.6.23, f. 16v: Velmans (1971), fig. 26.
[188] For the identification of this scene, and its incorrect inscription, see chapter 6.
[189] Paris.gr.923, f. 211r: Weitzmann (1979a), 163–164, figs. 408–409.
[190] Velmans (1971), figs. 21, 203; Omont [n.d.], pls. 15, 107.

Fig. 173 Mount Athos, Pantokrator 61, f. 144r: Christ healing the demoniac and two others

reflect a visual account of Matthew, where the healings of the centurion's servant and of Peter's mother-in-law were conjoint;[191] if so, the Tokalı painter used the composition to illustrate a different female healing.

The healing of Peter's mother-in-law (Matthew 8:14–15, Mark 1:30–31) completes the second register. The woman, identified by inscription (Η ΠΕΝΘΕΡΑ ΠΕΤΡΟΥ), is dressed in brown with a white headdress. She leans against a red and gold pillow; her lower body, wrapped in a green blanket, rests on a gold bed with

[191] Cf. chapter 6 note 128.

Fig. 174 Florence, Laurenziana plut.6.23, f. 16v: Christ healing the demoniacs; shepherds recount
the episode as Christ and disciple sail away

red and white undercurtains. A gold stepping stool sits next to the bed, which
extends at a forty-five degree angle from a house in the background – presumably to
indicate that this is an interior scene – and thus parallels the bed of the centurion's
servant. Peter's mother-in-law extends her hand to Christ, who touches her wrist in
accordance with the gospel account; he is otherwise indistinguishable from his
other portrayals on the page. Peter, shown as usual in Paris.gr.510 with a short light
beard and hair that dips down over his forehead, stands between the two in a pink
robe. As noted earlier, the episode of Peter's mother-in-law shares a margin with the
healing of the leper and of the centurion's servant in the *Sacra Parallela* (fig. 172),
and, like the healing of the leper, that of Peter's mother-in-law closely resembles the
version in Paris.gr.510.[192] Though Peter has been omitted for lack of space and the
furniture has been simplified, the relationship between architecture and bed is
identical, the bed extends at the same forty-five-degree angle, Christ stands in the
position he adopts on f. 170r, and he grasps the woman by the wrist exactly as in
Paris.gr.510. The middle Byzantine tetraevangelia continue the pattern found in
the two ninth-century manuscripts.[193]

[192] So too Weitzmann (1979a), 164.
[193] Velmans (1971), figs. 22, 130, 194; Omont (n.d.), pl. 15.

Fig. 175 New Tokalı: Christ healing the man with dropsy and the centurion's servant; the raising of Jairus' daughter

The lowest register is devoted to an expansive composition showing Christ walking on water and rescuing Peter (Matthew 14:25–31). Eleven apostles, the fore-most identified by his curly hair as Andrew, huddle together in a boat floating on a dark blue sea, its waves indicated by overlapping spirals, that melts almost imperceptibly into the blue sky beyond. Christ stands to the far left and grasps Peter's wrist just as he had his mother-in-law's in the preceding scene. Peter, now clad in a pink himation over a blue chiton, has half sunk in the water and gestures toward Christ with his free hand. The inscription above his head indicates that we see 'Peter sinking into the sea' (Ο ΠΕΤΡΟC ΕΝ ΤΗ ΘΑΛΑCCΗ ΒΥΘΙ-ZOMENOC). As noted long ago by Otto Demus, the depiction of this scene did not admit much variation and its iconography remained stable from the early

Fig. 176 Rome, San Saba: Peter rescued by Christ

Christian through the late Byzantine period.[194] The moment is illustrated in the Florence tetraevangelion,[195] but the composition closest to that on f. 170r appears earlier, in the eighth-century wall paintings at the San Saba monastery in Rome (fig. 176).

Folios 3r, 87v, and 170r are representative of the gospel scenes as a whole, and illuminate two patterns found throughout Paris.gr.510. First, compared with the Old Testament scenes, there are fewer examples of gospel iconography that have been manipulated to underline a particular visual argument; instead, visual com-

---

[194] Demus (1949), 278, see also pl. 85B.
[195] Velmans (1971), fig. 63.

mentary is provided by the juxtaposition of scenes. A thematic arrangement governs the selection of scenes on f. 87v, where we correspondingly find only one scene – Christ and Nathanael – that seems to display morphological revisions designed to complement the point of the page; the same is true of f. 170r, where scenes interpreted as anti-heretical are grouped together with only one evident change to highlight the connection: the garments of the men being healed are identical. While Old Testament narratives tend to remain intact, with commentary spun by alterations within an episodic sequence, New Testament narratives fragment into themes.[196] Perhaps for this reason, there are fewer anomalous New Testament images in Paris.gr.510, though the calling of Nathanael (f. 87v; fig. 16), the dream of the Magi (f. 137r; fig. 18), perhaps the Dives and Lazarus sequence (f. 149r; fig. 20), and the healing of the bent woman (f. 310v; fig. 31) do appear to have been invented for the manuscript.

Some gospel scenes – notably the healings of the paralytic and the woman with the issue of blood (f. 143v; fig. 19), and the miracle of the loaves and fishes (f. 165r; fig. 21) – replicate early formulae. Some – the visitation (f. 3r; fig. 6), Matthew following Christ (f. 87v; fig. 16), Christ among the doctors (f. 165r; fig. 21), Christ saving Peter (f. 170r; fig. 22), and the raising of Lazarus (f. 196v; fig. 24) – present generic iconography that changed little over the centuries. But a second pattern evident amongst the gospel scenes in Paris.gr.510 is the appearance of transitional forms. On f. 87v (fig. 16), the scene of Christ and Zachias exemplifies this: both Paris.gr.510 and the marginal psalters ultimately relied on an older composition represented by the Augustine Gospels, but modified that scheme in different ways, and the version adapted on f. 87v prevailed in the middle Byzantine tetraevangelia. Two more scenes – Christ calling the four apostles and Christ with the rich youth – also find comparisons in the middle Byzantine gospel cycle in Florence (figs. 168, 171), and the first of these, along with the image of Matthew as tax collector, recurs in similar form in the Cappadocian church of New Tokalı (figs. 167, 169). Whether or not any of these scenes existed in monumental form, the miniatures we have just examined suggest that gospel imagery was being revised, and new formulations germinated, in ninth-century Constantinople.[197] The frescoes at New Tokalı intimate that some of these modifications were widely familiar by the middle of the tenth century; they were collected into the tetraevangelia in the eleventh.

The largest group of gospel scenes in Paris.gr.510 is related most closely to ninth-century Byzantine work. Some scenes follow patterns apparently formulated slightly earlier in the century. Two images – the parable of the Good Samaritan (f. 143v; fig. 19) and the healing of the leper (f. 170r; fig. 22) – find their closest counterparts in the *Sacra Parallela* (fig. 64); the healing of the two men born blind (f. 310v; fig. 31) also resembles the *Sacra Parallela* (fig. 113), though a similar scene recurs in

---

[196] See Brubaker (1996a), esp. 17–19.

[197] R. Nelson (1980), 97–107, suggests the same for the creation of prefatory illustrations to the gospels. See also Frolow (1945); Mütherich (1987); Elsner (1988), 476.

the middle Byzantine tetraevangelia. The visitation (f. 3r; fig. 6) and the conversion of the Samaritan woman (f. 215v; fig. 25) repeat formulae established in the marginal psalters (figs. 110, 111, 166); the deposition and entombment (f. 30v; fig. 7) also follow the psalters (fig. 118), as does the fresco at Old Tokalı (fig. 119). Paris.gr.510 groups with the marginal psalters, Old Tokalı, and the early ninth-century reliquary crosses in its image of the presentation (f. 137r; fig. 18) and the crucifixion (f. 30v; figs. 7, 116), though in the latter scene some more recent details, later found at New Tokalı (fig. 117), were appended. The transfiguration (f. 75r; fig. 14) resembles its pendants in the Khludov Psalter (fig. 122) and, apparently, the Apostoleion; the temptations of Christ (f. 165r; fig. 21) recall the marginal psalters (fig. 69) and anticipate New Tokalı (fig. 70). The annunciation (f. 3r: fig. 6), though similar to the earlier wall paintings at Sta Maria Antiqua in Rome (figs. 162, 163), was perhaps more immediately influenced by the Apostoleion, from whence it also seems to have travelled to New Tokalı (fig. 165). Another parallel with the Apostoleion appears on f. 30v (fig. 7), where, as also in the Church of the Virgin of the Source, the chairete appeared rather than the increasingly common anastasis. A number of additional gospel scenes directly anticipate New Tokalı: the calling of Peter, Andrew, James, and John, and the calling of Matthew (f. 87v; fig. 16); the healing of the centurion's servant and of Peter's mother-in-law (f. 170r; fig. 22); and the healing of the man with the withered arm (f. 310v; fig. 31) all find parallels there (figs. 112, 167, 169, 175) and seem to reflect the most up-to-date compositions being produced in Constantinople.[198]

Finally, a number of gospel scenes show general similarities with the middle Byzantine tetraevangelia. These include Christ and Zachias, and Christ and the rich youth (f. 87v: figs. 16, 171); the healing of the man with dropsy and the healing of the demoniacs (f. 170r; figs. 22, 174); the supper at Simon's and the entry into Jerusalem (f. 196v; fig. 24); the healing of the ten lepers (f. 215v; fig. 25); and the healing of the blind man at Siloam (f. 316r; fig. 32). Though Paris.gr.510 influenced a few later Byzantine manuscripts, its general impact was minimal; parallels with the later tetraevanglia intimate that the Homilies painters had familiarity in some way with a fairly extensive repertoire of gospel scenes and suggest that documented monumental gospel sequences, such as that at the Church of the Virgin of the Source, did not stand in isolation.

Acts

The three images from Acts have already been discussed: the martyrdom of James (f. 32v; fig. 8) and Pentecost (f. 301r; fig. 30) in chapter 6; the conversion of Saul (f. 264v; fig. 28) in chapter 5. The first two were familiar and liturgically important scenes that appeared in diverse contexts throughout the Byzantine period; they

---

[198] For an early assessment of the relationship between Paris.gr.510 and New Tokalı, see Jerphanion (1938a). See also chapter 2 note 29.

seem to have existed independently of a text-bound narrative cycle. The last scene appears as part of a martyrdom sequence that was also detached from Acts, which, indeed, relates only one of the twelve martyrdoms pictured.

New Testament Apocrypha

The Acts of the various apostles (f. 32v; fig. 8) were considered in chapter 6; the flight of Elizabeth and John the Baptist, and the martyrdom of Zacharias (f. 137r; fig. 18), both from the Protevangelion, were discussed in chapter 2.

PARIS.GR.510 AND OTHER SURVIVING PROGRAMMES

The survival of earlier imagery

The pattern established by the gospel scenes continues throughout Paris.gr.510. A few isolated scenes repeat early formulae that look quite different from their conventional middle Byzantine renderings,[199] and two narratives duplicate early sequences otherwise unattested after Iconoclasm: the scenes from the infancy of Christ (f. 137r; fig. 18) seem to have come as a unit from an early source heavily influenced by the Protevangelion (fig. 62), while the Joseph scenes (f. 69v; fig. 12) find their closest relatives in the eighth-century frescoes at Sta Maria Antiqua (figs. 127, 132).

There are also a few images in Paris.gr.510 that seem to echo Byzantine developments during the period of Iconoclasm. The frontispiece crosses and portraits (figs. 2–5) assimilated and perpetuated iconoclast ideas about the importance of the cross and of dynastic succession. The *vita* of Constantine (fig. 45) also sustains pictorialized ideas that would have been familiar to iconoclast emperors, while the image of the martyrdom of the Makkabees on f. 340r (fig. 34) probably follows a fresco cycle commissioned during the period between the two phases of Iconoclasm by Tarasios, patriarch from 784 to 806; the martyrdom of apostles sequence on f. 32v (fig. 8) may also have been inspired by a work from this period.

Finally, in addition to the gospel scenes already mentioned, Moses receiving the laws (f. 52v; fig. 10), Jacob's dream (f. 174v; fig. 23), and the tower of Babel (f. 360r; fig. 37) resemble early counterparts, but also find parallels in later Byzantine art; the Homilies miniaturists evidently replicated a living tradition rather than consciously reverting to old forms.

Ninth-century formulations

Most images in Paris.gr.510, however, are tied very firmly to the post-iconoclast ninth century. Comparisons between Paris.gr.510 and, particularly, other ninth-

---

[199] E.g. the fall of Jericho (f. 424v; fig. 41).

century manuscripts indicate that familiar Byzantine scenes such as the three Hebrews in the fiery furnace (f. 435v; fig. 43) acquired specific and short-lived ninth-century configurations (fig. 158); others, for example the healing of the two men born blind (f. 310v; fig. 31), suggest the existence of a ninth-century gospel or christological cycle that no longer survives. The similar compositions shared by Paris.gr.510 and later extensively illustrated gospel cycles in Paris (gr.74 and 115) and Florence (Laur.plut.6.23) intimate that at least part of this ninth-century sequence was ultimately incorporated into middle Byzantine compilations.

The miniatures of Paris.gr.510 hint at the existence of two additional cycles otherwise unattested in the ninth century. The martyrdom of the apostles series on f. 32v (fig. 8), which recurs in later monuments produced by artisans unlikely to have been familiar with Paris.gr.510 (figs. 107, 108, 109), probably indicates that this cycle also was current in the ninth century, and later parallels with the epitomized Adam and Eve sequence on f. 52v (figs. 10, 124, 126) suggest that this grouping too might have existed and circulated by the 880s.

The later impact of Paris.gr.510

The later impact of the Homilies illustrations was, on the whole, restricted to a small group of Constantinopolitan manuscripts, three of which, like Paris.gr.510, demonstrate secure links with Byzantine court circles. The miniaturists of the Leo Bible, probably produced around 940, and the Paris Psalter, which apparently represents a slightly later reworking of a mid-tenth-century original, seem to have consulted Paris.gr.510 directly,[200] as, apparently, did the illustrators of the Psalter of Basil II and Dumbarton Oaks 3. Evidently, and for obvious reasons, Paris.gr.510 was not available for consultation to a broad audience. Indeed, aside from the miniaturists responsible for the manuscripts just mentioned, who may be assumed to have had access to the imperial library, the only other work that may demonstrate the direct influence of Paris.gr.510 is the imperial ivory of Leo VI, which, just as f. Cv shows Gabriel crowning Basil in the Homilies (fig. 5), shows the Virgin accompanied by an archangel crowning Basil's son Leo (fig. 177).

THE TRANSMISSION OF ICONOGRAPHY

Once the scenes to be presented had been selected, and the specific requirements imposed by visual exegesis had been worked out, the miniaturists blocked out the page; most of the time, they replicated, with modifications, conventional and familiar iconography. *How* was this iconography familiar?

[200] For the connections between the Leo Bible and Paris.gr.510, see the discussions of ff. Bv–Cr, 52v, 71v, 174v, 264v; on the Paris Psalter (Paris.gr.139), see the discussions of ff. 3r, 52v, 174v, 264v, 435v and chapter 2 note 190.

Fig. 177 Berlin, Staatliche Museen, ivory with Leo VI, the virgin Mary, and an archangel

Paris.gr.510 points the way to several responses to this question, both negative and positive. The most obvious negatives are that we do not find here evidence for blind and unthinking copying of some canonical model(s); nor do we find evidence that workshop training, whatever that may have consisted of, indoctrinated painters with a set of particular iconographic formulae that they then reproduced regardless of context. The Homilies miniaturists *never* provide us with an obvious example of straightforward copying; and we have also seen that the same miniaturist was quite capable of producing iconographies that we have been taught to view as having distinct pedigrees. Such versatility was not restricted to the miniaturists responsible for Paris.gr.510: even within the coherent and self-referential family of the marginal psalters there are differences, and sometimes profound ones, between picture sequences. Further, when it can be demonstrated that one manuscript copies another, it is clear that revisions were normal:[201] miniaturists who specifically intended to copy a picture cycle did not view 'copying' as mechanical reproduction.[202]

But Paris.gr.510 did not 'copy' any monolithic earlier cycle. The evidence that its miniatures – and those in the Vatican 'Christian Topography', the marginal psalters, and the *Sacra Parallela* – provide primarily supports awareness of single images and occasionally of small thematic or episodic sequences.

Though the exegetical role played by the Homilies miniatures allowed few coherent iconographical sequences to appear, those that exist display a clear pattern. There are an equal number of Old and New Testament narratives, but the Old Testament sequences are, on average, over twice as long; New Testament imagery tends to be collected together thematically rather than episodically. Old Testament and New Testament scenes were apparently viewed differently, were joined together in distinct ways, and played contrasting roles in the ninth century.[203] Despite their usually thematic arrangement, however, the New Testament scenes suggest that gospel imagery in particular was being revised and reconsidered in the ninth century.

Many of the scenes we have just considered find their closest links with other ninth-century images, but relatively few of them present the same episode identically. This suggests that the scenes in question were familiar, and therefore mutable, for familiarity encourages inclusion and modification to accommodate a given audience. It also suggests that painters were far more aware of what their compères were doing than we might think; rather than looking exclusively and passively at older objects, as art historians must, they had the option of learning from each other.

There are two implications enmeshed in the foregoing discussion. The first of these recapitulates a familiar theme: there is a symbiotic relationship between artisan, image, audience, and text. The second is that there also seems to be a symbiotic relationship between images and images. Miniatures exist in a complex dialogue with their audience and the text they accompany, but just as the audience has a life beyond that shaped by texts or images, and texts exist independently of one particular reader or picture cycle, so too images and their makers intersect with each other in ways outside the confines of text and audience. To put it in literary terms, images speak the language of images, not the language of texts. Attempts to circumscribe the relationship between pictures and words too tightly ignore both the painter and the language of images.

[201] See Lowden (1982), Anderson (1991), and Lowden (1992).
[202] See further Vikan (1989).   [203] Brubaker (1996a).

9

Conclusions

The miniatures of the Paris Homilies reinterpreted Gregory's words in ways that reveal ninth-century Constantinopolitan attitudes, and in ways tailored to (or by) individuals who had their own slant on those attitudes. The miniatures contextualized the text; but often, too, the sermons served as springboards for virtually autonomous visual commentaries directed to the eyes of a small élite, and sometimes for two men alone.

Many of the messages layered into the miniatures of Paris.gr.510, and the attitudes that underpin them, are predictable; some of them are not. We have looked at the micro-messages: chapter 4 detailed the ways that the miniatures of Paris.gr.510 visualized imperial panegyric, and moulded it to the Emperor Basil I; chapter 5 dealt primarily with the visual expression of Photios' patriarchal concerns, and some of his private preoccupations; chapter 6 examined how the parameters of the holy and the heretical were defined pictorially in the late ninth century; and chapter 7 considered the importance of showing interaction between the divine and the human. We shall return to the personalized dialogue sketched out in these earlier chapters; first, though, I should like to look at two of the macro-messages: the broad cultural ones that transcend personalities.

MATERIAL PRESENCE AND PHYSICAL APPEARANCE

The most obvious, overarching, message conveyed by Paris.gr.510 is that images mattered: material presence had meaning. The importance of material presence – and material representation – was not, of course, invented in the ninth century.[1] The issue took on, however, a certain amount of ideological baggage at the hands of iconophile theologians, who, understandably enough, followed Maximos the Confessor's arguments that the spiritual was fused to the material as the soul to the body.[2] As we saw in chapter 1, John of Damascus argued that 'It is impossible for us

---

[1] See e.g. Gordon (1979).   [2] This line of reasoning has been clearly explicated by Parry (1989).

to think immaterial things unless we can envisage analogous shapes';[3] and he also noted that 'the mind which is determined to ignore corporeal things will find itself weakened and frustrated'.[4] But although similarly polemical defences of material representation continued to be made – and by Photios, especially – well into the second half of the ninth century,[5] the polemical point itself was never explicitly made by the miniatures of Paris.gr.510, which instead demonstrated the value of material presence by example.

This value was demonstrated not only by the profusion of miniatures, head-pieces and painted initials – which by their presence alone legitimized the value of material imagery – but also, as we saw in chapter 1, by the emphasis on colour and expensive materials. It was also demonstrated, though in a somewhat different way, by the intermingling of human and divine figures in the miniatures considered in chapter 7, and by the emphasis on physical appearance in Paris.gr.510.

The portrait of the archangel Gabriel with the Emperor Basil (f. Cv; fig. 5), with the two figures standing on the same level and wearing the same costume, suggests just how important physical appearance, or physical presentation, was in ninth-century Byzantium. This was not a new concern: physical appearance had had meaning in preceding centuries and would continue to have it in later ones.[6] It was implicated in the theoretical bases of image veneration, for the concept on which so much iconophile theory was based – that honour given to the image passes to its prototype – required the viewer to recognize the saint depicted, and that recognition was dependent on the physical appearance of the saint por-trayed.[7] Iconophile pleas to continue traditional visual formulae do not only mark the importance of tradition *per se*: they also underscore the significance of physical presentation.

A similar emphasis on physical appearance surfaced in social interactions.[8] In a culture that reserved certain dye colours for the imperial house, and that claimed to mistake female saints for males when they simply adopted men's clothing, we should not be surprised when, to denigrate monks, iconoclasts denigrated monas-tic clothing: the clothing alone was credited with the power to evoke hatred.[9] In a

---

[3] John of Damascus, 'Against those who attack divine images' III,21: ed. Kotter (1975), 128; trans. Anderson (1980), 76. Nikephoros made a similar point: 'knowledge of the primary form [archetype] is obtained through the figure [image]' (*Antirrheticus* 1,30; Mondzain-Baudinet [1990], 110–112; Alexander [1958], 200).

[4] John of Damascus, 'Against those who attack divine images' I,11 (cf. III,21): ed. Kotter (1975), 85 (129); trans. Anderson (1980), 20.   [5] See e.g. Thümmel (1983); additional citations in chapter 1.

[6] See e.g. Maguire (1989).   [7] See Dagron (1991); Maguire (1996).

[8] The importance of physical appearance was not restricted to Byzantium: see e.g. van Dam (1985), 64–66.

[9] On the murex dye, restricted to the imperial house until at least the tenth century, see Muthesius (1992), esp. 244–247. On (male reports of) female saints dressed as men, see e.g. Herrin (1983), 179, and the seminal Patlagean (1976). For more on the importance of clothing, see Cameron (1987), 130–131, and Mango (1982), esp. 342 (actresses and actors forbidden, under Justinian, to wear monastic clothing), 349 (men and women forbidden, by the Council *in Trullo*, to cross-dress).

culture that believed that facial disfigurement disbarred one from the throne, we should not be surprised by the punishment meted out to the iconophile brothers Theodore and Theophanes in 836 by the iconoclast Emperor Theophilos: their faces were tattooed with an insultingly ill-written text (thereby endowing them with their epithet, the Graptoi).[10] As punishment for iconophile leanings, monks, we are told, were forced to parade publicly with women, and divested of their outward signs of sanctity: their robes and beards.[11] Whatever the germ of truth in these accounts may be, it is clear that their authors were convinced of the power of clothing – monastic garments were ridiculed *and* removed – and of that other external sign of monasticism, hair. For, our informants tell us, not only were monks forcibly shaved: the iconoclast Emperor Constantine V ordered all citizens to shave so that the monks still hirsute stood out dramatically.[12] Even those who did not accept the power of religious imagery, in other words, understood and manipulated the power of visual appearance. Whether or not one was willing to transfer the importance of physical appearance to the importance of material presentation, the former was apparently a universally accepted value.

As such, the physical appearance of the figures in the miniatures of Paris.gr.510 is, indeed, significant,[13] and as the preceding discussion might lead us to expect, garments are important indicators of meaning. Paris.gr.510 goes beyond the conventions of portraying the imperial family and women in red shoes, and of dressing Christ in purple: we have already examined the significance of the shared costume worn by the archangel and the emperor on f. Cv (fig. 5). Beyond this, shifts in status are conveyed by shifts in clothing. Though the miniaturists of Paris.gr.510 were perfectly capable of portraying children, on f. 104r (fig. 17) St Basil has the same face as a child hiding in a cave in the Pontos mountains as he does as an adult cleric: the inscribed name was apparently not, in this case, considered sufficient to ensure recognition of Basil as child. His change of status is indicated not by physiognomy but entirely by a change of clothes, from civilian garments to ecclesiastical vestments. Cyprian before his conversion wears a toga (see too the togate philosopher of Athens on f. 104r); after his baptism he affects the apostolic chiton and himation (f. 332v; fig. 33). Clothes label status in more general ways as well. Gregory's brother Kaisarios, who was an imperial official, wears clothing carefully distinguished from that of his ecclesiastic brother and father (ff. 43v, 452r; figs. 9, 46); the small figure standing next to Jacob on f. 69v (fig. 12) and the youth lying on a bed on f. 170r (fig. 22) are identified as a young males by their costumes (and uncovered hair); changes

---

[10] See the Life of Michael the Synkellos, 20, 23: ed. Cunningham (1991), 84–89, 94–95. For other examples of facial disfigurement, McCormick (1986), 142–143, who connects the 'fascination with the human face' with the cult of icons.

[11] An excellent analysis of this process as expressed in the Life of Stephen the Younger appeared in Rouan (1981).

[12] Relevant documents for all these actions have been collected and discussed by, among others, Gero (1977a); Gero (1977b); and Alexander (1977).   [13] Cf. Brubaker (1989b), 79–81.

in Joseph's costume in the last two scenes of f. 69v signal the imperial implications of the miniature. Colour can have meaning, too, even when it is not applied to garments. In images of conflict, the horses of the good are white; those of the bad are black: witness Merkourios and Julian (f. 409v; fig. 40), or Constantine and Maxentius (f. 440r; fig. 45).

Finally, just as the physical relationship of figures within the composition of any one miniature has been seen to carry meaning time and time again, so too the physical position of individual figures can be an important indicator. Sleeping heroes, for example, look the same: Jonah (f. 3r; fig. 6), Jacob (f. 174v; fig. 23), and Constantine (f. 440r; fig. 45) follow the same pattern. But while certain configurations recur throughout Paris.gr.510, a given figure type rarely recurs on a single page:[14] when such repetition occurs, the replication itself carries meaning – we need only recall, for example, the duplications of figures in the presentation and the adoration of the Magi on f. 137r (fig. 18). We saw in chapter 2 that backgrounds remain subservient to the figures, who act out their roles in the immediate foreground. The neutralized space – which keeps the setting firmly in place as a backdrop or frame – allows the viewer to focus on the physical appearance of these figures and to concentrate on details of their clothing, hair, and position that evidently had considerable significance in Paris.gr.510.

WOMEN, MEN, AND FAMILY

One of the more striking features of the anti-Jewish images in Paris.gr.510 is the role of women in them: every one of those miniatures balances women against men. The healing of the centurion's servant joins the healing of Peter's mother-in-law on f. 170r (fig. 22); Christ and the Samaritan woman is paired with the healing of the ten lepers below the judgment of Solomon, also a mixed-gender scene, on f. 215v (fig. 25); the healing of the man with the withered arm balances the healing of the bent woman on f. 310v (fig. 31); the healing of the blind man at Siloam is linked with the parable of the widow's mite, and the healing of the paralytic at Capernaum with the raising of the widow's son at Nain, on f. 316r (fig. 32). As we saw in chapter 6, the miniaturist sometimes manipulates the composition of the page or deviates from established iconographical formulae to achieve this balance. Attempts at gender balancing are not, however, restricted to the anti-heretical miniatures: a related pairing appears on f. 143v (fig. 19), in the lowest register of which are joined the healings of the paralytic and of the woman with the issue of blood, which, although sometimes linked in anti-Jewish polemic, do not seem to function pri-

---

[14] Aside, of course, from the five pages that present formal group portraits on ff. Br and Cv (the imperial family; figs. 2, 5), f. 43v (Gregory and his family; fig. 9), f. 71v (Gregory, Basil, and Gregory of Nyssa; fig. 13), and f. 285r (Helena and Paraskeve; fig. 29).

marily in this capacity here.[15] Though it would be structurally tidy to find women associated primarily with anti-heretical images – for Byzantine wives were consistently charged with maintaining a pious domestic atmosphere and were held responsible for the morals and orthodoxy of their households[16] – the miniaturists do not here oblige us. Throughout Paris.gr.510 there is a greater emphasis on women than one might expect from reading accounts of now-lost mural programmes or from leafing through other contemporary manuscripts: nearly two-thirds of the miniatures include them.[17] Unlike other examples of Byzantine visual gender balancing (which are in any case later, and less extensive), Paris.gr.510 does not restrict itself to a demonstration of Christ's impartiality toward women and men.[18] Crowd scenes, for example, virtually always incorporate both sexes: women form a distinct group in the audience for Gregory's sermon on the hailstorm (f. 78r; fig. 15), and mingle with men at Christ's multiplication of loaves (f. 165r; fig. 21), and at his entry into Jerusalem (f. 196v; fig. 24); men and women together appear as well in Old Testament scenes of the exodus such as Moses striking water from the rock (f. 226v; fig. 26) or the crossing of the Red Sea (f. 264v; fig. 28), which also includes Miriam dancing, something that not all ninth-century representations of the scene do.

The sheer number of females incorporated in Paris.gr.510 is notable; it is equally striking that, in a large percentage of cases, women play a prominent role, and few – Potiphar's wife (f. 69v; fig. 12) and Delilah (f. 347v; fig. 35) are the lone examples – are cast as forces of evil.[19] Men and women are, in fact, rarely presented in opposition in Paris.gr.510, which may help explain the unusual omission of the weeping mothers in the massacre of the innocents (f. 137r; fig. 18): male/female conflict was avoided by showing the soldiers killing the children without any female spectators at all.

Byzantine visual conventions lead us to expect the Virgin Mary in scenes of Christ's infancy (ff. 3r, 137r, 165r; figs. 6, 18, 21) and of his death (f. 30v; fig. 7). Even here, however, her role in Paris.gr.510 sometimes oversteps conventional bounds. The scene of Christ in the temple (f. 165r), for example, repeats the standard Byzantine formula of showing Mary and Joseph entering from the left to find Christ in the temple. But the Homilies miniaturist inserts the very rare scene of Mary embracing Jesus,[20] and thus stresses the emotional bonds between mother

---

[15] On f. 143v, see chapter 2. For the use of the two healings in anti-Jewish polemic, see Hennecke and Schneemelcher I (1963), 457.

[16] For ninth-century expressions of this sentiment see e.g. Gouillard (1982), esp. 449–450.

[17] Females appear in twenty-seven miniatures; they are omitted from nineteen.

[18] On which see Maguire (1981), 74–83.

[19] On the Byzantine tendency to use women to embody evil, see esp. Galatariotou (1984/5) and Harvey (1990).

[20] As we saw in chapter 2, the embrace does not recur until the late Byzantine period, and even then it is unusual. It may have appeared at the Kariye Camii, and is preserved at the Brontochion at Mistra: Lafontaine-Dosogne (1975), 237–238. A textual parallel appears in the apocryphal Gospel of Thomas: Hennecke and Schneemelcher I (1963), 396.

and son. The miniaturist also included the figures of Mary and John the evangelist in the scene of Christ's deposition (f. 30v). In this case, however, the Homilies version of the scene found contemporary textual analogues – in, especially, George of Nikodemia's influential homily on the death of Christ, which emphasized Mary's role at the deposition[21] – and seems to have been part of a wider Byzantine development: two slightly later versions of the scene, those in Old and New Tokalı, increase the emphasis on Mary; the grouping eventually was transformed into the lamentation over the dead body of Christ.[22] As we saw in chapter 7, the appearance of both visual and written descriptions of the deposition in the ninth century followed the iconophile insistence on Christ's human nature.[23] Indeed, Ioli Kalavrezou convincingly argued that Mary's earlier epithet, *theotokos* (the bearer of God), shifted to *meter theou* (the mother of God) in the ninth century because the iconophile emphasis on Christ's humanity suggested a parallel stress on Mary as mother; she also suggested that the inclusion of Christ's words to his mother on f. 30v – one of the anomalous inscriptions in Paris.gr.510 that go beyond simple description – was motivated by the same desire.[24] The miniatures in Paris.gr.510 that show a new awareness of Mary's emotional bonds with her son find, in other words, a solid context in ninth-century religious thought.

But Mary is not the only woman emphasized in Paris.gr.510, nor is she the only mother. Salomone appears with the Makkabees (f. 340r; fig. 34); Gregory's mother and sister are portrayed in two of the biographical miniatures (ff. 43v, 452r; figs. 9, 46); and the widow whom Basil defended is shown in that saint's pictorial *vita* (f. 104r; fig. 17). While none of these examples is particularly unusual, the inclusion of St Basil's mother in the latter sequence is almost unparalleled. Eve may nominally be the central figure in her own creation but, as we have seen, she nonetheless usually appears as a half-figure emerging from Adam's side rather than sitting next to him, legs and all, as on f. 52v (fig. 10), a configuration for which there are precious few parallels. Similarly, Mary and Martha are normally present at the raising of their brother Lazarus, but they are usually minimized as tiny figures; in Paris.gr.510, they are portrayed as (almost) full-sized women (f. 196v; fig. 24). Helena and Paraskeve represent a female incursion into a male vision (f. 285r; fig. 29); Justina takes up nearly a quarter of the space devoted to the life of Cyprian (f. 332v; fig. 33). The portrait of Eudokia with her sons (f. Br; fig. 2) furthers the dynastic emphasis of the frontispiece sequence, but Helena did not need to be included in the history of Constantine (f. 440r; fig. 45); the flight of Elizabeth was motivated neither by

---

[21] See Maguire (1981), 97–101; additional bibliography, and discussion, appear in chapter 7.

[22] See esp. Weitzmann (1961); Maguire (1981), 96–108. For Tokalı, Epstein (1986), figs. 38, 85.

[23] See Kartsonis (1986), 137, 229.

[24] Kalavrezou (1990), esp. 168–170; see further chapter 1. I would also suggest that the unusual image of Christ's various progenitors in the Vatican 'Christian Topography' fulfils the same function: it demonstrates Christ's ties on earth, and in so doing emphasizes his human nature and the importance of the incarnation. Vat.gr.699, f. 76r: Stornajolo (1908), pl. 41.

Gregory's sermon nor by the internal commentary supplied by the miniature as a whole (f. 137r; fig. 18); and there is no traditional grounding for the inclusion of Job's wife in what is essentially an image devoted to Job and his (male) friends (f. 71v; fig. 13): as we saw, this combination is unprecedented in Byzantine Job manuscripts.

What nearly all of the gender-mixed scenes – those that conventionally included women and those that did not – stress is family relationships: wife and husband, or mother and son. Even the anti-Jewish images, which already balance a female healing against a male one, reveal a tendency toward mother/son (or, in one case, son-in-law) or husband/wife images: the healing of Peter's mother-in-law (f. 170r; fig. 22), the raising of the widow's son at Nain (f. 316r; fig. 32), and Christ the bridegroom who has come to the Samaritan woman (f. 215v; fig. 25) perpetuate the theme of family relationships.

The portraits of Basil, Eudokia, Leo and Alexander on ff. Br and Cv (figs. 2, 5) show this overtly; they are, however, dynastic portraits and, as such, stress only a particular strand of family ties: children outside the line of succession were not included. Helena's inclusion in the history of Constantine miniature (f. 440r; fig. 45) furthers the mother/son motif, as does the introduction of a small boy tugging at his mother's hand in the entry into Jerusalem (f. 196v; fig. 24); so, too, does the inclusion of Elizabeth in the cave with John the Baptist (f. 137r; fig. 18) and this image is paralleled by the image of St Basil and his mother (and father) safe in a cave in the Pontos mountains (f. 104r; fig. 17). In this latter case, as in the frontispiece miniatures, we can see that the importance of families runs in tandem with the female/male pairings of mother/son and wife/husband.

The last miniature still preserved in Paris.gr.510 – the pictorial life of Gregory on f. 452r (fig. 46) – has already demonstrated another way that the significance of family ties could be visually expressed. We saw in chapter 3 that the scene of Gregory leaving his family on the shore and sailing off to an unidentified destination on the right side of the register does not illustrate any particular moment in Gregory's life, but is instead a symbolic encapsulation of Byzantine ideas about the strength of family ties. Gregory's sea voyage away from his family metaphorically signifies his moral strength and intellectual fortitude; the miniaturist shows us that for the sake of the church, Gregory gathered the courage to leave the security and comfort of his family.

Fathers, of course, appear in family groupings as well: Joseph is included in all scenes of Christ's infancy (ff. 137r, 165r; figs. 18, 21); Basil's parents both accompany him in the cave (f. 104r; fig. 17); Gregory's father joins the family groups on ff. 43v and 452r (figs. 9, 46). Though there is only one instance of a father/daughter grouping (Jairus and his daughter on f. 143v; fig. 19), fathers and sons regularly appear without accompanying women, as do brothers.[25] Non-familial forms of male

[25] Gregory and his father stand before the Nazianzus monks (f. 52v; fig. 10) and before the community after the hailstorm (f. 78r; fig. 15); Abraham and Isaac appear together on f. 174v (fig. 23). Jacob

kinship are visualised on ff. 32v and 426v (the apostles; figs. 8, 42), f. 71v (Gregory with Basil and Gregory of Nyssa), and f. 149r (Gregory and Basil).

Male communities thus appear with some regularity.[26] To this, however, female parallels are virtually non-existent. Aside from groups wherein the entire family is portrayed, the miniaturists of Paris.gr.510 never show us mother/daughter relationships. There are no female kinship groups (unless we count the cluster of women attending Gregory's sermon on the hailstorm on f. 78r; fig. 15); there are no nuns or groups of women in any way comparable with the apostles; and sisters appear together only in the visitation, the chairete, and the raising of Lazarus (ff. 3r, 30v, 196v; figs. 6–7, 24).[27] Women, with rare exceptions such as the portraits of Paraskeve and Helena on f. 285r (fig. 29), are visually valued primarily in their roles as wives and mothers of sons.[28] In this, the miniatures of Paris.gr.510 duplicate the conventional Byzantine attitudes expressed in legal codes, hagiography, and other texts;[29] but the accent on women as mothers and wives only serves to highlight the extraordinary emphasis on family groupings in the manuscript: well over half of all the miniatures play into the family theme.[30]

On the strength of these examples, we can scarcely avoid concluding that family ties were a recognized and important attribute of the lives of ninth-century Byzantines. The visual evidence provided by Paris.gr.510 finds a strong corollary in the findings of social historians: Evelyne Patlagean in particular has observed that the real family – or, perhaps even more essentially, the metaphorical family – had become the fundamental social and political model in Byzantium by the ninth century.[31] The miniatures of Paris.gr.510 that picture family units appear to corroborate Patlagean's observation, but it remains the case that other ninth-century manuscripts do not exhibit this visual recognition of contemporary models to the same degree. The dynastic emphasis evident in the opening pages of the manuscript suggests that the miniaturists responded to a micro-climate wherein family currents were likely to be picked up. As important, however, the full-page format consistently adopted by the Homilies miniaturists permitted the inclusion of relevant social details in a way that the marginal (or text column) format used for most other ninth-century miniatures did not. The relatively loose conceptual relationship between Gregory's sermons and the miniatures that accompany them – which

---

and Joseph are joined by the rest of Jacob's sons (f. 69v; fig. 12); David and Jesse are accompanied by all but the eldest of David's brothers (f. 174v; fig. 23). Other images of brothers include Gregory and Kaisarios (f. 43v; fig. 9); and Basil and Gregory of Nyssa (f. 71v; fig. 13).

[26] On which see e.g. Mullett (1988), who considers almost exclusively male friendships, for the good reason that male alliances were what (male) Byzantine authors tell us about.

[27] Brothers and sisters together are equally rare: Gregory and Gorgonia (f. 43v; fig. 9) and Mary, Martha, and Lazarus (f. 196v; fig. 24).   [28] See Harvey (1990) and Bynum (1984).

[29] For the ninth century see e.g. Gouillard (1982), and Beaucamp (1977), esp. 164–176; and on the low status of unmarried daughters, Grosdidier de Matons (1967), 28–31.

[30] Twenty-nine of the forty-six miniatures of Paris.gr.510 (63%) have been considered in this discussion.   [31] Patlagean (1986), esp. 427.

is presumably connected with the decision to adopt a full-page format – and the use of images alone to communicate complex messages (rather than images explained by inscriptions) also freed the miniaturists from the need to produce images mediated through words. Having dispensed with the constraints imposed by relying on ideas that could be formulated using familiar patterns of verbal construction, the miniaturists could communicate different things. One thing that they communicate is the importance of families and kinship groups.

TEXT AND IMAGE

The interaction of image and text has been one of the main themes of this book: discussion of the relationship between a miniature and the text that it introduces – which, in the case of the frontispiece miniatures, meant the relationship of this sequence to the whole book – has in many respects dominated the way in which I have set out Paris.gr.510. This approach was intentional, for while I believe that the images in the Homilies communicate differently from the text that they accompany and from other texts as well, I also believe that whenever we deal with a medium that juxtaposes images and words we must respect that combination, and this means that we must come to terms with the way the two interacted. There are a number of levels on which this relationship seems to have worked in Paris.gr.510; perhaps the clearest way to summarize these is to compare the combination of images and words in the Homilies and in another ninth-century manuscript closely associated with it, the Khludov Psalter (figs. 57, 85, 103, 104, 110, 118, 122, 125, 131, 142, 143, 151, 166). These two manuscripts, as we have seen, are alike in several important ways. Both bear witness to a re-thinking of the relationship between text, image, and audience. Kathleen Corrigan has indicated how this process worked in the Khludov Psalter;[32] and in Paris.gr.510, as we saw in chapter 3, the process of this re-evaluation is still vaguely discernible in the biographical miniatures, which chart the shifts from illustration, to supplementary images, and then to full-blown visual exegesis. Most importantly, both the Psalter and the Homilies use images to recontextualize the words of David's psalms and Gregory's sermons, respectively, and to reinterpret and re-frame them for a specific ninth-century audience. But the precise way the miniaturists of each manuscript achieved this end is different in each case, and the differences between the two manuscripts tell us something important about Paris.gr.510.

The principal physical difference between the way that image and word interact in the Homilies and the Psalter is obvious: Paris.gr.510 contains full-page, framed miniatures that introduce the text but remain separate from it; the Khludov Psalter

[32] Corrigan (1992).

positions unframed scenes in the margins of the text itself. The location of the Psalter miniatures was itself enough to identify them as potential commentaries, for the wide margins ruled for them by the scribes replicated the space left by other contemporary scribes for the newly instituted textual commentary on a manuscript text, the catena.[33] This parallel positioning, vis-à-vis the main body of the text, of commenting texts and commenting images is surely not coincidental: Corrigan persuasively suggested that marginal signs, whether words or images, signalled 'commentary' in the ninth century.[34] The Khludov Psalter was made forty years before Paris.gr.510, in the years immediately following the end of Iconoclasm when conflict and opposition were still very much to the intellectual fore. Corrigan saw this climate of opposition inscribed on the miniatures – which present orthodox Christians in debates with iconoclasts, Jews, and Muslims – and linked, too, the atmosphere of debate with the marginal format used in the Khludov Psalter, as well as with the confrontational composition of many of its marginal images.[35] The marginal format of the Psalter was, in short, an appropriate construct for the visual debate about the proper interpretation of the psalm texts, just as it was a fitting format for the 'proof' images of the *Sacra Parallela* florilegion and the Milan Gregory.[36] The immediacy of the image–text dialogue in the Khludov Psalter has been lost in the inherently more reflective miniatures of Paris.gr.510. As we have seen throughout this book, the visual arguments of the Homilies miniatures relied more on antithesis, alignment, and metaphor than on conflict and debate. These structures depended upon combinations of scenes, and meaningful juxtaposition of scenes more or less demanded the full-page format that we find in Paris.gr.510. Whether the synthetic argument developed in the Homilies was a consequence of the full-page format selected, or whether that format was chosen with this model of visual argument in mind, is a moot point. The important issue here is that the difference between the physical relationship of image and text in the Khludov Psalter and the Paris Homilies is paralleled by a difference in the structure of the visual argument in each book.

In contrast with the Psalter, the miniatures of Paris.gr.510 distance themselves from words in another way as well. While one of the most striking features of the Khludov Psalter is its incorporation of inscriptions that help the viewer interpret the pictures ('this image means . . .' or 'David says that . . . ' [see fig. 110]), the inscriptions within the Homilies miniatures are, normally, laconic and purely descriptive. Even the titles written in red on the gold frames of the miniatures only twice go beyond simple identification: the heading to Habakkuk's vision (f. 285r; fig. 29) was taken from the opening words of Gregory's sermon; that introducing the mission of the Apostles (f. 426v; fig. 42) supplies a quotation from Matthew 28:19. Of the 205 narrative scenes preserved in Paris.gr.510, a mere nine

---

[33] Ibid., esp. 108–111.   [34] Ibid.   [35] Ibid.   [36] See chapter 1.

retain inscriptions that go beyond naming the characters or identifying the scene, and even these nine differ from the interpretative inscriptions of the Khludov Psalter.

Two of the inscriptions that go beyond simple identification are quotations from the bible spoken by the protagonist of the image that signal a liminal moment in her or his life: Gorgonia's recitation of a psalm verse at her death (f. 43v; fig. 9) and Gregory's father recounting the psalm verse that he heard in a dream to his wife (f. 87v; fig. 16) are both recorded in the inscriptions. The rest of the inscriptions that transcribe spoken words document conversations not recorded in Gregory's sermons. Twice we are given a genuine exchange: Nathan's with David (f. 143v; fig. 19), and Joshua's with the archangel (f. 226v; fig. 26). Otherwise, the conversations are one-sided: the inscriptions quote Christ's dying words to Mary and John (f. 30v; fig. 7), Isaiah's order to Hezekiah (f. 435v; fig. 43), God's command to Moses (f. 264v; fig. 28), Christ's question of Saul (also f. 264v), and, against the Septuagint, Ezekiel's of God (f. 438v; fig. 44). Five of these conversations were inscribed to make specific points, but these points were not, as in the Khludov Psalter, about the proper interpretation of the image. Christ's words to Mary and John fit within the larger theme of family ties in Paris.gr.510; Joshua's conversation with the archangel, Ezekiel's question to God, God's words to Moses, and Christ's to Saul were all elements in another leitmotif of the Homilies, the importance of human/divine interaction. The remaining conversations – that between Nathan and David and Isaiah's words to Hezekiah – correspond with a third subplot of the manuscript: the proper relationship between a ruler and his spiritual advisor. I shall return to this theme shortly; for now, it suffices to note that all of the conversation inscriptions in Paris.gr.510 follow the same pattern. Their primary strategy is not to authorize a particular interpretation of the image, but rather to contextualize it.[37]

The differences in the relationship between image and text in the Homilies and the Khludov Psalter are essentially structural. The Psalter miniaturists, on the whole, favoured a direct approach; the ninth-century modifications of, and additions to, the traditional core of psalter illustration introduced a new format that physically juxtaposed text and commentary miniatures, and added images that individually interacted with the adjacent text passages. The Khludov Psalter demonstrates that the importance of the visual, and the particular ways that the visual communicated with a certain segment of ninth-century Byzantine society, did not mean that words were rendered obsolete. The one-to-one approach characteristic of the Khludov Psalter, however, is not what we find in Paris.gr.510, where the visual polemic of the Psalter was normally abandoned as a visual strategy; it was instead internalized, and re-emerged as visual exegesis. Rather than inserting contemporary debates bodily into images of the past, as we find in the Psalter

---

[37] The material in this paragraph was developed more fully in Brubaker (1996b).

images, the Homilies miniatures tend to recast the past into a metaphor of contemporary life.

The past that we are talking about here is a past still essentially dependent on text: the miniatures of Paris.gr.510 re-frame, after all, Gregory's sermons. To understand what the images meant in the ninth century, too, we must rely heavily on information conveyed by words. But it is important to recognize not only the impact of the words on the images, but the impact of the images on the words. For once images have attached themselves to a narrative, they change the way an audience interprets the story. *The Tale of Peter Rabbit* is a text familiar to most middle-class American and English children, and can be understood perfectly well as a written narrative; once seen, however, Beatrix Potter's illustrations of Peter Rabbit become inextricably interwoven with our understanding of the account. To Anglo-Americans who were brought up on the book even the name 'Peter Rabbit' immediately conjures up a mental image of a bunny in a blue jacket. Images can indelibly recontextualize what is written.

In Paris.gr.510, however, images do more than recontextualize: many of them are almost independent commentaries on subjects only nominally linked to the topic of the sermon that they accompany. While no text miniature is ever entirely divorced from Gregory's words,[38] there are miniatures in the Homilies that develop messages of relevance to the ninth-century audience of the manuscript from a single phrase in the adjacent sermon. Though the relevant phrases are almost always marked with initials or marginal signs, unlike the Khludov Psalter Paris.gr.510 offers no inscriptions to explain that 'this means that . . .'.

The process of recontextualization and the creation of new meaning through quasi-autonomous commentary have been followed through the course of this book. We have seen, too, that the participating audience was limited. Paris.gr.510 was not a public monument: it was a manuscript for the private use of a restricted group, and many of the messages it conveyed were personal ones. Indeed, to return to the point at which we started this chapter, the audience to whom Paris.gr.510 was directed sometimes seems to have consisted only of two men, the Emperor Basil I and the patriarch Photios. Robin Cormack has argued that information about the personality of a patron is of questionable value,[39] and while I would agree that Photios and Basil acted from within a particular social and intellectual framework, I would also argue that if we did not know to whom Paris.gr.510 was given, and if we could not establish beyond reasonable doubt by whom it was commissioned, our understanding of the Paris Homilies would be flawed: the individual predilections and agendas of Basil and Photios are crucially involved in the meaning of Paris.gr.510. Their particular self-interests stamp the manuscript, and it is to the working out of those self-interests that we shall now turn.

---

[38] Though, as noted earlier, f. 435v remains enigmatic.   [39] Cormack (1986b), esp. 617–618.

PHOTIOS AND BASIL

The relationship between the images of Paris.gr.510 and the text that they accompany was ignored or denied by the earliest commentators precisely because, as we have known since Sirarpie Der Nersessian published her seminal article in 1962, it is a complex relationship. Following ground broken by André Grabar in 1957, Der Nersessian's conclusions changed the face of Byzantine art-historical scholarship: she demonstrated, for miniature after miniature, that the images in Paris.gr.510 often functioned as visual commentary rather than as illustration. This type of relationship presupposes an extremely close reading of Gregory's sermons, and Der Nersessian's assumption has been borne out in this study. But while the messages communicated by the miniatures of Paris.gr.510 are complex, they are also focused. The Homilies was not created for public consumption, and the issues resolved in the miniatures of Paris.gr.510 were largely self-imposed: Photios used Gregory's anti-heretical sermons as a platform from which to harangue his own demons; he manipulated Gregory's panegyrics into flattery directed at Basil I. We have already examined how this was done in chapters 4 and 5; here I should like to look at some of the broader implications, and consider the fundamental question of why Photios commissioned a copy of Gregory's sermons as a gift for Basil I.

We may dismiss Basil's own interests as a motive. Even the eulogizing *Vita Basilii* admits that Basil did not have 'commerce with letters',[40] and we certainly have no indication that he had any interest in the sermons of Gregory of Nazianzus. Byzantine emperors, in any event, followed Roman precedent and achieved renown through public (architectural) patronage rather than through any occasional commissions of books that few would have seen: Basil perpetuated this model.[41] Paris.gr.510 incorporated imperial ideology, but it was not first and foremost an imperial statement.

The personalized messages of Paris.gr.510 indicate, instead, a manuscript designed for Basil by Photios – the one person, as we saw in chapter 5, who had the knowlege to create them, the resources to afford to express them in such a luxurious format, the reason to present such a sequence to the emperor, and the access to that emperor to explain them. Margaret Mullett has described how letter bearers conveyed personalized messages along with the letters that they carried; and she has noted that these verbal messages were intended to contextualize the words for the recipient of the letter.[42] I would speculate that this pattern was followed as well when Photios presented the book we now know as Paris.gr.510 to Basil and his family.

[40] *Vita Basilii* 89: ed. Bekker (1838), 333–334; see chapter 4 note 47. See also Magdalino (1996), 27–28.

[41] On the building campaigns, *Vita Basilii* 76–94: ed. Bekker (1838), 319–341; see chapter 4 note 47.

[42] Mullett (1990).

But I would also suggest that it was not just flattery that underpinned Photios' presentation. For one theme that runs throughout the miniatures is the proper behaviour of rulers, and in particular the wisdom of rulers who follow the counsel of their religious advisors. The balance of power between church and state was, as is well known, a favourite theme of the patriarch Photios;[43] and as we have seen it works itself out in the miniatures of Paris.gr.510 with some regularity. Here I would only note two instances mentioned earlier in this chapter but not yet fully considered. These return us to the anomalous inscriptions that record conversations, in this case that between Nathan and David (f. 143v; fig. 19), and the one-sided remarks of Isaiah to Hezekiah (f. 435v; fig. 43).

The first of these has David claiming 'I have sinned against the Lord' (HMAP-TIKA TΩ K[YPI]Ω) to Nathan's response 'and the Lord has put away thy sin' (KAI K[YPIO]C AΦHΛE[N] TO AMAPTHMA COY); the second reads 'Isaiah said to Hezekiah, Give orders concerning thy house' (HCIAC ΛEΓΩN TΩ EZEKIA · TAΞE ΠEPI TOY OIKOY COY). Both provide biblical precedents for the authority of spiritual advisors over their rulers after those rulers had sinned. Historical precedent, as we saw in chapter 5, was one of Photios' preferred means of dealing with contemporary situations; these two instances of a religious leader demonstrating his authority over a ruler cannot, given the rarity of such extensive inscriptions in Paris.gr.510 and Photios' predilection for historical precedent, be ignored. Nor can the fact that both religious leaders deal with rulers who have sinned: Nathan pardons David; Isaiah tells Hezekiah how to redeem himself. Photios was patriarch under the joint rule of Michael III and Basil, and thus headed the church when Basil murdered Michael; he was deposed immediately after the murder, for reasons no one has properly explained, to be reinstated only a few years later. Whatever the reasons for Photios' temporary exile, he had to propitiate Basil I in order to restore his own position, and once he had done so, he could balance that precarious position against the undeniable advantage of moral superiority. The flattery is obvious in Paris.gr.510, but on ff. 143v and 435v the other side of Photios' relationship with Basil seems to come out as well.[44]

Why Photios selected Gregory's sermons as a vehicle for his various messages is an unanswerable question. Perhaps in part because he was the first patriarch since 843 who had never had connections with iconoclasts, Photios linked himself with the iconophile cause throughout his career.[45] It is possible that his commission of the Homilies forms a part of this chain, for Gregory was often cited in iconophile polemic, and seems especially to have been favoured by Theodore of Stoudion.[46] But Gregory and Basil of Caesarea were the patristic fathers most often quoted by Byzantines of all periods; it may simply have been Gregory's undisputed orthodoxy

---

[43] See the discussion of the *Eisagoge* in chapter 4.   [44] See further Brubaker (1996b), 105–109.

[45] I thank Patricia Karlin-Hayter for this point; see also Mango (1977b) and Thümmel (1983).

[46] See Dvornik (1933), 33–34.

– augmented by the iconophile tendencies with which he was credited in the eighth and ninth centuries – that recommended his sermons to Photios. The sermons' consistent attacks on heresy can, given Photios' own agenda, only have been an advantage. Certainly, Photios admired Gregory: he commented upon and paraphrased his works more often than any of the church fathers save John Chrysostom;[47] he may have written a praise-text in his honour;[48] and the fact that Leo VI modelled his eulogy to Basil I on Gregory's funeral oration for St Basil suggests that he was taught from Gregory by his tutor Photios.[49] It has also to be remembered that Paris.gr.510 was apparently not originally meant to have illustrations.[50] At its initial (unillustrated) conception, it would have anticipated the large, elegantly written and unillustrated editions commissioned by Arethas – possibly Photios' student – a generation later.[51] In that form, the manuscript may not even have been destined for the emperor: the choice of Gregory's Homilies for the weighted miniatures that they now accompany could be in part fortuitous. What prompted the decision to include miniatures is irretrievable: we can speculate that the text from which Paris.gr.510 was adapted contained pictures and inspired the thought of an illustrated book;[52] we can speculate that Photios had succeeded in pleasing Basil with an earlier illustrated book and believed that another and even more luxurious one would have the same effect;[53] we can even speculate that Paris.gr.510 was directed to Photios' pupil Leo as well as to Leo's father Basil. We can speculate any number of things, but in the end it may not matter so much which text Photios ultimately gave; the significant point is that he chose to commission a text, large and sumptuously illustrated, for the emperor and his family. With something as big and costly as Paris.gr.510 in his hand as a prompt for exegesis or commentary, Photios may have reasoned that his didactic duty to the imperial family was in hand.

PARIS.GR.510: A REPRISE

Paris.gr.510 was a luxury manuscript that advertised its status in overt ways. The size, the use of archaic and expensive uncial, the decorated initials and gilded marginal signs, the full-page and boldly coloured miniatures, all speak to the consciously sumptuous quality of the manuscript. What one might call the self-consciousness of the manuscript extends to its introduction of painted letters, which link text and image as well as embellishing the pages of the book; to its use of pictures to supplement and comment on the text in ways of particular relevance to

[47] For a list of the citations of Gregory in Photios' letters and the *Amphilochia*, see ed. Westerink VI,2 (1988), 17–18; for Chrysostom, ibid., 15–16.   [48] Dvornik (1933), 33–34.   [49] Adontz (1933b).
[50] See Introduction.   [51] See e.g. Wilson (1983), 120–130.   [52] See Introduction.
[53] See chapters 4 and 5.

its circumscribed audience; to its manipulation of the compositions and details of individual miniatures to underscore the interpretive role those images played; and to the autonomous exegesis that many of the miniatures ultimately develop.

The consistency with which Paris.gr.510 fulfils its goals implies the careful coordination of three distinct groups of workers: the scribes, the illuminators, and the miniaturists. This indicates that one person supervised the production of the book. We can identify the person who did with virtual certainty: the patron of Paris.gr.510 was the patriarch Photios. The particular concerns of his career or his personal interests inform many pictures in the book; and while Photios' patriarchal and personal preoccupations may have been shared by others in his immediate circle, only he had both the access to the resources necessary to produce Paris.gr.510 and the need to marshal these resources to commission a gift of this sort for Basil I.[54]

For all of its peculiarities, Paris.gr.510 nonetheless was a product of its time, and fits within its late ninth-century context. Images that supplement the accompanying text appear in other manuscripts of the period, notably the Khludov Psalter and the *Sacra Parallela*. While neither of these manuscripts contains miniatures as autonomous and self-sufficient as those in Paris.gr.510, both use pictures as more than simple illustrations. In the Psalter, inscriptions often tell us precisely how the marginal images function as interpretations of the text, while in the *Sacra Parallela* the miniatures either extend the narrative by picturing scenes not specifically described in the florilegion text or authenticate the accuracy of the quotations copied in it.[55] While Paris.gr.510 expands the role of miniatures expressed in both of these manuscripts by liberating its pictures from the confines of the text margins and by omitting explanatory captions so that images carry the whole weight of interpretation, the fundamental relationship between the Paris Homilies and these ninth-century books is clear.

Conceptually, formally, and iconographically, Paris.gr.510 fits within a well-defined cultural structure. Even its sumptuousness conforms with prescriptions that art be 'made from the purest and most splendid material'.[56] From within this structure, and in part because of it, Photios' voice nonetheless speaks to us in the miniatures of Paris.gr.510. The language is ninth-century Constantinopolitan, but the dialect remains isolated and distinct. The miniaturists communicate to us too, but less clearly, for they lack the benefit of subsidiary texts to amplify their messages to a modern scholarly public more used to reading beneath the surface of texts than to seeing beneath the surface of images. All the same, whether or not we yet have the tools to see through images with the same confidence that literary critics can unpick texts, it seems to me clear that the miniatures in Paris.gr.510 tell us one very important thing: not just that images can communicate differently from words,

[54] On the benefits of art as an élite gift, see Cormack (1992), esp. 228–230. [55] See chapter 1.
[56] Nikephoros, *Logos*, 772; see Travis (1984), 37, for commentary.

but that the people involved in the Paris Homilies knew and believed that images could and should do this. Images in the Paris Homilies were not substitutes for words; they were chosen instead of words and they insist on that separation by their format and by their nearly unanimous lack of explanatory captions. The miniatures of Paris.gr.510 do not provide a pictorial supplement to written exegesis, as the images in the marginal psalters normally do; they *are* visual exegesis, and that is a different thing.[57] Though there are times when the miniatures parallel written interpretations closely, there are more examples that, while operating from within the same frame of reference as contemporary written words, communicate ideas not expressed in extant texts. In Paris.gr.510, the miniaturists convey messages primarily through manipulating the composition of the page and through the juxtaposition of scenes; they weave independent threads of interpretation (often but not always paralleled in written form) together to create new meaning that co-existed with, but was in important ways independent of, the texts with which their visions were bound.

[57] Cf. Kessler (1991/2), 57; Zambouli (1995), 87.

APPENDIX A

Inventory of the miniatures

The following inventory lists the forty-six miniatures in the order that they now appear in Paris.gr.510 and briefly identifies the subject matter of each picture. When a page is composed of more than one register, these have been indicated by small letters (a to e); when a single sequence extends over more than one register, the small letters are separated by a dash: the a–b following f. 52v below, for example, means that the creation and fall narrative fills the first two registers. Standard biblical and literary references have been incorporated; citations in Gregory's sermons appear in the discussions of the relationship between text and image for each miniature. A list of the textual references for the scenes appears in Appendix B.

1	Av		Christ enthroned
2	Br		Empress Eudokia flanked by Leo and Alexander
3	Bv		Cross
4	Cr		Cross
5	Cv		Emperor Basil I flanked by Elijah and Gabriel
6	3r	a	Annunciation and visitation, 2 scenes (Luke 1:26–45; see also the Protevangelion)
		b	Jonah sequence, 5 scenes (Jonah 1:1–4:6)
7	30v	a	Crucifixion (Matthew 27:33–56, Mark 15:22–41, Luke 23:33–49, John 19:18–34; see also the Acts of Pilate)
		b	Deposition and entombment, 2 scenes (John 19:38–42; see also Matthew 27:57–60, Mark 15:42–46, Luke 23:50–53)
		c	Chairete (Matthew 28:9–10)
8	32v	a–d	Martyrdom of the apostles, 12 scenes (Acts 12:2; Acts of Andrew, John, Paul, Peter, Thomas etc.)
9	43v	a	Gregory and his family
		b	Funeral of Gregory's brother, Kaisarios
		c	Death of Gregory's sister, Gorgonia
10	52v	a–b	Creation and expulsion sequence, 8 scenes (Genesis 1:26–3:25; see also the *Vitae Adae et Evae*)

417

		b	Healing of the centurion's servant (Matthew 8:5–13)
			Healing of Peter's mother-in-law (Matthew 8:14–15, Mark 1:30–31)
		c	Christ walks on water (Matthew 14:25–31)
23	174v	a	Sacrifice of Isaac, 2 scenes (Genesis 22:5–13)
		b	Jacob's struggle with the angel (Genesis 32:24–30)
			Jacob's dream (Genesis 28:10–15)
		c	Anointing of David (1 Kings 16:3–13)
24	196v	a	Raising of Lazarus (John 11:1–44)
			Supper at Simon's (John 12:1–8; see also Matthew 26:6–13, Mark 14:3–9, Luke 7:36–50)
		b	Entry into Jerusalem (Matthew 21:1–9, Mark 11:1–10, Luke 19:29–38, John 12:12–15)
25	215v	a	Judgment of Solomon (3 Kings 3:16–27)
		b	Conversion of the Samaritan woman (John 4:5–26)
			Healing of the ten lepers (Luke 17:11–19)
26	226v	a	Moses strikes water from a rock (Exodus 17:1–7)
		b	Joshua stops the sun and moon (Joshua 10:12–14)
			Joshua meets the angel (Joshua 5:13–15)
27	239r	a	Gregory and the Emperor Theodosios
		b	Gregory leaves Constantinople
28	264v	a	Moses and the burning bush (Exodus 3:1–5)
			Conversion of Saul (Acts 9:3–5)
			Ascension of Elijah (4 Kings 2:11–13)
		b	Crossing of the Red Sea with the dance of Miriam (Exodus 14:21–31, 15:20–21)
29	285r		Vision of Habakkuk
30	301r		Pentecost (Acts 2:1–13)
31	310v	a	Healing of the man with the withered arm (Matthew 12:10–13, Mark 3:1–5, Luke 6:6–10)
			Healing of the two men born blind (Matthew 20:30–34)
		b	Healing of the bent woman (Luke 13:11–16)
			Parable of the withered fig tree (Matthew 21:18–21, Mark 11:12–14, 20–25)
32	316r	a	Healing of the blind man at Siloam (John 9)
			Parable of the widow's mite (Mark 12:41–44, Luke 21:1–4)
		b	Healing of the paralytic at Capernaum (Matthew 9:1–8, Mark 2:3–12, Luke 5:17–26)
			Raising of the widow's son at Nain (Luke 7:11–16)
33	332v	a–b	Life of Cyprian, 5 scenes (see Eudokia Augusta's *vita* of Cyprian)
34	340r	a–c	Martyrdom of the Makkabees, 9 scenes (4 Makkabees)
35	347v	a–b	Samson sequence, 5 scenes (Judges 15:15–16:30)

		c	Gideon and the fleece (Judges 6:36–40)
			Martyrdom of Isaiah (see Martyrdom of Isaiah)
36	355r		Council of 381
37	360r	a	Tower of Babel (Genesis 11:1–9)
		b	Noah's ark (Genesis 8:6–11)
38	367v	a–c	History of the Arians
39	374v	a–c	History of Julian the Apostate, part I
40	409v	a–c	History of Julian the Apostate, part II (see Pseudo-Amphilochios' *vita* of Basil)
41	424v	a	Fall of Jericho (Joshua 6)
		b	Israelites' victory over the Amalekites (Exodus 17:8–13)
		c	Gregory writing
42	426v	a–d	Mission of the apostles, 13 scenes (Matthew 28:19)
43	435v	a	Daniel in the lions' den (Daniel 14:31–39)
			Three Hebrews in the furnace (Daniel 3:26–88)
		b	Manasses (see 4 Kings 21:1–18, 2 Chronicles 33:1–20, 2 Baruch)
			Isaiah and Hezekiah (Isaiah 38:1–3)
44	438v		Ezekiel in the valley of the dry bones, 2 scenes (Ezekiel 37:1–14)
45	440r	a–c	History of Constantine and Helena, 3 scenes (*vita* of Constantine)
46	452r	a–c	Life of Gregory of Nazianzus, 4 scenes (Gregory the Presbyter, *vita* of Gregory of Nazianzus)

APPENDIX B

Textual references for the scenes in Paris.gr.510

Sequences confined to a single miniature are here listed as a unit, with the inclusive text cited; the number of individual scenes incorporated is indicated by the numbering on the far left. The first line below, for example, refers to an eight-scene sequence that illustrates events narrated between Genesis 1:26 and 3:25. A more fastidious break-down, linking particular verses with specific scenes, is not always possible in Paris.gr.510; when such precision is feasible, references appear in the discussion of individual miniatures. Supplementary texts follow the main biblical citation, and the synoptic gospel accounts have been grouped together as appropriate.

OLD TESTAMENT

1–8	Genesis 1:26–3:25; creation and expulsion sequence (f. 52v)
	See also the *Vitae Adae et Evae*
9	Genesis 8:6–11; Noah's ark (f. 360r)
10	Genesis 11:1–9; tower of Babel (f. 360r)
11–12	Genesis 22:5–13; sacrifice of Isaac (f. 174v)
13	Genesis 28:10–15; Jacob's dream (f. 174v)
14	Genesis 32:24–30; Jacob's struggle with the angel (f. 174v)
15–28	Genesis 37:13–41:43; Joseph sequence (f. 69v)
29	Exodus 3:1–5; Moses and the burning bush (f. 264v)
30	Exodus 14:21–31, 15:20–21; crossing of the Red Sea with the dance of Miriam (f. 264v)
31	Exodus 17:1–7; Moses strikes water from a rock (f. 226v)
32	Exodus 17:8–13; Israelites' victory over the Amalekites (f. 424v)
33	Exodus 34:4–5; Moses receives the laws (f. 52v)
34	Joshua 5:13–15; Joshua meets the angel (f. 226v)
35	Joshua 6; fall of Jericho (f. 424v)
36	Joshua 10:12–14; Joshua stops the sun and moon (f. 226v)

37	Judges 6:36–40; Gideon and the fleece (f. 347v)
38–42	Judges 15:15–16:30; Samson sequence (f. 347v)
43	1 Kings 16:3–13; anointing of David (f. 174v)
44	2 Kings 12; penitence of David (f. 143v)
	See also Psalm 51 and the *Palaia historica*
45	3 Kings 3:16–27; judgment of Solomon (f. 215v)
46	4 Kings 2:11–13; ascension of Elijah (f. 264v)
47	Job 2; Job on his dungheap (f. 71v)
48	Isaiah 6:1–7; vision of Isaiah (f. 67v)
49	Isaiah 38:1–3; Isaiah and Hezekiah (f. 435v)
	For the martyrdom of Isaiah, see scene 151 below.
50	Jeremiah 38:7–13; Jeremiah raised from the pit (f. 143v)
51–52	Ezekiel 37:1–14; Ezekiel in the valley of the dry bones (f. 438v)
53	Daniel 3:26–88; three Hebrews in the furnace (f. 435v)
54	Daniel 14:31–39; Daniel in the lions' den (f. 435v)
55–59	Jonah 1:1–4:6; Jonah sequence (f. 3r)

NEW TESTAMENT

60	Matthew 2:1–11; adoration of the Magi (f. 137r)
61	Matthew 2:12; dream of the Magi (f. 137r)
62	Matthew 2:26; massacre of the innocents (f. 137r)
63–65	Matthew 4:1–11; temptation of Christ (f. 165r)
66	Matthew 4:18–22; calling of Peter, Andrew, James, John (f. 87v)
67	Matthew 8:2–4, Mark 1:40–44, Luke 5:12–14; healing of the leper (f. 170r)
68	Matthew 8:5–13, Luke 7:2–10; healing of the centurion's servant (f. 170r)
69	Matthew 8:14–15, Mark 1:30–31; healing of Peter's mother-in-law (f. 170r)
70	Matthew 8:28–32; healing of the demoniacs (f. 170r)
71	Matthew 9:1–8, Mark 2:3–12, Luke 5:17–26 healing of the paralytic at Capernaum (f. 316r)
72–73	Matthew 9:9, Mark 2:14, Luke 5:27–28; calling of Matthew (f. 87v)
74–75	Matthew 9:18–26, Mark 5:22–43, Luke 8:41–56; healing of the woman with the issue of blood; raising of Jairus' daughter (f. 143v)
76	Matthew 12:10–13, Mark 3:1–5, Luke 6:6–10; healing of the man with the withered arm (f. 310v)
77	Matthew 14:13–21, Mark 6:31–44, Luke 9:10–17, John 6:1–13; multiplication of the loaves and fishes (f. 165r)
78	Matthew 14:25–31; Christ walks on water (f. 170r)
79	Matthew 17:1–10, Mark 9:2–9, Luke 9:28–32; transfiguration (f. 75r)

80	Matthew 19:16–22, Mark 10:17–22; Christ and the rich youth (f. 87v)
81	Matthew 20:30–34; healing of the two men born blind (f. 310v)
82	Matthew 21:1–9, Mark 11:1–10, Luke 19:29–38, John 12:12–15; entry into Jerusalem (f. 196v)
83	Matthew 21:18–21, Mark 11:12–14, 20–25; parable of the withered fig tree (f. 310v)
84	Matthew 27:33–56, Mark 15:22–41, Luke 23:33–49, John 19:18–34; crucifixion (f. 30v) See also the Acts of Pilate
85	Matthew 28:9–10; chairete (f. 30v)
86–98	Matthew 28:19; mission of the apostles (f. 426v)
99	Mark 12:41–44, Luke 21:1–4; parable of the widow's mite (f. 316r)
100	Luke 1:26–38; annunciation (f. 3r) See also the Protevangelion
101	Luke 1:40–45; visitation (f. 3r)
102	Luke 2:25–35; presentation (f. 137r)
103–105	Luke 2:41–49; Christ among the doctors (f. 165r)
106	Luke 7:11–16; raising of the widow's son at Nain (f. 316r)
107–110	Luke 10:30–37; parable of the Good Samaritan (f. 143v)
111	Luke 13:11–16; healing of the bent woman (f. 310v)
112	Luke 14:2–4; healing of the man with dropsy (f. 170r)
113–117	Luke 16:19–31; Dives and Lazarus (f. 149r)
118	Luke 17:11–19; healing of the ten lepers (f. 215v)
119	Luke 19:1–5; Christ and Zachias (f. 87v)
120	John 1:44–49; conversion of Nathanael (f. 87v)
121	John 4:5–26; conversion of the Samaritan woman (f. 215v)
122	John 5:2–15; healing of the paralytic at Bethesda (f. 143v)
123	John 9; healing of the blind man at Siloam (f. 316r)
124	John 11:1–44; raising of Lazarus (f. 196v)
125	John 12:1–8 (Matthew 26:6–13, Mark 14:3–9, Luke 7:36–50); supper at Simon's (f. 196v)
126–127	John 19:38–42 (Matthew 27:57–60, Mark 15:42–46, Luke 23:50–53); deposition and entombment (f. 30v)
128	Acts 2:1–13; Pentecost (f. 301r)
129	Acts 9:3–5; conversion of Saul (f. 264v)
130	Acts 12:2; martyrdom of James (f. 32v)

APOCRYPHAL BOOKS

| 131–141 | Acts of Andrew, John, Paul, Peter, Thomas etc.; martyrdom of the apostles (f. 32v) |

142–150   4 Makkabees; martyrdom of the Makkabees (f. 340r)

151   Martyrdom of Isaiah; martyrdom of Isaiah (f. 347v)

152–153   Protevangelion; the flight of Elizabeth and John the Baptist; the martyrdom of Zacharias (f. 137r)

OTHER TEXTS

154–196   Gregory of Nazianzus, Homilies; various scenes (ff. 43v, 52v, 67v, 71v, 78r, 87v, 104r, 149r, 239r, 285r, 332v, 367v, 374v, 409v, 424v)
See also Eudokia Augusta's *vita* of Cyprian for f. 332v; and Pseudo-Amphilochios' *vita* of Basil for f. 409v

197–200   Gregory the Presbyter, Life of Gregory of Nazianzus; life of Gregory of Nazianzus (f. 452r)
See also Gregory of Nazianzus' autobiographical writings

201–204   *Vita* of Constantine; Constantine's dream and victory at the Milvian bridge; Helena's discovery of the cross (f. 440r)

SCENES WITHOUT A TEXTUAL REFERENCE

205   Penitence of Manasses (f. 435v)
See 4 Kings 21:1–18, 2 Chronicles 33:1–20, 2 Baruch

206   Council of 381 (f. 355r)
See also the Acts of this council

207–211   Frontispiece sequence (ff. Av, Br, Bv, Cr, Cv)

APPENDIX C

Quire diagrams

Greek number below each gathering = quire signature
no parentheses or brackets = a signature in the original ninth-century hand
(parentheses) = a Palaiologan signature
[brackets] = a hypothetical signature
E.g. quire K (20) retains its original signature and displays a later one as well; quire MA (41) shows no signature.

Arabic numbers = total number of enlarged initials on the page
Most are gold; if a second number appears below the first it indicates how many of the initials on that page were painted rather than gilded.
E.g. on f. 5r there are five initials, four gold and one painted.

H = headpiece
These are numbered; the surviving numbers are enclosed in (parentheses) immediately below the H; [brackets] indicate that the number no longer survives. Compare ff. 1r and 33r.

C = colophon (see f. 2v)

M = miniature (see f. 3r)

ø = blank page (see f. Ar)

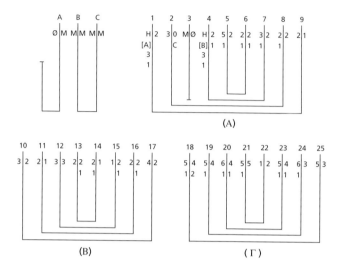

f. Av	Miniature: Christ enthroned
ff. B–C	Reversed bifolium (correct order = Cr, Cv, Br, Bv)
f. Br	Miniature: Empress Eudokia, Leo, Alexander
f. Bv	Miniature: cross
f. Cr	Miniature: cross
f. Cv	Miniature: Emperor Basil I, Elijah, Gabriel
f. 1r	'On Easter' (Homily 1)
f. 3r	Miniature: annunciation; visitation; history of Jonah
f. 4r	'Apology' (Homily 2)

Quire diagrams

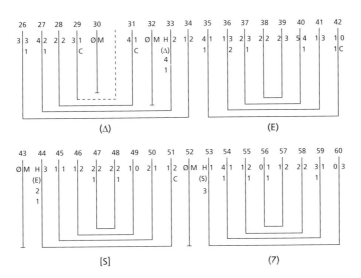

f. 30v   Miniature: crucifixion; deposition; entombment; chairete

f. 31r   'To those who had invited him' (Homily 3). The first five paragraphs (=
          SC 247, 242–248 line 4) are missing; with headpiece 3 (Γ) the lost text
          originally occupied a folio between ff. 30 and 31

f. 32v   Miniature: martyrdom of the apostles

f. 33r   'Funeral oration on Kaisarios' (Homily 7)

f. 43v   Miniature: Gregory of Nazianzus and his family; funeral of Kaisarios;
          death of Gorgonia

f. 44r   'Funeral oration on Gorgonia' (Homily 8)

f. 52r   Later quire signature Z

f. 52v   Miniature: history of Adam and Eve; Moses receiving the laws; Gregory
          and his father with the Nazianzus religious community

f. 53r   'On Peace' I (Homily 6)

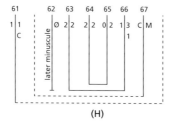

(H)

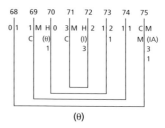

(θ)

f. 61r	Small crosses (in ink of text) in upper lateral margins
f. 62	Replacement leaf, s.xiv-xv, with beginning of 'On Peace' II (Homily 23). The replaced text (SC 270, 280–282 line 13), with headpiece 7 (Z), would originally have occupied one side of the folio only.
f. 67v	Miniature: vision of Isaiah; Gregory's consecration as bishop of Sasima
f. 68r	'Apology to his father' (Homily 9). The beginning of the text (SC 405, 300–306 line 5) is lost; with headpiece 8 (H), it originally occupied a folio between ff. 67 and 68.
f. 69v	Miniature: life of Joseph
f. 70r	'Apology after his flight' (Homily 10)
f. 71v	Miniature: Basil, Gregory of Nyssa, Gregory of Nazianzus; Job on the dungheap
f. 72r	'To Gregory of Nyssa' (Homily 11)
f. 75r	Miniature: transfiguration
f. 75v	'To his father' (Homily 12)

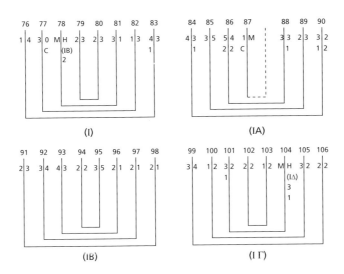

(I)

(IA)

(IB)

(IΓ)

f. 78r	Miniature: hailstorm; Gregory preaching
f. 78v	'On the plague of hail' (Homily 16)
f. 81	Outer margin excised
f. 87v	Miniature: conversion of Peter, Andrew, James, and John; Christ and Zachias; conversion of Matthew; Christ and the rich youth; conversion of Nathanael; conversion of Gregory's father
f. 88r	'Funeral oration on his father' (Homily 18). The beginning of the text is lost (*PG* 35:985–989A6); with headpiece 13 (IΓ), it originally occupied a folio between ff. 87 and 88.
f. 104r	Miniature: life of Basil
f. 104v	'Funeral oration on Basil' (Homily 43)

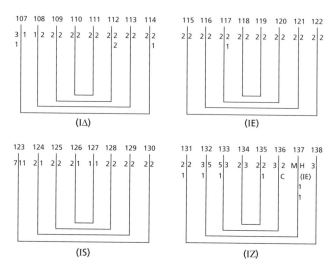

f. 137r   Miniature: adoration of the Magi; massacre of the innocents; presentation

f. 137v   'To Julian the tax-collector' (Homily 19)

f. 138   Outer margin excised

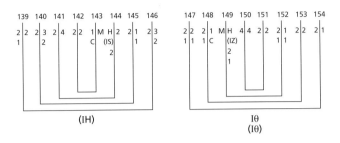

(IH)

Iθ
(Iθ)

---

f. 143v Miniature: Jeremiah released from the pit; penitence of David; parable of the good Samaritan; Christ healing the paralytic and Jairus' daughter

f. 144r 'To the people of Nazianzus and the prefect' (Homily 17). Headpiece 15 (IE) is excised.

f. 144v Text on reverse of excised headpiece (*PG* 35:968A3–8) missing

f. 149r Miniature: Gregory and Basil in Basil's hospital; parable of Dives and Lazarus

f. 149v 'On the love of the poor' (Homily 14)

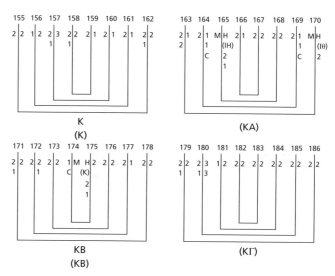

f. 155r   Original quire signature K preserved but overwritten

f. 158   Outer margin excised

f. 163r   Base of original quire signature KA preserved

f. 165r   Miniature: Christ among the doctors; temptation of Christ; miracle of the loaves

f. 165v   'On dogma' (Homily 20)

f. 170r   Miniature: Christ healing the leper, the man with dropsy and two demoniacs; Christ healing the centurion's servant and Peter's mother-in-law; Christ walks on water

f. 170v   'Against Eunomios' (Homily 27)

f. 171r   Original quire signature KB preserved but overwritten

f. 174v   Miniature: sacrifice of Isaac; Jacob's vision; anointing of David

f. 175r   'On theology' (Homily 28)

f. 179r   Base of original quire signature KΓ preserved

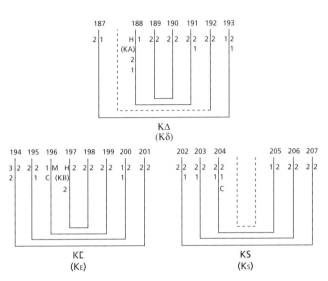

f. 187r   Original quire signature KΔ preserved but overwritten

f. 187v   Text terminates in the middle of the last paragraph of the homily (at SC 250, 172 line 25). The lost text originally occupied the recto of a folio between ff. 187 and 188.

f. 188r   'On the Son' I (Homily 29)

f. 194r   Original quire signature KE preserved but overwritten

f. 196v   Miniature: raising of Lazarus; supper at the house of Simon; entry into Jerusalem

f. 197r   'On the Son' II (Homily 30)

f. 201   Outer margin excised

f. 202r   Original quire signature KS preserved but overwritten

f. 205r   'On the Holy Spirit' (Homily 31). The first five and a half paragraphs of text are lost (SC 250, 276–286 line 10); with headpiece 23 (KΓ), the lost text originally occupied three sides of a bifolium between ff. 204 and 205. The fourth side (originally facing f. 205r) was not needed for text.

433

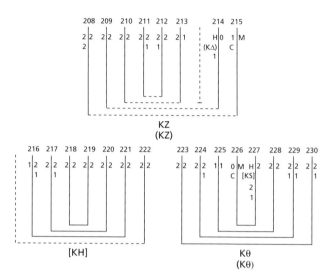

KZ
(KZ)

[KH]

Kθ
(Kθ)

ff. 208–215 Quire 27 apparently originally contained nine leaves, the exact disposition of which is unclear.

f. 208r   Original quire signature KZ preserved but overwritten

f. 213v   Text terminates near the beginning of the last paragraph of the homily (SC 250, 340 line 19); the remaining text originally occupied the recto of a folio between ff. 213 and 214 (the stub is visible).

f. 214r   'On virginity' (poem)

f. 215v   Miniature: judgment of Solomon; Christ and the Samaritan woman; Christ healing the lepers

f. 216r   'On moderation' (Homily 32). The folio opens with the last word of the third paragraph; with headpiece 25 (KE), the lost text (SC 318, 82–88 line 20) originally filled a folio between ff. 215 and 216.

f. 226v   Miniature: Moses striking water from the rock; Joshua halts the sun and moon; Joshua before the archangel

f. 227r   'On himself . . . and the bishopric of Constantinople' (Homily 36)

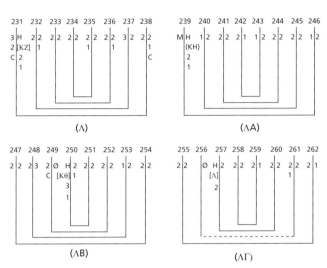

(Λ) (ΛA)

(ΛB) (ΛΓ)

f. 231r	Portion of final paragraph of Homily 36 (SC 318, 266 line 18–268 line 3) excised along with headpiece on verso
f. 231v	'On himself' (Homily 26); headpiece 27 (KZ) excised
f. 239r	Miniature: Gregory and Theodosios; Gregory leaves Constantinople. Later quire signature ΛA in margin
f. 239v	'Valedictory oration' (Homily 42)
f. 249v	Blank
f. 250r	'On the nativity' (Homily 38)
f. 256	Replacement leaf, s.xiv-xv, with last paragraph of Homily 38. The replaced text (SC 358, 146 line 6–148 line 7), with colophon, would originally have occupied one side of the folio only.
f. 257r	'On light' (Homily 39)
f. 262	Outer margin excised

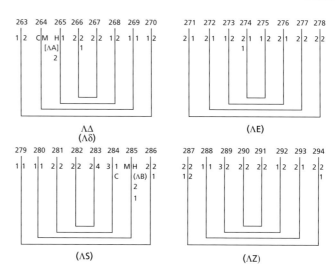

263	264	265	266	267	268	269	270
1|2	C|M	H|1	2|2	2|2	1|2	1|1	1|2
	[ΛΑ]		1				
	2						

ΛΔ
(Λδ)

271	272	273	274	275	276	277	278
2	1	2	1	1	2	2	1	1	2	2	1	2	2	2	2
			1				

(ΛΕ)

279	280	281	282	283	284	285	286
1|1	1|1	2|2	2|2	2|4	3|1	M|H	2|2
					C	(ΛB)|1	
						2	
						1	

(ΛS)

287	288	289	290	291	292	293	294
2	2	1	1	3	2	2	2	2	2	1	2	2	1	2	2
1	2							1

(ΛZ)

f. 264v   Miniature: Moses and the burning bush; conversion of Saul; ascension of Elijah; crossing of the Red Sea

f. 265r   'On baptism' (Homily 40)

f. 285r   Miniature: vision of Habakkuk, with Helena and Paraskeve

f. 285v   'On Easter' (Homily 45)

f. 289   Outer margin excised

f. 292   Outer margin excised

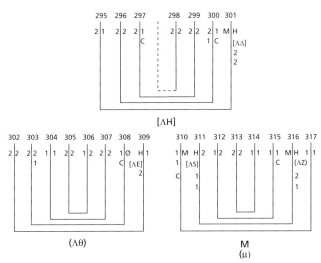

f. 295   Outer margin excised

f. 298r   'On New Sunday' (Homily 44). The opening paragraphs of text are missing; with headpiece 33 (ΛΓ), the lost text (*PG* 36:608A–C4) originally occupied one side of a folio between ff. 297 and 298.

f. 300   Outer margin excised

f. 301r   Miniature: Pentecost

f. 301v   'On Pentecost' (Homily 41)

f. 308v   Blank

f. 309r   'To Nektarios' (Epistle 88)

f. 310v   Miniature: Christ healing the man with the withered hand and the two blind men of Jericho; Christ healing the bent woman; the parable of the withered fig tree

f. 311r   'To Kledonios' I (Epistle 101)

f. 316r   Miniature: Christ healing the blind man at Siloam; the parable of the widow's mite; Christ healing the paralytic at Capernaum and raising the widow's son at Nain

f. 316v   'To Kledonios' II (Epistle 102)

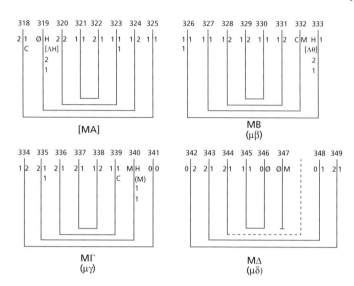

f. 319r   Blank

f. 319v   'Funeral oration on Athanasios' (Homily 21)

f. 332v   Miniature: life of Cyprian

f. 333r   'In praise of Cyprian' (Homily 24)

f. 340r   Miniature: martyrdom of the Makkabees

f. 340v   'On the Makkabees' (Homily 15)

f. 346   Outer column of text excised along with last six lines of homily; verso blank

f. 347r   Blank

f. 347v   Miniature: history of Samson; Gideon and the fleece; martyrdom of Isaiah

f. 348r   'In praise of Heron' (Homily 25). The opening paragraphs of text are missing; with headpiece 41 (MA), the lost text (SC 284, 156–162 line 4) originally occupied a folio between ff. 347 and 348

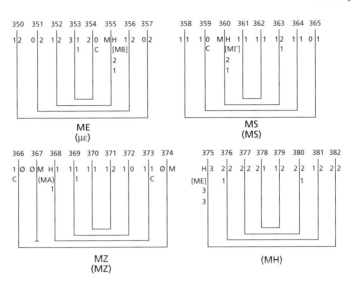

f. 355r	Miniature: Council of 381 at Constantinople
f. 355v	'On the arrival of the Egyptians' (Homily 34)
f. 360r	Miniature: tower of Babel (partially excised); Noah's ark
f. 360v	'On Peace' III (Homily 22); headpiece excised
ff. 366–374	The reconstruction of quire 47 is tentative
f. 366v	Blank
f. 367r	Blank
f. 367v	Miniature: the Arians persecute the orthodox
f. 368r	'Against Arianos' (Homily 33)
f. 374r	Blank
f. 374v	Miniature: history of Julian the Apostate I
f. 375r	'Against Julian the Apostate' I (Homily 4)

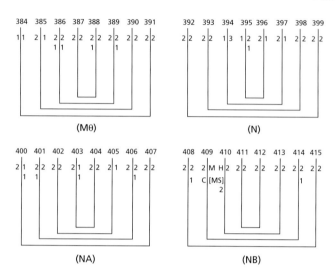

(Mθ)

(N)

(NA)

(NB)

f. 384r   Text continues uninterrupted from f. 382v: 383 omitted by modern pag-
inator

f. 409v   Miniature: history of Julian the Apostate II

f. 410r   'Against Julian the Apostate' II (Homily 5)

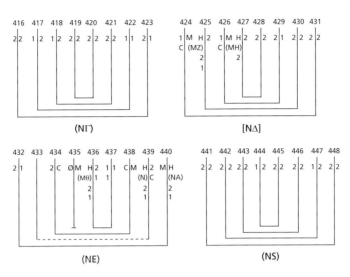

f. 424v   Miniature: Joshua at Jericho; Moses defeats the Amalekites; Gregory writing

f. 425r   'On the consecration of Eulalios' (Homily 13)

f. 426v   Miniature: mission of the apostles

f. 427r   'On the words of the gospel' (Homily 37)

f. 433   Replacement leaf, s.xiv–xv (SC 318, 308 line 7–314 line 9)

f. 435r   Blank

f. 435v   Miniature: Daniel in the lions' den; three Hebrews in the furnace; Manasses; Hezekiah and Isaiah

f. 436r   'To Evagrios' (Epistle 243, spurious?)

f. 438v   Miniature: Ezekiel in the valley of dry bones

f. 439r   *Significatio in Ezechielem* (spurious)

f. 440r   Miniature: history of Constantine and Helena

f. 440v   'Metaphrase of Ecclesiastes' (Gregory Thaumaturgos)

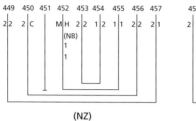

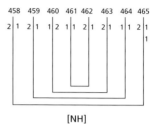

(NZ)   [NH]

f. 451	Inserted leaf, s.xiv–xv, with 'On martyrs and against Arians' (Homily 35; spurious): see SC 318, 77
f. 452r	Miniature: life of Gregory of Nazianzus
f. 452v	'Life of Gregory of Nazianzus' (Gregory the Presbyter)
f. 465v	Text terminates in midst of *vita* (at *PG* 35:288C2); rest of manuscript lost

Bibliography

Authors with the same last name who published concurrently are cited with first initials or, occasionally, full names in the notes (e.g. Jules Leroy and Julien Leroy); authors with the same last name whose cited works are chronologically separated are not (e.g. E.J. Martin and J.R. Martin are both cited as Martin).

Accorinti (D.) 1990: 'Sull'autore degli scoli mitologici alle orazioni di Gregorio di Nazianzo', *Byzantion* 40, 5–24.

Adontz (N.) 1933a: 'L'âge et l'origine de l'empereur Basile I (867–886)', *Byzantion* 8, 475–500.

Adontz (N.) 1933b: 'La portée historique de l'oraison funèbre de Basile I par son fils Léon VI le Sage', *Byzantion* 8, 501–513.

Adontz (N.) 1934: 'L'âge et l'origine de l'empereur Basile I (867–886)', *Byzantion* 9 (1934), 223–260.

Ainalov (D.) 1961: *The Hellenistic Origins of Byzantine Art.* Trans. E. and S. Sobolevitch. New Brunswick. Originally published in Russian, 1900–1901.

Alexakis (A.) 1994: 'A Florilegium in the Life of Nicetas of Medicion and a Letter of Theodore of Studios', *Dumbarton Oaks Papers* 48, 179–197.

Alexander (P. J.) 1953: 'The Iconoclastic Council of St. Sophia (815) and Its Definition (Horos)', *Dumbarton Oaks Papers* 7, 37–66.

Alexander (P. J.) 1958: *The Patriarch Nicephorus of Constantinople. Ecclesiastical Policy and Image Worship in the Byzantine Empire.* Oxford.

Alexander (P. J.) 1962: 'The Strength of Empire and Capital as seen through Byzantine Eyes', *Speculum* 37, 339–357.

Alexander (P. J.) 1977: 'Religious Persecution and Resistance in the Byzantine Empire of the Eighth and Ninth Centuries: Methods and Justifications', *Speculum* 52, 238–264.

Anastos (M. V.) 1954: 'The Ethical Theory of Images Formulated by the Iconoclasts in 754 and 815', *Dumbarton Oaks Papers* 8, 151–160.

Anderson (D.) 1980: *St John of Damascus, On the Divine Images: Three Apologies Against Those Who Attack the Divine Images.* Crestwood NY.

Anderson (F.) 1977: *An Illustrated History of the Herbals.* New York.

Anderson (J. C.) 1975: 'An Examination of Two Twelfth-Century Centers of Byzantine Manuscript Production'. PhD dissertation, Princeton University.

Anderson (J. C.) 1982: 'The Seraglio Octateuch and the Kokkinobaphos Master', *Dumbarton Oaks Papers* 36, 83–114.

443

Anderson (J. C.) 1987: 'The Common (Studite) Origin of the Moscow Menologium and the Jerusalem Gregory', *Byzantion* 57, 5–11.

Anderson (J. C.) 1991: 'The Illustrated Sermons of James the Monk: Their Dates, Order, and Place in the History of Byzantine Art', *Viator* 22, 69–120.

Anderson (J. C.) 1994: 'The Palimpsest Psalter, Pantokrator Cod. 61: Its Content and Relationship to the Bristol Psalter', *Dumbarton Oaks Papers* 48, 199–220.

Anderson (J. C.) 1995: 'The Byzantine panel portrait before and after Iconoclasm', in R. Ousterhout and L. Brubaker, eds., *The Sacred Image East and West*, Illinois Byzantine Studies 4. Urbana, 25–44.

Astruc (C.) 1974: 'Remarques sur les signes marginaux de certains manuscrits de S. Grégoire de Nazianze', *Analecta Bollandiana* 92, 289–95.

Astruc (C.), (W.) Wolska-Conus, (J.) Gouillard, (P.) Lemerle, (D.) Papachryssanthou, and (J.) Paramelle 1970: 'Les sources grecques pour l'histoire des pauliciens d'Asie Mineure', *Travaux et mémoires du Centre de recherche d'histoire et civilisation byzantines* 4, 1–227.

Auzépy (M.-F.) 1987: 'L'iconodoulie: défense de l'image ou de la dévotion à l'image?', in F. Boespflug and N. Lossky, eds., *Nicée II 787–1987, douze siècles d'images religieuses*. Paris, 157–165.

Auzépy (M.-F.) 1988: 'La place des moines à Nicée II', *Byzantion* 58, 5–21.

Auzépy (M.-F.) 1990: 'La destruction de l'icône du Christ de la Chalcé de Léon III: propagande ou réalité?', *Byzantion* 40, 445–492.

Babić (G.) 1969: *Les chapelles annexes des églises byzantines. Fonction liturgique et programme iconographique*, Bibliothèque des Cahiers Archéologiques 3. Paris.

Baldwin (B.) 1988: 'Nicholas Mysticus on Roman History', *Byzantion* 58, 174–178.

Baldwin (B.) 1990: 'A Note on Late Roman and Byzantine Caricature', *Byzantion* 40, 429–431.

Barber (C.) 1991: 'The Koimesis Church, Nicaea. The Limits of Representation on the Eve of Iconoclasm', *Jarhbuch der Österreichischen Byzantinistik* 41, 43–60.

Bardy (G.) 1936: 'Faux et fraudes littéraires dans l'antiquité chrétienne', *Revue d'Histoire Ecclésiastique* 32, 5–23, 275–302.

Barnard (L.) 1977: 'The Theology of Images', in Bryer and Herrin, eds. (1977), 7–13.

Baumstark (A.) 1904: 'Il mosaico degli Apostoli nella chiesa abbaziale di Grottaferrata', *Oriens Christianus* 4, 121–150.

Baumstark (A.) 1926/7: 'Ein illustriertes griechisches Menaion des Komnenenzeitalters', *Oriens Christianus*, ser.3, 1, 67–79.

Beaucamp (J.) 1977: 'La situation juridique de la femme à Byzance', *Cahiers de Civilisation Médiévale* 20, 145–176.

Bechow (S. M.) 1975, 1976: 'Culture, History, and Artifact', *Canadian Museums Association* 8, 13–15 and 9, 24–27. Reprinted in T. J. Schlereth, *Material Culture Studies in America*. Nashville, 1982, 114–123.

Bekker (I.), ed. 1838: *Theophanes Continuatus, Chronographia*. Corpus Scriptorum Historiae Byzantinae. Bonn.

Bekker (I.), ed. 1842: *Leo Grammaticus, Chronographia*. Corpus Scriptorum Historiae Byzantinae. Bonn.

Bellinger (A. R.) 1956: 'The Coins and Byzantine Imperial Policy', *Speculum* 31, 70–81.

Belting (H.) 1962: *Die Basilica dei Ss. Martiri in Cividale und ihr frühmittelalterlicher Freskenzyklus*. Forschungen zur Kunstgeschichte und christlichen Archäologie V. Wiesbaden.

Belting (H.) 1968: *Studien sur beneventanischen Malerei*. Forschungen zur Kunstgeschichte und christlichen Archäologie VII. Wiesbaden.

Belting (H.) 1974: 'Byzantine Art Among the Greeks and Latins in Southern Italy', *Dumbarton Oaks Papers* 28, 3–29.

Bergman (R.) 1973: 'Portraits of the Evangelists in Greek Manuscripts', in Vikan (1973), 44–49.

Bergman (R.) 1974: 'A School of Romanesque Ivory Carving in Amalfi', *Metropolitan Museum Journal* 9, 163–186.

Bernabò (M.) 1978: 'Considerazioni sul manoscritto Laurenziano plut. 5.38 e sulle miniature della *Genesi* degli *Ottateuchi* bizantini', *Annali della Scuola Normale Superiore di Pisa*, ser.3, 8, 135–157.

Bernabò (M.) 1979: 'La Cacciata dal Paradiso e il lavoro dei progenitori in alcune miniature medievali', *La miniatura italiana in età romanica e gotica*. Storia della miniatura, Studi e documenti 5. Florence, 269–281.

Bernardakis (V. P.) 1901/2: 'Le culte de la croix chez les Grecs', *Echoes d'Orient* 5, 193–202, 257–264.

Bernheimer (R.) 1952: 'The Martrydom of Isaiah', *Art Bulletin* 34, 19–34.

Bianchi Bandinelli (R.) 1961: 'La composizione del diluvio nella Genesi di Vienna', *Archeologia e cultura*. Milan, 343–359.

Binon (S.) 1937a: *Documents grecs inédits relatifs à S. Mercure de Césarée*. Louvain.

Binon (S.) 1937b: *Essai sur le cycle de Saint Mercure*. Paris.

Blum (P. Z.) 1969: 'The Middle English Romance "Iacob and Iosep" and the Joseph cycle of the Salisbury Chapter House', *Gesta* 8/1, 18–34.

Boeckler (A.) 1953: *Die Bronzetüren des Bonanus von Pisa und des Barisanus von Traini*. Berlin.

Bogyay (T. von) 1960: 'Zur Geschichte der Hetoimasie', *Akten des XI. Internationalen Byzantinisten-Kongresses*. Munich, 58–61.

Boojamra (J. L.) 1982: 'The Photian Synod of 879–880 and the Papal Commonitorium (879)', *Byzantine Studies/Etudes byzantines* 9, 1–23.

Bordier (H.) 1885: *Description des peintures et autres ornements contenus dans les manuscrits grecs de la Bibliothèque Nationale*. Paris.

Breckenridge (J. D.) 1980/1: 'Christ on the Lyre-Backed Throne', *Dumbarton Oaks Papers* 34/35, 247–260.

Brehier (L.) 1940: 'Les peintures du rouleau liturgique no.2 du monastère de Lavra', *Seminarium Kondakovianum* 11, 1–19.

Brenk (B.) 1971: 'Die Wandmalerei im Tempio della Tosse bei Tivoli', *Frühmittelalterliche Studien* 5, 401–412.

Brightman (R. E.) 1901: 'Byzantine Imperial Coronations', *Journal of Theological Studies* 2, 359–392.

Brinkmann (A.) ed. 1895: *Alexandri Lycopolitani Contra Manichaei opiniones disputatio*. Corpus Scriptorum Historiae Byzantinae. Bonn.

Brock (S.) 1971: *The Syriac Version of the Pseudo-Nonnos Mythological Scholia*. Cambridge.

Brown (P.) 1973: 'A Dark-Age Crisis: Aspects of the Iconoclastic Controversy', *English Historical Review* 346, 1–34.

Brown (P.) 1981: *The Cult of the Saints. Its Rise and Function in Latin Christianity*. Chicago.

Browning (R.) 1975: *Byzantium and Bulgaria: a Comparative Study Across the Early Medieval Frontier*. Los Angeles.

Browning (R.) 1978: 'Literacy in the Byzantine World', *Byzantine and Modern Greek Studies* 4, 39–54.

Brubaker (L.) 1977: 'The Relationship between Text and Image in the Byzantine MSS of Cosmas Indicopleustes', *Byzantinische Zeitschrift* 70, 42–57.

Brubaker (L.) 1981: 'The Tabernacle Miniatures of the Byzantine Octateuchs', *Actes du XVe Congrès International d'Etudes Byzantines II: Art et Archéologie.* Athens, 73–92.

Brubaker (L.) 1983: 'The Illustrated Copy of the Homilies of Gregory of Nazianzus in Paris (Bibliothèque Nationale, cod.gr.510)'. PhD dissertation, The Johns Hopkins University.

Brubaker (L.) 1985: 'Politics, Patronage and Art in Ninth-Century Byzantium: The *Homilies* of Gregory of Nazianzus in Paris (B.N.gr.510)', *Dumbarton Oaks Papers* 39, 1–13.

Brubaker (L.) 1989a: 'Perception and Conception: Art, Theory and Culture in Ninth-Century Byzantium', *Word & Image* 5/1, 19–32.

Brubaker (L.) 1989b: 'Byzantine Art in the Ninth Century: Theory, Practice, and Culture', *Byzantine and Modern Greek Studies* 13, 23–93.

Brubaker (L.) 1991: 'The Introduction of Painted Initials in Byzantium', *Scriptorium* 45, 22–46.

Brubaker (L.) 1992: 'The Vita Icon of Saint Basil: Iconography', in B. Davezac, ed., *Four icons in the Menil Collection.* Austin, 70–93.

Brubaker (L.) 1994: 'To Legitimize an Emperor: Constantine and Visual Authority in the Eighth and Ninth Centuries', in P. Magdalino, ed., *New Constantines: the Rhythm of Imperial Renewal in Byzantium, 4th–13th Centuries.* Aldershot, 139–158.

Brubaker (L.) 1995: 'Originality in Byzantine Manuscript Illumination', in A. R. Littlewood, *Originality in Byzantine Literature, Art and Music. A Collection of Essays.* Oxbow monograph 50. Oxford, 1995, 147–165.

Brubaker (L.) 1996a: 'Miniatures and Liturgy: Evidence from the Ninth-Century Codex Paris.gr.510', *Byzantion* 66, 9–34.

Brubaker (L.) 1996b: 'When Pictures Speak: the Incorporation of Dialogue in the Miniatures of Paris.gr.510', *Word & Image* 12/1, 94–109.

Brubaker (L.) and (A.) Littlewood 1992: 'Byzantinische Gärten', in M. Carroll-Spillecke, ed., *Der Garten von der Antike bis zum Mittelalter.* Kulturgeschichte der antiken Welt 57. Mainz a.R., 213–248.

Bryer (A. A. M.) 1986: 'Byzantine Agricultural Implements: the Evidence of Medieval Illustrations of Hesiod's *Works and Days*', *Annual of the British School of Archaeology at Athens* 81, 45–80.

Bryer (A. A. M.) and (J.) Herrin, eds. 1977: *Iconoclasm.* Birmingham.

Bucher (F.) 1970: *The Pamplona Bibles.* New Haven.

Buchthal (H.) 1938: *The Miniatures of the Paris Psalter.* London.

Buchthal (H.) 1957: *Miniature Painting in the Latin Kingdom of Jerusalem.* Oxford.

Buchthal (H.) 1963: 'Some Notes on Byzantine Hagiographical Portraiture', *Gazette des Beaux-Arts* 62, 81–90.

Buchthal (H.) 1966: 'Some Representations from the Life of St Paul in Byzantine and Carolingian Art', *Tortulae, Studien zu altchristlichen und byzantinischen Monumenten.* Römische Quartalschrift, suppl. 30. Rome, 43–48.

Burgin (V.) 1986: *The End of Art Theory, Criticism and Postmodernity.* Houndsmills.

Buschausen (H.) 1980: 'Die Katacombe an der Via Latina zu Rom', *Jahrbuch der Österreichischen Byzantinistik* 29, 293–306.

Bussagli (M.) 1985/6: 'Sul contacio della natività di Romano il Melodo', *Rivista di studi bizantini e neoellenici* n.s. 22–23, 3–49.

Bynum (C. Walker) 1984: 'Women's Stories, Women's Symbols: A Critique of Victor Turner's Theory of Liminality', in R. L. Moore and F. E. Reynolds, eds., *Anthropology and the Study of Religion*. Chicago, 105–125.

Byzance 1992: *Byzance. L'art byzantin dans les collections publiques françaises*. Paris.

Calofonos (G.) 1984/5: 'Dream interpretation: a Byzantine superstition?', *Byzantine and Modern Greek Studies* 9, 215–220.

Cameron (Al.) 1973: *Porphyrius the Charioteer*. Oxford.

Cameron (Av.) 1979: 'Images of Authority: Elites and Icons in Late Sixth-Century Byzantium', *Past and Present* 84, 3–35. Reprinted in Av. Cameron, *Continuity and Change in Sixth-Century Byzantium*. London, 1981, essay XVIII.

Cameron (Av.) 1987: 'The Construction of Court Ritual: the Byzantine *Book of Ceremonies*', in D. Cannadine and S. R. F. Price, eds., *Rituals of Royalty: Power and Ceremonial in Traditional Societies*. Cambridge, 106–136.

Cameron (Av.) 1989: 'Virginity as Metaphor: Women and the Rhetoric of Early Christianity', in Av. Cameron, ed., *History as Text: the Writing of Ancient History*. London, 184–205.

Cameron (Av.) 1990: 'Models of the Past in the Late Sixth Century: the Life of the Patriarch Eutychios', in G. Clarke, ed., *Reading the Past in Late Antiquity*. Canberra, 205–223.

Cameron (Av.) 1992a: 'Byzantium and the Past in the Seventh Century. The Search for Redefinition', in J. Fontaine and J. Hillgarth, eds., *The Seventh Century: Change and Continuity / Le septième siècle: changements et continuités*. Studies of the Warburg Institute 42. London, 250–271.

Cameron (Av.) 1992b: 'The Language of Images: the Rise of Icons and Christian Representation', in D. Wood, ed., *The Church and the Arts*. Studies in Church History 28. Oxford, 1–42.

Cameron (Av.) 1992c: 'New Themes and Styles in Greek Literature: Seventh–Eighth Centuries', in Av. Cameron and L. Conrad, eds., *The Byzantine and Early Islamic Near East I: Problems in the Literary Source Material*. Studies in Late Antiquity and Early Islam 1. Princeton, 81–105.

Cameron (Av.) 1992d: *The Use and Abuse of Byzantium, An Essay on Reception*. Inaugural lecture delivered 15 May 1990. London.

Cameron (Av.) and (J.) Herrin, eds. 1984: *Constantinople in the Early Eighth Century: The Parastaseis Syntomoi Chronikai*. Columbia Studies in the Classical Tradition 10. Leiden.

Camille (M.) 1985: 'Seeing and Reading: Some Visual Implications of Medieval Literacy and Illiteracy', *Art History* 8, 26–49.

Camille (M.) 1992: review of H. Belting, *Bild und Kult: Eine Geschichte des Bildes vor dem Zeitalter der Kunst*, in *Art Bulletin* 74, 514–517.

Carr (A. Weyl) 1976: 'Chicago 2400 and the Byzantine Acts Cycle', *Byzantine Studies / Etudes byzantines* 3/2, 1–29.

Catafygiotu-Topping (E.) 1977: 'Romanos, On the Entry in Jerusalem: A Basilikos Logos', *Byzantion* 47, 65–91.

Cavallo (G.) 1977: 'Funzione e struttore della maiuscola greca tra i secoli VIII–XI', *La paléographie grècque et byzantine*. Colloques Internationaux du Centre National de la Recherche Scientifique, no. 559. Paris, 95–110.

Cavallo (G.) 1982: 'La cultura italo-greca nella produzione libraria', in G. Cavallo, V. von Falkenhausen, R. Farioli Campanati, M. Gigante, V. Pace, F. Panvini Rosati, *I Bizantini in Italia*. Milan, 497–612.

Cavallo (G.), (V.) von Falkenhausen, (R.) Farioli Campanati, (M.) Gigante, (V.) Pace, and (F.) Panvini Rosati 1982: *I Bizantini in Italia*. Milan.

Cavallo (G.), (J.) Gribomont and (W. C.) Loerke 1987: *I vangeli di Rossano: Le miniature / The Rossano Gospels: The miniatures*. Rome.

Cecchelli (C.) 1944: *La Cattedra di Massimiano ed altri avorii romano-orientali*. Rome.

Cecchelli (C.), (G.) Furlani, and (M.) Salmi 1959: *The Rabbula Gospels*. Olten.

Charles (R. H.) 1913: *The Apocrypha and Pseudepigrapha of the Old Testament*. 2 vols. Oxford.

Christou (P.) 1971: 'The Missionary Activity of the Byzantine Emperor', *Byzantina* 3, 277–286.

Christou (P. C) *et al.* 1991: Π.Κ. Χρήστου, Χ. Μαυροπούλου-Τσιούμη, Σ.Ν. Καδᾶς, and Α. Καλαμαρτζῆ-Κατσαροῦ. *Οἱ Θησαυροὶ τοῦ ἁγίου ὄρους* 4. Athens.

Clédat (J.) 1902: 'Notes archéologiques et philologiques', *Bulletin de l'Institut Français d'Archéologie Orientale du Caire* 2, 1–30.

Connor (C. L.) 1984: 'The Joshua Fresco at Hosios Loukas', *Abstracts of Papers*, Tenth Annual Byzantine Studies Conference. Cincinnati, 57–58.

Connor (C. L.) 1991: *Art and Miracles in Medieval Byzantium*. Princeton.

Cormack (R.) 1967: 'Byzantine Cappadocia: The Archaic Group of Wall Paintings', *Journal of the British Archaeological Association*, ser.3, 30, 19–36.

Cormack (R.) 1968: 'Ninth-Century Monumental Painting and Mosaic in Thessaloniki'. PhD thesis, Courtauld Institute of Art, University of London.

Cormack (R.) 1977a: 'The Arts During the Age of Iconoclasm', in Bryer and Herrin, eds. (1977), 35–44. Reprinted in Cormack (1989), essay III.

Cormack (R.) 1977b: 'Painting after Iconoclasm', in Bryer and Herrin, eds. (1977), 147–163. Reprinted in Cormack (1989), essay IV.

Cormack (R.) 1981: 'Interpreting the Mosaics of S. Sophia at Istanbul', *Art History* 4/2, 131–149. Reprinted in Cormack (1989), essay VIII.

Cormack (R.) 1985: *Writing in Gold, Byzantine Society and its Icons*. Oxford.

Cormack (R.) 1986a: 'New Art History vs Old Art History: Writing Art History', *Byzantine and Modern Greek Studies* 10, 223–231.

Cormack (R.) 1986b: 'Patronage and new programs of Byzantine iconography', *The 17th International Byzantine Congress, Major Papers*. New York, 609–38. Reprinted in Cormack (1989), essay X.

Cormack (R.) 1989: *The Byzantine Eye: Studies in Art and Patronage*. London.

Cormack (R.) 1992: 'But Is It Art?', in J. Shepard and S. Franklin, eds., *Byzantine Diplomacy*. London, 218–236.

Cormack (R.) and (E.) Hawkins 1977: 'The Mosaics of St. Sophia at Istanbul: the Rooms Above the Southwest Vestibule and Ramp', *Dumbarton Oaks Papers* 31, 177–251.

Corrigan (K.) 1978: 'The Ivory Scepter of Leo VI: A Statement of Post-Iconoclastic Imperial Ideology', *Art Bulletin* 60, 407–416.

Corrigan (K.) 1992: *Visual Polemics in the Ninth-Century Byzantine Psalters*. Cambridge.

Corrigan (K.) 1995: 'An Icon of the Crucifixion at Mt. Sinai', in R. Ousterhout and L. Brubaker, eds., *The Sacred Image East and West*, Illinois Byzantine Studies 4. Urbana, 45–62.

Cotsonis (J.) 1989: 'On Some Illustrations in the Lectionary, Athos, Dionysiou 587', *Byzantion* 59, 5–19.

Coulie (B.) 1985: *Les richesses dans l'œuvre de Grégoire de Nazianze, Etude littéraire et historique.* Publications de l'Institut Orientaliste de Louvain 32. Louvain-le-Neuve.

Cramer (J. A.) 1844: *Catenae Graecorum Patrum in Novum Testamentum IV: In Epistolam S. Pauli ad Romanos.* Oxford.

Crehan (J. H.) 1966: 'Patristic Evidence for the Inspiration of Councils', *Studia Patristica* 9. Texte und Untersuchungen 94. Berlin, 210–215.

Cunningham (M. B.) 1991: *The Life of Michael the Synkellos: Text, Translation and Commentary.* Belfast Byzantine Texts and Translations I. Belfast.

Cutler (A.) 1974: 'The Spencer Psalter: A Thirteenth Century Byzantine Manuscript in the New York Public Library', *Cahiers Archéologiques* 23, 129–150.

Cutler (A.) 1975: *Transfigurations. Studies in the Dynamics of Byzantine Iconography.* University Park and London.

Cutler (A.) 1976: 'The Aristocratic Psalter: The State of Research', *Rapports et co-rapports, XVe Congrès international d'études byzantines III: art et archéologie.* Athens, 229–257.

Cutler (A.) 1984: *The Aristocratic Psalters in Byzantium.* Bibliothèque des Cahiers Archéologiques 13. Paris.

Cutler (A.) 1985: 'Apostolic Monasticism at Tokalı Kilise in Cappadocia', *Anatolian Studies* 35, 57–65.

Cutler (A.) 1987: 'Under the Sign of the Deesis: on the Question of Representativeness in Medieval Art and Literature', *Dumbarton Oaks Papers* 41, 145–154.

Cutler (A.) 1992: 'ΠΑΣ ΟΙΚΟΣ ΙΣΡΑΗΛ: Ezekiel and the Politics of Resurrection in Tenth-Century Byzantium', *Dumbarton Oaks Papers* 46, 47–58.

Cutler (A.) 1994: *The Hand of the Master. Craftsmanship, Ivory, and Society in Byzantium (9th–11th Centuries).* Princeton.

Cutler (A.) and (N.) Oikonomides 1988: 'An Imperial Byzantine Casket and its Fate at a Humanist's Hands', *Art Bulletin* 70, 77–87.

Dagron (G.) 1979: 'Le culte des images dans le monde byzantin', in J. Delumeau, ed., *Histoire vécue du peuple chrétien* I. Toulouse, 133–160. Reprinted in Dagron (1984b), essay XI.

Dagron (G.) 1981: 'Quand la terre tremble...', *Travaux et mémoires du Centre de recherche d'histoire et civilisation byzantines* 8, 87–103. Reprinted in Dagron (1984b), essay III.

Dagron (G.) 1984a: *Constantinople imaginaire. Etudes sur le recueil des Patria.* Bibliothèque Byzantine, Etudes 8. Paris.

Dagron (G.) 1984b: *La romanité chrétienne en Orient.* London.

Dagron (G.) 1991: 'Holy Images and Likeness', *Dumbarton Oaks Papers* 45, 23–33.

Dagron (G.) 1994: 'Lawful Society and Legitimate Power: Ἔννομος πολιτεία, ἔννομος ἀρχή', in A. Laiou and D. Simon, eds., *Law and Society in Byzantium, Ninth–Twelfth Centuries.* Washington, 27–51.

van Dam (R.) 1985: *Leadership and Community in Late Antique Gaul.* Transformation of the Classical Heritage 8. Berkeley.

Daniélou (J.) 1950: *Sacramentum futuri.* Paris.

Daniélou (J.) 1956: *The Bible and the Liturgy.* Notre Dame.

Daniélou (J.) 1960: *From Shadows to Reality: Studies in the Biblical Typology of the Fathers.* Westminster.

Davis-Weyer (C.) 1966: 'Die Mosaiken Leos III. und die Anfänge der karolingischen Renaissance in Rom', *Zeitschrift für Kunstgeschichte* 29, 111–132.

Declerck (J.) 1976: 'Five unedited Greek Scholia of Ps.-Nonnos', *L'antiquité classique* 45, 181–9.

Declerck (J.) 1977: 'Les commentaires mythologiques du Ps.-Nonnos sur l'homélie XLIII de Grégoire de Nazianze. Essai d'édition critique', *Byzantion* 47, 92–112.

Declerck (J.) 1978/9: 'Contribution à l'étude de la tradition grecque des "Histoires Mythologiques" du Ps.-Nonnus', *Sacris Erudiri* 33, 177–190.

Deichmann (F. W.) 1958: *Frühchristliche Bauten und Mosaiken von Ravenna.* Baden-Baden.

Delehaye (H.) 1921: 'Cyprien d'Antioche et Cyprien de Carthage', *Analecta Bollandiana* 39, 314–322.

Demus (O.) 1949: *The Mosaics of Norman Sicily.* London.

Demus (O.) 1979: '"The sleepless watcher". Ein Erklärungsversuch', *Jahrbuch der Österreichischen Byzantinistik* 28, 241–245.

Demus (O.) 1984: *The Mosaics of San Marco in Venice.* 2 parts in 4 vols. Chicago and London.

Demus-Quatember (M.) 1974: *Est et alia pyramis.* Rome.

Der Nersessian (S.) 1926/7: 'Two Slavonic Parallels of the Greek Tetraevangelia: Paris 74', *Art Bulletin* 9, 222–274.

Der Nersessian (S.) 1955: 'The Illustration of the Metaphrastian Menologium', in K. Weitzmann, ed., *Late Classical and Mediaeval Studies in Honor of Albert Mathias Friend, Jr.* Princeton, 222–231.

Der Nersessian (S.) 1962: 'The Illustrations of the Homilies of Gregory of Nazianzus, Paris gr. 510', *Dumbarton Oaks Papers* 16, 197–228.

Der Nersessian (S.) 1965: 'A Psalter and New Testament Manuscript at Dumbarton Oaks', *Dumbarton Oaks Papers* 19, 155–183.

Der Nersessian (S.) 1970: *L'illustration des psautiers grecs du moyen âge II: Londres, Add.19352.* Bibliothèque des Cahiers Archéologiques 5. Paris.

Der Nersessian (S.) 1975: 'Program and Iconography of the Frescoes of the Pareclession', in P. Underwood, ed., *The Kariye Djami* 4. Princeton, 305–349.

Der Nersessian (S.) 1987: 'Two Miracles of the Virgin in the Poems of Gautier de Coincy', *Dumbarton Oaks Papers* 41, 157–163.

Der Nersessian (S.) and (II.) Vahramian 1974: *Aght'amar.* Documents of Armenian Architecture 8. Milan.

Deshman (R.) 1989: 'Servants of the Mother of God in Byzantine and Medieval Art', *Word & Image* 5/1, 33–70.

Diebold (W. J.) 1992: 'Verbal, Visual, and Cultural Literacy in Medieval Art: Word and Image in the Psalter of Charles the Bald', *Word & Image* 8/2, 89–99.

Diller (A.) 1962: 'Photius' Bibliotheca in Byzantine Literature', *Dumbarton Oaks Papers* 16, 389–396.

Dindorf (L.) 1831: *Chronographia.* Bonn.

Dinkler (E.) 1964: *Das Apsismosaik von S. Apollinare in Classe.* Wissenschaftliche Abhandlungen der Arbeitsgemeinschaft für Forschung des Landes Nordrhein-Westfalen 29. Cologne.

Dinkler (E.) 1970: *Der Einzug in Jerusalem: Ikonographische Untersuchungen im Anschluss an ein bisher unbekanntes Sarkophagfragment.* Arbeitsgemeinschaft für Forschung des Landes Nordrhein-Westfalen, Geistwissenschaften 167. Opladen.

Dölger (F.) 1943: 'Europas Gestaltung im Spiegel der fränkisch-byzantinischen Auseinandersetzung des 9. Jahrhunderts', in T. Mayer, ed., *Der Vertrag von Verdun*. Leipzig, 203–273.

Downey (G.) 1957: 'Nicholaos Mesarites: Description of the Church of the Holy Apostles at Constantinople', *Transactions of the American Philosophical Society*, n.s. 47, pt. 6, 855–924.

Duffy (J.) and (J.) Parker, eds., 1979: *The Synodikon Vetus*. Corpus Fontium Historiae Byzantinae XV, Dumbarton Oaks Texts 5. Washington DC.

Dufrenne (S.) 1964: 'Le psautier de Bristol et les autres psautiers byzantins', *Cahiers Archéologiques* 14, 159–182.

Dufrenne (S.) 1965: 'Une illustration "historique" inconnue du psautier du Mont-Athos, Pantokrator 61', *Cahiers Archéologiques* 15, 83–95.

Dufrenne (S.) 1966: *L'illustration des psautiers grecs du moyen âge* I. Bibliothèque des Cahiers Archéologiques 1. Paris.

Dufrenne (S.) and (P.) Canart 1988: *Die Bibel des Patricius Leo. Codex Reginensis Graecus IB*. Codices e Vaticanis Selecti 75. Vatican City.

Duggan (L.) 1989: 'Was Art Really the "Book of the Illiterate"?', *Word & Image* 5/3, 227–251.

Dujčev (I.) 1952: 'Au lendemain de la conversion du peuple bulgare. L'épître de Photius', *Mélanges de Science Religieuse* 8, 211–226.

Dujčev (I.) 1962: *Miniatiurite na Manasievata Istoris*. Sophia.

Duncan-Flowers (M.) 1990: 'A Pilgrim's Ampulla from the Shrine of St John the Evangelist at Ephesus', in R. Ousterhout, ed., *The Blessings of Pilgrimage*. Illinois Byzantine Studies 1. Urbana, 125–139.

Dvornik (F.) 1933: *Les Légendes de Constantin et de Méthode vues de Byzance*. Byzantinoslavica, Supplementa 1. Prague.

Dvornik (F.) 1948: *The Photian Schism, History and Legend*. Cambridge.

Dvornik (F.) 1958: 'The Patriarch Photius in the Light of Recent Research', *Berichte zum XI. internationalen Byzantinisten-Kongress*. Munich, 1–56. Reprinted in Dvornik (1974), essay VI.

Dvornik (F.) 1966: *Early Christian and Byzantine Political Philosophy*. 2 vols. Washington DC.

Dvornik (F.) 1970: *Byzantine Missions Among the Slavs*. New Brunswick.

Dvornik (F.) 1974: *Photian and Byzantine Ecclesiastical Studies*. London.

Ebersolt (J.) 1926: *La miniature byzantine*. Paris.

Efthymiadis (S.) 1991: 'On the Hagiographical Work of Ignatius the Deacon', *Jahrbuch der Österreichischen Byzantinistik* 41, 73–83.

Eleen (L.) 1977: 'Acts Illustration in Italy and Byzantium', *Dumbarton Oaks Papers* 31, 255–278.

Elsner (J.) 1988: 'Image and Iconoclasm in Byzantium', *Art History* 11, 471–491.

Epstein (A. W.) 1977: 'The "Iconoclast" Churches of Cappadocia', in Bryer and Herrin, eds. (1977), 103–111.

Epstein (A. W.) 1982: 'The Rebuilding and Redecoration of the Holy Apostles in Constantinople: A Reconsideration', *Greek, Roman and Byzantine Studies* 23, 79–92.

Epstein (A. W.) 1986: *Tokalı Kilise: Tenth-Century Metropolitan Art in Byzantine Cappadocia*. Washington DC.

Ericsson (K.) 1968: 'The Cross on Steps and the Silver Hexagramma', *Jahrbuch der Österreichischen Byzantinischen Gesellschaft* 17 (1968), 149–164.

Fabre (P.) 1921/2: 'Le développement de l'histoire de Joseph dans la littérature et dans l'art au cours des douze premiers siècles', *Mélanges d'Archéologie et d'Histoire* (Ecole Française de Rome) 39, 193–211.

Fälschungen 1988: *Fälschungen im Mittelalter.* Internationaler Kongress der Monumenta Germaniae Historica. 5 vols. Hanover.

Featherstone (J. M.) 1980: 'The Praise of Theodore Graptos by Theophanes of Caesarea', *Analecta Bollandiana* 98, 93–150.

Ferrua (A.) 1960: *Le pitture della nuova catacomba di Via Latina.* Vatican City.

Filov (B. D.) 1927: *Les miniatures de la Chronique de Manassès à la Bibliothèque du Vatican (cod. Vat. Slav. II).* Codices e Vaticanis Selecti, series major XVII. Sophia.

Folda (J.) 1976: *Crusader Manuscript Illumination at Saint-Jean d'Acre, 1275–1291.* Princeton.

Follena (G.) and (G. L.) Mellini 1962: *Bibbia istoriata padovana della fine del trecento.* Venice.

Follieri (E.) 1964: 'L'ordine dei versi in alcuni epigrammi bizantini', *Byzantion* 34, 447–467.

Forsyth (G. H.) and (K.) Weitzmann, n[o] d[ate]. *The Monastery of Saint Catherine at Mount Sinai: the Church and Fortress of Justinian.* Ann Arbor.

Frantz (A.) 1934: 'Byzantine Illuminated Ornament', *Art Bulletin* 16, 43–76.

Frazer (M. E.) 1973: 'Church Doors and the Gates of Paradise: Byzantine Bronze Doors in Italy', *Dumbarton Oaks Papers* 27, 145–162.

Freeman (A.) 1985: 'Carolingian Orthodoxy and the Fate of the *Libri Carolini*', *Viator* 16, 65–108.

Friedman (M.) 1989: 'More on the Vienna Genesis', *Byzantion* 59, 64–77.

Friend (A. M. Jr.) 1927: 'The Portraits of the Evangelists in Greek and Latin Manuscripts', *Art Studies* 5, 115–147.

Frolow (A.) 1945: 'Deux églises byzantines d'après des sermons peu connus de Léon VI le Sage', *Revue des Etudes Byzantines* 3, 79–85.

Frolow (A.) 1956: 'IC XC NIKA', *Byzantinoslavica* 17, 98–113.

Frolow (A.) 1961a: 'Le culte de la relique de la croix', *Byzantinoslavica* 22, 320–339.

Frolow (A.) 1961b: *La relique de la Vraie Croix.* Archives de l'Orient Chrétien 7. Paris.

Frolow (A.) 1962: 'La renaissance de l'art au IXe siècle et son origine', *Corso di cultura sull'arte ravennate e bizantina* 9, 269–293.

Frolow (A.) 1963: 'Le Christ de la Chalcé', *Byzantion* 33, 107–120.

Frolow (A.) 1965: *Les reliquaires de la Vraie Croix.* Archives de l'Orient Chrétien 8. Paris.

Furlan (I.) 1978: 'Contributo alla ritrattistica agiografica bizantina attraverso nuove minature della Biblioteca Marciana', *Arte veneta* 32, 5–9.

Gaehde (J.) 1974: 'Carolingian Interpretations of an Early Christian Picture Cycle to the Octateuch in the Bible of San Paolo Fuori Le Mura in Rome', *Frühmittelalterliche Studien* 8, 351–384.

Gagé (J.) 1933: '*Stauros nikopoios*: la victoire impérial dans l'empire chrétien', *Revue d'Histoire et de Philosophie Religieuses* 13, 370–400.

Galatariotou (C.) 1984/5: 'Holy Women and Witches: Aspects of Byzantine Conceptions of Gender', *Byzantine and Modern Greek Studies* 9, 55–94.

Galatariotou (C.) 1993: 'Travel and Perception in Byzantium', *Dumbarton Oaks Papers* 47, 221–241.

Galavaris (G.) 1969: *The Illustrations of the Liturgical Homilies of Gregory Nazianzenus.* Studies in Manuscript Illumination 6. Princeton.

Galbraith (K. J.) 1965: 'The Iconography of the Biblical Scenes at Malmesbury Abbey', *Journal of the British Archaeological Association* 28, 39–56.

Gallay (P.) 1943: *La vie de saint Grégoire de Nazianze*. Paris.

Garidis (M.) 1969: 'La représentation des "nations" dans la peinture post-byzantine', *Byzantion* 39, 86–91.

Garrison (E. B.) 1961: 'Note on the Iconography of the Fall of Man in Eleventh- and Twelfth-Century Rome', *Studies in the History of Medieval Italian Painting* IV. Florence, 201–210.

Garrucci (P. R.) 1879: *Storia dell'arte cristiana* V. Prato.

Gatch (M.) 1975: 'Noah's Raven in Genesis A and the Illustrated Old English Hexateuch', *Gesta* 14/2, 3–15.

Gauthier-Walter (M.-D.) 1990: 'Joseph, figure idéale du Roi?', *Cahiers Archéologiques* 38, 25–36.

Geertz (C.) 1983: *Local Knowledge: Future Essays and Interpretive Anthropology*. New York.

Gero (S.) 1973a: *Byzantine Iconoclasm during the Reign of Leo III, with Particular Attention to the Oriental Sources*. Louvain.

Gero (S.) 1973b: 'The Libri Carolini and the Image Controversy', *Greek Orthodox Theological Review* 18, 7–34.

Gero (S.) 1975: 'The Eucharistic Doctrine of the Byzantine Iconoclasts and its Sources', *Byzantinische Zeitschrift* 68, 4–22.

Gero (S.) 1977a: *Byzantine Iconoclasm during the Reign of Constantine V with Particular Attention to the Oriental Sources*. Corpus Scriptorum Christianorum Orientalium 384, Subsidia 52. Louvain.

Gero (S.) 1977b: 'Byzantine Iconoclasm and Monomachy', *Journal of Ecclesiastical History* 28, 241–248.

Gero (S.) 1992: 'The Alexander Legend in Byzantium: Some Literary Gleanings', *Dumbarton Oaks Papers* 46, 83–87.

Gerstinger (H.) 1931: *Die Wiener Genesis*. Vienna.

Gerstinger (H.) 1979: *Dioscorides, Codex Vindobonensis med.gr.1*. Graz.

Giakalis (A.) 1994: *Images of the Divine. The Theology of Icons at the Seventh Ecumenical Council*. Leiden.

Gjuzelev (V.) 1976: *The Adoption of Christianity in Bulgaria*. Sophia. Reprinted in V. Gjuzelev, *Medieval Bulgaria, Byzantine Empire, Black Sea-Venice-Genoa*. Villach, 1988.

Gjuzelev (V.) 1986: 'La Bulgarie médiévale et l'Europe occidentale (IXe–XIe s.)', *Byzantinobulgarica* 7, 89–101. Reprinted in Gjuzelev, *Medieval Bulgaria, Byzantine Empire, Black Sea–Venice–Genoa*. Villach, 1988.

Goar (J.) 1730: Εὐχολόγιον *sive Rituale Graecorum*. Venice. Reprinted Graz, 1960.

Goldschmidt (A.) and (K.) Weitzmann 1930: *Die byzantinische Elfenbeinskulpturen*. 2 vols. Berlin.

Gombrich (E.) 1969: *Art and Illusion, a Study in the Psychology of Pictorial Representation*. Bollingen Series 35:5. Second edn Princeton.

Gordon (R. L.) 1979: 'The Real and the Imaginary: Production and Religion in the Graeco-Roman world', *Art History* 2, 5–34.

Gouillard (J.) 1960: 'Une œuvre inédite du patriarche Méthode: la Vie d'Euthyme de Sardes', *Byzantinische Zeitschrift* 53, 36–46.

Gouillard (J.) 1966: 'Fragments inédits d'un antirrhétique de Jean le Grammairien', *Revue des Etudes Byzantines* 24, 171–181.

Gouillard (J.) 1967: 'Le synodikon de l'orthodoxie, édition et commentaire', *Travaux et mémoires du Centre de recherche d'Histoire et Civilisation Byzantines* 2, 1–316.

Gouillard (J.) 1968: 'Aux origines de l'iconoclasme: Le témoignage de Grégoire II?', *Travaux et mémoires du Centre de recherche d'Histoire et Civilisation Byzantines* 3, 243–307.

Gouillard (J.) 1969: 'Art et littérature théologique à Byzance au lendemain de la querelle des images', *Cahiers de Civilisation Médiévale* 12, 1–13.

Gouillard (J.) 1971: 'Le Photius du Pseudo-Syméon Magistros', *Revue des Etudes Sud-est Européennes* 9, 397–404.

Gouillard (J.) 1982: 'La femme de qualité dans les lettres de Théodore Stoudite', *Jahrbuch der Österreichischen Byzantinistik* 32/2, 445–452.

Grabar (A.) 1936: *L'empereur dans l'art byzantin.* Strasbourg.

Grabar (A.) 1943a: *Les miniatures du Grégoire de Nazianze de l'Ambrosienne (Ambrosiana 49–50).* Paris.

Grabar (A.) 1943b: *Martyrium. Recherches sur le culte des reliques et l'art chrétien antique.* 2 vols. Paris.

Grabar (A.) 1953: *Byzantine Painting.* New York.

Grabar (A.) 1957: *L'iconoclasme byzantin. Dossier archéologique.* Paris.

Grabar (A.) 1958: *Les ampoules de Terre Sainte.* Paris.

Grabar (A.) 1960: 'Une pyxide en ivoire à Dumbarton Oaks', *Dumbarton Oaks Papers* 14, 123–146.

Grabar (A.) 1965: 'Quelques notes sur les psautiers illustrés byzantins du IXe siècle', *Cahiers Archéologiques* 15, 61–82.

Grabar (A.) 1968a: 'L'art religieux et l'empire byzantin à l'époque des Macédoniens', *L'art de la fin de l'antiquité et du moyen âge* I. Paris, 151–168.

Grabar (A.) 1968b: 'Le schéma iconographique de la Pentecôte', *L'art de la fin de l'antiquité et du moyen âge* I. Paris, 615–627.

Grabar (A.) 1969: 'La précieuse croix de la Lavra de S. Athanase au Mont Athos', *Cahiers Archéologiques* 19, 99–126.

Grabar (A.) 1972: *Les manuscrits grecs enluminés de provenance italienne (IXe–XIe siècles),* Bibliothèque des Cahiers Archéologiques 8. Paris.

Grabar (O.) 1977: 'Islam and Iconoclasm', in Bryer and Herrin, eds. (1977), 45–52.

Graeven (H.) 1900: 'Typen der Wiener Genesis auf byzantinischen Elfenbeinreliefs', *Jahrbuch der Kunsthistorischen Sammlungen in Wien* 21 (1900).

Grant (R.M.) 1960: 'The Appeal to the Early Fathers', *Journal of Theological Studies* n.s. 11, 13–24.

Gray (N.) 1949: *Jacob's Ladder.* London.

Gray (P.) 1982: 'Neochalcedonianism and the Tradition: from Patristic to Byzantine Theology', *Byzantinische Forschungen* 8, 61–70.

Grégoire (H.) 1933: 'Etudes sur le neuvième siècle', *Byzantion* 8, 515–550.

Grierson (P.) 1962: 'The Tombs and Obits of the Byzantine Emperors (337–1042)', *Dumbarton Oaks Papers* 16, 3–63.

Grierson (P.) 1973: *Catalogue of the Byzantine Coins in the Dumbarton Oaks Collection and in the Whittemore Collection* III, 1–2. Washington DC.

Grishin (A.D.) 1985: 'The Aght'amar wallpaintings: some new observations', *Parergon* 3, 39–51.

Grosdidier de Matons (J.) 1967: 'La femme dans l'Empire byzantin', in P. Grimal, ed., *Histoire mondiale de la femme* III. Paris, 11–43.

Grumel (V.) 1922: 'L'iconologie de S. Germain de Constantinople', *Echos d'Orient* 21, 165–175.

Grumel (V.) 1936: *Les regestes des Actes du Patriarchat de Constantinople I: Les actes des patriarches.* Fasc. II. Istanbul and Paris.

Grumel (V.) 1937: 'Jean Grammaticos et saint Théodore Studite', *Echos d'Orient* 36, 180–9.

Grumel (V.) 1958: *La chronologie.* Traité d'études byzantines 1. Paris.

Grumel (V.) 1959: 'Les douze chapitres contre les iconomaques de saint Nicéphore de Constantinople', *Revue des Etudes Byzantines* 17, 127–135.

Grüneisen (W. de) 1911: *Sainte Marie Antique.* Rome.

Grüneisen (W. de) 1922: *Les caractéristiques de l'art copte.* Florence.

Guilland (R. J.) 1969: *Etudes de topographie de Constantinople byzantine.* 2 vols. Berliner byzantinische Arbeiten 37. Berlin.

Guillou (A.) 1979: 'Deux ivoires constantinopolitains datés du IXe et Xe siècle' in S. Dufrenne, ed., *Byzance et les slaves. Etudes de civilisation. Mélanges Ivan Dujčev.* Paris, 207–211.

Gutmann (J.) 1953: 'The Jewish Origin of the Ashburnham Pentateuch Miniatures', *Jewish Quarterly Review* n.s. 44, 55–72. Reprinted in J. Gutmann, *No Graven Images.* New York, 1971, 329–346.

Gutmann (J.) 1977: 'Noah's Raven in Early Christian and Byzantine Art', *Cahiers Archéologiques* 26, 63–71.

Gutmann (J.) 1984: 'The Sacrifice of Isaac: Variations on a Theme in Early Jewish and Christian Art', *Thiasos ton Mouson: Studien zu Antike und Christentum. Festschrift für Josef Fink zum 70. Geburtstag.* Vienna, 115–122.

Hahn (C.) 1989: 'Purification, Sacred Action, and the Vision of God: Viewing Medieval Narratives', *Word & Image* 5/1, 71–84.

Hahn (C.) 1990: 'Picturing the Narrative: Narrative in the *Life* of Saints', *Art History* 13/1, 1–33.

Haldon (J.) 1986: 'Everyday life in Byzantium: Some Problems of Approach', *Byzantine and Modern Greek Studies* 10, 51–72.

Haldon (J.) 1990: *Constantine Porphyrogenitus, Three Treatises on Imperial Military Expeditions.* Corpus Fontium Historiae Byzantinae 28. Vienna.

Hamann-MacLean (R.) and (H.) Hallensleben 1963: *Die Monumentalmalerei in Serbien und Makedonien vom 11. bis zum frühen 14. Jahrhundert.* Giessen.

Hanfmann (G. M. A.) 1951: 'Socrates and Christ', *Harvard Studies of Classical Philology* 60, 205–233.

Harvey (S. Ashbrook) 1990: 'Women in Early Byzantine Hagiography: Reversing the Story', in L. Coon, K. Haldane, and E. Summers, eds., *'That Gentle Strength': Historical Perspectives on Women and Christianity.* Charlottesville, 36–59.

Haugh (R.) 1975: *Photius and the Carolingians, The Trinitarian Heresy.* Belmont.

Heikel (I.A.) ed. 1891: *Ignatii Diaconi Vita Tarasii Archiepiscopi Constantinopolitani.* Acta Societatis Scientiarum Fennicae 17. Helsinki.

Hemmerdinger (B.) 1962: 'Une mission scientifique arabe à l'origine de la Renaissance Iconoclaste', *Byzantinische Zeitschrift* 55, 66–67.

Hemmerdinger (B.) 1964: 'La culture grècque classique du VIIe au IXe siècle', *Byzantion* 34, 125–133.

Hendy (M.) 1985: *Studies in the Byzantine Monetary Economy c.300–1450.* Cambridge.

Hennecke (E.) and (W.) Schneemelcher 1963: *New Testament Apocrypha.* 2 vols. Philadelphia.

Henry (P.) 1976: 'What was the Iconoclastic Controversy All About?', *Church History* 45, 16–31.

Henry (R.) ed. 1959–1977: *Photius, Bibliothèque.* 8 vols. Paris.

Herbert (J. A.) 1911: *Illuminated Manuscripts*. New York.

Hergenröther (J.) 1867–1869: *Photius, Patriarch von Constantinopel. Sein Leben, seine Schriften und das griechische Schisma*. 3 vols. Regensburg.

Herrin (J.) 1977: 'The Context of Iconoclast Reform', in Bryer and Herrin, eds. (1977), 15–20.

Herrin (J.) 1983: 'In Search of Byzantine Women: Three Avenues of Approach', in A. Cameron and A. Kuhrt, eds., *Images of Women in Antiquity*. London, 167–189.

Hesseling (D. C.) 1909: *Miniatures de l'Octateuque grec de Smyrne*. Leiden.

Holum (K.) 1982: *Theodosian Empresses. Women and Imperial Dominion in Late Antiquity*. Berkeley.

Huber (P.) 1973: *Bild und Botschaft. Byzantinische Miniaturen zum Alten und Neuen Testament*. Zurich.

Hussey (J. M.) 1986: *The Orthodox Church in the Byzantine Empire*. Oxford.

Hutter (I.) 1972: 'Paläologische Übermalungen im Oktateuch Vaticanus graecus 747', *Jahrbuch der Österreichischen Byzantinistik* 21, 139–147.

Hutter (I.) and (P.) Canart 1991: *Das Marienhomiliar des Mönchs Jakobos von Kokkinobaphos, Codex Vaticanus Graecus 1162*. Codices e Vaticanis Selecti 79. Vatican City.

Ihm (C.) 1960: *Die Programme der christlichen Apsis-malerei vom vierten Jahrhundert bis zur Mitte des achten Jahrhunderts*. Forschungen zur Kunstgeschichte und christlichen Archäologie 4. Wiesbaden.

Ishizuka (A. M.) 1986: 'The Penitence of David in Paris, Bibl.Nat., Cod.gr.510. Iconography and its Place in Byzantine Manuscript Illustration', *Machikaneyama Ronso* 20, 3–22.

Jacopi (G.) 1932/3: 'Le miniature dei codici di Patmo', *Clara Rhodos* VI/VII, 573–591.

Jaeger (W.) 1947: 'Greek Uncial Fragments in the Library of Congress in Washington', *Traditio* 5, 79–102.

James (L.) 1991: 'Colour and the Byzantine Rainbow', *Byzantine and Modern Greek Studies* 15, 66–94.

James (L.) 1996: '"Pray Not to Fall into Temptation and Be on Your Guard": Pagan Statues in Christian Constantinople', *Gesta* 35/1, 12–20.

James (L.) and (R.) Webb 1991: '"To Understand Ultimate Things and Enter Secret Places": Ekphrasis and Art in Byzantium', *Art History* 14/1, 1–17.

James (M. R.) 1921: *Illustrations of the Book of Genesis: Being a Reproduction in Facsimile of the Manuscript, British Museum Egerton 1894*. Oxford.

Janin (R.) 1969: *La géographie ecclésiastique de l'empire byzantin I,3: Les églises et les monastères*. Second edn. Paris.

Jeffreys (E.) and (R.) Scott trans. 1986: *The Chronicle of John Malalas*. Melbourne.

Jeremias (G.) 1980: *Die Holztür der Basilika S. Sabina in Rom*. Tübingen.

Jerphanion (G. de) 1930: 'Quels sont les douze apôtres dans l'iconographie chrétienne?', *La voix des monuments*. Paris, 189–200.

Jerphanion (G. de) 1936: *Les églises rupestres de Cappadoce* II,1. Paris.

Jerphanion (G. de) 1938a: 'La date des plus récentes peintures de Toqale Kilisse en Cappadoce'. *La voix des monuments*. Rome and Paris, 222–225.

Jerphanion (G. de) 1938b: 'Histoires de Saint Basile dans les peintures cappadociennes et dans les peintures romaines du moyen âge', *La voix des monuments*. Rome and Paris, 153–173.

Jolivet-Levy (C.) 1987: 'L'image du pouvoir dans l'art byzantin à l'époque de la dynastie macédonienne', *Byzantion* 57, 441–470.

Jolivet-Levy (C.) 1989: 'Les programmes iconographiques des églises de Cappadoce au Xe siècle. Nouvelles recherches', *Constantine VII Porphyrogenitus and His Age*. Second International Byzantine Conference, Delphi 1987. Athens, 247–284.

Josi (E.), (V.) Federici, and (E.) Ercadi 1967: *La porta bizantina di San Paolo*. Rome.

Jugie (M.) 1939: 'Origine de la controverse sur l'addition du *Filioque* au symbole', *Revue des Sciences Philosophiques et Théologiques* 28, 369–385.

Kalavrezou (I.) 1989: 'A New Type of Icon: Ivories and Steatites', *Constantine VII Porphyrogenitus and His Age*. Second International Byzantine Conference, Delphi 1987. Athens, 377–396.

Kalavrezou (I.) 1990: 'Images of the Mother: When the Virgin Mary Became *Meter Theou*', *Dumbarton Oaks Papers* 44, 165–172.

Kalavrezou-Maxeiner (I.) 1977: 'Eudokia Makrembolitissa and the Romanos Ivory', *Dumbarton Oaks Papers* 31, 305–325.

Kalavrezou-Maxeiner (I.) 1978: 'The Portraits of Basil I in Paris gr.510', *Jahrbuch der Österreichischen Byzantinistik* 27, 19–24.

Kaplan (M.) 1991: 'Maisons impériales et fondations pieuses: réorganisation de la fortune impériale et assistance publique de la fin du VIIIe siècle à la fin du Xe siècle', *Byzantion* 61, 340–364.

Kaplan (M.) 1992: *Les hommes et la terre à Byzance du VIe au XIe siècle, propriété et exploitation du sol*. Byzantina sorbonensia 10. Paris.

Karlin-Hayter (P.) 1966: 'Quel est l'empereur Constantin le nouveau commémoré dans le synaxaire au 3. Septembre', *Byzantion* 36, 624–626.

Karlin-Hayter (P.) 1977: 'Gregory of Syracuse, Ignatios, and Photios', in Bryer and Herrin, eds. (1977), 141–145.

Karlin-Hayter (P.) 1991: 'L'enjeu d'une rumeur. Opinion et imaginaire à Byzance au IXe s.', *Jahrbuch der Österreichischen Byzantinistik* 41, 85–111.

Karpp (H.) 1966: *Die frühchristlichen und mittelalterlichen Mosaiken in Santa Maria Maggiore zu Rom*. Baden-Baden.

Kartsonis (A.) 1986: *Anastasis, The Making of an Image*. Princeton.

Kazhdan (A.) 1984: 'The Aristocracy and the Imperial Ideal', in M. Angold, ed., *The Byzantine Aristocracy, IX to XIII Centuries*. BAR International Series 221. Oxford, 43–57.

Kazhdan (A.) 1987: 'Constantin imaginaire. Byzantine Legends of the Ninth Century about Constantine the Great', *Byzantion* 57, 196–250.

Kazhdan (A.) and (G.) Constable 1982: *People and Power in Byzantium, An Introduction to Modern Byzantine Studies*. Washington DC.

Kazhdan (A.) and (H.) Maguire 1991: 'Byzantine Hagiographical Texts as Sources on Art', *Dumbarton Oaks Papers* 45, 1–22.

Kessler (H. L.) 1973: 'Paris.gr.102: A Rare Illustrated Acts of the Apostles', *Dumbarton Oaks Papers* 27, 211–216.

Kessler (H. L.) 1977: *The Illustrated Bibles from Tours*. Studies in Manuscript Illumination 7. Princeton.

Kessler (H. L.) 1979: 'Scenes from the Acts of the Apostles on Some Early Christian Ivories', *Gesta* 18/1, 109–119.

Kessler (H. L.) 1985a: 'Pictorial Narrative and Church Mission in Sixth-Century Gaul', *Studies in the History of Art* 16, 75–91.

Kessler (H. L.) 1985b: 'Pictures as Scripture in Fifth-Century Churches', *Studia Artium, Orientalis et Occidentalis* II/1, 17–31.

Kessler (H. L.) 1990: 'An Apostle in Armor and the Mission of Carolingian Art', *Arte medievale*, ser. 2, 4/1, 17–39.

Kessler (H. L.) 1991/2: '"Pictures Fertile with Truth": How Christians Managed to Make Images of God without Violating the Second Commandment', *Journal of the Walters Art Gallery* 49/50, 53–65.

Kessler (H. L.) 1992: 'A Lay Abbot as Patron: Count Vivian and the First Bible of Charles the Bald', *Committenti e produzione artistico-letteraria nell'alto medioevo occidentale*. Settimane di studio del Centro italiano di studi sull'alto medioevo 39. Spoleto, 647–675.

Kislinger (E.) 1983: 'Eudokia Ingerina, Basileios I, und Michael III', *Jahrbuch der Österreichischen Byzantinistik* 33, 119–136.

Kitzinger (E.) 1973: 'Observations on the Samson Floor at Mopsuestia', *Dumbarton Oaks Papers* 27, 135–144.

Kitzinger (E.) 1974: 'A Pair of Silver Book Covers in the Sion Treasury', in U. E. McCracken *et al.*, eds, *Gatherings for Dorothy E. Miner*. Baltimore, 3–17.

Kondakoff (N.) 1886, 1891: *Histoire de l'art byzantin considerée principalement dans les miniatures*. 2 vols. Trans. M. Trawinski. Paris. Reprinted New York, 1970.

Kotter (B.) ed. 1975: *Die Schriften des Johannes von Damaskos* III: *Contra imaginum calumniatores orationes tres*. Patristische Texte und Studien 17. Berlin.

Kraeling (C.) 1956: *The Excavations at Dura-Europos. Final Report VIII, Part I. The Synagogue*. New Haven.

Krautheimer (R.) 1983: *Three Christian Capitals, Topography and Politics*. Berkeley.

Kravari (V.) 1991: 'Note sur le prix des manuscrits (IXe–XVe siècle)', in V. Kravari, J. Lefort, and C. Morrisson, eds., *Hommes et richesses dans l'Empire byzantin* II, *VIIIe–XVe siècle*. Réalités Byzantines 3. Paris, 375–384.

Kresten (O.) 1994: 'Leon III. und die Landmauern von Konstantinopel', *Römische Historische Mitteilungen* 36, 21–52.

Künzle (P.) 1961/2: 'Per una visione organica dei mosaici antichi di S. Maria Maggiore', *Atti della Pontificia accademia romana di archeologia, Rendiconti* 34, 154–190.

Kustas (G. L.) 1962: 'The Literary Criticism of Photios, A Christian Definition of Style', *Hellenika* 17, 132–69.

Kustas (G. L.) 1964: 'History and Theology in Photius', *Greek Orthodox Theological Review* 10, 37–74.

Ladner (G. B.) 1953: 'The Concept of the Image in the Greek Fathers and the Byzantine Iconoclastic Controversy', *Dumbarton Oaks Papers* 7, 3–34.

Lafontaine (J.) 1959: *Peintures médiévales dans le temple dit de la Fortune Virile à Rome*. Brussels and Rome.

Lafontaine-Dosogne (J.) 1968: 'Théophanes – visions auxquelles participent les prophètes dans l'art byzantin après la restauration des images', *Synthronon. Art et archéologie de la fin de l'antiquité et du moyen âge*. Bibliothèque des Cahiers Archéologiques 2. Paris, 135–143.

Lafontaine-Dosogne (J.) 1975: 'Iconography of the Cycle of the Infancy of Christ', in P. Underwood, ed., *The Kariye Djami* IV. Princeton, 197–241.

Lafontaine-Dosogne (J.) 1987a: 'L'illustration du cycle des mages suivant l'Homélie sur la Nativité attribuée à Jean Damascène', *Le Muséon* 100, 211–224.

Lafontaine-Dosogne (J.) 1987b: 'Pour une problématique de la peinture d'Eglise byzantine à l'époque iconoclaste', *Dumbarton Oaks Papers* 41, 321–337.

Laourdas (B.) ed. 1959: *Φωτίου ὁμιλίαι*. Thessaloniki.

Laourdas (B.) and (L. G.) Westerink, eds. 1983, 1984, 1985: *Photii Patriarchae Constantinopolitani, Epistulae et Amphilochia*, vols. 1–3 (Epistulae). Bibliotheca Scriptorum Graecorum et Romanorum Teubneriana. Leipzig.

Lassus (J.) 1973: *L'illustration byzantine du Livre des Rois*. Bibliothèque des Cahiers Archéologiques IX. Paris.

Lassus (J.) 1979: 'La création du monde dans les octateuques byzantins du douzième siècle', *Monuments et Mémoires, Fondation Eugène Piot* 62, 85–148.

Lazarev (V.) 1967: *Storia della pittura bizantina*. Turin.

Legrand (E.) ed. 1896: 'Description des œuvres d'art et de l'église des Saints Apôtres de Constantinople, poème en vers iambiques par Constantin le Rhodien', *Revue des Etudes Grècques* 9, 32–103.

Lehmann (K.) 1945: 'The Dome of Heaven', *Art Bulletin* 27, 1–27.

Lektionar 1994: *Lektionar von St Petersburg: vollständige Faksimile-Ausgabe im Originalformat des codex gr. 21, gr. 21a des Russischen Nationalbibliothek in St Petersburg*. 2 vols. Graz.

Lemerle (P.) 1943: *Le style byzantin*. Paris.

Lemerle (P.) 1952: 'Psychologie de l'art byzantin', *Bulletin de l'Association Guillaume Budé* ser. 3, 1, 49–58. Reprinted in P. Lemerle, *Essais sur le monde byzantin*. London, 1970, essay VII.

Lemerle (P.) 1965: 'L'orthodoxie byzantine et l'œcuménisme médiéval: les origines du "schisme" des églises', *Bulletin de l'Association Giullaume Budé* ser. 4, 2, 228–246. Reprinted in P. Lemerle, *Essais sur le monde byzantin*. London, 1970, essay VIII.

Lemerle (P.) 1973: 'L'histoire des Pauliciens d'Asie Mineure d'après les sources grècques', *Travaux et Mémoires du Centre de recherche d'histoire et civilisation byzantines* 5, 1–144.

Lemerle (P.) 1986: *Byzantine Humanism, the First Phase. Notes and Remarks on Education and Culture in Byzantium from its Origins to the 10th Century*, Byzantina Australiensia 3. Trans. H. Lindsay and A. Moffat. Canberra. Rev. edn of P. Lemerle, *Le premier humanisme byzantin. Notes et remarques sur enseignement et culture à Byzance des origines au Xe siècle*, Bibliothèque Byzantine, Etudes 6. Paris, 1971.

Leroy (Jules) 1964: *Les manuscrits syriaques à peintures conservés dans les bibliothèques d'Europe et d'orient*. Institut Français d'Archéologie de Beyrouth. Bibliothèque Archéologique et Historique 77. Paris.

Leroy (Jules) 1974: *Les manuscrits coptes et coptes-arabes illustrés*. Institut Français d'Archéologie de Beyrouth. Bibliothèque Archéologique et Historique 96. Paris.

Leroy (Julien) 1961: 'Un témoin ancien des Petites Catéchèses de Theodore Studite', *Scriptorium* 15, 36–60.

Leroy (Julien) 1974: 'Note codicologique sur le Vat.gr.699', *Cahiers Archéologiques* 23, 73–78.

Leroy (Julien) 1976: *Les types de réglure des manuscrits grecs*. Paris.

Leroy (Julien) 1978: 'Les manuscrits grecs d'Italie', *Codicologia* 2, 52–71.

Lipsius (R.) 1883: *Die apokryphen Apostelgeschichten und Apostellegenden* I. Brunswick.

Ljubinković (R.) 1965: 'Sur le symbolisme de l'histoire de Joseph du narthex de Sopoćani', *L'art byzantin du XIIIe siècle*, Symposium de Sopoćani. Belgrade, 207–237.

Lokin (J. H. A.) 1994: 'The Significance of Law and Legislation in the Law Books of the Ninth to Eleventh Centuries', in A. Laiou and D. Simon, eds., *Law and Society in Byzantium, Ninth–Twelfth Centuries*. Washington DC, 71–91.

Loos (M.) 1964: 'Le mouvement paulicien à Byzance', *Byzantinoslavica* 25, 258–86.

L'Orange (H. P.) 1935: 'Sol-Invictus Imperator. Ein Beitrag zur Apotheose', *Symbolae Osloenses* 14, 86–114.

Lowden (J.) 1982: 'The Production of the Vatopedi Octateuch', *Dumbarton Oaks Papers* 36, 115–126.

Lowden (J.) 1988: *Illuminated Prophet Books. A Study of Byzantine Manuscripts of the Major and Minor Prophets*. University Park.

Lowden (J.) 1990: 'Luxury and Liturgy: the Function of Books', in R. Morris, ed., *Church and People in Byzantium*. Birmingham, 263–280.

Lowden (J.) 1992: *The Octateuchs. A Study in Byzantine Manuscript Illumination*. University Park.

Ludwich (A.) ed. 1897: *Eudociae Augustae, Procli Lycii, Claudiani Carminum Graecorum Reliquiae*. Leipzig.

Maas (M.) 1990: 'Photius' Treatment of Josephus and the High Priesthood', *Byzantion* 40, 183–194.

MacCormack (S.) 1981: *Art and Ceremony in Late Antiquity*, The Transformation of the Classical Heritage 1. Berkeley.

McCormick (M.) 1986: *Eternal Victory: Triumphal Rulership in Late Antiquity, Byzantium and the Early Medieval West*. Past and Present Publications. Cambridge.

McGeer (E.) 1988: 'Infantry versus Cavalry: The Byzantine Response', *Revue des Etudes Byzantines* 46, 135–145.

McGrath (R. L.) 1965: 'The Martyrdom of the Makkabees on the Brescia Casket', *Art Bulletin* 47, 257–261.

McGucken (J. A.) 1985: 'The Patristic Exegesis on the Transfiguration', *Studia Patristica* 18, 335–341.

McKitterick (R.) 1990: 'Text and Image in the Carolingian World', in R. McKitterick, ed., *The Uses of Literacy in Early Mediaeval Europe*. Cambridge, 297–318.

Macrides (R.) 1992: 'Dynastic Marriages and Political Kinship', in J. Shepard and S. Franklin, eds., *Byzantine Diplomacy*. London, 262–280.

Macrides (R.) and (P.) Magdalino 1988: 'The Architecture of Ekphrasis: Construction and Context of Paul the Silentiary's Ekphrasis of Hagia Sophia', *Byzantine and Modern Greek Studies* 12, 47–82.

de Maffei (F.) 1974: *Icona, pittore e arte al concilio Niceno II*. Rome.

Magdalino (P.) 1987: 'Observations on the Nea Ekklesia of Basil I', *Jahrbuch der Österreichischen Byzantinistik* 37, 51–64.

Magdalino (P.) 1988: 'Basil I, Leo VI, and the Feast of the Prophet Elijah', *Jahrbuch der Österreichischen Byzantinistik* 38, 193–196.

Magdalino (P.) 1996: *Constantinople médiévale. Etudes sur l'évolution des structures urbaines*. Travaux et Mémoires du Centre de recherche d'histoire et civilisation de byzance, Monographies 9. Paris.

Maguire (H.) 1974: 'Truth and Convention in Byzantine Descriptions of Works of Art', *Dumbarton Oaks Papers* 28, 113–140.

Maguire (H.) 1977: 'The Depiction of Sorrow in Middle Byzantine Art', *Dumbarton Oaks Papers* 31, 123–174.

Maguire (H.) 1980/1: 'The Iconography of Symeon with the Christ Child in Byzantine Art', *Dumbarton Oaks Papers* 34/35, 261–269.

Maguire (H.) 1981: *Art and Eloquence in Byzantium*. Princeton.

Maguire (H.) 1988: 'The Art of Comparing in Byzantium', *Art Bulletin* 70, 88–103.

Maguire (H.) 1989: 'Style and Ideology in Byzantine Imperial Art', *Gesta* 28/2, 217–231.

Maguire (H.) 1990: 'Garments Pleasing to God: The Significance of Domestic Textile Designs in the Early Byzantine Period', *Dumbarton Oaks Papers* 44, 215–224.

Maguire (H.) 1992: 'Byzantine Art History in the Second Half of the Twentieth Century', in A. Laiou and H. Maguire, eds., *Byzantium, a World Civilization*. Washington DC, 119–155.

Maguire (H.) 1995: 'A Murderer among the Angels: the Frontispiece Miniatures of Paris gr.510', in R. Ousterhout and L. Brubaker, eds., *The Sacred Image East and West*. Illinois Byzantine Studies 4. Urbana, 63–71.

Maguire (H.) 1996: *The Icons of their Bodies. Saints and their Images in Byzantium*. Princeton.

Malickij (N.) 1926: 'Remarques sur la date des mosaiques de l'église des Saints-Apôtres à Constantinople décrites par Mésaritès', *Byzantion* 3, 123–151.

Mango (C.) 1958: *The Homilies of Photius, Patriarch of Constantinople*. Dumbarton Oaks Studies 3. Washington DC.

Mango (C.) 1962: *Materials for the Study of the Mosaics of St Sophia at Istanbul*. Dumbarton Oaks Studies 8. Washington DC.

Mango (C.) 1963: 'A Forged Inscription of the Year 781', *Zbornik Radova* 8, 201–207.

Mango (C.) 1972: *The Art of the Byzantine Empire 312–1453*. Sources and Documents in the History of Art. Englewood Cliffs.

Mango (C.) 1973: 'Eudocia Ingerina, the Normans, and the Macedonian Dynasty', *Zbornik Radova* 14/15, 17–27.

Mango (C.) 1975: 'The Availability of Books in the Byzantine Empire, AD 750–850', *Byzantine Books and Bookmen*. New York, 29–45.

Mango (C.) 1977a: 'Historical Introduction', in Bryer and Herrin, eds. (1977), 1–6.

Mango (C.) 1977b: 'The Liquidation of Iconoclasm and the Patriarch Photios', in Bryer and Herrin, eds. (1977), 133–140.

Mango (C.) 1982: 'Daily Life in Byzantium', *XVI. Internationaler Byzantinistenkongress. Akten I/1 = Jahrbuch der Österreichischen Byzantinistik* 32/1, 337–353. Reprinted in C. Mango, *Byzantium and its Image*. London, essay IV.

Mango (C.) 1990a: 'Constantine's mausoleum and the translation of relics', *Byzantinische Zeitschrift* 83, 51–62, 434.

Mango (C.) 1990b: *Nikephoros, Patriarch of Constantinople, Short History*. Corpus Fontium Historiae Byzantinae XIII, Dumbarton Oaks Texts 10. Washington DC.

Mango (C.) and (E. J. W.) Hawkins 1965: 'The Apse Mosaics at St Sophia at Istanbul', *Dumbarton Oaks Papers* 19, 115–151.

Mango (C.) and (E. J. W.) Hawkins 1972: 'The Mosaics of St Sophia at Istanbul. The Church Fathers in the North Tympanum', *Dumbarton Oaks Papers* 26, 3–41.

Mango (C.) and (I.) Ševčenko 1973: 'Some Churches and Monasteries on the Southern Shore of the Sea of Marmara', *Dumbarton Oaks Papers* 27, 235–277.

Markopoulos (A.) 1992: 'An Anonymous Laudatory Poem in Honor of Basil I', *Dumbarton Oaks Papers* 46, 225–232.

Marković (J.) and (M.) Marković 1995: 'Genesis Cycle and Old Testament Figures in the Chapel of St Demetrios', in V .J. Djurić, *Zidno slikarstvo manastira Dečana* (Wall paintings of the monastery of Dečani). Belgrade, 323–350. In Serbian with English summary at 351–352.

Martin (E. J.) 1930: *A History of the Iconoclastic Controversy*. London.

Martin (J. R.) 1950: 'An Early Illustration of the Sayings of the Fathers', *Art Bulletin* 32, 291–295.

Martin (J. R.) 1954: *The Illustration of the Heavenly Ladder of John Climacus*. Studies in Manuscript Illumination 5. Princeton.

Martin (J. R.) 1955: 'The Dead Christ on the Cross in Byzantine Art', in K. Weitzmann, ed., *Late Classical and Mediaeval Studies in Honor of Albert Mathias Friend Jr*. Princeton, 189–196.

Marx (K.) 1973: 'The Eighteenth Brumaire of Louis Bonaparte', in D. Fernbach, ed., *Surveys from Exile, Political Writings* 2. Harmondsworth, 143–249.

Mateos (J.) 1963: *Le typicon de la Grande Eglise*. 2 vols. Orientalia Christiana Analecta 166–167. Rome.

Mathews (T. F.) 1993: *The Clash of Gods, a Reinterpretation of Early Christian Art*. Princeton.

Matthews (J. T.) 1980: 'Reflections of Philo Judaeus in the Septuagint Illustrations of the Joseph Story', *Byzantine Studies / Etudes Byzantines* 7, 35–56.

Mazal (O.) 1984: *Josua-Rolle. Vollständige Faksimile-Ausgabe im Originalformat des Codex Vaticanus Palatinus Graecus 431 der Biblioteca Apostolica Vaticana*. Graz.

Meijer (J.) 1975: *A Successful Council of Union: A Theological Analysis of the Photian Synod of 879–880*. Analekta Blatadon XXIII. Thessaloniki.

Menologio 1907: *Il menologio di Basilio II (cod. Vaticano greco 1613)*, Codices e Vaticanis Selecti VIII. Turin.

Miles (M. R.) 1985: *Image as Insight. Visual Understanding in Western Christianity and Secular Culture*. Boston.

Millet (G.) 1910: 'Les iconoclastes et la croix: à propos d'une inscription de Cappadoce', *Bulletin de Correspondance Hellénique* 34, 96–109.

Millet (G.) 1916: *Recherches sur l'iconographie de l'Evangile aux XIVe, XVe et XVIe siècles*. Paris.

Millet (G.) 1920: 'L'art byzantin', in A. Michel, ed., *Histoire de l'art depuis le premiers temps chrétiens jusqu'à nos jours* I/1. Paris.

Miniature 1905: *Miniature della Bibbia Cod. Vat. regin. greco I e del Salterio Cod. Vat. Palat. greco 381*. Collezione paleografica vaticana, fasc. I. Milan.

Mitius (O.) 1897: *Jonas auf den Denkmalern des christlichen Altertums*. Freiburg i.B.

Moffat (A.) 1977: 'Schooling in the Iconoclast Centuries', in Bryer and Herrin, eds. (1977), 85–92.

Mondzain-Baudinet (M. J.) 1990: *Nicéphore, Discours contre les iconoclastes*. Paris.

Moorhead (J.) 1985: 'Iconoclasm, the Cross and the Imperial Image', *Byzantion* 55, 165–179.

Moravcsik (G.) 1961: 'Sagen und Legenden über Kaiser Basileios I', *Dumbarton Oaks Papers* 15, 59–126.

Moravcsik (G.) ed. and Jenkins (R. J. H.) trans. 1967: *Constantine Porphyrogenitus, De Administrando Imperio*. Dumbarton Oaks Texts 1, Corpus Fontium Historiae Byzantinae 1. Washington DC.

Moreland (J.) 1991: 'Method and Theory in Medieval Archaeology in the 1990's', *Archeologia Medievale* 18, 7–42.

Morey (C. R.) 1929: 'Notes on East Christian Miniatures', *Art Bulletin* 11, 5–103.

Morris (R.) 1976: 'The Powerful and the Poor in Tenth-Century Byzantium: Law and Reality', *Past and Present* 73, 3–27.

Morris (R.) 1995: *Monks and Laymen in Byzantium 843–1118*. Cambridge.

Mossay (J.) 1973: 'Notes sur l'herméneutique des sources littéraires de l'histoire byzantine', *Recherches de Philologie et de Linguistique*. Louvain, 39–51.

Mossay (J.) 1982: 'Le signe héliaque. Notes sur quelques manuscrits de S. Grégoire de

Nazianze', in L. Hadermann-Misguich and G. Raepsaet, eds., *Rayonnement grec. Hommages à Charles Delvoye*. Brussels, 273–284.

Mullett (M.) 1988: 'Byzantium: A Friendly Society?', *Past and Present* 118, 3–24.

Mullett (M.) 1990: 'Writing in Early Mediaeval Byzantium', in R. McKitterick, ed., *The Uses of Literacy in Early Mediaeval Europe*. Cambridge, 156–185.

Mundell (M. C.) 1975: 'A Sixth-Century Funerary Relief at Dara in Mesopotamia', *Jahrbuch der Österreichischen Byzantinistik* 24, 209–227.

Muñoz (A.) 1907: *Il Codice Purpureo di Rossano*. Rome.

Mütherich (F.) 1987: 'Das Verzeichnis eines griechischen Bilderzyklus in dem St Galler Codex 48', *Dumbarton Oaks Papers* 41, 415–423.

Mütherich (F.) and (J.) Gaehde 1976: *Carolingian Painting*. New York.

Muthesius (A.) 1992: 'Silken Diplomacy', in J. Shepard and S. Franklin, eds., *Byzantine Diplomacy*. London, 237–248.

Narkiss (B.) 1979: 'The Sign of Jonah', *Gesta* 18/1, 63–76.

Narkiss (B.) 1987: 'The "Main Plane" as a Compositional Element in the Style of the Macedonian Renaissance and its Origins', *Dumbarton Oaks Papers* 41, 425–441.

Nelson (J.) 1976: 'Symbols in Context: Rulers' Inauguration Rituals in Byzantium and the West in the Early Middle Ages', *Studies in Church History* 13, 97–119.

Nelson (J.) 1990: 'Literacy in Carolingian Government', in R. McKitterick, ed., *The Uses of Literacy in Early Mediaeval Europe*. Cambridge, 258–296.

Nelson (R.) 1980: *The Iconography of Preface and Miniature in the Byzantine Gospel Book*. New York.

Nelson (R.) 1995: 'The Italian Appreciation and Appropriation of Illuminated Byzantine Manuscripts, ca. 1200–1450', *Dumbarton Oaks Papers* 49, 209–235.

Neuss (W.) 1912: *Das Buch Ezekiel in Theologie und Kunst bis zum Ende des XII. Jahrhunderts*. Münster.

Nimmo Smith (J.) 1992: *Pseudo-Nonniani in IV orationes Gregorii Nazianzeni Commentarii*. Corpus Christianorum, Series Graeca 27, Corpus Nazianzenum 2. Turnhout.

Nobbs (A. E.) 1990: 'Philostorgius' View of the Past', in G. Clarke, ed., *Reading the Past in Late Antiquity*. Oxford, 251–264.

Noble (T. F. X.) 1987: 'John Damascene and the history of the Iconoclastic Controversy', in T. F. X. Noble and J. J. Contreni, eds., *Religion, Culture, and Society in the Early Middle Ages. Studies in Honor of Richard E. Sullivan*. Studies in Medieval Culture 23. Kalamazoo, 95–116.

Nordenfalk (C.) 1970: *Die spätantiken Zierbuchstaben*. Die Buchornamentik der Spätantike 2. Stockholm.

Nordhagen (P. J.) 1965: 'The Mosaics of John VII (705–707 A.D.)', *Acta ad Archaeologiam et Artium Historiam Pertinentia* 2, 121–166.

Nordstrom (C.-O.) 1955/7: 'Some Jewish Legends in Byzantine Art', *Byzantion* 25/27, 487–508.

Obolensky (D.) 1971: *The Byzantine Commonwealth, Eastern Europe 500–1453*. London.

Oikonomides (N.) 1985a: *Byzantine Lead Seals*. Washington DC.

Oikonomides (N.) 1985b: 'Some Remarks on the Apse Mosaic of St Sophia', *Dumbarton Oaks Papers* 39, 111–115.

Oikonomides (N.) 1986: 'L'artiste-amateur à Byzance', in X. Barral i Altet, ed., *Artistes, Artisans et Production Artistique au Moyen Age*. Paris, 45–50.

Omont (H.) 1902: *Miniatures du Psautier de S. Louis*. Leiden.

Omont (H.) 1909: 'Peintures de l'Ancien Testament dans un manuscrit syriaque', *Monument Piot* 17, 85–98.

Omont (H.) 1927: 'Miniatures des homélies sur la Vierge du moine Jacques (MS grec 1208 de Paris)', *Bulletin de la Société Française de Reproductions de Manuscrits à Peintures* 11, 1–24.

Omont (H.) 1929: *Miniatures des plus anciens manuscrits grecs de la Bibliothèque Nationale, du VIe au XIVe siècle*. Paris.

Omont (H.) n[o] d[ate]: *Evangiles avec peintures byzantines du XIe siècle*. 2 vols. Paris.

Onians (J.) 1980: 'Abstraction and Imagination in Late Antiquity', *Art History* 3, 1–23.

Ortner (S. B.) 1984: 'Theory in Anthropology since the Sixties', *Society for Comparative Study of Society and History* 26/1, 126–166.

Osborne (J.) 1981a: 'A Note on the Date of the Sacra Parallela (Parisinus graecus 923)', *Byzantion* 51, 316–317.

Osborne (J.) 1981b: 'The Painting of the Anastasis in the Lower Church of San Clemente, Rome: a re-examination of the evidence for the tomb of St Cyril', *Byzantion* 51, 255–287.

Ötüken (Y.) and (R.) Ousterhout 1989: 'Notes on the Monuments of Turkish Thrace', *Anatolian Studies* 39, 121–149.

Ouspensky (L.) 1960: 'Quelques considérations au sujet de l'iconographie de la Pentecôte', *Messager de l'exarchat du patriarche russe en Europe occidentale* IX, 33–34, 45–92.

Pächt (O.) 1943: 'A Giottoesque Episode in English Medieval Art', *Journal of the Warburg and the Courtauld Institutes* 6, 51–70.

Pächt (J.) and (O.) Pächt 1954: 'An Unknown Cycle of Illustrations of the Life of Joseph', *Cahiers Archéologiques* 7, 35–50.

Pallas (D. I.) 1971: 'Eine Differenzierung unter den himmlischen Ordnungun (ikonographische Analyse)', *Byzantinische Zeitschrift* 64, 55–60.

Pallas (D. I.) 1974: 'Eine anikonische lineare Wanddekoration auf der Insel Ikaria. Zur Tradition der bilderlosen Kirchenausstattung', *Jahrbuch der Österreichischen Byzantinistik* 23, 271–314.

Pallas (D. I.) 1978: 'Une note sur la décoration de la chapelle de Haghios Basileios de Sinasos', *Byzantion* 48, 208–225.

Panofsky (E.) 1939: *Studies in Iconology*. Oxford.

Parker (E. C.) 1978: *The Descent from the Cross: its Relation to the Extra-Liturgical 'Depositio' Drama*. New York.

Parry (K.) 1989: 'Theodore Studites and the Patriarch Nicephoros on Image-Making as a Christian Imperative', *Byzantion* 59, 164–183.

Parry (K.) 1996: *Depicting the World. Byzantine Iconophile Thought of the Eighth and Ninth Centuries*. The Medieval Mediterranean 12. Leiden.

Patlagean (E.) 1968: 'Ancienne hagiographie byzantine et histoire sociale', *Annales. Economies, Sociétés, Civilisations* 1, 106–126. Reprinted in E. Patlagean, *Structure sociale, famille, chrétienté à Byzance, IVe–XIe siècles*. London, 1981, essay V. English trans. 'Ancient Byzantine Hagiography and Social History', in S. Wilson, ed., *Saints and their Cults: Studies in Religious Sociology, Folklore and History*. Cambridge, 1983, 101–121.

Patlagean (E.) 1976: 'L'histoire de la femme déguisée en moine et l'évolution de la sainteté féminine à Byzance', *Studi Medievali*, ser.3, 17, 597–623. Reprinted in E. Patlagean, *Structure sociale, famille, chrétienté à Byzance*. London, essay XI.

Patlagean (E.) 1979: 'Discours écrit, discours parlé, niveaux de culture à Byzance aux

VIIIeme–XIeme siècles', *Annales. Economies, Sociétés, Civilisations* 12, 264–278. Reprinted in E. Patlagean, *Structure sociale, famille, chrétienté à Byzance, IVe–XIe siècles.* London, 1981, essay VI.

Patlagean (E.) 1984: 'Les débuts d'une aristocratie byzantine et le témoignage de l'historiographie: système des noms et liens de parenté aux IXe–Xe siècles', in M. Angold, ed., *The Byzantine Aristocracy, IX–XIII centuries.* BAR International Series 221. Oxford, 23–42.

Patlagean (E.) 1986: 'Familles ct parentèles à Byzance', in A.Burguière *et al.*, eds., *Histoire de la famille I: Mondes lointains, mondes anciens.* Paris, 421–441.

Patlagean (E.) 1992: 'De la chasse et du souverain', *Dumbarton Oaks Papers* 46, 257–263.

Pelekanides (S. M.) *et al.* 1973, 1975: S. M. Pelekanides, P. C. Christou, C. Mauropoulou-Tsioumis, and S. N. Kadis. *The Treasures of Mount Athos. Illuminated Manuscripts*, vols. 1 and 2. Athens.

Pelekanides (S. M.) *et al.* 1979: Σ.Μ. Πελεκανίδου, Π.Κ. Χρήστου, Χ. Μαυροπούλου-Τσιούμη, Σ.Ν. Καδᾶς, and Α. Κατσαροῦ. *Οἱ Θησαυροὶ τοῦ ἁγίου ὄρους*, vol. 3. Athens. (Vol. 4 appears under Christou [P. C.])

Petković (V.) 1941: *Dečani* II. Belgrade.

Pincus (D.) 1996: 'The Stones of Venice in the Baptistery of San Marco: Eastern Marbles in Western Mosaics', in C. L. Striker, ed., *Architectural Studies in Memory of Richard Krautheimer.* Mainz, 137–141.

Pitra (J. B.) ed. 1858: *Spicilegium Solesmense Complectens Sanctorum Patrum Scriptorumque Ecclesiasticorum Andecdota Hactenus Opera . . .* 4. Paris.

Porcher (J.) 1964: 'Aux origines de la lettre ornée mediévale', *Mélanges Eugène Tisserant* 5, Studi e Testi 235. Vatican City, 273–276.

Ratkowska (P.) 1964: 'The Iconography of the Deposition without St John', *Journal of the Warburg and the Courtauld Institutes* 27, 312–317.

Reinink (G. J.) 1992: 'Ps.-Methodius: A Concept of History in Response to the Rise of Islam', in Av. Cameron and L. Conrad, eds., *The Byzantine and Early Islamic Near East I: Problems in the Literary Source Material.* Studies in Late Antiquity and Early Islam 1. Princeton, 149–187.

Restle (M.) 1967: *Byzantine Wall Painting in Asia Minor.* 3 vols. Greenwich.

Reuss (J.) 1957: *Matthäus-kommentare aus der griechischen Kirche aus Katenenhandschriften gesammelt und herausgegeben.* Texte und Untersuchungen 61. Berlin.

Riddle (M.) 1981: 'Illustration of the "Triumph" of Joseph the Patriarch', *Byzantine Papers* I (1981), 69–81.

Rizzo (J. J.) 1976: *The Encomium of Gregory Nazianzen by Nicetas the Paphlagonian.* Subsidia Hagiographica LVIII. Brussels.

Rodley (L.) 1983: 'The Pigeon House Church, Çavuşin', *Jahrbuch der Österreichischen Byzantinistik* 33, 301–339.

Rodzianko (V.) 1957: 'Filioque in Patristic Thought', *Studia Patristica* II. Texte und Untersuchungen 64. Berlin, 295–308.

Romanelli (P.) and (P. J.) Nordhagen 1964: *S. Maria Antiqua.* Rome.

Ross (M. C.) 1957: 'A Byzantine Gold Medallion at Dumbarton Oaks', *Dumbarton Oaks Papers* 11, 247–261.

Roth (C. P.) 1981: *St Theodore the Studite, On the Holy Icons.* Crestwood NY.

Rouan (M.-F.) 1981: 'Une lecture "iconoclaste" de la Vie d'Etienne le Jeune', *Travaux et Mémoires du Centre de Recherche d'Histoire et Civilisation Byzantines* 8, 415–436.

Ruggieri (V.) 1991: *Byzantine Religious Architecture (582–867): its History and Structural Elements*. Orientalia Christiana Analecta 237. Rome.

Sahas (D. J.) 1986a: *Icon and Logos. Sources in Eighth-Century Iconoclasm*. Toronto.

Sahas (D. J.) 1986b: 'What an Infidel Saw that a Faithful Did Not: Gregory Dekapolites (d.842) and Islam', *Greek Orthodox Theological Review* 31, 47–67.

Sansterre (J.-M.) 1982: 'Les missionaires latins, grecs et orientaux en Bulgarie dans la seconde moitié du IX siècle', *Byzantion* 52, 375–388.

Sansterre (J.-M.) 1994: 'La parole, le texte et l'image selon les auteurs byzantins des époques iconoclaste et posticonoclaste', *Testo e immagine nell'alto medioevo*. Settimane di studio del Centro italiano di studi sull'alto medioevo 41. Spoleto, 197–240.

Ščepkina (M. V.) 1977: *Miniaturi Khludovskoi Psalt'iri*. Moscow.

Schamp (J.) 1987: *Photios, historien des lettres. La Bibliothèque et ses notices biographiques*. Bibliothèque de la Faculté de Philosophie et Lettres de l'Université de Liege 248. Paris.

Schapiro (M.) 1949: 'The Place of the Joshua Roll in Byzantine History', *Gazette des Beaux-Arts* ser. 6, 35, 161–176.

Schapiro (M.) 1952: 'The Joseph Scenes on the Maximianus Throne in Ravenna', *Gazette des Beaux-Arts* ser.6, 40, 27–38.

Schermann (T.) 1907: *Propheten- und Apostellegenden*. Leipzig.

Schiller (G.) 1971: *Iconography of Christian Art*. 2 vols. Trans. J. Seligmann. Greenwich.

Schminck (A.) 1985: '"Rota tu volubilis", Kaisermacht und Patriarchenmacht in Mosaiken', in L. Burgmann, M. T. Fögen, and A. Schminck, eds., *Cupido Legum*. Frankfurt am Main, 211–234.

Schminck (A.) 1989: '"In hoc signo vinces" – aspects du "césaropapisme" à l'époque de Constantin VII Porphyrogénète', *Constantine VII Porphyrogenitus and His Age*, Second International Byzantine Conference, Delphi 22–26 July 1987. Athens, 103–116.

Schnasse (C.) 1869: *Geschichte der bildenden Kunste* III/1. Düsseldorf.

Schönborn (C.) 1976: *L'icône du Christ: Fondements théologiques*. Paradosis. Etudes de Littérature et de Théologie Anciennes 24. Second edn. Fribourg.

Schreiner (P.) 1991: 'Réflexions sur la famille impériale à Byzance (VIIIe–Xe siècles)', *Byzantion* 61, 181–193.

Schultze (B.) 1982: 'Zur Ursprung des Filioque: Das Filioque und der römische Primat', *Orientalia Christiana Periodica* 48, 5–18.

Schwartz (E.) 1972/3: 'A New Source for the Byzantine Anastasis', *Marsyas* 16, 29–34.

Sears (E.) 1986: *The Ages of Man. Medieval Interpretations of the Life Cycle*. Princeton.

Ševčenko (I.) 1962: 'The Illuminators of the Menologion of Basil II', *Dumbarton Oaks Papers* 16, 245–276.

Ševčenko (I.) 1965: 'The Anti-iconoclastic Poem in the Pantocrator Psalter', *Cahiers Archéologiques* 15, 39–60.

Ševčenko (I.) 1977: 'Hagiography of the Iconoclast Period', in Bryer and Herrin, eds (1977), 113–131.

Ševčenko (I.) 1978: 'La biographie de l'empereur Basile Ier', *La civiltà bizantina dal IX all'XI secolo, Aspetti e problemi* 2. Bari, 91–127.

Ševčenko (I.) 1984: 'A Program of Church Decoration Soon After 787 According to the *Vita Tarasii* of Ignatius the Deacon', abstract and translation distributed at the symposium *Byzantine Art and Literature around the Year 800*, Dumbarton Oaks.

Ševčenko (I.) 1992a: 'Re-reading Constantine Porphyrogenitus', in J. Shepard and S. Franklin, eds., *Byzantine Diplomacy*. Aldershot, 167–195.

Ševčenko (I.) 1992b: 'The Search for the Past in Byzantium around the Year 800', *Dumbarton Oaks Papers* 46, 279–293.

Ševčenko (N. P.) 1973: 'Cycles of the Life of St Nicholas in Byzantine Art'. PhD dissertation, Columbia University.

Ševčenko (N. P.) 1983: *The Life of Saint Nicholas in Byzantine Art*. Turin.

Ševčenko (N. P.) 1990: *Illustrated Manuscripts of the Metaphrastian Menologion*. Studies in Medieval Manuscript Illumination, Chicago Visual Library Text-Fiche Series, no. 54. Chicago.

Ševčenko (N. P.) 1991: 'Icons in the Liturgy', *Dumbarton Oaks Papers* 45, 45–57.

Ševčenko (N. P.) 1993/4: 'The Representation of Donors and Holy Figures on Four Byzantine Icons', Δελτίον ser. 4, 17, 157–164.

Shepard (J.) 1985: 'Information, Disinformation and Delay in Byzantine Diplomacy', *Byzantinische Forschungen* 10, 233–293.

Sheppard (C. D.) 1969: 'Byzantine Carved Marble Slabs', *Art Bulletin* 51, 65–71.

Shorr (D. C.) 1946: 'The Iconographical Development of the Presentation in the Temple', *Art Bulletin* 28, 17–32.

Simon (D.) 1994: 'Legislation as Both a World Order and a Legal Order', in A. Laiou and D. Simon, eds., *Law and Society in Byzantium, Ninth–Twelfth Centuries*. Washington DC, 1–25.

Sinko (T.) 1917, 1923: *De traditione Orationum Gregorii Nazianzeni*. 2 vols. Cracow.

Spain (S.) 1979: 'The Promised Blessing: the Iconography of the Mosaics at S. Maria Maggiore', *Art Bulletin* 61, 518–540.

Spatharakis (I.) 1974: 'The Portraits and the Date of the Codex Par.gr.510', *Cahiers Archéologiques* 23, 97–105.

Spatharakis (I.) 1976: *The Portrait in Byzantine Illuminated Manuscripts*. Leiden.

Spatharakis (I.) 1981: *Corpus of Dated Illustrated Greek Manuscripts to the Year 1453*. Leiden.

Spatharakis (I.) 1989: 'A Note on the Imperial Portraits and the Date of Par.gr.510', *Jahrbuch der Österreichischen Byzantinistik* 39, 89–93.

Speck (P.) 1986: 'Die Ursprünge der byzantinischen Renaissance', *The 17th International Byzantine Congress, Major Papers*. New York, 555–576.

Speck (P.) 1987: 'Anthologia Palatina I,1 und das Apsismosaik der Hagia Sophia', *ΠΟΙΚΙΛΑ BYZANTINA* 6, Varia 2, 287–329.

Speyart van Woerden (J.) 1961: 'The Iconography of the Sacrifice of Isaac', *Vigiliae Christianae* 15, 214–255.

Speyer (W.) 1971: *Die literarische Falschung im heidnischen und christlichen Altertum*. Munich.

Spiegel (G. M.) 1990: 'History, Historicism, and the Social Logic of the Text in the Middle Ages', *Speculum* 65, 59–86.

Squilbeck (J.) 1966/7: 'La tentation du Christ au désert et le Bellinger insignis', *Bulletin des Musées Royaux d'Art et d'Histoire de Bruxelles* ser. 4, 38/39, 118–152.

Starr (J.) 1939: *The Jews in the Byzantine Empire 641–1204*. Athens.

Stavropoulou-Makri (A.) 1990: 'Le thème du massacre des innocents dans la peinture post-byzantine et son rapport avec l'art italien renaissant', *Byzantion* 40, 366–381.

Stein (D.) 1980: *Der Beginn des byzantinischen Bilderstreites und seine Entwicklung bis in die 40er Jahr des 8. Jahrhunderts*. Miscellanea Byzantina Monacensia 25. Munich.

Steiner (M.) 1962: *La tentation de Jésus dans l'interprétation patristique de Justin à Origène*. Paris.

Stern (H.) 1953: *Le calendrier de 354*. Paris.

Stern (H.) 1960: 'Les peintures du Mausolée "de l'Exode" a El-Bagaouat', *Cahiers Archéologiques* 11, 93–120.

Stichel (R.) 1974: 'Außerkanonische Elemente in byzantinischen Illustrationen des Alten Testaments', *Römische Quartalschrift* 69, 159–181.

Stornajolo (C.) 1908: *Le miniature della Topografia Cristiana di Cosma Indicopleuste. Codice vaticano greco 699*. Codices e Vaticanis Selecti X. Milan.

Stornajolo (C.) 1910: *Miniature della Omilie di Giacomo Monaco (cod. Vatic. gr. 1162) e dell'Evangeliario greco urbinate (cod. Vatic. Urbin. gr. 2)*. Codices e Vaticanis Selecti, series minor I. Rome.

Striker (C. L.) and (Y.) Doğan Kuban 1971: 'Work at the Kalenderhane Camii in Istanbul: Third and Fourth Preliminary Reports', *Dumbarton Oaks Papers* 25, 251–258.

Striker (C. L.) and (Y.) Doğan Kuban 1997: *Kalenderhane in Istanbul. The Buildings, their History, Architecture, and Decoration*. Mainz.

Strong (D.) 1976: *Roman Art*. Middlesex.

Strunk (O.) 1955: 'St Gregory Nazianzus and the Proper Hymns for Easter', in K. Weitzmann, ed., *Late Classical and Mediaeval Studies in Honor of Albert Mathias Friend, Jr.* Princeton, 82–87.

Styger (P.) 1914: 'Die Malereien in der Basilika des Hl. Sabas auf dem Kl. Aventin in Rom', *Römische Quartalschrift* 18, 49–96.

Taft (R.) 1980/1: 'The Liturgy of the Great Church: an Initial Synthesis of Structure and Interpretation on the Eve of Iconoclasm', *Dumbarton Oaks Papers* 34/35, 45–75.

Talbot Rice (D.) 1950: 'The Leaved Cross', *Byzantinoslavica* 11, 72–81.

Teteriatnikov (N.) 1992: 'The Frescoes of the Chapel of St Basil in Cappadocia: Their Date and Context Reconsidered', *Cahiers Archéologiques* 40, 99–114.

Thierry (N.) 1966: 'Le costume épiscopal byzantin du IXe au XIIIe siècle d'après les peintures datées, miniatures, fresques', *Revue des Etudes Byzantines* 24, 308–315.

Thierry (N.) 1980/1: 'Le culte de la croix dans l'empire byzantin du VIIe siècle au Xe dans ses rapports avec la guerre contre l'infidèle', *Rivista di studi bizantini e slavi* I. Miscellanea Agostino Pertusi. Bologna, 205–228.

Thierry (N.) 1982: 'L'iconoclasme en Cappadoce d'après les sources archéologiques. Origines et modalités', in L. Hadermann-Misguich and G. Raepsaet, eds., *Rayonnement grec. Hommages à Charles Delvoye*. Brussels, 389–403.

Thierry (N.) 1983: 'Le cycle de la création et de la faute d'Adam à Alt'amar. Notes préliminaires', *Revue des Etudes Arméniennes* 17, 289–329.

Thierry (N.) 1989: 'La peinture de Cappadoce au Xe siècle. Recherches sur les commanditaires de la nouvelle église de Tokalı et d'autres monuments', *Constantine VII Porphyrogenitus and His Age*, Second International Byzantine Conference, Delphi 1987. Athens, 217–246.

Thümmel (H. G.) 1983: 'Eine wenig bekannte Schrift zur Bilderfrage', in H. Köpstein and F. Winkelmann, eds., *Studien zum 8. und 9. Jahrhundert in Byzanz*. Berlin, 153–157.

Thümmel (H. G.) 1992: 'Kreuze, Reliquien und Bilder im Zeremonienbuch des Konstantinos Porphyrogennetos', *Byzantinische Forschungen* 18, 119–126.

Tikkanen (J. J.) 1933: *Studien über die Farbgebung in der mittelalterlichen Buchmalerei*. Helsinki.

Tobias (N.) 1969: 'Basil I (867–886), the Founder of the Macedonian Dynasty: a Study of the

Political and Military History of the Byzantine Empire in the Ninth Century.' PhD dissertation, Rutgers University.

Tobias (N.) 1976: 'Basil I and Byzantine Strategy', *Byzantine Studies / Etudes Byzantines* III/1, 30–55.

Totev (T.) 1987: 'L'atelier de céramique peinte du monastère royal de Preslav', *Cahiers Archéologiques* 35, 65–80.

Tougher (S. F.) 1994: 'The reign of Leo VI (886–912). Personal relationships and political ideologies.' PhD thesis, St Andrews.

Townsley (A. L.) 1974: 'Die Präsentationsszene in der St-Martins-Kirche in Zillis: Anzeichen eines möglichen vorikonoklastischen Einflusses', *Zeitschrift für Schweizerische Archäologie und Kunstgeschichte* 31, 22–30.

Tozzi (R.) 1933: 'I mosaici del Battistero di S. Marco a Venezia e l'arte bizantina', *Bollettino d'arte* 26, 418–432.

Travis (J.) 1984: *In Defense of the Faith. The Theology of Patriarch Nikephoros of Constantinople.* Brookline.

Treadgold (W.) 1980: *The Nature of the Bibliotheca of Photius.* Dumbarton Oaks Studies 18. Washington DC.

Trimarchi (M.) 1978: 'Per una revisione iconografica del ciclo di affreschi nel Tempio della "Fortuna Virile"', *Studi medievali* ser. 3, 19, 653–679.

Tsuji (S. G.) 1983: 'Destruction des portes de l'Enfer et ouverture des portes du Paradis. A propos des illustrations du Psaume 23, 7–10 et du Psaume 117, 19–20', *Cahiers Archéologiques* 31, 5–33.

Underwood (P.) 1959: 'The Evidence of Restorations in the Sanctuary Mosaics of the Church of the Dormition at Nicaea', *Dumbarton Oaks Papers* 13, 235–242.

Underwood (P.) 1975: 'Some Problems in Programs and Iconography of Ministry Cycles', in P. Underwood, ed., *The Kariye Djami* 4. Princeton, 243–302.

Underwood (P.) and (E. J. W.) Hawkins 1961: 'The Mosaics of Hagia Sophia at Istanbul. The Portrait of the Emperor Alexander', *Dumbarton Oaks Papers* 15, 187–217.

Uspensky (F.) 1907: *L'Octateuque de la Bibliothèque du Serail à Constantinople.* Sophia.

Vaccaro (A. M.) 1967: 'Sul sarcofago altomedioevale del Vescovato di Pesaro', *Alto medioevo* 1, 111–138.

Van den Ven (P.) 1955/7: 'La patristique et l'hagiographie au concile de Nicée en 787', *Byzantion* 25/27, 325–362.

Vasiliev (A. A.) 1948: 'The Monument of Porphyrius in the Hippodrome at Constantinople', *Dumbarton Oaks Papers* 4, 27–49.

Velmans (T.) 1971: *Le Tétraévangile de la Laurentienne.* Bibliothèque des Cahiers Archéologiques 6. Paris.

Velmans (T.) 1974: 'Le dessin à Byzance', *Monuments et Mémoires, Fondation Eugène Piot* 59, 137–170.

Velmans (T.) 1979: 'La couverture de l'Evangile dit de Morozov et l'évolution de la reliure byzantine', *Cahiers Archéologiques* 28, 115–36.

Vercleyen (F.) 1988: 'Tremblements de terre à Constantinople. L'impact sur la population', *Byzantion* 58, 155–173.

Vezin (G.) 1950: *L'Adoration et le cycle des Mages dans l'art chrétien primitif, étude des influences orientales et grècques sur l'art chrétien.* Paris.

Vikan (G.), ed. 1973: *Illuminated Greek Manuscripts from American Collections.* Princeton.

Vikan (G.) 1976: 'Illustrated Manuscripts of Pseudo-Ephraim's Life of Joseph and the Romance of Joseph and Aseneth.' PhD dissertation, Princeton University.

Vikan (G.) 1979: 'Joseph Iconography on Coptic Textiles', *Gesta* 18/1, 99–108.

Vikan (G.) 1989: 'Ruminations on Edible Icons: Originals and Copies in the Art of Byzantium', *Studies in the History of Art* 20, 47–59.

Vikan (G.) 1990: 'Art and Marriage in Early Byzantium', *Dumbarton Oaks Papers* 44, 145–163.

Vileisis (B.) 1979: 'The Genesis Cycle at Sta. Maria Antiqua.' PhD dissertation, Princeton University.

Vogt (A.) 1908: *Basile Ier Empereur de Byzance (867–886) et la civilisation byzantine à la fin du IXe siècle*. Paris.

Vogt (A.) ed. 1967a: *Constantin VII Porphyrogénète, Le Livre des Cérémonies*, second edn. 2 vols. Paris.

Vogt (A.) ed. 1967b: *Constantin VII Porphyrogénète, Le Livre des Cérémonies. Commentaire*, second edn. 2 vols. Paris.

Vogt (A.) and (T.) Hausherr eds. 1932: *L'oraison funèbre de Basile I par son fils Léon VI le sage*. Rome.

Volbach (W. F.) 1976: *Elfenbeinarbeiten der Spätantike und des frühen Mittelalters*, second edn. Mainz.

Volbach (W. F.) and (M.) Hirmer 1961: *Early Christian Art*. London.

von Falkenhausen (V.) 1988: 'San Pietro nella religiosità bizantina', *Bisanzio, Roma e l'Italia nell'alto medioevo* 2, Settimane di studio del Centro italiano di studi sull'alto medioevo 34. Spoleto, 627–658.

Waagen (M.) 1939: *Kunstwerke und Künstler in England und Paris* III. Berlin.

Waetzoldt (S.) 1964: *Die Kopien des 17. Jahrhunderts nach Mosaiken und Wandmalerei in Rom*. Vienna.

Walter (C.) 1970a: 'Heretics in Byzantine Art', *Eastern Churches Review* 3, 40–9. Reprinted in C. Walter, *Studies in Byzantine Iconography*. London, 1977, essay VII.

Walter (C.) 1970b: *L'iconographie des conciles dans la tradition byzantine*. Archives de l'orient chrétien 13. Paris.

Walter (C.) 1971: 'Liturgy and the Illustration of Gregory of Nazianzen's Homilies. An Essay in Iconographical Methodology', *Revue des Etudes Byzantines* 29, 183–212.

Walter (C.) 1972: 'Un commentaire Enluminé des Homélies de Grégoire de Nazianze', *Cahiers Archéologiques* 22, 115–129.

Walter (C.) 1975: 'The Coronation of a Co-emperor in the *Skyllitzes Matritensis*', *Actes du XIV Congrès International des Etudes Byzantines*. Bucharest, 453–458.

Walter (C.) 1976a: 'Death in Byzantine Iconography', *Eastern Churches Review* 8, 113–127.

Walter (C.) 1976b: 'The Significance of Unction in Byzantine Iconography', *Byzantine and Modern Greek Studies* 2, 53–73.

Walter (C.) 1978: 'Biographical Scenes of the Three Hierarchs', *Revue des études byzantines* 36, 233–260.

Walter (C.) 1979: 'The Earliest Representation of Mid-Pentecost', *Zograf* 8, 15–16.

Walter (C.) 1980: 'An Iconographical Note', *Revue des Etudes Byzantines* 38, 255–260.

Walter (C.) 1981: 'Saints of the Second Iconoclasm in the Madrid Skylitzes', *Revue des Etudes Byzantines* 39, 307–318.

Walter (C.) 1982: *Art and Ritual of the Byzantine Church*. Birmingham Byzantine Series I. London.

Walter (C.) 1986: 'Christological Themes in the Byzantine Marginal Psalters from the Ninth to the Eleventh Century', *Revue des Etudes Byzantines* 44, 269–287.

Walter (C.) 1987: '"Latter-Day" Saints and the Image of Christ in the ninth-century Byzantine marginal psalters', *Revue des Etudes Byzantines* 45, 205–22.

Walter (C.) 1989: 'The iconography of the prophet Habakkuk', *Revue des Etudes Byzantines* 47, 251–60.

Walter (C.) 1990: 'The Aristocratic Psalters and Ode Illustration in Byzantium', *Byzantinoslavica* 51/1, 43–52.

Warner (G.) 1912: *Queen Mary's Psalter*. London.

Weaver (D.) 1983: 'From Paul to Augustine: Romans 5:12 in Early Christian Exegesis', *St Vladimir's Theological Quarterly* 27, 187–206.

Weaver (D.) 1985: 'The Exegesis of Romans 5:12 Among the Greek Fathers and its Implication for the Doctrine of Original Sin: the 5th–12th Centuries', *St Vladimir's Theological Quarterly* 29, 133–159, 231–257.

Weitzmann (K.) 1929: 'Der Pariser Psalter MS.Gr.139 und die mittelbyzantinische Renaissance', *Jahrbuch für Kunstwissenschaft* 6, 178–194. Reprinted in K. Weitzmann, *Byzantine Liturgical Psalters and Gospels*. London, 1980, essay I.

Weitzmann (K.) 1935: *Die byzantinische Buchmalerei des IX. und X. Jahrhunderts*. Berlin.

Weitzmann (K.) 1942/3: 'Illustrations for the Chronicles of Sozomenos, Theodoret and Malalas', *Byzantion* 16, 87–134.

Weitzmann (K.) 1947: *Illustrations in Roll and Codex. A Study in the Origin and Method of Text Illustration*. Studies in Manuscript Illumination 2. Princeton. Revised edn, 1970.

Weitzmann (K.) 1948: *The Joshua Roll, a Work of the Macedonian Renaissance*. Studies in Manuscript Illumination 3. Princeton.

Weitzmann (K.) 1951a: *The Fresco Cycle at S. Maria di Castelseprio*. Princeton.

Weitzmann (K.) 1951b: *Greek Mythology in Byzantine Art*. Princeton.

Weitzmann (K.) 1959: 'Ein kaiserliches Lektionar einer byzantinischen Hofschule', in O. Benesch *et al.*, eds., *Festschrift Karl M. Swoboda zum 28. Januar 1959*. Vienna and Weisbaden, 309–320.

Weitzmann (K.) 1960: 'The Mandylion and Constantine Porphyrogennetos', *Cahiers Archéologiques* 11, 163–184.

Weitzmann (K.) 1961: 'The Origin of the Threnos', in M. Meiss, ed., *De Artibus Opuscula XL. Essays in Honor of Erwin Panofsky*. New York, 476–490.

Weitzmann (K.) 1969: 'A Metamorphosis Icon or Miniature on Mt. Sinai', *Starinar* 20, 415–421. Reprinted in K. Weitzmann, *Byzantine Liturgical Psalters and Gospels*. London, 1980, essay XIII.

Weitzmann (K.) 1970: 'Ivory Sculpture of the Macedonian Renaissance', in V. Milojčić, ed., *Kolloquium über spätantike und frühmittelalterliche Skulptur* 2, 1–12. Reprinted in K. Weitzmann, *Classical Heritage in Byzantine and Near Eastern Art*. London, 1981, essay IX.

Weitzmann (K.) 1971a: 'The Illustration of the Septuagint', in H. L. Kessler, ed., *Studies in Classical and Byzantine Manuscript Illumination*. Chicago, 45–75. Orig. published as 'Die Illustration der Septuaginta', *Münchner Jahrbuch der bildenden Kunst* 3/4, 1952/53, 96–120.

Weitzmann (K.) 1971b: 'A 10th-Century Lectionary. A Lost Masterpiece of the Macedonian Renaissance', *Revue des Etudes Sud-est Européennes* 9, 617–640. Reprinted in K. Weitzmann, *Byzantine Liturgical Psalters and Gospels*. London, 1980, essay X.

Weitzmann (K.) 1972: *Catalogue of the Byzantine and Early Mediaeval Antiquities in the Dumbarton Oaks Collection* III. Washington DC.

Weitzmann (K.) 1974: 'An Illustrated Greek New Testament of the Tenth Century in the Walters Art Gallery', in U. E. McCracken, L. M. C. Randell and R. H. Randell, Jr., eds., *Gatherings in Honor of Dorothy E. Miner*. Baltimore, 19–38.

Weitzmann (K.) 1975: 'The Selection of Texts for Cyclic Illustration in Byzantine Manuscripts', *Byzantine Books and Bookmen*. Washington DC, 69–109. Reprinted in K. Weitzmann, *Byzantine Book Illumination and Ivories*. London, 1980, essay II.

Weitzmann (K.) 1976: *The Monastery of Saint Catherine at Mount Sinai. The Icons I: From the sixth to the Tenth Century*. Princeton.

Weitzmann (K.) 1977: *Late Antique and Early Christian Book Illumination*. New York.

Weitzmann (K.) 1978: 'The Classical Mode in the Period of the Macedonian Emperors: Continuity or Revival?', *Byzantina kai Metabyzantina. The Past in Medieval and Modern Greek Culture*. Malibu, 71–85. Reprinted in K. Weitzmann, *Classical Heritage in Byzantine and Near Eastern Art*. London, 1981, essay X.

Weitzmann (K.) 1979a: *The Miniatures of the Sacra Parallela, Parisinus graecus 923*. Studies in Manuscript Illumination 8. Princeton.

Weitzmann (K.) ed. 1979b: *Age of Spirituality. Late Antique and Early Christian Art, Third to Seventh Century*, Catalogue of an Exhibition at The Metropolitan Museum of Art, November 19, 1977 through February 12, 1978. New York.

Weitzmann (K.) 1982: 'Some Remarks on the Sources of the Fresco Painting of the Cathedral of Faras', *Studies in the Arts at Sinai*. Princeton, 187–210. Orig. published in *Kunst und Geschichte Nubiens in Christlicher Zeit*. Recklinghausen, 1970, 325–340.

Weitzmann (K.) and (G.) Galavaris 1990: *The Monastery of Saint Catherine at Mount Sinai. The Illuminated Greek Manuscripts I: From the Ninth to the Twelfth Century*. Princeton.

Weitzmann (K.) and (H. L.) Kessler 1986: *The Cotton Genesis, British Library Codex Otho B. VI*, The Illustrations in the Manuscripts of the Septuagint I. Princeton.

Weitzmann (K.) and (H. L.) Kessler 1990: *The Frescoes of the Dura Synagogue and Christian Art*. Dumbarton Oaks Studies 28. Washington DC.

Weitzmann (K.) and (I.) Ševčenko 1963: 'The Moses Cross at Sinai', *Dumbarton Oaks Papers* 17, 385–398. Reprinted in K. Weitzmann, *Studies in the Arts at Sinai*. Princeton, 1982, essay IV.

Westerink (L. G.), ed. 1986, 1987: *Photii Patriarchae Constantinopolitani, Epistulae et Amphilochia*, vols. 4–6 (*Amphilochia*). Bibliotheca Scriptorum Graecorum et Romanorum Teubneriana. Leipzig.

White (D.) 1974: 'Photios' Letter to the Bishops in Exile', *Greek Orthodox Theological Review* 19, 113–129.

White (D.) 1981: *Patriarch Photios of Constantinople, his Life, Scholarly Contributions, and Correspondence Together with a Translation of Fifty-two of his Letters*, The Archbishop Iakovos Library of Ecclesiatical and Historical Sources 5. Brookline.

White (D.) and (J. R.) Berrigan, Jr. 1982: *The Patriarch and the Prince. The Letter of Patriarch Photios of Constantinople to Khan Boris of Bulgaria*. Brookline.

Wieczynski (J. L.) 1974: 'The Anti-Papal Conspiracy of the Patriarch Photios in 867', *Byzantine Studies* 1, 180–189.

Wilkinson (J.) 1977: *Jerusalem Pilgrims Before the Crusades*. Warminster.

Willoughby (H. R.) 1932: *The Rockefeller-McCormick New Testament*. Chicago.

Wilson (N. G.) 1967: 'The Libraries of the Byzantine World', *Greek, Roman and Byzantine Studies* 8, 53–80.

Wilson (N. G.) 1983: *Scholars of Byzantium*. Baltimore.

Wilson (N. G.) 1994: *Photius, The Bibliotheca, a selection translated with notes*. London.

Winkelmann (F.) 1978: 'Das hagiographische Bild Konstantins I. in mittelbyzantinischer Zeit', in V. Vavřinek, ed., *Beiträge zur byzantinischen Geschichte im 9.–11. Jahrhundert*. Prague, 179–203.

Winkelmann (F.) 1987: *Quellenstudien zur herrschenden Klasse von Byzanz im 8. und 9. Jahrhundert*. Berlin.

Wolska (W.) 1962: *La Topographie Chrétienne de Cosmas Indicopleustes, Théologie et science au VIe siècle*. Paris.

Wolska-Conus (W.) 1980: 'Un programme iconographique du patriarche Tarasios', *Revue des Etudes Byzantines* 38, 247–254.

Wolska-Conus (W.) 1989: 'Stéphanos d'Athènes et Stéphanos d'Alexandrie: Essai d'identification et de biographie', *Revue des études byzantines* 47, 5–89.

Wolska-Conus (W.) 1990: 'La "Topographie Chrétienne" de Cosmas Indicopleustès: hypothèses sur quelques thèmes de son illustration', *Revue des Etudes Byzantines* 48, 155–191.

Wormald (F.) 1973: *The Winchester Psalter*. London.

Wortley (J.) 1982: 'Iconoclasm and Leipsanoclasm: Leo III, Constantine V and the Relics', *Byzantinische Forschungen* 8, 253–279.

Wright (D.) 1980: 'The School of Princeton and the Seventh Day of Creation', *University Publishing* 9, 7–8.

Wright (D.) 1985: 'The Date of the Vatican Illuminated Handy Tables of Ptolemy and of its Early Additions', *Byzantinische Zeitschrift* 78, 355–362.

Zacos (G.) 1984/5: *Byzantine Lead Seals* 2. Compiled and edited by J. Nesbitt. Basel.

Zacos (G.) and (A.) Veglery 1972: *Byzantine Lead Seals* 1. Basel.

Zoubouli (M.) 1995: 'L'Esthétique et le sacré: l'icone dans la pensée spéculative et dans la vie quotidienne', *Etudes Balkaniques* 2, 71–102.

Index

References to individual miniatures in the Paris Homilies are listed under Paris.gr.510; *references in* **bold type** *indicate primary discussions. References to folios without illustrations have not been indexed; nor have footnotes. Biblical citations for scenes pictured in Paris.gr.510 all appear in Appendix B.*

Aaron: 343, 346–347

Abgaros of Edessa, king: 169

Abraham, Old Testament patriarch: 16, 131–132; *see also* Paris.gr.510, f. 174v

Achilles: 182

Acre: 182

Acts: 253, 255–256; *see also* iconography, New Testament

Adam: 292

Adam and Eve: *see* Paris.gr.510, f. 52v; ivory caskets of: 310, 313, 316

adoration of the Magi: *see* Paris.gr.510, f. 137r

Adrianople: 161

Aegeates: 248

Aght'amar: 310, 367

Agrippa: 247

akakia: 162

Alexander, emperor: 5–6; *see also* Paris.gr.510, f. Br

Alexander, Paul: 52

Alexander of Lykopolis: 216

Alexander the Great: 161, 172, 199

Alexandria: 245

Amalekites: *see* Paris.gr.510, f. 424v

Amorites: *see* Paris.gr.510, f. 226v

Amphilochios, metropolitan of Kyzikos: 203

Anastasios of Sinai: 48

anastasis: 291, 301–302

Anastasius, emperor: 172

Anderson, Jeffrey: 360

Andrew, apostle 242, 245, 248, 251 (*see also* Paris.gr.510, f. 87v); acts of: 248, 417, 423

annunciation: *see* Paris.gr.510, f. 3r

anointing of David: *see* David, anointing of

anti-Islamic polemic: 24, 28, 43, 154, 167, 239, 288, 293, 409

anti-Jewish imagery: 264, 269–270, 273, 275–277, 279, 403, 406

anti-Jewish polemic: 24, 28, 43, 78, 154, 167, 239, 262–263, 266, 269–271, 273, 275, 288, 293, 403, 409

Antioch: 229, 245

Antioch, relief from: 131

Antiochos: 258

antithesis: 264–265, 272, 277, 289, 409

Apollinarios: 211–212, 214–216, 270, 275

Apollo: 229

apostles baptizing: *see* Paris.gr.510, f. 426v

apostles, martyrdom of the: 262; *see also* Paris.gr.510, f. 32v

apostles, mission of the: *see* Paris.gr.510, f. 426v

appearance, importance of: 59, 400–403